FOR EVER GODARD

EDITED BY
MICHAEL TEMPLE
JAMES S WILLIAMS
MICHAEL WITT

Black Dog Publishing

82124

Black Dog Publishing
© 2004 Black Dog Publishing Limited, the artists and authors
All rights reserved

Edited by Michael Temple, James S Williams and Michael Witt
Designed by Zoé Roman with Emilia Gómez López and David Ottley at BDP
Picture research by Michael Temple and Michael Witt
Picture research assistants: Teresa Castro and Vicky Fox
Produced by Duncan McCorquodale and Catherine Grant

agnès b.

Printed in Italy by Litosei, Bologna

Black Dog Publishing Limited
Unit 4.04 Tea Building
56 Shoreditch High Street
London, E1 6JJ

Tel: +44 (0)20 7613 1922
Fax: +44 (0)20 7613 1944
Email: info@bdp.demon.co.uk
www.bdpworld.com

All opinions expressed within this publication are those of the authors and not necessarily of the publisher.

British Library Cataloguing-in-Publication Data.

A catalogue record for this book is available from the British Library.

ISBN 1 901033 69 4

Every effort has been made to trace the copyright holders, but if any have been inadvertently
overlooked the publishers will be pleased to make the necessary arrangements at the first opportunity.

ACKNOWLEDGEMENTS

We would like to thank the following for their invaluable help during this project: Martin Brady for translating Chapter Nine; Mary Lea Bandy of the Museum of Modern Art, New York; Raymond Bellour; Pierre Bourdy of Aux Films Du Temps; Nicole Brenez; Andrew Brighton of Tate Modern; Agnès Calatayud; Vicki Callahan; Steve Cannon; Teresa Castro; Philippe Dubois for generously giving us free access to his collection of photographs; Manfred Eicher of ECM Records; Harun Farocki; Corine Faugeron of Gaumont; Catherine Fröchen of *Cahiers du cinéma*; Vicky Fox at Black Dog Publishing; Gérard Fromanger; Florian Ganslmeier of ECM Records; Guillaume Gaubert of *L'Avant-Scène Cinéma*; Jean-Luc Godard; Emilia Gómez López of Black Dog Publishing; Vérène Grieshaber; Nina Harding of British Film Institute Stills; Vinzenz Hediger; Trace Hollenbeck; Junji Hori; George Kaltsounakis of Ontario Cinematheque; Fumiaki Kimura of Kinokuniya; Roland-François Lack; Olivia Lahav of Tate Modern; Waltraud Loges of the National Film Theatre; Ken Lyndon of University of Surrey, Roehampton; Colin MacCabe; Vibeke Madsen of POL for permission to translate "Le Paradoxe de Godard" by Serge Daney; Jann Matlock for translating Chapter Eight; Anne-Marie Miéville; Valerie Orpen for translating Chapters One, Five and 14, "The Written Screen" and occasional short pieces of French, and also for producing the Index; Marc Ramey; Rebecca Reinhart of *agnès b.*; Zoé Roman of Black Dog Publishing for the design of the book; Jonathan Rosenbaum; Hilary Smith of the National Film Theatre; Muriel Tinel; Agnès Troublé; Cécile Verguin of Bibliothèque du Film et de l'Image (BIFI); Alexandra Witt. We would also like to thank the following companies and institutions for their generous financial support: *agnès b.*; Birkbeck College London; Kent Institute of Arts and Study of Humanities (KIASH), University of Kent; University of Surrey, Roehampton. Finally, we would like to offer special thanks to Catherine Grant of Black Dog Publishing for her calm efficiency, and above all to the publisher Duncan McCorquodale for his initial enthusiasm for the project and his inspiration throughout.

Cover: **Godard during the making of** *Alphaville* **in 1965.**

WORK AND WORKS

FORM AND FIGURE

SOUND AND MUSIC

HISTORY AND MEMORY

NOTES ON CONTRIBUTORS

Raymond Bellour has published widely on film as well as romantic and contemporary literature. His books include *L'analyse du film*, 1979, *Passages de l'image*, 1989, *L'Entre-Images: Photo, Cinéma, Vidéo*, 1990, *Jean-Luc Godard: Son+Image 1974-1991*, 1992 and *L'Entre-Images 2*, 1999.

Christa Blümlinger is Maître de Conférences at the Film Studies Department of the University of Paris-III. Her most recent publications include an edition of the writings of Serge Daney entitled *Von der Welt ins Bild. Augenzeugenberichte eines Cinephilen*, 2000, and an edition of writings by Harun Farocki, *Reconnaître/ Poursuivre*, 2002.

Nicole Brenez is Maître de Conférences in Cinema Studies at the University of Paris-I. She is the curator of the Cinémathèque Française's experimental and avant-garde film programme. Her many publications include *Shadows de John Cassavetes*, 1995, and *De la Figure en général et du Corps en particulier. L'invention figurative au cinéma*, 1998.

Vicki Callahan is Associate Professor and program coordinator of Film Studies in the English Department at the University of Wisconsin-Milwaukee. Her book on the films of Louis Feuillade, *Zones of Anxiety: Movement, Musidora, and the Crime Serials of Louis Feuillade*, will be published in 2004.

Monica Dall'Asta teaches Film Theory at the University of Bologna. She is the author of a book on Maciste and other muscle men of the Italian silent cinema entitled *Un cinéma musclé*, 1992 and of *La macchina delle alternative. La serialità nel cinema muto*, 2001.

Serge Daney was, until his death in 1992, one of France's foremost film critics. He was Chief Editor of *Cahiers du cinéma* 1974-1981, film critic for *Libération* during the 1980s, and co-founder with Raymond Bellour of the film journal *Trafic*.

Antoine de Baecque writes for *Libération*. His published works include *François Truffaut*, 2001, *Cahiers du cinéma: histoire d'une revue*, 1991, and *La Nouvelle Vague: portrait d'une jeunesse*, 1998.

Philippe Dubois is Professor of Cinema Studies at University of Paris-III. His published works include *L'acte photographique*, 1993, *Cinéma et dernières technologies*, 1998 and *Recherches sur Chris Marker*, 2002.

Catherine Grant lectures in Film Studies at the University of Kent. She is currently completing a book on the body of international documentaries and fiction films about the South American "Disappeared".

Vinzenz Hediger is a research fellow in Film Studies at the University of Zürich. His publications include a book on movie trailers, *Verführung zum Film. Der amerikanische Kinotrailer seit 1912*, 2001, as well as two anthologies on cinema and culture in Switzerland.

Leslie Hill is Professor in the Department of French Studies at the University of Warwick and the author of *Marguerite Duras: Apocalyptic Desires*, 1993, *Blanchot: Extreme Contemporary*, 1997, and *Bataille, Klossowski, Blanchot: Writing at the Limit*, 2001.

Junji Hori is a JSPS Research Fellow at the Department of Interdisciplinary Cultural Studies, University of Tokyo. He is co-editor of a collection of essays on *Histoire(s) du cinéma* entitled *Godard, Image, History*, 2001, and has collaborated on a complete annotated Japanese DVD version of the series.

Laurent Jullier is Professor of Film Studies at the University of Metz, France. He is the author of *L'écran post-moderne*, 1997, *Les images de synthèse*, 1998, *L'analyse de séquences*, 2002, and *Qu'est-ce qu'un bon film?*, 2002.

Roland-François Lack teaches literature and film in the Department of French at University College London. He is currently writing a monograph on Godard and the Book and is the author of *Lautréamont: poetics of the pretext*, 1998.

Trond Lundemo is Associate Professor at the Department of Cinema Studies at Stockholm University, as well as Visiting Professor and researcher at Seijo University, Tokyo (in 2002 and 2004). He is currently engaged in research on the films and philosophy of Jean Epstein.

Colin MacCabe is Distinguished Professor of English and Film at the University of Pittsburgh and Professor of English at the University of Exeter. His most recent book is *Godard: A Portrait of the Artist at 70*, 2003.

Adrian Martin is film critic of *The Age* (Melbourne). He is the author of *The Mad Max Movies*, 2003, *Once Upon a Time in America*, 1998, and *Phantasms*, 1994, as well as co-editor of *Movie Mutations*, 2003, and the on-line journal *Rouge* (www.rouge.com.au).

James Quandt is Senior Programmer at Cinematheque Ontario, Toronto. He has organised touring retrospectives of the films of Kenji Mizoguchi, Shohei Imamura, Kon Ichikawa, Robert Bresson, Alexander Sokurov, and Nicholas Ray, and has edited monographs on Bresson, Imamura, and Ichikawa.

Jacques Rancière is Emeritus Professor of Aesthetics and Politics at the University of Paris-VIII. His most recent books include *Le partage du sensible. Esthétique et politique*, 2000, *L'Inconscient esthétique*, 2001, *La Fable cinématographique*, 2001, and *Le Destin des images*, 2003.

Keith Reader is Professor of Modern French at Glasgow University and is the author of numerous studies of French cinema, including a book on Robert Bresson for Manchester University Press, 2000.

Libby Saxton is Lecturer in French and Film Studies at Queen Mary, University of London, and is completing her doctoral thesis for the University of Cambridge. She is the co-editor of *Seeing Things: Vision, Perception and Interpretation in French Studies*, 2002.

Michael Temple teaches at Birkbeck College, London, and is the author of *The Name of The Poet*, 1995, editor of *Meetings with Mallarmé*, 1998 and is currently writing a book about Jean Vigo.

James S Williams is Senior Lecturer in French and Comparative Literature at the University of Kent. He is the author of *The Erotics of Passage: Pleasure, Politics, and Form in the Later Work of Marguerite Duras*, 1997, and co-editor of *Gay Signatures*, 1998, *The Cinema Alone*, 2000, and *Gender and French Cinema*, 2001. He is currently completing a monograph on the cinema of Jean Cocteau.

Michael Witt teaches Cinema Studies at the University of Surrey, Roehampton. He is the co-editor with Michael Temple of *The French Cinema Book*, 2004, and is completing a study of Godard as cinema historian.

FOR EVER DIVIDED

RAYMOND BELLOUR   It is through the filmmaker Jean-Luc Godard that the history of cinema–
understood as the history of the twentieth century–was forever divided.

Before: cinema in its tireless diversity seemed always to be moving
towards its own essence, inventing and reinventing itself, almost
unconsciously and without any real awareness of the gaze of television.

After: cinema remains full of life and, even into the next century,
is sustained by so many new and powerful films, but it is now just one
medium among others, in the accelerated history, the upstream and
downstream, of moving images–albeit a medium that has succeeded
unlike any other.

Between the before and the after: Godard has lived his whole life moving
between these two moments in time, and he has made the present, which
for many he personifies, into both a prophetic anticipation and a nostalgic
reinterpretation. Two formulas by Alain Bergala have captured this furious
and frustrated movement: "the art of the balancing act" and "none better
than Godard".

From the opening shot of his first feature film, the hero in the guise of
a *film noir* double looks straight at the spectator and speaks to camera, as if
he were a female television announcer. And now Godard is preparing for
2004-2005 his first quasi-installation, a kind of satellite connecting his
isolated bunker in Rolle to the Georges Pompidou National Centre for Art
and Culture in Paris. The project is called *Collage de France*. A title that is
both a nod to the learned institution of the Collège de France and a further
realisation of cinematic montage, which he has famously described as "my
beautiful care". Similarly, he once reworked the classic school-text *The Tour
of France by Two Children* into *France/tour/détour/deux/enfants*, which among
all his great films was the first television masterpiece, before *Histoire(s) du
cinéma* broke down all the categories and gave cinema the systematic yet
overwhelmed consciousness that it had been waiting for.

He may thus be the last Romantic. The final incarnation of the Jena school
of Romanticism. In the early nineteenth century, literature experienced a
similar great divide, thanks to an increased self-consciousness and a
transformation of its means of expression, shifting from the essay and the
novel to the fragment. In this self-portrait of Jean-Luc Godard as Friedrich
Schlegel, we can even find the same projected perfection of the image of
Lucinde, that luminous female presence, source of an obsession which
Godard has ceaselessly retransformed, rendering it for all of us, men and
women, singularly cruel.

LA OU C'ETAIT, JE SERAI

LA OU JE SERAI, J'AI DEJA ETE

Where it was, I shall be
Where I shall be, I have already been

LĀ OŪ ÇA IRA, ON SERA MIEUX

When it's OK, we shall be better

Opposite and above: **Collage composed by Godard for the**
May 1981 issue of *Cahiers du cinéma.*

INTRODUCTION

This volume is inspired by the successful four day international conference *For Ever Godard* held in London at Tate Modern in June 2001. This event was the first of its kind ever to be devoted to Jean-Luc Godard's work in the UK, and it brought together specialists and writers from around the world working in different fields and disciplines, including film and television, history, philosophy, feminism, cultural studies, art and art history, music and literature. Longstanding commentators of Godard's work entered into new and exciting dialogue on Godard's 50 years of work in the cinema with an emerging generation of younger critical voices. The sessions were based around screenings of Godard's recent work, including the UK premiere of *The Old Place*, 1999, made in collaboration with Anne-Marie Miéville, and the rare screening of a short film by the artist Gérard Fromanger, *Le Rouge*, made in 1968 with Godard's technical assistance (now held at the Musée d'Art Moderne in Paris). The many interventions and round-table discussions also addressed more general theoretical questions such as historical memory, technological change and the future of cinema. The Godard that emerged from these fertile debates was a unique kind of multi-media artist, a prodigious experimenter of forms who has redefined–and continues to redefine–what a contemporary engaged filmmaker is and what are the appropriate terms of his reception.

The present collection of essays is faithful to the genuinely interdisciplinary nature and interrogative spirit of the conference, yet it is not a simple proceedings volume. Of the 22 chapters included, 10 are based on papers delivered at Tate Modern and these have themselves been expanded and revised in the light of discussion during and after the conference. With one exception–an important short text by Serge Daney entitled "The Godard Paradox" first published in the *Revue Belge du Cinéma* in 1986 and until now only available in French–the other 11 chapters are completely new essays which we have commissioned to enhance the book's critical range beyond the mainly late focus that characterised the conference agenda. With this additional material the collection explores further primary areas of enquiry such as historiography and film history, yet it also establishes a fresh agenda of issues, including Godard as entrepreneur and producer, his extensive collaborative practice, in particular with Anne-Marie Miéville, the importance of voice and music, museology and the sacred, the influence of Walter Benjamin and Maurice Blanchot, and the lyrical aspects of his work.

One of the major aims of *For Ever Godard* is to help to initiate a reconfiguration of the Godard corpus, since filmographies of Godard's work reproduce more or less the same list of titles. These are usually confined to the feature films, film shorts and larger video works and television series, whereas a distinctive feature of Godard's prolific output has been his interest in experimenting with different formats. This has produced numerous short pieces on video ("letters", "notes", "video scripts", etc.) as well as occasional works for television, often in collaboration with Anne-Marie Miéville. To this "other" list we might also add the films that were abandoned for creative, financial or censorship-related reasons, and which therefore come to us only in the form of ideas, projects or incomplete fragments. In fact, Godard's own many unrealised projects could be said to constitute a parallel corpus to his completed works, whether film proposals (e.g. *La Formation de l'acteur en France*, 1992), proposals for serials (e.g. *Naissance (de l'image) d'une nation*, 1977-1979), longstanding cherished projects (e.g. *Moi je*, 1972-1975), abandoned footage (*One A.M.*, 1968, *Jusqu'à la victoire*, 1969-1972), or extra-cinematic practical projects (collaboration with Aäton on the 35/8 camera, 1979-1984, a montage studio at the French National Film School (FEMIS), 1989-1991, etc.). At the time of writing, who can say what will become of works planned or in progress such as *Notre Musique* (a collaboration with Manfred Eicher of ECM Records), *Champ contre champ* (a contribution to a compilation film about Paris), and, perhaps most fascinatingly, *Collage de France* (a multi-media exhibition at the Centre Georges Pompidou in Paris)? The many unrealised projects which have never made it into the official Godard filmography will doubtless inflect our critical understanding of the more visible body of work. Certainly, to consider their importance is already to move beyond the thorny issue of periodisation that has marked Godard studies, since the whole "Godard story" is not finished and is always in the process of correcting itself. There can be little point, therefore, in dividing it up into conveniently chronological slices. Indeed, perhaps a more useful way of trying to bring together Godard's different ventures in film, video and television, as well as in other visual formats such as photography and collage (in the case of *Histoire(s) du cinéma*, this includes even an art-book), would be to consider all of his works as essentially "incomplete", and the sum of his work as still to be decided. This "essayistic" model immediately offers a more open, flexible and above all dynamic means of thinking about the Godard corpus in its diversity of forms, materials, motifs and textures. It is a model that may also contribute to a general rethinking of the relations between the visual arts, cinema and other contemporary media that Godard's work always encourages.

For Ever Godard is divided into four main thematic sections. Part I, "Work and Works", comprises six chapters that re-examine in different ways the range and conception of Godard's work across five decades. It begins with Serge Daney's provocative analysis of the Godardian paradox and continues with an examination of Godard's intermittent engagement with politics and contemporary events, his role as producer and entrepeneur, the evolution of his extensive artistic collaboration since the early 1970s with Anne-Marie Miéville, his approach to cinema both in the museum and as a new form of museum, and finally the practical issues encountered in assembling Godard's work for a retrospective. Part II, "Form and Figure", features another six chapters that discuss some major pathways through this potentially reconfigured landscape: Godard's reinvention of the trailer, the different modes of interrogation in his work, the recurring figure of the parade and procession, the connection between Godard's use of cinematic form (e.g. the camera frame) and aesthetic notions of the sacred, Godard's approach to filming the body in motion and series, particularly on video, and the terms of his remarkable investment in Hitchcock as an artistic model. The four chapters of Part III, "Sound and Music", pursue in detail one pathway which has been relatively underexplored, sound and music, and together they open up an original field of research. Among the subjects analysed are the different forms of lyricism in Godard's films, the importance of ECM Records to his progressively more involved experimentation with music, Godard's ideas of, and for, music and its link with other processes in his work such as love and memory, and the nature and role of voice (notably his own) and the speaking subject. Finally, the five essays that comprise Part IV, "History and Memory", investigate an area that has come directly to the fore only in the last 15 years with *Histoire(s) du cinéma*, and which has been largely responsible for the thorough rethinking of Godard's work that we have made central to this collection. The contributors discuss not only the complex nature and philosophical ambition of Godard's historiographal project but also related aspects such as the function of cinema as historical record and testimony, the significance of Godard's work for reassessing film as cultural resource and archive, Godard's practice and theory of montage, and his overlapping strategies of literary and philosophical citation. Each of the four Parts is prefaced by a short introduction describing briefly the chapters and providing a general context and theoretical framework for the issues to be discussed.

Today Godard remains a pioneering visual and graphic artist, and a principal aim of this volume is to do critical justice to the full sweep of his artistic interests and preoccupations. The 22 chapters deploy illustrative images from the different films under discussion, arranged in a variety of forms and combinations in relation to the texts. These images are also contextualised by visual material from other sources, especially non-Godardian films, as a way of balancing the critical discussion of Godard with visible evidence of the work's wider commerical and cultural existence. Included in this further body of material are press books, published and unpublished screenplays, written notes, letters and projects, lobby cards, artworks and posters, special issues of journals, records and CDs, and extracts from Godard's own published work. The volume features, in addition, two exclusively visual sections. The first is an illustrated filmography that lists the essential production credits for all Godard's films and multi-media work over the last 50 years. Not only will this serve to provide a clear perspective of the multiple contours of the Godard corpus, but also it will afford the reader a valuable point of reference for those chapters which move freely across the decades. The second visual section takes the form of an essay of images by Philippe Dubois entitled "The Written Screen", which focuses on the continual tension across Godard's work between the written word and the visual sign. The volume concludes with a selective bibliography, with a particular emphasis on works available in English.

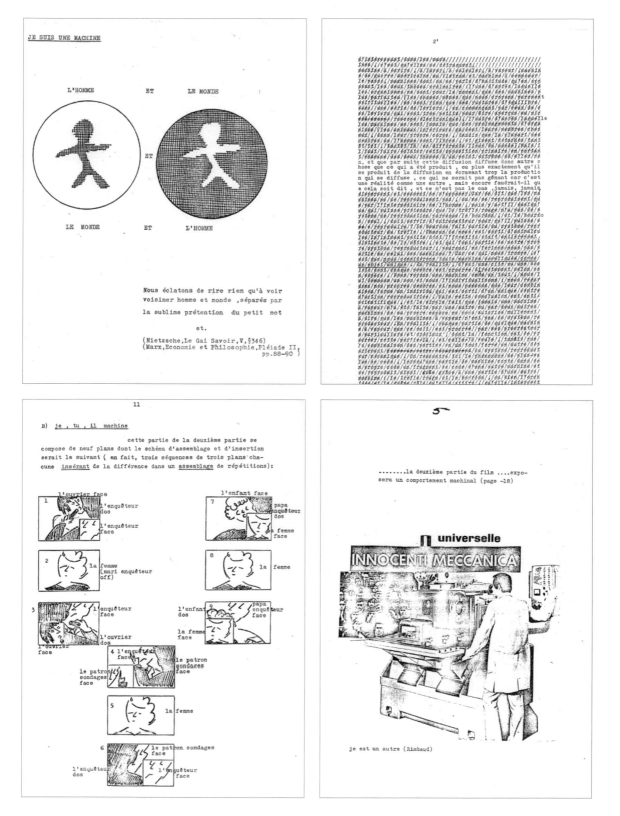

Above: **Pages from the 1973 script of *Moi je*.**

ILLUSTRATED FILMOGRAPHY

Voici le bilan d'une expérience.
Paul Éluard

This illustrated filmography provides brief details of all of Godard's known audiovisual work. In line with our belief that the shorts, video essays, television work, and occasional commissions are no less interesting or significant than the feature films, indeed that they are central to an appreciation of Godard's trajectory and achievement as an artist to date, each work is here accorded equal space, irrespective of length or format. The date given for each work is generally the release date. If there was a significant delay between the date of production and of distribution, the date given is that of production, although the release date is also noted. We are indebted to those who have compiled Godard filmographies in the past, especially Alain Bergala, Julia Lesage, and Sally Shafto. Besides providing a chronological reference guide for the reader, the aim of this filmography is to give a visual account of the Godardian corpus through a variety of materials, including photographs, press books, posters, and lobby cards. English language release titles are given where they exist; otherwise, a non-italicised English translation of the French title is given in inverted commas. Where the soundtrack of a work has been released as a separate artwork, details are given in brackets. Godard's written output is listed in the Bibliography.

Many of Godard's well-known features, especially those of the 1960s and 1980s, have long been available on video. The past decade has seen the release of a range of less visible and more recent works on video or DVD with English subtitles in the USA and UK, including *Comment ça va?*, *Ici et Ailleurs*, *Numéro Deux*, *King Lear*, *Soigne ta droite*, *2x50 ans de cinéma français*, *For Ever Mozart*, and *Hélas pour moi*. Expansion of the DVD market, especially in France, Japan, and the USA has led to the re-release of many familiar features (*Le Petit soldat*, *Pierrot le fou*, *Made in USA*, *Week-end*, *Passion*, *Prénom Carmen*, etc.) alongside a range of hitherto comparatively rare titles, including *Vent d'est*, *Lettre à Freddy Buache*, *Allemagne année 90 neuf zéro*, *JLG/JLG: autoportrait de décembre*, *For Ever Mozart*, *Histoire(s) du cinéma*, and *Éloge de l'amour*. A number of the Japanese DVD releases include video essays as part of the package (e.g. the discs for *Passion* and *Je vous salue, Marie* include *Scénario du film Passion* and *Petites notes à propos du film Je vous salue, Marie* respectively). Note however that Japanese DVDs do not generally include English subtitles. The following list of web addresses gives a selected guide to some key on-line sources.

FRANCE

Alapage: www.alapage.com (French)
Amazon: www.amazon.fr (French)
CPEDERF: www.cpederf.com
(Paris-based company which can supply
university students or teachers anywhere in
the world with any video or DVD
commercially available in France–site is in
English, Staff are bilingual)
FNAC: www.fnac.com (French)

JAPAN

Amazon: www.amazon.co.jp (Japanese)
CD Japan: www.cdjapan.co.jp
(English language site specialising in Japanese
DVDs)

USA

Amazon: www.amazon.com
CineFile video: www.cinefilevideo.com
(specialises in hard to find and out-of-print
videos and DVDs)
Facets: www.facets.org
(invaluable distributor and store)
New York Film Annex:
www.nyfavideo.com
(catalogue includes several Godard titles,
including *Le Gai savoir*)
US Videoflicks: www.videoflicks.com

UK

Amazon: www.amazon.co.uk
**British Film Institute video and DVD
publishing:** www.bfi.org.uk
Grant and Cutler: www.grantandcutler.com
(supplier of foreign language materials)
MovieMail: www.moviem.co.uk

GERMANY

ECM Records: www.ecmrecords.com
(English–site of the company that released
Nouvelle Vague and *Histoire(s) du cinéma* on
audio CD)

19
55

Opération béton
English: "Operation Concrete"
Script: Jean-Luc Godard
Camera: Adrien Porchet
Sound: Jean-Luc Godard
Editing: Jean-Luc Godard
Producer: Jean-Luc Godard
Production: Actua Film
Format: 20 min, 35mm, b/w, documentary

19
56

"You have no idea how funny it was to watch her doing her thing, or rather her business. Sometimes she would shut the window and I'd see a gentleman walking up and down outside. This meant that she'd got her man, hook, line and sinker. [...] I got out my opera glasses to take a closer look at her method. Oh, it was very simple: first a quick look, then a smile, then a nod of the head that meant: 'Are you coming up?' But it was so subtle, so slight, so discreet, that you had to be pretty smart to do it as well as she did. I began to wonder if I could do it as well, that little movement of the head, up and down, bold and subtle. It really was very subtle, her little sign. I went to try it in front of the mirror. My dear, I did it better than her, I did it much better than her! [...] So I said to myself: 'Suppose I gave them the sign, me, an honest woman, do you think they would understand?' [...] It's stupid, I know, but I believe we have the souls of monkeys, women like us. Besides, I have it on good authority (it was a doctor who told me) that the brain of a monkey is very similar to ours. We always have to imitate someone. We imitate our husbands, when we still love them, in the first months of marriage, then it's our lovers that we imitate, then our girlfriends, then our priest if he's any good. We take on their way of thinking, their way of speaking, their words, their gestures, everything. It's stupid."

Extract from Guy de Maupassant's *The Sign*, source for *Une femme coquette*.

Une femme coquette
English: "A Flirtatious Woman"
Script: Hans Lucas (Jean-Luc Godard)
Camera: Hans Lucas
Editing: Hans Lucas
Producer: Jean-Luc Godard
Cast includes: Jean-Luc Godard,
Maria Lysandre, Roland Tolmatchoff
Format: 10 min, 16mm, b/w, short fiction

19 57

Tous les garçons s'appellent Patrick, a.k.a.
Charlotte et Véronique
English: *All Boys Are Called Patrick*
Script: Éric Rohmer
Camera: Michel Latouche
Sound: Jacques Maumont
Editing: Jean-Luc Godard, Cécile Decugis
Producer: Pierre Braunberger
Production: Les Films de la Pléiade
Cast includes: Nicole Berger,
Jean-Claude Brialy, Anne Colette
Format: 21 min, 35mm, b/w, short fiction

19 58

Une histoire d'eau
English: *A Story of Water*
Co-director: François Truffaut
Script: Jean-Luc Godard, François Truffaut
Camera: Michel Latouche
Sound: Jacques Maumont
Editing: Jean-Luc Godard
Producer: Pierre Braunberger
Production: Les Films de la Pléiade
Cast includes: Jean-Claude Brialy,
Caroline Dim
Format: 18 min, 35mm, b/w, short fiction

19
58

Charlotte et son Jules
English: *Charlotte and her Boyfriend*
Script: Jean-Luc Godard
Camera: Michel Latouche
Sound: Jacques Maumont
Editing: Jean-Luc Godard
Producer: Pierre Braunberger
Production: Les Films de la Pléiade
Cast includes: Jean-Paul Belmondo,
Gérard Blain, Anne Colette
Format: 20 min, 35mm, b/w, short fiction
(first distributed 1961)

19
60

À bout de souffle
English: *Breathless*
Script: Jean-Luc Godard,
from an outline by François Truffaut
Camera: Raoul Coutard
Sound: Jacques Maumont
Editing: Cécile Decugis, Lila Herman
Producer: Georges de Beauregard
Production: Société Nouvelle de
Cinématographie, Productions Georges
de Beauregard
Cast includes: Jean-Paul Belmondo,
Liliane David, Jean-Pierre Melville,
Jean Seberg
Format: 90 min, 35mm, b/w, fiction feature

19 60

Le Petit soldat
English: *The Little Soldier*
Script: Jean-Luc Godard
Camera: Raoul Coutard
Sound: Jacques Maumont
Editing: Agnès Guillemot,
Nadine Marquand, Lila Herman
Producer: Georges de Beauregard,
Carlo Ponti
Production: Productions Georges de
Beauregard/Société Nouvelle de
Cinématographie, Rome-Paris Films
Cast includes: Henri-Jacques Huet,
Anna Karina, Michel Subor, Laszlo Szabo
Format: 88 min, 35mm, b/w, fiction feature
(banned until 1963)

19 61

Une femme est une femme
English: *A Woman is a Woman*
Script: Jean-Luc Godard,
based on an idea from Geneviève Cluny
Camera: Raoul Coutard
Sound: Guy Villette
Editing: Agnès Guillemot, Lila Herman
Producer: Georges de Beauregard,
Carlo Ponti
Production: Rome-Paris Films
Cast includes: Jean-Paul Belmondo,
Jean-Claude Brialy, Catherine Demongeot,
Anna Karina
Format: 84 min, 35mm, colour, fiction feature

**19
62**

La Paresse (episode in *Les Sept péchés capitaux*)
English: *Sloth* (in *The Seven Capital Sins*)
Script: Jean-Luc Godard
Camera: Henri Decaë
Sound: Jean-Claude Marchetti,
Jean Labussière
Editing: Jacques Gaillard
Producer: Joseph Bergholz
Production: Films Gibé/Franco-London
Films/Titanus
Cast includes: Eddie Constantine,
Nicole Mirel
Format: 15 min, 35mm, b/w, short fiction

**19
62**

Vivre sa vie
English: *It's My Life*, a.k.a. *My Life to Live*
Script: Jean-Luc Godard
Camera: Raoul Coutard
Sound: Guy Villette
Editing: Agnès Guillemot
Producer: Pierre Braunberger
Production: Les Films de la Pléiade
Cast includes: Anna Karina, Peter Kassovitz,
André S Labarthe, Brice Parain
Format: 90 min, 35mm, b/w, fiction feature

19 63

Le Nouveau monde (episode in *RoGoPaG*)
English: *The New World*
(in *Let's Have a Brainwash*)
Script: Jean-Luc Godard
Camera: Jean Rabier
Sound: André Hervé
Editing: Agnès Guillemot, Lila Lakshmanan
Producer: Alfredo Bini
Production: Société Lyre
Cinématographique/Arco Film/Cineriz
Cast includes: Jean-Marc Bory,
Michel Delahaye, Jean-André Fieschi,
Alexandra Stewart
Format: 20 min, 35mm, b/w, short fiction

19 63

Les Carabiniers
English: *The Riflemen*, a.k.a. *The Soldiers*
Script: Jean-Luc Godard, Jean Gruault,
Roberto Rossellini, based on *I Carabinieri* by
Benjamin Joppolo
Camera: Raoul Coutard
Sound: Jacques Maumont, Bernard Orthion
Editing: Agnès Guillemot, Lila Lakshmanan
Producer: Georges de Beauregard,
Carlo Ponti
Production: Rome-Paris Films/Laetitia/Les
Films Marceau/Cocinor
Cast includes: Geneviève Galéa, Albert
Juross, Marino Masé, Catherine Ribeiro
Format: 80 min, 35mm, b/w, fiction feature

**19
63**

Le Grand escroc (episode in *Les Plus belles escroqueries du monde*)
English: *The Great Swindle* (in *World's Greatest Swindles*)
Script: Jean-Luc Godard
Camera: Raoul Coutard
Sound: André Hervé
Editing: Agnès Guillemot
Producer: Pierre Roustang
Production: Ulysse Productions/LUX-CCF/Primex Films/Vidès Cinematografica/Toho-Toawa/Caesar Film Productie
Cast includes: Charles Denner, Jean Seberg, Laszlo Szabo
Format: 25 min, 35mm, b/w, short fiction (released 1964)

**19
63**

Le Mépris
English: *Contempt*
Script: Jean-Luc Godard, from the novel *Il disprezzo* by Alberto Moravia
Camera: Raoul Coutard
Sound: William Sivel
Editing: Agnès Guillemot, Lila Lakshmanan
Producer: Joseph Levine, Carlo Ponti
Production: Rome-Paris Films/Les Films Concordia/Compagnia Cinematografica Champion
Cast includes: Brigitte Bardot, Fritz Lang, Jack Palance, Michel Piccoli
Format: 110 min, 35mm, colour, fiction feature

Bande à part
English: *Band of Outsiders*, a.k.a.
The Outsiders
Script: Jean-Luc Godard, based on
Fool's Gold by Dolores and Bert Hitchens
Camera: Raoul Coutard
Sound: René Levert, Antoine Bonfanti
Editing: Agnès Guillemot, Françoise Collin
Producer: Jean-Luc Godard
Production: Anouchka Films/Orsay Films
Cast includes: Claude Brasseur, Anna Karina,
Sami Frey, Ernest Menzer
Format: 95 min, 35mm, b/w, fiction feature

Une femme mariée
English: *The Married Woman*
Script: Jean-Luc Godard
Camera: Raoul Coutard
Sound: Antoine Bonfanti, René Levert,
Jacques Maumont
Editing: Agnès Guillemot, Françoise Collin
Producer: Jean-Luc Godard
Production: Anouchka Films/Orsay Films
Cast includes: Roger Leenhardt, Philippe
Leroy, Macha Méril, Bernard Noël
Format: 98 min, 35mm, b/w, fiction feature

Montparnasse-Levallois (episode in
Paris vu par...)
English: *Montparnasse-Levallois*
(in *Six in Paris*)
Script: Jean-Luc Godard
Camera: Albert Maysles
Sound: René Levert
Editing: Jacqueline Raynal
Producer: Barbet Schroeder
Production: Les Films du Losange/
Les Films du Cyprès
Cast includes: Serge Davri, Philippe Hiquilly,
Johanna Shimkus
Format: 18 min, 16mm, colour, short fiction

19
65

Alphaville,
une étrange aventure de Lemmy Caution
English: *Alphaville,*
a Strange Adventure of Lemmy Caution
Script: Jean-Luc Godard
Camera: Raoul Coutard
Sound: René Levert
Editing: Agnès Guillemot
Producer: André Michelin
Production: Chaumiane/Filmstudio
Cast includes: Eddie Constantine,
Anna Karina, Laszlo Szabo, Akim Tamiroff
Format: 98 min, 35mm, b/w, fiction feature

19
65

Pierrot le fou
English: *Pierrot Goes Wild*, a.k.a. *Crazy Pete*
Script: Jean-Luc Godard, from the novel
Obsession by Lionel White
Camera: Raoul Coutard
Sound: René Levert, Antoine Bonfanti
Editing: Françoise Collin, Andrée Choty
Producer: Georges de Beauregard,
Dino de Laurentiis
Production: Productions Georges de
Beauregard/Rome-Paris Films/Dino de
Laurentiis Cinematografica
Cast includes: Jean-Paul Belmondo,
Raymond Devos, Anna Karina, Dirk Sanders
Format: 110 min, 35mm, colour,
fiction feature

19
66

Masculin Féminin
English: *Masculine Feminine*
Script: Jean-Luc Godard, based on *Le Signe*
and *La Femme de Paul* by
Guy de Maupassant
Camera: Willy Kurant
Sound: René Levert, Antoine Bonfanti
Editing: Agnès Guillemot, Geneviève Bastid
Producer: Anatole Dauman
Production: Anouchka Films/Argos
Films/Svensk Filmindustri/Sandrews
Cast includes: Michel Debord, Chantal Goya,
Marlène Jobert, Jean-Pierre Léaud
Format: 110 min, 35mm, b/w, fiction feature

19 66

Made in USA
Script: Jean-Luc Godard, based on the novel
The Jugger by Richard Stark
Camera: Raoul Coutard
Sound: René Levert, Jacques Maumont
Editing: Agnès Guillemot,
Géneviève Letellier
Producer: Georges de Beauregard
Production: Anouchka Films/Rome-Paris
Films/SEPIC
Cast includes: Anna Karina, Philippe Labro,
Jean-Pierre Léaud, Laszlo Szabo
Format: 90 min, 35mm, colour, fiction feature

19 67

Deux ou trois choses que je sais d'elle
English: *Two or Three Things I Know*
About Her
Script: Jean-Luc Godard
Camera: Raoul Coutard
Sound: René Levert, Antoine Bonfanti
Editing: Françoise Collin, Chantal Delattre
Production: Anouchka Films/Argos Films/Les
Films du Carosse/Parc Film
Cast includes: Christophe Bourseiller,
Blandine Jeanson, Raoul Lévy, Marina Vlady
Format: 90 min, 35mm, colour,
fiction feature

1967

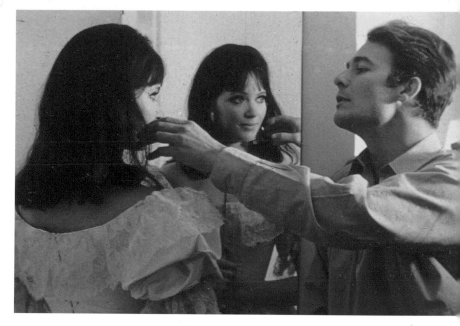

***Anticipation*, a.k.a. *L'Amour en l'an 2000*
(episode in *Le Plux vieux métier du monde*)**
English: *Love Through the Centuries*
(in *The Oldest Profession*)
Script: Jean-Luc Godard
Camera: Pierre Lhomme, Armand Marco
Editing: Agnès Guillemot,
Geneviève Letellier
Producer: Joseph Bergholz
Production: Francoriz Films/Les Films
Gibé/Rialto Films/Rizzoli Editore
Cast includes: Jacques Charrier,
Anna Karina, Jean-Pierre Léaud, Marilù Tolo
Format: 20 min, 35mm, colour, short fiction

1967

La Chinoise
English: "The Chinese Woman"
Script: Jean-Luc Godard
Camera: Raoul Coutard
Sound: René Levert, Antoine Bonfanti
Editing: Agnès Guillemot, Delphine Destons
Production: Anouchka Films/Les Productions
de la Guéville/Athos Films/Parc Films/
Simar Films
Cast includes: Juliet Berto, Omar Diop,
Jean-Pierre Léaud, Anne Wiazemsky
Format: 90 min, 35mm, colour, fiction feature

19 67

Caméra-oeil (episode in *Loin du Vietnam*)
English: *Camera-Eye* (in *Far From Vietnam*)
Script: Jean-Luc Godard
Camera: Armand Marco, Alain Levent
Sound: Antoine Bonfanti
Editing: Chris Marker,
Jacqueline Meppiel, Ragnar
Producer: Jean-Luc Godard, Chris Marker
Production: SLON/Sofracima
Cast includes: Jean-Luc Godard
Format: 15 min, 16mm, colour, essay

19 67

*L'Aller et retour andate e ritorno des
enfants prodigues dei figli prodighi,* a.k.a.
L'Amour (episode in *Vangelo 70,* a.k.a.
Amore et Rabbia, a.k.a. *La Contestation*)
English: "Love" (in *Love and Anger*)
Script: Jean-Luc Godard
Camera: Alain Levent, Armand Marco
Sound: Guy Villette, Antoine Bonfanti
Editing: Agnès Guillemot, Delphine Desfons
Producer: Carlo Lizzani
Production: Castoro Films/Anouchka Films
Cast includes: Nino Castelnuovo, Christine
Guého, Catherine Jourdon, Paolo Pozzesi
Format: 26 min, 35mm, colour, short fiction

19 67

Week-end
English: *Weekend*
Script: Jean-Luc Godard
Camera: Raoul Coutard
Sound: René Levert, Antoine Bonfanti
Editing: Agnès Guillemot, Odile Fayot
Production: Films Copernic/Ascot
Cineraïd/Comacico/Lira Films
Cast includes: Mireille Darc, Jean-Pierre
Kalfon, Jean-Pierre Léaud, Jean Yanne
Format: 95 min, 35mm, colour,
fiction feature

19 68

Le Gai savoir
English: *The Joy of Knowledge*, a.k.a.
Joyful Wisdom
Script: Jean-Luc Godard, loosely inspired by
Rousseau's *Émile*
Camera: Georges Leclerc
Editing: Germaine Cohen
Production: originally ORTF, later Anouchka
Films/Gambit/Bavaria Atelier
Cast includes: Juliet Berto, Jean-Pierre Léaud
Format: 95 min, 35mm, colour, essay
(first distributed in 1969)

1968

Ciné-tracts
Camera: Jean-Luc Godard
Editing: film edited in camera
Format: 2-4 min each, 16mm, b/w (it is
generally agreed that tract numbers 7, 8, 9,
10, 12, 13, 14, 15, 16, 23 and 40 were made
by, or in collaboration with, Godard. He also
acted as technical advisor on Gérard
Fromanger's *Ciné-tract No.1968*, a.k.a.
Le Rouge)

1968

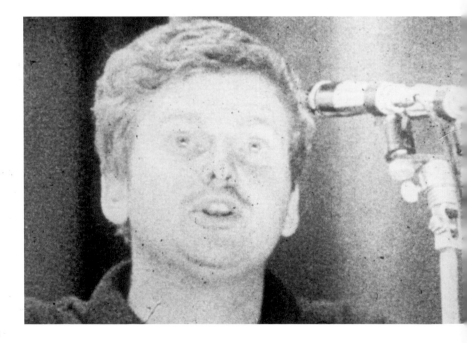

Un film comme les autres
English: *A Film Like Any Other*
Camera: William Lubtchansky,
Jean-Luc Godard
Editing: Jean-Luc Godard
Production: Anouchka Films
Cast includes: three militant students from
Nanterre and two workers from the Flins
Renault factory (incorporates footage of
May 1968 shot by the ARC group)
Format: 100 min, 16mm, colour and
b/w, essay

19 68

One Plus One, a.k.a. *Sympathy for the Devil*
Script: Jean-Luc Godard
Camera: Tony Richmond
Sound: Arthur Bradburn, Derek Ball
Editing: Ken Rowles, Agnès Guillemot
Producer: Iain Quarrier, Michael Pearson
Production: Cupid Productions
Cast includes: The Rolling Stones,
Frankie Dymon Jnr, Iain Quarrier,
Anne Wiazemsky
Format: 99 min, 35mm, colour, essay

19 68

One American Movie, a.k.a. *One A.M.*
Script: Jean-Luc Godard
Camera: Donn Pennebaker, Richard Leacock
Sound: Mary Lampson, Robert Leacock,
Kate Taylor
Production: Leacock-Pennebaker Inc
Cast includes: Jefferson Airplane,
Eldridge Cleaver, Tom Hayden, Rip Torn
Format: Unfinished. A 90-minute
compilation of the footage shot for
One A.M., and of a film being shot on
the making of *One A.M.*, was edited by
Pennebaker and released as *One P.M.*
in 1971.

19
69

British Sounds, a.k.a. *See You at Mao*
Co-director: Jean-Henri Roger
Script: Jean-Luc Godard, Jean-Henri Roger
Camera: Charles Stewart
Sound: Fred Sharp
Editing: Christine Aya
Producer: Irving Teitelbaum, Kenith Trodd
Production: Kestrel Productions for
London Weekend Television
Cast includes: Michael Lonsdale, students
from Oxford and Essex, British Motor Co.
production line workers (Cowley, Oxford),
militant workers from Dagenham
Format: 52 min, 16mm, colour, essay

19
69

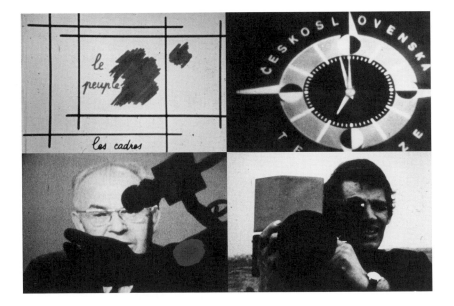

Pravda
Co-director: Paul Bourron, Jean-Henri Roger
Script: Groupe Dziga Vertov
Editing: Jean-Luc Godard, Christine Aya
Producer: Claude Nedjar
Production: Centre Européen
Cinéma-Radio-Télévision
Format: 58 min, 16mm, colour, essay

19 69

Vent d'est

English: *Wind From the East*, a.k.a.
East Wind
Co-director: Jean-Pierre Gorin,
Gérard Martin
Script: Daniel Cohn-Bendit, Jean-Luc Godard,
Jean-Pierre Gorin
Camera: Mario Vulpiani
Sound: Antonio Ventura,
Carlo Diotalevi
Editing: Christine Aya
Production: CCC/Poli Film/Film
Kunst/Anouchka Films
Cast includes: Daniel Cohn-Bendit, Glauber
Rocha, Gian Maria Volonte,
Anne Wiazemsky
Format: 100 min, 16mm, colour, essay

19 70

Lotte in Italia

French title: *Luttes en Italie*
English: *Struggles in Italy*
Co-director: Jean-Pierre Gorin
Script: Groupe Dziga Vertov
Camera: Armand Marco
Sound: Antoine Bonfanti
Editing: Christine Aya
Production: Anouchka Films/Cosmoseion for
Radiotelevisione Italiana
Cast includes: Christiana Tullio Altan,
Jérôme Hinstin, Paolo Pozzesi,
Anne Wiazemsky
Format: 76 min, 16mm, colour, essay

19
71

Vladimir et Rosa
English: *Vladimir and Rosa*
Co-director: Jean-Pierre Gorin
Script: Groupe Dziga Vertov
Camera: Armand Marco, Gérard Martin
Sound: Antoine Bonfanti
Editing: Christine Aya, Chantal Colomer
Production: Munich Tele-Pool/
Grove Press Evergreen Films
Cast includes: Yves Alfonso, Jean-Luc
Godard, Jean-Pierre Gorin, Anne Wiazemsky
Format: 103 min, 16mm, colour, essay

19
72

 TOUT VA BIEN

Tout va bien
English: *All's Well*
Co-director: Jean-Pierre Gorin
Script: Jean-Luc Godard, Jean-Pierre Gorin
Camera: Armand Marco
Sound: Bernard Orthion, Antoine Bonfanti
Editing: Kenout Peltier
Producer: Alain Coiffier, Jean-Luc Godard,
Jean-Pierre Rassam
Production: Anouchka Films/Vicco
Film/Empire Film
Cast includes: Vittorio Caprioli, Jane Fonda,
Yves Montand, Jean Pignol
Format: 95 min, 35mm, colour,
fiction feature

19
72

Letter to Jane
Co-director: Jean-Pierre Gorin
Script: Jean-Luc Godard, Jean-Pierre Gorin
Camera: Jean-Luc Godard, Jean-Pierre Gorin
Editing: Jean-Luc Godard, Jean-Pierre Gorin
Producer: Jean-Luc Godard,
Jean-Pierre Gorin
Format: 52 min, 16mm, colour, essay

19
74

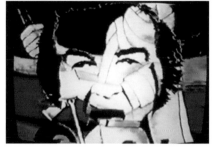

Ici et Ailleurs
English: *Here and Elsewhere*
Co-director: Anne-Marie Miéville
(Jean-Pierre Gorin for the footage from the
abandoned Groupe Dziga Vertov project,
Jusqu'à la victoire)
Script: Jean-Luc Godard,
Anne-Marie Miéville
Camera: William Lubtchansky (Armand
Marco for the original rushes of *Jusqu'à
la victoire*)
Editing: Jean-Luc Godard,
Anne-Marie Miéville
Producer: Jean-Luc Godard,
Anne-Marie Miéville, Jean-Pierre Rassam
Production: Sonimage/INA/Gaumont
Cast includes: Jean-Pierre Bamberger
Format: 50 min, 16mm, colour, essay
(first distributed in 1976)

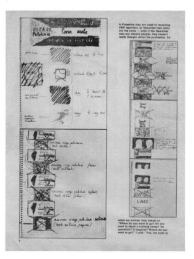

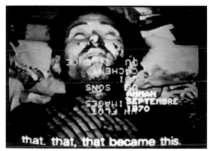

that. that. that became this.

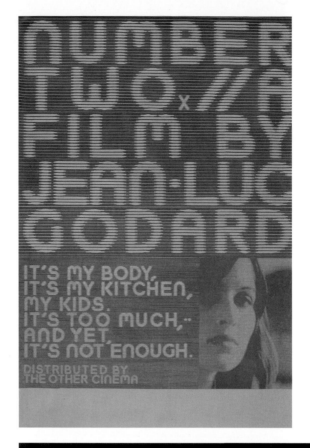

Numéro Deux
English: *Number Two*
Script: Jean-Luc Godard,
Anne-Marie Miéville
Camera: William Lubtchansky (film),
Gérard Martin (video)
Technicians: Milka Assaf, Gérard Martin,
Gérard Teissèdre
Sound: Jean-Pierre Ruh
Editing: Jean-Luc Godard,
Anne-Marie Miéville
Producer: Georges de Beauregard,
Jean-Pierre Rassam
Production: Sonimage/Bela/SNC
Cast includes: Sandrine Battistella,
Pierre Oudry, Alexandre Rignault,
Rachel Stefanopoli
Format: 88 min, 35mm and video, colour,
fiction feature

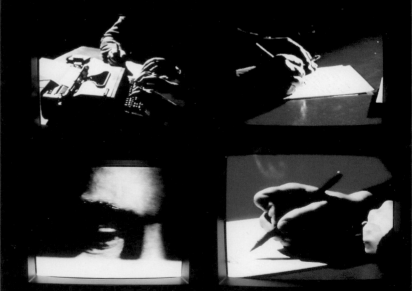

Comment ça va?
English: *How Is It Going?*
Co-director: Anne-Marie Miéville
Script: Jean-Luc Godard,
Anne-Marie Miéville
Camera: William Lubtchansky
Editing: Jean-Luc Godard,
Anne-Marie Miéville
Producer: Jean-Luc Godard,
Anne-Marie Miéville, Jean-Pierre Rassam
Production: Sonimage/Bela/SNC
Cast includes: Michel Marot,
Anne-Marie Miéville
Format: 78 min, 16mm and video, colour
(first distributed in 1978)

19 76

Six fois deux (Sur et sous la communication)
English: "Six Times Two (On and Under Communication)"
Co-director: Anne-Marie Miéville
Script: Jean-Luc Godard, Anne-Marie Miéville
Camera: William Lubtchansky, Dominique Chapuis
Technicians: Henri False, Joël Mellier, Philippe Rony, Gérard Teissèdre
Editing: Jean-Luc Godard, Anne-Marie Miéville
Producer: Michel Raux, Jean-Luc Godard
Production: Sonimage/INA for FR3
Format: 12x50 min, video, colour, 12-episode television series: 1a: *Y'a personne*, 1b: *Louison*, 2a: *Leçons de choses*, 2b: *Jean-Luc*, 3a: *Photos et cie*, 3b: *Marcel*, 4a: *Pas d'histoire*, 4b: *Nanas*, 5a: *Nous trois*, 5b: *René(e)s*, 6a: *Avant et après*, 6b: *Jacqueline et Ludovic*

19 78

Faut pas rêver
English: "Dream On"
Camera: Jean-Luc Godard
Editing: Jean-Luc Godard
Cast includes: 'Camille', voice of Anne-Marie Miéville
Format: 2 min, video, colour (illustration of a Patrick Juvet song, broadcast in 1978 on the programme *On ne manque pas d'airs*)

Mother:	*Are you going to Olivia's this afternoon?*
Daughter:	*Yeah, sure!*
Mother:	*Have you done the exercises she asked you to do?*
Daughter:	*Well, yes, everything!*
Mother:	*Yes, because you've got to work a little in between classes, the classes alone aren't enough.*
Daugher:	*Yeah... but God... I practice my scales anyway and I study anyway!*
Mother:	*Did you go swimming this morning?*
Daughter:	*Uh-huh*
Mother:	*What did you do? Competitive [...] things like that?*
Daughter:	*We swam a few kilometres, it took ages... You know, it was... it's a 25 metre swimming-pool so when you do twenty lengths... it takes a while.*
Mother:	*For the... er... modern competition system.*
Daughter:	*There were only four of us who managed a kilometre.*
Mother:	*Why do you do it then, do you like it?*
Daughter:	*Yeah, I suppose... I don't... I dunno... Well, I managed 900 metres, I had another... 100 metres to do, and after that, you forget you're swimming, so...*
Mother:	*Okay, we should put away the crockery from time to time, because it's all very well leaving it to dry, but it mounts up, and then... there's... there's loads and it's always me who puts it away, I'm sick of it!*
Daughter:	*Listen, I'll do it later, I've got to watch this.*
Mother:	*You always say you'll do it later, you watch TV, you've always got something to do and you don't do it, and I end up doing it! It's not fair!*
Daughter:	*That's not true...*
Mother:	*Yes it is!*

France/tour/détour/deux/enfants
English: *France/Tour/Detour/Two/Children*
Co-director: Anne-Marie Miéville
Script: Jean-Luc Godard,
Anne-Marie Miéville, loosely based on
G Bruno's *Le Tour de la France par Deux
Enfants: Devoir et Patrie* (1884)
Camera: William Lubtchansky,
Dominique Chapuis, Philippe Rony
Technician: Pierre Binggeli
Editing: Jean-Luc Godard,
Anne-Marie Miéville
Production: Sonimage/INA for Antenne 2
Cast includes: Betty Berr, Albert Dray,
Arnaud Martin, Camille Virolleaud
Format: 12x26 min, video, colour,
12-episode television series

Scénario vidéo de Sauve qui peut (la vie)
English: "Video Scenario for *Sauve qui peut
(la vie)*"
Script: Jean-Luc Godard
Editing: Jean-Luc Godard
Production: Sonimage/
Télévision Suisse Romande
Cast includes: photographs of Isabelle
Huppert, Miou-Miou, Werner Herzog
Format: 20 min, video, colour, essay

19 80

Sauve qui peut (la vie)
English: *Every Man for Himself*,
a.k.a. *Slow Motion*
Script: Jean-Claude Carrière,
Anne-Marie Miéville
Camera: Renata Berta, William Lubtchansky,
Jean-Bernard Menoud
Sound: Jacques Maumont, Luc Yersin,
Oscar Stellavox
Editing: Jean-Luc Godard,
Anne-Marie Miéville
Producer: Jean-Luc Godard, Alain Sarde
Production: Sara Films/MK2/Saga
Productions/Sonimage/CNC/ZDF/SSR/ORF
Cast includes: Nathalie Baye,
Jacques Dutronc, Isabelle Huppert,
Cécile Tanner
Format: 87 min, 35mm, colour, fiction feature

19 81

*Passion, le travail et l'amour: introduction à
un scénario, a.k.a. Troisième état du
scénario du film Passion*
English: "*Passion*, the Work and Love:
Introduction to a Script"
Script: Jean-Luc Godard
Editing: Jean-Luc Godard
Production: Sonimage
Cast includes: Jean-Claude Carrière,
Isabelle Huppert, Jerzy Radziwilowicz,
Hanna Schygulla
Format: 30 min, video, colour, essay
(for a description of this little seen work,
see *Cahiers du cinéma*, May 1982)

19 82

Lettre à Freddy Buache
English: *Letter to Freddy Buache*
Script: Jean-Luc Godard
Camera: Jean-Bernard Menoud
Sound: François Musy
Editing: Jean-Luc Godard
Production: Sonimage/Film et Vidéo
Production Lausanne
Cast includes: Jean-Luc Godard
Format: 11 min, video transferred to 35mm,
colour, essay

19 82

Passion
Script: Jean-Luc Godard
Camera: Raoul Coutard
Sound: François Musy
Editing: Jean-Luc Godard
Producer: Alain Sarde
Production: Sara Films/Sonimage/Films
A2/Film et Vidéo Production SA/
SSR Télévision Suisse
Cast includes: Isabelle Huppert,
Michel Piccoli, Jerzy Radziwilowicz,
Hanna Schygulla
Format: 87 min, 35mm, colour, fiction feature

19 82

Scénario du film *Passion*
English: "Scenario of the Film *Passion*"
Script: Jean-Luc Godard
Collaboration: Anne-Marie Miéville,
Pierre Binggeli, Jean-Bernard Menoud
Production: Télévision Romande/JLG Films
Cast includes: Jean-Luc Godard,
Isabelle Huppert, Jerzy Radziwilowicz,
Hanna Schygulla
Format: 54 min, video, colour, essay

19 82

***Changer d'image*, a.k.a. *Lettre à la bien-
aimée* (episode in *Le changement à plus
d'un titre*)**
English: "Change of Image"
(in "Change in More Than Name")
Script: Jean-Luc Godard
Production: INA/Sonimage
Cast includes: Jean-Luc Godard,
Jacques Probst, voice of
Anne-Marie Miéville
Format: 10 min, video, colour, essay

1983

Prénom Carmen
English: *First Name: Carmen*
Script: Anne-Marie Miéville
Camera: Raoul Coutard
Sound: François Musy, Oscar Stellavox
Editing: Jean-Luc Godard,
Suzanne Lang-Villar
Producer: Alain Sarde
Production: Sara Films/JLG Films/Films A2
Cast includes: Jacques Bonnaffé,
Maruschka Detmers, Hyppolite Girardot,
Myriem Roussel
Format: 84 min, 35mm, colour,
fiction feature

1983

*Petites notes à propos du film Je vous
salue, Marie*
English: "Little Notes on the Film *Je vous
salue, Marie*"
Script: Jean-Luc Godard
Camera: Jean-Luc Godard
Editing: Jean-Luc Godard
Production: JLG Films
Cast includes: Jean-Luc Godard, Myriem
Roussel, Thierry Rode, Anne-Marie Miéville
Format: 25 min, video, colour, essay

19 85

Je vous salue, Marie
English: *Hail Mary*
Script: Jean-Luc Godard
Camera: Jean-Bernard Menoud,
Jacques Firmann
Sound: François Musy
Editing: Jean-Luc Godard
Production: Pégase Films/JLG Films/Sara
Films/Channel 4/Gaumont/
SSR Télévision Suisse Romande
Cast includes: Juliette Binoche,
Philippe Lacoste, Thierry Rode,
Myriem Roussel
Format: 72 min, 35mm, colour, fiction feature

Détective
Script: Anne-Marie Miéville, Alain Sarde,
Philippe Setbon
Camera: Bruno Nuytten
Sound: Pierre Gamet, François Musy
Editing: Marllyne Dubreuil
Producer: Alain Sarde
Production: Sara Films/JLG Films
Cast includes: Nathalie Baye,
Claude Brasseur, Alain Cuny,
Johnny Hallyday
Format: 95 min, 35mm, colour, fiction feature

19 85

Soft and Hard (Soft Talk On a Hard Subject Between Two Friends)
Co-director: Anne-Marie Miéville
Script: Jean-Luc Godard,
Anne-Marie Miéville
Video: Pierre Binggeli
Editing: Jean-Luc Godard,
Anne-Marie Miéville
Producer: Tony Kirkhope
Production: JLG Films/
Deptford Beach Productions for Channel 4
Cast includes: Jean-Luc Godard,
Anne-Marie Miéville
Format: 52 min, video, colour, essay

19 86

Grandeur et décadence d'un petit commerce de cinema, a.k.a. *Chantons en choeur*
English: *Grandeur and Decadence of A Small-Time Filmmaker,* a.k.a. *The Rise and Fall of a Small Film Company*
Script: Jean-Luc Godard, from the novel *The Soft Centre (Chantons en choeur)* by James Hadley Chase
Camera: Caroline Champetier
Sound: François Musy, Pierre-Alain Besse
Editing: Jean-Luc Godard
Producer: Pierre Grimblat
Production: Hamster Productions/TF1/
Télévision Suisse Romande/RTL/JLG Films
Cast includes: Jean-Luc Godard, Jean-Pierre Léaud, Jean-Pierre Mocky, Marie Valéra
Format: 90 min, video, colour, telefilm (broadcast in the 'Série Noire' series on TF1 in May 1986)

19 86

Meetin' WA, a.k.a. *Meeting Woody Allen*
Script: Jean-Luc Godard
Editing: Jean-Luc Godard
Sound: François Musy
Production: JLG Films
Cast includes: Jean-Luc Godard,
Woody Allen, voice of Annette Insdorf
Format: 26 min, video, colour, essay

19 87

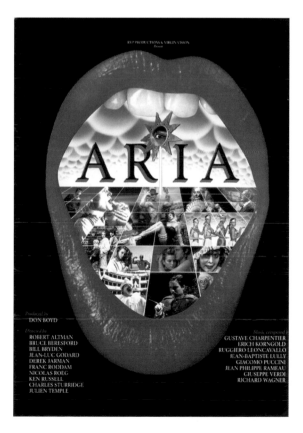

Armide (episode in *Aria*)
Script: Jean-Luc Godard
Camera: Caroline Champetier
Sound: François Musy
Editing: Jean-Luc Godard
Producer: Don Boyd
Production: Boyd's Company/Lightyear
Entertainment/RVP Productions/
Virgin Vision
Cast includes: Valérie Alain, Luke Corre,
Jacques Neuville, Marion Petersen
Format: 12 min, 35mm, colour, short fiction

19 87

Soigne ta droite, a.k.a.
Une place sur la terre comme au ciel
English: *Keep Your Right Up*
Script: Jean-Luc Godard
Camera: Caroline Champetier
Sound: François Musy
Editing: Jean-Luc Godard, C Benoit
Producer: Jean-Luc Godard,
Ruth Waldburger
Production: Gaumont/JLG Films/Xanadu
Films/RTSR
Cast includes: Jane Birkin, Michel Galabru,
Les Rita Mitsouko, Jacques Villeret
Format: 81 min, 35mm, colour, fiction feature

19 87

King Lear
Script: Jean-Luc Godard
Camera: Sophie Maintigneux
Sound: François Musy
Editing: Jean-Luc Godard
Producer: Yoram Globus, Menahem Golan
Production: Cannon
Cast includes: Woody Allen, Burgess
Meredith, Molly Ringwald, Peter Sellars
Format: 90 min, 35mm, colour, fiction feature

**19
88**

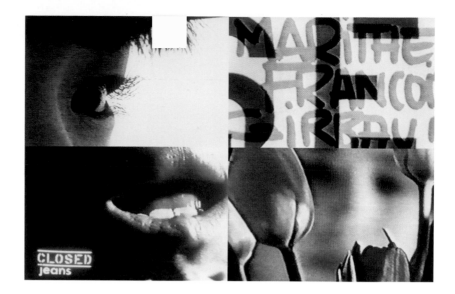

Closed
Camera: Caroline Champetier
Sound: François Musy
Editing: Jean-Luc Godard
Production: JLG Films/
Marithé et François Girbaud Design
Cast includes: Girbaud models Keshi,
Suzanne Lanza, Luca, Marc Parent
Format: 10x15 sec, video, colour,
television advertisements

**19
88**

On s'est tous défilé
English: "We All Stole Away"
Script: Jean-Luc Godard
Camera: Caroline Champetier
Sound: François Musy
Editing: Jean-Luc Godard
Production: Marithé et François
Girbaud Design
Cast includes: Marithé and François
Girbaud, models presenting the 1988
MFG collection
Format: 13 min, video, colour, essay

1983

Puissance de la parole
English: *The Power of Words*
Script: Jean-Luc Godard
Camera: Caroline Champetier
Sound: François Musy, Pierre Binggeli
Editing: Jean-Luc Godard
Production: France Télécom/
JLG Films/Gaumont
Cast includes: Lydia Andréi, Jean Bouise,
Laurence Côte, Jean-Michel Iribarren
Format: 25 min, video, colour, essay

1983

Le Dernier mot
(episode in *Les Français vus par...*)
English: *The Last Word*
(in "The French Seen By...")
Script: Jean-Luc Godard
Camera: Pierre Binggeli
Sound: Pierre Camus, François Musy
Editing: Jean-Luc Godard
Producer: Anne-Marie Miéville
Production: Erato Films/Socpresse/JLG
Films/*Le Figaro magazine*/Antenne 2
Cast includes: André Marcon,
Hanns Zischler, Catherine Aymerie,
Pierre Amoyal
Format: 12 min, video, colour, short fiction

19 89

Histoire(s) du cinéma (initial versions of chapters 1A, *Toutes les histories,* and 1B, *Une Histoire seule*)
English: *Histories of the Cinema* (1A "All the Histories", 1B "A Solitary History")
Script: Jean-Luc Godard
Video: Pierre Binggeli
Sound: Jean-Luc Godard, Pierre-Alain Besse, François Musy
Editing: Jean-Luc Godard
Producer: Jean-Luc Godard, Ruth Waldburger
Production: CNC/Canal Plus/La Sept/FR3/Gaumont/JLG Films/Vega Films/RTSR
Format: 2x52 min, video, colour, essay (first broadcast on Canal Plus in May 1989, these chapters, especially 1B, were significantly re-edited over the course of the 1990s)

19 89

Le Rapport Darty
English: "The Darty Report"
Co-director: Anne-Marie Miéville
Script: Jean-Luc Godard, Anne-Marie Miéville
Camera: Hervé Duhamel
Sound: Pierre-Alain Besse, François Musy
Editing: Jean-Luc Godard, Anne-Marie Miéville
Production: Gaumont/JLG Films
Cast includes: voices of Jean-Luc Godard and Anne-Marie Miéville
Format: 50 min, video, colour, essay

19 90

Nouvelle Vague

English: *New Wave*
Script: Jean-Luc Godard
Camera: William Lubtchansky
Sound: Pierre-Alain Besse, Henri Morelle,
François Musy
Editing: Jean-Luc Godard
Producer: Alain Sarde
Production: Sara Films/Périphéria/Canal
Plus/Véga Film/Télévision Suisse
Romande/Antenne 2/CNC/DFI/Sofica
Investimage/Sofica Creations
Cast includes: Alain Delon, Domiziana
Giordano, Roland Amstutz, Laurence Côte
Format: 89 min, 35mm, colour, fiction
feature (the soundtrack of this film was
released by ECM Records in 1997 as a
two-CD set)

19 91

L'Enfance de l'art

**(episode in *Comment vont les enfants*,
a.k.a. *"...et les gosses dans tout ça?"*)**
English: *The Childhood of Art*
(in *How Are the Kids?*)
Co-director: Anne-Marie Miéville
Script: Jean-Luc Godard,
Anne-Marie Miéville
Camera: Sophie Maintigneux
Sound: Pierre-Alain Besse
Editing: Jean-Luc Godard
Production: JLG Films/UNICEF
Cast includes: Nathalie Kadem,
Antoine Reyes, Michel Boupoil, Denis Vallas
Format: 8 min, 35mm, colour, essay

**19
91**

Allemagne année 90 neuf zéro
English: *Germany Year 90 Nine Zero*
Script: Jean-Luc Godard
Camera: Christophe Pollock
Sound: Pierre-Alain Besse, François Musy
Editing: Jean-Luc Godard
Producer: Nicole Ruelle
Production: Antenne 2/Brainstorm/
Gaumont/Périphéria
Cast includes: Eddie Constantine, Hanns
Zischler, Claudia Michelsen, Nathalie Kadem
Format: 62 min, 35mm, colour, essay

Pour Thomas Wainggai
(episode in *Écrire contre l'oubli*)
English: "For Thomas Wainggai"
(in "Against Oblivion",
a.k.a. "Lest We Forget")
Co-director: Anne-Marie Miéville
Script: Jean-Luc Godard,
Anne-Marie Miéville
Camera: Jean-Marc Fabre
Sound: Pierre-Alain Besse, François Musy
Editing: Jean-Luc Godard
Production: Amnesty International PRI/
Vega Film
Cast includes: André Rousselet,
Véronique Tillmann
Format: 3 min, video, colour, documentary
(broadcast in December 1991 on all French
channels apart from TF1)

19 93

Hélas pour moi
English: *Oh, Woe Is Me*
Script: Jean-Luc Godard
Camera: Caroline Champetier
Sound: François Musy, Pierre-Alain Besse
Editing: Jean-Luc Godard
Producer: Alain Sarde
Production: Vega Film/Les Films Alain
Sarde/Canal Plus/Télévision Suisse Romande/
Périphéria
Cast includes: Marc Betton, Roland Blanche,
Gérard Depardieu, Laurence Masliah
Format: 84 min, 35mm, colour, fiction feature

19 93

Les Enfants jouent à la Russie
English: *The Kids Play Russian*
Script: Jean-Luc Godard
Camera: Caroline Champetier
Sound: Stéphane Thiébaud
Editing: Jean-Luc Godard
Producer: Alessandro Cecconi, Ira Barmak,
Ruth Waldburger
Production: Worldvision Enterprises
(N.Y.)/Cecco Films/RTR/Vega Film/JLG Films
Cast includes: Bernard Eisenschitz,
Jean-Luc Godard, André S Labarthe,
Laszlo Szabo
Format: 63 min, video, colour, essay

19
93

Je vous salue, Sarajevo
English: "Hail, Sarajevo"
Script: Jean-Luc Godard
Editing: Jean-Luc Godard
Format: 2 min, video, colour, essay

19
95

JLG/JLG: autoportrait de décembre
English: *JLG/JLG: Self-Portrait in December*
Script: Jean-Luc Godard
Camera: Yves Pouliquen
Sound: Pierre-Alain Besse
Editing: Jean-Luc Godard,
Catherine Cormon
Production: Périphéria/Gaumont
Cast includes: Jean-Luc Godard, Denis Jadot,
André S Labarthe, Geneviève Pasquier
Format: 62 min, 35mm, colour, essay

19
95

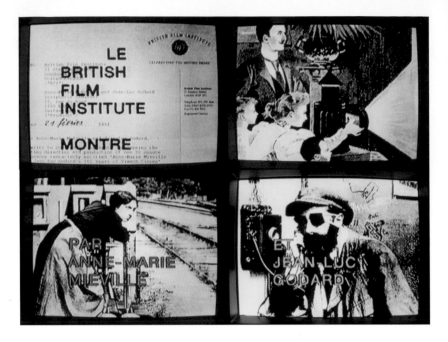

2x50 ans de cinéma français
English: *2x50 Years of French Cinema*
Co-director: Anne-Marie Miéville
Script: Jean-Luc Godard,
Anne-Marie Miéville
Camera: Isabelle Czajka
Sound: Stéphane Thiebaud
Editing: Jean-Luc Godard
Producer: Colin MacCabe, Bob Last
Production: British Film Institute/Périphéria
Cast includes: Jean-Luc Godard,
Estelle Grynspan, Michel Piccoli,
Cécile Reigher
Format: 49 min, video, colour, essay

19
96

Untitled
Script: Jean-Luc Godard
Editing: Jean-Luc Godard
Format: 3 min and 1 min, video, colour
(two montage sequences broadcast on
France 2 in the framework of the
programme *Le Cercle de Minuit* in
January 1996)

1996

1996

For Ever Mozart
Script: Jean-Luc Godard
Camera: Christophe Pollock
Sound: François Musy
Editing: Jean-Luc Godard
Producer: Alain Sarde
Production: Avventura Films/Périphéria/Vega
Film/CEC Rhône-Alpes/France 2 Cinéma/
Canal Plus/CNC/TSR/Eurimages/DFI/
ECM Records
Cast includes: Bérangère Allaux,
Madeleine Assas, Ghalya Lacroix,
Vicky Messica
Format: 85 min, 35mm, colour, fiction feature

Adieu au TNS
English: "Farewell to the Théâtre National
de Strasbourg"
Script: Jean-Luc Godard
Editing: Jean-Luc Godard
Cast: Jean-Luc Godard
Format: video, colour, essay

Farewell to the TNS

Good evening Ladies and Gents too
The following is the fond adieu
Of one who homeless vainly erred
In hope upon this stage to find
A friendly shelter in the Word

Receive, young friends, with open mind
The sad tale of the undersigned
Whose quest to save a lost princess
Concluded thus in tragedy
Before the doors of the TNS

The Fool believed most fervently
That should the damsel Liberty
In dismal Europe still survive
Her heart and soul by actors' speech
Would magically be kept alive

The finest texts their minds to reach
And pictures that their eyes might teach
With love were sent but coldly spurned
In silence and indifference
Each gift to sender was returned

Extract from text read by Godard

19 96

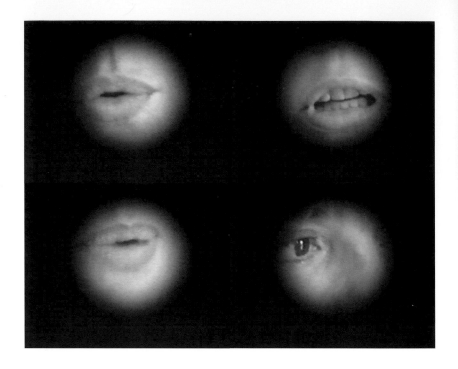

Plus Oh!, a.k.a. **Plus Haut!**
English: "Higher Still"
Camera: Jean-Luc Godard
Editing: Jean-Luc Godard
Cast: France Gall
Format: 4 min, video, colour, music video

19 98

Histoire(s) du cinéma
English: *Histories of the Cinema*
Script: Jean-Luc Godard
Editing: Jean-Luc Godard
Production: Gaumont/Périphéria
Cast includes: Juliette Binoche, Alain Cuny, Serge Daney, Julie Delpy
Format: 214 min, video, colour, 8-part series of essays:
1A *Toutes les histoires*/"All the Stories" (51 min)
1B *Une histoire seule*/"A Solitary History" (42 min)
2A *Seul le cinéma*/"The Cinema Alone" (26 min)
2B *Fatale beauté*/"Fatal Beauty' (28 min)
3A *La Monnaie de l'absolu*/"The Twilight of the Absolute" (26 min)
3B *Une vague nouvelle*/"A New Wave" (27 min)
4A *Le Contrôle de l'univers*/"The Control of the Universe" (27 min)
4B *Les Signes parmi nous*/"The Signs Amongst Us" (38 min)
(Gallimard published a box set of four art books derived from the
series in 1998. A remixed version of the soundtrack was released by
ECM Records on five audio CDs in 1999, accompanied by four art
books with text from the soundtrack given in French, German,
and English.)

19 99

The Old Place
Co-director: Anne-Marie Miéville
Script: Jean-Luc Godard,
Anne-Marie Miéville
Editing: Jean-Luc Godard,
Anne-Marie Miéville
Producer: Mary Lea Bandy, Colin MacCabe
Production: Museum of Modern Art,
New York/Périphéria
Format: 49 min, video, colour, essay

20 00

L'Origine du vingt et unième siècle, a.k.a
De l'origine du vingt et unième siècle
(pour moi)
English: "The Origin of the
Twenty-First Century"
Script:: Jean-Luc Godard
Camera: Julien Hirsch
Sound: François Musy
Editing: Jean-Luc Godard
Production: Canal Plus/Vega Film
Format: 15 min, video, colour, essay

20 01

Éloge de l'amour
English: *In Praise of Love*
Script: Jean-Luc Godard
Camera: Julien Hirsch, Christophe Pollock
Sound: François Musy, Christian Monheim
Editing: Jean-Luc Godard
Producer: Alain Sarde, Ruth Waldburger
Production: Avventura Films/Périphéria/
Canal Plus/Arte/Vega Film/TSR
Cast includes: Bruno Putzulu, Cécile Camp,
Jean Davy, Françoise Verny
Format: 98 min, 35mm and video, b/w and
colour, fiction feature

20 02

Dans le noir du temps (episode in *Ten
Minutes Older: The Cello*)
English: "In the Darkness of Time"
Script: Anne-Marie Miéville
Camera: Julien Hirsch
Sound: François Musy
Editing: Jean-Luc Godard,
Anne-Marie Miéville
Song: Anne-Marie Miéville
Producer: Ulrich Felsberg,
Nicolas McClintock, Nigel Thomas
Production: Matador Pictures/
Odyssey Films/Périphéria/Road Movies
Format: 10 min, video, colour, essay

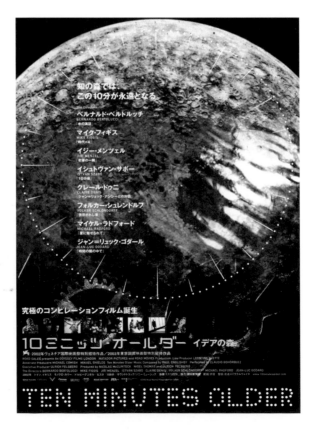

20
02

  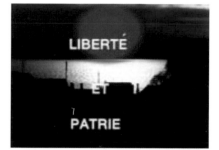

Liberté et Patrie
English: "Freedom and Fatherland"
Co-director: Anne-Marie Miéville
Script: Jean-Luc Godard,
Anne-Marie Miéville
Producer: Ruth Waldburger
Production: Vega Film/Périphéria
Format: 16 min, video, colour, short fiction

WORK IN PROGRESS:

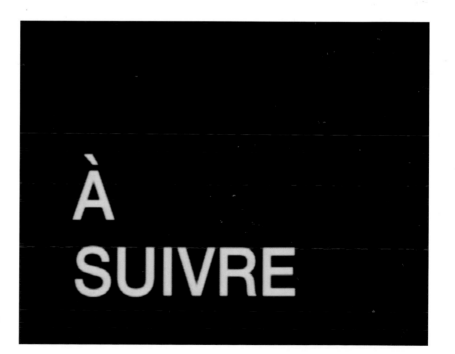

Notre Musique
"Our Music"
A collaboration with Manfred Eicher of
ECM Records.

Champ contre champ
"Shot, Counter Shot"
A short film about the 11th district of Paris
for a collective film about the city.

Collage de France
"Collage of France"
A multi-media installation at the Pompidou
Centre, Paris, planned for Autumn 2004.

WORK AND WORKS

WORK
AND WORKS

The six chapters that comprise this first section offer different ways of approaching the Godard corpus in its entirety. In particular, they explore the continuities (and discontinuities) of Godard's work, how it has been established as a corpus, and the complex links between Godard's working practices and the works produced. The films discussed are various, but a common set of related questions are addressed, either implicitly or explicitly. For example, what actually makes Godard such a different filmmaker? How does he engage with the present and contemporary events? To what degree is he essentially a collaborative artist? What is the cultural status of Godard's work, granted that he works with institutions and has precise views on what the museum, for instance, might be? None of these issues is fully resolved, yet taken together they allow us to enter Godard's oeuvre afresh in unexpected and productive ways.

In "The Godard Paradox", Serge Daney argues that despite conflicting appearances Godard is a filmmaker tied firmly to the present and reality. Godard achieves this by manipulating contradictions, or through a mysticism of the image. For this reason, Daney argues, Godard should be viewed much less as a revolutionary filmmaker than as a "radical reformer", since reformism always concerns the present. According to Daney, the utopia represented by Godard is not about doing totally new things, but about doing things differently even while continuing as before.

In "Godard and Asynchrony", Keith Reader considers another Godardian paradox. On the one hand, Godard, particularly in his earlier work, has the reputation of being one of French cinema's leading chroniclers of his period. On the other, Godard is the author of the (in)famous phrase: "It's not a just image, just an image", which would appear to deny the existence of the referent altogether. Yet at the root of Godard's statement, Reader argues, is an awareness of the subversive value of "asynchrony" that gives Godard's work its often unnervingly prescient quality. According to Reader, Godard deals with key historical, political and cultural crises ahead of–or after–their time, in the process shedding a necessarily different light on them.

In "The Commerce of Cinema", Colin MacCabe focuses on the neglected topic of Godard as producer and entrepreneur. Informed by his own experience of commissioning works by Godard such as *Soft and Hard*, 1985, and *2x50 ans de cinéma français*, 1995, MacCabe explores Godard's working methods and his role as a *petit commerçant* in a broadly economic perspective. In particular, he considers how Godard has managed to produce so much work, despite the apparent commercial failure of most of his feature films, and assesses whether Godard's working relationship with money, producers and the industry has changed over the years.

In "Home-Movies: the Curious Cinematic Collaboration of Anne-Marie Miéville and Jean-Luc Godard", Catherine Grant explores another instance of Godard's collaborative practice, his working relationship since the early 1970s with the Swiss filmmaker, Anne-Marie Miéville. While collaborating couples are far from unknown in the history of cinema, the nature and extent of Godard and Miéville's work together (more than ten co-directed films since *Ici et Ailleurs*, 1974, often under the auspices of the production company "Sonimage" which they set up together) is highly unusual. It is characterised by at least three discernibly separate strands: joint projects (co-directed, co-scripted, and co-signed); appearances as actors together and alone in each other's films; and other forms of aesthetic and political parallelism in the work which they have directed alone, and which are less straightforward to characterise. Grant examines aspects of each of these three strands, arguing that the notion of parallelism is vital to reach a proper understanding of the aesthetics of Godard and Miéville's separate-but-parallel tracks of dialogical authorship.

In "Godard in the Museum", Antoine de Baecque shows that Godard has always been interested not only in art and its exhibition but also in the development of museology and the ideology of its vision. In films such as *Bande à part*, museums are first represented as institutional, cultural and ideological spaces. Later, they are seen as an imaginary site that can encourage editing, which itself offers a means of rebuilding the aura surrounding works of art by inserting them into cinema, and thus history. Finally, museums are presented as the most authentic and moving embodiment of History. De Baecque argues, however, that Godard's ideal museum seems a largely impossible dream, since there is an insoluble contradiction between the exhibition and conservation space of the execrated classical museum, the ultimate dream of the museum as imaginary editing, and the museum as embodiment of the century's history.

In the last chapter of this section, "Here and Elsewhere: Projecting Godard", James Quandt examines his personal experience of organising a comprehensive Godard retrospective (*Godard For Ever*) in Toronto in 2001. According to Quandt, it was like an act of resurrection, and the challenges he faced reflect Godard's own concern with the recovery of the past. Quandt argues that the success of a Godard retrospective depends uniquely on the retrieval of both material and memory, i.e. not merely projectable copies of all Godard's work, but also a sense of their influence and importance, as well as of the cultural and political knowledge required for their enjoyment and understanding.

THE GODARD PARADOX[1]

SERGE DANEY

Winter 1985. Having just published a large collection of his writings for *Cahiers du cinéma*, Jean-Luc Godard agreed to a promotional "one-man show" taking the form of a cinema masterclass for members of the Cinémathèque française, who, it goes without saying, were already won over. Among a number of overly reverential questions, which he had no difficulty answering, two young men asked two rather disjointed questions: why did Godard not make adventure blockbusters that everybody wanted to see, and for that matter, why did he no longer communicate his great love of cinema in his films? Godard was naturally able to answer the first question (he had already answered it in his video *Scénario du film Passion*, 1982), but he was somewhat taken aback by the second one and paused. When it comes to a love of the cinema, cinephilia, fond citations from old movies, he believed (as did everybody else) that he's "been there, done that". To such an extent in fact that his name is now emblematic of a passion which even his detractors have had to concede, namely a passion for the cinema. The name "Godard" (after Welles, Fellini, Kubrick or more recently Wenders) designates an auteur but it is also synonymous with a tenacious passion for this region of the world of images that we call cinema.

A love of the cinema desires only cinema, whereas passion is excessive: it wants cinema but it also wants cinema to become something else, it even longs for the horizon where cinema risks being absorbed by dint of metamorphosis, it opens up its focus onto the unknown. In the early years of cinema, filmmakers believed that the art that they were inventing would be a resounding success, that it would play an incredible social role, that it would save the other arts and would contribute towards civilising the human race, etc.. For Gance and for Eisenstein, nothing had been decided. For Stroheim or the young Buñuel, on the face of it, nothing was

Opposite: **Orson Welles, Roberto Rossellini, Marguerite Duras, François Truffaut.**

DZIGA VERTOV

Above: **The 1965 French translation of N Abramov's study of Dziga Vertov.**

impossible. The evolution of cinema had not yet been indexed to the evolution of the Hollywood studio talkies, the war effort, the introduction of quality criteria (which, with hindsight, make studio productions look like the hand-crafted harbingers of industrial TV movies). As soon as that happened, the future of cinema was no longer anybody's passion (even on a theoretical level). It was only after the war, after the early warning signs of an economic recession, followed by the New Wave kamikaze patch-up job, that the idea of another cinema, one that would open onto something else, was possible again.

Possible, yes, but no longer with the conquering optimism of the early years ("you've seen nothing yet, cinema will be the art of the century"). Instead, it is accompanied by a lucidity tinged with nostalgia ("we've seen many films, cinema has indeed proved itself to be the art of the century, but the century's almost over"). There is an awareness that for a moment a perfect balance was struck (with Hawks, for instance), but that trying to reproduce it would be pointless, that new media are emerging and that the material nature of the image is mutating. What is ambiguous about Godard, as well as his New Wave friends, is that his cinema straddles this change of direction. In a way, he knows too much.

For he is not just a great filmmaker. Once again, he excels at being the filmmaker who expects everything from cinema, including "that cinema should free him from cinema", to paraphrase Maître Eckhart. He foils our calculations and disappoints those who worship him too readily; Godard has always kept moving, in every sense of the word, within a film-world that is still big enough to allow you to move about and to show your restless energy. He is a philosopher, a scientist, a preacher, an educator, a journalist, but all this as an amateur; he is the last (to date) to have been the (coherent) witness and the (moral) conscience of what's afoot in cinema.

One could argue that all contemporary filmmakers, provided they feel strongly enough about certain issues, can come to terms with both the "death" of cinema and its future metamorphoses. Judging from the radicalism of Duras and Syberberg, the technological utopias of Coppola, not to mention the submerged iceberg of "experimental" filmmakers or video artists, it is clear that these filmmakers have accepted the notion that cinema belongs to the past. If Godard, like Rossellini in his day, had given up his starting point (cinema) and had let himself be proclaimed a preacher or a prophet, his image would be more clear-cut. But he has consciously resisted being categorised in this way.

For it should not be forgotten that there is a difference between prophets and inventors. Using established forms as a starting point, Godard "invented" (indeed cobbled together) the current shape of our perception of images and sounds. He has always been a little ahead of his time, but nothing has protected him from the average illusions of his day (and when his films became more political, crafty though he was, he came up against the same naivety and dead-ends as any other "Maoist" of the age). Vertov was a prophet and Godard is, strictly speaking, his contemporary. The aesthetic strokes of genius of his early career simply allowed him to be slightly ahead of his audience (and for a little longer than anticipated). Otherwise, like many formal inventors, he advances back-to-front, apprehensively, facing what he is leaving behind. He is not so much the man who opens doors as the one in whose gaze a previously familiar and natural landscape changes with hindsight; he is worn down by an alarming feeling of alienation and overcome by the mystery that occurs when one feels that one no longer knows how to do things.

This sums up the Godard paradox. He is caught between a recent past and a near future (unlike prophets who can easily combine archaism and the future), he is crucified between what he can no longer do and what he cannot yet do, in other words, he is doomed to the present. Despite his strong sense of dialectic, we should not forget this sharp and voluntarist taste for the present, to which he is inextricably bound. He is able to find this present through a tremendous manipulation of contradictions, or, to save time, through a mysticism of the image, the ultimate in reality. Godard is too Bazinian to commit himself to the loss of "reality", which is replaced by a generalised interplay of references from one image to another, or to an acceptance that the image can no longer be used as a human means of communication, even negatively.

Godard has been so easily described as an "enfant terrible", an "avant-garde filmmaker", an "iconoclast" and a "revolutionary" that we have failed to notice that, right from the start, he respected the rules of the game (unlike Truffaut). In fact, Godard is troubled by the absence of rules. There is nothing revolutionary about Godard, rather, he is more interested in radical reformism, because reformism concerns the present. He never implicates the audience, financial profits or producers, or even certain ways of making films. His own utopia is to demand that people open themselves up to the possibility of doing things "differently" even while continuing as before. This utopia is less about doing something different than about doing the same thing, differently. At that price, it continues to bear fruit.

GODARD AND ASYNCHRONY

Elvis died the day he went into the army.
John Lennon

KEITH READER

There are few filmmakers in whose work the theme of asynchrony looms so large as in Godard's. On a formal level, from *À bout de souffle*, 1960, onwards, his films have been marked by a systematic (if constantly varying) disjunction of sound and image. This chapter argues through reference to six films from different phases of Godard's career that such formal asynchrony is accompanied by an equally asynchronous relationship between the contexts in which it is made and the topics it represents.

Asynchrony, seen as a temporal form of alterity, is a key trope in post-structuralist thinking, exemplified by Geoffrey Bennington's view of deconstruction as "a radical, non-dialectisable alterity at the heart of the same".[1] The non-coincidence of sound and image in Godard has much in common with the endless deferral of Meaning (with a capital M) in Derrida; it is no coincidence that these two most cited, hagiographised and reviled of contemporary thinkers on meaning should find common ground here, in an absence of what would normally be perceived as groundedness. Texts do not exist in the absence of contexts–something very well understood by both Godard and Derrida, if sometimes forgotten by certain of their acolytes. There is a widespread misperception in relation to both Godard and the indefatigably *engagé* Derrida that their work marks a lofty and/or disabused disconnection from the social and historical realities in which it is on the contrary firmly, if often perversely and sometimes turgidly, rooted. My analysis here will focus on the context of the six films I have chosen, stressing the "and then" component of Michael Witt's assertion that "the cinema, for Godard, has fulfilled the function of visionary scientific instrument, foreseeing patterns of emergent social change before they occur, and then confronting and testifying to the reality and/or atrocity of those events".[2] The "and then" here has much in common with

opus

INTERNATIONAL

2

l'œil vérité

the "betweenness" identified by Kaja Silverman and Harun Farocki as a crucial element in *Passion*, 1982, a film which for them represents a "larger experimentation with asynchronicity".[3] The asynchrony, the non-coincidence, in *Passion* are ascribed an explicitly political value, as in the meeting of woman trade unionists at the factory in which Godard's experimentation with sound/image disjunction means that the words "float once again 'between' all of those present".[4] What is interesting for us here is the persistence of this kind of politicised sound/image dissociation into the early 1980s, the time at which such experiments in superstructural revolution, and indeed belief in the possibility of socialist revolution *tout court*, were beginning (at least) to run out of steam. Asynchrony, that is to say, is there on both sides of the camera, in the time and conditions of the film's making and reception quite as much as in the formal strategies it deploys.

I have quoted John Lennon on Elvis, who became a *petit soldat* more or less as Godard was shooting his film of that title, for two reasons. One is that in my more rebarbative days I was wont to compare Godard and Truffaut to the Lennon and McCartney of New Wave filmmaking–though the analogy of course broke down, indeed became asynchronous, when the "wrong one" died prematurely. The other, more serious reason is that Lennon's remark suggests a Manichean view of Elvis's work–the good earlier years and the bad later ones–similar to "the crude digest of images and stereotypes purveyed by much contemporary Godard scholarship" denounced by Michael Temple and James S Williams:

The story is well known: something political happened around 1968 which led to a series of unwatchable films, before Godard then headed for the French provinces to make TV, returning to cinema only in the early 1980s with *Sauve qui peut (la vie)*. This produced in the early 1980s some late masterpieces by an Old Master, after which the old fool isolated in his Swiss retreat appeared to lose the plot.[5]

The crucial difference, of course, is that Elvis's post-Army records continued to be widely heard and to sell in vast numbers, despite their well-nigh universal critical dismissal and neglect. Godard's more recent films have experienced the opposite fate, being extremely difficult to see, often extremely difficult to watch, but it sometimes seems all but impossible to avoid reading about. The (at best) restricted availability of virtually all his work over the past decade and a half has not stemmed the torrent of words devoted to it–rather the reverse. It is almost as though those words represented a verbal compensation for the inaccessibility (in two senses) of the images to which they relate. The asynchrony that is so important in the filmic texts seems to have bled out into the time and conditions of their reception, which can be seen as constituting something very like a *mise en abyme* of the sound-image dissociation characteristic of all his work, but most markedly of the later years. This is illustrated by the notorious *bon mot* from *Vent d'est*, 1969: "Ce n'est pas une image juste, c'est juste une image" ("It's not a just image, it's just an image"), often taken by those hostile to Godard as a distillation of the supposed postmodernist view that no text can ever actually refer to anything at all, but (I hope) to be given slightly subtler treatment here.

The Godard industry began in earnest in the aftermath of 1968, when Godard ostentatiously withdrew from the production and distribution circuits of the art-house cinema. The major theoretical developments of the ensuing decade, centring around *Cahiers du cinéma* in France and *Screen* in Britain, represented something like a high noon of political formalism in which the disruption of the viewing subject's relationship to the filmic text was the *sine qua non* of a revolutionary cinema. Godard, with or without Jean-Pierre Gorin or Anne-Marie Miéville, was a totemic figure in this context. The fact that his

Opposite: **Cover of the 1976 Godard Special Issue of L'Avant-Scène Cinéma.**

LES CARABINIERS 1963 PARIS
JEAN-LUC GODARD FILMS

LES CARABINIERS 1963 PARIS
JEAN-LUC GODARD FILMS

films were difficult to watch acted as proof of their revolutionary seriousness, while given the metropolitan bias of both *Cahiers* and *Screen* the fact that, especially before the spread of video, they were difficult to see scarcely seemed to count for anything. Thus it was that what René Prédal was to term "the incense of the fundamentalist chapels dedicated to the cult" began to burn.[6] If we disregard the bizarre mixing of religious metaphors, Prédal's comment, like his later reference to "le god-art", is not unjustified.[7] He goes on to explain that Godard's work "has become so rarefied today that the figure who at one time symbolised aggressive provocation now finds himself cast in the role of last resort".[8] The provocative quality which at different times caused figures as disparate as Robert Benayoun, Raymond Durgnat and François Truffaut to direct ferocious invective against him has now, because his more recent work has been largely invisible as well as because of significant changes in the political climate, come to seem considerably more muted. Yet it has always, I would argue, been present, often–asynchronously–where we might least expect to find it. The hagiographic attention latterly given to much of his more recent work in particular has perhaps served to mask the provocative nature of the discontinuities by which it is permeated.

What I now propose to do is to take six films from differing periods of Godard's career and focus on some of the asynchronies–less of sound and image than of text and referent–that characterise them. The films will be dealt with in three groups of two. *Les Carabiniers*, 1963, and *Bande à part*, 1964, are chronologically close and both feature a duo of male protagonists whose sometimes coarse ingenuousness throws their political and cultural context into relief. *La Chinoise* and *Week-end*, both 1967, deal with the events of May 68 before they happened–surely the classic, because the

Above: **Japanese flyers for *Les Carabiniers*.**

Opposite: **Sami Frey, Claude Brasseur, and Anna Karina in *Bande à part*.**

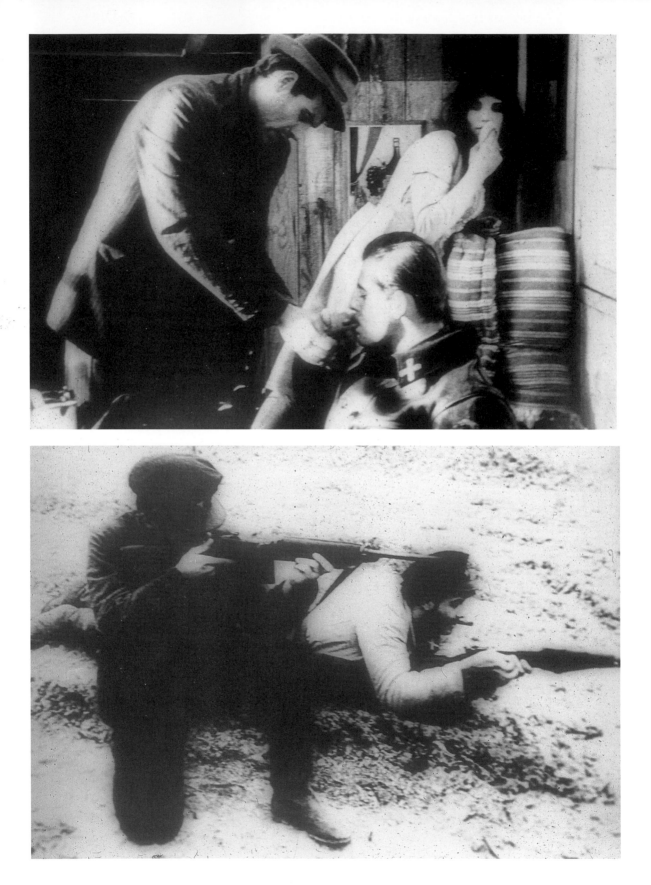

most extraordinary, instance of asynchrony in the entire oeuvre. *Numéro Deux*, 1975, and *Grandeur et décadence d'un petit commerce de cinéma*, 1986, while more widely separated in time, both set before us in grimly elegiac mode the (terminal?) crisis of the cinematic medium whose narrative and representational strength has often been thought to reside in its bringing together of image and word. The treatment of these films will necessarily be brief, but I hope that it will provide an accurate image, rather than just an image, of how asynchrony is built, with often unnerving percipience, into their diverse strategies.

Les Carabiniers and Bande à part

Godard has famously denounced cinema–notably in *Histoire(s) du cinéma*–for its failure to bear visual witness to the horror of the Second War and the Final Solution, much as Adorno asked himself from Californian exile how poetry was still possible after Auschwitz. Such a denunciation might be thought to apply to Godard's own work too (he is, after all, practised in the art of palinode), at least until 2001 and *Éloge de l'amour* which abounds in overt references to the Occupation and the Resistance. This, however, would be to reckon without *Les Carabiniers*–a film that touches more than incidentally on the then taboo subject of occupation and collaboration. The two conscripted soldiers–Ulysse/Marino Masé and Michel-Ange/Albert Juross–who are the film's central characters are lumpen proletarians, living with their companions Vénus/Geneviève Galéa and Cléopâtre/Catherine Ribeiro in a shanty-town of the kind that was common in the France of the time, though soon to be replaced by the tower-blocks that loom so large in *Deux ou trois choses que je sais d'elle*, 1967. The disparity between the loftiness of the characters' names and the squalor of their existence is plain enough, and reinforced when the soldiers who come to draft Ulysse and Michel-Ange into the army tell them that "soldiers can do anything provided it's in the King's name". On one level this can be read as a sardonic allusion to the high-handedness of the Gaullist regime then in its pomp. On another, however, it operates retrospectively, as an ironic evocation and demolition of the military chivalry mourned by Renoir a quarter-century before in *La Grande illusion*, 1937. Between the First World War–backdrop for *La Grande illusion*–and de Gaulle's France, there had of course been the Second World War and the German invasion, to which the recruiting soldiers' uniforms and the flags that fly on the tanks and other military vehicles make clear reference. It was not until a decade later, with Louis Malle's *Lacombe Lucien*, 1974, that a fiction film was to call into question the hitherto unchallenged myth of omnipresent French resistance to the occupier. Malle's film attracted widespread attention (both positive and negative) largely because its central character was depicted as oblivious to the wider context of his decision to join the Milice collaborators. Lucien's desire for an exciting escape from the tedium of his day-to-day existence and rapidly acquired taste for the material fruits of collaboration are surely pre-echoed in the profiteering of Ulysse and Michel-Ange, markedly less successful though that is.

That lack of success, culminating in their shooting at the end, is most notoriously figured in the scene when they return home bearing their booty–postcard photographs of monuments ranging from the predictable (the Taj Mahal) to the esoteric (the Chicago Aquarium). Here as so often subsequently, Godard acts as a kind of cultural soothsayer, prefiguring the age of mass intercontinental tourism which was not to develop until a decade and more later. The triumphant brandishing of photographs strikingly prefigures Guy Debord's assertion in *La Société du spectacle*, four years later, that "this society which does away with geographical distance interiorises distance as the separation of spectacle".[9] Ulysse and Michel-Ange's cartoon character-like

Opposite above: **The King's soldiers come recruiting in Les Carabiniers.**

Below: **Ulysse and Michel-Ange (Marino Masé and Albert Juross) go into battle.**

stylisation acts to place them between the unreflecting collaboration of Lucien Lacombe and the perhaps no less unreflecting consumerism of the latter-day tourist industry–out of synch with both, but precisely thereby drawing a powerfully implicit parallel between them.

Bande à part was for long widely regarded as a minor Godard, but has attracted more critical attention over the past decade, culminating in the recent reissue of a new print. Barthélémy Amengual's 1993 monograph marked an important reevaluation of the film, describing it as at once Godard's most realistic and his most classic work.[10] It may well have been these very qualities that led to the film's comparative neglect at the time when the formal-political experimentation of the Dziga Vertov period dominated discussion of Godard. Yet the "quite deliberate discrepancies" that for Amengual characterise the film unobtrusively prefigure the more florid asynchronies of much of the later work.[11] The "minute's silence" observed by the three central characters, one of whom says that it "can last an eternity", in fact lasts for only about 45 seconds. Amengual also draws attention to other significant asynchronies in the film, during the Madison dance sequence and in Godard's various voice-over interventions–these in what he has described as "the most realistic of Godard's films, if not the only one".[12] Amengual's prolonged deconstruction of that realism serves to show how the coincidence of word and image that is an important part of any conception of cinematic realism is continually undercut from within.[13]

That coincidence is "an important part of cinematic realism", but not the only one, for it leaves out of account the referential dimension. Godard may have invited us to do this with his proclamation of intent "not to make political films, but to make films politically", but acceptance of such an invitation is not obligatory, and is almost bound to impoverish our reading of his work. After all, the Godardophile "Cahiers/Screen orthodoxy" of the 1970s finally, and ironically, fell foul of developments in the 'real world'–most notably the waning of belief, including Godard's own, in the possibility of revolutionary social change–and now appears, for all the excellent work it produced and its undeniable importance in promoting serious debate on the moving image, as flawed by its symmetrical occlusion of on the one hand the referent, on the other the audience. Bande à part clearly reached a much wider audience than virtually all Godard's post-1968 work, and draws upon a largely popular-cultural set of referents–one reason maybe why it influenced Quentin Tarantino who pays tribute to the Madison sequence in Pulp Fiction, 1994. Yet this "popular" world is systematically intruded upon by, and in its turn intrudes upon, the more "serious" worlds of high culture and (post-) colonial politics–not in the postmodern form of pastiche (which apart from anything else is arguably all but impossible in black and white), but rather by way of an approach akin to montage, deriving its effects from the collision of habitually asynchronous or incompatible elements.

Five years after Bande à part, the explosion of May 1968 was to bring the politics of culture to the fore. Godard's foretelling of this in La Chinoise and Week-end is itself foretold in the farcical English lesson in Bande à part, where the rote-learning approach to Shakespeare–albeit in a private language school rather than in the State academy–figures the dreary centralisation of the French educational system. The cultural dereliction of the suburbs, not yet even partially redeemed by the advent of rap and tagging as in Kassovitz's La Haine of 1995, is almost as inescapable a backdrop to this film as it was to Les Carabiniers and would be–moved several degrees up-market–in Deux ou trois choses. The ethos of cultural consumerism is memorably lampooned in the sequence where the trio visit the Louvre in record time, beating the previous-American-best of nine minutes and 43 seconds. (I have no evidence to

Opposite: **Geneviève Galéa and Catherine Ribeiro during the making of Les Carabiniers.**

suggest that this "record" really existed, but *se non è vero è ben trovato*.) But the film's political frame of reference is not confined to the cultural, as the invocation of committed writers such as Jack London and Louis Aragon may suggest. It also contains a number of references to colonialism and the post-colonial epoch, in that respect constituting an intertext with *Les Carabiniers* with its *mise en scène* of the supplanting of colonialism by tourism. Franz/Sami Frey says after the English class that the United Kingdom is finished as a world power and that its place will be taken by China. The cousin of Arthur/Claude Brasseur was at Diên Biên Phu, the battle which in 1954 put paid to the French colonial presence in South-East Asia. In anecdotal, almost throwaway form these allusions refer to major sites of Godard's political concerns in the decade ahead: Vietnam from 1965 and *Pierrot le fou*, China of course from *La Chinoise* of two years later.

More striking to an audience today, however, is the reference to the former Belgian colony of Rwanda. This occurs when Arthur and Franz are waiting idly outside Odile/Anna Karina's house, reading passages from the newspaper to each other to pass the time. A couple of banal *faits divers* are followed by a story about ethnic conflict between Hutus and Tutsis in Rwanda, which had obtained its independence only the previous year. I saw this film for the first time at London's National Film Theatre in 1994, when the conflict was at its fiercest and featured prominently in the broadsheet press, and the sharp intake of audience breath was clearly perceptible. What is perhaps most powerful about this reference is the banality of the context in which it is embedded. Ethnic cleansing–to use a term not then invented–is placed on an everyday, uneventful footing, as though in support of Debord's theses on the levelling, banalising effects of the spectacle. (The visual metaphor of spectacle is essentially a dead one for Debord, whose analyses do not particularly privilege the moving image over other types of mass media such as the press.) It would, I think, be difficult even to argue that the violence described in the article serves as some kind of contrast to the violence of the film's final shoot-out, which as almost always in Godard is stylised and choreographed. The characters' lack of response to the article is so marked, and the shoot-out so distant from the earlier scene in time, that the two "killing fields" are radically, and as it were unhelpfully, other, refusing any assimilation into a political context that would become Godard's only from about 1965, which is as good a date as any to situate the onset of his *engagé* period. *Pierrot le fou* makes explicit connections between its central couple's crime spree and the violence in Vietnam, most clearly when Pierrot/Ferdinand/Jean-Paul Belmondo and Marianne/Anna Karina stage a satirical playlet about Vietnam for the benefit of some American sailors. *Bande à part*, by contrast, has more in common with the widely-observed nihilism of *Le Petit soldat*, 1960. The film's asynchronous universe is one in which violences of different kinds sit side by side without connecting tissue, whether humanistic ("this is the dreadful world in which we live") or dialectical ("these are only apparently dissimilar aspects of the dominance of capitalism in which its fall is also inscribed"). To that extent, *Bande à part*'s asynchronies make it, I would argue, a darker and less good-natured film than its overall tone may seem to suggest.

La Chinoise and *Week-end*

The one characteristic of the May 68 events on which all observers agree is their unexpectedness. Pierre Viansson-Ponté famously opined in *Le Monde* of 15 March 1968 that "France is bored", and even when student protests at the new university of Nanterre, in the western suburbs of Paris, spread to the Sorbonne and rapidly brought all French universities to a halt it was difficult to imagine that within a few weeks the very survival of the Fifth Republic

Opposite: **Anne Wiazemsky as Marie in Robert Bresson's *Au hasard, Balthazar*, 1966.**

Above: **German poster for *La Chinoise*. Mireille Darc during the making of *Week-end*.**

Opposite: **Exterminating Angel Joseph Balsamo (Daniel Pommereulle) terrorises Corinne and Roland (Jean Yanne and Mireille Darc) in *Week-end*. They in turn loot helpless car crash victims. And the affluent young (Juliet Berto) encounter the rural working class.**

would be called into question.[14] While May brought about immense changes in the cultural and educational worlds, the cinema, despite the (successful) outcry over Henri Langlois's dismissal from the Cinémathèque in February and the closure of the Cannes Festival, remained oddly insulated from these, not least because the difficulty of producing any kind of master narrative of May meant that it did not lend itself readily to the kind of fictionalisation that directors such as Melville or Tavernier might have produced.[15] Jean-Pierre Jeancolas's statement that Godard "did not make afterwards the kind of films he had been making before" thus distinguishes him from almost all other French filmmakers–an exception all the more remarkable given that *La Chinoise* and *Week-end* so strikingly prefigure the events.[16] Biographical coincidence appears to have been at the root of this, for Godard had met Anne Wiazemsky (who was to become his second wife) when she was filming Bresson's *Au hasard, Balthazar* the previous year, and began visiting her at Nanterre where she was a student. Nanterre was from the outset an epicentre of *gauchisme*–an overdetermined conjuncture of radical faculty (including the heterodox ex-Communists Henri Lefebvre and Francis Jeanson, who plays himself in the film), inadequate facilities (the university opened before its library was finished) and minimal transport links to Paris.[17]

It was thus not surprising that it was there that the first of the student occupations so characteristic of 1968 took place, nor that the university's students, who included Daniel Cohn-Bendit, played a leading role in the events and their aftermath. This means that it can sometimes take a positive effort to remind oneself, viewing *La Chinoise* 35 years down the line, that the film was made at a time when the radical potential of Nanterre would have been seen as (at best) a mildly interesting, or even grotesque, footnote to the real political debates of the time. This is the line taken by Jeanson in a

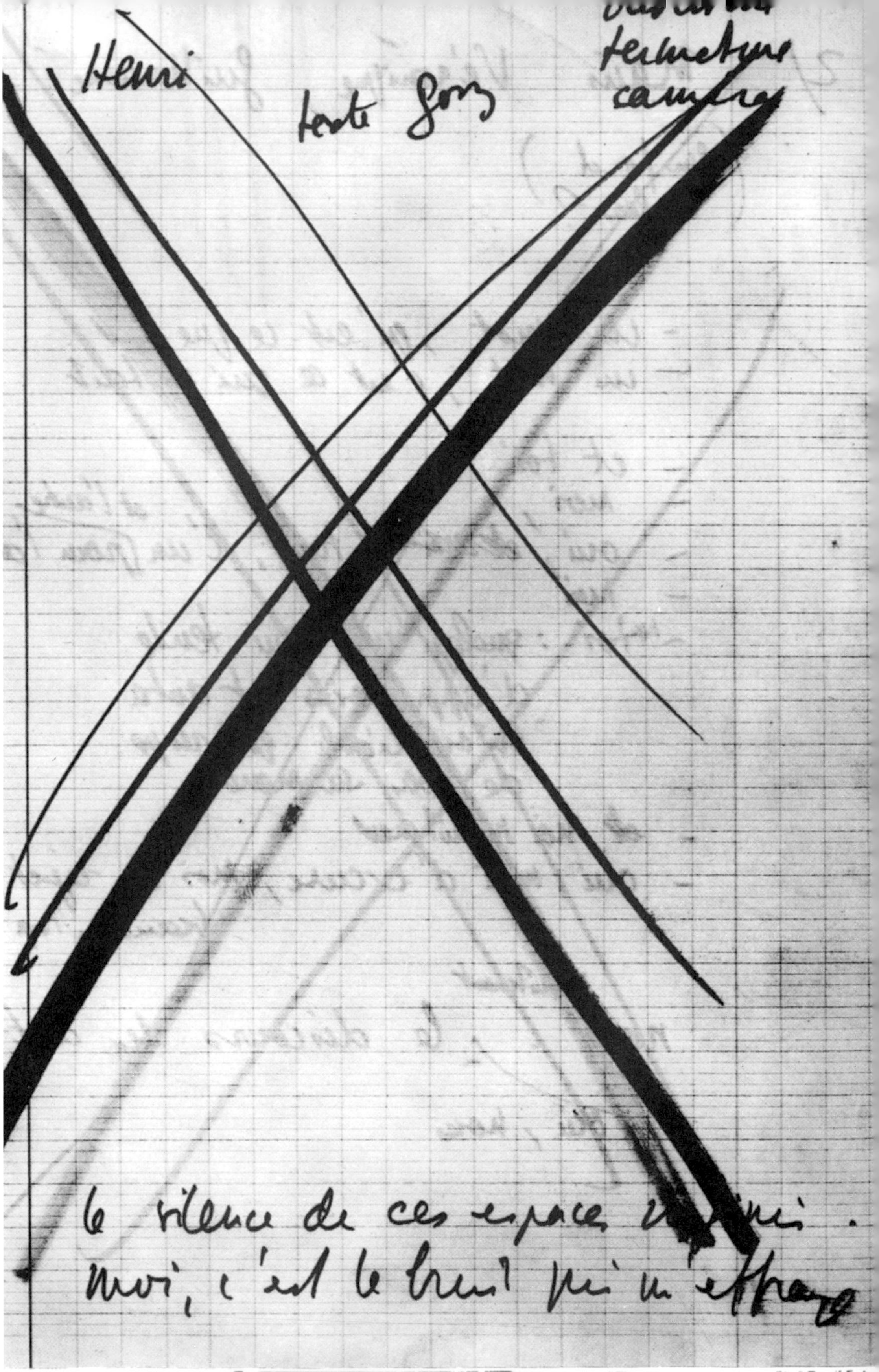

Henri

tente fort

fermeture
caméra

le silence de ces espaces infinis.
moi, c'est le bruit qui m'effraye

2/ Mais Véronique Guillaume
(sur fond)
préalea ?

- un mot, qu'est-ce que
- un mot, c'est ce qui existait

- et toi
- moi,
- oui, c'était toi, l'un pour l'autre et l'autre
- moi
- et toi : quelqu'un qui tente
  d'apprendre cet autre
  la ou ligne qui risque
  de sa, sa marche
- et moi maintenant
- oui mot d'excuse, moi de rejet,
                        beaucoup trop
        en tchant
  nou . le discours des autres
        -
  oui, nous

1 . La Chinoise . Juliet Berto joue le Vietnam sous le napalm extra du tigre en papier.

conversation with Véronique/Anne Wiazemsky on a train journey from Paris to Nanterre, the name of whose then only rail station–La Folie ("Madness")–is quizzically lingered on by the camera well before it was to become a byword for the media. Véronique's cell of Maoist militants, who squat a flat in a well-off area of Paris and lead a rigorously not to say parodically communal existence, advocate violent acts of terrorism as the only effective way of overcoming the bourgeoisie. For Véronique this may even mean bomb attacks on the university–a stance benignly contested by Jeanson (who had been a *porteur de valise* during the Algerian War). For Jeanson such individualistic acts of "adventurism"–to use a phrase numbingly characteristic of the PCF (the French Communist Party) at the time–can be no substitute for the arduous task of building a mass movement.

The assumptions and presuppositions of this conversation are so far removed from the political issues and realities of the incipient twenty-first century that viewers watching the sequence today are likely to respond with a bemusement which all but screens out any other response. It is thus probably worth making the point that this conversation, if it is a "realistic" one (Wiazemsky was a student at Nanterre and Jeanson plays Jeanson), is so in the Brechtian mode characteristic of Godard at the time. The characters, that is to say, articulate positions that have their equivalents in the real world of the late 1960s, but in a manner that distances the audience from them and thereby renders them problematic. The film was generally perceived on its release as a satire on Maoism rather than a polemical embracing of it, as Godard implicitly acknowledged in *Combat* on 5 September 1967 stating that the film had "annoyed the staff of the Chinese Embassy in Paris" as well as "young French Communists, whether pro-Chinese or not". Such a reading is given credibility by the fact that the group's attempted assassination of a visiting Soviet minister is bungled because the comrade selected to perform the task goes to the wrong hotel room.

To see *La Chinoise* as the *premier coup d'archet* of Godard's "Maoist years", as *Cahiers* were to call them, is thus an over-simplification. His submergence for much of the ensuing decade in the Dziga Vertov Group and Sonimage collectives can after all be read as a justification, in his own sphere of work, of Jeanson's insistence on the need for patient groundwork in the revolutionary struggle. Furthermore, the most sympathetically delineated member of the cell is Henri–a former Communist who as the film ends is contemplating rejoining the Party, as a good many ex-*gauchistes* did in the 1970s. Godard's view of the possible consequences of "adventurism" may have been a misplaced one so far as France was concerned, but it is uncannily prophetic of the often murderous antics of the Baader-Meinhof group in Germany and the Red Brigades in Italy. If Godard is out of synch here, it is spatially and geographically rather than chronologically. Richard Roud opines apropos Renoir's *La Règle du jeu*, 1939, that "if France were destroyed tomorrow and nothing remained but this film, the whole country and its civilisation could be reconstructed from it".[18] It would perhaps be an exaggeration to make a similar statement about *La Chinoise* and the France of 1968, but not much of one, and this is all the more remarkable considering that such a construction would be on the basis of precognitive–hence asynchronous–evidence.

Week-end is a companion-piece to its predecessor in a way that strikingly anticipates what was specific to the "French 1968" compared to similar events in many other countries: the twin-pronged onslaught on the ossification of the bourgeois university (dealt with as we have seen in *La Chinoise*) and on the consumer society, which had become a reality in the France of the previous decade. *Week-end*'s central couple–Corinne/Mireille Darc and Roland/Jean Yanne–display, in their internecine greed and braying solipsism, the vices of

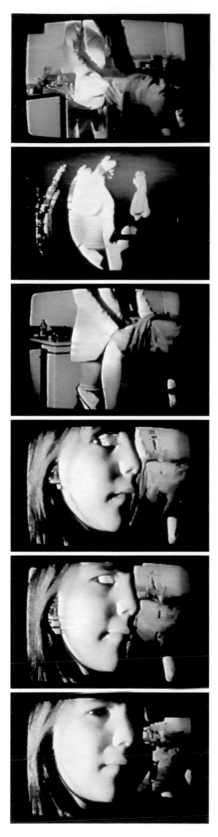

that society in caricatural, indeed cartoon-like form. There is no evidence that either of them has experience, or even awareness, of the educational world; yet the sundry literary and historical characters they encounter in their peregrinations (Saint-Just, Emily Brontë, Alice in Wonderland), like so many refugees from Truffaut's *Fahrenheit 451* of the previous year, form part of the symbolic décor of that world, and their reciprocal incomprehension prefigures the cultural abyss at the heart of May. Truffaut can lay claim to being the first filmmaker to foreshadow the educational and social turmoil of *les événements*, when his schoolteacher in *Les 400 Coups* (filmed in 1958) shouts exasperatedly at his class: "I feel sorry for France in ten years' time." Members of that class could, we might imagine, have gone on to form the "Seine-et-Oise Liberation Front" whose nihilistic, and ultimately cannibalistic, antics close the action of *Week-end*. That group (whose real-life equivalents would later be found in Germany, Italy or Japan rather than in France) represents a wholesale, neo-Dostoevskian rejection of bourgeois culture with which, despite appearances, Roland and Corinne actually have far more in common than they do with the iconic figures they have met on their earlier travels.

The sheer ugliness of this bourgeoisie is what rescues *Week-end*'s diatribe against the consumer society from being pious–something perhaps more obvious now, in a much more acquisitive and designer-conscious era, than when the film was made. Jean-Louis Bory, writing in the left-of-centre weekly *Le Nouvel Observateur*, links *Week-end* not only with *La Chinoise* but also with 1966's *Made in USA* and *Deux ou trois choses*, as part of what he terms "a spectral analysis of Gaullist France", and goes on to describe Godard as "the pamphleteer of a generation seeking its way between two forms of revolution that may wind up supporting each other". Those two forms of revolution–schematically, the ideological self-reflexiveness of *La Chinoise* and the visceral (anti-) consumerism of *Week-end*–were to coincide, if not to fuse, in the upheaval of May that Godard so strikingly prefigured. The battle between what Godard famously called "the children of Marx and Coca-Cola" (*Masculin Féminin*, 1966) is popularly supposed to be long over; but the "spectral analysis" referred to by Bory has recently surfaced in the famously asynchronic work of Jacques Derrida (*Marx et fils*, 2000, and of course *Spectres de Marx*, 1993), and the anti-globalisation movement can be seen as picking up where May left off, or at any rate suspended trading. Godard's 1968 outstrips its eponymous year even more and further than the prefigurations of *La Chinoise* and *Week-end* may suggest.

Numéro Deux and *Grandeur et décadence d'un petit commerce de cinéma*

The period after 1968 marked Godard's withdrawal from the production and distribution circuits of the cinema industry into first agit-prop 16mm filmmaking (the *Ciné-tracts* and Dziga Vertov Group films), then collaborative work on video with Miéville. The "unviewable" Godard and the Godard incessantly and hagiographically written about began their separate, yet, linked existences at about this time. Like in a very different way Renoir after he left France for the United States, Godard is often seen as henceforth having lost touch with the structures and workings of the society that had inspired his major films.[19] Yet I would contend that this is true only on a narrowly chronological reading, and for a filmmaker so deeply impregnated with the spirit of 1968 things could perhaps scarcely have been otherwise. It is difficult, if perversely entertaining, to imagine Godard as the quasi-official filmmaker of the French Socialist Party that a figure such as Tavernier was to become.

réalisé par
JEAN-LUC GODARD

NUMÉRO DEUX

un film produit par
Anne-Marie Miéville
et **Jean-Luc Godard**

avec **Sandrine Battistella**
Pierre Oudry
Alexandre Rignault
Rachel Stéfanopoli

INTERDIT AUX MOINS DE 18 ANS

...tu vois, Pierrot, la cuisine, les enfants, le cul, c'est à la fois trop et pas assez...

ingénieur vidéo : Gérard Teissedre
collaboration technique :
Milka Assaf et Gérard Martin

une co-production Sonimage/Bela/SNC
distribution
SNC / PARIS

HUREL

Godard's flirtations with the American film industry in the early 1980s–the varyingly abortive collaborations with West and East Coast in the respective shapes of Coppola and Woody Allen–provide the clue to the next major referential asynchrony that at the time of writing remains dominant in his oeuvre. From the pervasive pessimism of *Numéro Deux*, 1975, through to the petition calling for *The Matrix* to be translated into Breton in *Éloge de l'amour*, the failure of cinema, epitomised as we have seen in its inability to deal with Auschwitz, is emblematic of the onward march of globalisation. That term of course became common currency only in the aftermath of the Soviet bloc's collapse, yet its preconditions had been around for some considerable time before, and as with May 1968 if less spectacularly it can be argued that Godard foresaw a major socio-political movement significantly in advance of its time.

Numéro Deux, set on a housing estate in Grenoble that might be the successor to that in *Deux ou trois choses*, is structured as a number of intersecting mini-narratives of dysfunction–political, institutional, bodily and affective. The film is set at a time of political downturn for the Left, just after Giscard d'Estaing's victory in the 1974 presidential elections, and epitomised on the international scale by the failure of a woman living on the estate to interest the film's main (and only named) character, Sandrine, in coming to a Chile solidarity meeting. Sandrine's elderly father, meanwhile, recounts his memories of the class struggle and the International in a tone as exhausted as his naked body. Bodily dysfunction generally takes the form of blockage; Sandrine's constipation is paralleled by the blocked toilet in the family's flat, while her husband's fatigued impotence is relieved only when he forcibly sodomises her (in the sight of their daughter) after learning that she has been unfaithful. This grimly comic litany–a desolating string of asynchronies– perhaps matters less for our purposes than its (re)presentation. To quote Raymond Lefèvre: "We know nothing of the characters outside their present situation. No psychological explanation, no supporting plot, no chronological progression. All these situations are just the elements of a discourse Godard addresses to himself first, and to us thereafter–a soliloquy through which he lays claim to a solitude which is also a call to communicate."[20] That discourse takes the form of a montage of video images, itself framed by footage of Godard at an editing table before which we see him slumped in the film's final shot, as though in despair at his own impotence to provide any kind of dialectical closure or resolution.

The implied equation of Godard's failure to resolve the issues his film has raised with cinema's broader failure to address the key issues of the years since Auschwitz certainly does not lack authorial pretension, but a less cynical view of it may be suggested by the idea of work, constantly present in *Numéro Deux* as so often elsewhere in Godard. Godard stated in an interview entitled "*Numéro Deux*, a different kind of film" that: "People don't go to the cinema to work. The idea of work is no longer an interesting one. People do stupid jobs, so they don't want to work. And they'd rather have stupid pleasure than stupid work, which leads to an exploitation of pleasure quite as intense as that of work." "Stupid pleasure" surely evokes–albeit in a somewhat Manichean way–the world of Hollywood which predates the globalised pleasure industry of the early twenty-first century, that world that can only be countered by "low-budget films […] the only realistic way out".[21] Godard's despair may thus be less solipsistic than it appears, directed at the global hegemony of "stupid pleasure" rather than at his own demiurgic efforts, and doubtless distilling the sense of powerlessness that must afflict any attempt at countering such a hegemony.

The 1986 television film *Grandeur et décadence d'un petit commerce de cinéma* is perhaps Godard's most striking distillation of such powerlessness. The title has overtones of Balzac's *Splendeurs et misères des courtisanes* and Vigny's *Servitude et grandeur militaires*–nineteenth century narratives of prostitution, war and decadence that place the decline and fall of cinema in a grand Romantic tradition. The two central characters–Jean Almereyda (Vigo's father's alias) and Gaspard Bazin, in an allusion to two of French cinema's great figures both of whom died young–are played by Jean-Pierre Mocky, last French anarchistic defender of low-budget independent filmmaking, and New Wave icon Jean-Pierre Léaud, whose career was in a trough at the time. Godard makes an appearance as (some avatar of) himself, only to be run over and killed in suspicious circumstances along with Almereyda towards the close. The "petit commerce" the three have been running has degenerated into a television casting agency, whose members tranquilly go their unspecified ways as the film ends.

As a *mise en scène* of the crushing of cinematic independence, and by implication the triumph of globalisation, the film could scarcely be more desolate. This is all the more remarkable since the then only recently, and temporarily, dispossessed Socialist government, in particular its Culture Minister Jack Lang, had invested much, both literally and symbolically, in the French film industry. Yet Godard, in one of the more curious blind spots of his career, has shown remarkably little interest in Jack (as opposed to Fritz) Lang or indeed in the Left-Right vicissitudes of French governments since 1981. If there is anything positive to be read into the film, it is, as Alain

Bergala suggests, in the posthumous reconciliation it effects between Godard and Truffaut. Sartre famously said on Camus's death: "We had quarrelled, but it was a way of being together." The bilious exchanges between Truffaut and Godard may well recall those between the *engagé* Sartre and the liberal humanist Camus (or indeed Lennon's anti-McCartney diatribe *Whatever Gets You Through The Night?*). Truffaut's name, never mentioned in the course of *Grandeur et décadence*, nevertheless haunts the film. Bergala comments that "we constantly have the feeling that this film was for Godard a way of turning the clock back to before the interruption of death, of taking up once more [...] his dialogue with Truffaut". It is as if, in the draining fight against the global hegemony of "stupid pleasure", Godard needed to renew links with former, and now dead, allies–the logical conclusion perhaps of his earlier use of elderly filmmakers playing themselves (Fritz Lang in *Le Mépris*, 1963, Samuel Fuller in *Pierrot le fou*, 1965). Thus it is that *Grandeur et décadence* is Godard's way of showing, "in his own way, without pious images or ceremony, at once seriously and funnily, that the cinema they had loved together in the early days, and whose tradition Truffaut kept alive far more than the iconoclastic Godard, is now well and truly dead".[22] Such an elegiac vein is not surprising for a Godard by now well into the spiritual transcendental phase that can be said to have begun with *Passion* in 1982, but its repercussions reach considerably further. Godard and Truffaut along with Chabrol, Rivette and Rohmer had all met in the 1950s at Henri Langlois's Cinémathèque, to pay tribute to and embark on creative dialogue with actors and filmmakers many of whom were already dead. *Histoire(s) du cinéma*, the great project that Godard was to begin shortly after *Grandeur et décadence* and that was to occupy him for upwards of a decade, is surely among other things a revisiting of and homage to–most strikingly a reediting of–those early Cinémathèque years, deriving its poignancy from the gulf that separates the Godard of the 1980s and 1990s from the Godard of 30 or 40 years before. The ultimate Godardian asynchrony is perhaps the dialogue with the dead–his own earlier selves, needless to say, prominent among their number.

Opposite: **Jean-Pierre Léaud and Jean-Luc Godard during rehearsals for** *Grandeur et décadence d'un petit commerce de cinéma.*

THE COMMERCE
OF CINEMA

COLIN MacCABE

In one of the interviews he gave at Cannes about *Éloge de l'amour*, 2001, Godard made a distinction between commissions from others and commissions that he undertook himself. The language of the *petit commerçant*, of the skilled artisan for which Switzerland is legendarily famous is now very familiar. It is one of the major discourses which has guided the creation and development of Sonimage with Anne-Marie Miéville and it has been a constant self-description since the Maoist period. It has been my great good luck to bring three such commissions to him over the last two decades and a brief account of this experience may aid an understanding of Godard's working methods and indicate the importance of *The Old Place*, 1999, for both his and Miéville's work.

The first commission arose out of the financing for *Je vous salue, Marie*, 1985. Godard needed a final $100,000 to complete the money needed for the film and I found myself acting as the initial interface between Channel Four and Rolle. Channel Four were willing to provide the $100,000 but they wanted something else–an original documentary for which they were willing to pay an additional £40,000 (approx. $68,000). It was agreed that Godard and Miéville would make a documentary on Britain–a "British Images" to complement his *British Sounds* of 16 years earlier. There then followed a prolonged period of procrastination which ended with Godard and Miéville making a documentary reflecting on their own lives in Rolle (*Soft and Hard*, 1985). The process by which Godard transformed the commission from one topic to another is instructive. It would be easy to take the cynical view and claim that considerations of cost, and even more of time, meant that the British topic was always a mere fiction, but I think one could equally well argue that the British topic never engaged his full interest. The suggestion had been mine and although he had pursued it for

Opposite: **Outline of the "Images of Britain" project that would become Soft and Hard, 1985.**

Images of Britain

An ordinary outline script cannot be sustained as usual
since our method is to
              see first , and to
              talk after .

The main sequences may nevetherless be already named and
thought the following way :

1- old super eight

2- to day VHS

3- still stills

5- queen police tea

6- windows and gardens

7- shakes and pear

8- the language of the empire

9- james and Virginia

1o-1984 is behind them (or us)

s.a.r.l. au capital de 300.000 f. - siège social : 99, avenue du roule, 92200 neuilly - r.c. 64 b 574 - siren 305809360

the time, it never really captured his interest. The one page he produced on the topic for Channel Four hardly suggests a man with a topic burning to be filmed. If you follow this logic, then the passage from Godard and Miéville reflecting on Britain to Godard and Miéville reflecting on their own lives was not a devious or hypocritical one but a genuine pursuit of a subject that would engage them. In fact, I think that the cynical and the friendly interpretation are not genuine alternatives but two sides of an indivisible coin.

This was even clearer when, a decade later, I asked Godard and Miéville to contribute the French programme to a 16-part series occasioned by the 100th anniversary of the cinema. There was little doubt that, on this occasion, the commission immediately engaged his interest but under the sign of counter identification. If the general idea of the series was a celebration of cinema in its national and regional varieties, Godard saw very little to celebrate as the luckless Michel Piccoli found out. He was gently roasted by Godard for having accepted the presidency of the committee overseeing the French centenary celebrations. Indeed, Godard made clear his distance from the animating idea of the series with his title *2x50 ans de cinéma français*. From the first treatment it was clear that Godard and Miéville were not going to be celebrating the centenary. But Godard's negative work on the original commission was much more radical than that. From a producer's point of view *The Century of Cinema* was a massive exchange of clip licences, each film had their film clips cleared globally and for 20 years. We were particularly concerned that Godard would devote sufficient time and money to these clip clearances and we therefore elaborated a particularly complicated clause in the contract which specified that over a third of the budget would be reserved for clip clearances. Halfway through the production Godard informed us that as he did not intend to use clips for they ran counter to his aesthetic purpose, the clause did not apply. Once again a cynic would say that this decision was motivated by a desire to save time and money. A friend would point out that Miéville and Godard's decision did have real aesthetic point; their clipless film produces a very different account of film history from the other 15 episodes. Once again the cynical and friendly explanation are impossible to disentangle–the deep interpenetration of art and money, of films and contracts, are woven deeply into Godard's discourse as into his life.

It is this which undoubtedly has given Godard the reputation in French film circles of someone who is unreliable and greedy about money. My own experience suggests quite the contrary–I have always found Godard fair about money. But these rumours reflect a very important aspect of Godard's film production. Godard is the only filmmaker that I know of who really functions as a *petit commerçant*. He takes orders at prices fixed by the market and then decides himself how much time and money he will devote to the production of the artefact. He will not tie himself to a detailed budget, instead a price will be arrived at and then he will decide how his resources will be allocated. One could read this as a cynical ploy to accumulate more money but to do so is to ignore the fact that the money is endlessly recycled into other projects. When, for example, Godard made a contribution to Don Boyd's multi-authored film *Aria*, 1987, he was dissatisfied with his original contribution and, despite the fact that Boyd had accepted it, Godard insisted on shooting and editing a second and more satisfactory version at his own cost. Boyd was convinced that by any normal accounting the final results had cost more than the agreed fee. One of the reasons why Godard was able to make a second version of *Armide* was the fact that Miéville and Godard's company has almost all the equipment to shoot and edit both video and film. And this equipment has largely being acquired with monies saved on other projects.

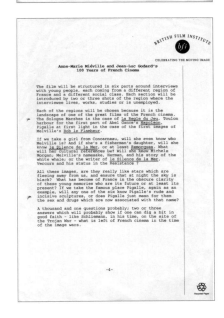

Above: **Godard and Miéville's proposal for *2x50 ans de cinéma français*, 1995.**

There is thus a very complicated internal accounting within Miéville and Godard's company which is entirely their decision. But it is a fair guess that *Je vous salue, Marie, Histoire(s) du cinéma, 1988-1998*, and *Éloge de l'amour* were subsidised by other less personal projects. What is interesting about *The Old Place* is that it began as a commission from outside but ended up as a personal project. As Miéville and Godard started work on their commission Godard rang me to make clear that the project had changed status for both of them as they found the question that had been posed was one that they needed to ask for themselves. This mixed origin of the work is signalled early on when Godard reads from the underlying contract. This attention to the financial and legal basis of the work is a constant emphasis of Godard from the prominence granted in the early films to the visa number which is the State's authorisation of the film to the famous sequence at the beginning of *Tout va bien*, 1972, when the cheques which constitute the financial reality of the film make up the credits sequence. The clause that Godard reads out is not the clause that appears in the legal document, but it represents a formulation that makes clear the double origin of the film, both in a question posed from outside and in the new meaning that the questions has provoked inside: "The producers shall examine any object or subject, ordinary or extraordinary in order to reveal, by chance and with painstaking care any trace that may remain of what we call art. That is to determine if art is myth [*légende*] or reality."

So much for a little of the context of *The Old Place*, but what of the film itself? I say "film", and that indeed is how Godard refers to it, but of course *The Old Place* is produced on video, and although Godard had, from his earliest films, played with text and image, it is doubtful if one could envisage the particular form of *The Old Place* without the experiments with the then new video technology which Miéville and Godard had carried out in the 1970s. *The Old Place* continues a conversation begun with *Ici et Ailleurs* in the early 1970s and which forms a continuous musical accompaniment to the work of the last 30 years. The particular importance of *The Old Place* can be grasped by the appearance of both Godard and Miéville in that scene so familiar to us from *Numéro Deux*, 1975, onwards, which shows Godard at work in his studio. That we finally see them together after 25 years shows the importance which they both accord to this piece.

It is tempting, and not inaccurate, to call this work an essay for it is Godard who has single handedly developed an essay style beginning with *Le Gai savoir*, 1968, further developed in the television work with Miéville, and which is now instantly recognisable. But it is perhaps more accurate to call it a poem, remembering Roman Jakobson's definition of poetry as an act of signification which focuses on the act of signifying itself. But one would need to integrate into Jakobson's definition the concept of montage, the juxtaposition of unrelated meanings to produce new meanings, to really grasp the nature of Miéville and Godard's work. In many ways *The Old Place* defies comment. The complexity of the references to painting, music, philosophy, literature and film would daunt any individual. Godard has spent a life immersed in art from his early childhood, and he may well have thought harder about the cinema than anyone else alive. What Jean-Marie Straub calls Jean-Luc's "discothèque" encompasses an astonishing range of music, and from his initial forays into anthropology Godard has assiduously tracked developments in twentieth century thought. When one adds to this a saturation in classic literature (his grandfather was Paul Valéry's private secretary), one is faced with a formidable range of reference. And that is before one also takes into account Miéville's own impressive musical culture, her training as a photographer and her own investigation of the philosophical canon.

軽蔑

監督 ジャン＝リュック・ゴダール

出演 ブリジット・バルドー ミシェル・ピコリ
フリッツ・ラング

MORAVIA
LE MÉPRIS

But it would be wrong to bury *The Old Place* beneath an avalanche of necessarily pedantic learning. The film is composed out of the most complex stands of reference but the composition makes sense in its own terms. It is explicitly and continuously a discourse on art and, as such, continues a discourse that marks Godard's work from his very earliest publications. It is well to remember that to claim the status of art for the Hollywood cinema in 1950 was not the simple evidence that it has become. And it is even more important to recall that for Godard and Éric Rohmer, perhaps theoretically the closest of his New Wave collaborators, part of the attraction of the cinema was that with its established codes and universal audience, it could proclaim itself the art which inherited the mantle of classicism. The paradoxes of modernism, the problem that one could not identify either artist or audience, could be ignored. This early optimism was early challenged. No sooner had the theory been elaborated than Hollywood went into the crisis of the late 1950s and by *Le Mépris*, 1963, Godard analyses the situation as "en pleine catastrophe". From this perspective the Maoist period can be seen as a final defence against modernism; a desperate attempt to avoid that collapse into individual subjectivity which modernism's loss of an audience threatens. *Ici et Ailleurs* offers a completely new solution which finds its justification neither in the audience (classicism) nor in the artist (modernism) but in conversation.

It is this conversation which sustains *The Old Place*, a conversation so serene in its rhythms that it is able to confront any topic. The basic topic is simple: like Major Amberson, like Godard, like the millennium, we confront a death which poses the most urgent questions about art and the film/documentary/essay/poem then pursues a series of possible deaths of art. But these deaths are not elaborated from a pessimistic point of view. This period of Godard's work might well be grouped under the rubric of elegy. But these elegies, these celebrations of the dead, do not look back but forward. The way forward is above all by new forms of juxtaposition, the bringing together of things distant and near, to echo the quotation from Pierre Reverdy which recurs in so much of Godard's work of the last 20 years. The penultimate section of the work sketches a history of twentieth century art which confirms the classicism of Godard's position. The breaking of conventions merely leads to a simple commercialisation of art in which the image is reduced to its contextual discourse. This potentially pessimistic emphasis is undercut both by the film itself and by the simple affirmation, significantly in Miéville's voice: "Still something will resist, something primal. The origin will always be there and will always resist." This cycle of the death of art and its rebirth is finally recaptured in the story of the A Bao A Qou constantly repeating its endless cycle. The beast lights up in colour when following a visitor up the stairs of the Tower of Victory at Chitor, turning even into a brilliant blue, only to return to its lethargic, semi-conscious state at the bottom when the visitor leaves and it has to wait for the next. This is the story of *The Old Place*.

Opposite left: **Japanese flyer for
Le Mépris, 1963.**

Right. **The 1955 French paperback
edition of Alberto Moravia's *Il Disprezzo*.**

Below: **Michel Piccoli and Brigitte Bardot
in *Le Mépris*.**

HOME-MOVIES: THE CURIOUS CINEMATIC COLLABORATION OF ANNE-MARIE MIÉVILLE AND JEAN-LUC GODARD

> The Straubs work in tandem, on the same bicycle, him in front, her behind. We have two bicycles.
>
> Jean-Luc Godard

> **Who am we?**[1]
>
> Sherry Turkle

CATHERINE GRANT

La Cinémathèque de Toulouse

2001

janvier

Anne-Marie Miéville

Wim Wenders

Claudia Cardinale

Positif

While collaborating couples are far from unknown in the history of cinema, the nature and extent of Anne-Marie Miéville and Jean-Luc Godard's work together is highly unusual. Unlike Jean-Marie Straub and Danièle Huillet, the French-born couple working in Germany to whom Godard refers above, who have had a very consistent approach to collaboration in their filmmaking over the years, Godard and Miéville's extensive body of film and video work together is characterised by at least three discernably separate strands: joint projects (co-directed, or co-signed, co-scripted and/or co-edited); appearances as personages or actors, together and alone, in each other's films; and forms of parallelism in the works they have directed alone, which are much less straightforward to characterise.[2] In this essay I shall examine aspects of these collaborative strands, focusing in particular on the case of one of their jointly made films *Sauve qui peut (la vie)*, 1980, directed by Godard but co-scripted and co-edited by Miéville, as well as on their appearances as actors in two films directed by Miéville (Godard in *Nous sommes tous encore ici*, 1997, and, especially, Godard and Miéville in *Après la réconciliation*, 2000).[3] These films have been chosen because their narratives all seem to revolve, to a greater or lesser extent, around the central figure of a creative couple, and have been used by other writers and researchers into Godard and Miéville's work to posit and sometimes to explore issues concerning their personal and professional partnership. It should quickly become obvious that my focus here derives itself less from my own curiosity about Godard's collaboration with Miéville on these projects–and much less from a belief that practical questions concerning, say, "who did what?", "who contributed what?", and "who influenced whom?" can be straightforwardly or even really usefully addressed in these and other cases–than it does from my interest in this

wider curiosity their collaboration has provoked in academic and journalistic discourse.[4] This kind of auteurist curiosity verging on, if not always openly entering, what might be regarded as the terrain of the name and not the work, has often coalesced around the figure of Godard. This is especially the case in France where, as Michael Temple and James S Williams write, "there exists a curious cultural paradox whereby 'Godard' the media icon (i.e. name plus face) is universally recognisable and yet totally unknown".[5] My objective, therefore, will be to explore how "Miéville" (name plus face plus work) factors itself into this paradox, but also why certain questions about her collaboration with her partner have been raised by commentators at particular times and in particular ways, as well as by Godard and Miéville themselves; these latter in their published and quoted words as well as, seemingly, in their films.

Jean-Luc Godard has a history of artistic collaboration with his romantic partners: Anna Karina, whom he married in 1961, appeared in seven of his early films; his second wife, Anne Wiazemsky, appeared in six, the last of these, *Tout va bien*, released in 1972.[6] This second marriage disintegrated at around the same time that Godard's working relationship with Jean-Pierre Gorin, his principal collaborator in the Dziga Vertov collective, came to grief. Godard and Miéville probably first met when she was manager of the Palestine bookstore in Paris, and he was preparing a video film on the Palestinian struggle with Gorin, to be titled *Jusqu'à la victoire*. This film was never completed, in part because of Godard's serious motorcycle accident in 1971, but he would later radically rework it in collaboration with Miéville as co-director. As an article in *Le Monde* put it: "she was first of all his interlocutor, then his collaborator, and finally the co-signatory of *Ici et Ailleurs* [1974]".[7]

Following the dissolution of the Dziga Vertov Group, and in convalescence after his accident, Godard moved with Miéville to Grenoble in the French

Above: **Godard and Miéville during the making of *Sauve qui peut (la vie)* in 1980.**

Opposite: **Programme for the Miéville retrospective held at the Cinémathèque de Toulouse in 2001.**

Alps, taking with them "Sonimage", the small studio or workshop that Godard had just previously established in Paris. They began experimenting with video and made a number of works in this medium, usually for French television and normally with equal billing in their credits as the constituent members of Sonimage. These works (*Ici et Ailleurs*; *Comment ça va?*, 1978; *Six fois deux (Sur et sous la communication)*, 1976; and later *France/tour/détour/deux/enfants*, 1979) are primarily concerned with the technological, economic and ideological "subjection" of humans and their "communications" by (and through) the modern media industries, in particular television.

While one project from this period that they co-produced on video and then reshot on 35mm was released for cinematic distribution (*Numéro Deux*, 1975), in the latter part of the 1970s Godard, assisted by Miéville, clearly directed his energies away from the specific cultural and economic field in which he had made his name in the previous decade.[8] This shift was consolidated by another geographical move that took Godard and Miéville even further away from the commercial mainstream of Francophone audio-visual production and nearer to their ideal of artisanal autonomy. The two took Sonimage to Rolle, a small town between Geneva and Lausanne in Switzerland, the country where both had grown up. As Colin MacCabe wrote of this distancing at the time: "It is from Rolle that Godard's most recent projects have originated and while concerns with information persist, such concerns are more and more inflected by an investigation of the constitutive terms of our subjectivity: the family and the opposition between the city and the country, between factory and landscape."[9] Godard himself described his and Miéville's move as follows: "We achieved the common purpose of our double solitude and of a new

Above: **Miéville and Godard fielding questions from secondary school students at the Sarlat Festival in 2000.**

Opposite: **Danièle Huillet (behind camera) and Jean-Marie Straub (wearing hat) shooting** *Dalla nube alla resistenza*, **1979.**

relationship with the world, with our selves, with our craft and profession, a little better here [in Switzerland], bi-national as we are."[10]

If Sonimage (including the subsequent move to Switzerland) is regarded metaphorically by commentators as, in Michael Witt's words, "a site of *transit*" in Godard's work, Miéville's role in this shift was not widely questioned in academic or journalistic discourse until after the couple made *Sauve qui peut* in 1980, the first film entirely shot and distributed on 35mm that they produced from their new base. Just as the Dziga Vertov label seemed to function to veil, rather than to promote, Gorin's contributions, in the face of Godard's greater fame as a filmmaker (as if the Maoist, collectivist politics of the films had not been believed, by commentators, to extend fully through the actual processes of their production), it can be argued that the Sonimage signature acted similarly to point up the notion that this new collective was simply Godard's latest venture. Like Gorin, Miéville had no track record of her own in filmmaking before beginning work with Godard. Yet recent research by Michael Witt has clearly established that, from the outset, she was no passive "assistant". He writes:

> It is tempting to overcompensate for critical neglect of Mieville's contribution by suggesting that hers was perhaps the more significant voice of the two. It would certainly be possible to argue that she was the [Sonimage] enterprise's principal creative force, supplying many of the thematic concerns that recur from work to work, and that Godard occupied a more reactive role, channelling her ideas into audio-visual form. In reality, of course, there is little to be gained from pursuing such an argument. The Sonimage work generally [...] was the fruit of full, equal collaboration.[11]

Witt's last comment is clearly pertinent, given the weight of his evidence, in terms of the artisanally produced Sonimage video work. The different industrial and commercial contexts of the jointly produced film work, however, where the couple were working with much larger numbers of collaborators and with the different financial imperatives of outside producers and distributors, clearly open up the question of the equality of their collaboration once more. Despite his radical, maverick history, Godard was a known entity who could raise feature-film finance as a writer-director; Miéville, at this time, was not. So the title sequence of *Sauve qui peut* records a different division of labour from that of most of the Sonimage video work. While that was completely 'collective' (the programmes and films were usually co-produced, co-written, co-directed and co-edited by the couple), Godard is credited as having "composed" this film ("composé par Godard").[12] Meanwhile, Miéville is credited as co-scenarist, with Godard and Jean-Claude Carrière, and as the film's co-editor with Godard.[13]

While Godard himself certainly seemed to be at pains to single out Miéville's contribution to *Sauve qui peut*, most prominently in the comment attributed to him that "she is at least 50% of this film",[14] he had also spoken in interviews of Miéville's contribution to *Numéro Deux*,[15] as well as to the other, earlier work. Researchers only really took up his insistence that she was an important collaborator once an obvious turn was detected in the work, a turning back to cinema, to actors and stars, and to prominent themes of sexual difference. Despite the fact that *Numéro Deux* is at least as resolutely concerned with these themes as *Sauve qui peut*, it doesn't seem to have operated to link them to the question of Godard/Miéville's collaboration in quite the way that the later film has. Even though Godard places himself (as a "real" subject) within the diegesis of *Numéro Deux*, it is what many have interpreted as the fictionalised self-portraiture of *Sauve qui peut*, set in a city and a small rural community in the Swiss countryside,

Above: **UK release poster for** *Sauve qui peut (la vie)*, **1980.**

Opposite: **"Anne-Marie, I invent stories through your channel."** *Nous trois*, **episode 5a of** *Six fois deux (Sur et sous la communication)*, **1976.**

that has attracted much greater attention.[16] This vein is carried in the film by two out of its three main figures in a series of connected micro-narratives: a filmmaker Paul Godard (Jacques Dutronc) and his writer-girlfriend and co-worker Denise Rimbaud (Nathalie Baye).[17] They are linked, in addition by the character of Isabelle Rivière (Isabelle Huppert), a prostitute whose own story flows between and around that of the couple, who, during the course of the film, become completely estranged, ending their troubled romantic and professional partnership (Denise leaves Paul and the city to write in the country). The film concludes with the comic/symbolic "death" of the irascible, cigar-smoking, bespectacled Paul Godard, in a road accident.

While numerous critics reviewing the film at the time couldn't help but notice the resemblance between the "two Godards" (and many noted that the film character is given the name of Jean-Luc's father), it took a newly prominent, contemporaneous critical audience to ask differently inflected questions of the film's authorship, as well as of its portrait of a collaborating couple.[18] Feminist film critics, especially Anglo-American theorists who had been writing about sexual difference in Godard's work for some time, seized upon *Sauve qui peut*. While some damned the seeming misogyny of the film's portrayal of violence against women, others, more sympathetic to Godard's cinematic project, went beyond crude forms of content analysis to investigate what might lie beyond the purview of such observations.

In their introduction to a special issue of the feminist journal *Camera Obscura* published in 1982 on Godard's work, the members of the editorial collective wrote:

The following three articles by the editors are intended as a preface to this special issue on Jean-Luc Godard's work in film, television and criticism. Taking as their point of departure Godard's latest film to be released in the US, *Sauve qui peut (la vie)*,

they are meant to be read as related pieces. We chose this way of raising certain issues with respect to the film (violence and enunciation, pornography and eroticism, the citation of the work of Marguerite Duras and her fictional inclusion in the film) in order to give readers a sense not only of the importance that we afford to Godard's work, but also the complexity of our relation to that work as it bears on our own project, namely, the examination of women and representation in film and the other arts.[19]

The editors closed their introductory remarks with the following comments:

Like many others, we have been very curious about Anne-Marie Miéville's contribution to the more recent films and television programs, where her role as collaborator has been readily, if a little vaguely, acknowledged by Godard. We tried to communicate with her directly, by sending questions about her views on these projects, her working methods, and her film, photographic, video or written work apart from Godard. Unfortunately, there was no response. We still hope to discover more about her contribution, clearly a considerable one, and publish this in a future article or review.[20]

If Godard has been (irritatingly?) vague about Miéville's contribution to "their" work, he has presumably been equally as vague about the limits of his own contribution in the statements to which the editors refer. But they don't say that they have attempted to contact Godard, or that they would be interested in so doing.[21] Only Miéville, it seems, can clear these matters up and she is silent.[22] It appears that, according to some kind of unstated auteurist default, Godard's contribution is not what is really in question.

Yet, as the last paragraph of the editorial introduction makes clear, part of *Camera Obscura*'s political project requires that Miéville must now be taken into account, not just as any collaborator with Godard but as one who may well be an author in her own right, whether or not she co-directs "his" films. By the time *Sauve qui peut* was distributed, it was known, again rather vaguely, that Miéville had been involved in certain filmmaking projects outside of her collaboration with Godard.[23] Despite the fact that the late 1970s and early 1980s saw the apogee of academic debates about the "death of the author", it can be seen that feminist film theory needed female filmmakers in its theorising of "women and representation in film and the arts". At the very least, it could not allow them to continue to be sidelined or ignored. In representing this desire the editorial introduction unavoidably bespeaks some of the contradictions of the debates about the practices of critical auteurism at this time.[24]

But what exactly does *Camera Obscura* want from Miéville? While the editors do not set out collectively to prove that Godard's work has changed with *Sauve qui peut*, and that therefore Miéville's role in this change should be investigated, two out of their three individually authored articles on the film do explore these ideas tangentially. In her article on the film, entitled "Pornography, Eroticism", Constance Penley (noting, along with other critics that "Paul Godard is a fictional character but he is also meant to be Godard") writes that "[i]n the masochistic fantasy of this film Paul Godard is destroyed by the women, or at least by his passivity in relation to their greater readiness to seek change".[25] She continues:

Women, then, in this schema, acquire a certain superiority, but it is at the price of a difference defined as essential (in their nature) and as necessarily bound to extinguish its opposite. The film offers a strikingly different narrative repartition of the terms of masculinity and femininity, but because it leaves unquestioned what it sees as the natural fascination of women, these terms sort themselves out, finally, according to a logic of male masochism as the response to a failed aggression against these idealised women. *Sauve qui peut* begins with a celebration of femininity in its essential difference –Denise in stop-action riding her bicycle in the country […]–and ends with the imagined consequences of this difference for men–Paul dying in the street.[26]

Opposite: **Isabelle Huppert, Roland Amstutz, Jacques Dutronc, and Nathalie Baye in *Sauve qui peut (la vie)*, 1980.**

While Penley does not mention Miéville in her account of this "strikingly different narrative repartition", Janet Bergstrom is somewhat less reticent in her offering on the film for the special issue.[27] She is also more positive about *Sauve qui peut*'s portrayal of sexual difference than Penley. Like Penley, though, she argues that

a large part of the sense of frustration and loss generated by the film comes from the way it extends beyond the usual boundaries of fiction. Godard is surely meant to be closely identified with his protagonist, Paul Godard, and the function of quotation here (the Duras episode, for example) is only a more pointed use of this *extending* strategy very familiar from Godard's earlier films.[28]

Bergstrom's greater optimism about the film's figuration of sexual difference, however, is linked to her idea that it manages to introduce a split into the overall logic of its enunciation:

While we follow mainly Paul's story, we are also given several important women characters with their own narrative trajectories who provide us with an array of examples of resistance to male narrative logic at the level of characters, as well as moments given over to a woman alone (Denise at the window-seat with her notebook) or women together (Denise and Isabelle in the car) that are significantly different from scenes to which they might be compared from earlier Godard films. In part, this is because of the way they are inaccessible to the male protagonist, even via the overlay of Romanticism and idealisation that has characterised the position of the desired woman within the logic of the enunciation in most of Godard's films.[29]

This enunciative split is not simply achieved, for Bergstrom, at the level of the narrative (plot, characters), though, but also through the film's form, which is finally achieved in the editing process, and in particular through the separation and pacing of the different stories or moments alone in *Sauve qui peut* through cutting, slow motion and stop-action. Of the image of Denise with her notebook, she argues that

She appears no less lovely than the other women photographed earlier as stills by Godard [such as Karina and Wiazemsky], but her seriousness in her writing, as an activity, as a direction, is at least equally evident. Therefore, we have a woman character who is unreachable for the male protagonist, but not to us, since we are given other views of her that show a separate logic of desire being pursued in the face of difficulties, uncertainty, fragility.[30]

In her only mention of Miéville, Bergstrom reiterates this idea of the divergent expressions of desire represented in the film by and through the characters of Paul and Denise. She argues that these expressions are "imagined by Godard and Miéville here, masculine/feminine. (Anne-Marie Miéville's exact contribution cannot be determined; we know that she collaborated on the conception, writing and shooting of the film with Godard.")[31] The idea that this shift in Godard's representation of sexual difference might be related to the film's actual co-authorship (even if this is not credited as co-direction) is raised by Bergstrom, only to be hastily toned down, parenthetically, by a lack of real evidence for the assertion.[32] And even though she draws a direct link, in these passages, between Paul Godard and Denise Rimbaud's different desires being 'imagined' by the extra-cinematic, masculine/feminine partnership of Godard and Miéville, she stops short of stretching her discussion of the film's strategy of "extension beyond the bounds of fiction" to suggest that the diegetic couple may be interpreted as co-author "surrogates".

This degree of reticence about making unequivocal statements on the relationship between metaphorical and actual film authorship seems not to have afflicted writers who are less burdened with the chronic academic

Opposite above: **Harriet Kraatz in Miéville's *How can I love (a man when I know he don't want me)*, 1984.**

Below: **Anny Romand and Hanns Zischler in Miéville's *Mon cher sujet*, 1989.**

queasiness around auteurism that was especially characteristic of the early 1980s. For example, Claire Pajaczkowska, a feminist researcher and filmmaker examining *Sauve qui peut* in the late 1980s, writes of the film that:

Godard is collaborating with Miéville in a deliberate and politically informed way, making collaboration a theme of the film itself in the relationship between Paul Godard and Denise Rimbaud [...] Whereas Denise and Paul's collaboration is represented as violent and 'impossible', Godard and Miéville collaborated successfully. The question of authorship raised in the film seems to be "What is it that prevents men and women from working and living together as equals?" From where does the 'impossibility' of progressive collaboration emanate?[33]

Here, Pajaczkowska's invokes quite openly, if rather crudely, Godard and Miéville's collaboration in relation to their potential fictional delegates. But even here such speculations have nowhere to go. Miéville is barely mentioned in the rest of the article. And the writer really doesn't seem to know what more to do with the stark fact that the film's story is the opposite of what she professes in passing to "know" about Godard and Miéville's partnership, beyond her suggestive concluding remarks that

we could ask what the film reveals about the difficulties of such work [artistic collaboration between the sexes]. The most basic difficulty, clearly shown in the film, is that of recognising and accepting the full extent of subjective reality and its influence on external reality. The unconscious meaning of the mother has a particularly significant effect on male subjectivity, and unless the Oedipus complex is recognised and accepted as a subjective reality men will continue to misrecognise and to misunderstand women.[34]

Even here, Pajaczkowska's thoughts on the collaboration are collapsed back on to a psycho-textual reading of the film's putative theme.

Despite the fact that this might be all that it was possible to say, and certainly to theorise, about Godard and Miéville's collaboration in the 1980s, there is something unsatisfactory about the way that all these accounts of *Sauve qui peut* invoke actual film authorship in relation to Godard's narrative representations of it. Why do they raise the question of collaboration at all if they don't wish to, or don't know how to, make these elements link up?

The most successful attempt to establish the kind of mediatory conceptual framework that is missing from these earlier feminist accounts is that of Kaja Silverman who has studied Godard's invocation of authorship in his films in her recent article "The Author as Receiver". In this work, she examines not only a range of fictional author 'surrogates' in Godard's films but also the films of his in which he makes an appearance, most notably *JLG/JLG: autoportrait de décembre*, 1995. While she doesn't consider his collaboration with Miéville, Silverman's use of Godard's own characterisation of *JLG/JLG* not as an autobiography but as a "self-portrait" might be usefully considered in relation to the narrative representations of collaborating couples.[35] Arguing that Godard allies his cinematic project with painting, over and against literature (producing self-portraits "in the sense that painters had practised this exercise; not by narcissism, but as an interrogation on painting itself"), Silverman re-examines the issues of Godard's supposed masochism in his self-representations as author.[36] She writes that "[b]iographical erasure might seem radically incommensurate with the idea of an artistic self-portrait, but it is Godard's very phenomenological idea that the artist is not properly a creator, but rather the site where words and visual forms inscribe or install themselves".[37] Of the constant repetition in Godard's films of these figurations of "self-erasure", Silverman concludes that:

SOFT TALK ON A HARD SUBJECT BETWEEN TWO FRIENDS

All those projects to grow, to be enlarged into subjects?

Where has it all gone?

Above: **The closing sequence** of **Soft and Hard**.

Like all egoic structures, biographical authorship is also not something from which anyone can emerge; as Lacan tells us in his first seminar, we can enter the imaginary register, but we cannot leave it. The death of the author is thus better understood as an ongoing process rather than as a realisable event.[38]

In the final part of my discussion, I would like to go on to consider some of these arguments in relation to Godard/Miéville's most recent collaboration on Miéville's latest two films. If a Godardian self-portrait "has no 'me'", as both Silverman and Godard himself have argued, can anything be made of the procedure of looking for an "us" in "their" dual self-portraiture?[39]

In an interview in 1973, at the outset of the Sonimage project in its initial incarnation in the Avenue du Maine in Paris, Godard affirmed the importance of the subjective in his new work:

As for me, I've become aware, after 15 years of cinema, that the real "political" film that I'd like to end up with would be a film about me which would show to my wife [Anne Wiazemsky] and daughter what I am, in other words a home-movie—home-movies represent the popular base of the cinema.[40]

This connection between cinema and home-movies is reprised, this time by both Godard and his next partner, Miéville, in their own "home-movie", the 1985 video film *Soft and Hard (Soft Talk on a Hard Subject Between Two Friends)*. In this co-directed work for Channel Four Television, the couple film themselves and are filmed in their daily routine as they discuss questions of communication in television, art, the cinema, as well as in their own joint and separate work, and their everyday life.[41] The film represents Godard's characteristic irascible vulnerability as well as Miéville's somewhat brittle and, occasionally, confrontational style. The couple seem to disagree more than they agree on certain topics.[42] Nonetheless, towards the end of the film, they join together as they recall what brought both of them to the cinema. While Godard notes that he became interested in cinema quite late, Miéville recounts that, as a young girl, she used to shut herself up in her bedroom and project images of her family from photographic negatives on to the wall. The film closes with a melancholic meditation on the difference between the projects of cinema and television, as a sequence from Godard's *Le Mépris*, 1963, is projected on to the wall, and we see the silhouettes of the arms of Godard and Miéville. As Michael Temple and James S Williams write of this climactic gesture, "the interweaving of the personal and the impersonal [is] most eloquently illustrated".[43]

While Miéville's first feature films as a solo director, *Mon cher sujet*, 1989, and *Lou n'as pas dit non*, 1994, do not employ anything resembling the home-movie form, the themes of the films certainly turn primarily on "domestic" issues: love (and the daily labours of love), the couple, the family, childhood, ageing, and the difficulties of communication between genders and across both professional and personal lives.[44] Her last two feature films, however, while continuing with the same themes as her earlier work, have been interpreted by critics as bearing some greater relation to Miéville's personal life. Given that the films themselves have become less naturalistic, this can only be because they contain performances from either Godard (*Nous sommes tous encore ici*) or Miéville and Godard (*Après la réconciliation*), a new feature for her solo projects on which much journalistic commentary picked up. The healthy level of interest in these two films (compared with the relative lack of interest in the first two, outside of academic circles) is unsurprising considering the curiosity that still exists in France and other Francophone countries about Godard, and in particular about the rather more reclusive figure of "late Godard".[45] But there is also the expression of a certain prurient interest in

après
la réconciliation
UN FILM DE Anne-Marie Miéville
AVEC Claude Perron Anne-Marie Miéville
Jacques Spiesser Jean-Luc Godard

Godard and Miéville as a couple, to which I shall briefly refer in relation to Godard's performance as one half of a longstanding, though bickering couple in *Nous sommes tous encore ici*.[46] Many of the reviews, interviews and articles on this film tell of how Godard ended up in the role of Lui/Him "by accident", replacing another actor at the last minute.[47] Some carry quoted comments from Godard disavowing a personal connection with his character. For example, he tells a *Le Monde* interviewer: "My character doesn't resemble me, and I don't identify with him."[48] But despite these efforts to derail "personal" interpretations, the curiosity of reviewers was undoubtedly aroused by the third, most naturalistic part of the film (with its dialogue entirely scripted by Miéville), which features Godard as a grumbling, somewhat fragile old man who visits his partner (played by Aurore Clément, bearing a striking resemblance to Miéville) in her separate apartment. For example, Claire Vassé writes in *Positif* that

in [the last part of the film where the couple comes together], the relationship to the text becomes personal. We are all ears, so much does it seem to speak to us directly, inscribing us into the very life of words lived by these two characters. Words that sometimes lay them bare, revealing them to us unreservedly, even with a certain shamelessness, in moments when one can't stop thinking of the real couple, just beneath the surface, the one made up of the filmmaker and her filmmaker/actor partner. In any case, Him and Her [the characters] are aware of this risk: "It's true that one no longer speaks of the work, just of the person... The person has become a work in him/her self." [quoted from the film's dialogue] In this film, there is something of an intimate diary in two voices.[49]

Although critics do not reflect much, if at all, on the nature of the story that *Nous sommes tous encore ici* might be telling them about Godard, or about Godard/Miéville as a couple, the *desire* to read the film in this way, as a story about them, is frequently expressed. And this reaction is intensified in the reviews of *Après la réconciliation*, when the two act together as a couple for the first time (since *Soft and Hard*, at least). For reviewers, it seems, the films potentially provide a biography (authored by Miéville) that doesn't otherwise exist, providing an interpretative key to reading the films, and, of course, giving them something accessible and engaging to write about in relation to otherwise "difficult" art cinema artefacts.

As for Miéville and Godard, they have said more together about their collaboration as a couple in relation to these films than they have in the rest of their careers. In response to the frequent questions about how well they work together, Godard generally replies with a variation on the following, fairly blunt statement: "Like two filmmakers who get on well, who make things together and separately."[50] Yet he also often speaks of his "escapist" pleasure in acting in *Après la réconciliation* (which interrupted the more troubled shooting of his own feature, *Éloge de l'amour*, 2001): "Working for the other [*l'autre*], especially if you love them, allows one to occupy a more modest place than that of filmmaker. I liked being part of the game outside of the name that is normally assigned to me."[51] Miéville also often invokes love when describing the harmonious atmosphere of the film's production:

I used to find that my family was a place where I didn't often see lots of displays of love because we never used to do anything together. There was, then, in this film a great deal of care in the preparation, in order to bring the right people in, where they were happy to be. With cohesion and support. This is a very important part of the vigour and style of the film. So, yes, in that sense, love works.[52]

Opposite: **Godard and Claude Perron in the poster for Miéville's *Après la réconciliation*, 2000.**

If Godard and Miéville seem happier, together, to discuss their personal collaboration in relation to *Après la réconciliation*, this could be because the film

AURORE CLÉMENT
BERNADETTE LAFONT
JEAN-LUC GODARD

nous sommes tous encore ici

UN FILM DE
ANNE-MARIE MIÉVILLE

UNE PRODUCTION ALAIN SARDE - PERIPHERIA - LES FILMS DU LOSANGE - VEGA FILM AVEC LA PARTICIPATION DE CANAL+, LE SOUTIEN DE LA FONDATION VAUDOISE POUR LE CINÉMA
LA COPRODUCTION DE LA TELEVISION SUISSE-ROMANDE - DISTRIBUTION LES FILMS DU LOSANGE

itself is framed more overtly as a "self-portrait" than any of Miéville's other films. It opens with what might be described as a home-movie styled *scénario-vidéo* that acts as a teaser for the film that will follow.[53] This pre-credit sequence begins with handheld video camera shots taken by Miéville of her grandchildren (she tells us they call her "Minnie" and that she doesn't see them very often). There are shots of the house where she filmed *Nous sommes tous encore ici*, lent to her by relatives, accompanied by her voiceover which tells of the shoestring budget she had for that film. There are shots (sketches) of the locations from the film to come. There are images of Miéville working at a desk (reminiscent of some moments in *JLG/JLG*). She speaks on the phone, possibly of Godard and of the financial problems with making the film.[54] Then there are black and white rushes from the film that follows, including some enticing yet fleeting images of Godard in one of the film's early scenes in the car before he snaps his clapperboard and "goes into character". The segment is threaded through with Miéville's opaque, metaphysical meditation on waiting at, or advancing across, thresholds, and the possibility of reconciliation. The whole prologue is teasing us, of course, in its ambivalence about communicating something of the meaning of the film that will follow. But, most of all, it teases us with the idea that Miéville is showing and telling us something of her intimate life. When we watch them again, these disjointed scenes can reveal no rounded, explicable "me", no "us"–there is no real exposition or "exposure". And in any case they are tempered at the end with Miéville's voiceover telling us "not to trust the storyteller, trust the story". This gesture of authorial divestiture, familiar to us from Godard's work, only reveals that, whatever will happen in the rest of the film, the prologue provides precisely the kind of reflection on the processes of self-portraiture of which Silverman speaks.[55]

The rest of the film also teases us, this time with its recognisable real people "acting" while still bearing the demeanour with which we may be familiar from their other film appearances. This onscreen couple play out a troubled relationship through philosophical and literary aphorisms, which work in abstract counterpoint to the scenes of everyday life in which they are uttered. She (Femme 1/Woman 1) briefly leaves her partner Robert to kiss another man, Arthur (Jacques Spiesser).[56] He (Robert) resists the sexual advances of another of the film's characters, Cathos (Claude Perron). Alone and reunited, he infuriates her with his inability to say "the phrase" she needs him to say; she, in turn, makes him cry with her furious insistence on this (an astonishing moment: "Godard" weeps). Together they establish an uneasy "reconciliation":

Robert: We'll no longer escape from one another.
Femme 1: Oh shut up! The other [*l'autre*], his solitude, his difference. Will it be like this until the end?

The film itself seems to conclude, in its brittle dialogue as well as in its beautiful final images and music, that the "splendour" of love between "two different creatures" can only last for an instant, although one should remain open to this possibility and work for it.[57]

Interestingly, despite the relatively non-naturalistic dialogue and staging of Miéville's last two films, the representation of sexual difference in both of them seems less schematic, and certainly less prominent than in either Godard's or her earlier films.[58] When her male/female couples are embodied by recognisable figures (Godard/Miéville), they seem less founded along masculine/feminine fault-lines; other, less socially (though no less psychically) entrenched forms of difference take precedence. In this case, the casting as actors of people about whom we think we "know" something renders the real couple's co-subjects (love, solitude and sexual difference) personal and metaphysical at one and the same time.[59] While creating this tension between

Opposite: **Godard and Aurore Clément in the poster for Miéville's *Nous sommes tous encore ici*, 1997.**

naturalism and non-naturalism, personalisation and de-personalisation has been Miéville's cinematic strategy for some time, and certainly since *Lou n'a pas dit non* with its Rilkean premiss that "love will no longer be the commerce of a man and a woman but of one humanity with another", it reaches its peak, so far, in *Après la réconciliation*.[60]

Of course, home-movies are not usually made to be seen by those outside an immediate circle of family and friends. So why make these films, and talk about them, in ways that will almost inevitably be interpreted as personal? The answer is probably that these are the films that can be made; they both respond to and create a demand for putative biographical stories. But they are also part of a longstanding project to make "subjective" cinema. As Michael Witt writes:

The Sonimage work is essentially the result of a collaborative venture played out between Godard and Miéville. It revolved around the attempt to live out a working practice in which the divisions of labour and of the sexes were dissolved in a reflection on the implications of finding pleasure in one's own work whilst collaborating with a partner one loves (to love work, and work at love).[61]

What should we be looking for if we seek out "Godard/Miéville" in their films, or in their published words? Perhaps simply to explore the idea, as they constantly do, that (whether coupled or single) film artists are not properly individual creators but, rather, particular embodied sites where words and audio-visual forms inscribe or install themselves. For Godard and Miéville, this plural site starts with Sonimage,[62] the beginning of the collective creative ferment[63] that frames all their later work, together and apart, and (re)creates them as "different" filmmakers and dual authors.

Opposite: *Lou n'a pas dit non*,
Anne-Marie Miéville, 1994.

GODARD IN THE MUSEUM

ANTOINE de BAECQUE

Jean-Luc Godard has always been interested in art and its exhibition, the development of exhibition space design and museology, and the ideology of its vision. In this respect, some of his films (as early as *Les Carabiniers*, 1963) have invited us to consider museums, be they imaginary (stemming from his fascination with André Malraux) or material (ranging from the visit to the Louvre's Great Gallery in *Bande à part*, 1964, to the recent filmed essay on the Museum of Modern Art in New York, *The Old Place*, 1999). My concern here is with the "destabilisation of museums" inherent in cinema and Godard's philosophy. This constitutes a destruction that leads to both revelation and loss, resulting in *Histoire(s) du cinéma*, 1998, which can be viewed and interpreted as a destruction of the Museum (the numerous paintings seem to have been ripped out) as well as its reconstruction (the constant alternation between films and paintings restores dignity and richness to the exhibition of art).

Editing in Godard's films is a means of rebuilding the aura surrounding works of art by inserting them into cinema, or in other words into the history of the twentieth century. In his films, whether earlier or more recent, museums are represented as institutional, cultural and ideological spaces; later they are seen as an imaginary site that can encourage and nurture editing, which is key to Godard's cinema; finally, museums are the most authentic and moving embodiment of History.

I should stress that, from the outset, Godard has always entertained an initial polemical relationship with museums; to him they are derisory sites of great learning, which is inherited, defunct and conservative. This relationship is illustrated in *Bande à part* with the famous speeded-up dash through the Louvre's Great Gallery. It takes Franz, Arthur and Odile exactly nine minutes and 43 seconds to tear through the greatest exhibition rooms

Above: **The race through the Louvre in** *Bande à part*, **1964.**

Opposite: **"A soldier salutes an artist!" Michel-Ange (Albert Juross) salutes Rembrandt in** *Les Carabiniers*, **1963.**

in the world and thus beat the former record by two minutes. In the film, this race takes up 24 seconds of screen time, during which time we are able to glimpse David's monumental paintings and the *Victory of Samothrace*.

These citations place Godard squarely within the French tradition of considering art and museums as antagonistic, whether these museums are conservation spaces or political institutions. Diderot and Baudelaire did not champion museums which they considered predators of artworks, but it was Quatremère de Quincy in particular who acted as Godard's direct ancestor by lambasting museums at the end of the eighteenth century and under Napoleon. According to Quatremère's *Lettres à Miranda*, museums entail the removal of works of art from their cultural and political contexts, thereby disfiguring the works and destroying their aesthetic meaning. Museums displace, lock away and appropriate artworks. They are an imposture.

This idea of the museum as theft can be found in *Éloge de l'amour*, 2001, where a line of dialogue attacks the directors of great classical museums: "We know what these people are like; the director of the Louvre doesn't just want to safeguard the *Victory of Samothrace*, he wants to take credit for this protection, so as to be on an equal footing with Phidias." Later, still in *Éloge*, one hears a similar assertion: "My dear boy, once a thief, always a thief, even a national museum." Because the director of the Louvre pretended to be the artist, this imposture is a blatant act of theft, the theft of the work's aura. In a sense, Godard turns Benjamin's seminal theory on its head: the physical presence of art in museums does not mean that art is restored; this is utopian, because its aura has been stolen by museums which do not restitute it to our gaze since they neutralise it, lock it away and kill it. The traditional museum is, for Godard, a large-scale abduction of art.

How can one retrieve the aura of a work of art? Godard suggests looking at it from the point of view of Malraux/Langlois. He creates a work of art by

Above: **André Malraux and Sergei Eisenstein in Moscow circa 1935.**

using the imaginary form of the museum: his ideal museum, following in the footsteps of Malraux, and later Langlois, is where artworks are brought together. It becomes a montage, following Malraux's assertion that "we are able to feel only through comparisons". Godard confirms that he has espoused this comparative approach by explaining with Anne-Marie Miéville the following in their voice-over commentary to *The Old Place*:

We mentioned the exercise of artistic thought. The general idea here is connections. In the same way as stars get closer, even when they're moving away from each other, driven by laws of physics, for example, to form a constellation, so certain thoughts come together to form one or more images. Therefore, to understand what is happening between the stars, between the images, one first needs to examine simple connections. Consequently, everything is far. But at the same time, everything is near. And between the infinitely small and the infinitely great, one will probably find a mid-point. The mid-point is the average man. What has already been will be and what will be has already been. Because an image is not just an atom, it is part of, it has been part of, it will be part of the image. And what of the image of the image? And the image of all these possibles? To create artistically does not only mean observing, accumulating experimental data, from which to draw a theory, a painting, a novel, a film, etc.. Artistic thought begins with the invention of a possible world, or a fragment of a possible world, which needs to be confronted with the outside world through experience, through work, painting, writing, filming. This never-ending dialogue between imagination and work allows an increasingly acute representation of what is commonly called reality.

The juxtaposed images in *The Old Place* suggest an editing process inherent to Godard's ideal museum: two female tennis players, a man kowtowing, people working, a Virgin Mary, a cinema auditorium, Lascaux and Picasso face to face, a *pietà* scene, Adam and Eve, and Pialat's Van Gogh uttering the words, "Hey, there's that other fellow!", by way of conclusion. This key sequence in *The Old Place*, which sheds rare light on Godard's conceptual thought, is matched by a praise of juxtaposition in *Éloge*: "Here's *Le Petit Chose*. We often tend to forget that classical painters worked solely through connections. That's the fundamental issue and it's Delacroix or Matisse who can supply the answer." A riposte to the imposture of classical museums can thus be found in this connective approach, borrowed from Malraux's imaginary museum. *Histoire(s) du cinéma* is probably the greatest exponent of Malraux and Langlois's theories.

It is difficult to ascertain to what extent *Histoire(s)* has been influenced by Malraux's *Les Voix du silence*, 1947-1965. The interstices between shots, frames and paintings form a space of comparison. It is only in that space that comparative thought can blossom, as Godard clearly explains:

In my opinion, films are hardly ever seen any more, since "seen" suggests to me the possibility of making comparisons. By that I don't mean comparing two things, or one image to the memory that one has of that image. Rather, I mean comparing two images and, at the moment of viewing them, highlighting certain links between them. For instance, if one claims that Eisenstein's parallel editing echoes a style of editing traditionally ascribed to Griffith, then one would need to project them simultaneously, with Griffith on the left and Eisenstein on the right. It would be like a trial and one could be sure of the accuracy of the claim. And one could discuss it. It would be technically difficult to place two cinema screens side by side, but video playback is now available so videotapes could be viewed side by side and compared.

In an article published in *Art Press* in 1996 (no. 221), Dominique Païni drew a parallel between this Godardian belief and Malraux's *Les Voix du silence* and also noted their common ambition: the ideal museum should separate artworks from the profane world and bring them together with contrasting, rival and distinct artworks. For both Malraux and Godard, this museum is a "confrontation" before being a conservation, a confrontation of metaphors and metamorphoses. By subjecting film extracts, shots and sequences to confrontation and comparison, Godard is developing a series of hypotheses in the same way as Malraux did in his imaginary museum, using photography to contrast works and corroborate his claims. The two projects are equally insane: Malraux shuffled some 7,000 years' worth of images, without any scientific legitimacy, convinced that these juxtapositions would give meaning to a history/histories of art. Similarly, Godard has edited together hundreds of sequences, extracts, photos, texts in over six hours of video. Malraux used photography, Godard prefers video, that is to say, exactly the medium which can destroy the aura of works of art, but in this instance it is used to recover some of the meaning (and thus also the aura) through comparisons. He behaves like Langlois, who was programmer at the Cinémathèque in Paris, bringing together, mixing, contrasting very different films. Langlois too inserted "silences" between the films and the *auteurs* he screened. Malraux's imaginary museum, Langlois's Cinémathèque, Godard's cinema are exceptional mental spaces where works of art recover their aura through the incessant interplay of comparisons. Malraux, Langlois and Godard are consequently the three theoreticians and practitioners of what could be called "museum-montage". Malraux turned this into a book, Langlois transformed it into film programming, Godard made a video. Godard makes the best use of the resources of his video museum by resorting to slow-motion, freeze frames, stop-motion cinematography, commentaries and operatic music, in other words, all the strategies that produce the fetish of the aura, and of which neither Malraux nor Langlois were able to avail themselves.

This method of creating a tool for comparison, namely video, is also a museographic device, since Godard also takes the liberty of removing paintings or images from traditional museums to "edit" them into film. That said, this imaginary place, hinted at in *Histoire(s)* and *The Old Place*, is only made possible because it also offers an embodiment of history. Godard's imaginary museum is not a spiritual flight of fancy, on the contrary, it is a vision of the history of the twentieth century. What ultimately emerges from these films is that they bear witness to the cinema through snippets of memory, which are fragments snatched from the history of an art at once personal and universal: these are film moments, gestures, bodies, sentences, movements which act as fetishistic objects and which make up a sort of vision leading to a visual, sacred or gnostic recollection of the universe. Thus the twentieth century is encapsulated in one of Bogart's looks, one of Keaton's gestures, one of Renoir's flashes of lightning, one of Malick's landscapes, a word from one of Bergman's films; this constitutes a theory of privileged fragments which brings us closer to a cinematic understanding of a perception of the twentieth century universe by paying homage to privileged moments where memories of historic images surface.

Similarly, Godard uses and juxtaposes fragments in the eight episodes that make up *Histoire(s)*. To these filmic fragments, which he selects and draws from his own memories and cinephile vision, he adds fragments of life. First of all, his own life, by his continual presence: he is the artist working on his own editing, offering his own interpretations, his own choice of archive material, using his own voice, either a seemingly whispered voice from beyond the grave or an assured voice speaking with oracle-like certainty. Secondly, there are the fragments of the lives of twentieth century men, through hundreds of photographs, archive footage, extracts from speeches and archive material which constitute the visual history of our time. Most of these fragments are shaped by the artistic and technical resources of video: freeze-frames, stop-motion cinematography, double exposures, photo montages, special effects, inserted titles and sentences, mixing black and white and colour photography, mixing paintings, photos, texts and film. *Histoire(s)* seems to have been made in a laboratory, a crypt or a workshop: a place where an artist, a sorcerer's apprentice, a historian, or a high priest, has created a new form. Made up of these fragments, sounds and voices, edited together to create contradictory and staccato movements, giving out a light that evokes the end of the world but which is also reminiscent of its beginning, this form is essentially operatic. Godard's prophecy, where the cinematic form undertakes to embody the history of the century, is a personal epic, the confession of a child of the century who is also a son of the cinema (*ciné-fils*), and vice versa. It is a prosopopeia: I, the cinema, speak, or more precisely: I, Jean-Luc Godard, who embody cinema, narrate the history of my twentieth century.

This magnum opus, which runs for over four hours, edits and reveals what made cinema and this century. Unrivalled in terms of its ambition, and aesthetically peerless, it is the culmination of our time. If one claims that the twentieth century began with the projection of a Lumière film coupled with the irruption of *Les Demoiselles d'Avignon* on to the art scene, one could argue that it ends with *Histoire(s) du cinéma*, which is the final destination of the Lumière train and the aesthetic manifesto of the art of editing together fragments and snippets launched by Cubism. If you haven't seen *Histoire(s)*, you've missed the century's exit.

Godard has thus created a confession, but which can be applied to all of us. "I'm telling my story", he emphasises, "while feeling that it's not really mine, but I can only tell it from my own perspective. It is a very simple story, one that is mediated through cinema." We are faced with a cinematic

form which embraces everyone's autobiography, where a man, in seeking his reason for being in his own life-story, ultimately discovers the reasons for history. Thanks to this "museum-montage", thanks to cinema, Godard is able to fashion historiographical logic: he is a historian in his museum. This is why he has no place in the classical museum: the comparative virtues of editing make his imaginary museum a workshop as much as a laboratory of history. I would call this the shift of the Museum from art museum to history museum. Hence the idea that the history of an art and the history of a century are linked, more so than being simply an archive store or just reflecting circumstances–it has now become obvious that the 1917 revolution, the 1929 crash, the Nazi takeover in 1933, May 68 and the Gulf War can be viewed on a screen, perhaps more than anywhere else, and these matters are personal and corporeal. This is the ultimate lesson to be learned from *Histoire(s)*: the imaginary museum is also an embodied museum, i.e. the cinema has made flesh the history of this century. It is a body in every sense of the word: a place where the century could take faces, movements and gestures, genitals and utterances. It could also take ideas, references, works, concepts, so as to enable the century to think. It is an embodied body and a corpus: for the century, cinema has been, and still is, a tangible surface revealing history and the knowledge of where to seek its great representations.

Histoire(s) shapes the history of the twentieth century but with its own weapons, rather like the novel shaped the nineteenth century. Cinema is linked to great events (there isn't a single significant date of the twentieth century which isn't also a cinematic watershed) and it offers tools (constantly altered and reinvented, like a vision of the world). Like the novel in the nineteenth century, but also most probably the theatre in the seventeenth century, the dictionary in the eighteenth century, and what one could call the "grand narratives", the revealing form of cinema becomes, at one point,

Above: *L'Arrivée d'un train à La Ciotat*, Auguste and Louis Lumière, 1895.

the cultural practice which is consistent with the life of a century and, more specifically, its concept of reality. For the man of the nineteenth century, reality is literary. It can be described, analysed and imagined following the suggestions of literature. The man of the twentieth century is quite different: he describes, analyses and imagines only through cinema. Even literature conceives the world in cinematic terms: it is made up of montages, of shots, of visual affects. By forging its own visual processes, its effects, its techniques, cinema quickly became the century's tool-box. Effects, shots, editing, technicolor, double exposures, slow-motion, flash-backs, split-screens, point-of-view shots, but also burlesque comedy, cinephilia, back projection and insert titles: all these strategies have a history which ranges from their emergence to their revival, and all have played a role in the history of the century. Each artist, writer, ideologist, advertising executive, anyone could have used them, borrowing them from the screen, using them to live, to write, to think, to create during this century. Understanding and allowing others to understand this cinematic form of the history of the century is the prime focus of Jean-Luc Godard's imaginary museum.

The culmination of this formal understanding of history is suggested by Godard in his analysis of *mise en scène* in Hitchcock's films, in Chapter 4A of *Histoire(s)* entitled *Le contrôle de l'univers*. The four minutes devoted to Hitchcock seem to resume, condense, and achieve the critical work and formal ideas deployed by the young New Wave critics (that is, before they turned their hand to filmmaking) between 1949 (the French release date of *Rope*) and 1966 (the publication of François Truffaut's interview-book on Hitchcock). This segment of film is a meticulous, explosive and creative confrontation of Hitchcock's images and words, including clips with Godard quoting reviewers' comments in voice-over. Images and words have become fetishised, chanted like a vision of history, and visually and aurally they restore the role Alfred Hitchcock played in the New Wave Young Turks' lives: for them, he was the greatest formal creator of the twentieth century and he thus represented the infancy of their art.

Godard's ideal museum seems to be an impossible dream, since there is an insoluble contradiction between the exhibition and conservation space of the execrated classical museum, the ultimate dream of the museum as imaginary editing, and the museum as embodiment of the century's history. There nevertheless exists a place which, according to Godard, can bring together these three contradictory museums, as well as Alfred Hitchcock: it is the exhibition *Hitchcock et l'art: coïncidences fatales*, mounted in Montreal in 2000 and then at the Pompidou Centre in Paris, and curated by Dominique Païni and Guy Cogeval. On the invitation card, Godard wrote, "Perhaps the only museum I've ever loved". He seemed to have found the "practical exercises" of art which he referred to in *The Old Place*.

Opposite: **Henri Langlois with chronophoto-graphic rifle on the cover of the April-May 1968 issue of** *Cahiers du cinéma.*

HERE AND ELSEWHERE: PROJECTING GODARD

JAMES QUANDT

"Advance warning: I am also working on a Jean-Luc Godard bonanza for next year. The programme is quite frightening but I am not panicking yet–I may ask you some questions about it in due course." This portentous e-mail from Waltraud Loges, programme researcher for London's National Film Theatre, arrived while I was recovering from organising a touring retrospective of the films of Robert Bresson and editing its accompanying monograph for Cinematheque Ontario.[1] The message was sent a mere year before the "bonanza" was scheduled to coincide with the *For Ever Godard* conference at Tate Modern in London in June 2001. It had taken me more than twice that time to prepare the Bresson retrospective–securing the funding, negotiating complex film and literary rights, getting prints made and subtitled, navigating ancient contentions and cultural differences every step of the way. The challenges of mounting a complete Godard retrospective, then, seemed not just daunting but impossible, his corpus being several times the size of Bresson's, and comparatively fractious and variegated. Panic seemed appropriate.

Loges's famously methodical and meticulous research and the National Film Theatre's remarkable connections, coupled with my own cache of information from organising three previous Godard shows, allowed the two of us to collect his vast oeuvre, a tessera or two aside, over the following months. (Predictably, the Torquemadas of the tesserae focused on those missing pieces.) As this account suggests, the process of assembling the Godard retrospective, like that of making a film in *Le Mépris*, 1963, came to reflect the director's view of cinema and the world, characterised by venality, greed, and uncaring; while that of exhibiting the work proved the opposite, an exhilarating instance of classic cinephilia in which films widely considered too dense or demanding for contemporary audiences managed to create a world apart, "in harmony with our desires".

Opposite: **Programme booklets for the Godard retrospective held at the Cinematheque Ontario in 2001-2002.**

Is there a place for Godard's cinema, itself so desperate to be included in the great tradition of Western art, in this world of *mémoire courte*, in which the contours of history and culture have taken on the chimerical shimmy and insubstantiality of the digital image derided in the second half of *Éloge de l'amour*, 2001? When New York's Museum of Modern Art mounted in 1992 a retrospective of Godard's work post-*Sauve qui peut (la vie)*, 1980, Jonathan Rosenbaum wrote an essay entitled "Eight Obstacles to the Appreciation of Godard in the United States".[2] The eighth impediment cited by Rosenbaum, "hermeticism and declining interest in intellectual cinema", has only escalated in the intervening decade. Mocked, ignored or reviled, Godard's late work has suffered increasingly limited exhibition, even as his films from *À bout de souffle*, 1960, to *Week-end*, 1967, have become canonic. The early films, however, exist mostly in a televisual universe of cropped Scope, murky resolution, and, when broadcast, commercial interruption, and have been subsumed into postmodernist culture as hip tropes of violent knowingness. Never easy to see, the films from the Dziga Vertov period have all but disappeared from availability, and are rarely discussed any more.

To organise a comprehensive Godard retrospective is an act of resurrection, and the challenges facing the curator who dares this task reflect, indeed manifest, Godard's own concern with the recovery of the past. Its success depends on the retrieval of both material and memory–not merely projectable copies of all of his films and videos, but also of a sense of their influence and importance, and of the cultural and political knowledge required for their understanding. At a time when the two corrupt mercenaries of *Les Carabiniers*, 1963, would probably be running for election to the US Senate, and when our numb culture–malled, wired, and logoed–is not so far from that of *Deux ou trois choses que je sais d'elle*, 1967, in which, Godard once said, "dead objects are always alive and live people are often already dead", this trinity of retrieval would seem a dubious, if not hopeless, undertaking.

Détective: "Cinema projected, and men saw that the world was there." The liturgical meaning Godard assigns the cinema, especially in *Scénario du film Passion*, 1982, might suggest that the projected light that bodies forth his buried, lost, or perished images in a retrospective is an act of transubstantiation. But that "miracle" is made possible only when its material is available, and few directors pose as daunting obstacles to exhibition as Godard. His prolific output over more than four decades in many formats and media, including a profusion of commissioned and sponsored works, some of them with uncertain or disputed rights, combined with the increasing emphasis on the marketable of both film distribution and film preservation, has resulted in a state of near unattainability. Like one of Godard's many hapless detectives, the curator must first wend his way through an Orphic maze of fashion houses (Marithé et François Girbaud) and corporations both public and private (France Telecom, Darty), international aid agencies (UNICEF) and rights organisations (Amnesty International), American studios (Paramount, MGM/UA, Columbia) and private collectors, government cultural institutes (the Swiss Pro Helvetia and French Ministry of Foreign Affairs), cinematheques, libraries, and archives on several continents (including Asia and Australia), the estates of obscure writers and the internecine, highly coded world of French film production and distribution (Gaumont, Canal Plus, INA, *et al*). Some works listed in the master filmography turned out to be apocryphal or non-extant, while one or two others were withheld by their commissioners. Others belonged to Godard himself, some only by default. In the case of *Nouvelle Vague*, 1990, one of his greatest films and scandalously undistributed in Britain or the United States, the producer originally refused me permission

Opposite above: **"Le Tout Godard" retrospective, Paris 1989.**

Below: **1960s "Revolte Phantasie & Utopie" season, Berlin 2002.**

to include it, and then agreed only if Godard gave his authorisation. "I am a man of my word", Godard growled at me from his office in Paris, insulted by my request for the necessary approval in writing, "Au revoir, Monsieur." Two days later, my imploring fax was returned with his scrawled OK. That was enough, but the close call was one of many.

The cornucopia of André Malraux's "museum" was possible because imaginary, whereas Godard's is elusive because real. Its copious contents, the findings and observations of a self-described "explorer", must be salvaged, scavenged, ransomed, purloined. Godard has often ignored the niceties of copyright clearance for the music and film clips he uses–*Histoire(s) du cinéma*, 1998, in particular, has been celebrated for its rampant sampling without attendant rights[3]–which made screening the withdrawn France Gall video *Plus Oh!*, 1996, impossible.[4] Similarly, Godard's habit of "basing" films on minor novels leads to baroque rights negotiations (*Grandeur et décadence d'un petit commerce de cinéma*, 1986, ostensibly based on James Hadley Chase's *The Soft Center*) or a dead-end (*Made in USA*, 1966, supposedly derived from Donald Westlake's *The Jugger* although owing more to Hawks's *The Big Sleep*). For every happy instance of Godard's blithe appropriation of texts and materials, such as his "retroactive purchase" at a Los Angeles racetrack of the rights to seven texts by Charles Bukowski which he used for Denise's journal entries in *Sauve qui peut*, there are those which have consigned certain of his works to a legal labyrinth or limbo. The gumshoe work on *Grandeur et décadence* alone took over one hundred e-mails that traced a projectable, subtitled tape source through dozens of curators, translators, and scholars in France, Australia, the United States, Canada, and Britain; once widely distributed, it had seemingly vanished. The attempt to secure authorisation for the screening led first to three of the film's original production companies in Paris, none of which turned out to hold any rights, then to an organisation which claimed ownership but replied that they could not afford to renew rights with the "original author" of the novel, so the film could not be shown. Using clues on a website that showed the original cover of the novel, I tracked down the agent for James Hadley Chase's estate in London, who was extremely co-operative, but the Parisian rights-holder denied this representative was the one with whom they were negotiating. In the end, when the belated permission arrived after more corkscrews and roundabouts, only a last minute loan of an archival subtitled tape from a colleague I had once helped on a Chris Marker project made the screening possible, one of many such "favours" needed to make the retrospective complete.

In many cases Cinematheque Ontario relied on different materials, both film prints and video copies, than the National Film Theatre, and in two instances we were forced to purchase new prints to ensure that major films were not shown in the battered, faded prints that were the only ones available. Both were owned by Gaumont and striking the prints was simple enough, but the subtitling of one, *Sauve qui peut*, quickly became vexing. The American and British translations of the film differed considerably, the latter bowdlerised enough to take the sting out of Godard's most shocking lines.[5] (The soundtrack of the gorgeous print of *Le Gai savoir*, 1968, bore the signs of actual censorship, loud beeps drowning out the soundtrack at various junctures; we presented it with electronic subtitles including the text that was suppressed, so the audience was aware of what was missing.) Those who had translated *Sauve qui peut* for its North American release graciously consented to loan their translation, but it could not be retrieved from "deep storage" in the Napa valley; done in the pre-computer age, the subtitles were typewritten and no word file existed. Only French language

Opposite above: **"For Ever Godard" conference, Tate Modern 2001.**

Middle: **Retrospective, Turin 1990.**

Below: **"The Godard Film Forum", Hull 1973.**

1 3 0

for ever godard

agnès b.

JEAN-LUC GODARD

Jean-Luc Godard

Centre Culturel Français de Turin

GODARD FORUM

ONE

spotting sheets survived at the original lab in Paris, whose sales agent wanted a fortune for them, and the materials for the British release print were never found. I finally cobbled together a translation from various sources, refashioning the language to reflect the more scabrous lines of the original French, and had the print subtitled in New York to avoid another flood of euros into French bank accounts.

Godard's cynical view of movie-making was repeatedly confirmed in organising the retrospective. To secure his work *in toto*, palms had to be greased, blind eyes turned, old debts called in and new ones accrued. Contrary to the apothegm in his *King Lear*, 1987, the money must flow faster than the images. Greed and indifference trump any sense of altruism, aesthetic heritage and patrimonial fealty, or dedication to greatness, especially in his once home country. The joke in the second half of *Éloge de l'amour* about the Breton version of *The Matrix* seems like a dig at both Hollywood hegemony and cultural parochialism, but the plaints of the French film industry about American domination are hard to countenance when faced with the extraordinary impediments French studios, producers, and sales agents place in the way of those attempting to organise exhibitions of their cinema: by charging exorbitant fees for rights, caring little about the lack of good or subtitled prints, and focusing exclusively on the commercial exploitation of their properties. (Ironically, American studios often rush to restore or strike new prints for important retrospectives; in a strange inversion, they now seem to care more about *l'histoire du cinéma* than do the French.)

INA, the Alphaville-sounding Institut National de l'Audiovisuel, which proclaims its mandate as the "preservation of the national audiovisual heritage […] valorising the archives for scientific, educational, and cultural purposes", in my experience seemed concerned less with valour than value, extracting as much money as possible from the Godard works it controls. France's Ministry of Foreign Affairs, which had fully supported the Bresson project, proved derelict on Godard; despite being implored on such recalcitrant issues as a new subtitled print of *La Chinoise*, 1967 (as essential a Godard as any), the Ministry demurred, preferring instead to disseminate a retrospective of the films of Jean-Paul Rappeneau, a director whose sense of history is more attuned to the times. Gaumont, which has assiduously amassed the rights to many of Godard's films and videos, was similarly apathetic, though Godard is reportedly considered their new house master the way his beloved Perret and Feuillade were in the silent era (both, of course, liberally quoted in *Histoire(s)*). Godard himself might have been bemused by the alacrity with which Gaumont accumulated the newly introduced euro, symbol of the very unified culture the director has railed against, on the basis of his back library, while ignoring all attempts to produce prints of long unavailable material.

Perhaps the French have given Godard up as Swiss. The obdurate heart of Euroland, itself fragmented into contentious *cantons* and linguistic domains, Switzerland has little of the passionate pride in *le patrimoine* that has long characterised French culture. Even the Swiss, however, managed to organise a companion retrospective of films, all in new prints, by Godard's partner Anne-Marie Miéville, and, through the auspices of the cultural agency Pro Helvetia, made it available free of charge to North American film institutes. One would think, as in the case with Godard, if whole swathes of Proust or Picasso were suddenly withdrawn from public access, or were available only in a degraded state, or their availability precluded by private accumulation, surely the French government would recognise the crisis and act accordingly. There is no programme of preservation, restoration,

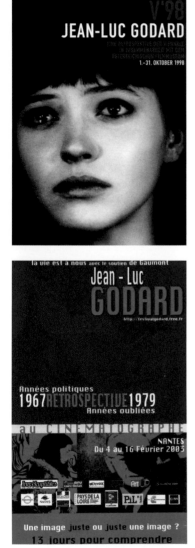

and diffusion for the works of Jean-Luc Godard, as has been undertaken by previous Italian governments for the work of that country's greatest auteurs (and even some quite minor: Zurlini, Petri, Ferreri). Instead, his work has been abandoned to market forces, resulting in its dereliction, its invisibility.

The mummy in the museum

A "child of the cinematheque", Godard has seen his own work take up home in the museum of Musidora, as perhaps the only place where it can be seen in its recondite entirety. The "museumification" of Godard's cinema signals for many its mummification. In the 1960s, the argument goes, his films both aped and shaped popular culture; were, despite their occasional abstruseness, demotic in their playful engagement with and anticipation of cultural trends. Lost during the Dziga Vertov period, and never regained even after Godard "landed in this beautiful country of narrative" with *Sauve qui peut*, the director's connection with a general audience vanished, leaving his work the domain of academic exegetes and cultural theorists. And, when the mummy moves, of cinematheques or film museums, his first homeland.

Cinematheque Ontario's retrospective largely belied this account. No need to reconfigure the corpus for an audience who have only a vague or iconic understanding of Godard's importance, and little effort to sustain interest beyond the 1960s classics. Aside from extensive contextual material (two essays and copious notes) in our programme guide, a simple chronological ordering of the career, the delicate deployment of euphemism ("challenging"), and the crafty inversion of the Tate conference's title to "Godard For Ever," thereby turning essentialism into celebration, the only impetus necessary to induce a kind of rebirth of 1960s-style cinephilia was to emphasise the very real rarity of the works. The irrelevance or invisibility of Godard seemed a fiction for the two exhausting months of the Toronto retrospective, which witnessed line-ups down the block in inclement winter weather, sell-outs–even ticket scalping!–for both the familiar (*À bout de souffle*) and the esoteric (a double bill of *Pravda*, 1969, and *British Sounds*, 1969); dewy youths toting books both classic and recent on Godard; animated, sometimes vehement post-screening discussions; and surprisingly affective responses to such supposedly thorny works as *Le Gai savoir*, *Lotte in Italia*, 1969, and *Ici et Ailleurs*, 1974. The wave of emotion that overtook the jam-packed theatre at the end of Chapter 3A of *Histoire(s) du cinéma*–elation, astonishment, even tears–was galvanic. For a brief moment, in this admittedly rarefied and circumscribed setting, Godard's cinema seemed to pack both the box-office and emotional power of his nemesis Steven Spielberg.

Godard early and late is one matter, but the Dziga Vertov period, that no man's land that lies between *Week-end* and *Sauve qui peut*, has long been neglected and thought to be unshowable. Certainly, the films from this period are the most difficult to secure, especially in subtitled versions, though Gaumont owns many of the rights. (One of my accidental finds was a version of *Vladimir et Rosa*, 1971, that has derisive commentary on the film by members of the Chicago Eight intercut with Godard's footage –more Brechtian than Godard might have imagined or wanted.) Godard did not make it easy for anyone to follow him out of the conflagration of *Week-end*; the zip, wit, and beauty, the linguistic and formal *jeux* of his 1960s films became increasingly suspect, if not anathema, in his post-68 cinema. But the retrospective decisively proved that the popular view of Godard sinking into a morass of Maoism, his poetry turning into polemics, his play into puritanism, is as simplistic as it is tempting. His auto-critiques can lapse into masochism, but amid the harangues and cant, the seemingly unGodardian surety of the "correct" ideology and image, the old Godard–of ambiguity, beauty, humour, and lucidity–peers through.

Films of this period proved to be the revelation of the retrospective, often very funny, lovely, and startlingly prescient. As with Godard's work of the 1960s, they have more to say about the way we live now than much contemporary cinema–*Lotte in Italia* could serve as a primary text for anti-globalisation groups–and the surprisingly young audience they drew (often in droves) initially came out of curiosity about work so long out of circulation, and returned repeatedly, obviously surprised that these legendarily abstinent works offered so many pleasures. *Ici et Ailleurs*, which has its origins in the Dziga Vertov period, uses brute juxtapositions to make its pro-Palestinian point, but seems genuinely sorrowful and uncertain, something critics rarely remark upon; it is "too simple and too easy to divide the world in two" we are told in the coda, surely not a sign of Manichaean thought. The film's complex, layered text and imagery, its anguish and scepticism all confute its agit-prop approach, and the result is as touching and beautiful as it is incensing. (The camera treats a Palestinian woman who is not who she pretends to be with the same tender but wary regard accorded the face of Anna Karina in *Vivre sa vie*.) Inhibiting the Barthesian density of cultural allusion and textual play of his 1960s films, Godard nevertheless could not suppress his magpie impulse, nor his wit or devotion to beauty. Just as the revolutionaries of *La Chinoise* always seem about to break into Jacques Demy formation–the "Mao! Mao!" pop song all but calls for Arthur Freed and colour-coded frocks–the chaste or hectoring tone of the Dziga Vertov essays keeps succumbing to puns and word play ("L O V E" gets teased out of *All about Eve* in *One Plus One*, 1968), to wry personal observation and visual abstraction. The circular shuttle of streetcars in *Pravda*, for example, reminds us that no one shoots traffic more exquisitely than Godard. Ever a dialectician, Godard managed, if uneasily, to be both ideologue and aesthete.

The Eternal Return: "History keeps repeating–it's one long stutter."
Doubtless, the Dziga Vertov films benefited from the flanking panels of the retrospective, their meanings more easily extruded and images more simply parsed in the context of Godard before and after. Each film of the 1960s seemed to portend a later one, each late work seemed to subsume all those previous. (One thinks of Chris Marker's comment on the photographs of Denise Bellon: "Each shows a past, yet deciphers a future.") Indeed, the compressed experience of viewing all of Godard in a relatively short span revealed the common taxonomy of his work, in three discernible periods, to be at best convenient, at worst reductive. For example, *Deux ou trois choses* gives the lie to the customary contention that Anne-Marie Miéville introduced the domestic world of kitchen and children to Godard's work–it has numerous parallels and echoes with *Numéro Deux*–and anticipates his "transcendental" period in Juliette's epiphany about being one with the world, as she moves through nature accompanied by a fragment of Beethoven's String Quartet 16, opus 135.

The retrospective became one long stutter, its experiential density emphasising the stammering persistence of Godard's first concerns. The way Godard lingers over the last shot of *À bout de souffle*–the "origin" of his career, "the wonder of a beginning"–in *L'Origine du vingt et unième siècle*, 2000, illustrates how marked is the shuttle of allusion, affinity, and citation between his early work and late. Certain motifs emerged or became more pronounced–blindness and incest, for instance–while the "civilisation of the ass" which Belmondo cites in *Pierrot le fou*, 1965, is transformed into a

Opposite above: **Godard and Miéville retrospective, Cinémathèque Suisse 1991-1992.**

Middle: **Retrospective, Vienna 1998.**

Below: **1967-1979 retrospective, Nantes 2003.**

fixation on anality, constipation, and shit—"coming at things from behind", as it were—in the later work. But evolution was less apparent than perseverance. Hanna Schygulla's regard for her Japanese car in *Passion*, 1982, echoes her consumerist sisters in *Les Carabiniers* and *Week-end*, while the connection of polyglot and the workings of international capital make twins of *Le Mépris* and *Nouvelle Vague* (which have markedly similar endings). The startling references to the Rwanda massacres in *Bande à part*, 1964, prefigure the slaughters and ethnic cleansing in *L'Origine*, as does the treatment of war as absurdist spectacle in *Les Carabiniers* the offhand portrait of the Bosnian conflict in *For Ever Mozart*, 1996 (both films employing Godard's motif of trains). The Cocteau references in *Armide*, 1987, and *King Lear*, 1987, mirror those in *Charlotte et son Jules*, 1958, and *Alphaville*, 1965, the lovely Lumière-like street scenes in *Une femme est une femme*, 1961, and *Masculin Féminin*, 1967, are classicised in *Éloge de l'amour*, while the hotels of *Anticipation*, 1967, *Vivre sa vie*, 1962, and *Alphaville* presage the proliferation of hotel settings (points of transit, instability, commerce) in *Sauve qui peut*, *Passion*, *Détective*, 1985, and *2x50 ans de cinéma français*, 1995. The assertion in *For Ever Mozart* that "knowledge of the possibility of representation consoles us for being enslaved to life. Knowledge of life consoles for the fact that representation is but shadow", recalls Roger's assertion in *Deux ou trois choses*: "It is not the real that we think. It is a ghost of the real." And the Hollywood deal-making of *Éloge de l'amour* looks back to that of *Le Mépris*. In both films, European myth, history, and culture are sold, plundered, and falsified by an American producer.

The catalogue of continuities between early and late Godard, both glancing and substantial, could run to volumes, but the retrospective made strikingly apparent his persistent concern with the Holocaust and its representation. His rebuking of Spielberg and Boltanski in *Éloge de l'amour* and *The Old Place*, 1999, for their usurpation of the trauma of the Holocaust, his obsessive return to the Holocaust as rupture—of politics, art, consciousness, history—in *Histoire(s) du cinéma* and *Éloge* have their antecedents in many of Godard's films of the 1960s: the tattooed numbers on the women in *Alphaville*; the brief discussion of the camps and German guilt in the café in *Masculin Féminin*; and, most markedly, the "Memory" sequence in *Une femme mariée*, 1964, in which Roger Leenhardt plays an investigator in the trial of Auschwitz perpetrators. As a filmmaker, theorist, and mentor to André Bazin, Leenhardt seems to represent for Godard an ideal of cultural memory, which is forever lost by the time we reach *Éloge de l'amour* more than three decades later. The married woman of the title confuses Auschwitz and thalidomide, the clutter of ads and articles in her head having rendered historical memory obsolete, whereas Berthe, the despairing heroine of *Éloge*, cannot escape memory—historical (the Resistance, the Holocaust) or personal (her role in the Hollywood deal)—and kills herself. "The image", she tells us, "the only thing capable of denying nothingness, is also the gaze of nothingness on us."

1.33 Mon beau souci
The image, that "gaze of nothingness", also returns to its origins in late Godard. Like Jean-Marie Straub and Danièle Huillet, Godard makes films that assume that his audience shares, or *should* share, his own vast knowledge of history, art and philosophy, and, like them, he continues to make the formal assumption that there is still room for the old and beautiful—the squarish classicism of the 1.33 aspect ratio (also employed in some of Bresson's late work)—in a world that is literally and metaphorically ill-equipped for it. Long outmoded, the 1.33 or 1.37 ratio (ironically also known as Academy ratio) can no longer fit the multiplex screen; few

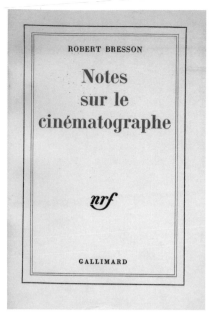

contemporary art houses, and even fewer commercial cinemas, are outfitted for it. 1.33 images are quite literally *misfits*, and as such bespeak an insular, oppositional aesthetic.

In a famous sequence in *Masculin Féminin*, the purist, pedantic Jean-Pierre Léaud berates a projectionist for showing a film in the wrong ratio: "The aperture should correspond to the format 1.65 or 1.75, as provided for during the shooting of the film", he recites from a manual. "The 1.85 format should not be exceeded under any circumstances, in conforming with the stipulations of ISO international standards." Increasingly in the 1960s, the visual pow of Godard's films naturally tended to the horizontal sprawl of CinemaScope, the ads, texts and intertitles, cars, guns, and consumer goods swarming his screen like in a James Rosenquist mural. One senses that Godard was drawn to Scope not just for its affinities with Nicholas Ray, Frank Tashlin, and Otto Preminger, and with the American musical, but also because he could stuff more signs, slogans, faces, products, more things and thoughts into its stretched frame. In late Godard "the time for action has passed, the time for reflection has come"; the pop, urban cornucopia of the Scope frame seems inimical to the melancholy, pastoralism and interiority of his post-1980 work.

Godard's preoccupation with "correct language" (Jean-Louis Leutrat) and "proper framing" (Jacques Fieschi) suggests exactitude, a search for precise placement and meaning, so a disturbing discovery of the retrospective was how frequently the full-frame compositions of Godard's late films have been ignored and overruled. Many of the prints are clearly marked by the lab with the widescreen ratios of 1.66 or (the almost standard) 1.85, and their subtitles are printed in the frame at the height indicated by those standards. Our meticulous projectionist Kate McKay experimented with whole reels of films, showing them first in 1.33 and then in the prescribed wider screen ratio, revealing the violence done to the compositions when shown the latter way. Some instances are ambiguous. *Numéro Deux*, 1975, though horizontally composed to take in the various video screens, for example, decapitates the standing Godard in the early sequences when not shown in 1.33, a perhaps intentionally startling effect. *Passion*, *Je vous salue, Marie*, *Nouvelle Vague*, *Hélas pour moi*, and *For Ever Mozart*, however, are abjectly constricted when shown 1.85; their open frames feel scrunched and suffocated, close-ups especially tight, sliced, or excised. Perversely, Godard shot *Armide*, his contribution to the anthology film *Aria*, in 1.33, the only sequence in that 10-part work not 1.85. His cubist cramming of flesh into tightly packed frames in *Armide* seems not to be an aesthetic choice; in Academy ratio, his images of bodybuilders and sirens are less violent. (Again, the term "misfit" springs to mind when one thinks of Godard in formal opposition to the nine other directors of *Aria*.) Disturbed by some oddly cropped compositions in *Éloge de l'amour*, which result in seemingly unintentional beheadings and concretions, I consulted Godard by fax about the aspect ratio and he confirmed that it was indeed, as stated, 1.66 (rather old-fashioned in its own way). That he occasionally still seems to be jamming a 1.33 composition into a frame that cannot accommodate it suggests his instinctual preference for the open image.[6]

Godard's predilection for the 1.33 frame could be the heritage of all the 16mm shooting he did during the Dziga Vertov period, or the television standards imposed by his and Miéville's video works, or a reversion to the look of his earliest films (a return to origins). Most likely, they embody a late classicism, one that arranges images like many of the paintings he admires. The mural splay of Scope has been displaced by the more "natural" framed space of painting, perhaps to avoid fragmentation, to see and show things—faces and bodies especially—fully. Again, Godard is both radical,

sur JEAN LUC GODARD
16 JANVIER — 11 FÉVRIER 86
LIBRAIRIE GALERIE DU JOUR AGNÈS B. 6 RUE DU JOUR PARIS 42 33 43 40

refusing the homogenising dictates of the predominant image (1.85, the filmic equivalent of the euro), and reactionary, clinging to antique, obsolete beauty.

This unnerving discovery, which suggests that some of late Godard has been shown and seen, therefore taught and analysed, inexactly, was compounded by the vexing issues that surround projecting *Histoire(s) du cinéma*. Legendary in its absence in North America, where it has been unavailable since the initial versions of various chapters were shown then withdrawn, *Histoire(s)* poses many problems for a retrospective. Should it be shown with subtitles for an audience that does not speak French? Godard has balked at the possibility, and has dragged his feet on providing an English translation. And, if it *is* shown with subtitles, how to translate the text, both written and spoken, with its poetic density and word-play, its tight braid of invective and aphorism, and how to elide and condense so that the eye and mind are not entirely preoccupied with reading? (The text, after all, is for him the enemy.) Moreover, should the work be projected at all, given that ephemerality tends to make the experience occlusive or overwhelming, especially for a neophyte audience? Exegesis of *Histoire(s)* has often depended on a denial of its very being, i.e. montage, isolating and arresting images or moments or texts that, when projected as they are intended, come as a flood tide of thought and philosophy, a sluice of teeming text and imagery that flashes, stutters, and dissolves, which surely cannot be apprehended or absorbed in a "no going back, no pausing or stopping" single viewing.

Polyphonic, structured by refrain and counterpoint, with chorale-like sequences, Godard's impossibly profuse and associative opus calls to mind such idiosyncratic musical works as Sorabji's *Opus clavicembalisticum*, Nancarrow's *Studies for Player Piano*, or Messaien's *Catalogue d'oiseaux*. Its sheer omnivorousness and the simultaneity of its many modes make it the summum of Godard's work. Encompassing, even oceanic, it comes closest to his dream of possessing and remaking the world through the medium and material of cinema. However, *Hélas pour nous*, is a work that forfeits its essence when its montage is suppressed in close analysis, and all but precludes anything but fugitive comprehension when projected for a first time audience. The unwary may respond to this monster of montage, this onslaught of thought in a way opposite to the viewers who sat, transfixed then frightened, by the oncoming trains in Lumière's film (invoked in Michel-Ange's innocent reaction in *Les Carabiniers*)–initially confused and apprehensive, then, as they submit to its daunting inundation, mesmerised: ironically for a work of such intellectual density, a reaction approaching rapture, non-thought.

Bonjour Tristesse

The forlorn and mournful are more common in late Godard, however, nowhere more so than in *Éloge*, which anchored the second half of the retrospective. The film's distributor, recognising that it had limited commercial appeal, readily agreed to make our exhibition the sole Toronto release, and its great success–all five screenings sold out–led to a subsequent, albeit brief and unprofitable, art-house engagement.

Cultural and political memory are synonymous in *Éloge*. Contentious as ever, Godard has produced, as the film's title suggests, a requiem for a world of art, politics, and philosophy that has been colonised and subdued by international capital, and a bitter screed against a state in which resistance is impossible and everything is for sale, even history and the individual "gaze". Its first half filmed in black and white, in images of such clarity, density, and lustre that they seem to have been shot on nitrate stock, *Éloge* employs a series of settings charged with political meaning (e.g. the old Renault factory

Opposite: *agnès b.* exhibition, Paris 1986.

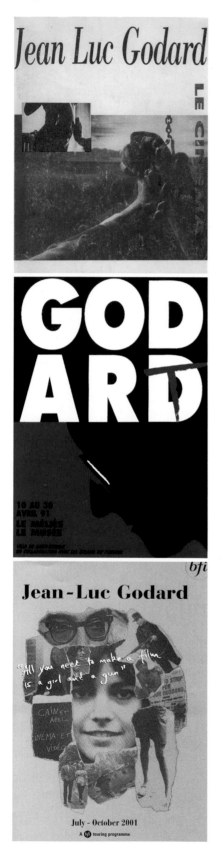

on the *île Seguin* in the Seine) and a postcard succession of gorgeously illumined monuments to turn Paris into the capital of melancholy. The second half of the film, set two years earlier and largely on the Brittany coast, was shot in digital and in colour. Godard inverts cinema's traditional presentation of the past in black and white, the present in colour–"I wanted to find a way of intensifying the past", he says–as well as his own romantic representation of the city and nature. Paris has never been more beautiful than in the first half of *Éloge* (Godard said he wanted to make it look "timeless"), and nature has rarely looked so noxious as it does in the colour-manipulated DV second half, which renders the Brittany landscapes in a conflagration of sulphurous oranges, bilious blues, and pestilential yellows, keyed hot and toxic, their lava-like whorls magnifying the innate swimminess of the digital image.[7]

The effect of this midway switch to digital has been called painterly or Fauvist, and it does occasionally recall the garish palette of Van Dongen Kees or Alexei Jawlensky. But the transition has as much thematic import as aesthetic effect. Godard famously called film and video Cain and Abel in *Sauve qui peut*, and one senses his doing the same with film and digital in *Éloge*. In his lament for a lost culture (stolen paintings, the films of Bresson) and for a time of political heroism (the French Resistance), Godard assigns an elegiac beauty to the 35mm imagery of Paris and the present, which is both lambent and weighty, while that of the immediate past (and of nature) is a contaminated flux, its digital imagery associated with commerce, historical amnesia, and cultural imperialism.

Éloge seems to follow, if unconsciously, the formal schema of Preminger's *Bonjour Tristesse*, 1958. In both *Éloge* and *Tristesse*, the recent past, in which a disastrous decision leads to a suicide, is set at the seaside (Brittany and the Côte d'Azur, respectively) and presented in fervid colour, while the present is set in Paris and is shot in black and white–albeit ashen and weightless in *Tristesse* to suggest the spectral lives of Cécile (Jean Seberg) and her roué father (David Niven). (A Godardian coincidence: the lead actress in *Éloge* is Cécile Camp.) That *Éloge* refashions the film that inspired Godard's first feature, *À bout de souffle* being a sequel of sorts to *Bonjour Tristesse*, suggests how the retrospective revealed the constant *revenance* of his cinema, its eternal return to origins.

A *revenant* cinema

Pathos and self-pity, spirituality and spite adhere in Godard's intensifying identification of the death of art, of cinema, memory, and history, with his own feeling of abandonment and mortality.[8] From the "left for dead" denouement of *Sauve qui peut* to the alarum of cinema's peril in *Lettre à Freddy Buache*, 1982, through the photograph of the filmmaker as a child "already in mourning for myself" in his self-portrait, *JLG/JLG: autoportrait de décembre*, 1995, to the incantation of "nothing was said" and theme of suicidal futility in *Éloge*, Godard's work post-1980 repeatedly meets surcease, the director's once impish wit soured by despondency and shadowed by death.

The sense of *revenance* in Godard's late cinema, explicit in its many references to resurrection and redemption–"the image will come at the time of the resurrection", a caption states in *Histoire(s) du cinéma*–paradoxically coincides with an emphasis on the imminent demise of the art. Godard's vatic voice, in such works as *L'Origine*, bids us adieu from the ruins, cataloguing the barbarities of the just finished century and prophesying more to come; "Politics today is the voice of horror", he opines in *Je vous salue, Marie*, recalling Edgar Typhus's list of historical atrocities in *Made in*

USA. But more like Géricault's raft than Goya's war, Godard's rendering of madness and suffering shocks not with journalistic or realistic detail but with sheer ravishment. Ironically, as with Bresson's colour films, especially *Le Diable probablement*, 1977, and *L'Argent*, 1983, the more dire or abject Godard's vision of the twentieth century, the more sumptuous, even ecstatic his films became in their awe of the world's beauty. Cultural memory, rampart against the flux and effluvia of time, against the tide of mercantilism that is sweeping away the last vestiges of artistic and political resistance, is signified in Godard's late work by the loving rearrangement (or derangement) of key literary works and paintings. Conversely, cultural amnesia is everywhere apparent–in the newspapers that displace books in *Nouvelle Vague*, in which the masters read about the market while the slaves (Cécile) read Schiller; in the American purchase of a European past in *Éloge*; in the parade of chambermaids in *2x50 ans de cinéma français* who know more about new Hollywood movies than old French films.

The *gris* of late Godard, its velvety impasto bearing intimations of purity and death, is more Manet than the Corot evoked in *Bande à part*; and the figure who best expresses the director's world-weariness is the very grey mafia don played by Alain Cuny in *Détective*. Severe, worn, taciturn, Cuny has iconic potency, both as symbol of resistance–he did not, as Godard emphasises in *Histoire(s)*, join his fellow actors on the train to the UFA studios in 1942, and starred in Carné's anti-Nazi allegory *Les Visiteurs du soir*–and of cultural memory (European cinema in general, as both star and director). Embodied by Cuny, who died in 1994, both forces are near expiry, and *Éloge* spells their end. It is Cuny who delivers the long Élie Faure text in Chapter 4A of the *Histoire(s)* which concludes with the image of the "march towards death", another of Godard's late references to the surcease of his self and of cinema. But the stuttering of history, the eternal return of cinema to its origins, manifested in the *revenance* of a retrospective, holds out hope for the inconsolable Godard. His images, like those of Manet and Rembrandt (the true subject of the Faure text), are regained and gathered in the museum, but unlike theirs rely on light to give them brief, transubstantiated life.[9] "That which plunges into the light is the repercussion of that which the night submerges", says Faure, and it is the encroaching night Godard's images resist, and invite.

Opposite above: **Retrospective, Brussels 1986.**

Middle: **Retrospective, Saint-Étienne 1991.**

Below: **Touring programme, UK 2001.**

FORM AND FIGURE

FORM AND FIGURE

The six chapters of this section explore some major pathways of the new critical landscape opened up in Part I. The various forms and figures analysed, from the trailer and figure of the parade to the cinematic frame line and stop-action photography, reveal the scale of Godard's interest in new formats and processes, as well as his continual focus on the human body and its multiple projections. Perhaps more than in any other section of the volume, we see here the benefit and indeed necessity of considering together the feature films and the so-called "minor" works for video and television. What this establishes in particular is that Godard's progression as a filmmaker can only really be understood in the wider terms of artistic practice and the development of modern and contemporary art.

In "A Cinema of Memory in the Future Tense: Godard, Trailers, and Godard Trailers", Vinzenz Hediger explores in Godard's work the "logic" of the trailer, in its aspect both as a technique of anticipated memory and as a technique of beginning. Hediger analyses not simply the trailers to Godard's films, many of which Godard produced himself, but also the use in the early work of stylistic features specific to the trailer, such as textual inserts and discontinuous montage. In these films, Hediger argues, the cinematic technique of the beginning extends to the entire film and thus transforms the feature film from the cinematic equivalent of the nineteenth century realist novel into the Romantic concept of the infinite work.

In "The Forms of the Question", Nicole Brenez explores the philosophical foundations of Godard's experimental practice of the question. This consists initially of Godard putting into practice a filmic problem in such a way that the question appears as a solution, first of a narrative, plastic order, then of an ethical and formal order. Brenez maps out the principal ways in which questions are given form in Godard's work, from the lesson to the torture scene, focusing in particular on the "Question-Image" which, she argues, has become Godard's most significant means of invention and generates new aesthetic forms. Brenez demonstrates that the evolution of Godard's work takes us from a simple *mise en scène* of the question to a transformation of the image itself into a pure formal problem.

In "Procession and Projection: Notes on a Figure in the Work of Jean-Luc Godard", Christa Blümlinger examines the figure of the *défilé* in Godard's work, notably in *On s'est tous défilé*, 1988, a video short about a fashion parade. According to Blümlinger, the *mise en scène* of a number of bodies passing through the frame embodies the idea of the *défilement* or "succession" of the image in movement. Blümlinger analyses, in addition, the links between Godard's filmic reflection on this subject and a text by Serge Daney entitled "Du défilement au défilé". She reveals that Godard deploys the figure of the *défilé* in order to reintroduce into the recording of the human figure a dialectic between emotion and distanciation.

In "'Gravity and Grace': On the 'Sacred' and Cinematic Vision in the Films of Jean-Luc Godard", Vicki Callahan proposes that Godard's work since *Passion*, 1982, represents a new effort to engage with issues of gender and sexuality by formal means. According to Callahan, Godard's use of cinematic form, notably the frame line in films such as *JLG/JLG: autoportrait de décembre*, 1995, is aligned with a longstanding aesthetic history and practice, whereby the art object presents the opportunity to see and think the world anew. In this sense, Godard follows Kandinsky for whom form becomes a conscious and selected area of demarcation by the artist rather than an essential, fixed entity. As with Kandinsky, Callahan argues, Godard's investment in form bespeaks a sacred attention to how we draw, and redraw, the boundaries of thought and experience, including those of sexual difference.

In "Altered Motion and Corporal Resistance in *France/tour/détour/deux/ enfants*", Michael Witt examines in close detail the second of Godard and Miéville's collaborations for television, the 12-part video series *France/tour/détour/ deux/enfants*, 1979. Engaging both with Foucauldian theory and the pre-cinematic science of Étienne-Jules Marey, Witt foregrounds the representation and decomposition of the corporal by means of altered motion. His account of Godard/Miéville's political anatomy of the body contextualises it in terms of the general movement of film history, from cinema's belated adolescence (the New Wave) to a new "post-television" maturity. The formal ramifications of this videographic treatment of the body can be traced in both Miéville's solo films and the metaphysical lyricism of Godard's subsequent work.

In "Godard, Hitchcock, and the Cinematographic Image", Jacques Rancière analyses the particular terms of Godard's presentation of Hitchcock as "the greatest creator of forms of the twentieth century" in *Histoire(s) du cinéma*, Chapter 4A, *Le contrôle de l'univers*. Rancière reveals that to argue his case, Godard has to change not only the signification but also the very nature of Hitchcock's images in order to make them "forms" as he understands them. Rancière investigates what exactly is at stake in Godard's "recreation" of certain famous Hitchcockian shots by referring to the specific nature of cinematographic images and the relationship between narrativity and plasticity. He proposes that Godard's "symbolist", as opposed to dialectical, strategy of reconnecting images is part of a general symbolist shift in contemporary art.

A CINEMA OF MEMORY IN THE FUTURE TENSE: GODARD, TRAILERS, AND GODARD TRAILERS

It is a sublime taste always to prefer things that have been raised to the second power. For example, reproductions of imitations, critiques of reviews, postscripts to addenda, commentaries on notes. We Germans indulge in it where prolongation is sought, the French where brevity and vacuity are favoured.
Friedrich Schlegel, Athenäums-Fragment 110, 1798

Taste is not only a part and an index of Morality–it is the ONLY morality.
John Ruskin, *Traffic*, 1864

VINZENZ HEDIGER

In a statement from his *Introduction à une véritable histoire du cinéma*, 1980, Jean-Luc Godard reveals that in the future, he might actually prefer to make trailers instead of films, only his trailers would be four to five hours long. Looking back over his oeuvre of the last 25 years, one is tempted to ask whether this famous adage may have been more profoundly ironic than is usually suspected. *Histoire(s) du cinéma*, for one, a compilation of film excerpts interspersed with titles and spoken texts composed between 1988 and 1998, resembles nothing so much as the long, long trailer Godard announced as one of his possible coming attractions in 1978, except that it exceeds the original project in length by a factor of two. But one is also justified in asking whether Godard's desire for the very long trailer may not have informed the director's earlier work as well. What indeed if Godard had been making trailers all along, only they were, on average, just 90 minutes long? And what if it was simply too obvious for anyone to notice? For the evidence was certainly not lacking. Take the final title card of *La Chinoise*, for instance. It reads: "This is the end of a beginning (not a trailer)." A straightforward statement, to be sure, but one which it is also quite easy–maybe too easy–to read as a text-book case of what Freud calls "Verneinung", of admission coupled with denial (a denial apparently shared by both author and audience). And what about passages like the one from *Numéro Deux*, in which, after 15 minutes of film, a female voice on the soundtrack announces: "*Numéro Deux*. A film produced by Anne-Marie Miéville and Jean-Luc Godard. *Numéro Deux*. Showing soon on this screen. Or on another."? At this point, the film clearly turns on to itself and into its own announcement, deferring itself towards other sites and coming projections, while at the same time hinting at the possibility that these projections will forever remain imaginary. That was in 1975.

Opposite: **Trailer for *À bout de souffle*, 1960.**

La Chinoise, on the other hand, was made in 1967, ten years before the Montreal lectures and 30 before *Histoire(s)* was completed.

Maybe now, at a time when Godard the author is more undead than ever and *Histoire(s) du cinéma* is about to enter the textbooks of film history as a work of art *sui generis* (and not a trailer), the moment has come to state the obvious truth and proclaim that Godard's films are, in fact, a lot like trailers, even beyond *Histoire(s)*. Let me establish the equation by starting with Godard's trailers. Godard trailers are, in most cases, also Godard films. Godard has in fact been making his own trailers since *À bout de souffle*, 1960, which is not entirely unusual for a director. What is unusual is that most of his trailers have actually been used. Making effective trailers requires a detachment from the material which directors usually lack. Witness Michael Cimino's trailer for *Heaven's Gate*, 1980, or Steven Soderbergh's for *sex, lies and videotape*, 1989, both incoherent, confused mumblings, the first of which was used (the film flopped and wrecked United Artists) and the second was not (the film was a hit and set Miramax on track to become a major force in Hollywood). Not so Jean-Luc Godard, a director who is not only a former film critic, but also an alumnus of Fox's publicity department in Paris, and whose mindset apparently is akin to that of a maker of trailers.[1] But if Godard trailers are Godard films, Godard films are also trailers. Clearly, as unmistakably Godardian as the films usually are, the format they most closely resemble in their style, their temporal and narrative structure and their mode of address, are trailers. It could in fact be argued that to the extent that Godard's films deconstruct mainstream cinema, they do so by resembling mainstream trailers rather than by not resembling mainstream films. Viewed from this perspective, Godard films are less a radical alternative to mainstream cinema than its continuation by its own means, albeit in a different direction—in the direction of a cinema where trailers no longer announce films, but dis- and replace them.

Writing about *Histoire(s)*, Jacques Rancière observes that Godard's handling of the materials of classical cinema is not just one of *découpage* and collage, of montage in the Vertovian sense. Rather than simply deconstructing classical cinema, *Histoire(s)* reassembles the fragments and excerpts into a montage, or rather anti-montage, which brings to the fore "their belonging to a same world of images".[2] Four elements characterise this anti-montage: strips of black film inserted between the actual excerpts, a disjunction between sound and image (the spoken words may or may not refer to the images we see), the use of the voice on the soundtrack, which gives the same world of images its homogeneity and depth, and finally, the use of video superimposition of images and quick alternating cuts between images, of what has been termed "image beats" ("battements d'images") by Nicole Brenez. In discussing the four elements of anti-montage, Rancière might as well have been talking about the montage of contemporary trailers.

1. Black strips of film

Excerpts fading in on a background of black and titles lighting up on black film are quite the rage in trailers from the 1990s.[3] It is precisely an effect of suggesting a world of images, an infinite and indeterminate background from which images and films emerge which the use of these elements suggests in trailers. The black strips seem to be suggesting that in trailers there's always more where this came from, thus always already pointing the audience even further ahead than just to the coming attraction, or further back than to the previous one, for that matter.

2. Disjunction between sound and image

Since the 1970s, it has become customary in trailers to completely separate sound and image tracks. The continuity of the trailer is now usually a continuity of the soundtrack, i.e. the plot résumés, on which the majority of trailers are now based, are constructed through the juxtaposition of dialogue fragments rather than through a sequence of images. Images are coupled freely with sound, and they may well anticipate or even contradict what is being said on the soundtrack rather than simply illustrate dialogue. Thus the disjunction of sound and image in trailers does not just deconstruct and deplete the original sense and meaning of the images, but more often than not makes the images speak in new and innovative ways.

3. Creating homogeneity and depth via the use of a voice

The majority of contemporary trailers use voice-over in the presentation of their materials. A specific vocabulary is employed by these voices. Insistently, we hear words like "now", designing either a turning point in the story of the film and/or the event/advent of the film, or formulas like "in a world where" uttered by the voice-over, also known as "narration" in industry parlance. Occupying the site of enunciation (to put it the French way) and setting every film "in a world where", the voice again underscores the notion of a world of images and simultaneously gives homogeneity and depth to that world.

4. Video superimposition of images and quick alternating cuts between images

In the realm of film, something like Godard's image beats were quite unheard of before *Histoire(s)*. In trailers, such editing techniques have been in use for some time, or rather they became widespread at about the time Godard started working on *Histoire(s)*. With the introduction of the MacIntosh-based AVID editing software in 1993, the marginal costs of any given decision in film editing have been significantly reduced. Since new opportunities are usually seized upon at least initially, this lead to a significant reduction of the average shot length not only in mainstream films, but also, and particularly so, in trailers. While in classical trailers, the average shot length was about half that of the corresponding films, it decreased to one third in the 1970s. In the late 1990s, the average shot length in trailers was less than one second, which is partly due to the fact that trailers tend to include sections where alternating images are juxtaposed in a manner very much reminiscent, to the connoisseur, of Godard's image beats (or *vice versa*).

If the anti-montage of *Histoire(s)* works along the same lines as the montage of contemporary trailers, Godard's earlier films betray a stylistic affinity with what you might call the logic of the trailer as well. Combinations of written text and images are wide-spread in the media. Pictures in magazines and news features on television are anchored with captions. Advertising billboards combine strong imagery with catchy slogans. Title sequences of movies are supposed to convey the atmosphere of the film through their choice of typography. With regard to film genres and film formats, however, there is only a limited number which are intrinsically characterised by the simultaneous use of written text and image. Newsreels spring to mind, advertising films, instructional and propaganda films, and, of course, trailers and Godard films. (In France the "Godard" is actually a genre, and major stars have to make at least one Godard to round out their filmographies. Looking back on the not altogether happy experience of shooting *Hélas pour moi* with Godard in 1993, Gérard Depardieu said in a interview on French television, "At least now I have made my Godard.") In classical trailers, superimposed titles are the primary means of address to the audience. In fact, you easily recognise a classical trailer by the superimposed titles. Roughly nine tenths of all American trailers from the pre-1960 period use superimposed titles to convey their

message: to list the stars, to describe the qualities of the films, to give some hints about the story and situate the excerpts shown in terms of genre. Contemporary trailers use titles less frequently–mostly, if they do, in lieu of voice-over narration–but textual elements still characterise the format to a large extent. Like titles in trailers, textual motifs in Godard films often build up across several title cards. Where in contemporary trailers, graphic elements often form abstract patterns across a series of cuts from title cards to images, only to eventually morph into the title of the film, in Godard films characters are added or omitted from one title card to another to create new words and meanings, or reveal new words hidden in old ones. In both classical and contemporary trailers as well as in Godard films, however, it would be a mistake to pretend that the textual elements are mere inserts, or that they establish a discourse *about* images, for that matter. Rather, text occurs on a par with images to form what Raymond Bellour, inverting Maurice Blanchot's formula of *parole d'écriture*, calls an *écriture de parole*–a discourse in which writing, instead of simply anchoring the image in some linguistic system of meaning, entertains, via *parole*, a dynamic, vital, at times tumultuous and hurtful relationship with the image.[4] Such an *écriture de parole*, such a "writing of the (spoken) word", implies that one has the power to treat writing like an image, and the image, the screen, like a page on which to write. What Bellour has to say with regard to Godard films again pertains to the trailer. Word, image and text are largely interchangeable in trailers. Textual elements occur in lieu of, or in conjunction with, the voice in contemporary trailers, or they set the theme in the introduction of classical trailers and prepare the ground for the voice to take over (which it usually does by confirming what has come before with a formulaic "yes, …"). Sometimes, however, the voice handles the introduction and the titles take over for the main part of the trailer). Through

Above: **Trailer for *Détective*, 1985.**

Opposite: **Press book.**

their typography, textual elements in trailers more often than not exemplify the experiental qualities displayed in or conveyed by the images, while in a similar fashion the hue of the voice usually confers certain generic qualities onto the visual materials it accompanies. The relationship between word, image and text in trailers remains as dynamic and conflictual as it is in Godard films, however. Not only do elaborate, expressive typographies tend to absorb writing into the iconic code, to phrase it in well-weathered semiotic terms, but writing and spoken words also tend to literalise the image when juxtaposed or confronted with it.[5]

The list of similarities and analogies could, of course, be expanded almost at will. Think of a discussion of quoting and citation in trailers and Godard films, for instance. There, one could talk about the fact that Godard films liberally quote from films, whilst trailers are basically made up of quotes from the films they belong to, or one could mention the fact that *Histoire(s)* is made up of almost nothing but quotes from other films, which in a way makes them a trailer which belongs to all the films it quotes. But I believe the point is now clear. Godard trailers, if anything, further underline the kinship between Godard films and trailers. As I've pointed out, Godard trailers are in most cases Godard films. Also, judging by the standards of other director-made trailers, they are quite simply too good not to come from someone with a deep understanding of what trailers are and how they work. As befits trailers which are also *auteur* films, Godard trailers are more than just trailers. Apart from announcements for coming attractions, they are usually also presentations of the poetics of the film. Furthermore, they can be read as a critique of the trailer; they are about what the trailer is about. And finally, and crucially, they are a laboratory for the aesthetics of the films.

Announcements for coming attractions

Godard trailers run the gamut of trailer rhetoric, from trailers made up of lists of attractions to trailers with song-like structures which convey the rhythm of the film to montage pieces, combining rebus structures with atmospheric passages, and specially shot trailers which sell the film without using material from the film. Plainly, there is nothing in the way of trailers Godard cannot do. The trailer for *Bande à part*, 1964, is a good example. A 110 second montage consisting of 56 shots, which means there is a cut every two seconds, strictly in sync with the rhythm of the popular song on the sound track. Few trailer makers would have had the audacity to be so abstract, and it is hard to imagine another director treating his own material with such equanimity (let alone effectiveness). Nor do Godard's trailers lack a sense of *Zeitgeist*. After his return to the big screen in the early 1980s, Godard managed to reposition himself in the context of French cinema as something of the cool daddy of the Mitterrand/Lang socialist era new wave of Beineix, Besson *et al* with films such as *Détective*, released in 1985, or *Soigne ta droite* from 1987, which stars the then ultra-chic pop duo, Les Rita Mitsouko. Such at least is the message of the trailer for *Détective*, Godard's take on the hotel film, with a touch of *noir* thrown in for good measure. In the trailer, we see Michel Galabru, who is not among the cast of the film, talking to a beautiful blonde lying on a hotel bed. Dressed in a *faux*-Bogart trench-coat, he resembles a contemporary comic book character. "Let's go now", he says; "No, I'm staying", she retorts. "Let's go", he says; "No, I'm staying", she insists, browsing through an illustrated magazine. "Let's go", he pipes again. "No, I'm staying", she says, visibly annoyed, whereupon he pulls a gun, shoots her, turns to the camera and says, "Don't make the same mistake. Go see *Détective*, the new film by Godard."

Presenting the poetics of the film

The trailer for *Éloge de l'amour*, 2001, is 84 seconds long, roughly the first half of which consists of a montage of digital video shots dyed in orange and blue alternating with black and white shots from the first part of the film (in Hollywood parlance, this kind of montage in trailers is called a "grid"). A dialogue fragment on the sound track delivers an instruction which may also be understood as an *avis au lecteur* directed at the audience: "I didn't tell you to watch. I told you to listen. Listen, listen." Another dialogue fragment, discussing various aspects and meanings of the notion of love and its moral implications, establishes the theme of the film. After a brief silence, a male voice says: "You wanted to tell me something?" On "something", the title of the film, *Éloge de l'amour* (of love), flashes on to the screen, white characters on black background. A female voice says: "The image, sir, alone capable of negating nothingness, is also the look nothingness directs on us." On "Negating nothingess", the title is flashed on to the screen once again, followed by another excerpt. On "the look nothingness directs on us", a title reads "Of something". The title is brought on again, and alternating with excerpts, two more title cards reading "Of love" follow. A final title card reads "A film by Jean-Luc Godard". Visual materials exposing the painterly quality of (digital) video in which Godard has long been interested, male and female voices dialoguing about the nature of the image, juxtapositions of image, text and sound in the "writing of the word" mode: a declaration of aesthetic principles at work in the film as much as just an announcement of the coming attraction.[6]

Critique of the trailer

While Godard's previews differ from classical Hollywood trailers in tone (and by virtue of the fact that they often use female voice-over narration, a thing not done in Hollywood), they reprise some of the basic patterns of these trailers. Hollywood trailers, particularly of the classical era, often feature lists. They list the attractions of the film, they list important collaborators, and they include titles of other successful films of the same genre. The trailer for *À bout de souffle* also consists of a list. A female voice on the sound track names what we see, delivering (once again) a formula for the film ("the woman, the man, the gun"). In the final section of the film, the female voice reads a list of film titles—*Du rififi chez les hommes, Le Diable au corps, Et Dieu créa la femme, Scarface*—accompanied by images from Godard's film (there is no other sound on the soundtrack). Godard's voice intervenes at four moments in the trailer when the title of the film interrupts the series of images, naming first the screenwriter (François Truffaut), then the director of production (Claude Chabrol) and finally the director (himself), only to conclude the trailer with yet another intervention, claiming, over the title of the film, that it is "the best film currently playing". Where Godard's films offer a critique of cinema, his trailers offer a critique of previews, if you will. Trailers for other New Wave films such as *Les Parisiennes* or *Les 400 coups* are quite conventional, following the structural patterns established by classical Hollywood trailers: there is an introduction presenting the theme of the film or the stars, followed by the title, a middle section showing excerpts, and a conclusion which again gives the title of the film. The trailer for *À bout de souffle*, on the other hand, gives us an idea of what a good classical trailer essentially is: a cinematic list poem about a film.

Laboratory for films

Hollywood trailers–or French trailers of the pre-1980 period, for that matter–almost never use female voice-over. Godard trailers do, starting with the trailer for *À bout de souffle*. While in that trailer, the female voice-over reads the list while Godard steps in to anchor her delivery by speaking over

Opposite: **Trailer for** *Éloge de l'amour*, **2001.**

BIENTÔT SUR CET ECRAN

Soon   This   Screen

The woman.   The man.   Italy.   The movies.

LE MÉPRIS

Starring Brigitte Bardot
and Michel Piccoli.   The Alfa-Romeo.   The variety show.   The Greek statue.

The revolver.   LE MÉPRIS

The new traditional film
by Jean-Luc Godard.   The slap.   The bedroom.

The kiss.   The bathroom.   LE MÉPRIS   LE MÉPRIS

With Jack Palance,
Giorgia Moll and Fritz Lang.   With Jack Palance,
Giorgia Moll and Fritz Lang.

LE MÉPRIS

With Jack Palance,
Giorgia Moll and Fritz Lang.   The crazy man.   The starlet.   The old man.

The sea.   LE MÉPRIS LE MÉPRIS LE MÉPRIS

Based on the famous novel
by Alberto Moravia.   Based on the famous novel
by Alberto Moravia.   Based on the famous novel
by Alberto Moravia.

the title of the film, male and female voice-over reappear on a more equal footing in the trailer for *Le Mépris*, another list poem. "Bientôt/sur/cet/écran" ("Showing soon on this screen") are its first four title cards, which are read aloud simultaneously by a male and a female voice. The female voice goes on to again name the visual materials that we see, while the male voice steps back in when more titles appear. Raymond Bellour points out the importance of the female other in and to Godard's work.[7] The Other, Bellour argues, is every other which Godard uses in his work–producer, technician, collaborator–but also the other who becomes an element of the image and at the same time guarantees the image to/of its creator. The Other can be every other, but it is preferably the woman, and particularly the loved one. It is the *femme lumière* (the woman of light/enlightenment), the female counterpart to the Romantic male intellectual. Kaja Silverman proposes to read Godard's inclusion of the Other in its various guises (technician, producer, etc.) but most notably of his female collaborator, Anne-Marie Miéville, in his work since the 1970s as an attempt to shed and undermine his own role as *auteur*.[8] If *JLG/JLG: autoportrait de décembre*, 1995, figures as a point of culmination in such a progressive development, *Le Gai savoir*, 1968, could be said to mark one of its crucial early stages. This is essentially a film consisting of a critical conversation: a man and a woman speak to each other across/about the image, or rather about the film. "In order to solve problems", one of the characters says at one point in the film, "you have to dissolve…. In this case, we dissolve images and sounds." Dissolving images and sounds, separating sounds from images and reassembling them in new ways in order to point out the problem of the film is what a trailer does. Assigning the work of dissolving the images of the film to a male and a female speaker/analyst is the particularity of the trailers for *À bout de souffle* and *Le Mépris*, 1963. The set-up of *Le Gai savoir* can thus be traced back to these trailers, with the Brechtian difference that in the 1968 film, the set-up of the trailer is put on view: we don't just hear the male and female analysts converse about the images and sounds and name them, we also see them doing it. From this perspective, *Le Gai savoir*, and the work that follows it, which includes *Numéro Deux*–a film by Godard and Miéville in which a female voice-over can be heard to say that it will soon be shown on this screen, or another–are variations on a theme, and a structure, established by the trailers for *À bout de souffle* and *Le Mépris*.

But trailers are advertising and Godard films are not, one might object. True, but then again, the audience doesn't seem to consider trailers to be advertising. People will tend to complain about advertising for cigarettes or other consumer products in theatres. In fact audiences in America have objected to advertising in theatres with such consistency that exhibitors have only recently begun to sell screen time to commercial advertisers on a regular basis. But while nobody will like all of the trailers all of the time, hardly anybody objects to the fact that they are there and shown before movies. Trailers are in fact, as Nico de Klerk puts it, part of the programme.[9] They draw the audience's attention to the films coming soon to a theatre near you, or rather to the one you're already sitting in. ("Demnächst in diesem Kino" is the German formula, "Prochainement sur cet écran" the French, which Godard likes to use in his own trailers, and in his films, as we know). Trailers thus refer to a theatre's programme as much as they do to an individual film, and they appeal not only to the basic desires of the audience, but also to their taste and knowledge, inviting them to make visits to this particular cinema a habit. With regard to the film they advertise, one could argue that trailers are preliminary presentations of the film within a program of which the film itself will be the continuation. Trailers, then, let the film begin before it actually begins.

Curiously, moviegoers hardly ever seem to blame the trailer if they end up not liking the film.[10] The cardinal rule of trailer making in Hollywood, as it

Opposite: **Trailer for *Le Mépris*, 1963.**

can be found in trailer-makers' statements from the classical era to this day, is that trailers simply have to be better than the film. Audiences seem to take it for granted that they are, at least judging by the fact that they let themselves be persuaded by trailers time and again, despite the many tales of disappointments every moviegoer has to tell. Apparently, it is not the trailer's fault if the film does not live up to the expectations created by the trailer. Rather, it is the film's fault if it does not keep the promise of the trailer. In broader, somewhat more philosophical terms, one could characterise this wide-spread psychological phenomenon as the triumph of the beginning over the middle and the end. Every beginning, and every trailer, by its nature holds such promise that no middle, end or full-length feature film could ever live up to it. The beginning is where infinite possibility dwells, where the world, and the world of images, is all it can be.

Among the chief proponents of a philosophy of the triumph of the beginning over the middle and the end in the realm of art is Jean-Luc Godard. "I am much more interested in beginnings than in middles or endings", Godard states in one interview, and there is some evidence to back him up.[11] Consider that Godard's films usually just stop rather than end, consider that *One Plus One*, 1968, basically consists of a series of attempts by the Rolling Stones to get a studio recording of *Sympathy for the Devil* right, or that *Nouvelle Vague*, 1990, begins all over again in the middle of the film, or remember the final title card of *La Chinoise* which insists that this is just the end of a beginning, and one gets an idea of the degree to which Godard's interest in beginnings informs his entire work. While apparently fully in tune with how movie audiences feel about the trailer and the promise of the beginning, Godard's concern with beginnings has a particular intellectual ring to it as well. Discussing Godard's debt to the German Romanticism of Novalis, the Schlegel brothers and their circle has now become commonplace, as Jacques Aumont points out.[12] One tends to agree with him, however, that it is still plainly justified, not least because like so many other things Godard's taste in beginnings may actually be traced back to the intellectual legacy of German Romanticism. In his *Blütenstaub Aphorism* no. 66, Novalis coins what German philosopher and legal historian Carl Schmitt calls a formula for Romanticism: "To the truly spiritual being, every encounter, every event, would figure as the first in an infinite series, as the beginning of an infinite novel."[13] The Romantic mind, instead of submitting to factual reality as it is, turns every occurrence into an occasion for aesthetic production. The infinite novel is the form that contains the world in so far as it is taken as the occasion for aesthetic production, but since the world and the number of occasions it presents are essentially infinite, the Romantic novel has to be constantly re-invented, which is best done in an infinite series of new beginnings. An echo of Novalis's formula may be found in a text Godard wrote in 1967: "In the course of a film–in its discourse, that is in its discontinous course–I feel like doing everything: something on sport, on politics, even on selling food." The film, its discourse, its discontinuous run is a form in which everything appears as an occasion for aesthetic production. "You can put everything in a film", Godard continues, "You have to put everything in a film."[14]

Which is, of course, impossible. "Romanticism is dead", Bellour writes with a view to a contemporary world in which the spread of mass media representations of the world in television and newspapers has basically rendered obsolete the idea of the individual as the source of a novel, or another artistic representation encompassing the world in its entirety.[15] It is useful to remember, however, that the modern mass media, particularly the newspaper, emerge at about the same time that the Jena circle of Romantics formulate their ideas about the aesthetic and the Romantic mind. Novalis's formula for the Romantic mind is always already attuned to a world in which, and of which, there is a potentially infinite number of representations. It is in true Romantic fashion, therefore, that Godard continues his argument in the text cited above:

> If someone asks me why I talk, or make people talk, about Vietnam, about Jacques Anquetil, about a woman who cheats on her husband, I refer the person who asks me the question to her habitual daily life. Everything is there. And everything is there right next to each other. This is why I'm attracted so much by television. A television newscast composed of carefully edited documentary features would be extraordinary. It would be even more so if one brought all the editors in chief of newspapers to handle the television newscasts.

Rather than making the novel obsolete, television and newspapers are just so many tools and materials for the creation of an infinite novel, which takes as its point of departure, but is not limited to, the cinema ("It's for this reason that, rather than talking about cinema or television, I prefer to use the more general terms of sounds and images", Godard's text concludes). While Jacques Rancière is right in claiming that *Histoire(s) du cinéma* is the most stunning contemporary manifestation of the Romantic poetics of "Alles spricht" ("Everything speaks"), one could also argue that Godard's films have always been manifestations of Novalis's infinite novel, firmly subscribing to its aesthetics of infinite beginnings.[16] While it may not be possible, strictly, speaking, to include everything in a film, one has to hold on to that possibility and devise an aesthetic that is still capable of answering to the imperative of "[y]ou have to put everything in a film". And be it just to avoid the disappointment expressed by the Jean-Pierre Léaud character in *Masculin Féminin*, 1966, when he talks about going to the movies. Everytime he and his girlfriend (another couple of a cinephile and his other) go to the movies, they are disappointed by the film they see, he says. What was needed instead was the total film: "This total film which was everyone's dream. This film that we would have wanted to make. Or rather to live." Another name for this film would be the infinite cinematic novel (which, as in *Le Gai savoir*, can also take the form of an infinite conversation about film, a *"romantisches Gespräch"* between the cinephile and his other).

Transposed to the realm of cinema, however, the idea of the infinite novel can get you into trouble. Quoted in full, the Godard statement about beginnings reads like this: "I'm much more interested in beginnings than in middle parts or endings, but what you still explore and are searching for cannot be sold." Or can it? True: a cinema of sustained intellectual inquiry seems to be necessarily at odds with the commercial logic of cinema. But while there is little doubt that you cannot market unfinished films, you can always co-opt the rhetoric of selling, and more specifically the rhetoric of the trailer, if you don't want to finish the film. At least that is what Godard did, and still does. After all, the rhetoric of the trailer is not only a marketing tool; it is also the cinematic technique of the beginning par excellence ("l'enfance de l'art cinématographique", as it were). Trailers are the only reliable manifestation of the Romantic idea of infinite beginnings within the commerical logic of cinema, a logic which Godard has, if not always closely adhered to, then certainly always been acutely aware of. Here, then, is a formula for the Godard: how do you make sure of the triumph of the beginning over the middle and the end? Extend the technique of the beginning to the entire film, i.e. turn your films into trailers. You will thereby transform the film from the cinematic equivalent of the nineteenth century realist novel into that of the infinite novel of Romanticism, and you will have safely vanquished middle and end, while at the same time firmly reinserting yourself into the commercial logic of cinema. Albeit, judging by the box office records, you will achieve the latter in a mostly symbolic fashion. But at least you give it a try. As you should. After all, even Godard films cost money.

The trailer is not only the cinematic technique of the beginning par excellence, it is also a technique of memory, or rather of virtual memory: a technique of rememberance of things to come. According to Lacan, the *futurum exactum* is the tense of desire, the tense of imaginary anticipation and of anticipated memory.[17] Feeding a little Lacan into the psychology of film advertising, one could argue that trailers create a desire to see the film by showing the film as one remembers it, or rather by showing the film one has not yet seen as one would remember it if one had already seen it, i.e. as a collection of excerpts of visually and emotionally strong moments. Furthermore, trailers underline the character of excerpts as virtual memory fragments by framing them with references to previous films of the same kind or genre, and by inserting them in what you might call a virtual fan discourse. When discussing the qualities of the star or the film, textual inserts and voice-over, particularly in classical trailers, will tend to employ a vocabulary which mimicks the language of enthusiastic fans recommending a film they have just seen. Thus, trailers suggest that what you're seeing just now, as well as what you will soon be seeing and hearing, are also already fond memories.[18] In that sense, trailers are actual films in the *futurum exactum* tense, a cinema of memory in the future tense.

Although contemporary trailers are usually based on story résumés, what counts in trailers is not the plot, but strong, dense moments, not narrative but aesthetic experience. In trailers, a logic of memory is at work of which, incidentally, a defense may be found in *Histoire(s) du cinéma* Chapter 4A, *Le contrôle de l'univers*, in a passage on Hitchcock:

One has forgotten why Joan Fontaine leans over the precipice
And what Joel McCrea went off to do in the Netherlands
One has forgotten about what Montgomery Clift keeps an eternal silence [...]
but one remembers a handbag
but one remembers a passenger coach in the desert
but one remembers a glass of milk, the wings of a windmill, a hair brush [...][19]

According to Godard, it is through these moments, the moments that linger on in memory when the plot is long forgotten, that Hitchcock succeeded where all great conquerors ("Alexander the Great, Julius Cesar, Napoleon") failed, namely at taking control of the universe. The key to the world of images lies in the power to create moments of enduring presence. That is also, if you will, the rule for trailers. Whether they succeed at unlocking the world of images for those they address, and whether they succeed at lastingly inscribing the film they present within the world of images, largely depends on whether their sounds and images are dense and strong enough to linger on, to insinuate themselves as "good" memories, memories one likes to have.

Histoire(s) itself is a defence of the primacy of aesthetic experience over its emplotment in stories and histories. In Jacques Aumont's words, it is a testament to what you might call the Orpheus complex, i.e. to a compulsion to return to the past, as well as to the Orphic powers of cinema, i.e. its power to write and rewrite history, to make History appear and disappear at a glance.[20] The glance, however, is by necessity a personal glance, a glance which renders History as memory. Following Godard's argument in *Histoire(s)*, cinema fails in the face of History where it fails to account for what happened in terms of memory, which is most notably the case for the concentration camps, where no cameras were present.

But if *Histoire(s)* exerts the Orphic powers of cinema on the History of cinema, History in the form of memories of films, of instances of "one remembers", features prominently in Godard's other films as well. From Belmondo's imitations of Bogart in *À bout de souffle* to the sudden outbursts of musical dancing in *Une femme est une femme*, 1961, by way of *Masculin Féminin*, which is the one Godard film Jean Rouch never made: folding what the films show into a memory of films seen at the expense of a coherent, linear narrative is a signature gesture of Godard's work since its inception. If one were to search for the roots of this gesture in the auteur's psyche, the Venice press conference on the occasion of the premiere of *Hélas pour moi* might provide some cues. Answering a journalist's question as to why he did not tell straightforward stories in his films, Godard said: "When I was a kid, whenever I told a lie, my mother would say, 'You mustn't tell stories [*histoires*]'." Thus instructed, the boy would never quite overcome the dichotomy of telling the truth and telling a story (it's the law of the mother, and after all, a boy loves his mother). Luckily for the young cinephile and aspiring director, however, the technique of the beginning and the Romantic strategy of continuous inception provided him with a way to sidestep the mendacious trajectory of the story told whole, while still remaining within the broader realm of Cinema with a capital C. As for that larger, ideologically more dangerous twin of story, History, it was precisely memory that provided a way out: memory as a reminder of the potentially coercive force of history, re-presented in the form of films in which what is shown is simultaneously, as in trailers, what is remembered, and what might be remembered by someone else.

An excerpt in a trailer, an excerpt in *Histoire(s)*, or a scene in a Godard film where someone, and the film along with her, remembers a film, may all in similar ways be considered as objective correlatives of memory. But if film as a mode of rememberance of films creates objective correlatives of memory, or memory-objects, the apparently random gesture of "putting everything in a film" has its objectivity as well. Romantic irony and the Romantic mind have come under attack from various sides over time, most notably from Hegel, who decried romantic irony as "hollow subjectivity", and from Carl Schmitt, for whom romantic irony is in essence secularised and subjective occasionalism.[21] Romanticism is largely about the invention of the aesthetic as a specific mode of experience. Hegel, as Karl-Heinz Bohrer points out, fails to grasp–or refuses to acknowledge–the specifity of aesthetic experience, insisting on the pedagogic function of art instead and requiring, in short, that art teach moral lessons rather than represent or engender a mode of being *sui generis*.[22] Schmitt, on the other hand, objects to Romanticism because the aesthetic in his estimate threatens to subvert traditional authority.[23] His charge of secularised occasionalism alleges that the Romantic mind puts itself in the position of the occasionalist god of eighteenth century philosopher Malebranche. Mimicking the occasionalist god, to whom the seemingly fixed dichotomies of the real world are mere occasions for creative intervention, for the *creatio continua*, the Romantic mind reduces the world to just so many occasions for aesthetic production. In that sense, the Godard film could truly be considered an example of God art. Godard, or his publicity people, have also toyed with the idea. The poster for *Hélas pour moi*, another example of "writing of the word", demonstrates that there is "god" in Godard, as there is "dieu" in Depardieu. The first three letters of Godard's name and the last four of Depardieu's are set in red, while the rest of the characters are blue. Indeed, since telling the truth and telling a story are two different things to Godard, he would not come off lightly in a Hegelian critique of his art, and since he insists that you have to put everything in a film (which makes your film akin to the Romantic novel), he also firmly casts himself as the enemy in Schmitt's scheme of things.

But Godard's morality, and the objectivity of his art, lie elsewhere: in his sublime taste in reinventing cinema at its margins, in making it resemble the peripheral discourse of the trailer more than the established discourse of the narrative fiction film.

The beauty of the Godard, as opposed to the trailer, of course is that in the discontinuous discourse of the Godard the promise given in the form of anticipated memories is never quite fulfilled, while the trailer leads us directly to the disappointment of the actual film. But then again, it doesn't necessarily do so. Contemporary trailers are actually meant to scare off that part of the audience for which the film is not intended, as one of the more seasoned practitioners of the craft once put it.[24] In that sense, declining to see a mainstream film on the basis of what the trailer tells you almost amounts to seeing a Godard film.

And then, of course, there is the trailer for *Soigne ta droite*, which resembles a Godard film in that it has obvious difficulty in ending. But if the Godard film-as-trailer feeds back into the Godard trailer at times, it is useful to remember that Godard trailers have always been part and parcel of the elaboration of the Godard film-as-trailer. The form of the infinite conversation, for instance, the analytical exchange between male and female voices, which was later to inscribe itself in Godard's films, was present in the trailer as early as *À bout de souffle*. Thus, while there is infinite conversation in Godard trailers and Godard films, there is also an infinite conversation between the Godard, the trailer and the Godard trailer. However, I would rather conclude by once again clearly pointing out the difference between a trailer and a Godard film. While mainstream trailers often contain all the best scenes from the movie, Godard's films contain all the best scenes that make up the trailer, because in them, as in so many cinematic realisations of Novalis's infinite novel, the film never entirely begins, and the trailer certainly never ends.

Opposite: **Gérard Depardieu and Laurence Masliah in the poster for *Hélas pour moi*, 1993.**

THE FORMS OF THE QUESTION[1]

For Raymonde Carasco

NICOLE BRENEZ

From the problem to the practical task

In *Éloge de l'amour*, 2001, Jean-Luc Godard uses the following phrase: "Every problem violates a mystery; in turn, the problem is violated by its solution." The work of analysis thus consists, ultimately, in rediscovering the mystery. But first, what is a question? As Gilles Deleuze reminds us in his *Abécédaire*, a question does not lead to an interrogation (whose answer goes without saying), but rather a question assumes at least two dynamics: a construction and a power of displacement. What, then, would be a question for the cinema? In relation to Godard, from the outset, three remarks seem imperative.

a. A classical belief in the virtues of the problematic

The founding Godardian model proves Socratic. *Introduction à une véritable histoire du cinéma*, 1980, establishes a parallel between Socrates and Roberto Rossellini:

Socrates was exactly the same kind of guy as Roberto, a guy they poisoned simply because he asked people questions. He accepted everything; all he wanted was to talk to people. And he was totally intolerable in Athens because, as a result not of asking questions but of talking to people, he pissed everybody off, just by simply expanding on things, by going a little farther. He had nothing of his own; he took from others and adapted things. One plus One, it went a lot further and people said to him: "We want to stay at One. We don't want to add 'plus One'."[2]

This formula can be seen as a pop remake of a text first published in 1953, whose title today seems in perfect resonance with the Godardian corpus, *Éloge de la philosophie*, 1953, where Maurice Merleau-Ponty makes Socrates the perfect model of the philosopher. For Socrates, philosophy "is not like

Opposite: *Faut pas rêver*, **1978.**

160

QUAND LA GAUCHE
AURA LE POUVOIR

QUAND LA GAUCHE
AURA LE POUVOIR
EST-CE QUE

QUAND LA GAUCHE
AURA LE POUVOIR
EST-CE QUE
LA TELEVISION

UAND LA GAUCHE
RA LE POUVOIR
T-CE QUE
TELEVISION
RA TOUJOURS

QUAND LA GAUCHE
AURA LE POUVOIR
EST-CE QUE
LA TELEVISION
AURA TOUJOURS
AUSSI PEU

QUAND LA GAUCHE
AURA LE POUVOIR
EST-CE QUE
LA TELEVISION
AURA TOUJOURS
AUSSI PEU
DE RAPPORT AVEC

QUAND LA GAUCHE
AURA LE POUVOIR
EST-CE QUE
LA TELEVISION
AURA TOUJOURS
AUSSI PEU
DE RAPPORT AVEC
LES GENS ?

RA LE POUVOIR
T-CE QUE
TELEVISION
RA TOUJOURS
SSI PEU
RAPPORT AVEC
ES GENS ?

EST-CE QUE
LA TELEVISION
AURA TOUJOURS
AUSSI PEU
DE RAPPORT AVEC
LES GENS ?

EST-CE QUE
LA TELEVISION
AURA TOUJOURS
AUSSI PEU
DE RAPPORT AVEC
LES GENS ?

an idol for which he would be the guardian and that he must keep in a safe place, but rather it exists in its living relationship to Athens. Always guilty by means of excess or by means of shortfall, always simpler and less succinct than the others, always more docile and less accommodating, he puts them in a state of discomfort; he inflicts on them that unpardonable offence of making them doubt themselves."[3] In this perspective, the task of Merleau-Pontian philosophy is intimately linked to the task of Godardian cinema: "philosophy awakens us to what is problematic in itself in the world's existence and in our own existence, to such an extent that we are never cured of seeking, as Bergson said, a solution 'in the notebook of the master'".[4] From the Socratic model, Godard therefore retains primarily two virtues of the problematic: first, a critical power; second, an experimental openness, which may also be traced to another model, non-dialogical but significant, in a less familiar but none the less fertile source, the Problemata of Aristotle.

b. The Problemata of Aristotle: the art of concrete questions
In Aristotle, one finds another way of using the question, a usage that is not included in a Socratic perspective, for this time it is not dialogical, oral, and developed through connections, but rather solitary, written, and accumulative: the 38 sections of the Problemata of Aristotle, a collection of concrete questions whose sometimes excessive or incongruous nature restores the practice of interrogation to its authentically experimental nature. Let's evoke, from among the hundreds of juxtaposed questions there, three brief examples among the Aristotelian Problemata. First, a classical example:

Why are men who are distinguished in philosophy, politics, poetry, or the arts, all apparently people in whom melancholia prevails? (Section XXX, question 1)

Then, an example to show that Aristotle, on one issue, had already thought a little bit beyond Nietzsche:

Why do doctors exercise their art only up to the point of a cure? Is it because it is impossible that something else might result beyond the point of healthiness? (Section XXX, question 8)

And finally, a very Godardian question: "Why is Eristic reasoning made up of gymnastics?" (Section XVIII, question 2) Let us recall that Eristics is the art of controversy, and that one can see here the beginning of a famous Godardian metaphor connecting dialogical exchanges in cinema with the exchange of shots in tennis, an exchange that *Vladimir et Rosa*, 1971, will thoroughly develop but that one finds throughout Godard's works, for example, in *Petites notes à propos du film Je vous salue, Marie*, 1985, in *Soigne ta droite*, 1987, and *JLG/JLG: autoportrait de décembre*, 1995. As a model, one can see working the essential virtues of the Godardian question in a relatively unknown work from 1978–a two-minute video clip for a popular song by Patrick Juvet, *Faut Pas Rêver*.

As is the case with all the brief forms invented by Godard, this little opus is not in the least a minor work. It is made up of two shots: first, a medium fixed shot of a little girl who is eating an apple for her afternoon snack after coming home from school; she is responding to her mother, whom we don't see (the voice of Anne-Marie Miéville is recognisable) and who asks her about her day, while the little girl watches, distractedly, a television set that is supposedly broadcasting the song of Patrick Juvet (whom we don't see either). Then, the second shot shows the following question appearing as text on a black background: "When the left is in power, will television still have so little of a relationship with people's lives?"

In this everyday dialogue, we find the emergence of a fundamental critical question that, in the mid-1970s, must have been perceived as quite violent (at that time we were right in the middle of the Giscardian regime, and it would take seven more years for the left to come to power). We also find here a little study on the problem of off-screen. The positioning out of frame, in turn, of the song, of the mother, and of the television set leaves room for an image of ordinary life, convincing particularly in proportion to its modesty and to its passive nature (the little girl is tired: she is relaxing; she is doing nothing; all the active elements remain at a distance). But this image of ordinary life cannot be the only image called for by the question written on the screen. The shot here possesses three layers of meaning: first, a polemical meaning, as the shot positions itself, in its simplicity, against false ideological images, since the frame obstructs the televised images and keeps them out of play; second, an actual and relative meaning, since the shot does not pretend to fulfil the programme that the critical question announces; third, the shot is a sample or a glimpse of an alternative, creating a gap in the ordinary stream of dominant images. In this way, the shot here turns into a "Problem" in the Godardian sense that we are trying to construct: that is to say, it is always at the same time polemical, prospective, and dialectical.

This experimental practice of the question, with its two principal historical sources, one oral and the other written, dialogical and technical, Socratic and Aristotelian, can be summed up in this formula from Merleau-Ponty (compare Godard's phrase "he had nothing of his own"): "He didn't know any more than they did. He only knows that there is no absolute knowledge and that it is by way of this absence that we are open to truth."[5] This gaping abyss is perhaps literally represented in the last shot of *Je vous salue, Marie*, 1985, by means of the wide open mouth of Myriem Roussel, or in the last shot of *Soigne*

Above: *Soigne ta droite*, 1987.

Opposite: **Godard and Jean-Pierre Gorin in *Vladimir et Rosa*, 1971.**

ta droite by means of the door wide open on to death–two final images signalling the dizzying approach of the Real.

c. The materiality of the question:
"Godard's discoveries pulverise all problematics." (Michel Delahaye)
The question is one of the most specific, persistent, and dynamic forms in the work of Jean-Luc Godard. Even the simplest interrogation, "How's it going?" ("Comment ça va?")–which Deleuze uses in his *Abécédaire* as the model of an amorphous interrogation–transforms itself into a concrete problem. The question, in effect, consists initially of a putting-into-practice of a filmic problem, in such a way as to have the question appear as a solution, first of a narrative, plastic order, then of an ethical and formal order. The evolution of Godard's work relating to this point takes us from the simple *mise en scène* of the question toward the transformation of the image itself into a pure formal problem.

We can trace a trajectory from *Tous les garçons s'appellent Patrick*, 1957, where Jean-Claude Brialy puts pretty girls to the question over and over without paying any attention at all to their answers, to *Histoire(s) du cinéma*, where all the explicit interrogative formulas begin to turn into affirmative slogans while at the same time, every image, sound, and superimposition raises a question. For the purposes of this essay, we shall now identify and categorise a range of examples, mapping out six principal ways in which questions are given form: 1. the interrogation; 2. the lesson; 3. the interview; 4. the dialogue; 5. the torture scene; and 6. the Question-Image. Of these, we will discuss especially the sixth, the most specific to the current research of Jean-Luc Godard.

1. Interrogation sequences (or the heuristic offering)
A random character, who is not in any way a professional in the art of questioning, meets another character, by chance, who is invested with knowledge and authority, and asks him to explain a number of phenomena. The sequence consists therefore of offering to the master the opportunity to put forth his world view. We might thus call this device the heuristic offering. This mechanism leads to some of the most famous Godardian sequences, including the following: the questions Jean-Paul Belmondo asks Samuel Fuller in *Pierrot le fou*, 1965; the questions Anna Karina asks Brice Parain in *Vivre sa vie*, 1962; the questions Anne Wiazemsky asks Francis Jeanson on the train in *La Chinoise*, 1967; the questions asked of Roger Leenhardt by the husband and wife in *Une femme mariée*, 1964.

2. The lesson
Another Godardian use of the figure of authority, this time non-dialogical, is that of the professor, and one might want to establish parallels between lesson sequences and interview sequences, each giving way to hybrid forms as, for example, in *La Chinoise*. Examples of lesson sequences include the classes in *Bande à part*, 1964, and in *Alphaville*, 1965, the one led by Jacques Dutronc/Paul Godard in *Sauve qui peut (la vie)*, 1980, with Marguerite Duras out of frame, and the course on the creation of the world in *Je vous salue, Marie*, 1985. Like the master-class that makes up the *Scénario du film Passion*, 1982, the first two episodes of *Histoire(s)* are organised according to a scenography of the lesson–but it is a lesson whose didacticism is nourished by the speculative virutes of fundamental research rather than by classical argumentation.

3. The fictions and mechanisms of the interview
Here, a professional in the art of questioning asks the person he has tracked

Above: **Eddie Constantine as Lemmy Caution** in *Alphaville*, **1965**.

Opposite above: **Omar Diop delivering a lecture on Marxism in** *La Chinoise*, **1967**.

Opposite below: **Jean Seberg filming the swindler (Charles Denner) in** *Le Grand escroc*, **1964**.

down to give him the answers he needs; the scenario appeals to two recurrent figures, both emblematic of B-movies: the journalist and the detective.

3a. Fictions of reporting

Here one finds the straightforward use of the figure of the journalist as a dramatic device, whether in relation to a sequence or to the whole of a film. Examples include: Jean Seberg interrogating Jean-Pierre Melville in *À bout de souffle*, 1960; the same Jean Seberg, this time a professional journalist (named Patricia Leacock), in the sketch *Le Grand escroc*, 1964; Philippe Labro in *Made in USA*, 1966; Jane Fonda in *Tout va bien*, 1972; the television crew interrogating Anne Wiazemsky in *One Plus One*, 1968; Michèle Halberstadt interrogating "The Professor", that is to say Jean-Luc Godard, in *King Lear*, 1987.

3b. Scenarios of investigation

Here, the opportunity to ask questions must be fought for by the investigator, either because the interviewee is evasive, or because by a reversal of roles the interviewer becomes the interviewee, or because the interviewee dissolves into the question itself. This is the relationship of Lemmy Caution (Eddie Constantine) to Alpha 60 in *Alphaville*. And again, 25 years later, it is the relationship of Lemmy Caution to his subject in *Allemagne année 90 neuf zéro*, 1991, where the detective no longer has an interlocutor and the very existence of Germany becomes a pure enigma and the existence of History a problem in itself.

Le Joli Mai

Above: **Jean Rouch and Edgar Morin in the Musée de l'Homme during the making of** *Chronique d'un été,* **1961.**

Opposite: *Le Joli mai,* **Chris Marker, 1963.**

4. Scenarios and mechanisms of dialogue

This time, the two interlocutors speak one after another, and the variants develop according to the forms their presence takes in the dialogue. There are at least four versions of this mechanism.

4a. The cinéma-vérité version: the questionnaire

This is the sociological side of the undertaking: the protagonists in a fictional work take up the positions of interviewer or interviewee. The exchanges are either relayed (a character retranscribes the filmmaker's oral questions, traces of which often remain in the mechanism), or direct (the character answers the camera straightforwardly). Models: television, but also Jean Rouch and Edgar Morin's *Chronique d'un été,* 1961, or Chris Marker's *Le Joli mai,* 1963. Examples include: the mutual interview of the characters in

Masculin Féminin, 1966; the direct interviews of the characters in *Une femme mariée*, 1964.

4b. Documentary version: the verification

This time the professional figure is the filmmaker, who interviews either a recognised expert or a "simple creature" treated as an expert on ordinary experiences. This arrangement often works in such a way that the stakes are neither in the accuracy of the answers nor in the beauty of the questions but in the unlikely and thus transgressive nature of the dialogue itself. This interview shouldn't have taken place. Nothing about the social situation of these figures made it possible. And that is exactly why it had to happen. Examples include: *Le Dinosaure et le bébé*, an interview between Godard and Fritz Lang where the very modest Lang proclaims the equal authority of the interlocutors; the project *One American Movie* (interviews with Eldridge Cleaver or with anonymous individuals who were to have been subsequently played by actors), a film ultimately completed by Leacock and Pennebaker; *Meetin' W A*, 1986, interview with Woody Allen; *Six fois deux (Sur et sous la communication)*, 1976, where the filmmaker, off-screen, questions in turn an amateur filmmaker, René Thom, a farmer, a woman.... In the episode *Jean-Luc*, Godard is in dialogue with a professional journalist, and this is without a doubt the clearest self-portrait we find of the artist as questioner since he takes up every position–of Socrates, of Aristotle, and of Merleau-Ponty; lastly, *France/tour/détour/deux/enfants*, 1979, doubtless the masterpiece of real dialogue, all the more so because each dialogue is reprised, commented upon, and given a broader perspective.

4c. Allegorical version: the colloquy

This version ensures the metaphysical dimension of the undertaking. It emerges most clearly in *Puissance de la parole*, 1988, structured by a dialogue out of Edgar Allan Poe, a discussion between two angels, Oinos and Agathos, which revolves around the origin of creation and the very possibility of knowing that origin.

4d. Home-movie version: the conversation

In *Un film comme les autres*, 1968, the debate between the opposing sides after May 68 represents the collective version of the dialogue. In *Soft and Hard (Soft Talk on a Hard Subject Between Two Friends)*, 1985, the dialogue between Godard and Miéville, which turns on the origin of images and the very possibility of making them, represents the private version.

5. The moments and thematics of torture

Such a thematic requires a particular treatment, for it proves particularly problematic, and thus influential and significant. Torture strips bare the violence inherent in the interrogation. It represents a real historical, anthropological, and political problematic, to such an extent that in Godard's work it cannot be reduced to its iconographic forms but instead constitutes a formal instrument, a pivotal lever. It appears early in Godard's work with the reversals between the Algerians and the French offered as a disposition in *Le Petit soldat*, 1960. It returns in the form of the thematic of hands attached to a train window during the interview between Anne Wiazemsky and the philosopher and hero of the Algerian War, Francis Jeanson, in *La Chinoise*, 1967. But we might not have noticed the preceding incident if this thematic had not been taken up again, notably in *Soigne ta droite*, 1987, or in *Changer d'image*, 1982, the latter particularly rich with regard to mechanisms of questioning since it creates associations between the

Above: **The torture of Bruno Forestier (Michel Subor) in *Le Petit soldat*, 1960.**

Opposite: **Filmmakers Jean-Luc Godard and Marcel Reymond, mathmatician René Thom, and farmer "Louison" in *Six fois deux (Sur et sous la communication)*, 1976.**

conversation (the exchange between Godard and Miéville), the colloquy (with Miéville remaining a voice-off), torture, and what we will call the "Question-Image". Torture, or "the ultimate question" (as it was called in the book by Henri Alleg on the practices of the French army during the Algerian War), constitutes perhaps the very model of the Question-Image. After *Le Petit soldat*, because of that first reversal of roles between victim and torturer–recalled in *Changer d'image*–an image could never again serve as the equivalent of its straightforward literal meaning: henceforth it would have to begin by existing as a response to its possible counter-shot.

6. The Question-Image

Here is the protocol for this aspect of the question: that the image, no longer just aurally but visually, becomes firstly a question, and secondly a critique. This form of the question no longer needs a character, no longer requires a questioner-figure even as a voice-off. Instead, the images become the protagonists themselves, direct and autonomous, of a debate, of an investigation, or of a mystery. The shot is no longer reduced to an illustrative role. It becomes performative: it is an act of displacement, a proposition, and an opening. Such a stylistics of the Question-Image has little by little taken on a major role in the work of Godard, to such an extent that it has become his most significant means of invention. One can identify four different periods in this process.

6a. Generalised reflexivity: criticised and critical images

Let's analyse a case in order to establish the clearest point of departure for the appearance of the Question-Image: in *Masculin Féminin*, the set of sequences during which the four protagonists eat lunch, observe a conversation between Brigitte Bardot and Antoine Bourseiller, then go to the movies, where they see a parody of a bad European art movie portraying a couple in crisis. Three basic observations can be made about this early example of dialogue between images. Firstly, its principal interest lies in the emotional suffering engendered by bad images. Hence the shattering gesture of Jean-Pierre Léaud closing his eyes because he cannot stand to watch a film that does not know how to represent love. Secondly, it is a critical *mise en abyme*, the bad film is criticised by the work of *Masculin Féminin* around it. Such a cinephiliac sequence connects with many others in the Godardian corpus, both before and after, and in particular one can think of similar scenes in *Les Carabiniers*, 1963, about understanding; *Vivre sa vie*, 1962, about emotion; *Soigne ta droite*, about the impossible; and the colour section of *Éloge de l'amour*, about the bad film (by Claude Berri) that was incapable of portraying the French Resistance.

Thirdly, if it is an encounter between critical images and criticised images, what is the relationship between the two types of images? Is the critical film the ideal, the counter-model, of the criticised film? In this example, criticised images possess three characteristics: they are badly projected; they are obscene; they are repetitive, already seen, they repeat other films. Here, "a man and a woman in a foreign city" recalls the synopsis of Rossellini's *Viaggio in Italia*, 1953, and also therefore *Le Mépris*, 1963, with which the criticised film shares the same formal attributes of the appearance of a couple moving around an apartment with white walls. It shares also, in part, the synopsis and iconography of Bergman's *The Silence*, 1963. Even as we reject these bad images, which leave us unable to do anything except close our eyes, they nevertheless profoundly belong to us. As for critical images, they also have three main characteristics.

Firstly, they develop in an obvious way a completely different set of gestures relating to love, turning on the caress between Chantal Goya and Jean-Pierre Léaud in the cinema (this relates to the problem of figurability that recurs throughout the cinema of Godard). Secondly, critical images are fragmentary, scattered, and untethered. Thus the editing in this set of sequences in *Masculin Féminin* features a number of surprising characteristics. This may be an unfinished shot, more or less a mistake (Jean-Pierre Léaud makes an error in his graffiti-writing, we hear the voice-off of the filmmaker and the shot cuts prematurely); or unconnected sounds, such as the sudden cry "Madeleine", Chantal Goya's interrupted song, the music coming out of nowhere at the end of the sequence involving the projectionist; or, by contrast, over-emphatic connections, such as the link between the movement of the man in the bad film going up a staircase and Léaud going down another, or the sound connection between the dialogues of the people in the cinema and those on the screen. Thirdly, critical images are heterogeneous. Thus we see in these sequences a typically Godardian confrontation between fictional, documentary, and reflexive images, such as the portraits of characters (Paul, Madeleine) that serve also as portraits of actors (Léaud, Goya), or the related sequence with Bardot rehearsing a play in a café with Bourseiller: here we have a problematic image of Bardot, who simultaneously "resembles" Brigitte Bardot, is Brigitte Bardot, and yet does not resemble the Brigitte Bardot who is customarily represented, since here she is working on a text both seriously and attentively (a superb

Above top: **Publicity flyer for Ingmar Bergman's *Tystnaden*, 1963.**

Above: **Japanese flyer for *Masculin Féminin*, 1966.**

Opposite: **Chantal Goya, Marlène Jobert, Jean-Pierre Léaud, Brigitte Bardot, and Antoine Bourseiller in *Masculin Féminin*.**

homage to an underestimated actress). We also find heterogeneous shots with dream-like connections, such as the shot of the gay men, which is practically a fantasmatic image evoked by the amorous situation that Paul is experiencing, and thus a mental image (the lovers do not move when he opens the door); or the shot of the straight couple with the prostitute in a far corner of the courtyard, which is like the background real for what is being projected inside on the screen. And finally, there are heterogeneous images that, if not completely impossible, are difficult to imagine, in an optative mood, as when we hear the voice of Léaud citing an extract from Georges Perec's *Les Choses*: "Often, we were disappointed. This wasn't the film that we had dreamt about, that each of us carried in ourselves, the total film that we would have liked to make, or, doubtless more secretly, that we would have wanted to live."

In answer to the disappointing nature of affective images, and to the inaccessible nature of the total film, there appears in *Masculin Féminin* the politics of graffiti, the cry of pure emotion, and the flowering of mental images, in other words a practice of images as scraps, as gestures, and as transferences. This is how, during this first period of deconstruction of classical cinema, Godard manages to problematise, firstly, the relationship of images to one another, never entirely foreign to each other, never just resembling one another; and secondly, the very nature of images, varying from one shot to the next with a subtle diversity, each time seeking a different answer to his fundamental concerns (How to find one's place in the cinema? What images should one make?), and each time, of course, announcing the general virtualisation of images that will explode the following year in *La Chinoise* ("a film to be made") and that will triumph in the 1990s.

6b. The stage of problematic literality: the blackboard
The end of the 1960s inaugurates a period of clarification as to the dialectical nature of images: "Language was not invented to affirm but to discuss"; "Images are not made to affirm, but to be discussed or to be themselves a discussion." During a large number of sequences, the pressing questions of the day are written out on blackboards, then the image jettisons such a staging and asserts itself directly as a blackboard. The ultimate Question-Image becomes in this way the black image. For example, the uses of black in chains of images possess at least four major meanings according to *Lotte in Italia*, 1970: firstly, a black image is an image that one does not want to make; secondly, a black image is an image that one must not accept ("Why this black in this chain of images? The voice of idealism is a lie, it puts black there"); thirdly, a black image takes the place of a just image; and fourthly, a black image indicates what is outside the film ("To see what there was before and after me on the screen"). In this way, the dialogue between different kinds of images accords an essential place to the virtual, to the conditional, to the absent, to the negative, to the unacceptable–in a word, to the problematic.

6c. From preparatory sketch to all-encompassing research
Here we encounter the form that Godard systematically explores and enriches, the cinematic sketch, structured by a series of questions, no longer just "what image are we going to make?" but also "what image must we make? what image has been made? what image are we discussing? what image are we critiquing?" These questions amount to the same thing: the film to be made is confused in turn with the film in the process of being made, with the film that has already been made, and with the film

that is impossible to make. The image becomes simultaneously optative, conditional, imperative, indicative. One could call this phenomenon of composition the integral sketch. It represents a first stage in Merleau-Ponty's program of "vindicating philosophy all the way down to its weaknesses". The most significant appearances of this are *Scénario vidéo de Sauve Qui Peut (la vie)*, 1979; *Lettre à Freddy Buache*, 1982; *Scénario du film Passion*; *Changer d'image*; *Petites notes à propos du film Je vous salue, Marie*. But the form of the integral sketch, which is given a certain autonomy as early as the time of the great reflexive fictions such as *Le Mépris*, later expands to the scale of the full-length films, such as *Grandeur et décadence d'un petit commerce de cinéma*, 1986, *Soigne ta droite*, *King Lear*. We even find a recent trace of it, increasingly problematic and polemical, in *Éloge de l'amour*, whose second colour section is a discussion about a film to be made about the Resistance, in relation to a film that has already been shot though nonetheless never named (Claude Berri's *Lucie Aubrac*, 1997).

In other words, each work becomes a pure problem of cinema. The origins of this esthetic paradox of inchoate form (everything is already done/everything is still to be done/everything is to begin or to begin again) derive from a complex constellation that brings together Hölderlin, Mallarmé, and Blanchot, the modernity of the unfinished work and of the "work to come"; Robert Bresson, when he writes: "Extreme complexity. Your films are essays, attempts"; and Theodor Adorno, for whom the figure of genesis is not simply an ethics, but especially a politics, of disintegration: "Art wants what has never yet existed; now, everything that is art has already been. It is incapable of projecting beyond the shadow of what it was. But what has not yet existed, that is the concrete."[6] Henri Langlois, one of whose Anti-Courses–given in Montreal in 1975 and constituting the archaeology of Godard's *Histoire(s) du Cinéma*–was devoted simultaneously to Andy Warhol and Jean-Luc Godard, and connected these two great inventors of forms precisely by the fact that they are both artists of the rough draft; and finally Chris Marker, whose *Sans Soleil*, 1982, constructs a notion of "total memory" that combines in one single gesture the project, its rejection, its fabrication, and its completion: "To make a futurist film, to say that one will not make it, to give it the title of the film that is made, which is the film itself."

6d. The total image and volumetric editing

We know today that an image is not equivalent to a shot, that is to say that it is not reducible to its iconographic literality. It possesses always, already and necessarily a relationship to other images; even before existing, it is inscribed in a history, and it is itself a history. The image is this volumetrics of the shot, this conjugation of the whole by which every image is called on by others, every image prefigures others, every image makes way for or obstructs the passage of others, whether they are similar (the simple version, as an exercise explains in *The Old Place*, 1999), antagonistic, or heterogeneous. Thus editing becomes a task of interweaving, not just between thematics, but between regimes of images. Editing becomes the mutual interrogation of one image by another image in the making, of the image as a trace by the image as an emerging form, of the familiar image by the image that has disappeared.... The difference between the sketch and the recapitulation has vanished, in other words editing thus redefined becomes an art of the presence of the image confronted by its own powers.

Le Rapport Darty, 1989, a film made to order, an industrial film like *Lettre à Freddy Buache* or *Puissance de la Parole*, proves exemplary from this point of view. It obeys the same structure as *Lettre à Freddy Buache*: a company, Darty

Above: *Éloge de l'amour,* 2001.

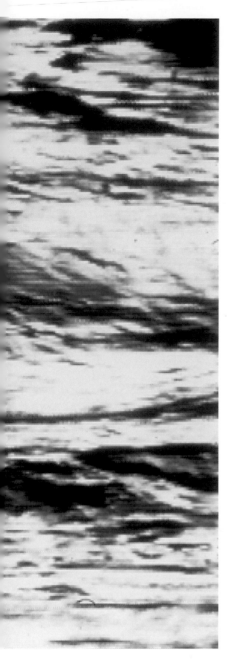

(a chain of popular stores that sell television sets and washing machines) orders a report from a production company. The filmmakers flee, leaving behind only a single secretary, Clio, and an old robot, Nathanaël. These two undertake to make the film but, halfway through the process, Darty sends them a letter rejecting their work. We see this letter on the screen and we hear the two protagonists reading it and discussing it. An essential essay on the relationship between business and the image, *Le Rapport Darty* develops before our eyes the state of the film: it brings together, superimposes, and confuses all at the same time the project, the rejection of that project, the execution, the exegesis, the evidence of the fabrication, and the disintegration of the finished product. (It is also a revealing work, since the film currently has been banned by Darty, who refuse to allow it to be distributed or shown.)

In praise of the wuestion

a. "At the conclusion of a reflection that first cuts him off, but in order to make him better feel the links of truth that attach him to the world and to history, the philosopher finds, not the abyss of the self or of absolute knowledge, but the renewed image of the world, and himself planted, among the others, in that world."[7] For Jean-Luc Godard, this would read "not the abyss of the self or of absolute knowledge", but the world renewed by the image.

b. We can detect at least four new aesthetic forms emerging from the principle of the Question-Image: the integral sketch; the negative composition, that is to say the composition conceived out of the absence of the image (the basis on which *Histoire(s) du cinéma* is structured); a general virtualisation of images; and volumetric editing.

c. The properties and potentialities of the image that is redefined in this way become visible over the course of an unbroken evolution. Rather than fixing chronological periods, one can trace the development of Godard's dominant concerns: from the image as a hypothesis (the image grasped in its exploratory qualities) to the image as mortgage ("reality has perhaps not yet emerged before anyone's eyes", says Kirilov in *La Chinoise*), and finally, to the image as a modern synthesis, that is to say having reintegrated the whole culture of the negative.

d. Merleau-Ponty: "the most determined philosophers always want the opposites: to realise, but by destroying; to get rid of things, but by preserving them." Such a trajectory through the properties of the question is therefore hard to imagine outside of a (crazed) Love of the Answer. The cinema of Jean-Luc Godard is, like philosophy according to Merleau-Ponty, "tragic, but not serious".

PROCESSION AND PROJECTION: NOTES ON A FIGURE IN THE WORK OF JEAN-LUC GODARD

CHRISTA BLÜMLINGER

In a number of films by Jean-Luc Godard a decisive figure emerges out of a dual movement of human forms and projected images (decisive in a formal rather than narrative sense). The *défilé*, as a *mise en scène* of a number of bodies crossing the field of view, conspicuously represents the idea of the passage of the moving, "living" image. Godard certainly did not invent this performative figure. It runs through film history from the outset and in early cinema already proved to be a popular motif. The cinematographers for the Lumière brothers were fond of capturing all kinds of things passing by their immobile cameras, be it by associating them with means of transport, as in *L'Arrivée d'un train à La Ciotat* ("Arrival of a train at La Ciotat"), or by filming amidst military parades, religious processions or other ritualised pageants. The term *défilé* crops up in the titles of numerous Lumière films, not only in the case of military regiments, but also in the context of cyclists, car drivers and young ladies from a girl's grammar school.[1] Usually the camera is positioned in such a way that the people move from the classical vanishing point deep within the image towards the viewer before filing past the camera and out of the field of view. In *Défilé de voitures de bébés à la pouponnière de Paris* ("Procession of Perambulators at the Day Nursery in Paris"), we see, for example, an almost perfectly marshalled file of prams advancing out of the image to the left.[2] Towards the end a little girl runs back and forth, thereby "disturbing" this sequence of events staged in time and space. It is the very sequence which the "first" film of the Lumière brothers, the *Sortie des usines* ("Workers Leaving the Factory"), had rehearsed in an exemplary way: the filling and emptying of a carefully framed field of view in the context of a predetermined duration.

The word *défilé* crops up in the title of a video by Godard which is in a sense a by-product of an advertising film for a Swiss designer. Like some

Opposite: *Tout va bien*, 1972.

other of Godard's commissioned or so-called "minor" productions, *On s'est tous défilé*, 1988, embraces a whole range of ideas, from the *dispositif* (the mechanism or set-up) of moving images through to the codes of representation of the human body. Taking as its starting point the idea of a fashion parade, this short video alludes to the idea of the procession in its title in a manner not unlike the Lumière films already referred to; moreover it formulates a paradox with the word play *défiler/se défiler* (to march past/to steal away) which draws a connection to fullness and emptiness and refers to both social (prefilmic) and technical (filmic) presentation. By means of this dual movement the fashion parade becomes a figurative crystallisation of a range of processions in Godard's work.

In Godard's earlier films processions already tend to dissociate themselves from the narrative in order to point up a paradoxical structure. In *Tout va bien*, 1972, for example, Godard's only militant feature film, there is an autonomous scene showing a chain of people which is figuratively not dissimilar to the Lumière parades in terms of framing, vanishing point and movement. The scene shows a fictitious parade of rebellious or striking workers controlled by the police, in which the workers' trade associations are represented by their places of work. Through the voice of an imaginary leader or presenter, these places ring out off-screen in the characteristic style of a collective presentation. Here the performative figure of the parade is shown to be a ritual capable of building a sense of community, but also, at the same time, one stripped of meaning, as a place of *communio* beyond communication. This interaction of speech and process makes plain that in this scene no new meaning is formed, but rather a form is repeated and adhered to.[3]

In French *défiler* not only means "to file" in the sense of to march past, but also, rather more generally and in a non-military sense, any moving past or passing by, including that of images. Alongside the parade, the *défilé*, the term *défilement* is also derived from the idea of filing past, initially a technical term which, in the language of cinema, refers to the passage of celluloid film though a projector, the succession of images. It is hardly a coincidence that French film theory has been particularly interested in this concept. If one conceives of the relationship of the audience to the filmic image in terms of the cinematic apparatus itself, then this relationship can be related theoretically to the phenomenon of *défilement*. In this context it is worth bearing in mind an early theoretical text by the video artist Thierry Kuntzel, which was published at the beginning of the 1970s alongside those texts which drove the so-called "apparatus debate",[4] and which bears the title *Le Défilement*.[5] Kuntzel is interested in the relationship between movement and stasis. He analyses the fact that the individual frames of a film successively "steal away" (*se défiler*) and as such remain obscured from the gaze of the spectator. In his analysis of an animated film Kuntzel demonstrates the function of the single frame as something simultaneously absent and present. Kuntzel thus locates the *filmic* neither on the side of movement nor of stasis but rather between the two, in the creation of the "film-as-projection" through the "film-as-strip" and in the disavowal of this material "film-as-strip" by the "film-projection".

How and why does this *défilement*, already apparent in the case of the Lumière brothers as a dual figuration of human bodies and filmic images, become so central to certain films by Godard? A decisive clue is to be found in the scattered writings of Serge Daney. Ten years after Kuntzel, Daney carries French theory's interest in the *défilement* to extremes in a text entitled "Du défilement au défilé".[6] In this short essay rich in ideas Daney analyses the relationship between the passage of the film strip (the *défilement*) and the filing past of figures in the film themselves (the *défilé*), like Kuntzel before him, as the relationship between mobility and immobility, between transport and stasis, but also between spectator and image. The "classic" cinema situation has often been described as a pacification of the audience for the sake of a more intense perception of the moving images. In his essay on the relationship between film and photography, Serge Daney deals with this classic relationship between inaction and mobility in order to invert Pascal Bonitzer's concept of "blocked vision" in the cinema by applying it to the contemporary situation. He construes the pacification of the cinema audience as a history of domestication which is undergoing a transformation. The more cinema ossified in order to become publicity through immobile or arrested images, the more the spectator, according to Daney, relinquished his or her passive seat in the cinema to become increasingly a consumer-*flâneur*. In the *dispositif* of television, but also in the realm of multi-media art, Daney identifies a return to the brightly lit shop window displays of the nineteenth century which the spectator would pass by. For Daney, TV shopping demonstrates most clearly the return of the moving image to consumption and advertising, away from representation towards the *presentation* of things. In so doing, however, cinema is seen to have reconciled itself with one of its original vocations.

What seems to be crucial about Daney's historical argument concerning the presentation of things–which, incidentally, appears to be related to Tom Gunning's reflections on the early "cinema of attractions"–is the link between the immobility of the "classic" audience and a form of representation of moving images which is ascribed to "classic narrative" film.[7] By contrast, in his "inverted" thesis on the crisis of film, Daney links a new mobility of the spectator to the immobilisation of the moving image. At first sight, this thesis may seem paradoxical. Because the link between the so-called "classical" and "post-classical" (or "modern") *dispositifs* is still the irrevocable invisibility of the single frames constantly in movement, their continuous withdrawal, their fundamental disappearance in the continual passage–the *défilement*–of the projector. The images are not halted during a film screening, which usually keeps the spectator tied to his seat for about one and a half hours without a break. As cinemagoers we subject ourselves to this temporal restraint and usually do not leave the auditorium, at least for the duration of the film; we remain chained, rather like the captives of Plato, with whose cave Jean-Louis Baudry has compared the *dispositif* of cinema. Thus we are, with a few exceptions, very rarely confronted with still images in the cinema. So what is Daney driving at with his apparently paradoxical thesis? His idea has to be understood in the context of a cinephile culture which understood cinema as an auratic space and which assumed a knowledge of film history (on the part of both the cinema-goers and the directors). Daney's idea of the stalling of images in the cinema does not refer so much to the freezing of images as a cinephile gesture of auteurist film (as in Truffaut), where it signifies the interruption of an unfolding series of events, but rather to the fact that large parts of mainstream cinema in the 1980s (he names Jean-Jacques Annaud and Luc Besson as examples) no longer remember film history, but instead appropriate prefabricated images that have ossified into clichés, in both senses of the word in French (the *cliché* as photographic reproduction and ideological matrix). Moving images cease to move when they are reproduced again and again in different media as visual trademarks and advertising. It is therefore a different kind of insight from the one we encounter in Godard, who in *Histoire(s) du cinéma* (in which he presents himself as an historian after all) exploits stasis in its most radical and cinephilic forms.

Opposite: *On s'est tous défilé*, **1988.**

The arrest of the moving image in the freeze-frame, the *arrêt-sur-image*, has become today, according to Daney, decades after Truffaut's *Les 400 coups* (which ends with one), a supreme gimmick:

When the last seconds of the film come we are no longer on the look out for the words The End (they don't usually appear anyway), but rather for the image which is most likely to be the last in the sequence, the one which will come up in slow motion like the number on which a roulette ball finally comes to rest. The very fact that it is the last one (destined to serve as a backdrop or curtain for the credits) confers on it a certain mystery and bluntness, a little (but how very little) of that "third sense" of which Barthes spoke.[8]

Thus, according to Daney, the imaginary arrest of the film image is a freezing that has become a cliché. It has nothing to do any more with the openness of Truffaut; instead it is the true essence of advertising: "[to] make the consumer focus his attention on a brand image. Focus the procession of commodities on one particular one (that is TV shopping)."[9] For Daney the image frozen for the purposes of advertising functions like *another poster*:

[…] still an integral part of the film, at the threshold between the darkness of the auditorium and the lights that come on again. As if the sequence of images drew up to a single image, one not content simply with summarising all the others but which genetically contained all the others (indeed always had done). As if a film were no longer a series of single frames but rather a unique, God-given image which came into being in one go, an "image" (in the sense of a petition) which poses for the sake of these moments of pause, which themselves have the greatest visibility.[10]

This form of presentation through brand images, through arrested advertising images, privileged consumer articles on the conveyor belt of cinematic movement, can, of course, be found in the earliest films of film history: for example, one of the Lumière files, a Swiss military parade, clearly displays a sponsor's advertising placard: "Sunlight" hangs resplendent on an advertising placard to the right of the frame and attracts the spectator's gaze away from the moving procession to the static brand name.[11] In a similar way Godard introduces a price list into a shot of passers-by in his video about the idea of the fashion parade, *On s'est tous défilé*.

It is thus not a coincidence that in *On s'est tous défilé*–as indeed previously in *Grandeur et décadence d'un petit commerce de cinéma*, 1986–Godard links the movement of figures (and that of a potential story) to the question of the marketplace and the cliché. Yet besides this connection identified by Daney there is also still a "classical" cinematic dimension to Godard's processions. For no sooner has Godard captured the commodification of the actor/model/image than he sets out to demonstrate how fiction is born (or reborn) and, along with fiction, emotion. In what follows I wish to use the figure of the procession or the *défilé* (a figure always linked to that of arrest) to analyse in certain films and videos of Godard this special facility for creating dialectical images.

A film dealing with movement itself, with the temporalisation of the image through movement, could constitute a counter-strategy to the ossification of the image diagnosed by Daney. It is telling that a classic of avant-garde film, Dziga Vertov's *The Man With a Movie Camera*, 1929, employs the freeze-frame in exactly this way, namely not as a single image which comes to rest at the end of the film in order to summarise it, but rather as a virtual single image, which as part of the "film-strip" (to use Kuntzel's term) is earmarked for the *défilement*, i.e. the movement in the projector, and which as such also disappears as soon as this *défilement* begins.

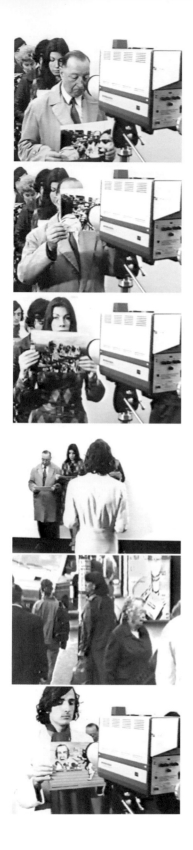

In a scene devoted to work at the editing table, Vertov shows a short strip of film consisting of a series of single images (a boy laughing in close-up) in order to bring this series of virtual single images to life, i.e. he has them disappear by replacing them with a single image of movement. Thus in the case of Vertov the single image is not at the end, but rather at the source of a movement, and the film emerges from stasis into action. In this way the ordinarily invisible *dispositif* of the *défilement*, the passage of images, is made visible.

So what is the relationship between *défilement* and *défilé* in Godard? It could be in a combination of Lumière and Vertov. In a pioneering film Godard connects the projection, Vertov's *défilement*, with the procession through the image, the *défilé*, as seen in Lumière. It has been noted that in *Ici et Ailleurs*, 1974, Godard's radical farewell to militant filmmaking, the film camera no longer simply records the way things take their course, but instead ordinary people, who queue up in front of an automatic video camera in order to produce for themselves their own, static self-image. Godard's pair of questions–"How is a chain organised?" and "How does one produce an image of oneself?"–are here coupled with a literal staging of the *dispositif* of projection and the *défilement*. The strength of this much-analysed film scene lies in the way that single images are virtualised by having them enlarged, filed past a video camera and thereby defined as the motionless element in an image of movement: cinema, according to Godard's famous sentence in *Le Petit soldat*, is truth 24 times a second.[12] Here a single figure is assigned to each single frame, the row of figures constitutes the row of images, and an invisible *défilement* has become a visible *défilé*.

From this point Godard repeatedly picks up on this idea of a connection between procession and projection. To a certain extent it is already anticipated in a scene from *Les Carabiniers*, 1963, in which the heroes leaf through a collection of postcards in order to talk about the world they have conquered during the war. *Sauve qui peut (la vie)*, 1980, one of the great symptomatic films with which Godard returned to the cinema after his extensive work on television, reflects in a highly articulate way on the *défilement*. In this film there is a series of temporal decompositions and reconfigurations which, as such, represent a visual attack on the *défilement*, the filmic flow of images. These dissections or decompositions into broken movements and series of image stoppages have frequently been described as a theoretical reflection. Thus Deleuze notes that Godard "can take as his starting point a continual gesture in order to decompose it into attitudes or categories. This is the case, for example, with the freeze-frames in *Sauve qui peut (la vie)*."[13] Raymond Bellour argues in a similar way, when he ascribes the power of this chain of frozen images without predetermined causality to an aspect of passionate feeling, namely the impossibility of bodies coming together, linked to the "almost neutral dimension of the gaze itself, its virtuality".[14] Hence, these "neutral" moments of dissection, right up to the final scene and Paul's hypothetical death, presuppose an activity on the part of the gaze, thereby privileging certain gestures and moments.[15]

In *Sauve qui peut*, time protracted in this manner is also a time which serves to evade the conveyor-belt of the factory and the rhythm of the machine. According to one of Isabelle's diary entries: "This breaking off–it is life clinging on" ("Ce décrochage–c'est la vie qui s'accroche"). The series of freeze-frames in *Sauve qui peut* culminates towards the end of the film in the virtual moment of death referred to above, and which Godard here literally–by means of the dialogue–connects back to the *défilement*. "I am not dying. My life has not yet passed before my eyes" ("ma vie n'a pas défilé devant mes yeux"), Paul says after he has been run over by a car.

Above: *Ici et Ailleurs*, 1974.

Above: *Grandeur et décadence d'un petit commerce de cinéma*, 1986.

The moment of impact is here shown, like the other essential and unrepresentable moments throughout the film, in slow motion, scenes which Bellour classifies as those of movement, of aggression or of passionate excitement.[16] Interestingly, the accident scene dissected in time is followed by a procession. Cécile, Paul's daughter, turns away from her father to follow her mother's call. We see her, accompanied by a slow tracking shot, walking along past some houses and a neatly arranged orchestra which is playing a ceremonial piece of music. Finally the camera stops and lets the two figures, mother and daughter, disappear into the background of the image. End of film.

What Godard does in this closing scene of *Sauve qui peut* is to associate an invisible *défilement* (life flashing past the inner eye of the dying man) with a visible *défilé* (the procession representing the farewell ceremony). The passage of the father's life remains invisible because it is unrepresentable and bound up with stopping, with death. The *défilé* of the daughter is visible because it is bound up with the fluidity of sound (with the music) and because it is assigned to a figure who does not want to see, who directs her gaze away from the sight of the dying man and towards the ritual.

For Godard, therefore, the *défilé* of bodies often points in a double movement to the social function of performative acts and the performative function of the cinematographic *dispositif*. Godard's figures of *défilement* are ultimately also linked to a third dimension of the filmic by way of the question as to the source of fiction. He does not locate this third dimension in the domain of the pre-filmic or of projection, but rather in the domain of recording. According to Godard, fiction ultimately has its starting point in documentary, in the filmic record of bodies passing by. The dissection of the movement of the image thus makes it possible to access the different attitudes of the body and the multiplicity of stories. Thus at the end of his video essay *Lettre à Freddy Buache*, 1982, Godard compares these image dissections with scientific studies and comments as follows on a slow motion image of passers-by in an urban setting: "What interests me is to find in the movements of these crowds a rhythm, the starting point for fiction."

If a film or video is stopped, if the filmic flow of images is freeze-framed or the electronic sequence halted, we are led by Godard, as we have seen, either to the idea of the moment or to the basic unit of the moving filmstrip. Freeze-frames and slow motion (the freezing and slowing down of moving images) serve to explain the genesis of a film. This analytical ability to return film to its constituent parts is, of course, not unique to Godard. But what distinguishes his position in such a remarkable way is, as Bellour puts it, his "metaphysical" ability to create a "vision of vision" by employing a number of different registers of image type simultaneously, namely silent film, classical and modern film.[17]

Thus in Godard's film essays the issue is not simply to present cinema or video as an apparatus of observation and registration, but also, at the same time, to be able to produce the emotional effects of a projected image of movement, effects which can readily be compared to those of the so-called "classical" feature film. These effects are generated by montage, in the lacunae of music, word and image, between the speech act and visual narration, between mobility and immobility. Godard's interventions into the illusion of homogeneous performativity are directed simultaneously at the physicality of the filmic figure and the materiality of the filmic image. They are also directed, in a third step, at the regime of fiction.

The Godardian connection between the figure of the projection (of images) and the figure of the procession of filmic forms in relation to the "vision of a vision" can be identified in a film which to some extent picks

Above: **Cécile Tanner in the closing sequence of *Sauve qui peut (la vie)*, 1980.**

Above: *Grandeur et décadence d'un petit commerce de cinéma*, 1986.

up where *Ici et Ailleurs* left off, *Grandeur et décadence d'un petit commerce de cinéma*. The moving image, Godard demonstrates here, is a system that is structured through the relationship between the visible and the invisible, between movement and stasis. Moreover, the cinematic process is one of power. In *Grandeur et décadence*, Godard employs the idea of a serial sequence of events–in this case a casting, a classic *défilé* of film production –in order to display the way in which cinematographic images function as "arresting" figures in the sense Daney uses the term. In the background of the *défilé* of extras, on the wall of the casting office, there is, tellingly, a film poster publicising Antonioni's *L'Avventura*. Thus Godard is not really aiming at the clichéd image, at a saleable brand image for a film. Rather he is searching for the image of a kind of film that thinks and remembers simultaneously, for example through the gestures and attitudes of an Antonionian body. Godard is therefore aiming from the outset at a body that is simultaneously created anew (because it stands at the beginning of a story, a fiction) and is also recreated (because it inscribes itself into a history of cinema).

The *défilés* in this film reiterate the *dispositif* of *Ici et Ailleurs*, one already introduced by the Lumière brothers and developed by others across the course of film history including contemporaries of Godard (such as Federico Fellini): a *défilé* of figures before a camera which is ever-present as an apparatus and which prompts the figures to address the audience directly. Two *défilés* in front of a film camera (with a camerawoman and not, as in *Ici et Ailleurs*, in front of an automatic and impersonal video camera) have a circle of figures step forward who in sequence recite whole sentences or text fragments following orders coming from beyond the field of view, from one of those famous Godardian voice-offs.

The first big *défilé* occurs after the sequential registration of the extras for the casting and represents a kind of pre-*défilé*: each time a name and telephone number, a ritualised act. The extras queue up "for the glory of it", each for himself. They are then called to appear for the first time in front of the camera. This first *défilé* scene introduces the casting room in accordance with a specific order: extras-camera-director. In contrast to the second *défilé* scene, in which the figures form a ring and recite a sequence of sentences which together relate a particular passage from a novel by Faulkner, each figure here only appears once in order to say one or two sentences (and not just parts of sentences) and each sentence comes from a different diegetic space.[18] During these initial recitations in front of the director the chain of sentences of the different figures does not follow any narrative order, and does not attempt to constitute a whole from a series of individual elements. The stringing together of attitudes here replaces the association of words. Bodies of this kind do not yet form part of a continuum, but instead set themselves apart one by one to become gesture or expression.

This introductory *défilé* is thus primarily about finding the *possibility* of fiction in gestures, expressions and postures by way of figures and faces. The desire for fiction is symbolically represented in both *défilé* scenes in the figure of the director. He is played by Jean-Pierre Léaud, who can be described, to use Deleuze's expression, as the exemplary actor of attitudes and positions.[19] Initially the desire for fiction is checked, or at least masked, by the serialisation of the figures. In a second step, however, towards the end of the first *défilé* scene, Godard conveys this desire by means of visual imagery.

As far as the structuring of the imagery is concerned, a crucial difference can be discerned between the two great *défilé* scenes: whilst the second *défilé* describes a continuous unfolding of events in time and space, reflected

in a syntactical continuum, Godard brings the first to rest on a female figure. Here Godard analyses the expression of one of his "actresses" who appears in front of the camera in the context of the *défilé*. "The only man I ever loved is dead", the actress shouts to the viewer. The director (Léaud) has the sentence she speaks repeated, while the *énonciateur* (Godard) slows down the image to a series of suspended poses that are lifted from the movement of a scream, before finally replacing the speech act with music. Through this progressive arrest the female figure ultimately becomes face and affect, and thus a virtual body-picture at the beginning of a cinematic story still to be shot.

The aim is to show how the advent of a film functions, the continuity of attitudes of waiting and exhaustion, of a series of points in time. Godard does not tell the story here of the pain of one figure, rather he presents the scream. He seems in this scene to be looking for the exhaustion behind the scream.[20] The inscription of the past into the body is initially suggested by a narrative fragment that is told in words. On being repeated the sentence conveyed by the scream is replaced by modern music for the Passion (Arvo Pärt) and the body is immobilised into poses. On the one hand this displaces the narration from the performance of verbal language on to the expression of the body, which thereby simultaneously gains both sound and visibility. On the other it shows that the voice is the trace of the body in language and how music functions as an expression of the unsayable.

In this scene the point is thus not, as was the case in the decompositions of movement in *Sauve qui peut* mentioned above, to prevent the bodies from joining together or to establish an undecidability of the image. Paradoxically, the imaginary interruption of the cinematic unfolding, of the *défilement*, does not generate in this case, for example, a brief subversion of narrative, but rather, on the contrary, releases a form of desire–previously held in check by

Above: *L'Avventura*,
Michelangelo Antonioni, 1960.

the serialisation–by generating the possibility of a fiction. The decomposed and recomposed shot of the crying woman thus becomes an image of the possible: Godard employs it in order to inscribe a past into a body, into a bodily posture communicated by gesture and facial expression. He thereby frees himself from the expectation of telling a story (with a before and an after). The idea is to show how a figure is constructed gesture by gesture, word by word, sound by sound.

Grandeur et décadence speaks, almost *en passant*, of the relationship between advertising and *défilé* as set out by Daney, for the moving images of the filmic bodies, even those of a "little cinema business", are expected to circulate profitably in other media as static images. This principle of advertising as the reification of bodies and figures is taken to an extreme by Godard in the little video mentioned at the outset, a kind of reflexive waste product from a (real) advertising film he made for a designer (the Swiss fashion team of Marithé et François Girbaud). Through a small series of freeze-frames, the *arrêts-sur-image* within a shot reminiscent of the images of the crowd in *Lettre à Freddy Buache*, one encounters again in *On s'est tous défilé* Daney's idea: the arrested film image, either immobile or barely moving, which for Daney constitutes like a "functional icon" or "portable idol" the "crux of the audiovisual industry", in which it becomes what he calls automaton bodies and images.[21] But at the same time Godard goes beyond this principle of fashion and advertising in mixing the body-idols of a fashion parade with the body-models (in the Bressonian sense) of a Parisian street. He is looking for the beginning or the possibility of a fiction and an emotion in these bodily postures.

Godard thus once more starts from the idea or a procession or parade, in this case a fashion parade. But here he no longer shows, as was the case in *Grandeur et décadence*, the passage of the figures as a sequence open to temporal alteration. In this video Godard literally destroys the continuity of the proto-filmic *défilement*, the succession of images, through the alternating flickering of different shots (as he had already done in *Puissance de la Parole,* a video commissioned by France Télécom and made in the same year).[22] The digital code is inscribed here as the cipher of the electronic image: in the age of computer images the *défilement* is no longer a matter of immobile single images linked together in a sequence, but rather a question of co-existing images. In addition, the sentence "On s'est tous défilé" is a play on words which I would like finally to draw attention to, without going down the etymological paths indicated by Godard himself in the film and analysed by Jean-Louis Leutrat from a Mallarméan perspective.[23] In the first instance, *défiler* means to undo something that has been threaded. *Se défiler* originally means "to protect oneself from enemy fire", but above all it means, in a figurative sense, "to steal away". This little video radicalises the connection between the *défilé* (of figures) and the *défilement* (of images) in the two senses of the verbs *défiler* and *se défiler*. *Défiler*: the figurative chain of images comes apart in Godard's work as soon as it encounters the digital. *Se défiler*: what seems to concern Godard above all, and as ever, is the power of the image (and of the body) that is recorded and then projected, but which in its very projection and movement constantly pulls back and remains, therefore, forever elusive.

"GRAVITY AND GRACE": ON THE "SACRED" AND CINEMATIC VISION IN THE FILMS OF JEAN-LUC GODARD

VICKI CALLAHAN

As a feminist intrigued by the invocation of the spiritual in the later works of Jean-Luc Godard, I am tempted to respond to the reputedly "predictable if not tiresome" female iconography in *Je vous salue, Marie*, 1985, with: "I know Godard is a misogynist, but all the same…".[1] My response is not so much a disavowal of the director's "problematic" sexual politics, but rather a gesture of confidence that Godard's films since *Passion*, 1982, represent a new effort to engage with the problem of sexual difference. Several critics have pointed to these later films and have seen a turn away from radical politics into a series of more strictly aesthetic, metaphysical or spiritual concerns. This interpretation presupposes that the aesthetic (or spiritual) and the political (material) are mutually exclusive terms, and I would ask feminists in particular if we are constructing a binary opposition precisely in a series of works that put such an oppositional structure into question. If past feminist critiques of Godard's films were primarily based on his presumed understanding of sexual difference as an essential difference, then I propose that a new understanding of difference might be at work in his later works. I am not therefore arguing with critiques of earlier films so much as suggesting that the past framework may not be useful to examine the later work.

One starting point for a discussion of the spiritual in Godard's later films might be to examine a very brief quotation from Wassily Kandinsky's *Concerning the Spiritual in Art*, 1911. Kandinsky notes:

Form, in the narrow sense, is nothing but the separating line between surfaces of colour. That is its outer meaning. But it also has an inner meaning, of varying intensity, and properly speaking, form is the outward expression of this inner meaning.[2]

Kandinsky is significant for our discussion of Godard both for the simplicity and elegance of his definition of form, "the separating line between surfaces…", and for his larger framework. That is, it is very clear that form is a conscious and selected area of demarcation by the artist (not an essential, fixed entity) that in turn produces not simply a beautiful object (it can be "discordant" not only harmonious or beautiful) but also *ideas*, which for Kandinsky are akin to the spiritual. Kandinsky's preoccupation with form is not with form in itself, but with how we draw the boundaries of thought and experience, and it is this guiding principle which then associates the artistic project with the sacred. Kandinsky sees the artist as a wilful force on a vital social mission:

I would remark that, in my opinion, we are fast approaching the time of reasoned and conscious composition, when the painter will be proved to declare his work constructive […] We have before us the age of conscious creation, and this new spirit in painting is going hand and hand with the spirit of thought towards an epoch of great spiritual leaders.[3]

Godard's explorations of aesthetics and the sacred, while not necessarily identical, are remarkably similar to those of Kandinsky.[4] To see this, we must first ask how Godard conceptualises the issue of form in cinema, what is his "mark" or "line" of demarcation? We can begin here with Godard's well-known attention to, and affection for, montage. In Chapter 4A of *Histoire(s) du cinéma*, 1998, Godard places on the sound track a segment of an interview with Alfred Hitchcock. Hitchcock notes:

We have a rectangular screen in a movie house. Now this rectangular screen has got to be filled with a succession of images. The mere fact that they are in succession that's where the ideas come from. One picture comes up after another. The public aren't aware of what we call montage, or in other words, the cutting of one image to another. They go by so rapidly so that they are absorbed by the content that they look at on the screen.

As we know, Godard repeatedly emphasises the point that montage is the essence of cinema and in a lecture at the French National Film School (FEMIS) in 1989, he stated that the popular art form of cinema was unique in that it:

[…] developed a technique, a style or a way of doing things, something that I believe was essentially montage. Which for me means seeing, seeing life. You take life, you take power, but in order to revise it, and see it, and make a judgement. To see two things and to choose between them in completely good faith.[5]

Thus, for Godard, the line of demarcation in cinematic form is at the point of the edit, that is, through the frame line. Montage produces a special form of seeing and a thought, indeed a judgement, a wilful shaping, discrimination, an ethics, and with it a certain confidence "in good faith". It is not one image alone that produces this kind of "sight", but rather at least two. In fact, the image alone, like the word alone, leads us into all sorts of errors and horrors as Godard suggests throughout *Histoire(s)* and numerous writings and interviews. It is the relationship between images, or rather, the movement from one image to another that is the key point for Godard.

While the questions of the frame line and movement are certainly consistent with Godard's earlier work, the later films, especially from *Passion* onwards, pursue more radically, rigorously, and indeed mathematically, the subject. What one finds in these films are almost mind-bogglingly diverse permutations and meditations on cinematic movement and form. That is, there might be the simple alternating montage across stories (between the work of factory and the work of the artist in *Passion*; between Eve's and Mary's narratives in *Je vous salue, Marie*), but then also across categories (the world of nature and world of humans in *JLG/JLG: autoportrait de décembre*,

1995, *Je vous salue, Marie*, and *Nouvelle Vague*, 1990). However, the pattern of alternation is also found within landscape shots, with an alternation of static and moving shots, and also with the contrast seen in static images with movement *within the frame itself*. Numerous shots of the outdoors in these films feature a stark and deserted setting where one might assume a still shot had been inserted for several frames, were it not for the movement of one element. For example, the sky alters, changing the shadows on the ground, or in other instances water flows in a stream or lake while everything else is still. The movement in the frame in these examples typically occurs across strict horizontal, vertical, or diagonal lines, accentuating all boundary lines and clearly extending beyond those lines (the frame) with that movement.

In the extraordinary opening sequence of *JLG/JLG*, one can begin to see the movement of the frame line itself in the frame–not the literal frame line, of course, but rather a poetic rendition of the process played out over his portrait. Shortly after the film opens we see a cameraman in silhouette looking through a door frame at a photograph of a young boy (a portrait of Godard) bathed in blue light. This monochromatic image then sets up the basic colour and graphic scheme for the rest of the film. Image after image in this sequence across internal and external spaces, across diverse objects (the human form, a chair, the lake) repeats the opening dark blue colour or its analogous shade accompanied by angular lines of objects and natural forms, all of which operate as our reminder of the frame line. The lengthy opening sequence winds down with a shot of a digital camera, the shape recognisable primarily through its blue screen as it is positioned to tape outside a window frame that looks on to an adjacent building of seemingly identical colour. This opening theme and variation of line and colour, which circulates in less explicit forms throughout *JLG/JLG*, concludes with the close-up of the window. The space begins in deep focus but is transformed by a zoom-in which leaves only the window frame itself in focus and a blue smearing of colour behind. This essentially abstract form of line and colour at the end of zoom-in is preceded by Godard's discussion of strict and immobile frame lines in a metaphorical sense. In this instance, Godard writes of the life of the rule (the fixed frame) and a life of lived exception (the shifting and mutable frame). The rule and the exception map out accurately the distinction between the life of culture and the life of art, and with the shift from the image of the window to the pure abstraction Godard renders the artist's responsibility both to move the frame lines and to note their potential movement. The entire sequence then concludes with several black frames reminding us of the line of division and the essential arbitrariness of that boundary.[6]

The "frame line" in *JLG/JLG* is produced by a shadow, that is, by the manipulation of light within–in fact, across–the frames. The workings of montage are thus logically revealed through its parallel processes in cinematography, for the frame line is constructed by the opening and closing of the photographic or cinematic lens, that is to say, where the light begins and ends. This attention to light/shadow is explicitly addressed throughout *Passion*, and throughout the film, Jerzy, the fictional director is obsessed with the correct lighting for the reproduced *tableaux vivants*. Moreover, the *tableaux* in question are especially noteworthy (both obviously and art historically) as dramatic explorations of light (e.g. Rembrandt and Goya). In his *Scénario du film Passion*, 1982, Godard's comments suggest what might be one motivation for his attention to light: "The work to be done is seeing… seeing the invisible become visible… and describing it." In other words, the difference between light and shadow is not oppositional, matter vs. void or

Above: ***JLG/JLG: autoportrait de décembre, 1995.***

Above: **JLG/JLG**

even known vs. unknown, but rather between seen and not yet seen, known and not yet known.

This discussion of cinematic form and movement can be further enriched by the German expressionist artist Ernst Ludwig Kirchner's thoughts on Rembrandt, which reveal another area of potential overlap between Godard and elements of a painterly aesthetic:

First of all I needed to invent a technique of grasping everything while it was in motion, and it was Rembrandt's drawings in the Kupferstichkabinett in Munich that showed me how. I practised seizing things quickly in bold strokes, where I was, walking and standing still, and at home I made larger drawings from memory and in this way I learned how to depict movement itself, and I found new forms in the ecstasy and haste of this work, which, without being naturalistic, yet represented everything I saw and wanted to represent in a larger and clearer way. And to this form was added pure colour, as pure as the sun generates it.[7]

Movement, pure light, the ecstatic, the creation of new forms, are all associations drawn from the work of Rembrandt by Kirchner. One might underline here also Kirchner's comments that the art work moves beyond the "naturalistic" or realistic representational form and moreover does not even need the object depicted to be visible before us (it can be taken "from memory") for the creative process to occur (and movement to be captured). This brings to mind the blind editor in *JLG/JLG* who edits via touch and her ability to "see" in her head, that is, abstractly. Or, at another point in the film, the abstraction that is put in the context of mathematics with the citation from Diderot's *Letter on the Blind*: "Men of geometry live their lives with their eyes shut." Or yet another variation in *JLG/JLG*, now within a musical context: a jazz song plays in the background without words but with its haunting melody, "I See Your Face Before Me". The melody reminds us of the lyrics which resonate powerfully in this context: "I close my eyes and there you are."

Passion, Nouvelle Vague and *JLG/JLG* all feature an ongoing interrogation of light and shadow. In each of these films dramatic lighting is frequently juxtaposed with the movement of the camera or lighting throughout or across a space–enticing us to explore and pointing not to a void, but to another space yet unseen. Moreover, the use of backlighting in each one of these films often produces an almost reversal effect of varying degrees, or what we might choose to call the "phantom image" following Godard's invocation of physics in *Hélas pour moi*, 1993, and his discussion of phantom matter. To summarise briefly the sequence in *Hélas pour moi* where the term occurs, Godard references the discovery by scientists of "the other half of the universe", the part that occurs "beyond images and beyond stories" and which he calls "phantom matter". The narration then clarifies the term as not something beyond, but rather something "this side of images, not stories." Like the poetic edit in the opening of *JLG/JLG*, the phantom image draws our attention to what the frame line–the form–tells us (both through the visible and the non-visible). Thus, what I call the phantom image will include both those areas non-illuminated, which might at a different point or time be illuminated, but also could include what the physicists call "dark matter", i.e. non-illuminated matter that can only be accessed via specialised instrumentation and inference (we cannot see it, but it is there). Like montage, the phantom image also has multiple variations (backlighting/silhouette, singular/stark illumination, the black frame) and even uses a kind of reversal effect in still(-like) images (i.e. landscape). The phantom image also appears even more dramatically in images that feature human beings and Godard himself. All of this is an extension of the

interrogation of the frame line and part of the movement of the frame line within the frame.

The movement of the frame line serves as a reminder or indeed recognition that all form/matter has the potential for movement and change, including human form. In *Nouvelle Vague*, when Roger Lennox (perhaps it is Roger although that is unknown at the time) returns from the watery grave where his lover, Elena, left him on an afternoon outing, this potentiality is visualised for us. Roger, now called Richard, is seen repeatedly in the second segment of the film as a "phantom image" (through backlighting he often appears as silhouetted form), yet it is particularly with his (re)introduction that a sort of double reversal takes place. Roger's return is presented in long shot, his reflection in the water dominates the image, and the colour scheme's limited palette of muted brown and green tones suggest a photographic negative seen from the perspective of a view camera, i.e. upside down. This presentation of the human "shadowy" zone is followed by the text "Je est un autre" for good measure.

What Godard is presenting is the human being as potential or process, or the passage from one place to another, and not an oppositional, Manichean or even "in-between" form. The in-between or border zone that Deleuze maps out, for instance, still implies a somewhat fixed space since it is "between two things", whilst Godard's efforts seem to be directed to our ongoing movement through those border zones.[8] Potentiality is demonstrated through the mobility of the form "line" around self, especially as light falls off a subject, thereby "highlighting" the non-rigidity of line. I would agree here with other critical work on later Godard, by James S Williams, and Kaja Silverman and Harun Farocki, that the crucial activity in place is one of transformation or transferral.[9] The passage can be found in the phantom image but also glimpsed in other cinematic techniques such as the dissolve, as can be seen in two very vivid examples from *Histoire(s)*. In Chapter 1A the sequence from Jean Vigo's *L'Atalante*, 1934, is cited when a young man in remorse has jumped into the river "searching" for his new bride after an argument and separation in town. He imagines he finds her and a dissolve shows us the couple "reunited" and joyous through their overlapping images. The dissolve moves from the masculine to the feminine image and back again. Importantly, Godard's version of this sequence alters the speed and stops the image during the dissolve/transformation.

The dissolve as transformation is also suggested by a citation from *The Wrong Man*, and while in the Hitchcock original we move from images of the spiritual to the wrongly accused to the guilty, in the alteration of the sequence in Chapter 4A of *Histoire(s)* the spiritual image of the sacred heart is replaced by the "miracle" of Hitchcock. So the transformative potential of human experience is revealed explicitly to us by montage and also by the artistic master of montage, Hitchcock. All three of these revelations about change–its very possibility, our knowledge and creation of change through the cinema, and the artist's responsibility to promote change (the life of the exception)–are therefore in the realm of the sacred.

Roger Lennox's return from the dead in *Nouvelle Vague* is certainly a form of resurrection, yet it is important to remember that his "rebirth" is accompanied by the phantom image. Hence, Godard's repeated use of the phrase in *Histoire(s)*: "The image will come at the time of the resurrection", takes on a rather interesting inflection if the crucial image is not simply the obvious one before us but extends necessarily beyond the "visible" form.[10] Roger's return repeats the miraculous hand of Hitchcock again with its suggestion of *Vertigo*, when Judy's appearance is, and is not, the return of Madeleine.[11] Scotty's misfortune is to believe both that the image can be

Above: *Nouvelle Vague.*

fixed and that he has the capacity to freeze it, a point eerily played out in Judy's makeover sequences where the entire process is driven by the instability of his own sanity and identity. Fixing Judy as Madeleine (and as essentially different) will thereby guarantee the couple and fix Scotty's ills. But the illusion of Scotty's belief is shattered by the discovery of Judy's "true" identity. Unfortunately, Scotty does not realise that the deception is not the false image but rather his very attachment to the image; thus, the second "death" of Madeleine condemns him to an endless repetition.

In *Nouvelle Vague* the formation of the couple (a classic Hollywood formula beyond *Vertigo* to be sure) can only come about with a not so standard Hollywood twist. For now it is Lennox's transformed/extended image that opens up the possibility of the couple, but this transformation questions the very forms of identity and gender. As the character Dorothy Parker reminds us earlier in the film, "Love speaks only to what is hidden in its object" (a quotation from Denis de Rougemont). Just before Lennox and Elena ride off together, Lennox notes the demarcation of self/other and masculine/feminine with a line that moves arbitrarily in space ("moi/toi"), once up and once down in the blink of an eye. The movement points towards the act of construction with a motion that mimics a shutter opening and closing (the riddle cited from Hawks's *To Have and Have Not*–"Have you ever been stung by a dead bee?"–furthers the play with gender). This moving frame line is a type of performance of the Vigo and Hitchcock dissolves discussed in *Histoire(s)* and it reproduces the construction or malleability of line and form and gender explicitly in the narrative. How we draw the line and the acknowledgement of our wilful participation in the process is revealed via the act of love, as is noted in *Nouvelle Vague*: "My love, it matters not that I am born; you become visible at the place where I am no more."

Above: **Jean Vigo's *L'Atalante*, 1934, in *Histoire(s) du cinéma*, 1998.**

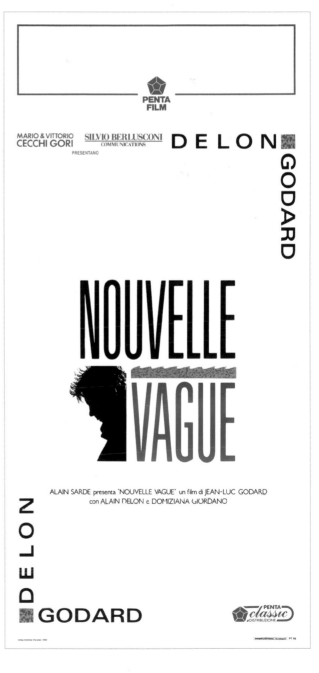

Above: **Japanese flyer for** *JLG/JLG.*

Right: **Italian poster for** *Nouvelle Vague.*

Above: *Je vous salue, Marie*, 1985.

Middle and below: *JLG/JLG*, 1995.

196

Ask rather
what is a government.

This sense of love as both self-recognition and self-loss moves us perhaps more explicitly into the spiritual, not in the sense of transcendence but rather as transformative and dependent upon choice: I must recognise the possibility of the non-visible space and be willing to move into that area. It requires a certain leap of faith, a confidence in both the certainty and uncertainty or indeterminacy of change. However, anxiety is also produced by this leap and is noted by Roger before his "resurrection" in the comment to Elena: "If I change I am not who I was and if I am not that...". The ellipsis in Roger's remarks points to a space without a name (and why his name technically speaking must change on his return) and a space without a fixed frame line or identity. Now the elegiac tone and the blue opening sequence of *JLG/JLG* can be read in the light of Roger's commentary. The over-narration of *JLG/JLG's* opening even points out that Godard is "already in mourning for myself", but perhaps now not so much mourning in the sense of age and a nostalgia for fleeting youth as mourning for an idea of the self that will invariably be left behind once committed to the idea of the mobile frame line (in both art and life). Godard continues that mourning is for his "sole and unique companion", and surely the distinctness of that companion must slip away with the emerging abstraction of the window/frame line. In the latter parts of *JLG/JLG*, the dispersal of the self is displayed as even Godard seems to disassemble before us–a match light points to his flickering presence conveyed only through script and later a blue monitor displays his image one step removed (an image of an image) shrouded in cigar smoke.

It could be argued that Roger Lennox's malleability merely reverses prior gender roles in Godard: woman as surface and appearance, usually dangerously so, as in the figure of the *femme fatale* (e.g. Jean Seberg in *À bout de souffle)*, with man as her passive victim. Many feminists have stated that these later films present woman as enigma and mystery, but with an important shift; rather than simply an ever-changing, unknowable being, woman has become a "transcendental cipher", an eternal myth, a reworking but replication of Godard's understanding of sexual difference as essential difference.[12] Perhaps the most controversial representation of woman from these later films is found in *Je vous salue, Marie*. While there are varying degrees of interest, distress, and disgust amongst feminists about the film, the consensus seems to be that for better or worse, Godard has invoked the most clichéd of patriarchal myths–the Virgin Mary. Moreover, a similar consensus seems to have been reached about Anne-Marie Miéville's short film, *Le Livre de Marie*, 1985, which was distributed in conjunction with Godard's film. That is, Miéville's film tells the feminist (i.e. good) version of Mary whereby she is the mediator and active agent), and Godard's the patriarchal, or evil one, according to which Mary is a passive receptacle of God's mystery, aligned with "mother" nature (e.g. the moon) and her body fragmented, fetishised, and ultimately desexualised.[13]

Most critics read Miéville's short film as a prologue to Godard's feature, with *Le Livre de Marie* giving us an account of Mary's life as a young girl. What is missed in this reading and the desire to see the two films as one continuing story line, whereby Mary grows up and falls into Godard's chauvinist *ciné-tract*, is the constructed and malleable frame line between authors and the opportunity to interrogate the privileged status of "woman" and "nature" as sacred images. If we look at the formal link between the two films, the phrase "en ce temps-là" ("at that time"), what we have in place is not a linear time so much as parallel times, setting up possible Marys and multiple authors for us. Not one then the other, but the two simultaneously. Yet how precisely is nature invoked at the very beginning

Above: *JLG/JLG.*

UN FILM DE JEAN-LUC GODARD
PASSION

Distribution : PARAFRANCE

VDC 9556

UN FILM DE JEAN-LUC GODARD
PASSION

Distribution : PARAFRANCE

VDC 9556

198

of *Je vous salue, Marie*? Does the association of woman with nature necessarily force us to examine gender and sexuality only within the tired clichés of "mother earth" or even woman's alternative "cyclical" time (woman/lunar cycles, etc.)? The opening titles are intercut with a static shot of water in movement and streaming with light, so that the light's dance upon the water gives us a double movement, illuminating the "invisible" spaces.

What seems to be important about nature and time in Godard is not so much a sort of essential "female time" as the presentation of competing notions of time. We have both human time and the time of nature, the time of the fixed image and the time of the moving image, the time of the visible and the revealed. The use of the landscape as a still-like image in the later work, broken by the movement of light, points us toward these two different times. It might be useful in thinking about these conflicting notions of time to recall Deleuze's notion of the distinction between history and Becoming: "What history grasps is an event in the ways it's actualised in particular circumstances; the event's becoming is beyond the scope of history."[14]

This does not mean, of course, that history is false and becoming is true (or *vice versa*), but rather that we are looking at different slices and segments of time. History can be thought of as akin to the photograph, the partially illuminated image that alters over time and shows us more through movement, that is, only with duration. It is the snapshot vs. duration, or to put this into more scientific terminology, with duration one can see the transformation of matter over time. That is what the cinema demonstrated to us, its unique and sacred talent, and what was taken away by synchronous sound, narrative and naturalistic illumination (the light which leads us to believe there is no other space to investigate). What is lost is not only duration but the possibilities and choices that we can make therein. These possibilities are not as apparent to us, and become less so in a world obsessed by the (fixed) image. As Einstein argued, while space and time are relative, light, or to be precise the speed of light, in the physical domain is our one absolute constant. It is therefore our best path of access to becoming and the possibilities which it opens up. If we can move our author frame line once more, let us go to the conclusion of *Le Livre de Marie* where the distraught Marie is consoled over the breakup of her parents' marriage by the mother's words: "Nothing can stay the same, it becomes. It becomes different. When a thing stops moving it is dead. You must have confidence, Marie." Thus we should not fear change but rather the cessation of light, that is, our ability to recognise and initiate changes around us. Let there be light, indeed.

ALTERED MOTION AND CORPORAL RESISTANCE II

FRANCE/TOUR/DÉTOUR/ DEUX/ENFANTS

MICHAEL WITT

The human body has always carried a high self-reflexive charge in Godard's work. In the 1950s and 60s, it reflected the phenomenological existentialism of Jean-Paul Sartre and Maurice Merleau-Ponty. In the late 1960s and 70s, it came to designate the materiality of cinema and the structuralist concern for the distortions inherent in all signifying processes. In the 1980s and beyond, as Laura Mulvey has noted, the female body came to represent the wider mysteries of cinema and lived experience.[1] While the meanings invested by Godard in the body have changed over the years, his exploration of the relationship between corporal movement and film form has remained a constant. When in 1958, in a review of Alexandre Astruc's *Une vie*, he described the "suddenness of gestures that gets the suspense moving every three minutes" and the "discontinuity latent in the continuity", he was charting a relationship between the human and cinematic body that has informed his project ever since.[2] Video technology allowed him and Anne-Marie Miéville to systematically explore this relationship in the 1970s, notably through the manipulation of tape speed. Since this time, they have deployed slow, stop-start, accelerated, and reverse motion extensively in their many collaborative ventures and individual projects. In extreme close-up, close-up, mid-shot, or long shot, the defamiliarised gestures of human bodies in motion are superimposed over or drawn into balletic interaction with those of other "bodies": people walking; cars passing; clouds moving; lights flashing; and so on. This longstanding videographic experimentation with altered motion can be traced back within Godard's oeuvre to the second of the two television series he made collaboratively with Miéville, *France/tour/détour/deux/enfants*, 1979. On one of the rare occasions that he discussed the use of altered motion in the series, it was to suggest a difference between the sequences involving the two

children, Camille and Arnaud, whose movements are 'decomposed' from episode to episode:

In *France/tour,* I had discovered an intuition, without pursuing it, as I would have needed to discuss it with colleagues and for them to share their experiences with me. We used slow motion and rhythm changes, what I prefer to call decompositions, employing the combined techniques of video and television. I had a little boy and a little girl at my disposal, and we did speed changes, semi-slowed down, semi-accelerated, semi-rhythmic, with loads of different possibilities. As soon as you stop one of 25 images (and which isn't enormous, it's five times the fingers on your hand, so something you can still conceive of), you realise that a shot you've filmed, depending on how you stop it, suddenly there are thousands of possibilities. All the possible permutations between these 25 images represent thousands of possibilities. I concluded that when you change the rhythms, and analyse a woman's movements, even movements as simple as buying a loaf of bread for instance, you realise that there are loads of different worlds inside the woman's movement. Whereas the use of slow motion with the little boy was a lot less interesting. We'd stop the image, and between each image was always the same guiding line. But with the little girl, even when she was doing extremely banal things, you'd go suddenly from profound anguish to joy a split second later. They were real monsters. And I, in my guise as a scientist who knows certain theories, had the impression that they were particles and different worlds, galaxies that were different each time and between which you moved via a series of explosions. Whereas the boy's movement was much more undulatory, with a point of departure, so that the use of slow motion was much less interesting plastically.[3]

As Jacques Aumont has suggested, *France/tour* is essentially "a film about the human body as very paradigm of representation and of expression".[4] This chapter pursues this line of thinking by analysing the series's videographic somatology through reference to the work of Michel Foucault and the pre-

Above: **Maria Schell in Alexandre Astruc's *Une vie*, 1958.**

cinematic science of Étienne-Jules Marey, arguing that the altered motion sequences exemplify a key aspect of Godard's wider project: the interrogation of the human body as a basis for cinematic renewal.

Sonimage

Godard first adopted the name "Sonimage" in late 1972. In early 1973 he established the first of the Sonimage studios (or "laboratories") in Paris, then in Grenoble, and finally in Rolle, Switzerland, where he and Miéville continue to live and work. While the venture ended in 1980, the company continued to exist officially until 1981, co-producing *Sauve qui peut (la vie)*, 1980, and *Passion*, 1982. Godard had always sought to work with a close-knit group of regular collaborators, but it is the encounter with Anne-Marie Miéville in the early 1970s that marks the beginning of one of modern cinema's great collaborations. Miéville's contribution has all too often been ignored or skated over, even when a piece is co-authored or co-directed. It is therefore important to stress that she co-directed, co-authored and co-edited all the Sonimage work with the exception of *Numéro Deux*, which she co-wrote. Their experiments in film, video, and television in this period constitute a self-contained and critically undervalued project. Their aim was clear: to put talk of audio-visual decentralisation into practice; work collaboratively; engage with television; and, through ownership of the necessary production equipment, take time to explore the technical and aesthetic potential of video as a compositional medium ("have a little bit of material with which to re-learn, and the time to compose with it").[5] Although their early ambition of producing as many as three low cost films per year proved unrealistic, the Sonimage experiment was astonishingly productive. Over six years, they made almost 19 hours of material for television broadcast or cinema release: three films (*Ici et Ailleurs*, 1974; *Numéro Deux*, 1975; *Comment ça va?*, 1978), and two monumental television series: *Six fois deux (Sur et sous la communication)*, 1976, and *France/tour/détour/deux/enfants*.

France/tour is a 12 part series with a total running length of a little over five hours. Each 26 minute programme (or "movement", as they are described), is introduced by two or three terms: 1 OBSCURE/CHEMISTRY, 2 LIGHT/PHYSICS, 3 KNOWN/GEOMETRY/GEOGRAPHY, 4 UNKNOWN/TECHNIQUE, 5 IMPRESSION/DICTATION, 6 EXPRESSION/FRENCH, 7 VIOLENCE/GRAMMAR, 8 DISORDER/CALCULATION, 9 POWER/MUSIC, 10 NOVEL/ECONOMY, 11 REALITY/LOGIC, and 12 DREAM/MORALITY. These loose generative metaphors frame the disparate material that follows: interviews with the children; altered motion sequences; mini documentaries; cryptic "stories"; and oblique discussions of the nature of television. In his influential 1974 commentary on television as technology and cultural form, Raymond Williams proposed the expression "planned flow" (or "programmed flow") to describe the predictable mosaïc of the programming grid.[6] Where Godard and Miéville's previous television series, *Six fois deux*, had intervened in the flow through a protracted process of amateurisation, *France/tour* simulates and parodies the conventions of televisual rhetoric. In their respective commentaries, albeit through different means, Godard-Miéville and Williams likewise foreground the question of proportion and mix in television programming. Tongue-in-cheek, Godard claimed to be playing the scheduling game: "Yes, I operated like the director of a channel, drawing up a programming grid. And then I began to shoot the follow-up shots. It was like a code, certain words of which you'd have, but whose logic had to be retrieved."[7] Each programme, designed for insertion into the flow on a weekly basis, mimics and lampoons the codes and forms of prime-time television. The usual ingredients are all available–the presenters; talking heads; direct address; reverse angles; bounce lighting; game shows; serials; news bulletins; interviews; and so on–but are redistributed according to obscure rules. As Jean-Paul Fargier observed, Godard and Miéville simply present "the whole of television simultaneously in each individual programme".[8]

Commissioned by the second French channel, Antenne 2, and made during 1977-1978 in Rolle, the series was immediately shelved for almost two years. Marcel Jullian, head of A2 when *France/tour* was commissioned, had been replaced by Maurice Ullich by the time it was complete. "There's no way we're broadcasting *that*", exclaimed Ullich on viewing the first 15 minutes of the series, "It's not at all the spirit of the channel."[9] Eventually broadcast in 1980 in three blocks of four programmes in Claude-Jean Philippe's *Ciné-Club* on A2 at 11 pm on Fridays, the series' serial logic and intended dynamic engagement with the codes, genres and figures of prime-time television were rendered almost wholly redundant. Understandably angry, Godard claimed sabotage, if not censorship: "They didn't know if it was cinema, television, or what. Whereas it was made to be broadcast just before *Aujourd'hui Madame* [...] The time of broadcast was intentionally chosen to damage my work."[10] With time, and despite these inauspicious beginnings, the importance of the programmes has become increasingly apparent, giving rise to something of a critical consensus ("probably the most profound and beautiful material ever produced for television", wrote Colin MacCabe).[11] An outstanding artistic achievement, the series represents the pinnacle of the Godard/Miéville collaboration in this period. It has also come to constitute an important reference point within the filmmakers' respective recent work, notably Miéville's *Après la réconciliation*, 2000, and *Histoire(s) du cinéma*, 1998.[12] In the context of Godard's evolution as an artist, its themes and forms pave the way for his third foray into the videographic serial genre, *Histoire(s)*. For film and television culture more generally, it remains a unique experiment in televisual composition and major contribution to theoretical reflection on the medium.

Unconscious optics

Experimentation and reflection in three areas converge in *France/tour*: the scientific impetus to the cinematograph; television theory; and historical research. I shall divide the remainder of my discussion into two principal sections: an analysis of the formal tool employed by Godard and Miéville, video, and a Foucauldian reading of their videographic decomposition of the body. Let me begin with a number of observations relating to the altered motion sequences. First, the brute material revisited, reworked temporally and re-presented is extremely diverse in colour, framing and camera movement. Second, tape speed is manipulated extensively throughout the series (in every movement, and on 19 separate occasions) but ultimately quite sparingly (the total quantity of such footage amounts to around ten percent of the total running time). Third, extracts vary greatly in length, from a little under 30 seconds to over three minutes. Fourth, a variety of bodies are surveyed and presented in many different poses/situations: clothed; naked; young; old; big; small; kissing; running; walking; at work; at play; and so on. Fifth, in no less than five of the movements, we encounter further altered motion sequences that are perhaps best considered short test cases. Here the body is examined and decomposed at work (in a café or supermarket, for instance), or as part of a procession or "flow" across or beneath the surface of the earth (on escalators; in tunnels; along streets). And sixth, on a general note, the effect of intervention in normal tape speed is such that it has tended to dominate how the series is remembered. Brief perusal of the journalistic commentaries written at the time of the series' initial broadcast in France almost give the impression that all 312 minutes unfold in slow motion. Discussion of altered motion in virtually

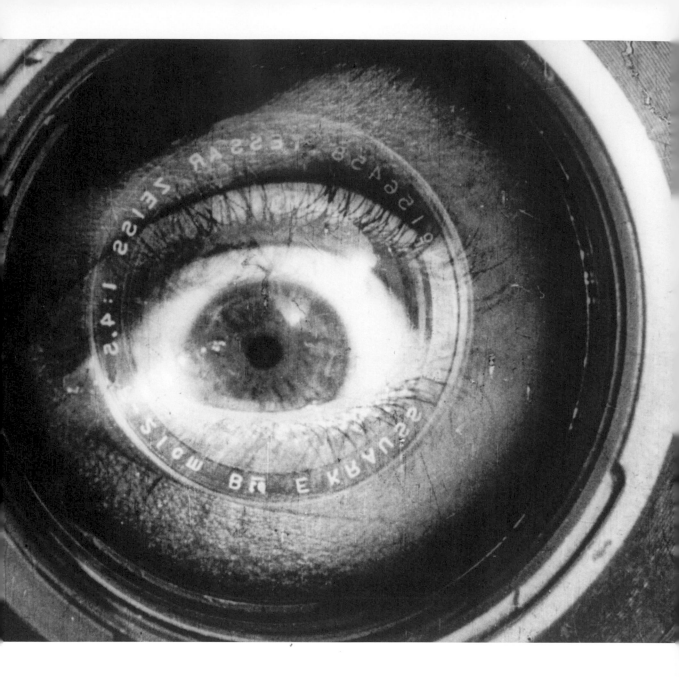

Above: *The Man With A Movie Camera,* Dziga Vertov, 1929.

Opposite: Twelth movement of *France/tour/détour/deux/enfants.*

every account, whether favourable or hostile, is in terms of technical trickery or aesthetic effect. In what follows, my aim is to relate Godard-Miéville's use of video to pre- and early cinema's experimentation with time and altered motion, and so to foreground its properly scientific heritage.

In contrast to many filmmakers of his generation, Godard had been eager to use video as early as 1967. When he did eventually begin to explore the medium, his experience would alter his cinema forever. He talks of its influence in terms of a profound and lasting democratising effect. By making the nascent image available to all members of cast and crew, video intrinsically challenges cinema's conventional divisions of labour:

I still consider myself to be a man who makes films. But I feel that the production apparatus that I've put together myself, with great difficulty, is something closer to a female organism: the way we organise the material, produce a film, or divide our time. There's a kind of democracy, whereas before it was more centrist.[13]

A major attraction of video, for Godard, as for many filmmaking collectives and community groups who invested in the new technology in the 1970s, was its capacity to by-pass the economic constraints of professional audio-visual production.[14] Etymologically, "video" simply means "I see". The combination of "video" with "scope" (from the Latin *scopium* and Greek *skopein*: to look at or examine) gives the term "videoscope". By placing video alongside other analogous "scopes" (microscope or telescope), the idea of the "videosocope" provides a good description of Godard and Miéville's use of the video camera.[15] The blend of slow, fast and stop-start motion in *France/tour* extends the time-honoured cinematographic tradition of influential precursors such as Dziga Vertov. Indeed the Sonimage studio might be seen as the belated realisation of the cinematic research laboratory dreamt of by Vertov. Like Godard-Miéville, Vertov was convinced of cinema's mysterious power to "make the invisible visible, the unclear clear, the hidden manifest, the disguised overt, the acted non-acted, the untruth truth".[16] In this context, it is worth recalling that Godard spoke explicitly at the end of the 1970s of having embarked on a conscious journey through the silent period in a quest for a fresh mode of sound filmmaking.[17] In the process, he and Miéville rediscover the explicitly scientific role for cinema outlined enthusiastically by Walter Benjamin in his 1936 essay, "The Work of Art in the Age of Mechanical Reproduction". In a passage that suggests a calling and form for cinema to which the Godardian project has ceaselessly aspired, Benjamin argues that cinema, especially the magic of slow motion, has revolutionised perception through the revelation of hitherto imperceptible processes and movements. He heralds the birth of an "unconscious optics" comparable in magnitude and import to Freud's account in *Psychopathology of Everyday Life* of the penetration of the unconscious by psychoanalysis:

The act of reaching for a lighter or a spoon is familiar from routine, yet we hardly know what really goes on between hand and metal, not to mention how this fluctuates with our moods. Here the camera intervenes with the resources of its lowerings and liftings, its interpretations and isolations, its extensions and accelerations, its enlargements and reductions. The camera introduces us to unconscious optics as does psychoanalysis to unconscious impulses.[18]

Perhaps even more influential for Godard and Miéville than the combined weight of Benjamin and Vertov is the pre-cinematic science of Étienne-Jules Marey. As a doctor whose early writings were devoted to the anatomy of the "human machine", Marey saw the photographic and cinematographic "camera-scope" as an incomparable scientific aid to the comprehension and demonstration of physical, physiological, mathematical and mechanical laws.[19]

As early as the 1880s, he was using his photographic rifle to stop and show the intermediate phases of rapid movement. In a letter to his mother in 1882, he expressed the surprising revelatory power of serial photography with disarming simplicity: "I have a photographic rifle which has nothing deadly about it, and which takes the image of a flying bird or running animal in a time of less than a 500th of a second. I don't know if you can imagine this speed but it's something surprising."[20] If the shot of the hovering seagull in the twelfth movement represents a discreet nod in Marey's direction, the principle of decomposition and recomposition at the heart of his analyses of animal and human movement in the latter half of the nineteenth century is the single most important point of reference for the videographic decomposition of body and image in *France/tour*. As early as 1878, Eadweard J Muybridge had begun to analyse animal movement through the use of photography at short intervals in San Francisco. Marey concentrated on the development of "chronophotography": the decomposition of motion into a series of discrete moments, and the reproduction of the resultant multiple exposures on a single photographic plate. "Chronophotography", explained Marey in terms that Godard and Miéville might equally have used to describe their practice three quarters of a century later, "is the application of instantaneous Photography to the study of movement; it allows the human eye to see the phases that it would not be able to see directly; and it allows one to carry out the reconstitution of the movement that has initially been decomposed."[21] Video allows Godard and Miéville to rediscover, and literally *animate*, Marey's spatial chronophotographs through an injection of saccadic movement. As Godard observed, video is a kind of intermediate technology between chronophotography and the cinematograph, making possible the unique, jerky, quasi-painterly vibratory visual slippages of *France/tour* that are neither exactly full-scale decomposition/recomposition (Marey), nor continuous reconstituted movement (Lumière):

It's the story of Marey, who filmed the decomposition of horses. And when he was told of Lumière's invention, he said: "Completely idiotic. Why film at normal speed what we can see with our eyes? I don't see the interest of a mobile machine". But the machine in between Marey and Lumière is missing, and there comes a time when you need to start again.[22]

As Marey was the first to acknowledge, chronophotography and "animated photography" were in an embryonic state at the time of his experiments.[23] He was also one of the first to express some disquiet at the excessively trivial uses to which moving images were already being put in the 1890s. But of one thing he was certain: they carried within them extraordinary scientific and pedagogical potential, and would lead to full knowledge of the mechanics of all physical movement. Such advances, he observed, depend on technical simplification and affordability, criteria amply met by video. On numerous occasions in *France/tour*, we are suddenly conscious that the human body, whether in isolation or viewed as part of a crowd, is being scrutinised in precisely the same way that a scientist examines particle motion through a microscope. Godard and Miéville's reinvention of chronophotography through video reclaims cinema's scientific heritage in the age of the television. We can rest assured that Marey too would have pounced on the videoscope with unbridled enthusiasm, delighting in the ease at which the tape can be manipulated through simple and quick post-production techniques.

Opposite above: **Chronophotograph by Étienne-Jules Marey, 1890.**

Below: **Serial photography by Eadweard Muybridge, 1887.**

Docile bodies

How might Foucauldian theory illuminate *France/tour*? The series examines the conditioning of the human infant as a docile subject of capitalism through a 24 hour trip to and from school that begins and ends with Camille and Arnaud preparing in turn for bed. A methodological fidelity to the rhythms of the children's day is therefore integral to the structure of the series. With this in mind, let us briefly review the contents of the altered motion and interview sequences involving the children. This imagery depicts often fleeting and private moments, and records transitional spaces where the children are not on show and television seldom goes to look. Three principal geographical places are represented: home (five sequences); school (four sequences); and various intermediate spaces between the two, notably the street (three sequences). The home and school imagery can be further divided into that which interrogates the children at rest in each of the locations (listening to music or watching television in the home; playing in the playground during a break at school) and that which shows them at work (in class or in detention). Following Foucault and Althusser, school is treated in *France/tour* not as a place for learning but for enforced incarceration. As suggested in *Leçons de choses*, episode 2a of *Six fois deux (Sur et sous la communication)*, children are really "political prisoners": detained in school, they are fed instructions and held in reserve for pre-designated future roles. "Learning and the assignment of social roles", as theorist-polemicist Ivan Illich has put it, "are melted into schooling."[24]

In an illuminating article, Constance Penley has discussed Godard and Miéville's relationship to Foucauldian theory in terms of a common concern for "the institutional organisation of space and time" and "the power of those spatial and temporal grids" in the normalising process, relating this to Philippe Ariès's influential account of the shift from the indeterminate education structures of medieval times to the rigorous, highly regimented modern age-based school system.[25] Power is located in the sum of the minutiae of the repetitious and regulatory daily, monthly and annual cycles into which the infant is inserted from birth: going to school; to work; on holiday; and so on. The nascent human animal is caught at the intersection of a series of divisions (between the sexes, labour and leisure, home and work) and repetitions (of the working day and week, of weekends, of holidays). Children are equated by both Foucault and Godard-Miéville with all manner of recording surfaces–"like paper, a recording surface", as formulated in the fifth movement–and decoded as open systems subjected to the effects of myriad socialising norms, which results in the production of an individual "programmed" to occupy a predetermined social position and function.

Traces of Foucault's *Discipline and Punish: The Birth of the Prison*, 1975, might almost be considered the scenario of the series, informing each of its component segments, as Godard and Miéville scrutinise the body and television through the videoscope.[26] It is certainly as important a source for Godard and Miéville as the celebrated nineteenth century school primer on which the series is ostensibly based, G Bruno's *Le Tour de la France par Deux Enfants: Devoir et Patrie*.[27] Indeed, Foucault might be seen as having provided the radical lens through which Bruno's pedagogical primer is read against the grain. Almost as a by-product of his account of the radical metamorphosis of the economy of punishment, and the emergence of the modern prison, Foucault postulates the formation of an all-pervasive "micro-politics of power" that subjects every body to a monotonous system of regulatory constraints, privations and obligations. Within this perspective, we are all

subject to a vast social *mise en scène*, wherein the body is exposed to a finely tuned, quasi-militaristic process of calibration.

Discipline and Punish is coterminous with the work of Sonimage and a major contribution to the intellectual climate of the 1970s. For Foucault, the classical age's discovery of the body as target of power is part of a larger collective intellectual interrogation of the body that developed during the eighteenth century. Borrowing the term "docility" from the general theory of corporal *dressage* proposed in La Mettrie's *L'Homme-machine*, Foucault charts the emergence of an insidious form of modern slavery located in the body, one achieved less by appropriation and ownership than the imposition of "docility-utility" through an accumulation of ostensibly non-ideological constraints, all veiled manifestations of a disciplinary monotony active throughout everyday life. A prime example given by Foucault of the regulated relationship between localised gesture and the overall position of the body, and explored visually by Godard and Miéville on numerous occasions in both *Six fois deux* and *France/tour*, is the "gymnastics" of handwriting. In a key passage, Foucault explains the effects of the disciplines on the docile body:

The historical moment of the disciplines was the moment when an art of the human body was born, which was directed not only at the growth of its skills, nor at the intensification of its subjection, but at the formation of a relation that in the mechanism itself makes it more obedient as it becomes more useful, and conversely. What was then being formed was a policy of coercions that act upon the body, a calculated manipulation of its elements, its gestures, its behaviour. The human body was entering a machinery of power that explores it, breaks it down and rearranges it. A "political anatomy", which was also a "mechanics of power", was being born; it defined how one may have a hold over others' bodies, not only so that they may do what one wishes, but so that they may operate as one wishes, with the techniques, the speed and the efficiency that one determines. Thus discipline produces subjected and practised bodies, "docile bodies" Discipline increases the forces of the body (in economic terms of utility) and diminishes these same forces (in political terms of obedience).[28]

For Foucault, therefore, daily life implies subjugation to modes of disciplinary control that are different only in intensity, not substance, from those formalised in the penal system proper. Disciplinary society teaches and imposes a series of specific gestures, thereby conditioning the human body as time-efficient machine. A contagious Taylorisation has spread far beyond the factory, infecting all gesture, from the most mundane (washing up) to the most intimate (love-making). We live a punishing routine.

The sequence depicting the technician repairing the video recorder in the fourth movement, or the reference in the sixth to René Clair's *À nous la liberté*, 1931–a film that deals explicitly with the advent of mechanisation, mass production and the subjugation of the body to the machine–serve to illustrate Sonimage's general critique of the power of machinery over the human body. Historically, of course, there is a direct relationship between the cinematograph and the calibration of the body. Integral to Marey's scientific exploration of movement was the question of energy efficiency. The principles that informed his experiments were soon adapted by Henry Ford to the elimination of inefficient movement and wasted energy on the factory production line. Godard and Miéville return to the mechanical impetus of Marey's experiments, giving these a political spin in the light of Foucauldian theory. Armed with the videoscope and the power of altered motion, they set out to conduct a kind of videoscopic ultrasound of the calibrated body, and so to cast in relief the work of the micro-powers in producing human docility-utility. Foucault draws on M de la Salle's prescriptive 1783 blueprint for a meticulous control of routine, elaborated

Above and opposite: **Sixth movement of France/tour/détour/deux/enfants.**

cahiers du CINEMA

Sur et sous la communication (Godard-Mieville)
Gilles Deleuze : Trois questions sur « Six fois deux »

La ligne générale
Le hors-cadre décide de tout
Les machines e(x)tatiques
Un rêve soviétique

Moi, Pierre Rivière ayant égorgé, etc. (Allio)
Notes de travail, critiques
Entretien avec Michel Foucault

LEÇON DE CHOSES
LEÇON DE CHOSES

N° 271   12 F

in *Traité sur les obligations des frères des écoles chrétiennes*, to argue that the methods of the timetable used throughout modern institutions (schools, workshops, hospitals)–with their established rhythms, specific operations, and regulated cycles of repetition–derive directly from the monastic model.[29] By relating modern disciplinary society directly to the model of the monastic cell, Foucault argues that disciplinary space is essentially cellular. "Is it surprising", he asks in a question that reverberates across the Sonimage imagery, "that prisons resemble factories, schools, barracks, hospitals, which all resemble prisons?"[30]

Such a model suggests the extent to which Godard was already Foucauldian in his art cinema of the 1960s. "Cellular theory", as we might call it, provides the logical extension and theoretical confirmation of a form of visual criticism characteristic of much of Godard's earlier work, especially from the mid-1960s onwards where, repeatedly, we encounter tales of solitude narrated through images of back-lit, silhouetted bodies. In *France/tour*, such characters have mutated into the slothful anonymous hulks or "monsters" who roam the underground passages of the *métro*. The saturation of the Sonimage imagery in frames and grids provides a visual shorthand for Godard and Miéville's indefatigable pursuit of ossified temporal and spatial relationships. Similarly, earlier films such as *Alphaville*, 1965, and *Deux ou trois choses que je sais d'elle*, 1967, had long since juxtaposed the soft, vulnerable forms and flesh of the human body against the harsh angles of the city. To put this another way, is Foucault as Godardian as Godard and Miéville are Foucauldian? Rather than assuming that Godard and Miéville are simply adopting Foucault, *Discipline and Punish* could be considered an extension of the tales of dehumanised automatons and manufactured desire in Godard's science-fiction films of the 1960s (*Le Nouveau monde*, 1963; *Alphaville*, 1965; and *Anticipation*, 1967). This proposition is perhaps a little far-fetched. But the point is that, in their respective projects, Godard-Miéville, Foucault, and indeed Deleuze/Guattari were all working on parallel tracks. Godard-Miéville's enterprise, however methodologically unconventional, is every bit as serious as that of their contemporaries. In his preface to Deleuze and Guattari's *Anti-Oedipus: Capitalism and Schizophrenia*, 1972, Foucault asks how we can begin to ferret out the traces of fascism ingrained in the body. "By casting in relief the physics of the regulatory micro-powers that subjugate the body to their rhythms through the videoscope", answer Godard and Miéville through their practice. To claim a place for filmmakers alongside philosophers, historians, and theoreticians will doubtless always be an uphill struggle. But in this period, as Deleuze himself noted enthusiastically in his oft-quoted commentary on *Six fois deux*, Godard and Miéville made a full and original contribution. It just happened to take audio-visual rather than bookish form. Through the videoscope, as Deleuze suggests, they combine a Foucauldian micro-politics of boundaries with systematic videographic revelation (Marey plus Vertov: rendering visible the imperceptible).[31]

Ultimately, Godard and Miéville might best be thought of as bringing Foucault's history up to date, using video as a tool through which to apply the findings of his historical research to Camille and Arnaud's repetitious cycle of home-school-home. They also employ it as a conceptual framework through which to theorise the programming grid of broadcast television. As Penley points out, Foucault's concern for the institutionalised compartmentalisation and capitalisation of space and time in daily life is eminently applicable to the superficiality and predictability of broadcast television: "The interrogation of the children's lives in the interviews ceaselessly points to the serialisation, the regulated flow and repetition of

Above: **Deleuze, Foucault, Godard, and Miéville in the November 1976 edition of *Cahiers du cinéma*.**

Opposite: **Fifth movement of *France/tour/détour/deux/enfants*.**

their domestic, school and leisure schedules."[32] As Godard has often suggested, if television is essentially a question of scheduling, it is the viewer who ends up "programmed". He goes to some length in dialogue with Arnaud in the tenth movement to draw an analogy between the passage of food and television through the body, via an exploration of the expression "ça fait chier" ("it makes you sick", or, literally, "it makes you shit"). The Foucauldian timetable is mapped by Godard and Miéville on to Raymond Williams's model of planned flow, and human bodies, dissected for traces of social programming, end up also representing television "programmes". This self-reflexive critique operates fluidly through the multiple connotations of terms such as *chaînes* ("channels", but also "chains") and *programmes*. As Godard suggested, television and the daily routine of the children mirror and figure one another: "The other logic was that of the day. The day of a worker, and so of a schoolchild, since children's work in Western countries is school. We begin at night, but night is just before daybreak, and we proceed to the rhythm of the two children's *programme*, until nightfall."[33] Here, as often in Godardian discourse, the flow (*défilé*) of people–in this case, that of those filing past the camera on political demonstrations, or making their way in waves to and from work–serves as a self-reflexive shorthand for the mechanical *défilement* of televisual or cinematic imagery. The slow motion sequences represent an active intervention in *both*, and foresee Godard's frequent return to the figure of the *défilé* in his subsequent work (see Christa Blümlinger's chapter in this book).

Resistance and recomposition

The centrality and weight of the critical dimension to the Godardian project, where every film and video, immaterial of ostensible subject matter, doubles as a running commentary on the state of cinema as artistic practice and cultural form, should never be underestimated. It is the intense self-reflexivity of the exploration of the body in the series that is of enduring significance for our understanding of the development of Godard's oeuvre, and of wider changes in cinema over the past 50 years. In this respect, Godard's commentary on his and Miéville's use of altered motion in *France/tour*, cited at the start of this chapter, is only partial. He omits any reference to such self-reflexivity, preferring to let the imagery speak for itself. And what we discover as we watch him and Miéville manipulating their material in the stop-start sequences is that the body *resists*. Much of the irrepressible vitality and optimism the series conveys derives from this conviction that the body–human and cinematic–can and does resist. Neo-Foucauldian denunciation of the disciplinary regulation of the body gives way to a systematic search for glimpses of the fissures and disjunctions–sudden and mysterious points of corporal resistance–concealed beneath superficial homogeneity and continuity. As Bérénice Reynaud has noted, this idea of the "resisting body" is central to Godard's art cinema of the 1980s:

Godard's concern has been to stress that there is an element that resists the geometry of contradictory texts and delineated spaces: the body. The body is this opaque substance that stops light; the body is what emits and receives discourse; the body of a woman is what escapes man's questions about it; the body is that mysterious object, endlessly questioned by philosophers ("One does not know what the body can", wrote Spinoza in the seventeenth century), castigated by some as the ultimate source of sin, overevaluated by others as the ultimate source of pleasure. The body, whose presence is tamed in traditional narrative cinema by the policed training of actors, or reduced to silence by the addition of the voice-over in well-meaning documentaries–the body is what resists becoming a pure signifier. It is thus both the real object of cinema and its more impure elements.[34]

The capacity of the body to evade wholesale machinal conditioning had already been hinted at in the startling flights of the dancing body in Marcel (episode 3b of *Six fois deux*), where we see Super 8 footage of a girl ice skating), and in the vitality and abandon of the young girl's dance that concludes episode 5b (*René(e)s*). These sequences prefigure the project systematised in *France/tour*, which in turn foresees the centrality of song and dance in Miéville's subsequent work. In particular, *Le Livre de Marie* might be considered an extended fictionalised case study based around the notion of a "resisting body": an account of how crisis (the emotional turmoil brought about by parental separation) traverses Marie's body, and of how the body fights back (the extraordinary cathartic dance sequence).

There is another form of resistance: that of the breathtaking beauty, vivid colours, and dense plasticity of the electronic imagery. Music appears to guide the movements of Godard and Miéville's intervention on the editing table, and often provides a rhythm for the unexpected on-screen choreography of everyday motion. But sometimes its sole function appears to be to further accentuate the aesthetic power discovered at the heart of ordinary imagery. Stripped of sound and extracted from the material in which they are couched, the 19 altered motion sequences that punctuate and complicate the smooth flow of *France/tour* constitute enormously potent self-contained, self-reflexive visual *essais* or *études* on the intertwined themes of human and audio-visual movement. Rooted in social theory, they veer rapidly and irreversibly into the sublime. The revelation of opera in the gestures of the waitresses in the fourth movement, or the celebration of colour in the free-jazz sketch of the children at play in the sixth, both point towards the invention of a unique form of animated painting rather than conventional television. The altered motion sequences carry within them the seeds of cinematic recomposition. Decomposition of the mechanics of an assortment of shapes and ages of human bodies throws up a whole new vocabulary of gesture, movement, and corporal interaction. Videographic intervention in television's planned flow leaves a trail of novel video-inflected forms. Together, they provide the basis for a revitalised mode of *mise en scène*, performance, and cinematic composition that will allow Miéville and Godard to recompose differently in images and sounds in the 1980s.

Returning to Godard's article on *Une Vie*, it is not hard to see how enthusiasm for the subversive and creative potential of unforeseen movement foreshadows the blend of formal disjunction and corporal liberation in his early work, perhaps nowhere more potently than in his manifesto of cinematic modernity, *À bout de souffle*, 1960. What has changed in the 20 years separating Godard's early criticism and *France/tour* is the nature of cinema itself. And the cinema of the early 1980s, as it mutated under economic domination and aesthetic infiltration by television, was in sore need of revitalisation. Where the Godard of *À bout de souffle* sought "discontinuity latent in continuity" as the basis for a belated and rather short-lived glimpse of cinematic modernity, the cinematic and corporal discontinuities revealed by the videographic anatomy of the body in *France/tour* interrogate the form, nature, and existence of filmmaking in the age of television and 'neo-television' (satellite, cable, VCRs). By identifying and collating moments of resistance, Godard and Miéville open a gap through which a mature form of cinema can pass. In the context of the development of Godard's work, the energy and sheer beauty of the sequences I have been discussing capture forever the oscillation, and ultimate irreversible slippage, from the primacy of the everyday to the new-found metaphysical lyricism of his subsequent work. In the wider

context of cinema history, they represent the final transition from cinema's belated adolescence (the New Wave) to a post-May 1968, post-television maturity. From a post-*Histoire(s)* vantage point, Godard's project might now be considered in terms of three major phases–the New Wave, the video-inflected art cinema of the 1980s, and the ongoing historical work–each one preceded by an extended period of reflection and preparation (written criticism in the 1950s, videographic research in the 1970s, and experimentation with audio-visual history in the 1980s and 90s), and each representing a fresh attempt to redefine and reinvent cinema in the face of emerging challenges, from television, neo-television, and digital technology respectively.

Above: *À nous la liberté*, René Clair, 1931.

Opposite: *Marcel*, episode 3b of *Six fois deux (Sur et sous la communication)*, 1976.

GODARD, HITCHCOCK, AND THE CINEMATOGRAPHIC IMAGE

JACQUES RANCIÈRE

Chapter 4A of Godard's *Histoire(s) du cinéma*, 1998, includes a specific episode entitled "Introduction à la méthode d'Alfred Hitchcock". There are three reasons for examining this sequence closely. First, it sounds like a manifesto. It at once enunciates and illustrates an idea concerning the nature of the cinematographic image which is not only the idea of a specific–and somehow maverick–author but sums up what I would call the standard avant-gardist view of the artistic nature of cinema. Second, the credit for the demonstration is granted to a director, Alfred Hitchcock, who is highly emblematic. But what does he emblematise exactly? In this sequence he epitomises the power of cinematographic form as a lost power. This sequence, in fact, is a kind of obituary that appears to be overseen by the funeral mask of the master. In Godard's view, this obituary is a mourning song dedicated to cinema as well, but it is also a descent into Hell, a descent into that realm of pure images from which cinema draws its power. In Deleuze's *Movement-Image* Hitchcock is simply emblematic, but he epitomises not so much the power of cinema as the breaking point between the two regimes of cinematographic image: the "movement-image" and the "time-image". That is to say, he epitomises both the perfection of the first regime and its limit, the point at which the "sensori-motor scheme" is struck by paralysis. Hitchcockian practice seems capable of epitomising at once the lost power of cinema now lying in its grave (Godard's thesis) and the power of an old cinema that for decades has been substituted for a new one (Deleuze). How and why can Hithcock's cinematographic practice sustain both statements, and what is the relation of that practice to an essence of the cinematographic image?

There is a third reason to focus on this short sequence. In the background, partly covered over by Godard's voice, we hear Hitchcock's voice, and what

he says suggests that he may not be in agreement with the ideas of cinema and modernity proferred by Godard and Deleuze. I am not interested in establishing who is right or who is wrong here. Rather, I wish to enter this debate to question further what we call the "image" in general and the "cinematographic image" in particular.

Let us start with Godard's statements in this sequence. He appears to make a very simple point: we never remember the plots of Hitchcock's films, for example, the reason why the American government hires Ingrid Bergman in *Notorious* or Joel McCrea in *Foreign Correspondent*, or why Joan Fontaine leans from a cliff in *Suspicion*, or why Janet Leigh stops at Bates Motel in *Psycho*. What we remember are merely images. More precisely, we remember shots focusing on some key objects: a shattering bottle of wine in *Notorious*, a glass of milk in *Suspicion*, the hand of Robert Walker trying to catch a key through the iron grate in *Strangers on a Train*, Marnie's bag, the hairbrush that Vera Miles brandishes against Henry Fonda in *The Wrong Man*, etc.. This privileging of visual presence over narration seems in line with the avant-gardist tradition. It echoes the statements already made in the 1920s by film pioneers such as Jean Epstein: "There are no stories. There never have been stories. There are only situations that have neither head nor tail; without beginning, middle or end, no right side or wrong side; they can be looked at from all directions; right becomes left; without limit in the past or the future they are the present."[1] This also reminds us of the opposition made by Robert Bresson in *Notes sur le cinématographe* between true cinematographic art based on fragmentation, and the old theatre-like tradition of narrative and expressive cinema. But the avant-gardist tradition seems to be taken up again here as a swan's song, a testimony to what cinema truly was or would have been if it had not been

Above: **Photograph of Hitchcock in** *Une femme mariée*, **1964.**

defeated by its enemy, the power of the text and narration which embody the deadly power of Commerce and Industry. Godard's introduction to Hitchcock's method in *Histoire(s)* also includes statements Godard made earlier in which he equated Hitchcock's death with the triumph of the Text, or Death, over the Image, Life.[2]

In order to substantiate his statement, Godard uses an apparently simple device. He divorces some of Hitchcock's images from their narrative embedding: the glass of milk, the shattering bottle of Pommard, the grate, the wings of the mill in *Foreign Correspondent*, the hairbrush in *The Wrong Man*.... Isolating them, he also makes new visual connections between them. For instance, the musical stave of *The Man Who Knew Too Much* loses its function of heralding the shooting and becomes instead merely a graphic grid paralleled thus with another grid–the grate through which Bruno seeks the lighter that he intends to use as a clue against Guy in *Strangers on a Train*. Dismissing the textual and commercial rationality of the plot, the power of cinema would lie in the power of these images, akin to that of Cézanne's apples or Renoir's flowers.

A blunt response to such a mighty statement might be that the opposition is pure sophistry. If the bottle of Pommard impresses us, it is because it has nothing to do with its plastic qualities but entirely with the logic of the plot. We are interested in the bottle precisely because it is filled with uranium. We are frightened by its collapse because Ingrid Bergman's husband, a Nazi spy (Claude Rains), is going down to the cellar to find champagne and soon will hear the noise, then notice that his wife stole the key from his bunch. In the same way, the glass of milk holds our attention because we know that Cary Grant needs to kill his wife in order to obtain her life insurance.

Godard opposes the old representational power of the text to the new supremacy of the image. But the plain opposition between text and image, representation and presence, might be a little too simplistic. What opposes the modern aesthetic regime of art to the regime of representation is, in fact, the way in which the two elements are linked together. Indeed, what characterises representational logic is a precise function of the images, an "expressive" function, subordinated to the causal relationality of the plot. In representational logic, the images are aimed at a surplus of visibility and expressivity. They must present visible effects inviting us to understand their causes and set in motion specific affects, thereby enhancing the perception of the cause-effect connection. Godard's statement is that cinematic images gain their independence from that expressive function. They become pure, autonomous blocks of sensibility that enter autonomously into a new connection, pushing to the background the narrative concatenation of events that constitute the "story".

Is this actually the case, though? By asking this question, I am not concerned whether Godard is right or wrong about Hitchcock's images. It is crucial instead to analyse fully the confrontation in order to understand a little better the exact nature of the cinematographic image. Let us look from this point of view at the sequence in *Suspicion* from which Godard extracted the glass of milk which he then reinserted between the torn wings of the mill in *Foreign Correspondent* and the key that Marnie's foot pushes into another grate. If Godard's fragment is juxtaposed with the whole Hitchcockian sequence, one is tempted to answer that the glass of milk functions as a perfect representational image. It merely puts under our eyes the object of Joan Fontaine's fear, who knows about both the interest of her husband in poison and his interest in her insurance policy. The glass of milk embodies her fear insofar as it embodies the possible object of Cary Grant's calculations; by materialising her fear it also enforces ours. Supporting an affect, the image thus consolidates the causal rationality of the plot. This has nothing to do, it seems, with the mere pictorial power of a white square on a white or black square or even of Cézanne's apples or Renoir's flowers. Hitchcock boasts of never having looked through a camera lens. The shot, he says, is in his mind and its effect must be in the mind of the viewer. This seems to be directly in keeping with the Aristotelian tradition whereby the plot is the primary concern and the "opsis" the last one. And in this very episode, Hitchcock seems to provide some evidence against Godard. Indeed, the voice of Alfred Hitchcock itself appears to deny that this is "his" method. Godard isolates the autonomous power of the grate, the bottle, the glass of milk, the key, and so on; he emphasises their nature as pure sensory blocks according to the tradition first outlined in the 1920s by pioneers like Jean Epstein, taken up again in the 1950s by artists or critics such as Robert Bresson and André Bazin, before being theoretically reformulated by Deleuze in the 1980s. Hitchcock, meanwhile, tells us that nothing is autonomous, that the visual elements are above all triggers that provoke identification, expectation, fear, etc.. Moreover, he tells us that all this goes so quickly that the viewer does not even notice the artifice of the montage through which he or she is propelled in motion.

So Hitchcock would seem to bolster the commonsensical idea that his images are in keeping with the tradition of representation, and that they have nothing to do with those icons Godard makes of them. However, this is not the whole story. Evidently, there is something else at work, for in spite of Hitchcock's insistence on the production of narrative pathos, his concern with issues of pictorialism remains clear. This point has recently been well documented by the exhibition at the Pompidou Centre in Paris, *Hitchcock et l'art: coïncidences fatales*.[3] But the main point is not to counter-oppose the pictorial dimension of his work with its apparent privileging of narration and pathos. Narration and pathos cannot be reduced to the plain Aristotelian pattern, and visuality and narrativity constitute a more complex relation. To take another glance at the glass of milk sequence: certainly, there is something counter-effectual here. After all, Joan Fontaine will not drink the milk and we shall never know whether there was poison in it or not. So the causal connection binding together events and affects seems to arrive at a counter-effect. How can we conceive of this counter-effect? How can we subsume it under the concept of "image"? That is to say, how can we assume a "modernity" of cinema in the use of that kind of the "image"?

It is important to acknowledge properly here that an image is never a pure visual presence. An image is an operation that binds together the demonstration of something visible and a mode of signification. What opposes a modern aesthetic art to a classical or representational art is the form of that linkage. The representational form shows the signification through the expression. This supposes–and this is what constitutes the order of representation–a whole system of correspondences between modes of expression and tenors of signification. In the classical order, the human face, voice and attitude are the agents of that correlation, for instance, the agents that equate their distorted expression with the signification "fear". Fear is a feeling conveyed by people who feel it.

Joan Fontaine–I mean Lina–is certainly scared. But you could hardly *fear her fear* by simply looking at her face or hearing her voice. Fear is actually conveyed by a glass of milk. Such a shift seems natural. Nevertheless, it supposes an overturning of the representational order that occurred first in the nineteenth century novel before fostering cinematographic narrative. In the new aesthetic regime of linkage between visibility and signification, not only has every hierarchy been overthrown so that vulgar objects assume as much importance as the actions and feelings of the heroes, but, even more so

Où est le cinéma à Orly?

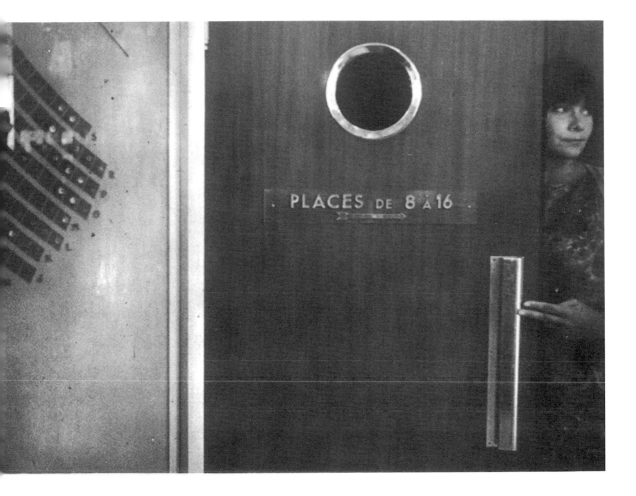

Above: **Double page from Godard and Macha Méril's** *Journal d'une femme mariée,* **1965.**

now, it seems that those best qualified to convey intense feelings are those inanimate objects which feel nothing. This law, first elaborated by the realist novelists, had been spelled out provocatively by an anti-realist stage director, Edward Gordon Craig, before it became a standard of cinema.

Mute objects convey feelings better than expressive faces. But they do it for opposing reasons. First, because they speak better. Signification is better embodied in their reality than in expressive faces, voice and attitudes. They don't think, they feel nothing, and they are unable to lie. Meanings are written directly on their body. This means that they fulfil the representative function–the matching of demonstration and signification–better than any discourse and gesture displaying the signs of fear. Second, they don't speak at all; they mean nothing. They are not signs, only things. As a consequence, they add to their function as reliable clues a contrary function, that of suspending any kind of decision, action or interpretation. There is no relationship between a glass of milk and a need for money or the fear of a crime. The glass of milk both enforces and suspends the causal plot.

But that is not all. There are two forms of suspension: one founded in representation and a properly aesthetic one. The representational form has long been summarised in the Aristotelian idea of catharsis, namely the purification of affect put into play. The glass of milk is a perfect case of catharsis. It first appears as a little white point, slowly growing as Cary Grant/Johnny climbs up the stairs. On the one hand, it is the vehicle of fear, but, on the other, it purifies that fear. Dapper as always, Cary Grant carries it while the orchestra ironically plays a Strauss waltz at a low tempo. This moving and expanding white spot is turned into an ironic question: do you think that this is poison? What's your guess? This means that the link made between the viewer's feeling and that of the lady is loosened slightly. The viewer moves to another position, that of a gambler for whom this terrible story is "only a story", a game promising either the satisfaction of having made the right guess about the riddle or the pleasure of having been fooled by the author in the right way. The muteness of the glass of milk makes it akin to the words possessing a double meaning in Greek tragedy. That form of suspension, the suspension of pathos by action, is still part of the logic of representation.

But there is another form of representation. In this second form, it is not a matter of "purifying" the affect in order to trace better the thread of the plot. Rather, it is a matter of not determining it, of rendering infinite the relationship between visibility and signification and thus paralysing the logic of action. Such is the aesthetic form of suspension, the suspension of action by pathos. Let us take a further look at the same episode from this point of view. We have left Lina in her elegant bedroom, the perfect setting for a domestic tragedy. According to the causal plot, we should now expect the cause of the anxiety: the poison brought by her husband. But this is not exactly what happens. We see first a white arrow on a grey circle, a kind of supremacist painting, which *visually* derives from nothing. Its abstract, two-dimensional space apparently bears no relation with Lina's bedroom. Slowly, of course, the abstract surface will be reset within the imaginary of the third dimension and the narrative connection. We are in the hall of the house. The light comes from the kitchen which Cary Grant is leaving while bearing the glass of milk. Nevertheless, a logic of disjunction has been set in motion and, as Grant climbs up the stairs, it is still at work in the play of light and darkness and the shading of the bars. A second logic has been induced by the cut between two shots, the white arrow on the grey circle. The white spot engenders a blank spot in representational logic. The logic of that "blank spot" spawns alongside the narrative thread, disconnecting the glass of milk from Lina's fear and

Johnny's will and reconnecting it with the white sheet that Lina draws upon herself as if to exit from the story. It suspends the action and paralyses the affect. The glass of milk will stay on the table untouched by Lina, only looked at, without this being related to any reflex action of self-protection or other debate in her mind. She withdraws from the causal connection and enters a form of passivity which is not that of the "victim" or the mere reflection of the "white" passivity of the glass, the sheet, etc..

This means that the glass of milk is an "image" in two opposed yet interconnected ways. First, it is an agent of condensation. It condenses in one single figure a set of representational relations of causes and effects, knowledge and ignorance, fear and the purification of fear. Second, it is the agent of dispersion. It sets in motion a secondary logic that both sustains and contradicts the first. According to this secondary logic, the passage from one shot to another redistributes the representational relations to another surface, a surface of disconnection. An image is, in fact, a combination of two image-functions. This is not specific to the cinematographic medium. It is a more general feature of what I would call aesthetic narration, a mode of narration that was first elaborated in the nineteenth century novel. The logic of the frame as both connection and disconnection might be documented, for example, through Flaubert's novels. The difference is that cinema is deprived of the subtracting power of literature, namely, the ability not to show what it "shows". Cinema still shows what it shows. As a consequence, it must enforce its capacity to withdraw the obviousness of what it shows.

There are no "pure" images, no pure "presences", to be opposed to the logic of representation. Nor is there a logic of the time-image that can be isolated in contrast with that of the movement-image. Cutting between the two shots always means binding and unbinding. But there are various ways of tying together the binding and unbinding function. What defines Hitchcock and, more generally, "classicism" within the aesthetic regime of art, is the capacity to have two functions matched so well that they become indiscernible. This is what makes Flaubert exemplary in literature. Each sentence of his novels both weaves the narrative thread and undoes it. And this is what makes Hitchcock exemplary in film: his shots are the materialising of mental representations calculated to maximise the affects linked to the causal plot. At the same time, they weave another thread made of "blank spots". But while a "modern" filmmaker would make the distance visible, both threads are rendered indiscernible in the same continuum of space-time

Let us compare, for instance, Hitchcock's episode with a parallel sequence in a "modern" film, Pedro Costa's *Ossos*, 1997. The aristrocratic glass of milk becomes here the gas cylinder found in a lumpen tenement and which is dragged in by the wretched young mother to enable the suicide of the whole family. We leave the mother, father and child lying apathetically next to the cylinder. But, as in *Suspicion*, when morning comes, nothing has happened and no explanation is offered about this non-event. Now Costa's *mise en scène* of the "same" episode moves exactly in the opposite direction. By using very long shots and playing on the distension of time and the absorbing power of the colour blue, it conveys a clear sense of disconnection between cause and effect; between a situation and any means of rationalising its causes and effects.

What happens when Godard divorces Hitchcock's fragments from their narrative continuum and binds them together in another? It could be answered that he makes them appear as he wants us to see them, that is to say, as icons of pure presence. He first isolates them with dark spots then connects them in various ways: formal comparisons parallel, for example, two grids or spirals, one made by blood spreading (*Psycho*), another by a hair bun (*Vertigo*). Superimpositions make the mask of Hitchcock, rather than the figure of James

Stewart, appear in the sequoia wood of *Vertigo*. Or Godard makes them flash on and off as if to make them in-between beings that come from the realm of shadows and shimmer for a brief moment in front of us, like a priest testifying to God's real presence.

Eventually it transpires that Hitchcock's images existed as if before his films, living their own life in a realm of pure images from which they could be borrowed and bound together in his work. Godard's introduction to Alfred Hitchcock's method performs a sort of ontological function aimed at disclosing what images truly are when freed from the constraints of narration. Once more, this attempt is not a matter of personal ideology. What Godard sets up here is nothing else than the aesthetic dream: the dream of "free" presence stripped of the links of discourse, narration, resemblance; stripped, indeed, of any relation to anything else except the pure sensory power that calls it to presence.

But images are never free and sensory power still remains a construct. Being an image still means being a link. The problem cannot be resolved through reference to the virtue of fragmentation. This has often been taken for granted as a hallmark of modernity, yet it has no subversive virtue in and of itself and can assume antithetical meanings. Bresson made it the key concept of anti-representational cinema and Godard often refers to Bresson's statements about the power of montage which allows one image to be connected with all other images. But in Bresson's films this means withdrawing power from the singular shot in order further to empower the overall connection of the shots within the film. This idea is still in keeping with the representational model of the work as an organic totality. In *Histoire(s)*, Godard's approach is the exact opposite, making each shot independent and giving it the power to enter into an indefinite number of relations with all sorts of fragments of other films, paintings, photographs, texts, sounds, etc..

We should not be led astray by Godard's emphasis on the purity of the image and by his statements that make it a kind of Veronica and which oppose the event of Godard's real presence to the dead power of the text. Montage remains the core of his theory and practice. His emphasis on the icon does not stand in contradiction to his practice of connecting anything with everything. It is the reverse side of the same coin. Freeing Hitchcock's images means tying them together by virtue of new links. Images must be turned into icons, torn apart from the representational story in order to deliver their true meaning, the testimony of "children" about their "parents". They must be sent back from stories to History. This idea of the purity of images is still an idea of their linking power, and conveys a sense of History. Fragmenting thus means unbinding and rebinding.

There are two main ways of effecting this rebinding: the dialectical way and the symbolist one. What I call here "symbolist" and what I call "dialectical" should be taken in a conceptual sense that crosses the boundaries of a particular doctrine. The dialectical way stresses the homogeneity of the elements that are placed together to reveal the connection of things hidden behind everyday reality. This "hidden" order may be the absolute reality of the dream and desire when undermining the routine of rational and bourgeois reality and which are embodied in the surrealist encounter of an umbrella and a sewing machine. It may be the power of the commodity hidden behind great ideals, or the violence of capitalism underlying the smooth course of everyday life, as embodied in Brechtian stories of cabbages or John Heartfield's X-ray images of capitalist gold in the throat of Adolf Hitler. The dialectical way sets up a clash, staging a strangeness of the familiar and testifying to a reality marked by antagonisms. Its politics consists of revealing the secrets of power.

Previous page:
Collage by Godard, 1979.

The symbolist way also brings together distant realities but it does so in order to produce an analogy, a familiarity of the strange and a witness to a common world where heterogeneous realities are woven in the same fabric and can still be related to one another by the linking of metaphor. Its politics consists of staging the "mystery" of co-presence. Mystery is the key concept of symbolism, just as the secret is the central concept of dialectics. Mystery does not mean enigma, nor does it mean religious mysticism. Since Mallarmé, mystery means the space of analogical practice: the possibility of recognising the thought of the poet in the feet of a dancer, the unfolding of a fan or the smoke of a cigarette. Cinematographic montage plays on the polarity of these two procedures. In so far as cinema is not merely an "aesthetic" art but a mixture of representational logic and aesthetic procedures, cinematic montage can be described as a negotiation between three logics: first, the representational logic of the causal plot with its grammar of expression and dynamic of emotions; second, the first aesthetic logic, the "dialectical" logic of tension between heterogeneous elements; third, the second aesthetic logic, the symbolist logic of association.

The dismissal of plot does not restore some sort of iconic virginity to images. It opens up the field for a shuttling between the dialectic and the symbolist poles. But this polarity is not established as an alternative. Not only can the two models overlap, but the very difference can become almost indiscernible. The Godardian "flash" might well embody the indiscernibility of the two procedures, since it is at the same time a break and a link. It is a signal of disconnection and the light of another world. Connecting one shot to another, a shot to a phrase, fresco, song, political speech, newsreel image or advertisement, etc., still means both staging a clash and framing a continuum.

The time-space of the clash and the time-space of the continuum have, in fact, the same name: History. Disconnecting images from stories, Godard assumes, is connecting them so as to make History. But history precisely means two different things. For some decades history has been plotted out as an open field of division and conflict. The historical connection of a cinematographic shot with a newsreel or an advertising image thus meant the demonstration of a contradiction and the appeal to the spectator as an agent in the process of historical conflict. On the other hand, history means the infinite continuum of co-presence whereby all experiences are held in store and can function as the metaphor for one another. During the 1960s, the Godardian practice of connecting anything to everything was spontaneously interpreted in the first manner. When in *Pierrot le fou*, 1965, a film without a clear political message, Belmondo played on the word "scandal" and the "freedom" that the Scandal girdle supposedly offered women, the context of a Marxist critique of commodification, of pop art derision at consumerism and of a feminist denunciation of women's false "liberation", was enough to foster a dialectical reading of the joke and the whole story.

The same cannot be said of another case of scandal that occurs in the opening chapter of *Histoire(s)* and which brings together, under the aegis of Giotto's Mary Magdalene, the happiness of Elizabeth Taylor in *A Place in the Sun*, 1951, with the dead of the Nazi concentration camps. Godard explains that this happiness was made possible because some years before, while accompanying the liberating Allied forces, George Stevens had used the first Kodachrome film to record the dead at Ravensbrück. In the 1960s or 1970s, the standard reading of the connection, and the standard sense of history which it carried, would have been the perception of the shameful secret of extermination underlying that American happiness: before having on their hands the blood of a crime on which their happiness depends, the two young lovers would have been soaking in the forgotten blood of the extermination of the Jews.

Anti-American though he is, Godard does not present the issue in this way. Elizabeth Taylor positively deserved her happiness because Stevens filmed the dead of the camps positively, and, by so doing, redeemed the art of cinema, i.e. its guilt at not having been there and documented the images of Nazi extermination. What the disconnecting connection of American romance and Nazi extermination foregrounds is no longer the shame of this egotistical American happiness when related to war time atrocities, as in Martha Rosler's photomontages of the 1970s, *Bringing War Home*. Rather, it is the redeeming power of filming the camps, the redeeming power of the descent into Hell.

This means that the practice of collage since the 1960s and 1970s has been thoroughly overturned. Collage is no longer a means of unveiling secrets; it has become a way of establishing a mystery. Elizabeth Taylor's happiness visible in the art of Stevens the filmmaker and the filming of the camps by Stevens the war reporter are tied together by the chain of mystery. They testify to the "mystery" of co-presence symbolised by the third element, the "Mary Magdalene" which Godard wrenched from the *Noli me tangere* ("Don't touch me") in order to reverse the meaning of the scene and have her symbolise the over-binding power born of fragmentation itself. Releasing "images" from stories thus means increasing their power of infinite interconnection within a space whose aesthetic name is mystery and whose political name is History –history as co-existence and inter-expression. Through contrary procedures, Godard ultimately achieves the same ends as Bresson: he uses fragmentation to further the power of connection, or, in his terms, the power of "redemption".

This point may be reinforced by another episode from *Histoire(s)* where Godard reconfigures the images of another filmmaker. Just after the Elizabeth Taylor episode, Godard reframes the end of Rossellini's *Germany Year Zero*, 1948. We know that this film and its filmmaker have been considered emblematic figures of "modernity". Rossellini is supposed to be the father of the New Wave and, according to André Bazin, the founding father of modern cinema along with Orson Welles. The "year zero" of Germany has been identified by Deleuze with the emergence, amidst the ruins of the Second World War, of a new cinema composed of "op-signs" and "sound-signs" disconnected from the "sensori-motor scheme", a cinema that bears witness to the loss of any capacity to react to such situations. It is debatable how far *Germany Year Zero* and Rossellini's cinema in general match the idea of a "disconnected" cinema.[4] In his own way, Rossellini also plays on the ambiguity of connection and disconnection. On the one hand, he builds a strong causal-ideological plot. At the beginning, we are told that the story will show the awful consequences of ideologies on childish minds. According to this plot, Edmund kills his father because he has been intoxicated with propaganda and commits suicide out of remorse. On the other hand, the *mise en scène* weaves a different thread: Edmund's act of murder is generated, in fact, within a frame of strong physical and affective relationships with his father. It is propelled by the dizzying discovery of the pure power of doing or not doing what is said in the words of others, of transforming the causal ideological plot into his own action, a free act of love and murder unrelated to anything else but his own decision or his own dizziness. But what interests me here is Godard's practice, which unfolds in a different way from the Hitchcock episode. I mean that, in this case, Godard, instead of loosening the bond between the images, strengthens it. Instead of restoring images to their independence, he over-binds them in another ideological plot.

In Godard's view, neorealism in general, and this film in particular, embody the resistance of Italian cinema against the American and Hollywood invasion of Europe. He explicitly makes this point in another episode Chapter 1A of *Histoire(s)*. The shots of *Germany Year Zero* are inserted between two charges of

American horsemen, the first evoking conquest, the second a retreat. But here the emphasis is placed not so much on "resistance" as on "redemption", although both are related. The only European cinema capable of resisting Hollywood was the only European cinema that achieved its own redemption. The enmeshing of this plot entails a significant restaging of the end of Rossellini's film. At the end of *Germany Year Zero*, when the Nazi teacher has absolved himself of any responsibility for Edmund's murder of his own father, the causal-ideological plot can be definitively dismissed. What remains is simply the second, vertiginous plot. Then comes the long quasi-mute sequence of Edmund's random wanderings. We see him balancing along the edge of the sidewalk, hopping from strip to strip, giving a passing kick to some other kids' ball, salvaging a fantasy gun to fire on squares of light, sliding down a chute meant for construction materials and eventually jumping into the void.

How is that redemption staged by Godard? He uses two principal procedures: superimposition and slow-motion. Superimposition in his hands means that Edmund is withdrawn from the loneliness in which Rossellini has him play his children's game prior to jumping into the void. He is no longer alone, no longer playing randomly, no longer mimicking suicide as a game before committing it. He is only putting his face in his hands before jumping. His figure appears superimposed over another icon of neorealist cinema, Giulietta Masina/Gelsomia, who is a kind of twin sister for Edmund but also a Mary Magdalene. In this context, Edmund's gesture, unreadable in Rossellini's film, becomes over-determined. First it appears as the illustration of a little fable, asking us to check our eyes with our hands rather than our hands with our eyes. Second, Edmond seems to ponder not only on his act but also on the meaning of his act; not on suicide but on redemption. When he takes away his hands he looks like a sleeper suddenly awakening. Similarly, we understand that cinema is waking up from the American nightmare.

This point will be confirmed by the end of Chapter 1A. Rossellini's last shot showed us Edmund's sister kneeling next to him in silent prostration, an image that did not allow for any interpretation. Godard cuts the end of the sequence and uses the slow-motion to build an entirely new plot. The sister who leant above her brother's corpse becomes an Angel of Resurrection slowly rising above the dead. Like Mary Magdalene in the preceding sequence, she embodies the redemptive power of the Image which will come at the time of the Resurrection. In this way, Godard has transformed a sequence of disconnection into a powerful historical connection. By stressing this reversal, I do not wish to accuse Godard of misunderstanding or distorting his colleagues' films. What is important to me is the sense of the distortion. Fragmentation as employed by Godard reveals two things. First, it demonstrates that a cinematographic image is actually a complex thing, a combination of several functions: the image connects *and* disconnects. It implements a representational function by subjecting the visual elements to the logic of a narrative or symbolic plot, *and* it engenders an aesthetic logic of suspension and infinitisation. In Deleuzian terms, I would say that each image functions both as movement-image and time-image. Every film is composed not of images but of image functions that both supplement and contradict each other. This is as true in the case of Hitchcock's classicism as it is in that of Rossellini's modernism. There is no shift from an *ancien régime* of cinema to a modern age. There are simply different ways of putting more or less into play the tension between different image-functions.

Second, fragmentation is by no means a "liberation" of images, restoring to them some pure essence. It is an operation of montage, or rather a combination of operations. As used by Godard, fragmentation and collage are ways of bringing to the fore disconnections that are usually erased in the construction

of a specific space-time. But these procedures can be implemented in antithetical ways. *Histoire(s)* bears witness to a radical shift in this regard. In Godard's recent films, collage may at first sight appear to be in line with the Surrealist, Brechtian or pop traditions, but it slowly shifted to the exact opposite. Another film, *Prénom Carmen*, 1983, already witnessed that shift in exemplary fashion. The fact of isolating Carmen's flower, in its plastic wrapping, from Bizet's aria and Mérimée's plot might look like a practice of derision in keeping with a Surrealist or Situationist strategy of dialectical *détournement*. But the break away from Bizet and Mérimée through a cock-and-bull narrative of terrorism allows Godard to encapsulate the relationship of two loving bodies within a stronger sensory interconnection, in such a way that Virginia Woolf's *The Waves* echoes Beethoven quartets through Impressionist pictures of deserted beaches, a sunrise at sea and foaming waves breaking on to the sand. Cinema has turned out to be a new form of *Gesamtkunstwerk*, staging an analogy between music, painting and literature as expressions of the same originary rhythm.

    Histoire(s) du cinéma is another kind of *Gesamtkunstwerk,* one that is more complicated and sophisticated and where collage does not aim to make the close and distant clash but rather to make them merge together. That is why there is no contradiction between the practice of disconnection that isolates Hitchcock's glass of milk or shattering bottle and the practice of connection that transforms Edmund's death or Elizabeth Taylor's happiness into symbols of the resurrection of Cinema. Contradictory as they may seem, the transformation of functional Hitchcockian images into pure icons, and the transformation of Edmund's wanderings into a process of Redemption, are part of the same story and produce the same result.

Above: *Going Forth By Day*,
Bill Viola, 2002.

Previous page: **Collage composed
by Godard in 1980 using images from
Rossellini's *Germania anno zero*, 1947,
and Hitchcock's *The Birds*, 1963.**

230

Hence, Godard's narrative of a lost battle of the cinematographic image against the power of text and plot–that is, the power of Industry and Capital–is not what matters, any more than his dream of iconic virginity. What is at stake is the idea and practice of linkage entailed in the very idea of purity, and the way in which Godard actually reframes the history of cinema by reconnecting his images, binding anew the connecting and disconnecting power of cinematographic images. The real battle is the one opposing the dialectical and symbolist ways of making this linkage. In this respect, we can say that the symbolist way has overcome the dialectical.

This shift should not be related merely to the melancholic mood of an individual, nor simply to a French ideological trend, i.e. mourning the death of the Image, Art, Thought, History, Politics, etc.. What I call the "symbolist shift" can be observed more widely in contemporary art. Sometimes it takes explicit and spectacular form, for instance when Matthew Barney creates the *Cremaster Cycle*, 1995-2002, as a contemporary *Gesamtkunstwerk*, symbolising the life of the embryo and "the potential of creative force" through narrative videos that revive Greek, Celtic or Masonic mythology and analogical plastic sculptures, photographs and music. But even when exhibitions of video art and photography, as well as video installations, still claim allegiance to the critical tradition of the 1960s, they now tend, rather than to disclose the relations of power hidden between things and images, to present us with sets of images and items that bear witness to the mystery of co-presence or to frame symbolic representations of the human condition. This shift was well documented by the recent *Moving Images* exhibition at the Guggenheim Museum in New York. For instance, Vanessa Beecroft's video showing nude women moving in the space of the museum was still supposed to "question" feminine stereotypes in art. But those mute figures gave stronger evidence of their inaptitude for any signification and for any conflict of significations. Their strangeness was put into a context of familiarity with the strange, documented by Sam Taylor Wood's polyptics, Gregory Crewdson's photographs of ordinary/strange suburbs, Rineke Djikstra's photographs of ambiguous teenagers on popular beaches, etc.. All these representations of the familiar strangeness of everyday life and common people seemed in turn to be symbolically summed up in Bill Viola's video-installation *Going Forth By Day*, 2002, which stages on the five walls of a dark room the course of human and cosmic destiny, the cycle of birth, life, death and resurrection, along with the cycle of the four elements. Viola refers in his work to the model of Giotto's frescoes, but it is much more in keeping with the great Symbolist and Expressionist cycles of the human condition.

Godard may well have thought of himself as the last of the Mohicans mourning the death of cinema and predicting the reign of darkness. Paradoxically, he might have foreshadowed something quite different: a new trend of symbolist art, this art of testimony that purports to reframe a sense of human community. How far this new trend is attuned to a situation where concerns with "humanity" and the "inhuman" are increasingly prevailing over political concerns goes beyond the scope of this chapter.

THE WRITTEN SCREEN: JLG AND WRITING AS THE ACCURSED SHARE

PHILIPPE DUBOIS

If one had to name a filmmaker for whom, throughout the last 50 years, every form of writing is organically and systematically present in (and around) the image, it would have to be Jean-Luc Godard. He may well be the only filmmaker that the general public have heard speak or whose words they have read more often than they have seen his films. This is a filmmaker who started out as a film critic (and whose reviews were written as if they were already films) before turning to directing (and approaching it in a writerly way). This is a filmmaker who has continuously insisted that writing is his "supreme enemy", that one should "see and not read", that "writing embodies the Law" and thus "death" (as opposed to the image, which embodies "desire" and "life"), yet simultaneously, written textual citation and literary borrowings have been the principal (if not exclusive) source of the voices in Godard's films. This is a filmmaker renowned for his rejection of carefully written, elaborate and rigid scripts, which he tends to pare down to a few lines or pages (combined with images) when he doesn't prefer to use video-essays, yet he is also very precise when writing dialogue, which he rigorously imposes on his actors, leaving them with very little leeway. In short, this is a filmmaker who, throughout his long career and in many different guises, has always asserted both his love and distrust of words, opening up his work to the complex and dialectic interplay between the order of the visible and that of the readerly.

It is chiefly in the body itself of his work that, with great perseverance and constantly renewed inventiveness, Godard has succeeded in using (some might say "over-using") "all" the possible ways of presenting written text in and through images. To name just a few of these recurring figures, in no particular order, there is the representation of the acts of reading (in every possible position) and writing (handwritten or typewritten),

L'ECRAN ECRIT

Philippe DUBOIS

epistolary videos and film-letters (to Jane Fonda or Freddy Buache), postcards (saturated with information and where both sides–written and photographic–complement each other), displayed book covers (conveying multiple meanings), newspapers, posters, fliers, neon signs inscribing their messages, graffiti sprayed on walls, carefully crafted credit titles, intertitles, inserts and surtitles, verbal collages that de- and re-construct language, electronic graphics "in the making", direct inscriptions which seem to turn the screen into a (black- or white-) board, thus allowing the Master's inimitable aphorisms to be visualised "pedagogically", the systematic practice of puns (as well as letter and image games, rebuses, etc.) which short-circuit or (re)generate shifts in meaning, and even the image-screen as "visual writing" (of the body, landscapes, paintings, etc.).

In short, whereas such film/text, image/writing, cinema/literature or visible/readerly dichotomies tend to be apprehended by others either from an overly territorial standpoint, or are perceived as having a competing legitimacy, or as dangerous in their transfers of competences and technologies, one could see these constantly shifting relationships as the very heart of Godard's working, thinking, and making (since, in his case, all three activities are indistinguishable). What follows is an attempt at a scripto-visual essay, composed solely of arrangements of frames taken from his films and which inscribe before our eyes a sense of writing conceived ultimately as a sort of accursed share of the world of images that is Godard's art.

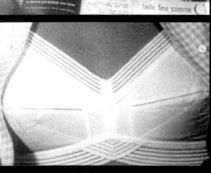

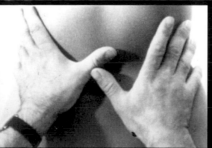

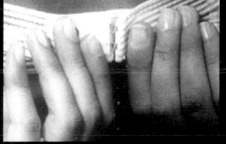

Du bas de ces Pyramides, on a regardé les quarante siècles d'Histoire qui nous contemplaient.

On laisse derrière nous des traces de sang et des morts. On vous embrasse tendrement.

$E=mc^2$

détruire
x 60
par elle-même
sauver ceux
celle qui
pleure nt
tuer K
tendresse

CE FILM
POURRAIT
S'APPELER

LES ENFANTS
DE MARX ET
DE COCA-COLA

LA TAUPE EST INCONSCIENTE,
MAIS ELLE CREUSE LA TERRE
DANS UNE DIRECTION DÉTERMINÉE

YET IT DIGS IN A SPECIFIC DIRECTION.

FÉMININ

F   IN

dix-huit leçons
sur la société
industrielle

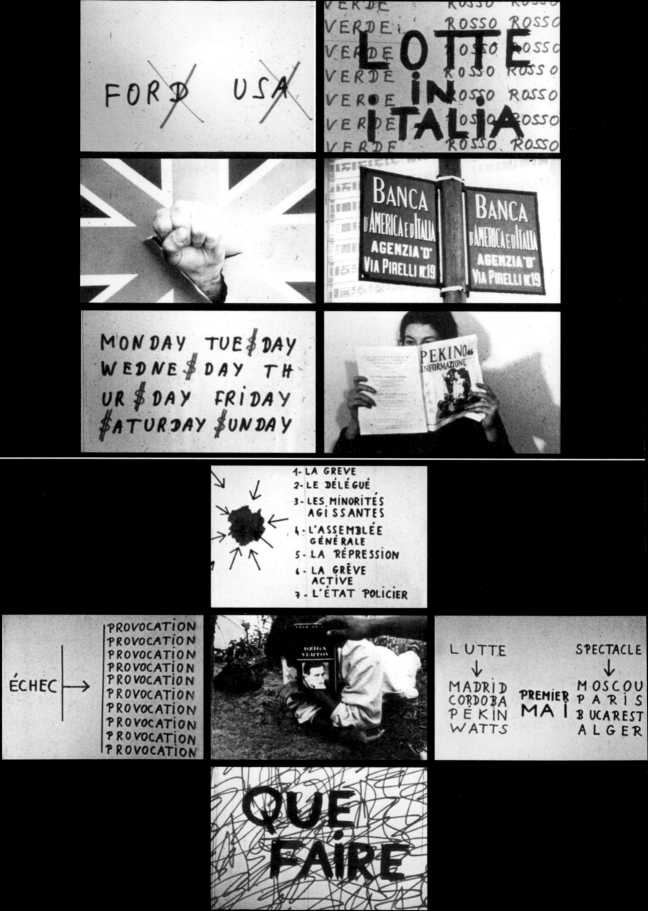

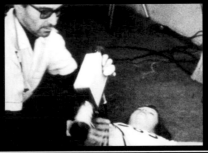

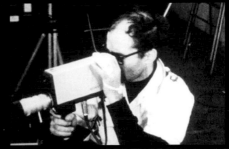

MUSIQUE MUSCHANDISE MARCHANDISE

PEUT-ETRE

LA MERDE PEUTERDE

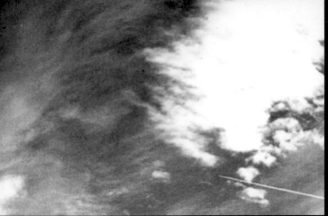

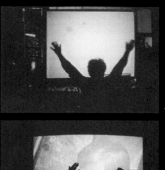

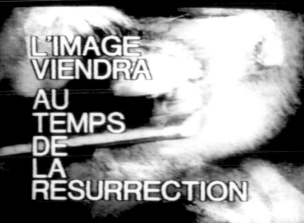

L'IMAGE
VIENDRA

AU
TEMPS
DE
LA
RESURRECTION

SOUND AND MUSIC

SOUND AND MUSIC

The relationship between sound and image in montage is one of the most crucial aspects of form in Godard's work, and it has inspired some of the best critical approaches, for example, Colin MacCabe's groundbreaking 1980 study, *Godard: Images, Sounds, Politics*. However, what if one were temporarily to bracket the term "image" and to concentrate exclusively on "sound"? Godard, after all, was one of the first exponents of live sound during the New Wave and has always held a fascination for the human voice in its different accents and tones. The singing voice and recorded song feature heavily throughout his work, in particular French chanson, whether Jean Ferrat in early films such as *Vivre sa vie*, 1962 (where Ferrat actually appears), or the recurring refrains of Léo Ferré in Godard's work since the late 1970s. In the case of music, Bach and Beethoven are already present in the early shorts, and modernist and contemporary classical music have become a key feature of Godard's work since the mid-1980s. However, Godard's use of music has remained a relatively untold story, due, in part, to the fact that Godard himself rarely talks about music and often professes to know little about it.

The four chapters in this section focus on specific aspects of the rich, polyphonic weave of voice, song and music that is present in some of Godard's most distinctive and influential work, notably *À bout de souffle*, 1960, *Vivre sa vie*, 1963, *Bande à part*, 1965, *Je vous salue, Marie*, 1985, *JLG/JLG: autoportait de décembre*, 1995, and *Histoire(s) du cinéma*, 1998. What stands out clearly, particularly in regard to his use of symphonic and instrumental music, is how Godard is always able to reveal and exploit the intrinsic qualities of his chosen medium.

In "Recital: Three Lyrical Interludes in Godard", Adrian Martin examines the special place poems and songs have in Godard's work. With less didactic intent than the other kinds of literary and cultural quotation employed by Godard, poems and songs allow a complex outpouring of effects and affects, creating both a heightened, breathtaking lyricism and a free-associative essayistic mode that could be called "sensuous thought". The chapter looks in descriptive detail at three films from one of the richest periods for poetic and musical interludes in Godard's oeuvre: *À bout de souffle*, *Bande à part*, and *Alphaville*, 1965.

In "JLG/ECM", Laurent Jullier explores the apparent symbiotic relationship that exists between Godard's sound-work and Manfred Eicher's German record label, ECM Records, which has released the soundtracks of a number of Godard's films. Jullier contends that if the soundtracks of Godard's films, and especially of *Histoire(s)*, play freely on the effects of unintelligibility and concealment, these same characteristics effectively disappear when they are transferred on to CD. The central question addressed is why music should appear to retain its integrity in Godard's work and is never subjected to the techniques of serialism, free-form jazz or cut-up. Jullier argues that Godard remains a fundamentally modernist filmmaker since his soundtracks never feature the musical equivalent of his manipulation of images, voices and noises.

In "Music, Love, and the Cinematic Event", James S Williams explores Godard's ideas of, and for, music. Taking as key instances of Godard's musical practice, *Je vous salue, Marie*, and *Nouvelle Vague*, 1990, Williams analyses Godard's use of melodic symphonic and instrumental music, and considers why Godard chooses to play and replay the beginning of a movement, air or theme, cutting or fading it out before it has time to develop or be modified as a variation. The listener is continually promised the advent of something new, a pure event. Williams argues that the endlessly renewable event of music functions, in fact, as the primary cinematic event for Godard, since it offers him the only means now by which to register a cinematic absolute. Moreover, as *Éloge de l'amour*, 2001, ultimately confirms, music provides a means both of conveying memory and of instantiating the annunciatory and revelatory power of love.

In "Sa Voix", Roland-François Lack considers the changing use Godard makes of his own voice. Lack argues that, concurrent with a career-long practice of manipulating and complicating the inscription of self as voice, a vocalised persona progressively develops in Godard's work: from early ironic self-depreciation through a more radical emptying-out of selfhood towards the fully formed, pathos-laden personality that authors *Histoire(s) du cinéma*. The chapter begins with brief expositions of how Godard's voice signifies in the earlier phases of his filmmaking, and then examines elements of the later work through the tension between Godard's evidently manipulated voice and a performance of vocal plenitude. Lack argues that the complex dialectical articulations of voice in *Histoire(s)* began with the contingent substituting of Godard's voice for that of Jean-Paul Belmondo in *Charlotte et son Jules*, 1958, and reached its fullness of affect in *Histoire(s)* through variants of that substitutive process.

RECITAL: THREE LYRICAL INTERLUDES IN GODARD

For the victory of the cinema resides in the defeat of coherent language, in the triumph of disorder, which only on occasion becomes, in those rare moments of joy during which the editing becomes lyrical, the inexpressible goal that is sought: lyricism, that harmony between being and language, can today only be instantaneous and ephemeral.

Marie-Claire Ropars-Wuilleumier[1]

In memory of Raymond Durgnat

ADRIAN MARTIN

A startling moment in Jean-Luc Godard's oeuvre: near the start of *Scénario du film Passion*, 1982, a piece of classical music–Fauré's *Requiem*–is heard from beginning to end, without rude interruptions, without chaotic, noisy overlays. This explosion of lyricism may be conventionally structured–accompanying, as it does, a montage of images from and around the feature film *Passion*, 1982, in the manner of a rock video or a song-interlude in a mainstream film. But its effect goes beyond the convention, precisely because of its uniqueness and specialness in Godard's work–indeed, it carries an air of the sacred.

Godard's cinema is the art of quotation, of collage. Any viewer of his work is used to the brevity and speed of most of his quotations, and their seemingly off-hand, scattershot delivery. One also quickly learns to sense their constellations, the patterns of similarity and difference which they form as they come at us in clusters. But there is a bridge, within the Godardian aesthetic, between the tiniest fragments (letters of words, corners of posters, details of paintings, stray bars of music) and that sole instance of plenitude in *Scénario du film Passion*. This bridge is comprised of the rare but powerful passages of recital in his work: poems quoted at some length, songs sung and danced. (More often for the latter than the former, Godard uses pastiche rather than quotation–songs composed in some "typical manner" or idiom–but note, for example the invented "never do two glances meet" poem spoken by Jean-Pierre Léaud at the start of *Masculin Féminin*, 1966.)

This essay does not offer an exhaustive list of such recitals, but instead concentrates on three key examples from Godard's first period: *À bout de souffle*, 1960, *Bande à part*, 1964, and *Alphaville*, 1965. It comprises part of a larger work on lyricism in Godard, and on the general fate of the lyrical

Above: **Mexican lobby card for**
À bout de souffle, **1960.**

mode in cinema within modernist forms of the musical.[2] It is also intended as a contribution to the study of Godard's life-long innovations in sound design, a rich but generally under-explored topic. Lastly, one of my concerns threaded through the discussions included here is the ways and means of critical analysis itself when applied to the often tricky case of Godard, in particular, the under-theorised practices of the processes of description, research, and segmentation that precede the act of interpretation *per se*.

À bout de souffle: Be careful, Jessica

As the rather inventive screenplays published by Lorrimer in the 1960s proved, it is easy to misdescribe what actually occurs on the image-tracks and soundtracks of Godard's movies. In particular, it is tempting, in the process of description, to normalise the films, "equalising" (as is said in sound recording and mixing) the diverse elements that co-exist in such a fragmented and free-floating state. Many commentaries on Godard invent lines of narrative-driven clarity and coherence, connection and inference, that are often simply not there. Or, if they are there, they exist in more of a suggestive, sketch-like way, waiting for the mind of the spectator to pull them (or not) into a *gestalt*. For Raymond Durgnat, this was, in fact, one of the most distinctive and radical achievements of Godard: the invention of what he termed the "notional" scene.[3]

Of course, we expect and can accept a degree (sometimes a very high degree) of descriptive error in accounts of films written before the age of VCR or DVD. However, not even the rigorous protocols of textual analysis have managed to save us from rampant impressionism where Godard's films are concerned.[4] And perhaps this phenomenon tells us something not merely about the mind's natural tendency to want to create order where there is sometimes only chaos (or at best the merest hint of–in Hollywood-speak–a "through line"), but also something about Godard's work, its complexity and its semantic porousness, its status not only as palimpsest but also Rorschach test for each and every viewer. How can, for example, the two scenes of performed songs in *Pierrot le fou*, 1965, strike me as deliberately flat, abrasive and disconnected, while to another critic (José Luis Guarner) they register as its "fullest moments–in their simplicity, two of the most beautiful moments of the film"?[5]

All the same, I want to attempt, in my initial example, to describe a famous moment from *À bout de souffle* a little more accurately than many critical accounts do. Michel (Jean-Paul Belmondo) and Patricia (Jean Seberg) stand in the street, it is a two-shot. She suggests: "Let's go to the cowboy film"; he replies: "Yes, but let's wait until dark". They exit the frame, and the presumably "real" people left milling in the background of the image look idly in their direction. Then, still over this shot, a discernibly "cowboy" soundtrack begins: a din of noises (horses, yells) culminating in two loud gunshots. This is indeed (I have checked) a fragment from the soundtrack of the film that Michel and Patricia go to see, Budd Boetticher's not terribly distinguished *Westbound*, 1959 (released in France as *Le Courrier de l'or*)–a detail we will only grasp afterwards, when they leave the theatre. From the street, cut to a close-up of the couple in profile, kissing for almost a minute, lights (as if from the movie screen) playing over their faces–an anthology moment often incorrectly cited as the only kissing scene in Godard's entire oeuvre. Off-screen–although what exactly constitutes off-screen sound here is, of course, a complex matter in a film featuring an extra-diegetic jazz score by Martial Solal that morphs into diegetic record-playing and radio-fiddling–we hear the following recital spoken, in alternate verses, by the voices of a man (Godard) and a woman (research has not turned up her identity):

Opposite: **Production photograph taken during the making of *Westbound*, Budd Boetticher, 1959.**

Be careful, Jessica
At the crossroad of kisses
The years pass too quickly
Flee flee flee
Broken memories

You're wrong, Sheriff
Our story's noble as it's tragic
like the grimace of a tyrant
No drama's chance or magic
No detail that's indifferent
Makes our great love pathetic

(Méfie-toi, Jessica
Au biseau des baisers
Les ans passent trop vite
Évite évite évite
Les souvenirs brisés

Vous faites erreur, Shérif,
Notre histoire est noble et tragique
Comme le masque d'un tyran
Nul drame hasardeux ou magique
Aucun détail indifférent
En rend notre amour pathétique)

The basic point or joke of this scene is not lost on the viewer: the flowery passages of romantic poetry seem to refer to–or even derive from–the B-western on screen, at the same time as they comment, in an ironic-prophetic way, on the eventually "tragic" love story of Michel and Patricia. (On a lower, less "thematic" level of cinephilic humour, the scene is presumably also a joke about the dubbing of American genre films prevalent within French commercial distribution at the time, thus constituting the first of many such gags in post-New Wave film history.) But first of all, before embarking on any further analysis or interpretation, a note on sources and their misreporting, for to study the cinema of Jean-Luc Godard and its attendant critical literature is truly to enter a labyrinth of misattribution, misdescription and misinformation.

The text collaged by Godard for *À bout de souffle* comprises citations from two distinct poems, respectively Louis Aragon's "Elsa je t'aime" ("Elsa, I Love You", one of many lyrical poems composed in honour of his wife) and "Cors de chasse" ("Hunting Horns") from Guillaume Apollinaire's *Alcools*.[6] Before each, Godard has invented a "cowboy" line to make the exchange of verses seem, comically, like a dialogue from Boetticher's western. Yet even this much basic information on the structure of this simple quotation/collage is hard to extract from the mountain of writing on the film. Tom Milne's normally scrupulous editorial apparatus for *Godard on Godard* helpfully points out the first appearance of the Aragon passage (with no date or title given for it) in a review by Godard from 1950 of Max Ophuls's *La Ronde*; however, he includes the prefatory line ("Méfie-toi, Jessica"/"Be careful, Jessica") as part of the poem itself![7] And where Milne seems to remember only Aragon figuring in the scene, Peter Wollen's recent collection *Paris Hollywood* (which gets itself into its own knot of "broken memories" by wrongly citing the film's release date as 1959) recalls only Apollinaire.[8]

This segment of *À bout de souffle* has been the subject of a lengthy, sophisticated and penetrating analysis by Marie-Claire Ropars-Wuilleumier in her Derridean phase.[9] She rightly describes the work of the scene using the

Opposite: **Jean Seberg and Jean-Paul Belmondo** in *À bout de souffle.*

Situationist term of *détournement*–a nuance possibly lost to those who read that as "diversion" in the available English translation–and this crucial allusion is worth corroborating. *Détournement* refers in one of its modes to the practice of wiping the original soundtrack of a "found" film-object and replacing it with another, usually parodic, ironic or straightforwardly critical. The embedded reworking of *Westbound*–which seems, in this regard, much more remarkable today than it must have to commentators and viewers in 1960–is in fact so much like the Situationist films by Guy Debord and others (westerns were, and still are, privileged fodder for *détournement* among Situationists and their predecessors, the Lettrists), that it is surely plausible to imagine that Godard was at least a little familiar with them at the time of making *À bout de souffle*. We know, for instance, that Éric Rohmer wrote on the principal Lettrist Isidore Isou in a 1952 issue of *Cahiers du cinéma*, while veteran *Positif* contributor Jacques Demeure recently recalled, looking back on his moviegoing experiences of that same era: "Thanks to the Studio de l'Étoile and the Latin Quarter ciné-club, I knew all the Lettrist films, and laughed like crazy at Guy-Ernest Debord's *Hurlements en faveur de Sade*."[10]

This recital is a notional scene. It is possible to misremember it–as I have myself done–as actually depicting what it only conjures through association: images of Boetticher's western in which Randolph Scott and his woman talk in the dubbed language of French poets, their hardboiled slang mixing with flowery, lyrical speech. Yet–and this is crucial to the figural economy of the scene–no clip from *Westbound* is actually included in the montage. Others misremember it in such a way as to almost miss the point or the fact of the *détournement* gag: they take the poetry to be what will rapidly become in Godard's work a typical authorial voice-over, an intrusion or interpellation (in the form of an urgent whisper, as in *Bande à part*) utterly "outside" the space of the fiction.

Ropars-Wuilleumier misses none of the subtle and intricate figural interweavings and "spacings" in the scene: the disjunctive meeting of lyrical quotation with generic pastiche, or the fact that male and female voices on the soundtrack correspond with–while being different from–the man and woman in the image (strikingly prefiguring, in this regard, the use of Tom Waits and Crystal Gale as lyrical, singing "doubles" of the characters on the soundtrack of Francis Ford Coppola's *One from the Heart*, 1982). Yet she also tends to render it as an example of "authorial interpellation" by virtue of not quite managing to mention several simple, technical aspects of Godard's sound work that are so crucial to its material effect, not to mention its humour. The reciting voices of Godard and his female companion are not treated distinctly from the rest of the sound-space–that is, they are not handled aurally in the manner of pure, narrating voices-off or voices-over. Rather they are mixed with a shallow, reverberant edge, to make them sound as they would to a spectator sitting in a movie theatre. (One should add the likely hypothesis that the snippet of *Westbound*'s ambient sound, in which of course none of the original American voices or their French dubbed equivalents appear, was recorded from exactly this position, "bootlegged" on to a secreted sound-deck from within a theatre rather than expensively gathered and remixed as is usually done professionally in such "citations"–even if the final effect is to be exactly the same, shallow and reverberant.) This small re-touching might seem, in another context, conventional–a way of "naturalising" the recited quotation–but in Godard it goes to the heart of the formal ambiguity that he, like Marguerite Duras, would explore extensively throughout his career: does a "voice-off" come from a "space-off" (a nearby or surrounding space), or some space that is more mysterious, magical, virtual, both of the scene and not of it? It is precisely within this measured, artfully controlled ambiguity that Godard finds the resources for his peculiarly modern lyricism, "instantaneous and ephemeral".

Opposite: **Spanish poster for *Alphaville*, 1965.**

eddie constantine
anna karina

akim tamiroff
howard vernon

fotografía
raoul coutard

montaje
agnès guillemot

sonido
renê levert

música
paul mizraki

MUSIDORA

CAPITALE
DE LA
DOULEUR

nrf

ALPHAVILLE
una película de jean-luc godard

Above and opposite: **Anna Karina, Howard Vernon, and Laszlo Szabo** in *Alphaville.*

Wollen's memoir testifies to the revolution that was *À bout de souffle*: here, in the festive meeting orchestrated by Godard of Apollinaire, Boetticher and Aragon, was the heady, historic collision of low and high culture long before postmodernism found its name and its theory. This particular scene also sets out the typical framework for Godard's lyrical interludes: in a moment or situation that is pointedly set out of time–usually, and with gallant discretion, the elided or suggested time of an amorous, sexual encounter–the film expands into a lyrical *rêverie*, and spoken poetry finds its best entrance point. In *À bout de souffle*, the interlude is still tentative, even terse; the film's clipped, jump-cut economy does not yet allow for those "rare moments of joy during which the editing becomes lyrical". None the less, Michel and Patricia's dive into a cinema halts the momentum of the plot long enough to carve out a multi-levelled, imaginary world in which different planes collide–thanks largely to the work of the soundtrack–and the diegetic couple fleetingly become not only the auteur and his feminine shadow, but also these liberated, cartoonish figures of the Sheriff and Jessica.

Alphaville: One Enchanted Evening

The use of Paul Éluard's poetry in *Alphaville* amounts to far more than a few quotations torn out of context and inserted into an ongoing collage; as Ropars-Wuilleumier suggested in 1967, part of the film's distinction comes from the fact that it "creates through the cinema a series of harmonious instants" in which Éluard's poetry "instead of being illustrated, seems to be recreated".[11] Since its release, commentators have taken the prominent visual display of an edition of the poet's *Capitale de la douleur* (*Capital of Pain*) as an indication of a respectful and fulsome homage to this particular work–and have immediately spun that reference into a key for the film's historically

Above: *Alphaville:* **a scene out of time.**

Surrealist dimension, since *Capitale* was written at a time in the 1920s when Éluard was very much a part of the Surrealist movement. The drift of such discussions is not exactly wrong but is certainly incomplete, and does reveal the traps that Godard's cagey method of quotation sets for the unwary analyst.

A complex 15 minute scene set in the apartment of Lemmy Caution (Eddie Constantine) has for its lyrical centrepiece a remarkably stylised segment which is perfectly "out of time" with the narrative–it appears to occur in a magical "fold", one entire, enchanted evening, that opens up between the moment that a police car arrives and the action, seconds later, when the cops burst into the apartment. It also breaks with the spatial or pictorial register of the film as a whole, rendering this night of love (with the customary Godardian tact) as a play of light and darkness over the figures of Lemmy and Natacha (Anna Karina), who are posed in dance-like postures, often facing and gazing into the camera. Visually, the scene rests on a beautiful ambiguity inherent to the medium of celluloid: the light which is born and dies, extinguished in darkness, or burns so bright that it whites out the image altogether, cannot be clearly, cleanly attributed to either an on-set, production process (manipulation of the lighting) or a post-production treatment (optical fades and dissolves). (This particular work on the ambiguous properties of light will be continued systematically by a post-New Wave filmmaker dazzled, in his youth, by his initial encounter with Godardian cinema via *Alphaville*: Philippe Garrel.)

Poetically, *Alphaville* is Godard's most coherent and organic film. This lyrical set-piece is, ultimately, less of a rupture of the film's space-time continuum than its fulfilment on a higher level of abstraction. (Indeed, close listening suggests that it may be accompanied by the only other musical piece in the Godardian oeuvre retained in its integrality beyond the Fauré in *Scénario du film Passion*–the lovely cue "Valse triste" from Paul Misraki's otherwise greatly hacked-about and reduced score.) Commentators including Gilberto Perez have teased out the many ways in which the figural values of light and darkness–and especially their mutual metamorphosis–inform every level of the film, from the switches into negative stock to the homages to German Expressionism.[12] This time, more romantically than in *À bout de souffle*, the lyrical transport provided by a poetic recital does not merely mirror the characters but directly transforms them: from a halting, uncomprehending delivery earlier in the scene, Natacha now magically moves to being a smooth, communicating vessel for verse (and Lemmy changes from a tough guy to a Bressonian model). Although the aural mode of this recital is far more obviously a traditional voice-over than the passage in *À bout de souffle*, the transition to the closely rendered, "pure" voice of Karina is, in this context, striking in its strangeness. Entering into Natacha's stream of consciousness (this would be one, imperfect way of placing the typically ambiguous or freeform status of Godardian voice-overs) through her dramatically altered vocal tone and delivery, is to leap with her into a whole new, hitherto unimagined state of being. The text that Karina recites runs as follows (its final phrases accompany a coda shot, still in the enchanted night, of Natacha walking through one of the apartment's rooms, circling and turning on a lamp):

Your voice, your eyes, your hands, your lips. Our silences, our words. Light that goes, light that returns. A single smile between us. In quest of knowledge, I watched night create day, while we seemed unchanged. O beloved of all, beloved of one alone. Your mouth silently promised to be happy. Away, away, says hate, closer, closer, closer, says love. A caress leads us from our infancy. Increasingly, I see the human form as a lovers' dialogue. The heart has but one mouth. Everything by chance. All words without thought. Sentiments adrift. Men roam the city. A glance, a word. Because I love you, everything moves. We must advance to live. Aim straight ahead towards those you love. I went toward you. I went endlessly towards the light. If you smile, it enfolds me all the better. The rays of your arms pierce the mist.[13]

Many commentators assume this is a recital from *Capitale de la douleur*. The assumption is understandable. As Harun Farocki and Kaja Silverman astutely point out, the famous, early morning image that follows this passage–of Karina in a Maya Deren-like pose at the window, holding a copy of Éluard's book–seems to function as a bibliographic "attribution". (An even more explicit pointer in the dialogue preceding the recital–Natacha reading aloud from the page in *Capitale* that Lemmy opens and shoves upon her–is, as we will see, even more misleading.) Unfortunately, everything else they go on to say about the use of Éluard in this section of *Alphaville*–such as their contentions that "only two of the passages seemingly imputed to *Capital of Pain* are direct quotations from it, and they are both poem titles: "death in conversation" and "to be trapped by trying to trap", and that "the other passages are more readings *of* than readings *from* the poems" is, despite being on the right investigative track, comprehensively wrong.[14] Julien d'Abrigeon is closer to the mark in his estimation that "this 'poem' is in fact a gigantic collage, by Godard, of several verses from Éluard taken from different poems", but he doesn't enumerate Godard's exact sources.[15]

It seems that few people who have studied the film have actually bothered to look up Éluard. Godard, on the other hand, obviously knows the poet's collected works very well. His collage is creative indeed–first of all, for its apparent seamlessness (it is possible to mistake it as an integral quotation of a single, Surrealist poem), and secondly for the fact that he even constructs new sentences from phrases taken from completely different poems (as in "Je vois de mieux en mieux la forme humaine/comme un dialogue d'amoureux"), indeed, any analyst must, as I have done, make his or her editorial decisions about how to transcribe and segment the phrases of this collage on a page. What even those commentators aware of the thoroughgoing collage method fail to clarify is that Godard is borrowing from all over Éluard's entire poetic oeuvre–assorted bits and pieces from *Capitale* (Farocki and Silverman miss two further titles woven into the apartment scene's dialogue, "Dying is Not Dying" and "Men Who Change", not to mention the image that scans almost the entire one page text of "Nudité de la vérité" ("Nakedness of the Truth")), and especially a late work that came decades after *Capitale*, namely *Le Phénix*, 1950. To give a sense of the supreme poetic logic of this collage, and the extremity of its rewriting-through-assemblage, I will gloss only four consecutive fragments that are derived from three poems in *Le Phénix*:

Il suffit d'avancer pour vivre, d'aller droit devant soi vers tous ceux que l'on aime ["La Petite enfance de Dominique"]. J'allais vers toi. J'allais vers la lumière ["La Mort, l'amour, la vie"]. Si tu souris, c'est pour mieux m'envahir ["Certitude"]. Les rayons de tes bras entrouvraient le brouillard ["La Mort, l'amour, la vie"].

Éluard's complete poetic oeuvre is the true "underwriting" of *Alphaville*, in an extensive and fully worked-out way that I believe is singular in Godard's career. A key example is the passage read out by Natacha seemingly from the open pages of *Capitale*.

We live oblivious to our metamorphoses
But this echo that runs throughout the day
This echo beyond time, anguish or caress
Are we near to our consciousness, or far from it

(Nous vivons dans l'oubli de nos métamorphoses
Mais cet écho qui roule tout le long du jour
Cet écho hors du temps d'angoisse ou de caresses
Sommes-nous près ou loin de notre conscience)

This text is not, in fact, from *Capitale*. It is a condensation in four lines of the first three verses (Godard's sharply creative reassemblage, again) of Éluard's 1946 poem, "Et notre mouvement" ("And Our Movement"):

We live oblivious to our metamorphoses
The day is lazy but the night is busy
A breath of air at midday the night filters and burns up
Night doesn't leave dust over us

But this echo that runs throughout the day
This echo beyond time of anguish or caress
This raw continuity of dull worlds
And of sensitive worlds its sun is double

Are we near to our conscience, or far from it
Where our limits are our roots our objective

(Nous vivons dans l'oubli de nos métamorphoses
Le jour est paresseux mais la nuit est active
Un bol d'air à midi la nuit le filtre et l'use
La nuit ne laisse pas de poussière sur nous

Mais cet écho qui roule tout le long du jour
Cet écho hors du temps d'angoisse ou de caresses
Cet enchaînement brut des mondes inspides
Et des mondes sensibles son soleil est double

Sommes-nous près ou loin de notre conscience
Où sont nos bornes nos racines notre but)

What Godard does not explicitly cite from this poem–and here we reach a subterranean, buried level of *Alphaville*'s generating matrix–might well have inspired the core imagery of the enchanted evening/impossible night segment, with its profile views, its dramatic comings and goings of the light, its "incensed forms" and "bodies without limits", as well as feeding into some of the more squalid, violent imagery elsewhere in the "real" world of the movie:

The long pleasure, however, of our metamorphoses
Skeletons moving around in the rotting walls
The appointments given to weird forms
With ingenious flesh to blind seers

The appointments given by the face to its profile
By suffering to health, by light
To the forest, by the mountain to the valley,
By the mine to the flower, by the pearl to the sun

We are hand-to-hand, we are down-to-earth
We are born everywhere, we are without limits

(Le long plaisir pourtant de nos métamorphoses
Squelettes s'animant dans les murs pourrissants
Les rendez-vous donnés aux formes insensées
À la chair ingénieuse aux aveugles voyants

Les rendez-vous donnés par la face au profil
Par la souffrance à la santé par la lumière
À la forêt par la montagne à la vallée
Par la mine à la fleur par la perle au soleil

Nous sommes corps à corps nous sommes terre à terre
Nous naissons de partout nous sommes sans limites)

Why the absence of a full disclosure by Godard in relation to such Éluard sources? Apart from the fact that he is an artist with due license and not an academic bibliographer, one can speculate about the positive ramifications of his devious collage method here. The cover of *Capitale* serves him well as a physical object because of the resonance of that title for the film's dystopian, sci-fi vision–and we know from Godard's other work, right through to *Histoire(s) du cinéma*, 1998, how he can productively regard a book's cover, in its words and graphics, as a sign autonomous from its inner, literary contents. But the foregrounding of this one misleading attribution obscures other connotations that arise from the Éluard association–thus displacing them into the deep structure of the text. (And I would have to add heretically here that I do not believe every Godard film actually possesses a deep structure, since I hold the old-fashioned view that those which do, like *Le Mépris*, 1963, and *Vivre sa vie*, 1962, as opposed to those that don't like *Les Carabiniers*, 1963, and *Made in USA*, 1966, are the richer works.)

To begin, the last poems of Éluard's life in the early 1950s are not the effusions of a young man drunk on the *rêverie* of Surrealist *amour fou*. He had recently been revitalised, after the death of his second wife Nush (Maria Benz), by the discovery of a new, younger love, Dominique. This resonates with the "May-September" casting of Constantine against Karina, bringing a special poignancy to the birth of love theme crucial to the film. Also involved here, no doubt, is Godard's autobiographical identification, in this period, with those modern, romantic poets (Éluard and Aragon) who eulogised their wives/muses; and possibly his own age difference (ten years) in relation to Karina.

On another, more profound level, there is a secretly political dimension–the trace of which we will again uncover in *Bande à part*–in Alphaville's adjustment of Éluard. Beyond his adventures in Surrealism, Éluard found a part of his fame as an activist-poet in the Resistance. As Su-Shuan Chen, Meredith Protas and Leah Doberne have pointed out, "the title 'And Our Movement' can signify the physical movement of the body, or an organisation like the Resistance or the Surrealist movement [...] the poem shows Éluard's transition between Surrealism and the Resistance [...] It is difficult to know of which he speaks: he is describing a general movement [...] the latter is more political, but it is still a movement."[16] All of these mixed associations–love, Surrealism, political resistance and rebellion–are fully in play in the futuristic parable that is *Alphaville*.

Bande à part: people and things

I am treating *Bande à part* out of chronological order because, in its magnificent métro scene between Odile (Karina) and Arthur (Claude Brasseur), it provides a bridge between the spoken and sung recitals in Godard's work. Stylistically, too, it is watershed in his career: it makes a sublime gesture of innocently recapturing the freshness and spontaneity of his first films, before heading off into more turbulent waters of negatory modernism and radical politics. *Bande à part* is, in many respects, Godard's most classical and linear film, especially on the levels of plot, character and theme–and also in the bittersweet affect it generates. Barthélémy Amengual, for instance, suggests that, within the global context of the entire fiction, the métro scene–with its abrupt culmination

Opposite: **Anna Karina, Sami Frey, Claude Brasseur, and Louisa Colpeyn in *Bande à part*, 1964.**

in a surprising shot of Odile and Arthur in bed, after what may well be her sexual initiation–"represents the coming night of love and takes its place, transposing it, anticipating the agonies, indecisions, sorrow and deception of Odile which the rest of the film evades".[17]

It is one of the most complexly organised sequences in Godard's oeuvre, one that belies his carefully cultivated legend of casual, on-set improvisation. Apart from the challenging logistics of shooting on trains, the soundtrack (if carefully listened to) gives ample evidence of the enormous technical and aesthetic preconceptualisation that must have gone into the scene. The sound montage of this scene–shortly after completing the film, Godard remarked that "people never attach any importance to sound, but that's what interests me most"–is a wonder of directly recorded and postsynchronised sounds, atmospheric touches blended into expressive modulations, realism and manipulation deftly combined–and all at the service of this voice which, as in the most refined Hollywood musical, will gradually pass from speech to "musicalised" recitation to full-blown song.[18] But with a Godardian twist: in the polyphonic, 'multi-channel' mode of image and sound montage which is his true trademark, even a voice in full lyrical flight can suddenly be left stranded without its underlying sonic "bed" or support–an effect which the scene deploys in a breathtaking manner.

The scene begins with a dialogue between Odile and Arthur that turns gradually from intimate matters–her shyness, her hopes for the future, his more aggressive, animal pursuit of pleasure–to the world immediately around them: the anonymous train passengers in their daily lives. Arthur offers a quick semiotic lesson on the malleability of appearances: depending on the background you supply, a particular guy can seem happy or sad. This folksy moment of deconstruction is important in implicitly setting the lyrical flight that follows into quotation marks, indicating it precisely as a way of seeing, and transforming, the quotidian world through art or discourse. Odile remarks: "It reminds me of a song. How does it go again?", and proceeds alternately to speak and sing the following text:

I hear their footsteps I hear their voices
Saying banal things
Like one reads in the newspaper
Like one says at home in the evening

What is done to you men women
Oh gentle stone so easily worn
And your broken appearances
Looking at you tears my soul

Things come and go as they do
From time to time the earth shakes
Disaster resembles disaster
It is deep deep deep

You would like to believe the sky is blue
I know this feeling well
I too believe in it at times [...]

I admit to you I believe in it sometimes
Such that I don't believe my ears
Ah we are truly alike
Ah I am truly like you

Like you like the grains of sand
Like the blood always spilled

Like the fingers always wounded
Ah I am truly your fellow man

(J'en ai tant vu qui s'en allèrent
Ils en demandaient que du feu
Ils en contentaient de si peu
Ils avaient si peu de colère

J'entends leurs pas j'entends leurs voix
Qui disent des choses banales
Comme on en lit sur le journal
Comme on en dit le soir chez soi

Ce qu'on fait de vous hommes femmes
Ô pierre tendre tôt usée
Et vos apparences brisées
Vous regarder m'arrache l'âme

Les choses vont comme elles vont
De temps en temps la terre tremble
Le malheur au malheur ressemble
Il est profond profond profond

Vous voudriez au ciel bleu croire
Je le connais ce sentiment
J'y crois aussi moi par moments [...]

J'y crois parfois je vous l'avoue
À n'en pas croire mes oreilles
Ah je suis bien votre pareil
Ah je suis bien pareil à vous

À vous comme les grains de sable
Comme le sang toujours versé
Comme les doigts toujours blessés
Ah je suis bien votre semblable)

This text has two sources, the latter of which, until recently, has rarely been mentioned or accounted for in Godardian criticism. It began life as the poem "J'entends j'entends" ("I Hear, I Hear") by Aragon. In 1961 it was set to music by the famous French singer-songwriter Jean Ferrat, and it is this setting which Karina performs–without, of course, musical accompaniment (Ferrat's rendition, with a full orchestra, sounds much jauntier than one might guess from *Bande à part*). As usual, Godard has performed what d'Abrigeon rightly calls an act of "ablation": there are five further verses lopped off, but once again this hidden part is not irrelevant to the film's performance-recreation of the song's sentiments.

Alongside the poetic materiality of Godard's lyrical passages, we must insist on their conceptual rigour–especially when it comes to "deep" sources like Godard's preferred poets and performers (apart from Ferrat–who had already figured in song and in person in *Vivre sa vie*–the list includes Léo Ferré, Leonard Cohen and Bob Dylan). Godard referred to *Bande à part* as "a French film with a pre-war atmosphere"–or, in some sense, a period film which is not a period film. What this means in effect–with a suitably expanded historical sense of what "pre-war" might mean for Godard in this context–is that he fills the film with the ambience of a historically wide-ranging poetic populism in French culture, of the sort we associate with Jean Renoir's Popular Front films, Jacques Prévert's "poetic realist" screenplays, and Raymond Queneau's novels. This is a popular culture–already the object of a certain, sentimental nostalgia in 1964 and more so today–which is fundamentally leftist in character. Aragon and Ferrat both were among this culture's heroes, its stars, its icons (one of Ferrat's hits was a hymn to the battleship Potemkin). Both were publicly associated with political activism: Aragon as a high-profile communist, Ferrat, in later life, as a progressive politician.

Godard's scene performs a poetic-realist account of everyday life. Its very setting–a train at peak hour, taking weary commuters from work to home–is a prime emblem of populist art and culture. (We could transpose on to it, from another time and place, The Kinks' song *Waterloo Sunset*.) So is its time frame, from dusk to dawn on a typical week day–those fleeting, precious, always endangered and enclosed hours of "free time" allowed those who are slaves to the industrial capitalist system (which is why populist art is so obsessed with the poignancy of weekends and holidays). Aragon's poem and Ferrat's song dramatise the moment of what we might call "populist identification": the process whereby the artist or intellectual, inevitably positioned in a more privileged sector of society, comes to empathise with ordinary people in their everyday plights-moving from a distant point of superior critique (banal things) to the eventual attempt to dissolve himself or herself into this mass of humanity ("Yes, I am one of you"). Aragon and Ferrat's deepest wish is, ultimately, political: to form and energise a human community which is aware of its own oppression (this is the explicit subject of the verses omitted by Godard). Yet the loneliness and atomisation of modern life counterpose a sadness to what the song calls (in its original, final verse) the "modest and mad dream" of oneness.

Godard achieves something special and perfectly poised in the way he takes on this lyrical, populist mode: he shares the dream, but underlines the melancholy and impossibility which face it. He speaks both *through* the lyric mode, in a fond appropriation/appreciation, and *about* that mode and its limits, critically. A comment he made at the time indicates both his identification with this mode and his appraisal of it precisely as a mode: the métro scene is "really my point of view in the film, that is, I'm interested in people, in things [....] That's the theme of Aragon's song."[19]

Cinematically, the scene is an outstanding (and rightly classic) piece of lyrical work. The scene begins by establishing, conventionally, the positions of various people in the train carriage, people who will figure later in the lyrical editing. Once Odile is into her song, the flight of the voice releases the images, which follow suit. The scene leaps off the train, viewing it from the outside, going out into the streets, flashing from day to night, no longer tied to any character's point of view. At the lyric high point of the scene, when Karina in close-up turns to look at the camera (a movement self-consciously reprised, in anthology mode, in *Histoire(s)*), we can no longer say exactly where we are on that train, or even that we are still in a train: every realistic index in the image has deliberately been blurred and abstracted by that point. We have definitively passed, in Pier Paolo Pasolini's terms, from cinema-prose to cinema-poetry in hardly a minute of screen time. Another way to conceive the logic of the scene is in its gradual drawing or circling of a community: the movement of the montage is from the couple to the surrounding individuals and groups; and even at the end, when we come back to the amorous twosome, Godard cuts to Franz (Sami Frey) also asleep in his bed, another reminder of a small-scale family or community, and another populist homage/allusion to Vigo's *L'Atalante*, 1934.

Then there is the work on the materiality, the phenomenology even, of sound, closely married to the structures of meaning and association created by the images. Like for Bresson, Godard (at least in this pre-Mao period) believes that sound communicates first as rhythm, tone and sensation before it registers as meaning. Paramount in this sonic system is the affective difference for the spectator between the sound of a voice recorded live (within the real ambience of a location) and that same voice re-recorded more "cleanly" in controlled conditions. The passage, the cut from live to pre-recorded voice, often precipitates a powerfully felt "interior turn" in a Godard film, an intensification of purpose.

In the métro scene, Godard and his team are mixing (to my ear) six distinct tracks of sound: two tracks devoted to voices and four to sound effects of train and street noises–and of these four, three are comprised of sounds recorded live, and the last is a minimal Foley track of stylised, recreated footsteps. In its complexity, this sound montage prefigures the elaborate work Godard would do in the 1980s and beyond with François Musy. There is a trick, an aural sleight of hand occurring in the scene, at the point where it passes from the live take of Karina's voice backed by real train sound, to a post-synchronised Karina backed by a manipulated montage of edited train sounds. Of course, all mainstream films today play these sorts of tricks, usually in the name of a seamless illusionism or naturalism. Godard, by contrast, assembles and then disassembles the sonic illusion–not for the sake of a facile deconstruction but in order to launch a poetic, lyric drama. I am referring again to that moment when the backing track drops out under Karina, leaving Odile's voice sailing alone and unaccompanied over the street-life images. This creates a tremendous "real time" effect of poignant suspension, fragility and vulnerability. Godard achieves this great audiovisual moment, but he also builds a total, rising lyric structure: each technical treatment of Odile's voice–the passage from live voice over train to pre-recorded voice over train and then finally only voice–places it at a more abstracted, purer level of sensation. This is a voice that–like all those celebrated birds in classical lyric poetry–soars away from the world, weightless, while longing, paradoxically, to be merged with it. It is a voice at once intimate and impersonal, belonging to no one and everyone.

Inside the recital of the Aragon/Ferrat text, Godard creates, on every stylistic level, the feeling of taking off from the strict, individualised space of the fiction into a wider, real world. Godard's lyrical raptures often aim at this: an impersonality or trans-personality which registers as a collective voice of experience. This is the sweet vertigo of cinematic lyricism at its giddy height: as spectators we momentarily lose our bearings, the characters float free of the plot that contains and constrains them, voices are torn asunder from bodies and narrative identities, there is born an impossible discourse about matters on which these creatures could not formerly express themselves.... And yet ultimately, within this cinema which, in its most profound gestures, bridges the modes of storytelling and essay–this cinema of 'sensual thought' wrought with the materials of images and sounds, landscapes and bodies–we come to rest on the wisdom which Ropars-Wuilleumier well identified long ago: that the greatness of Godard's best work lies in the fact that "it shows the difficult search for this lyricism, not its fulfilment".[20]

JLG/ECM

LAURENT JULLIER

If the title of this essay sounds like a wedding invitation, it is quite deliberate. In fact, Jean-Luc Godard phonetically wrote "Eux c'est aime" for ECM in the synopsis of the film he intended to direct about this German record company ("Eux c'est aime" is approximately equivalent in English to "Them, it is love").[1] This "marriage" has already been consummated (ECM has released the complete soundtracks of two of Godard's films, *Nouvelle Vague*, 1990, and *Histoire(s) du cinéma*, 1998, on CD, and conversely, Godard has used musical excerpts from the ECM catalogue in these two films), but this is nevertheless intriguing. The parties seem so different. On the one hand, we have the rough, staccato and self-reflexive audiovisual works of Godard. On the other, the homogeneous and polished records of ECM, renowned for their "nice" packaging. In a symbolic and typical example, the sunset which opens *Passion*, 1982, once it has been frozen on to David Darling's *Cello* CD cover, is transformed into a "pretty picture". But the *Passion* sunset is *not* pretty: Godard (who happened to be holding the camera that evening, while waiting for Coutard to finish his dinner) intentionally shot it bluntly, as if to denounce–in the usual modernist manner–the narcotic (not to say kitsch) beauty of this cliché.

Thus, this union raises certain aesthetic questions, which can be grouped under three headings. 1. In an analytic way, we can consider how the ECM tracks are chosen, edited and how they interact with the images. 2. On the "stylistic" side, we can examine the postmodern dimensions of the final audiovisual work. Does Godard's collaboration with ECM necessarily mean that a champion of modernism defected to the postmodern "enemy", similar to Philip Johnson's "scandalous" postmodern AT&T Manhattan skyscraper? 3. Finally, in a comparative way, we can focus on the CD format. Does bringing out an autonomous film soundtrack constitute the creation of a new work, comparable to a piece of concrete music, or is it

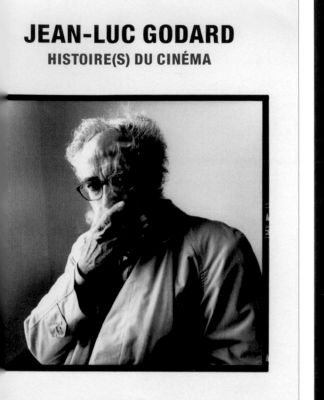

JEAN-LUC GODARD
HISTOIRE(S) DU CINÉMA

ECM NEW SERIES

JEAN-LUC GODARD
HISTOIRE(S) DU CINÉMA

ECM NEW SERIES

Above: **The ECM press book for the five-CD box-set of *Histoire(s) du cinéma*, and the cover of the box.**

a mutilation, in which the image is experienced as *lacking* from both the CD and the minds of the frustrated audience?

Both parties have commented on this union, but predictably, their discussions are not enlightening, since a theory of aesthetics cannot be based on the real authors' external assessments. Manfred Eicher, founder and president of ECM, mainly describes the artistic encounter between Godard and himself in terms of friendship. He expressed regret that my essay did not go into this dimension, but I prefer to take on the role of an unknowing spectator, so as to avoid "overreading" biographical details. As for Godard, he refused to theorise his collaboration with ECM, declaring: "One day, Anne-Marie [Miéville] and I received some CDs in the post.... We listened to them and liked some of them...", before adding in his usual provocative manner, "Besides, I don't know anything about music." Godard later fudged the issue by explaining that he used "ECM music because it is not film music", but ironically undermined his own choice, calling David Darling a "minor Bernard Herrmann", which is incorrect, since these two composers have absolutely nothing in common in terms of compositional and recording styles.[2]

In order to understand better this intriguing union, we must look elsewhere and focus on the works themselves. Broadly speaking there are two possible definitions of the term "postmodernism". In philosophical terms—the best-known being that of Jean-François Lyotard—postmodernism is a game without rules, celebrating language games. The theory of language games is inspired by Wittgenstein's posthumous *Philosophical Investigations*, which states that the meaning of a word is determined by its usage rather than by the object it denotes, with the result that language "has no outside".[3] Lyotard specifies that the legitimating discourses of knowledge and action which have prevailed since the Renaissance, and particularly since the Enlightenment, are no more than meta-narratives, or "Grand Narratives", now null and void (which is seen as positive since they have led to Auschwitz and the Gulag *inter alia*, "ultimate irrational events" which render the Law "unpresentable"), and that they have resulted in generalised nihilism, "delegitimation" and the decay of "forms of being-together", which is negative.[4] Regarding the arts, Lyotard's solution is to promote art in which "the main issue is to get close to fundamental matter. In other words, to get close to presence while avoiding the use of the means of presentation". The listener must "become open to the invasion of nuances, porous to tone".[5] There is also the more general meaning of postmodernism, which is an extension of the concept proposed by Robert Venturi in architecture in 1966, and which refers with reasonable precision to an artistic "style" based on playful spatio-temporal eclecticism. Depending on the context, the connotations of this can be either negative (relinquishing the modern drive to seek out the new, which is replaced by nostalgic quotations of forms from a lost past) or positive (the return to figural representation and tonality as sources of simple pleasures).

Histoire(s) du cinéma fits easily within Lyotard's definition. It uses the magnifying glass of the editing table to explore layers of representation from Giotto to Hitchcock, revealing the bankruptcy of the Grand Narratives that led to the Nazi extermination camps, which are themselves very present in the images. It also reveals the failure of the medium, the fact that cinema has been unable to capture the horror of the camps. At first glance, *Histoire(s)* does not obviously correspond to the second category of the everyday meaning of the term postmodern. Its playful allusions have little to do with spatio-temporal eclecticism, except for the inclusion of a few cabaret songs and clips from low-grade pornographic films. Rather, *Histoire(s)* focuses on the great art of the Western world. However, we need to look–and more importantly *listen*–a little more closely. Although the two aforementioned definitions may seem mutually exclusive (Lyotard praises Daniel Buren, an artist considered as a radical modernist by art lovers who know little of contemporary philosophy), they share a return to the "sensory" world, which is where Lyotard locates the "ineffable". He wrote in a rather Wittgensteinian manner: "We can say that the tree is green, but we have not put the colour into the sentence."[6] He contrasts the sensory world to "collective anaesthesia", namely a "growing insensitivity" to sensations and feelings.[7]

What I wish to argue here is that *Histoire(s)* is not so much a work of history as one of sensory experience, an attempt to reach the ineffable, mainly through the soundtrack. It appears initially as a web of associations, but it quickly puts the personal culture of the audience to such a test that they become saturated with recognitions and references and have to abandon this eminently cognitive game by succumbing to the experience of the audiovisual flow. So are we justified in speaking of a pop video effect here, even if that may sound disrespectful? To answer this question we must consider Godard's choice of composers.

The ECM label is not entirely devoted to postmodern music, which in this context means, neo-tonal or neo-Debussyist music (even if Manfred Eicher seems to consider the word "postmodern" as an insult), but Godard did not select the most overtly modernist composers in the catalogue. All

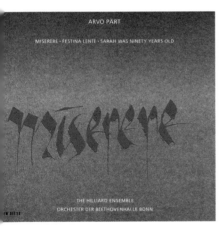

those who feature in the ECM-JLG box set have committed the sin (in the eyes of the modernists) of using the notes of *The Well-Tempered Clavier* (from which *Histoire(s)* uses a very famous extract), and most of them also use the consonant chords which the dodecaphonists and other exponents of serial music have borne in contempt for over a century. Before examining in detail the fundamental discord of the tonal system, let us consider whether there is any common aesthetic approach between the use of consonant chords and Godard's interwoven quotations.

At first glance, there appear to be no similarities. Historically, the French context has led to postmodern music being met with rejection or scorn by the intelligentsia. Patrick Szersnovicz couldn't be more elitist in his article in *Le Monde de la musique*. He aimed to provide an overview of current composition and, after the obligatory praise of Boulez, condemned the "primitive bland music" and other "over-rated traditional products" whose success with audiences does not "ensure either their validity or even their legitimacy".[8] There is a plethora of critics in France who "accuse a piece of being kitsch as soon as a dominant is heard".[9] However, if we look a little closer the gap is not so wide. Jean-Pierre Dambricourt writes that the music of Michael Nyman (the best known of the postmodern composers and almost certainly the most loathed and mocked by the modernists) "turns his creations into the signifiers of a lost object, for which they express both desire and mourning", and they "somewhat nostalgically take stock of the irreversible loss of any stable reference point", including a "sense of history".[10] The same could be said of some of Godard's works, such as *Le Mépris*, 1963 ("It's the end of cinema!", exclaimed Georgia Moll), *Nouvelle Vague* (which opens with the very Lyotardian words, "But I wanted this to be a story..."), and of course *Histoire(s)*.

Let us now consider four composers selected by Godard.

1. Arvo Pärt. *Festina lente*, completed in 1990, is an adagio for strings and harp, a truly archetypal piece of postmodern music. It is at once materially archaic (traditional instruments playing perfect harmonies) and structurally modern, using algorithms of repetitions and multiple intervals. As the CD booklet explains, the strings are split into five groups: three play the main melody, each in a different tempo, while the other two play a counterpoint, each in a tempo that is different again, twice as fast and twice as slow. The piece features the double coding of postmodern works, as Umberto Eco notes in a text written for a duo of Italian ECM artists.[11]

2. Paul Hindemith. *Symphony "Mathis der Maler"*, 1933-1934, is a three-movement symphony by Hindemith (1895-1963) that became the basis for the famous opera of the same name, first performed in Zürich in 1938. Mathis Gothardt Nithart was a Renaissance painter whose best known work is the *Isenheim Altarpiece*. Mathis and Godard have a number of things in common, despite the 450 year gap. Hindemith wrote the programme for the first performance, noting that Mathis "put up the greatest possible resistance against the pressure exerted by those in power, while at the same time clearly recording in his paintings how disturbed he was by the savagery of his time".[12] The opera recounts how he supported the peasants' revolt and subsequently became disillusioned. The peasants ultimately destroy the *Virgin Mary* painted by Mathis (Tableau 4, scene 1). This evokes Godard's difficulties with *Je vous salue, Marie*, 1985. The opera was written between 1932 and 1934, during the Nazi takeover of Germany, and Mathis's disillusion is also that of Hindemith as he watches the direction taken by the German people in their hopes for the future.

David Darling
Cello

Giya Kancheli Abii ne viderem

Kim Kashkashian   The Hilliard Ensemble
Dennis Russell Davies   Stuttgarter Kammerorchester   ECM

The Sea

Dino Saluzzi

Andina

ECM

Godard uses two extracts of the symphony in both *Histoire(s)* and *Nouvelle Vague*: from the third movement, "Temptation of St Anthony" (Tableau 6, scene 2 of the opera), in which Mathis, in the guise of St Anthony, dreams that all are accusing him one by one of having failed in his art; and from the second movement, the "Entombment" (Tableau 7, scene 1 of the opera), which shows the death of the painter's partner and his decision to give up painting. (The real Mathis ended up building windmills, which limits comparisons with Godard and, in the context of *Histoire(s)*, demonstrates the limitations of associations combined with a neverending search for metaphors.) Only the introductions have been retained; these are thematically very dark, mirroring the events they accompany–the end of creativity, the death of political ideals, the loss of loved ones. Hindemith was moreover castigated by supporters of musical modernism, and particularly by his compatriot Adorno, for his use of tonality.

Thus we can see here that the two artists share similar approaches. But there may also be formal similarities.

3. and 4. Meredith Monk: *Do you be* (used in *Nouvelle Vague*), and Giya Kancheli: *Abii ne viderem* (used in *Histoire(s)*). These two pieces clearly share the same structure: phrases separated by silence. Although they are very different in length and instrumentation, they are related through their fragmented nature. In contrast to the manipulation, fragmentation, editing and superimposition found in the image, the pieces of music chosen by Godard establish a showcase (Pärt, Hindemith) or a counterpoint (Monk, Kancheli). They either provide cohesion by bridging disparate and fleeting images (which seem all the more fragmentary for being seen against a background of continuity), or they mark out itineraries, establishing a rhythm that is never that of the image editing–although, as in *Festina Lente*, some overlaps give the illusion of isochrony or a large-scale link between cut and beat which never happens. In fact, a great many things do not happen in *Histoire(s)*, in the sense that here one of Godard's basic techniques is the suppression of one of the pair of two shots that form the shot/reverse shot structure, so that we see actors looking, but not what they are looking at. We shall see that this approach is linked to the idea of the open-ended work of completion to be carried out by the viewer.

Why did Godard choose tonal and melodic tracks, instead of, say, cut-up avant-garde jazz or dodecaphonic music? Why is the tonality so important? The American cognitivist Ray Jackendoff suggests that, in music consisting of notes, it is possible to distinguish between group structure (groups of notes forming motifs, which in turn form melodies, etc.), metrical structure (the accents and pacing involved in a particular time), and the structure of reduction (differentiation of melody and ornamentation, where possible; it is at this stage that the contrast between dissonance and harmony appears, and it is precisely this stage which is often lost through Godard's fragmentation). The recognition of these structures may be innate, or it may be learnt; in either case it is not necessary to be a musician to spot them. Not only do we expect to hear certain notes, we also expect them to occur at a particular time (harmonic expectancy).

There are also connections between mental imagery and music. Barbara Tillmann and others speak of "low-dimension representation" which captures the similarities and redundancies in a piece and result in a "topographic representation on two levels", the harmonic level and that of key in chromatic music.[13] At the same time a second link is established with motor and pre-motor imagery. Some pieces of music make us want to dance or to beat time; descending or rising harmonies set off imaginary movements with physical effects.[14] Hollywood composers are well aware of this, often accompanying narrative peaks and troughs with chromatic rises or falls. They exploit the viewer's propensity for "associative listening", or James Young's "hearing as", which is analogous to the associative sight or "seeing as" which makes us believe we can see faces in clouds.[15] This type of listening associates music with movement: attraction/repulsion, hesitation/impetuosity, and even more complex movements which are still centred on the listener's body, such as something "that is simultaneously pulled into two directions" or "that moves into the wind". The music can even "show what it is like to pursue some desirable but unattainable end [...]".[16] Such imaginary movements can create a certain euphoria, or sometimes some sophisticated feelings: "The repeated deferral of the expected pleasure of a resolution can result in impatience."[17] Every connoisseur of Godard's work here will recognise his preferred approach when he decides to play with tonal music.

Through such associations a child learns how music can be emotionally inflected by his or her cultural background. Of course, in absolute terms music does not "mean" anything. Mireille Besson recalls Stravinsky's statement that music expresses itself.[18] This top-down view, says Besson, was also expressed by Jean-Jacques Rousseau: "For it is not the ear that brings pleasure to the heart, but the heart that brings pleasure to the ear."[19] However, between the ages of three and eight Western children come to associate minor keys and slow tempos with sadness, major keys and fast tempos with happiness.[20] This emotional conclusion can be drawn more quickly (within half a second!) than a cognitive one (such as recognising the title or style of the piece), and unlike the latter, is not affected by the listener's musical culture.[21] The colossal number of opening bars in *Histoire(s)* may perhaps make the audience experience the flow in a more emotional way.

Adorno stresses that tonality and atonality go hand in hand: "Aural beauty and dissonance are not simple opposites; each annexes the other, just as the pleasure experienced by a gourmet eating a fine dish can border on disgust."[22] But at the same time he argues in favour of new music, whose aesthetically critical position, he says, is also a social position. He sees people consuming music like children, "held in a vice", with their low "intellectual level", and who "ask only to hear what they are given to hear and fear anything that brings them back to reality because it threatens a cosy existence that they themselves do not really believe in".[23] The compensatory happiness they "think they find" in tonal music is "child-like".[24] "My music is not lovely", the furious Schoenberg is said to have retorted to a Hollywood producer who wanted to hire him.[25] Adorno criticises tonal music for its ideological connotations of a mendacious humanism which "justified what was bad".[26] He rejects its debt to natural sound, since it dates only from the Florentine *ars nova*.[27] He looks to chance and randomness as the means to escape it, as in the work of Cage,[28] or to electronic music, which enables the creation of a far more complex scale than those produced by orchestral instruments.[29] Schoenberg also adopts a formalist perspective when he describes one of Verdi's melodies as unbearable "because the rhythm of the principal motif was obvious after four bars".[30] However, as we shall see, predictability, whether offered by the medium (CD) or the music itself (loops, recurrences), can be considered a way of shifting the listener's attention.

And what if Godard chose ECM's tonal and melodic tracks and edited and transposed them more spectacularly so as to highlight his manipulation of them? Let us turn to the notion of musical fragmentation and musical re-contextualisation. With the exception of two pieces, a cabaret song (*Nostra lingua italiana* by Riccardo Cocciante) and a piece just under half an hour to which we shall return later (*Abii ne viderem* by Kancheli), no piece of music is reproduced in its entirety on the soundtrack of the two films under discussion here. We can begin with a coldly commercial, albeit scandalous interpretation of this fact. According to Erkki Pekkilä, the extract is emblematic of the commercial, not only because musical works not originally written for commercials always exceed the 30 seconds of the ad itself, but more importantly because brief extracts foster a desire to prolong the pleasure (and so buy the associated product, or the CD).[31]

More significantly in this context, Jacques Aumont emphasises the aesthetic value of Godard's fragmentation of music.[32] "By preventing the melody from developing, he draws attention to a different musical quality", for example, in using Beethoven's 7th quartet in *Une femme mariée*, 1964. According to Aumont, Godard "gives the persistent rhythmic scansion its full power [...] by separating it from its function as an accompaniment".[33] Further, "a cut, however unexpected, analyses instead of dismembering".[34] This is also a way of giving music equal status to the other elements in the film, in the sense that all are liable to be cut. Adorno sees extracts as the ultimate reductive test: "There is no more severe test to which music can be subjected than that of extracting tiny fragments and seeing if they have meaning, if they can be played as they are."[35] However, this is not what Godard is doing, since his cuts do not correspond to musical "breathing".

This dissection into musical "shots" goes a long way towards making the musical material more cinematic and lessening the repetitive effect of the heterogeneity of these continual imports (none of the pieces was written expressly for the film), although (in contrast to what happens on the image track) the interruption usually takes the form of an aural fade-out rather than a cut. Aurally, the tactic of fragmentation has three consequences. 1. When the structure of reduction cannot be established, which often happens in *Histoire(s)*, the audience is required to listen to the music in an unfamiliar way–they must listen analytically, in the manner described by Aumont. 2. When the structure of reduction has time to appear, frustration always accompanies the final fade-out which deprives the listener of any resolution, however gentle the fade may be (although the smoothing over of sound is not a practice of Godard's, far from it). 3. There are a great many beginnings of pieces and very few codas. The emotional response is therefore privileged to the detriment of the cognitive response. There is more opportunity to savour the start of a musical journey than to respond to a game or test of recognition.

Noël Carroll stresses the reciprocity of the relationship between film and music.[36] The film anchors the "objectless" emotion carried by the music into a particular object (an operation of *indication*), while in return the music characterises the film object, sometimes to the point of changing it (operation of *modification*). When the selected music pre-dates the film, this dual operation is called *re-contextualisation*. The search for new combinations of this type is not new in Godard's work. In 1970, for example, the Dziga Vertov Group sought to produce a Marxist-Leninist cinema that "could be used as a weapon" for "new relationships between image and sound".[37] "We are not looking for new forms, we are looking for new relationships."[38] Almost 30 years later in *Histoire(s)*, Godard repeats his aim of "establishing links between things that have never been linked before and do not seem amenable to it" (Chapter 4B).

The lowest level of re-contextualisation of the piece of music being used involves retaining the identity of the "narrative" structure. Thus, the first bars of *Winter* (Dino Saluzzi) open *Nouvelle Vague,* while its coda closes the film. Are these semantic connections? Admittedly, the film takes place in winter, but the instruments evoke the Andes, which means that the degree of re-contextualisation involved is not above the minimum. By contrast, Monk's *Do you be* finds echoes through its instrumentation. In *Nouvelle Vague* it is associated with birdsong and with the following words, yodelled in Monk's piece: "The instinctive skill with which women adapt to the home! That serene confidence

48

C'est un disque
qu'il a rapporté de Berlin ouest
pour un de ses amis
de l'OTAN ici.

Pierre veut bien
que je l'écoute
si je suis gentille.

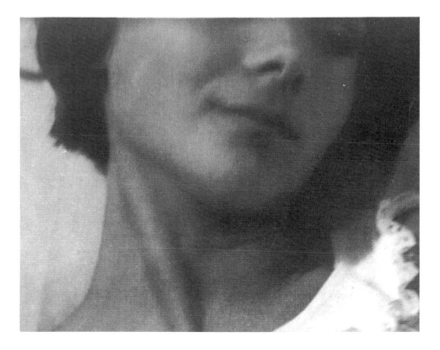

Je suis gentille.

in what love will bring!" (and later, women who "spread their wings before taking flight"). The semantic field seems homogeneous; it is natural–the *instinctive* skill. The title *Do you be* itself apes a primitive proto-langage. Furthermore, the vocalised yodels use unidentifiable phonemes, in a powerful voice synaesthetically linked to the (slightly sarcastic) enthusiasm of the actor who utters the words.

Kancheli's magnum opus, *Abii ne viderem*, is more problematic. It overlays almost the whole of Chapter 4A of *Histoire(s)*: the photographs of famous women and of the variations on the human hand, the eulogy of Hitchcock and the portraits of the "artists" of the New Wave (films such as *L'Année dernière à Marienbad*). So it certainly confers structural unity on something whose semantic unity is not all that apparent. However, on two occasions, Godard synaesthetically associates powerful moments in the music, using almost consonant chords, with famous moments from key films in the history of Western cinema: John Wayne carrying away Natalie Wood at the end of *The Searchers* and the close-up of the dying mother letting go of the celebrated pram in *Battleship Potemkin*. In these two instances, Kancheli's music adopts the habitual mantle of the Hollywood composer as cementer of empathetic identification. At other times the echoes are more conceptual, although paradoxically the recurring concept is that of innocence. The innocence of the postmodern composer, of the "infancy of art", of the primacy of the aforementioned sensorial: "And now that he *felt everything* he thought he *knew nothing*. And yet...." An impressive visual triptych clarifies matters, or confuses them, since these connections are threatened by polysemy: a close-up from a porn film/the silent laughter of a pinhead from *Freaks*/a skeletal corpse thrown into a mass grave during the liberation of the extermination camps. Is this the fate that awaits the innocent? The title of the piece itself, *Abii ne viderem* (I turned away so as not to see), refers to the attitude of the composer fleeing his native Estonia when "atrocities were about to be committed there".[39]

Now, before suggesting a possible interpretation of the JLG-ECM union, we must return to our initial question: does releasing an autonomous film soundtrack constitute the creation of a new work?

This is not the first time that a film soundtrack has been released on disc with all its background noise, dialogue and aural fade-outs.[40] However, the case of Godard is particularly interesting since his soundtracks tend to exploit the possibilities of deception and unintelligibility, characteristics which may lose some of their impact when transferred to CD (combined with a remix by François Musy for ECM). That said, the difference is not striking since any gain in clarity of sound is lost with the sight of on-screen lips speaking to camera, which is, of course, absent from the CD. The remix has also avoided any spatialisation of the simultaneous voices, which prevents auditory fission. Ultimately it is impossible to make quantitative comparisons. We hear different things, particularly in *Nouvelle Vague* since *Histoire(s)* contains far fewer polyphonies.

Theodore Gracyk emphasises the "original mystery" contained in a disc: are we hearing a virtuoso performance or the result of overdubbing?[41] We can never be sure. He recalls that some critics make a distinction between music heard live and sonic art on disc (including live recordings).[42] Lee Brown gives a three-point definition of the "work of phonography" to move the debate forward: 1. It is *replete*, in other words everything in it makes sense and the slightest detail remains the same each time it is heard. 2. It is created with an aesthetic rather than a documentary aim in view. 3. It cannot be "performed"; it is only "phono-accessible".[43] Criteria 2 and 3 are not valid: the terms "aesthetic" and "documentary" reflect usage as much as the intentions of the producers (a document can be heard as an aesthetic object and *vice versa*); the "performance" of works of phonography is a common practice in the world of techno music (everyone knows that a CD does not sound the same on a small car radio as on a huge sound system). But the first criterion is self-sufficient.

Gracyk sees the success of music videos as an alternative to musical performance, whose audience has become a minority in our society. This would explain why these videos show a great many dance routines and physical movements linked to the production of sound.[44] This is the illustration in reverse of the universal need for inter-sensorial confirmation (or cross-modal checking), already reflected in the fact that, long before cinema, spectacles involving projected images were always and everywhere accompanied by music. By suppressing the image, the shift from film to CD avoids the pitfalls of the music-video effect and synaesthesia. Another advantage is the ease of repetition, of rewinding, that has always been a feature of the disc medium. Howard Niblock sees the mechanical repetition of a recording on disc as debasing: "it has lost so much of its freshness that it almost ceases to be music".[45] Gracyk rightly retorts that the repetition argument does not apply to poems or paintings.[46] Furthermore, repetition makes it possible to explore details. This is another example of "reduced listening" as defined by Pierre Schaeffer, which considers the sound for itself and not for what it means or for what produced it, and which is facilitated by repetition.[47] Barthes noted this phenomenon in *S/Z* in relation to literature: "Those who do not bother to reread are obliged to read the same story everywhere."[48] Similarly, Aumont sees the repetition of musical fragments in Godard's work as an "act of profound and effective understanding", enabling the audience to "contrast the figure with another that could have replaced it".[49]

Michel Fano, of whom many critics have said that his film compositions for Gérard Vienne and Alain Robbe-Grillet had the makings of pieces of concrete music, has admitted that he refuses to allow recordings to be made of his film scores because they are pointless without the image.[50] The case of *Histoire(s)* is different in so far as nothing was written expressly for the film. Certainly, the collage of fragments was tailor-made but not the sources of these fragments. The case of *Nouvelle Vague* is more delicate. How can listeners cope with a storm, the cawing of crows and the isochronic rhythm of the actors' footsteps? Do they melt everything down into a piece of concrete music, either in a radical way, like John Cage listening round the clock to the world as one vast piece of music ("Noises everywhere. Concerts celebrating the fact that concerts are no longer necessary..."), or simply like the audience of a piece of concrete music?[51] Either approach is hard to adopt, since the fine, rich recording (particularly on the CD) tends towards the context-free replication of sound. For a musicologist such as Carl Dalhaus, a practitioner of concrete music "verifies the possible aestheticisation of acoustic phenomena which fulfil a pragmatic function in everyday life" and creates an "internal acoustic context which encourages listeners–instead of evoking running taps or the clicking of kitchen utensils–to observe the particularities and characteristics of sounds". Causal listening occurs "even if they have been modified by tape manipulation".[52]

In *Nouvelle Vague* there are no modifications and thus it is more or less impossible to disconnect causal listening. The indexical precision of the sounds combined with the lack of causal narrativity largely explains why the blind author of the booklet for the ECM box set can easily create her own "reinvented film".[53] So here we are truly dealing with a *second work* that is reconstructed by the viewer according to relatively loose enunciative directions (Godard: "The film lets you think whatever you like; it may suggest frameworks for thinking, which are in fact far more flexible than what I used to do."[54])

But there is the matter of the musical extracts, and particularly the ECM extracts. With concrete music everything is easy: the original is there, directly within earshot. Here, everything is different. The musical extracts in these two sets are presented to the listener as fragments of an original which can be purchased. Moreover, recordings on the ECM label very often have a *sound signature* in the form of a long, gentle reverberation which symbolically refers the connoisseur to sacred music (churches and cathedrals are temples of endless reverberations). This reverberation is a showcase in which most of the ECM music is presented. Even listeners who are not fans of the famous Munich label will note that the ECM extracts stand out, particularly when the background noise has been recorded and mixed in a rather flat way, as is the case in *Nouvelle Vague*.

Let us be a little iconoclastic here: is this two-headed film/CD product the typical video/CD pairing? On the subject of MTV, Lida Hujic discusses a meta-textual mode of operation into which other programmes slip (ultimately everything takes on the appearance of MTV, from commercials to news reports), and with which viewers experiment environmentally–it is aimed less at understanding than at feeling.[55] It is true that some moments in *Histoire(s)* could fit this description: everything blends into the twilight tones of the whole film. Other clues include a quasi-absence of sounds and distortions in the musical extracts (whereas the images are manipulated, slowed down and modified). To continue our iconoclastic approach, can these sets be described as ECM samplers? Could they be sets of samples from the Munich catalogue corresponding to film samples covering the period of cinema? Of course not. There are in fact very few overtly frustrating cuts, designed to make the listener want to hear or buy the complete work. Nor is Godard's selection representative of the aesthetic field covered by ECM (as any real sampler CD should be): there is no free jazz and no "hits" (Keith Jarrett and Jan Garbarek, for instance).

Instead, these CDs function to make their listeners work. This is hardly a surprise: the soundtracks of all, or almost all, of Godard's films reflect the idea of work which has been done or which is to be done, and Godard himself has long asserted this.[56] One such statement from 1975 will suffice: "The viewer's participation seems to me to be the first step [...] If a viewer says to me 'I saw a bad film', I will say, 'it's your own fault. What did you do to improve the dialogue?'"[57] I'm not alluding here to the work of recognition of the mysterious extracts, which always flatters the spectator, nor to attempts to graft on an inferential narrative logic ("What's going to happen next?"). Since the earliest days of his career, or almost, Godard's films have always combined perceptions and apperception, not only on the part of the characters (what they see, what they hear, what they suddenly think of, what they foresee, what they remember), but also on that of the utterance itself (the camera starts to look at the actor rather than the character; the director suddenly chooses to reflect on the nature of cinema, on showing, on narration, instead of continuing to tell the story as though there was no one pulling the strings; he recalls the history of cinema and its stories). Add to this complexity of the image an abundance of snatches of sound and, as Mauricio Kagel observed, "es geht alles". Any A combined with any B will ultimately always produce an interesting A+B combination.

I would like to conclude by focusing on a different kind of work. At first the release of the CD (whether of *Nouvelle Vague* or *Histoire(s)*) and the invitation to broaden the flow of sound invites listeners to carry out something they can barely attempt when faced with the images, namely to discover the *ineffable* aspect of musical sound, even before Jackendoff's group structure. This again is an instance of "reduced listening" which entails concentrating on certain parameters of the body of the sound itself.[58] Secondly, the CD is all the

Opposite: **Paulette Goddard in *The Great Dictator*, Charles Chaplin, 1940.**

Above: **The _Ruby's Arms_ sequence in _Prénom Carmen_, 1983.**

more useful to _Histoire(s)_ because it strengthens a hypothesis present throughout the film, that of the _innocence_ of cinema in relation to the two-fold crime it is accused of having committed: 1. failing to record the death camps, 2. failing to understand that it had already shown them (_La Règle du jeu_, _The Great Dictator_).

The question of sound-traces functioning as immanent proof is seldom raised in our society. (How many news reports consisting of sounds do we hear on the radio? Television news reports go so far as largely to erase them). Regarding the collapse of the Grand Narratives in the wake of Auschwitz mentioned earlier, Godard believes that sound is even more innocent and virginal. Hence the seductive bonus of consuming it separated from a tainted and dubious image. In _Histoire(s)_, over the horrific images from _The Passenger_, the 1963 Polish film about the camps where the absence of a Scope lens has the effect of symbolically turning bodies into skeletons, Godard superimposes a soothing song, _Addio Lugano bella_. The recorded song ostensibly crackles as we read the title, "Oh sweet miracle of our blind eyes [...]" Here, the crackles are surely more the result of a mechanical fault rather than a sound taken directly from the source, a "sample of the real world". Thus, any ECM recording which immediately presents itself as a phonographic object can only match this apparent logic (it cannot fail because it has not been designed to produce a sample of the real world).

At the very end of _Histoire(s)_, Godard combines a typically postmodern, or rather neo-romantic, ECM track called _The Sea_, by Ketil Bjørnstad, with the famous passage from _Anima Poetae_ by Samuel Coleridge: "If a man could pass thro' Paradise in a Dream, & have a flower presented to him as a pledge that his Soul had really been there, & found that flower in his hand when he awoke–Aye! and what then?"[59] "I was this man" ("J'étais cet homme"), answers Godard. This response is puzzling since _rêverie_, the delights of Paradise or the beauty of nature are not typically associated with his films. The extract from *The Sea*, which is played simultaneously, is fragmented many times. These cuts are easily noticeable, since to cut an ECM recording is almost always more spectacular than to cut any other kind of recording, because of the already mentioned long and gentle reverberation. The melody is truly butchered too, but a harmonic suite of perfect chords ultimately concludes the work without any alteration. According to modernist theory, this kind of neo-romantic music has sold out to the culture industry. It seduces a large audience because it "allows the listener to remember the happiness of childhood".[60] This is (almost the only) opportunity for the oppressed masses to "cry a little", which is why "they love the expression of nostalgia more than the expression of happiness"; it is "a kind of mass psychoanalysis, intended to circumvent people".[61]

When he butchered *Ruby's arms*, the sad and beautiful song by Tom Waits, in *Prénom Carmen*, Godard clearly followed this Brechtian way of thinking ("Say goodbye to Ruby's arms", sings Waits, i.e. say goodbye to Paradise). So the *doxa* of modernism appears neo-Platonic, associating the dangers of *rêverie* with the Freudian *principle of pleasure* (here we can hear consonant chords and a neo-romantic melody), and the revolutionary virtue of lucidity with the *principle of reality* (here, musical cut-up and the multiple frustrations of the expectations of tonal pleasure). Hindemith and Kancheli's works reflect this kind of rousing strategy which relies on "unexpected cadences and the absence of a leading tone", thereby engendering "a feeling of absence, the feeling that something is missing".[62] This "something", according to the Coleridge dream, is Paradise lost, or at best glimpsed. But in choosing nostalgia for a conceptual equivalent of Ruby's arms (i.e. a glimpsed Paradise), from a somehow post-mortem vantage point ("I *was* this man"), and finally letting *The Sea* develop its deliciously melancholic harmony, Godard seems more subdued, or at least he bids goodbye to this modernist dialectic knowing that the Grand Narrative is dead. Perhaps he needed the ECM showcase to allow a melody to have a pleasurable but nevertheless dangerous effect on the spectator–the kind of effect perhaps, which, when all is said and done, leads towards the Lyotardian ineffable of the sensory world.[63]

MUSIC, LOVE, AND THE CINEMATIC EVENT

La Treizième revient... c'est encor la première;
Et c'est toujours la Seule,–ou c'est le seul moment [...]
Gérard de Nerval, "Artémis"

If I speak in the tongues of mortals and of angels, but do not have love, I am a noisy gong or a clanging cymbal.
St Paul to the Corinthians, I:13

JAMES S WILLIAMS

1. The mystery of music

For a filmmaker so knowing and eloquent about his own method, Godard is singularly unenlightening about his use of music. When not simply silent on the matter, he often adopts a cavalier public attitude to what is without doubt a major creative resource. During a recent radio interview with Thierry Jousse actually devoted to music, Godard flaunts the fact that he is not a musician and repeats his by now standard line that it was Manfred Eicher of ECM records who suggested, and voluntarily supplied, much of the music in his films since the mid-1980s.[1] In addition, serial music such as Boulez is peremptorily dismissed, and even the contemporary composer David Darling, whose work is omnipresent in his later work, is downgraded and miscategorised as "minor" film music. This type of impatient reaction reaches a comic level with Godard's screen persona, notably in Anne-Marie Miéville's *Nous sommes tous encore ici*, 1997, where the irascible "Lui" complains that classical works are now played much faster than when originally performed and thus offer no comfort. In fact, whenever he can, Godard chooses to divert the discussion of music to questions of art and painting on which he has a well-honed discourse and possesses even practical experience (notably his collaboration with Gérard Fromanger during the late 1960s). It is as if Godard were absolving himself of any knowledge of music, as if his wide-ranging use of the Western musical canon were simply instinctive and beyond analysis. Composers he uses are credited in his films but this is often a half-hearted gesture, the lists of names remaining distinctly vague and incomplete. Ironically, the only real moment in his work where there is any serious attempt at a discourse on musical history occurs in *Week-end*, 1967, where, as the camera repeatedly tracks 360 degrees around the piano in the farmyard, the travelling musician Paul Gégauff explains that all modern music springs from Mozart. And

Above: *Le Rouge*, Gérard Fromanger, 1968. In the same year, Fromanger also made a three minute 16mm film version of this painting with Godard's technical assistance.

Mozart will remain uncontroversially the standard icon of Western music for Godard right up to *For Ever Mozart*, 1996, and beyond.

Why should Godard wish to draw such a marked veil over his musical practice, especially when his films over the last 20 years have become ever more musically dense and complex, often comprising whole swathes of the ECM catalogue?[2] This is a basic question that has been evaded by most critics, including myself, who consider Godard a remarkable exponent of film sound and yet who have preferred to follow his lead and approach him more as a painter of images.[3] This state of critical affairs is all the more unfortunate for the fact that soundtracks of recent works like *Nouvelle Vague*, 1990, and *Histoire(s) du cinéma*, 1998, are commercially available and ripe for analysis. Godard even remarks of *Nouvelle Vague*: "my film, if you listen to the soundtrack without the images, will turn out even better".[4] It is essential from the outset to emphasise the steady and frankly astonishing evolution in Godard's use of music. Bach, Beethoven and Mozart were all in play in the early shorts, of course, leading to their ironic dissection and counterpointing with contemporary images in the feature films of the 1960s (Bach, Vivaldi and Schubert mixed with Stockhausen in *La Chinoise*, for instance).[5] This was extended by Godard's calculated and parodic over-use of specially commissioned theme music in films like *Le Mépris* (Georges Delerue), *Pierrot le fou* and *Week-end* (both Antoine Duhamel). After his complete refusal to engage with music during the Dziga Vertov period on the grounds that it was bourgeois and elitist, Godard's return to commercial filmmaking in 1980 with *Sauve qui peut (la vie)* marked not simply a return to theme music (Gabriel Yared), which determines here the stop-start rhythm of the image, but the explicit formulation of a question that will haunt his subsequent work: "what is that music?" ("c'est quoi cette musique?") (the film's final section is expressly titled "Musique"). The works that follow are flush with music. In the timeless chords of the classics and

Opposite: **The Prat Quartet rehearsing Beethoven's string quartets in** *Prénom Carmen***, 1983.**

Church music in *Passion* (Ravel, Mozart, Beethoven, Dvořák, Fauré), it has a comforting function, helping to smooth over and render equal the opposed worlds of love and work, bosses and workers. *Prénom Carmen* presents in close-up the rehearsal of Beethoven string quartets, while *Je vous salue, Marie* features a kind of antiphony between Bach and Dvořák.

Coinciding with the first chapters of *Histoire(s)* in the late 1980s, however, a whole new set of composers emerged, from early modernists such as Paul Hindemith, Anton Webern, Béla Bartók, Arthur Honegger, Arnold Schoenberg and Dmitri Shostakovich, to contemporary composers and musicians such as Darling and Ketil Bjørnstad, Arvo Pärt, Heinz Holliger and Giya Kancheli. The same sets of chords, harmonic phrases and melodic tracks of these composers, by turns plaintive, strident, elegiac and menacing, are heard across the different works of the 1990s, giving a powerful sense of identity and coherence to the period. Hindemith, in particular, who is first heard in *Le Rapport Darty*, 1999, and who provides much of the initial steampower for *Histoire(s)*, constitutes a vital connecting link. Significantly, the chosen extracts are played usually from the beginning of a section or movement and are allowed to continue, even if they are temporarily silenced or halted in their progress. Which is to say, Godard's new respect for the integrity of the musical sample means that it now has time to install itself on the ear and register its own direction. This is particularly noticeable in *Histoire(s)* where, although Hindemith may be fragmented or Bach's *Prelude and Fugue in C major* interrupted three times in succession (to take just two examples), still the music manages to impose itself and often all the more clearly, resulting in sustained passages of music. In *Allemagne année 90 neuf zéro*, 1991, which is structured as a series of variations, composers like Bach and Webern not only prevail over a rapidly changing image-track but are also thematised in different ways. Gavin Bryars's doleful *After the Requiem* establishes early on the tone of the film which is both an elegy for the vanished ghosts of German culture and a celebration of German music that has been tainted by the War and the legacy of guilt created by Hitler.[6] To make a further small but crucial point, with the exception of the rehearsals by Les Rita Mitsouko in *Soigne ta droite*, 1987, this varied music is almost exclusively prerecorded and thus operates on a highly different level from that of *Sauve qui peut* and *Prénom Carmen*, say, where live music takes centre-stage in the image and as such can prove fatal.[7] (In the former, an orchestra plays Yared's theme music live on the side of the street following Paul Godard's car accident; in the latter, the string quartet arrives in time to accompany the death of Carmen at the hands of the police.) In short, music becomes in Godard's later work an index of continuity and perdurability.

Again, in view of such major shifts in experimentation whereby music assumes an increasingly concrete and plastic role in his work, why should Godard fall so silent on his use of music, making it almost an untouchable object? He is clearly not just being coy or strategic. Music *is* a mystery for him, and part of its unique power is that he feels unable to define or decipher it. It is ineffable; it simply *is*. Here is how Godard best attempts to describe it:

Music expresses the spiritual, and it provides inspiration. When I'm blind music is my little Antigone; it helps to see the unbelievable. And what has always interested me is the fact that musicians have no need for the image although people involved with images need music. I've always wanted to be able to pan or track during a war scene or love scene, in order to see the orchestra at the same time. And for music to take over at the moment when there is no more need to see the image. For music to express something else. What interests me is to see music–to try to see what one is hearing and to hear what one is seeing.[8]

The final chiastic twist of this passage is a familiar rhetorical move by Godard, of course, and it lies behind the aesthetic conceit elaborated in *Passion*, 1982,

Above: *Masculin Féminin*, 1966.

of "seeing" Fauré and "hearing" Rembrandt. The specifically Romantic implications of Godard's approach, which promotes music as primarily a state of feeling, have already been well noted by Jacques Aumont who runs with the idea of Antigone and accounts for Godard's obsessiveness with regard to music in terms of the maternal, since this involves immersion in an infinitely retold melody. According to Aumont, Godard is interested principally in the "idea" of music, or rather in the idea that he can make of the musical idea, and specifically in the "surging forth" (*"surgissement"*) of that idea. With each instance of music, Aumont writes, Godard is looking for an idea or feeling in its raw state and power.[9]

It would be tempting to pursue further the psychoanalytic implications of Godard's relationship with music, especially since he acknowledges that he came to music via his mother's interest in Schumann. It could certainly be argued, for example, that music represents another aspect of Godard's "heterosexual fix", since whatever period of classical music he chooses to engage with, it is most usually with instrumental and symphonic forms, occasionally choral, but very rarely the operatic which harbours gender instability and perversion. One thinks of the grotesque sequence at the very start of *Sauve qui peut (la vie)* where the male operatic voice-off segues into a scene of gay male paranoia, with Godard's alter ego Paul physically rebuffing a hotel concierge who pursues him into the hotel car-park with confused memories of the night before. Compare this counter-reaction with Jean-Pierre Léaud's shock and horror in *Masculin Féminin*, 1966, at glimpsing two men kiss in a toilet. Contrast it, too, with the scene of male narcissism and self-absorption in *Armide*, 1987, which generates joint fantasies of revenge in the women who have been ignored. The twin features here of male indifference and uncontrolled sound (the sequence of Lully's opera entitled "Enfin il est en ma puissance" is played almost uninterrupted in its entirety) recall, in turn,

the earlier video short *Changer d'image*, 1982, where Godard filmed himself being physically beaten by another man while classical music (possibly Beethoven but it remains deliberately indiscriminate) played on heartlessly in the background. The contemporaneous video short, *Lettre à Freddy Buache*, 1982, offers a counter-example: Godard films himself close to the turntable while listening attentively to the whole sweep of Ravel's *Boléro*, as if unwilling to relinquish any authorial control and thereby expose himself to unforeseen emotional or sexual danger.

Such a fixed thematic approach would, however, reduce Godard's rich and varied engagement with music to a single fantasy complex and suggest merely an ongoing Oedipus-like struggle with the classical Grand Masters. Indeed, according to this reading, Godard would still be stuck in the groove of Éric Rohmer's *Le Signe du lion*, 1958, where in a cameo-role he played a party-goer listening again and again to the same opening bars of the slow movement of Beethoven's *Ninth String Quartet*. To return to the passage cited above, it would also entirely overlook how Godard positions music as something both already "there" and "other", at the limits of his artistic practice. Music inspires him to create and beckons even when the visual image proves redundant. A concerted wish by Godard to negotiate and channel this apparently inexhaustible source of artistic desire might perhaps help to explain his increasingly involved investment in music over the last 20 years. Yet this is still to remain on the level of authorial motivation. Can one talk of a particular musical "idea" or theory in Godard?

Rather than attempt to answer this question by offering an exhaustive account of all the various kinds of music employed by Godard (including *chanson*, American popular song and free-form jazz), I shall limit myself to studying the evolution of Godard's engagement with the classical tradition. I will take two emblematic works of the last twenty years, *Je vous salue, Marie*, 1985, and *Nouvelle Vague*, 1990, and examine in detail a key musical turning-point in each film, which I shall then also relate to other films of the same period. I will argue that far from being a reassuring hook in his work (a way, for example, for the viewer to endure heavy subject matter and intensive montage), still less a supplementary tool of innate expression, Godard's use of predominantly tonal and melodic music goes to the very heart of his artistic and intellectual project, precisely because it allows him to move beyond the usual chiastic boundaries of his thinking.[10] Further, music–and Hindemith will be an exemplary case–comes to constitute what I shall be calling "the cinematic event", for it functions directly as the very index of cinema in its ideal Godardian form, marking the space where the cinematic as conceived by Godard in its specific relation both to human love and history–the two progressively central themes of the later corpus–is most able to reveal itself. I will conclude my discussion with a formal analysis of *Éloge de l'amour*, 2001, which marks the logical culmination of Godard's experimentation with music and its integral link to the primary processes of love and memory operating in his work.

2. Hail Mary, music of love

The first 15 minutes of *Je vous salue, Marie* offers a virtual medley of Bach's greatest hits, with extracts taken from a variety of forms both sacred and secular (Church music, piano, organ) (Godard has talked of the film being a kind of documentary on Bach's music).[11] In particular, the *Toccata in D Minor* and *Prelude and Fugue in C Major* burst forth repeatedly, even if temporarily thwarted by silence, and *Jesu, Joy of Man's Desiring* greets the birth of Jesus. Bach will eventually be joined by Dvořák, specifically the first and second movements ("Allegro" and "Adagio ma non troppo") of

Above: **Godard listening to Ravel in *Lettre à Freddy Buache*, 1982.**

Opposite: ***Armide*, 1987.**

Dvořák's highly romantic and stormy *Cello Concerto in B minor (op. 104)*, 1895. The solo cello of this concerto first arrives in the film when Gabriel and the child angel discover Mary's face and perform the Annunciation, and it will also figure extensively in the film's middle section. Like the Bach segments, Dvořák is taken *in medias res*, and together these two composers form a kind of cosmic pull in the film that matches the extraordinary sky/solar/moon-scapes without ever simply illustrating them (as was arguably the case with the self-consciously sublime set-piece sequences in *Passion* featuring, for instance, the "Agnus Dei" of Fauré's *Requiem*). Godard exploits the full dramatics of sound by fading the music in and out and by increasing or decreasing the volume of both the minor and major keys in an array of mounting crescendos and delicate diminuendos. The music is persistently barred from developing until the end of the film, when Bach's melodic phrase–the final "reconciliation" chorus of the *St Matthew Passion*–provides the climax. It is thus maintained in a state of perpetual annunciation and surprise, impelling Eva to declare: "It's a wonder that any phrase arrives. There could be nothing." As Godard himself puts it, the film is not about climaxes but rather "signs in the beginning. Signs in the sense of signals, the beginning of signs, when signs are beginning to grow. Before they have signification or meaning. Immaculate signs in a way."[12]

Through music a timeless zone of possibility and transition is produced in the film, and the action remains always *en ce temps-là*. Marie herself will make contact with this external continuum, if only fleetingly, during her agonising spiritual confrontation with God and when her body encounters her soul. As for Godard, he, too, is in search of a cinematic *kairos*, or what we might call more mechanically in view of Mary's job at the petrol station its necessary "biting point". This occurs in Marie's room just after she has instructed Joseph in the meaning of love. Instead of wishing to possess Marie as before, Joseph removes his hand from her abdomen, exclaiming "that's it, I love you" ("c'est ça, je t'aime"). By repeating the gesture, he comes to understand that love is also a question of letting go and welcoming the otherness of the Other. The film then records a new and unheralded type of event: the sudden and dramatic intercutting of Bach with Dvořák. We proceed from a shot of Marie's behind (Dvořák) to a shot of the sky, then forwards horizontally by means of a brief mini-zoom into the sky (Bach), before moving gently into an exploration of the clouds and further shots of nature (Dvořák). The frisson generated by this inter-musical sequence, a formal embrace (Dvořák/Bach/Dvořák) where the aural edit is always just slightly ahead of the visual, is registered directly by the forward thrust of the zoom.

How should we read this horizontal, musical movement forwards, which is evidently more than a simple counterpointing of the Baroque and Romantic? Godard talks in an interview with Katherine Dieckmann of privileging the horizontal when it comes to sound:

I try to work not with an idea of vertical sound, where there are many tracks distinct from one another, but horizontally, where there are many, many sounds but still it's as though every sound is becoming one general speech, whether it's music, dialogue or nature sound. *Je vous salue, Marie* had more of a documentary use of sound than other films I've done. It's simple in a way: there's dialogue, direct sounds, and music.[13]

This account of the horizontal leaves out, however, the play of the image. Another point Godard makes in the same interview, specifically about Bach, is more pertinent. After asserting that Bach was the music of Martin Luther who attacked the way the Catholic Church makes images, he states the following:

Bach's music can be matched to any situation. It's perfect. When you play it *in reverse*, it sounds almost same. It's very mathematical. You could play it in the elevator, like Muzak. It blends itself. Bach is the perfect musician for the elevator.[14] (my emphasis)

This ever so slightly scandalous notion of background classical music is confirmation that Bach constitutes the musical ground of *Je vous salue, Marie*. It also reveals that at this stage of his practice Godard is conceiving of Bach in predominantly reversible terms. By inserting Bach as it were horizontally within Dvořák to record a cinematic event and so reach the vital biting point (which, as we have said, is also the moment of human love and its recognition), the film moves, however, beyond the purely abstract or conceptual–the logic of reversibility–and arrives at something far more direct and immediately affective (leading Marie in a voiceover shortly after the zoom to talk of experiencing the light like a glowing fire).

This type of formal counter-manoeuvre along the horizontal axis is not new in Godard's work, of course. It occurred already very graphically in *Vivre sa vie*, 1962, a film that also showcases the purity of sound (both dialogue and background noise were recorded as direct sound). During the famous pendulum sequence, the camera metronomically crossing the dead space between Nana and Paul suddenly stopped mid-way between them, and the painful, frozen silence that ensued was broken only by a nervous laugh from Nana that immediately drove the camera horizontally back towards her, as if drawn magnetically by the love of Godard for his model and then wife, Anna Karina. But the manoeuvre is perhaps most visible in *Histoire(s)*, where it can be read more specifically as a matching of the vertical and metaphorical by the horizontal and metonymical. As I have argued elsewhere, dense, rhetorically motivated formations of montage (for instance, the superimposition within a single frame of shots of the concentration camps, a stop-started sequence from George Stevens's *A Place in the Sun*, 1951, and a *Noli me tangere* representation by Giotto), are off-set by non-discursive moments of association, confluence, contiguity, conjunction and coincidence, moments that trace the inter-relations of human form at the level of silhouette, shape and figure. These far more basic and spontaneous associations by Godard are material, proximate, local and specific. As such, they offer a pure, inclusive moment of seeing and feeling than the more mental act of cognition and interpretation.[15]

In short, by means of its horizontal cinematic event, music in *Je vous salue, Marie* is shown to partake of the same mystery as human (as opposed to divine) love, and as we have seen, and as Marie (previously a violinist in *Prénom Carmen*) herself acknowledges here, it is "always in advance of us". Furthermore, it retains its virginal and annunciatory force in the film even after the images have begun to fade following the birth of Jesus and have acquired a flat, National Geographic aspect. One could read the film more generally as a personal statement by Godard that music remains a locus of creativity and experimentation even after the visual shock of cinema (the period of the New Wave, for instance) has lost its aura and images have become simply clichés. By comparison, *Détective*, made quickly to finance the completion of *Je vous salue, Marie*, might appear a minor, almost throwaway Godard. Yet *Détective*, as free and generous in its use of Schubert and Honegger as it is restricted within the walls and mirrors of the Hôtel Concorde, lays the essential groundwork for *Je vous salue, Marie*. The film announces itself with Schubert's *Unfinished* even before the first image arrives, and the dense soundtrack of familiar classical bars and passages create real dramatic tension above the corny B-movie plot continues even after the final credits have fallen away. The concluding musical high underscores Ariel's parting words, a repetition of those she uttered at the very beginning: "[…] because love is eternal". As in *Je vous salue, Marie*, the music is already here, already there, unfolding of its own accord in a kind of inexorable *transparaître*, a continuous act of stereophonic love (*Détective* was actually Godard's first experiment with Dolby stereo). The use of Honegger's *Liturgical Symphony* (No. 3), 1945-1946, in particular the pounding, portentous military march of its third part "Dona

Opposite: *Je vous salue, Marie.*

298

nobis pacem", may seem completely unjustified and even inappropriate here, yet precisely for this reason it soars forwards and ever higher above the visual frame.

Détective and Je vous salue, Marie complement each other perfectly in their common project of "trying out" music, and they set the tone for much of Godard's production of the mid-to-late 1980s: works like On s'est tous défilé, 1988, a light, almost incidental parade of assorted music (Mozart, Honegger, Leonard Cohen, Barbara Streisand) that matches the interflashing of fashion images and art, and Puissance de la parole, 1988, a meditation on the vibrations of the cosmos where any musical connection is potentially possible between Ravel, Bach, Beethoven, Cohen and John Cage. In each case, what prevails is the inimitable capacity of music to spring to the fore and operate in the filmic present, rather than merely to vehicle prior meaning. The effect produced is of a creative act in the present tense. Compare such works with King Lear, 1987, a film "shot in the back", riddled with captions such as "fear and loathing", "no thing" and "everything over", and where a "violent silence" haunts the world. Even if William Shakespeare the Fifth is able to gather and even recreate for himself visual signs of the recent dead past (he flashes up images of cinematic icons as well as works by the Great Masters, projects spectral images within a camera obscura, lights sparklers, replays filmed sequences of resurrection from Cocteau's La villa Santo-Sospir, etc.), all the musical sounds employed in the film (Darling/Bach/Honegger/Ravel) are as if frozen and skewed in an indecipherable, base-line slur. "Edgar, it's a pity there is not music", Julie Delpy complains to Leos Carax near the end. Yet if, as Godard states, music is the most powerful of all the arts because it subtends everything, it is also the hardest to retrieve and restore to life once it has all but disappeared.[16]

Above: *Je vous salue, Marie.*

Opposite: **Cover of ECM *Nouvelle Vague* box-set and the list of source material used in the film.**

I	Nouvelle Vague	
00:05	Dino Saluzzi	Winter
02:46	David Darling	Far Away Lights
04:11	Patti Smith	Distant Fingers
05:58	Jean Schwartz	Charta Koa
09:53	David Darling	Solo Cello
13:00	Werner Pirchner	Kammer-Symphonie
15:02	Paolo Conte	Blue Tango
16:15	Meredith Monk	Do You Be
18:16	Werner Pirchner	Sonate vom rauhen Leben
24:04	Werner Pirchner	Do You Know Emperor Joe
29:37	Dino Saluzzi	Transmutation
34:24	Paul Hindemith	Mathis der Maler, *Grablegung*
42:54	Paul Hindemith	Trauermusik
46:03	Paul Hindemith	Mathis der Maler, *Versuchung des heiligen Antonius*
48:39	David Darling	Solo Cello
49:29	David Darling	Clouds

I	Nouvelle Vague	
00:05	Dino Saluzzi	Winter
02:46	David Darling	Far Away Lights
04:11	Patti Smith	Distant Fingers
05:58	Jean Schwartz	Charta Koa
09:53	David Darling	Solo Cello
13:09	Werner Pirchner	Kammer-Symphonie
15:02	Paolo Conte	Blue Tango
16:15	Meredith Monk	Do You Be
18:18	Werner Pirchner	Sonate vom rauhen Leben
24:04	Werner Pirchner	Do You Know Emperor Joe
29:37	Dino Saluzzi	Transmutation
34:24	Paul Hindemith	Mathis der Maler, *Grablegung*
42:54	Paul Hindemith	Trauermusik
46:03	Paul Hindemith	Mathis der Maler, *Versuchung des heiligen Antonius*
48:39	David Darling	Solo Cello
49:29	David Darling	Clouds

3. The tracks of love

Music returns in force three years later in *Nouvelle Vague* which begins with the caption "Lamentatio incipit", proceeds to "Acta est Fabula" and concludes with "Consummatum est". Something has happened during the course of the film, but what exactly? Music no longer seems to be simply annunciatory in the style of *Je vous salue, Marie* or even *Passion*, where the opening tracking of a plane's smoke through the clouds was accompanied by the romantic rush and yearning of Ravel (*Piano Concerto for the left hand*). Still less is it explicitly thematised as in *Je vous salue, Marie*, which told of the Annunciation of the Divine and the Cosmic. In the more fractured historical world of Godard's later work, the emphasis will now be on keeping the fragment of music intact and clear, but to what effect? *Nouvelle Vague* clearly bears the weight of the past, and not simply due to its title referring to the New Wave and Godard's own cinematic history. In its choice of location–the shores of Lake Geneva, Godard's childhood home–we detect the traces of Godard's slightly earlier video short, *Le Dernier mot*, 1988, his first and highly sombre attempt at historical reconstruction. Dedicated to the memory of Valentin Feldman, this film detailed the last moments of the young philosopher shot dead by the Nazis; the music employed was exclusively Bach. In *Nouvelle Vague*, on the other hand, the music encompasses Werner Pirchner, Hindemith, Heinz Holliger, Schoenberg, Dino Saluzzi, Meredith Monk and David Darling. Hindemith predominates, however, with extracts of varying length taken repeatedly from his 1933-1934 symphony *Mathis der Maler*, *Trauermusik* (for Viola and String Orchestra), 1936, and three different viola sonatas. Typically, while almost everything in the film is articulated and rendered discursive in the unremitting barrage of quotes and texts and captions, no mention whatsoever is made of the diverse music employed. The caption "Solo cello and voice", for instance, is not attributed to any composer or composition and simply floats by. For this reason, however, music is protected from the choking nets of discourse and knowledge and remains always an enigmatic and potent force. Moreover, however long they are played, the extracts are usually taken from their beginning and are often immediately repeated. "Entombment", for instance, is repeated six times in succession (not always swift) in the first half of the film. The effect of permanency created is thus all the greater, a fact recognised by the blind critic Claire Bartoli in her quite awestruck appreciation of the sound-track of *Nouvelle Vague*. She writes: "Beyond the realm of words, the music expressed as the inexpressible fluid enchantment returns like a memory, never to abandon us. It is also fragmented, inserting itself into the score of sound. And yet I feel its permanence, in slow waves [...] [the music] lunges forward with the spoken words, charging them with intensity."[17]

The film begins with Saluzzi's "Winter" from *Andina*, 1988, followed by Darling's "Far Away Lights" (from *Journal October: Solo Cello*, 1980), and closes with exactly the same works although in reverse order. This complements the film's other more evident chiastic features: it is divided into two parts, the first where Elena dominates Lennox, the second its reversal, each culminating in a boating accident on Lake Geneva. It hinges, too, on the possible resurrection/reincarnation of Roger Lennox (Alain Delon) in the form of his brother Richard Lennox (Alain Delon). The film's chiastic framing structure is further emphasised in the booklet of the 2-CD set produced in 1997, which offers a musical break-down of each CD on facing pages. In fact, the chiastic status of *Nouvelle Vague* is at once compounded and undermined by an error in this breakdown copyrighted

to Godard and endorsed by the *L'Avant-Scene Cinéma* special issue on *Nouvelle Vague* (nos. 396-397). It is an error that would have us believe that three different pieces of Hindemith are used in the last quarter of each CD. The problem is essentially this: on the second disc, after the use of *Sonate für Bratsche allein* (Opus 25/1), we are supposed to hear an extract from the second movement ("Entombment") of *Mathis der Maler* followed by an extract from *Trauermusik*. This would complement the three-part Hindemith series that occurred near the end of the first disc, which included extracts first from "Entombment", then *Trauermusik*, and finally "The temptation of Saint Anthony", the third movement of *Mathis der Maler*. Such symmetry would appear to exemplify Godard's chiastic compulsion. However, what we hear in the second disc are actually the first and second stages of the first movement ("Langsam") of *Trauermusik* (lasting three mins 41 seconds) separated by a pause of around 25 seconds. In other words, we witness a continuous development (albeit halted) of the same music, rather than a repetition or reversal engineered by Godard through montage. The lure of the chiasmus only affects the reader, therefore, not the listener of Godard's work who is able to appreciate more fully the sealing of difference by the final words of the film (spoken by Elena): "It's the same, it's another."

But more is at stake in Godard's non-chiastic use of Hindemith in *Nouvelle Vague*. *Trauermusik* initially occurred in the first half of the film, where it was repeated three times. What set it in motion was the command by Roger Lennox, "Think about it" ("Pensez-y"). When the piece appears again in longer and yet suspended form in the second half, it is to accompany the most extraordinary shot in the film, and surely one of the most remarkable Godard has ever filmed: the soaring lateral tracking shot above land and water that is triggered by Elena's reaching out to catch Richard Lennox's hand and thus save herself from drowning. The shot begins on a level with the water and shore and then

Above: **The lateral tracking shot that follows Elena's rescue in *Nouvelle Vague*. 1990.**

begins to rise, taking in Lennox as he runs up to join Elena and head back with her through the country estate, shouting to her in echo form, as if he were Eurydice to her Orpheus, "Don't turn round". The camera is still lifting slowly and smoothly high above them through the trees, laterally then frontally, and eventually abandons them on their return to the mansion. This glorious, ever upward and forward tracking shot, enhanced by the play of long shadows and silhouettes formed by the low angle of the sun, explodes the blockage of the film's earlier flat and less ambitious tracking shots. Even when the visual image is replaced by the printed caption "Omnia Vincit Amor", the music continues for another ten or so seconds. The sound-track, however, does not only feature Hindemith. Speaking in Italian, Elena recites in Dante-esque tones a passage that, in its second part, would appear to work against the image:

And then the fear diminished a little, that had lasted the whole night which I spent overwhelmed by so much compassion in the depths [literally "lake"] of my heart. It's like those who with anxious energy, having come out of the sea and reached the shore, *turn back and look at the dangerous water*; so did my soul which, still on the run, did turn back and look at the pass that never let anyone through alive. (my emphasis)

The baton is then passed on to Lennox who in French focuses our attention further on this stunning visual event and its composite of internal differences across nature, time, language and gender:

They had the impression of having already lived all that. And their words seemed to stop short in the traces [*Trauermusik* resumes] of other words from before. They paid no attention to what they were doing, but rather to the difference that meant their current actions were of the present, and that similar actions had been of the past... They felt tall, immobile, with the past and present above them like the identical waves of the same one ocean.

Nothing, of course, indicated that *Trauermusik*, a piece originally written for a specific historical occasion (the sudden death of George V on 20 January 1936), could inspire or sustain an elongated tracking shot of such magisterial force and elevation, one that swells time and space simultaneously and brings Elena and Lennox (Richard or Roger? both?) together with nature. The far more dramatic music employed a little earlier for suspense, Hindemith's *Sonate für Bratsche allein*, or even the nervous uncoiling and pounce of "The temptation of Saint Anthony" used for the earlier drowning scene in the film, might perhaps have been more appropriate. Yet in this series of inspired inversions by Godard, the gentle, measured sweep of viola and strings (temporarily suspended) proves exactly the right music for the slowly ascending and always evolving tracking. Pitching it a little higher, it is as though in this supremely musical moment, *Nouvelle Vague* had transcended time and being itself. Herein lies the crucial difference between Godard's use of music in *Nouvelle Vague* and *Je vous salue, Marie*. If, in the earlier film, music (Bach/ Dvořák) still operated romantically as a mode of the celestial sublime and lasted only for as long as it took to achieve the film's biting point, in *Nouvelle Vague* the sublime musical moment projects itself ever forward in time to the beat of Hindemith who eventually surpasses the visual image.

Such a proactive combination of music and tracking shot is found in other works by Godard of the 1990s. In *Allemagne*, specifically its fifth Variation, the first part of the second movement ("Allegretto") of Beethoven's *Seventh Symphony in A major*, 1813, takes us into the film's first major tracking shot, a brisk and brief lateral tracking from right to left past Lake Wansee as Lemmy Caution exclaims: "O beloved land, where are you?". The music is immediately replayed twice, the second instance transporting us over the boundary into the film's sixth variation ("The decline of the West"). This solemn, processional music is Beethoven at his (comparatively) more muted, taken at the very start of the movement before it reaches its inevitable crescendo. It is kept therefore at the stage of desire, eschewing completely the original resolution of the movement which imagined two lovers who must separate for a few moments in order to enjoy a greater bond (this could be read on one level as a highly ambivalent comment by Godard on German reunification). In *JLG/JLG: autoportrait de décembre*, 1995, the first camera movement of the film is instigated by the first movement of Hindemith's *Trauermusik*: a slow forward tracking through the house, then laterally past the video monitor showing a black and white film, before finally resting in front of the table where another video-camera lies. A little later, we ride a repeat of this tracking shot, now a lateral tracking inside past the bookshelves accompanied by the same Beethoven used in *Allemagne* (the tracking shot is then immediately reversed and matched with Darling in a contrapuntal musical form).

The key problem with *Hélas pour moi*, 1993, of course, a film acknowledged by Godard himself to be "inside out" because it proved an inversion of his original intentions (it ended up recording the presence rather than absence of God), is that it never achieves ignition, still less an adequate biting point, by means of a musical tracking. Indeed, as the film's key themes become ever more explicit and prosaic (e.g. Simon #2/God/Depardieu: "events are what happens and has a meaning"; Klimt: "the music is raising us all to this spot of light"), so the music is consigned to the background to join the phantom matter preached by Klimt (Godard, we know, introduced this inspector figure only as a last-ditch effort to salvage the film). Hence, the first tracking shot right to left that takes in a boat on the lake is accompanied by a short piece by Darling which began in the previous shot. The musical effect is dispersed and even mute, like the film's odd mixings of indeterminate music that achieve no real dramatic effect. Which is to say, the film's relentless concern with the events of the past (including even a double flash-back) is blurred and confused, like the repeated use of out-of-focus. No definitive or enduring sense of futurity through music is possible here. The result is a film that performs only negatively: something like *Je vous salue, Marie* (the varied use of Bach, the talk of body, love and the soul), something like *Nouvelle Vague* (the theme of return, the shores of Lake Geneva), yet neither.

4. The cinematic event

What "happens" in *Nouvelle Vague* and the other achieved films of Godard's later period like *Allemagne* and *JLG/JLG* is, of course, essentially an act of montage. Montage, as these works keep reminding us, brings together for the first time elements not predisposed to being linked, and if this involves normally opposed composers (Bach/Dvořák) it can also be as simple and as profound as matching the music of mourning (Hindemith) with the lightest of forward tracking shots. To invoke the repeated message of *Histoire(s)*: "What is great is not the image but the emotion which it provokes... The emotion thus provoked is true because it is born outside all imitation, all evocation, and all resemblance." This process of cinematic juxtaposition and substitution has always carried a distinctly musical charge for Godard, and it is already there in the Bazinian phrase cited with such graphic gusto in *Le Mépris*: "The cinema substitutes for our gaze a world in harmony [*qui s'accorde*] with our desires." But what *Nouvelle Vague* further demonstrates is that music can also generate formally of itself the originality and emotion of montage. As we have seen, the same piece of music may sound the same, yet each instance of its playing is different and unique. Moreover, unlike a textual quote, it cannot be replaced by, or substituted for, anything else. It is, as it were, irreducible, untranslatable and non-deconstructable, acquiring with each repeated play an even greater self-sufficiency and permanency. The fact that Godard chooses predominantly symphonic, orchestral or solo instrumental music means not just that the music safeguards its "natural" *élan* but that this process is never diverted or derailed by the tricks of discourse. That again would be to risk conventional textual citation and with it Godard's standard reflex of rhetorical reversibility. Just one musical note can be compellingly present, even momentous. As Marc Swed writes so movingly of *Histoire(s)*: "Listening, we linger, hang on to, fall in love with (whether for the first time or anew) every note [...] music that is so familiar and that we thought we 'knew', he [Godard] makes us feel for the first time."[18]

By taking a movement of music not at its climax but at its very beginning, and sometimes just the opening snippets or the prelude before the theme or leitmotif succumbs to variation, Godard maintains music invariably in its proleptic and revelatory mode, in a continual state of becoming. Which is to say, it will never run the risk of staleness or complication because it remains forever "open", like an eternal hope or promise. It thus incarnates the spirit of Mozart, and this even in the film *For Ever Mozart* where Mozart actually features very little. A classic Mozart flourish at the start of the film is cut up and rendered staccato before transmuting into the music of Darling and Bjørnstad, as if Godard were denying Mozart exclusive composer status precisely to capture the film's Mozartian essence. This is the case even when Godard is referring to twentieth century composers who were inextricably linked to the periods in which they were working (the rising tide of European fascism, The Second World War, the Cold War, etc.), and whose music was clearly affected by their own personal fates (one thinks in particular of Hindemith, Bartók, Webern and Shostakovich).[19] Indeed, however historically laden, sad and melancholic, music in late Godard always records a free and positive act of creation. By contrast, the image, as *Je vous salue, Marie* demonstrated so clearly, is ultimately no longer recuperable, and Godard knows this however hard he tries in *Histoire(s)* and elsewhere to reinscribe its original documentary qualities.

The notion of music as a creative "event" has always been present in Godard, of course. To return to *Week-end,* Gégauff's piano recital is presented explicitly as a "happening", an "ACTION MUSICALE". Yet in Godard's later work, the primacy, permanency and projection of music may actually be said to constitute *the* cinematic event, since it offers perhaps the only means now to register a cinematic absolute of the kind claimed in *Histoire(s)*, i.e. cinema's original capacity to "look at the world looking at it", and its unique ability to forecast and anticipate historical events (Renoir's *La Règle du jeu*, 1939, and Chaplin's *The Great Dictator*, 1940, are the favoured examples). Certainly, it has the status now of an ideal, like the Image continually promised during the silent era but never realised, namely the event of "montage". Moreover, it never operates less than as a mystery, which for Godard was cinema's essential function ("neither an art, nor a science, but a mystery"). In addition, emotion and lyricism, which once existed in silent cinema and then disappeared as if people were ashamed of it, are possible now only in the performance of the musical extract or, more rarely, when editing can itself rise to the level of a clear musical passage.[20] That so much of Godard's music of the later period is either sad or angry emphasises that in the very gesture of recovering the essence of cinema through another form (i.e. music), Godard is also mourning cinema's current impossibility. The extreme pathos of this situation finds its natural obverse in the bathos of the screeching birds that punctuate so much of the later work.

Yet if the unstoppable promise and direct summons of music inspires Godard's still burning passion for the cinema, evident in such disarming statements by Godard as "cinema remains for me a cause for hope", it is also because as a cinematic moment music is intimately linked to the call of love which can provide a form of continuity with the past.[21] We have already seen how both *Je vous salue, Marie* and *Nouvelle Vague* showcase the process of love as a recognition of the Other and the free giving of the gift of life.[22] Elena remarks at one point that what is not resolved by love remains forever in suspense, and I would argue that the climactic tracking shot of *Nouvelle Vague* does achieve this desired resolution. Indeed, music acquires such determining value in Godard precisely because it both conveys *and* instantiates the annunciatory and revelatory power of love. Again, it does so beyond all resemblance and imitation. Godard may be equally in awe of painting, but this can generate both creative excitement and nervous rivalry, leading him in *Passion*, for example, to stage the Grand Masters as *tableaux vivants* and then dismantle them. For as long as he is unable to compose or play music, it will never become something to try to copy or imitate. Not unexpectedly, his project in 1988-1990 to make a film entitled *La Neuvième Symphonie* (The Ninth Symphony) was eventually aborted.

I have been employing the term "event" deliberately for its echoes of the "Truth-Event" in the work of Alain Badiou, who uses it to account for that unpredictable moment when something is suddenly imposed on us from the outside by a traumatic encounter that shakes us to the very foundations of our being. This is an event of revelation occurring in a totally different dimension from that of Knowledge and the ontological order. Love as a singular encounter and process is a prime instance of the Truth-Event delineated by Badiou and further expounded by Slavoj Žižek in his recent work.[23] It reinscribes a properly metaphysical dimension, where the infinite Truth is eternal and *meta-* with regard to the temporal process of Being. For Badiou, *the* example of a "Truth-Event" is Christianity: the Event is Christ's incarnation and death, its ultimate God is the Final Redemption, and its subjects are the believers who search for signs of God. Here is how Žižek describes the event of Christian Truth:

The Christian Truth [...] is the one of Revelation [...] Truth is not inherent, it is not the (re)discovery of what is already in myself [the Socratic philosophical principle] but an Event, something violently imposed on me from the Outside through a traumatic encounter that shatters the very foundation of my being.[24]

Mindful that for the later Lacan love is no longer merely the narcissistic screen obfuscating the truth of desire but "the very way to come to terms with the traumatic drive", Žižek also equates the Christian Truth-Event with the psychoanalytic moment of "traversing the fantasy":[25]

[...] psychoanalytic treatment is, at its most fundamental, not the path of remembrance, of the return to the inner repressed truth, its bringing to light; its crucial moment, that of "traversing the future", rather designates the subject's (symbolic) rebirth, his (re-) creation *ex nihilo*, a jump through the "zero-point" of death-drive to the thoroughly new symbolic configuration of his being.[26]

Love, the greatest of the three Pauline principles of faith, hope and love since it marks a New Beginning and offers a way out of the deadlock of Law, its prohibition and its transgression (through desire), is defined by both Badiou and Žižek as fidelity to the Truth-Event.

Taken together, Badiou and Žižek allow us to understand how far Godard has reached in his practice since he expressed his consuming desire for music in the passage cited at the beginning of our discussion. By allowing music to enter freely into his work on its own terms and acquire the status of an original and unstoppable Event, he has traversed the "blind" fantasy whereby

he was Theseus to music's Antigone. The desire for music has now become the love of music which, as we have seen, operates as the very essence of cinema in its ideal form. *Histoire(s)*, we know, presents a Godard who, having been passively and indelibly marked by the Event of Cinema and so, as he put it, having no other home, remains utterly faithful to the unlimited mystery and potential of "the cinematic". "Believe, whatever happens" ("Crois, quoi qu'il arrive"), and "the story, not the person who tells it"), are just some of the recurring formulae of *Histoire(s)*, and they refer also to Godard's early days in the New Wave when "cinema" stood for the films that could not be seen and thus required faith in an invisible image. By personally "embodying" cinema in *Histoire(s)*, Godard performs an act of passionate devotion to the cinematic form. To take only one of the subjective stances towards the Truth-Event proposed by Badiou, that of the Master, we might say that Godard, as inventor of new forms of critical and historical montage, orchestrates formally the Event of Cinema in order to guarantee its continuity. As he explains during one particularly effusive moment: "The cinema is the love, the meeting, the love of ourselves and of life, the love of ourselves on earth, it's a very evangelical matter, and it's not by chance that the white screen is like a canvas… the screen as the linen of Veronica, the shroud that keeps the trace, the love, of the lived, of the world."[27]

The obvious question raised by such statements from Godard is whether his current use of music should be considered to some extent specifically Christian, especially when he can also refer with such case to an "honest and secular Christianity" while explaining the influence of Wittgenstein on the phrase just cited ("Believe, whatever happens").[28] After all, Hindemith and Pärt may be classed as modern Christian composers in the long line established by Mozart and Fauré, and in Pärt's case *Passio* is a defiant expression of the

Above: **Domiziana Giordano and Alain Delon** in *Nouvelle Vague.*

Catholic faith. Similarly, Honegger's *Symphony No.3* draws directly upon the liturgy of the Catholic mass for the dead. And as Jullier has noted, the long and gentle "reverberations" of music in Godard's work can relate symbolically for the enlightened listener to sacred music, even when non-overtly religious composers like Darling and Bjørnstad are being used. (Keith Jarrett is unusual in this respect in that the titles of the two hushed and eerie piano compositions from *Dark Intervals*, 1988, which Godard reprises throughout *Histoire(s)* and other recent works, are actually religious in nature–"Hymn" and "Ritual Prayer"–although significantly they refer to form rather than content.) Yet what we have witnessed is that Godard's artistic conscience is ultimately post-chiastic, and when he turns to Christian narratives and iconography he is operating more in the fluid realm of available aesthetic and cultural metaphor. The Christian legacy for Godard is primarily that of Western art guided by the notion of love as the defining event of human existence, and this absolute general principle also guides Godard's work. It is ultimately not the religious or sacred content of the music that matters to Godard, but rather its fundamental status as tonal music and its natural extension and projective qualities. The force of Godard's repeated Pauline message in *Histoire(s)* and elsewhere, that "the image will come at the time of the resurrection", lies solely in its *mode* of articulation in the musical tense of Godardian montage rather than in any strictly literal sense–Christian or otherwise–of the term "image" it may denote.

In the particular case of Hindemith, it is highly significant that Godard employs the original symphony *Mathis der Maler* rather than the subsequent opera. Which is to say, he uses the third movement of the symphony rather than the sixth scene of the opera, "The temptation of Saint Anthony", of which it forms the basis. There, following the vision in which Mathis sees himself as a latter-day St Anthony holding out against the temptations of wealth and power and of the heroism of war and sensual delight, St Paul the Apostle utters to the lost artist the redeeming and admonitory words: "Go forth and create." Certainly, Godard cannot escape the influence of the later opera which determines how one reads the symphony, but the urgent summons of its artistic message is conveyed formally in Godard's work through the performance and advance of the music, in the insistent, driving repetition of the opening passage of the symphony's third movement. For this experience alone Hindemith comes to function for Godard as a kind of perpetual Reveille, a call to artistic arms.

In the case of another contemporary composer, Giya Kancheli, a Georgian in exile from his native Tiflis and composer of major works such as *Trauerfarbenes Land* ("Land that Wears Mourning"), Godard refers throughout *Histoire(s)* (especially 2A and 3B) and *JLG/JLG* to the dramatic opening of *Vom Winde beweint*, 1992, a "liturgy" for solo viola and orchestra. This one shockingly loud and raw minor chord from the piano is held for a long minute, releasing into the air sound waves that are allowed to die away in their own time. Writing of another very similar piece by Kancheli entitled *Lament*, a work composed in 1994 for violin, soprano and orchestra, and where fragments disappear even before they fully appear and pass immediately into a *fortissimo* explosion, a violent cataclysmic *tutti*, Žižek remarks on the eruption of the Real in all its brutality and evil: "The subject takes the risk of putting himself forward; the Other strikes back with all ferocity."[29] In the particular way that *Vom Winde beweint* springs forth seemingly of its own accord in Godard's work, sometimes in silence, sometimes over other music, at times in quick succession, and always powerful enough to provoke a cut in the image, it is the pure and indefinable emotion created by the musical event that matters, and the fact that this nameless, almost unholy sound without apparent object continues to expand and consolidate itself through space and time.

Opposite: **Bruno Putzulu** in *Éloge de l'amour*, **2001.**

5. In praise of music

If all Godard's successful films are thus really to be conceived of formally as love melodies–for the cinema, art, the viewing public–only one, of course, explicitly bears that message in its title, *Éloge de l'amour*. Again, while there is endless discussion in the film of cinema (documentary film/Spielberg), art and painting, writing and philosophy (Georges Bataille, Simone Weil, etc.), music passes by almost unnoticed. What is new in Godard's work, however, is the degree to which the musical element has become distilled, for while there is some variation (the odd extract from Pärt and another ECM composer of largely string music, Karl Amadeus Hartmann, as well as occasional references to French film composers such as Georges Van Parys and Maurice Jaubert), one gentle, sparse and elegiac 25 second segment by Darling and Bjørnstad predominates. The tune is heard in truncated form at the very beginning of the film and then reproduced close to 20 times in different forms, tones and volumes, sometimes interrupted or suspended, but always there and always reappearing as if new.

Darling and Bjørnstad are able to "carry" *Éloge*, indeed to provide its very rhythm and backbone, because by this stage within the Godard corpus they have acquired their own history and significance. They seem to anticipate the flow of images and by themselves operate the cinematic event as we have defined it: a sustained chord of promise and futurity. If *Éloge* appears to some critics even to be composed formally like music (for Marie-Anne Guerin it is a "hymn" to the image, while for Amy Taubin it has the beating of a late Beethoven string quartet since the shards of images and black spacing, along with speech and music, are treated almost as individual notes and can coalesce into something akin to melodic phrases or harmonic textures), this is surely because of the continuous flow of the apparently slight but unstoppable bars of Darling and Bjørnstad.[30] The sudden spectacular switch one hour into the film from black and white 35mm to colour digital video is actually of secondary aesthetic importance, as is the obvious fact of the film's reversible structure whereby it comes around full circle, the ending meeting the beginning in the middle.[31] Likewise, the repeated chiastic use of the captions "De l'amour" and "de quelque chose" advance the film no further than other repeated captions such as "Deux ans avant" and "Archives" in the film's second part. Indeed, the film's structure functions far more humbly as a tool of character contrast between the young misguided filmmaker Edgar (Bruno Putzulu), attempting in vain to compose a cantata-cum-opera about Weil, and his more focused creator (Godard) who trusts, as always, only to instrumental or symphonic music in order to perform his cinematic act.

This is not at all to downplay the historical element of *Éloge* which features the story of two former Resistance fighters and is visually drenched in moody night time shots of Paris that radiate echoes of the Second World War (including even close-up shots of commemorative plaques), the New Wave and the French cinematic tradition in general (Vigo, Renoir, etc.). On the contrary, the use of music enacts history at both a concrete and metaphorical level, for the playing and replaying of the same few critical bars creates duration (the horizontal axis) and generates of itself the processes of memory (the vertical axis). Always moving forwards in linear fashion, music is the past recasting itself poetically into the future. As such, it manages to escape the fatal nexus of money, cinema (Hollywood) and history for sale that results in the film in the very betrayal of memory. In short, music in Godard is history, its mourning, *and* its transcendence.[32] The very title of Schoenberg's 1917 string sextet, *Transfigured Night*, much used in both *Nouvelle Vague* and *Histoire(s)*, signals this effect. Far more even than painting, music continually exemplifies the resurrectional status of art as defined by André Malraux and endorsed by Godard in *Histoire(s)*: "art is what is reborn in what has been burnt." It thus offers an aesthetic model for Godard, not only because it enables him to step down from the cross of his chiastic thinking, but also because it imprints itself within a larger, more intersubjective and inclusive process, that of memory. Like universal "sovereign" love, as *Éloge* now defines it following Georges Bataille, this relies on the recognition and respect of difference within the totality of the whole, of the kind that exists, for example, between the past and the present and between the loved one as object and the lover as subject, however much these instances overlap and can sometimes fuse.[33]

Éloge thus marks the most advanced sublimation yet of Godard's artistic desire for music. Moreover, it suggests that the love of/for music may not only offer a highly valuable means of creative thinking, but also constitute a potentially powerful ethical foundation. It will be interesting to see how Godard develops this exciting possibility. Certainly, when articulated verbally by Godard himself in works like *JLG/JLG*, the idea of love can become self-absorbed and inflated ("I said that I loved/there's the promise/right now/I must sacrifice myself/in order that through me/the word of love/ has a meaning/in order that there is love/on earth..."). In *Éloge*, too, it can become caught up chiastically as soon as Godard attempts to translate it into discourse (for example, with the phrase "La mesure de l'amour, c'est aimer sans mesure"). However, in the inimitable performance of music, which always arouses us as if for the first time, Godardian love and cinema finds its most original, consistent and open expression.

"SA VOIX"

The memory of a yellow rose seen at sunset.[1]

ROLAND-FRANÇOIS LACK

The aim of this essay is to describe the range of uses to which voice, mostly Godard's own, is put in his work, with emphasis placed on *Histoire(s) du cinéma*, 1998, as the culmination of certain trajectories.[2] By listening to the speaking subject in *Histoire(s)* and in ten or so other films by Godard, I will suggest a strategic reversal of the priority commonly accorded the image over sound. The argument that subtends this description is that sound is the primary level of signification in *Histoire(s)* and often in those other works too. Indeed, Godard is one of only a handful of filmmakers whose work would survive the end of images.[3]

Many readers of Godard's cinema, or of cinema in general, might prioritise the image as the place where things first are. We say *voice-off*, and are literal; to say *voice-on* to describe a voice produced from within the image is metaphorical. The voice is never *on*, just as the image is never *off*. But by that token, the ever-present image cannot signify presence. Throughout *Histoire(s)* the voice, through the image, by using the image, plays with the possibility of presence. It begins by being absent, as voice off, and present through synchronisation. At the end the voice is off, and still present: the closing images, a painting and a photograph, are at best the past metamorphosed–thanks to the fraternity of metaphors–into the present.

To speak of the voice's presence is also, of course, metaphorical. It is a device for imagining the unity of the speaking subject, a convenience for the purposes of this essay, whereas *Histoire(s)* demonstrates that "cet homme" (Godard) is, like his work, heteroglossic, polymorphic, multilingual, "irrepressibly multiplicitous" (to paraphrase Raymond Bellour). But these epithets apply also to voice, of course, and the object of this essay should be, more modestly, to make of this multiplicitous signifier a more singular presence.

"Sa voix", then, and not "son image". Not, certainly, his image in a photograph, the object of scrutiny in that other self-portrait of the period, *JLG/JLG: autoportrait de décembre*, 1995. Six photographic portraits of Godard are shown in *Histoire(s)*, plus two film stills of him and the photocopied photograph that in *JLG/JLG* is his portrait as a child.[4] These photographs, unlike the many moving images of Godard in *Histoire(s)*, cannot be made to speak, cannot be voice's instrument. Their muteness is at best a "voix du silence" but, unlike that of those subjects portrayed by Leonardo, Vermeer, Corot or Manet and displayed in Chapter 3A, *La monnaie de l'absolu*, unlike that of the child's photograph shown in *JLG/JLG*, it is left un-interrogated in *Histoire(s)* until perhaps at the very end.

"Sa voix", and not another's. The other voices heard relate only by association to the subject of this essay, though the association can be very strong. A montage of images and text in Chapter 1A, *Toutes les histoires*, brings together four filmmakers called "Jean" (Renoir, Vigo, Cocteau, Epstein), all admired by "Jeannot" (as Godard is called in *JLG/JLG* and in life). An associated voice, an actor's, speaks for these predecessors and, above all, for Godard, the actor of *Histoire(s)*: "Je suis l'erreur qui vit. Je suis Jean qui a toujours joué Le Vivant malgré lui."[5]

His voice, and not his silence. The word as image, printed on screen, lacks intonation, timbre, expression: everything that, in the voice, is also body. A text by Léon Bloy shown on screen in 3B and then spoken in 4B makes the point. The same point is made in the contrast between Charles Ferdinand Ramuz's expressive delivery in 1B, *Une histoire seule*, of his story "L'amour de la fille et du garçon" and the screen-text in 4B, *Les signes parmi nous*, that tells the story of another text by Ramuz (the novel *Les signes parmi nous*).[6] The gap between voice and text is all the more evident from the effort made, in this

Above: *Le Gai savoir*, 1968.

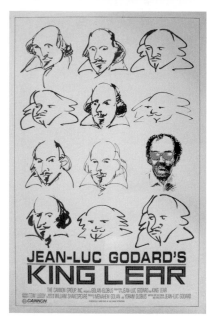

Above: **Self-portraiture in** *Prénom Carmen*, **1983,** *Numéro Deux*, **1975, and** *King Lear*, **1987.**

Opposite: **Peter Kassovitz in** *Vivre sa vie*, **1962; cover of the** *Avant-Scène Cinéma* **scenerio; source book for the film.**

screen-text version of a novel, to invest the words with vocal characteristics. Repetitions of phrase ("et dure des jours et des jours" x 3; "que c'est la fin du monde" x 4) suggest the hesitancy of Godard's vocal delivery, or the technical effects of delay (echo and reverb); vocal emphasis is represented by increases in point size of the last phrase:

CE COLPORTEUR C'ÉTAIT LE CINÉMA

C'ÉTAIT LE CINÉMA / C'ÉTAIT LE CINÉMA
C'ÉTAIT

C'ÉTAIT / C'ÉTAIT / C'ÉTAIT [7]

Text on screen is the degree zero of disembodied voice. Godard's vocal performances in *Histoire(s)* are situated at many different points along the scale from zero to complete identity of voice and body, though that point of plenitude is never, in fact, attained. Throughout Godard's work body and voice are signifiers apart, even when brought together forcibly, as in *Prénom Carmen*, 1983, of which he says that "je tenais à faire travailler mon corps et ma voix", and in several self-portraits painted before and after: *JLG/JLG*, of course, but also *Numéro Deux*, 1975, *Jean-Luc* from *Six fois deux*, 1976, *Soigne ta droite*, 1987, and *King Lear*, 1987.[8] At times that body and voice work together in *Histoire(s)*, though the harder worker overall is certainly the voice. In the recent *Éloge de l'amour*, 2001, as if exhausted, it falls silent; the body remains, a solitary figure on a Paris bench (reading) while conversation goes on around it, in the image and off.

Despite their occasional *rapprochements*, Godard's body and voice did not seem predisposed to be conjoined in his work.[9] The body can occasionally be glimpsed among the first films (in *À bout de souffle*, *Le Petit soldat*, *Le Mépris*); more often the voice works alone (in *Vivre sa vie*, *Bande à part*, *Deux ou trois choses que je sais d'elle* and *Made in USA*). In *Le Gai savoir*, 1968, a model for the practice of *Histoire(s)*, the voice is everywhere, but the image of the body is present only as a photograph of Godard (reading). A "zéro" is written over the body's only image ("juste une image"). Not until *Vladimir et Rosa*, 1971, do image and sound collaborate in a performance, and it is symptomatic that they do so heavily disguised, the body in police uniform, the voice in the exaggerated accents of Godard's homeland, the Swiss canton of Vaud.[10]

Voice is not the only medium for the self-portrait composed over the eight chapters of *Histoire(s)*. As well as the photographs of himself, taken by others, Godard uses stills and extracts from his own films (including images of himself from *Le Mépris*, *Caméra-oeil*, *Prénom Carmen*, *Soigne ta droite*, *King Lear*, *JLG/JLG*), cites his earlier writings ("Montage mon beau souci", "Pierrot mon ami"), has Serge Daney talk about him and, of course, films himself. These are discussed in passing, but this essay attends above all to voices, to one voice above all, the last to speak, the one that reflectively declares at the close: "j'étais cet homme".[11]

I choose to privilege voice here for three reasons. The first is that, on several occasions over more than 45 years of filmmaking, Godard's voice has been used to play novel and sometimes subtle variations on the old trope of cinematic self-reflexivity whereby the director's material presence in a film disrupts narrative illusionism. (Hitchcock is an obvious precedent, though largely in the visual field.) These vocal variations feature in this essay in their own right and as anticipations of Godard's practice in *Histoire(s)*.[12] The second reason is that, in those four last words that end *Histoire(s)*, voice seems to be presented, paradoxically, as the ultimate self-signifier. The paradox is that overall Godard's voice in his films has been a

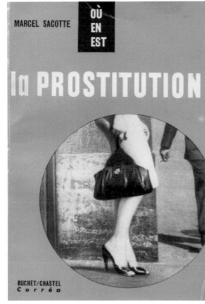

sign of absence from the image, of what is missing from the thing filmed, of the necessary supplement that montage must supply. The third reason is personal: the first thing I knew well of *Histoire(s)* was the set of CDs produced in 1999 by ECM. For almost two years all I attended to was this beautifully mixed montage of voices and music: when the image arrived, it was secondary, an illustration of or supplement to the primary object, sound. Though elsewhere I have sought to overcome this prejudice, I have allowed it to serve as a premise for the present essay.

This essay is primarily descriptive, and only theoretical in its implications.[13] The last section is a close reading of the sounds and images montaged in the last two minutes of *Histoire(s)*, read through an idea of identification. The preceding sections consider the work to which Godard's voice is put under four related headings: recitation, ventriloquism, diction and apparatus.

1. "Que dire alors?"–recitation

"Is this book yours?", asks Nana. "No, I found it here" replies a voice (Godard's). The question asked in *Vivre sa vie*, 1962, can be asked again every time text is heard or seen in a film by Godard. In *Vivre sa vie* it interrupts a recitation by Godard of Poe's "The Oval Portrait", and if his answer in 1962 declines to appropriate Poe's story, later the voice is inclined to keep what it has found: "all these histoires that now are mine" (*Histoire(s)* 2B). This may be a function of the place or mode of attribution. For the citation in *Vivre sa vie* the source–book title, author and translator–is shown on screen; for texts spoken by Godard in *Histoire(s)* the sources (author/name only) are rarely given on screen (Hugo's speech at the beginning of 3A is one exception), most are found only in an appendix to the Gallimard books, with minimal aids to the matching of source and citation. *Les signes parmi nous* (4B) moves from one mode to the other, beginning with unattributed passages from Bloy, Foucault, Laforgue and Aragon, to end with titles on screen identifying the texts spoken (Bernard Lamarche-Vadel, Hollis Frampton, Arthur Rimbaud, Georges Bataille, Maurice Blanchot, Emily Dickinson, Jorge Luis Borges).

The appropriation of the other's text is effected also by editing. *Vivre sa vie* delivers a reduced version of Poe's story, cutting away elements of the frame narrative to keep only details about portraiture, the vehicle of the analogy with the film itself (which has, effectively, become the frame narrative). The opening of *Histoire(s)* modifies the syntax and address of passages from Bresson, whose written texts–"While changing nothing, may all be different"; "Not to show all sides of things. Margin of the undefined"–are spoken as imperatives: "Change nothing so that all can be different"; "Don't go showing all sides of things, keep a margin of the undefined."[14]

As montage, voiced modifications appear more innocent, less interventionist than the re-editing of images from films, because the immediacy of vocal delivery sanctions minor slippages, lapses in memory. Godard's forgetful voice is differentiated here from those of the actors engaged, who are shown either reading their texts with exactitude–Julie Delpy's Baudelaire in Chapter 2A, Juliette Binoche's Brontë in 3A, Alain Cuny's Faure in 4A–or performing a text they have perfectly memorised (see Sabine Azéma's irritatingly complacent performance of Broch in 2B, *Fatale Beauté*).

Actorly exactitude is of course no guarantee of the text's integrity: Baudelaire's "Le voyage" is edited, much as was his translation of Poe, to preserve only those elements of analogy with the framing discourse; only those parts of Brontë's poem that fit the accompanying images are kept; the montage of fragments from different parts of Broch's *The Death of Virgil*

transforms the novel into a prose poem; Faure's description of Rembrandt is, as read by Cuny, transformed by simple substitutive montage into a description of cinema.

When the thing found is a book, the text is easily modified to serve new purposes. Modifying the found image requires more formal, apparatus-based interventions (of which *Histoire(s)* employs a spectacular variety). So should the modification of found voice, a forceful intertextual mode in *Histoire(s)*, though the examples on offer suggest a reluctance on Godard's part to manipulate this material. Where voices in the present (his own or his actors') may modify the past, voices from the past are left intact. Real voices, that is, those of Hitler, Pétain or de Gaulle, of Renoir or Hitchcock, of Ramuz, Freud, Braudel, Malraux, Sartre, Celan or Pound. Their performances may be edited, other sounds may be overlaid, but a higher degree of textual integrity is, necessarily, preserved. Also preserved, necessarily, is the delivery. The hieratic manner of Ramuz, Pound, Celan, above all of Malraux, matches the affect of their texts word for word.[15] Hitchcock's voice (in 4A), speaking in English and spoken over by Godard, is reduced for a moment to a form without content;[16] Freud's delivery (in 1B), also in English and also spoken over by Godard, is almost pure voice without meaning.[17]

The found voice is a dead voice. A reluctance to manipulate is simple respect for the dead, though this self-evidence has implications for the voices in *Histoire(s)* that still live: his own, for example, and Anne-Marie Miéville's. The last dead voice heard in *Histoire(s)* is Ezra Pound's, reciting a passage from the *Cantos* where, precisely, the dead are revived: by drinking sacrificial blood they recover their voices and speak with the living. Recitation of texts in Godard, by Godard or Miéville, is revival of this order. It is, in *Histoire(s)*, an important mode of dialogue with the dead.

Clockwise from top left: **Jean Vigo and Dita Parlo during the making of *L'Atalante*, 1934; Jean Cocteau in *Le Testament d'Orphée*, 1960; Jean-Luc Godard and Jean Renoir at the Théâtre de la Commune d'Aubervilliers in January 1968; Jean Epstein circa 1946.**

2. "ProDuIRE"—ventriloquism[18]

At the end of Chapter 3B, *Une vague nouvelle*, Godard is asked a question to which he answers "oui". The accompanying image is of a young Jean-Pierre Melville (now dead), nodding and saying "oui" in sync with the ventriloquist. The recitation of Poe's "The Oval Portrait" in *Vivre sa vie*, more than 30 years before, is also an act of ventriloquism, the montage of one man's body and another man's voice.[19]

The Poe episode is one among many expressions in Godard of the separation of body and voice. Earlier, in *À bout de souffle*, 1960, his body and voice were both put to work, but separately. His image in that film, famously, is that of the informer who recognises the photograph of Poiccard/Belmondo in the paper and points him out to the police.[20] The first shot of this 70 second sequence shows Godard cross the street and go out of frame, then his voice is heard asking, insistently, for a copy of *France Soir*. We hear him no more, but his image returns to be matched twice with that of Belmondo (both wear dark glasses). It is then shown going back across the street towards two policemen, to finish framed by the iris that closes the sequence: the return of the music precludes any possibility of hearing what he is seen to say.

The image-centred inscription of the self here is rightly remembered, though perhaps at the expense of the more complex uses to which the voice alone is put in *À bout de souffle*. The most striking of these is an elaborately mediated kind of ventriloquism. Michel and Patricia are at the cinema, ostensibly to see Budd Boetticher's *Westbound*, 1958, although nothing of the film is shown on screen. What we see is Belmondo and Seberg, kissing. What we hear is an exchange between "Jessica" and the "Sheriff" (characters from Samuel Fuller's *Forty Guns*). The dialogue is not from that film, however, but composed from fragments of poems by Aragon ("Elsa je t'aime") and Apollinaire ("Cors de chasse"). In this complex of intertextual substitutions the Sheriff's voice is Godard's, commenting on the on-screen kiss as he declaims Aragon's lines: "Be careful, Jessica/At the crossroad of kisses/The years pass too quickly/Flee flee flee/Broken memories" ("Méfie-toi, Jessica,/Au biseau des baisers/Les ans passent trop vite/Évite évite évite/Les souvenirs brisés").[21] A passage from *Histoire(s)* 3A montages the death of Jean Gabin in *Quai des brumes* (a pretext for Belmondo's death in *À bout de souffle*) with the same lines from Aragon, but this time mute, delivered as text on screen (though accompanied by Gabin's dying words, where kisses are solicited, and the "vite" of "évite" is repeated: "Kiss me, kiss me… Quickly [*vite*], there's not much time… quickly…").[22] If this is a (broken) memory of Aragon via the cinema-scene in *À bout de souffle*, it is also a memory of the voice from that scene, now barely audible in the intertext.[23] Nothing of *À bout de souffle* is remembered in *Histoire(s)*, save this trace of the voice.

Le Petit soldat, 1960, picks up and develops some modes of self-inscription from *À bout de souffle*, though again the best remembered is image-centred: at the railway station the matching of star and director is repeated from the 'informer' sequence, as Godard, in dark glasses, appears behind his actor Michel Subor, in dark glasses. The physical mismatch in each of these encounters appears to be ironised by the use, in other parts of *Le Petit soldat*, of a Godard lookalike: briefly when Bruno (Subor), disembarking from the ferry, pushes past a man dressed as Godard at the railway station (and carrying a camera); at greater length in the figure of a man first seen giving Veronica (Karina) a mechanical dog, then seen bringing to Bruno's captors a piece of equipment (known euphemistically as a telephone) for torturing with electric shocks. (Both men are less attractive stand-ins for

Godard who, in the course of shooting *Le Petit soldat*, won over the beautiful Karina and married her the next year.)

Against these peculiar examinations of his own image in *Le Petit soldat* can be read the inscription of the disembodied voice. When Bruno is investigated over an incident involving his car, the ventriloquist speaks for the arresting policeman. Instantly recognisable as not that of the actor on screen, Godard's voice draws attention to the radical separation of sound and image that is so important a factor in the post-synchronisation of *Le Petit soldat*. It also echoes an earlier manifestation, pre-*À bout de souffle*, when Godard dubbed his own voice on to the body of Belmondo in the 1958 short, *Charlotte et son Jules*, apparently because Belmondo was unavailable for the post-synchronisation. The earlier film made a virtue of necessity.[24] *Le Petit soldat* makes of vocal impersonation a feature of Godard's image-based self-reflexivity. Between *Le Petit soldat* and *Vladimir et Rosa*, Godard's physical presence in his films is almost wholly vocal. The interrogative, reflexive style of commentary now familiar in *Histoire(s)* is shaped in three films from the 1960s: *Bande à part*, *Deux ou trois choses que je sais d'elle* and *Le Gai savoir*. Listened to together they display changes of sonority over time, from 1964 to 1968, from deadpan through murmur to whisper, and form a narration-trilogy where the recurring voice (Godard's) attempts to shape our reception of the image, each time differently.

The variations played on the mode of narration or commentary begin with the reading of Poe in the last tableau of *Vivre sa vie*. This appears to be merely embedded narration, delivered by "le jeune homme", a character in the film's fiction. It becomes narration from beyond the fiction because the voice that delivers the story is not that of the actor Peter Kassovitz–*his* voice was heard in an earlier scene–but Godard's, superimposed on the image of the young man. If the trick seems familiar after *Charlotte et son Jules* and *Le Petit soldat*, the difference is the care taken to conceal Kassowitz's mouth beneath the book from which he is supposed to be reading, so that at no point is this a matter of synchronisation.[25] Rather, the anachronicity apparent in those earlier dubbings–and implicit in all post-synchronisation–is made the more explicit in this sequence by the dialogue written for the character of the young man (and delivered by Godard): "It's our story, a painter making the portrait of his wife." The painter here is not the young man (who likes art, but is not a maker of images): it is Godard, making a portrait of Karina. Not only has the matter of Poe's story been appropriated: the power to associate with stories has been usurped–a certain "puissance de la parole"–through the substitution of voice.[26]

At some distance in time from these examples, a voice (Godard's) heard in *Les signes parmi nous* comments on another substitution of voice:

And I understand more fully why I had so much difficulty in starting just now. I know now what voice it was that I might have wished to precede me, carry me, invite me to speak, and establish itself in my own discourse. I know now what was so intimidating about speaking in this place where I used to listen to him, and where he himself is no longer present to hear me.

The wished-for voice would precede the speaker, carry him, solicit his speech and make a home in his own discourse. Described thus, the voice is simply pretext, any text cited. Poe's for example: "The Oval Portrait" comes before *Vivre sa vie* in time (obviously), carries its narrative forward (announcing Nana's death), solicits response ("it's our story"), and becomes embedded in Godard's own discourse.[27] The wished-for voice is, also, for example, the text cited above, the end of Michel Foucault's *L'ordre du discours*, as heard in *Histoire(s)* for which it performs these same functions. But the second half of the text cited substitutes indicative forms for the past conditional, and substitutes for the feminine voice, "elle", a masculine subject, "lui", the body that had spoken in this place before. The body is absent, deceased, and can only be made present if a voice speaks in place of the voice it can no longer produce. In this ventriloquism the body has almost no substance. It is not Foucault, present only as a name in a list at the end of the published volume. Even less so is it Jean Hippolyte, the absent listener mourned by Foucault in his inaugural lecture at the Collège de France. At best it is the pretext, precedent in time and by that token lost to dialogue; what it cannot do is hear or understand. The pretext is dead text, as Hippolyte is dead for Foucault. Even when speaking the words of another, Godard is talking to himself.

3. "Dire sans rien dire"–diction

When Godard speaks in *Histoire(s)*, sometimes his body illustrates his speech, sometimes not. In speaking he does, mostly, one of four things: recite texts; list book or film titles; dialogue; narrate or comment.[28] Of the four, the major mode is the last, practised in all eight chapters, though it falls away after 3A and is little used in the last, 4B, where the recital of texts predominates. Changes of sonority are partly temporal and partly rhetorical. The voice is more flexible than the image, which is left to look the age it is at the moment of filming, whereas the voice's many guises may disguise the effects of age. Both signifiers are set in dramatic relief when the voice and image come from a distant past, as in the fragments of *Le Mépris* used in *Une histoire seule* (1B): the mere contrast in tone between the phrases muttered in 1988 and the "silence" shouted in 1963 gives the voice a history, just as what we are watching tells the history of an image, in the superimposition of Godard's face now on his body then.

The narrative or commentary mode has broad expressive range, and is also the mode most subject to technical process (echoes, reverb, slowing down, speeding up). The delivery of the recited texts varies little, consistently grave in tone, ranging only from the clipped inexpressivity of the Hugo speech in 3A to the mournful resignation at the close of 4B (reading Lamarche-Vadel, Frampton, Rimbaud, Bataille *et al*). Variations are introduced at a formal level, through the use of technical device (e.g. the echoing and reverberation for the Bloy, Foucault and Laforgue at the opening of 4B), and at the level of content, where the text cited is adapted (see the alterations to Bresson at the start of 1A), turning citation into commentary. Every one of these cited texts is delivered voice-off, without bodily illustration. A limit-case is the use in 4B of a text by Reverdy ("an image isn't strong because it's brutal or fantastic but because its association of ideas is far-reaching and true [*juste*]"), delivered in a passage taken from *JLG/JLG*. This is reasonable economy: there is no reason to recite the text again if Godard has only just used it a year or two before. But *Histoire(s)* also uses the image of the recitation in *JLG/JLG*, where the image is peculiarly placed at the limit of illustration: Godard is close to the camera, his back to us, watching television monitors as he speaks; we do not see his mouth as it speaks, we see only the body move, ever so slightly. This image of the difficult association of two distant realities, sound and image, is an image of montage.

The listing of titles is confined to the first half of *Histoire(s)*, and predominantly to the first chapter. 33 are given in 1A, 30 in 1B, only one in 2A, 14 in 2B.[29] The delivery in 1A and 1B varies in volume and otherwise little, a monotone backdrop to the more expressive vocalisations of commentary or recitation. The *mise en scène* provides a consistent visual backdrop, the body

Opposite: **Michel Subor and Anna Karina in *Le Petit soldat.***

reading the titles of books in his library. The monotony of delivery suits the seeming arbitrariness of the titles recited, but just as the choice of title can suddenly seem to fit what is happening elsewhere on the soundtrack or on screen, so may the delivery invest the title with the force to turn it into a comment. This happens with the first title spoken in 1A, *La Règle du jeu*, repeated three times, the last time in such a way as to turn "jeu" [game] into "je" [I], signalling an autobiographical subtext.[30] Similarly, the first two titles given in 2B reflect autobiographically upon the subject speaking (*Great Expectations... The Man Without Qualities...*).[31]

The voice enters into dialogue only twice (in 2A and 3B), but dialogue is an apt figure for montage in *Histoire(s)* for every kind of contact between distinct signifiers (sound and image, sound and text, text and image; one sound and another; one image and another, one text and another, etc.). The figurative force of dialogue is missing from the real exchange between Godard and Daney (who have almost the same "bobine" [reel or face]), unless the disparity between the parties ("one that fills up and one that empties") is itself a figure of dialogue's inherent inequalities, of dialogue between master and slave. The *mise en scène* of this video *plan-séquence* parodies classical composition in depth, with Daney (as Bazin) properly framed in the middle distance and Godard (with Wellesian cigar) in distorted close-up. True, nothing happens through the window at the farthest plane, but the video monitor placed between the window and Daney is a plane unto itself (offering, as *mise en abyme* of dialogue, images from television interviews).

The bodily illustration of the voice is synchronised with it, though the framing only just allows the mouth's movements to be visible. The slight echoing of voice (Daney's and Godard's) momentarily de-synchronises voice and image. The end of this first dialogue sequence is marked by an echoing that more fully desynchronises the two: "To me, big history is the history of the cinema [*du cinéma du cinéma du cinéma...*], it's bigger than the others [*que les autres que les autres que les autres...*] because it's projected [*projette projette projette...*]."[32] Dialogue becomes monologue (Godard on projection, paraphrasing a history of mathematics), and the illustration is entirely separate: Godard speaks off, and is shown on screen, silent, save for the one film or book title pronounced in this episode, *La Règle du jeu*.[33]

The second dialogue, in 3B, is a scripted, acted exchange on a subject similar to the first ("what was the New Wave?"), with Godard playing the guardian of the Museum of the Real, swapping lines with visitors to the Museum. The voice separates from the body in the last exchange, enabling the ventriloquism of Melville already noted, and shifting, it would seem, from fictional mode to the real. Godard is asked: "All the same, Becker, Rossellini, Melville, Franju, Jacques Demy, Truffaut, you knew them all?", and replies: "Yes, they were my friends."[34]

Narration or commentary, as already noted, is delivered mostly off screen, illustrated by found images. On occasion body and voice are present, but unsynchronised: the voice speaks and the body says nothing, or something else. Here the body is emblematic of the discourse delivered, an illustration of the absent speaking subject. At rare moments voice and body come together, synchronised, and then the body is emblematic of the voice's presence. If there is other illustration, it is superimposed or inserted; the voice maintains its presence in either case. The narrator is on screen, narrating, only on three occasions: in 1B, addressing the camera directly (with ironic counterpoint from the screen-text: "L'histoire, pas celui qui la raconte"–"the tale not the teller"); in 3A, briefly, and again with reference to story-telling ("What are the stories then?"); and in 3B, at length, when Godard delivers a lesson in cinema history through words and gesture. This manner of delivery is precisely not that of the historian Braudel, to whom Godard pays homage before beginning his own lesson, and whose image, speaking, he shows. (He even uses Braudel's voice to call his own class to order: "this time it's serious, the class is beginning".) Godard's performance, choreographed as comedy, like the dialogue that follows in the Museum of the Real, makes voice present in the image, but consigns it to the domain of fiction, of storytelling (when it had come so close to the real, to history).

4. "Cela s'enregistre"–apparatus [35]

A voice absent from the image can become present via apparatus (telephone, radio, tape recorder). The machine may make present, also, the apparatus of *mise en scène* and, more forcefully, of montage. The soundtrack of the cinema scene in *À bout de souffle* sets the manipulations of the editing suite against the simplicity of the thing filmed (a one-shot extreme close-up, with illusionistic flicker in the lighting). That the presence of montage is felt via a voice-off (Godard's) is no surprise to viewers of *Histoire(s)*, or to attentive audiences of *À bout de souffle*. Three earlier instances of the voice-off in that film are associated with some form of technological mediation, and are emblematic of montage. On the radio in Minouche's bedroom, pop music is interrupted by Godard announcing the time ("07.02"), then the Radio Luxembourg announcer gives the time of Eisenhower's arrival in Paris the next day, followed by more music, this time from outside the diegesis (Martial Solal's score for the film). Later, when Poiccard asks for Berutti on the telephone from Mansard's garage, Godard is heard replying that Berutti will be in one or other café at a certain time. His voice is heard again at the Orly press conference (asking "Are men more sentimental than women?"), a *mise en scène* opposing three modes of recording: pen and paper, film, audio-tape.[36] The last of these is the instrument of montage, which is the instrument of Godard's vocal self-inscription.

Technology as a mode of vocal self-inscription is deployed in *Le Petit soldat*. Fragments of radio broadcasts are heard in the course of the film, all making reference to the Algerian War as the broader context of events in Geneva. Some of these broadcasts can be connected to specific periods, either May 1958 or January 1960, intermingled in order to undermine any initial impression of chronological specificity in the film, and while some of the broadcasts are clearly authentic, off-air recordings (those associated with January 1960, particularly), others can be heard to be delivered by a performing voice, no doubt Godard himself.[37] Faked radio broadcasts, if they are to appear authentic, do not constitute the speaking self as spectacle to the same degree as, for instance, faking the dialogue of a Sam Fuller western. When, in *Pierrot le fou*, 1965, Marianne (Karina) responds at length to a radio broadcast about events in the Vietnam War, that it sounds like Godard's voice on the radio is perhaps incidental. Of greater consequence however, is the scene's re-inscription some 30 years later, when the voices of Godard and Karina are heard again in *Histoire(s)*, where every possible inflection of the voice is explored in a display of presence that is framed by such echoes of the past.

In most of these examples the absent voice is made present across space, over the telephone or radio. The apparatus in *Made in USA*, 1966, a tape recorder, makes the voice present across time, where the voice in the machine is a ghost, the dead fiancé of Paula (played by Karina), voiced by ex-husband Godard. The voice reads dead text, extracts from a redundant political polemic, and is finally effaced when Paula makes her own recordings, reciting live text from the year the film is made: Foucault's *The Order of Things* and Beckett's *Enough*.[38] Following on from a live exchange of poetry that echoes the cinema scene in *À bout de souffle* (though this time the verse is by Queneau), the apparatus scene here illustrates the impossibility of dialogue with the dead.

Above: **Cover of the 1967 UK edition of the scenario for Made in USA.**

Opposite: **Anna Karina, Ernest Menzer, Kyoko Kosaka, and Lazslo Szabo in Made in USA, 1966.**

The domestic drama figured in *Made in USA*, Godard's separation from Karina, is only a sub-genre of the tragic separation of present from past figured in *Histoire(s)*, though the death of sentiment is charged with a similar poignancy when evoked in the later work. Hear, for example, in 1A, Godard's listing of book titles over the image and voice of Karina from *Bande à part*, titles that comment on their love story: *L'école des femmes, Les liaisons dangereuses, On ne badine pas avec l'amour, Adieu ma jolie, Bonjour tristesse, L'éducation sentimentale*. Throughout *Histoire(s)*, the words and image of Karina are motifs of an autobiographical theme, developed mostly through reference to *Pierrot le fou*.[39] At the already discussed conjunction in 3A of Godard's voice on the car radio and Karina's in the image, Godard is an absent third party to the couple Karina-Belmondo. Near the beginning of 1A, likewise, a still from *Pierrot le fou* of Karina kissing Belmondo is contemplated by a third party, a Godard-like figure in silhouette.[40] In 4B, a montage of screen couples (Gene Kelly and Leslie Caron from *An American in Paris*, Tatsuya Fuji and Eiko Matsuda from *Ai No Corrida*, Max Schreck and Greta Schröder from *Nosferatu*) includes a shot from *Pierrot le fou*, with Karina standing in front of a Picasso portrait, cutting across the screen with scissors.[41] Here, too, a screen couple is signified, though at this point of *Pierrot le fou* the couple does not appear to be Karina and Belmondo but Karina and the dwarf she will kill with the scissors. Belmondo retrieves his place in the couple through sympathy with the victim, when he arrives and discovers the body: "a great, beautiful death for a little man". Godard is present here too, as third party, through identification: the dwarf is played by Jimmy Karoubi, fresh from Chabrol's *Le Tigre aime la chair fraîche*, where he played a dwarf-assassin called–a joke at Godard's expense–Jean-Luc. Karoubi in *Pierrot le fou* is, then, identifiable as self-mocking self-inscription, the filmmaker as victim.

Godard's absence from this image in *Pierrot le fou* is redressed not, in contrast with the car radio scene, through the presence of apparatus but by the elaboration of intertext, an intertext, moreover, whose signpost is entirely pro-filmic: the presence of an actor on screen, with a pair of scissors in his neck. It is hard to imagine that Godard's identification with "Jean-Luc le nain" is still active 30 years later, when the scissors are seen again in 4B. At that point other, stronger identifications are at work.

5. "J'étais cet homme"–identification[42]

"L'homme... L'homme... L'homme...": Godard's monologue in 4B begins with this portentous echoing. The phrase as a whole, from Léon Bloy ("Man has in his poor heart places that do not yet exist and in which pain enters so that they may exist"), repeats the screen-text of 3B where it had appeared over a photograph of Langlois and film of the couple from Murnau's *Sunrise*.[43] These associations appear to make of Langlois the particular subject of Bloy's general theory of human suffering, as part of the personal martyrology developing around the New Wave in 3B. In 4B the accompanying images (Masaccio's Adam and Eve expelled from paradise; a massacre from Eisenstein's *Alexander Nevsky*) invite a general application, as part of this episode's discourse on "l'homme" and "l'espèce humaine".[44]

"Cet homme", in the last words of *Histoire(s)*, is a different man, specified rather than generalised. He is identified, specifically, with the speaking voice, but it is not at all clear who is being identified by the voice. There are a number of candidates in the 110 seconds that form the closing sequence of *Histoire(s)*. "Cet homme" could be the man first described by Jean-Paul, translated by Coleridge, transcribed by Borges and recited by Godard: "If a man could pass thro' Paradise in a Dream, & have a flower presented to him as a pledge that his Soul had really been there, & found that flower in his hand when he awoke-Aye! and what then?" (Coleridge's text) But there is a gap to be overcome between the question asked and the four last words, "I was that man", that are not an answer.[45] Godard simply points to an element of the story, the man, and leaves to one side the material proof of paradise that for Jean-Paul, Coleridge and Borges might be supplied by the flower in his hand.

In a 1998 interview, Godard identifies himself with the man who passed through Paradise and the flower with cinema.[46] The flower found in *Histoire(s)* is a rose, remembering flowers already cited: Leslie Caron in *An American in Paris*, 1951, has a red rose in her hand; white roses (painted by Picasso) are visible behind Karina in the scissors shot from *Pierrot le fou*; earlier, Gozzoli's angel was seen proferring red roses in the "musée du réel" (3B). The first rose shown in *Histoire(s)* resembles most the last: Chaplin's rose is Godard's.[47]

The rose at the end of *Les signes parmi nous* is taken from Godard's *Allemagne année 90 neuf zéro*, 1991. As it passes to *Histoire(s)*, the rose undergoes a transformation, from white to yellow. The white rose of *Allemagne* is a memory of Sophie Scholl, the student beheaded by the Nazis for distributing tracts; the yellow rose of *Les signes parmi nous* is a forgetting of her death, and of history. The white rose, *sub specie mortalitatis*, is replaced by a rose *sub specie aeternitatis*. The type of flower evoked by Jean-Paul, Coleridge or Borges was not specified, but the yellow rose is Borgesian, the subject of a tale from 1960 describing the death of the epic poet Marino (heir to Homer and Dante), where the flower that a woman places by his bedside provokes a revelation: "Marino saw the rose as Adam might have seen it in Paradise."[48] Borges is troping on Dante (*Paradiso* XXX and XXXI), where the traveller through Paradise is shown a white and yellow rose as the preliminary to a vision of the divine splendour. Godard is more modest, troping only on Borges: *Histoire(s)* is a human, not a divine comedy.

The paradisial is the counterpart of the infernal. The *nekuia*, or Descent into the Underworld, is a framing motif in *Histoire(s)*. The first words on screen are "hoc opus hic labor est", Virgil's comment on how difficult it is to return from the Underworld, though the descent may be easy. References to Orpheus and Eurydice in 2B develop the theme, and the last voice sampled in *Histoire(s)* (before Godard recites Borges) is, as I have already mentioned, Ezra Pound, describing a *nekuia*. In this passage from the *Cantos*, Pound rewrites Virgil's pretext in Homer (*Odyssey* book XI), where Odysseus consults the dead in Hades: "But first Elpenor came, our friend Elpenor,/Unburied, cast on the wide earth./Limbs that we left in the house of Circe,/Unwept, unwrapped in sepulchre, since toils urged other./ Pitiful spirit." This passage repeats at the close of *Histoire(s)* the mourning for lost friends in *Une vague nouvelle*, with the added bitterness of regret. If Odysseus is Godard, Elpenor is Truffaut, "pitiful spirit". Pound's recitation brings a final differentiation to the *mise en scène* of voice: Pound's manner is everything Godard's is not, but Pound's relation to his pretexts is Godardian, faithful to the model while making it new.

More than Odysseus, Orpheus or Aeneas, Godard's guide is Dante who has passed through both Inferno and Paradiso. We remember an earlier identification, with the man and woman expelled from Paradise in Masaccio's painting. The screen couple is a recurrent motif in *Histoire(s)*. Against negative or tragic instances of failed couples (Welles-Hayworth, Godard-Karina) are set positive images, in particular a still from Bergman's 1948 film *Prison* where a man and woman are positioned each side of a projector, united in their work. The dedication to Anne-Marie Miéville and Godard himself is a variant of the motif.[49] The optimism associated with Miéville in

JEAN-PAUL BELMONDO · ANNA KARINA

pierrot le fou

Un film de JEAN-LUC GODARD

Productions
G. de Beauregard

TECHNISCOPE

EASTMANCOLOR

Histoire(s) might suggest that the couple motif will counter the despair over "l'espèce humaine" in 4B.[50] The couple in Bergman's *Prison* are shown as the screen lists twentieth century horrors ("Tu n'as rien vu à Hiroshima, Leningrad, Madagascar, Dresden, Hanoi, Sarajevo"), but a few minutes later we see only the man from that image, and in the closing sequence it is the tragic variant of the couple that returns.[51] In a painting, firstly: Gabrielle Münter's 1908 portrait of an art couple, Werefkin and Jawlensky, each turned from the other in an image of separation. Then in a film still: Jane abducted by Cesare, from Wiene's *Caligari*, and, finally, Desdemona and Othello, in a montage from Welles's film.

Of the men in these couplings the strongest identification would be with Welles, a reference omnipresent in *Histoire(s)* either, as here, as part of a tragic screen couple, or on his own as emblematic artist and "example to be followed"–also as here, since the citation of *Othello* shows Godard practising the art of cinema, constructing a new sequence from seven shots of Welles's film taken out of context and out of order. Welles's films are an important source of motifs throughout *Histoire(s)*, beginning with the second image shown in 1A, Mischa Auer and his magnifying glass from *Confidential Report*, 1955, illustrating Shakespeare's axiom: "Let every eye negotiate for itself."[52] This phrase is remembered in the closing sequence of 4B when a still of Auer with magnifying glass precedes Godard's negotiation for himself of Welles's *Othello*.

The couple is an autobiographical motif present in *Histoire(s)* and absent from the parallel "autoportrait" *JLG/JLG*, save in the sample of dialogue from *Johnny Guitar* ("lie to me, tell me all these years you've waited"), dialogue that has been emblematic of the tragic couple for Godard since it was first paraphrased in *Le Petit soldat* (and is still so when sampled in

Above: **Jimmy Karoubi and Anna Karina in** *Pierrot le fou*, 1965.

327

Histoire(s) 1B). *JLG/JLG* is a portrait of the artist's solitude, and supplies motifs for that theme when it is used in *Histoire(s)*, especially in 4B. An image of Godard cited from *JLG/JLG* in the closing sequence of 4B removes the people around him and their comments on the soundtrack, so that this is no longer "cet imbécile de JLG", it is the solitary artist, "l'homme", or rather "cet homme".

The voice at the end of *Histoire(s)* remembers the voice at the end of *JLG/JLG*, where a similar identification is offered: "a man, nothing but a man, who is worth no other man, but whom no other man is worth". This ending had in turn differentiated itself from an earlier (written) identification: "A man, made of all men, and who is worth them all and whom anyone is worth." This philosophical commonplace, Sartre's closing words in *Les mots*, is corrected in *JLG/JLG*, and the end of *Histoire(s)* rejects as explicitly the claim to universality.[53] An earlier sequence in 4B, on Sartre's criticism of Orson Welles ("*Citizen Kane* is not an example for us to follow"), had shown Sartre the militant in 1968, a period when Godard himself was a part of Sartre's biography. The biographical plenitude of Sartre's image here (*voix* and *visage* together) or of his words in *Les mots*, is, however, exactly the contrary of the self's *mise en scène* in *Histoire(s)*: Sartre is not an example followed by Godard.

An example that, in life, Godard did seek to follow, at least according to Alexandre Astruc (Sartre's biographer), also provides a gloss on the last images of *Histoire(s)*. In his autobiographical reminiscences, Astruc describes Godard's arrival in Paris: "We saw arrive in Paris from Geneva a sombre young man […] From the Gare de Lyon he went straight to the terrace of the Café de Flore. He'd say, holding a rose in his hand: 'I shall be the Cocteau of the new generation.'"[54] Whether or not the story is apocryphal, it would be appropriate that Godard's yellow rose in *Histoire(s)* be a memory of Cocteau.[55] Shots and stills from Cocteau's films are used throughout *Histoire(s)* (*Le Testament d'Orphée* in 1A, *Orphée* in 1B, *Le Sang d'un poète* in 2A, *La Belle et la Bête* in 2B and 3B); his photograph is seen in 2A and 4A; he is quoted in 2B and 3B. His voice is heard in the long sequence from *Orphée* and in the brief extract from *Le Testament d'Orphée* (combined with the image of the body in 1A, separated from it in 3A).

The yellow rose combines literary allusions (Borges and Dante) with this last cinema memory. The last memory of all in *Histoire(s)* is of a different order. Before the cutting and superimposition of yellow rose and Godard photograph, the painting of a man in a landscape is shown. This image returns after the rose to have the portrait of Godard slowly superimposed on it, and the last image of *Histoire(s)* is of photographed face and painted man combined. The accompanying sound is the phrase, "J'étais cet homme", but we are prevented from identifying "cet homme" with the man in the painting by the resemblance between this image and that of the Bible salesman, from Ramuz's *Les signes parmi nous*, subject to a different identification: "ce colporteur c'était le cinéma".[56]

Identifying the painting, at first sight, undoes that identification: the figure is Van Gogh, from Bacon's second *Study for a portrait of Van Gogh*, 1957. This is an image not of art but of *l'artiste*, like the series of artists displayed in 4A. They were, it is true, mostly filmmakers (Cocteau, Bresson, Truffaut…) represented by photographic portraits, but there was one painting, placed in a privileged position: Bonnard's 1920 *Self-portrait with beard*. Somewhere between the filmmakers and the painter in this montage from 4A an image is missing (Godard's), that of the artist who makes a portrait of himself in *Histoire(s)*. It would have been reasonable to see in Rembrandt's *Self-portrait with wide-open eyes*, 1630, shown in 1A, a

Above: *The Artist on the Road to Tarascon*, Vincent Van Gogh, 1888.

reflection of the wide-eyed Godard, and reasonable to see similar reflections in the Cézanne self-portrait in 1B, the Reynolds self-portrait in 2A or the Bonnard self-portrait in 4A. It is strange, then, that at the close of *Histoire(s)* the last picture shown is neither one of Bacon's many self-portraits, nor indeed one of Van Gogh's.

Bacon's *Study for a portrait of Van Gogh* brings a quite different set of associations into play. Van Gogh's painting *The artist on the road to Tarascon* was destroyed by fire in Magdeburg in April 1945, but the image is resurrected in Bacon's painting.[57] It represents, then, at this point of *Histoire(s)*, the memory of that which is irremediably lost, and the fantasy of its recovery. The Van Gogh painting, with the *colporteur*-like figure within it, is cinema; the Bacon painting is a story of cinema. It is a history lesson, not simply a modernist rewriting of the past (like Picasso's versions of Velázquez, Delacroix and Manet, or the Cézanne version of del Piombo's *Christ in Limbo*, shown earlier in 4B). New art's effort to retrieve its illustrious past is an impulse linking this last other image to the last other voice in *Histoire(s)*, Pound's version of Homer in the *Cantos*.

"J'étais cet homme." The phrase is the last of many identificatory gestures made in *Histoire(s) du cinéma*, but the only one to point explicitly to the other term. Even so, what is pointed to is not clear: the man in the text (whether Jean-Paul's, Coleridge's or Borges's) or the man in the painting (Van Gogh's or Bacon's). It is also, of course, the man in the photograph: the speaking subject points to an image of the man he was only recently, but as if it were an image of a lost former self–like the photograph in *JLG/JLG* of a child from the past who is no longer (if he ever was) the man who speaks in the present. The last four words of *Histoire(s)* say what the voice was, but they also ask the question: what, then, is the voice now? Or, to close by appropriating the closing question of Godard and Miéville's 1985 video, *Soft and Hard*, asked and answered in English there: "Where has it gone? It is hard to say."

HISTORY AND MEMORY

HISTORY AND MEMORY

The opening chapter of this section, "Godard's Two Historiographies" by Junji Hori, serves to introduce the major historiographical questions raised by *Histoire(s) du cinéma*, 1988-1998, the common point of focus for all the essays on history and memory included here. Hori underlines a key point: that Godard's historiographical approach is directly linked to issues of form. More specifically, by juxtaposing multiple, distant narratives through the process of montage, Godard is attempting to reveal the invisible aspects of history. This would be an application of the method of the "between" which Godard developed in his television work of the 1970s. Hori then locates two sources for Godard's central idea of cinema's misencounter with the Holocaust: the cinema as scientific instrument, and the cinema as Christianity. At their juncture lies Godard's key motif of the salvation of the Holocaust through the cinematographic image. According to Hori, there are two main genealogies of the image in Godard's historiography: the "euphoric image" based on a Bazinian faith in the image, and a Benjaminian "dialectical image" that flashes instantaneously through the effects of montage.

In "The (Im)possible History", Monica Dall'Asta explores in detail the Benjaminian aspects of Godard's historiographical project. Dall'Asta reveals the close convergence between *Histoire(s)* and Benjamin's particular concept of history as a construction (versus reconstruction) of the past. Inaugurated by Nietzsche's critique of historicism, this alternative approach to historical thought was most clearly formulated in Benjamin's short and enigmatic work, "Theses on the concept of history". Indeed, Dall'Asta shows that *Histoire(s)* can be interpreted as one of the most coherent realisations of the methodological aspects of Benjamin's text, even to the point of illustrating graphically certain problematic passages of the theory. Dall'Asta concludes that Godard's techniques of montage and quotation allow him to fulfil the programme of a truly materialistic form of historiography.

In "Anamnesis and Bearing Witness: Godard/Lanzmann", Libby Saxton focuses on the implications of Godard's assertion in *Histoire(s)* that the cinema failed to honour its ethical commitment to presenting the unthinkable barbarity of the Nazi extermination camps. She places this statement in the particular context of Claude Lanzmann's *Shoah*, 1985, which Godard barely acknowledges in his work. Indeed, Godard's "iconophiliac" agenda and his notion of the image as a vehicle of redemption appear completely opposed to Lanzmann's professed iconophobia. Yet both filmmakers have abandoned narrativity to explore cinema as a way of re-thinking time, memory and history when fractured by atrocity, and, most crucially, the charged relationship of aesthetics to ethics in the wake of an historical event of unprecedented violence. Saxton tests therefore the conviction that there is no common ground between Godard and Lanzmann and shows that the opposing ethical and aesthetic paradigms which they defend bring uniquely into focus a wider strand of ethico-philosophical discourse preoccupying thinkers from Adorno to Žižek.

In "The Index and Erasure: Godard's Approach to Film History", Trond Lundemo approaches the question of montage in *Histoire(s)* from the perspective of the archive and the search engines of databases. According to Lundemo, *Histoire(s)* is groundbreaking in its approach to segmentation and the forming of series because it employs multiple "search criteria", such as iconic matches, movement relations and sound juxtapositions, as well as more conventional archival searches based on linguistic criteria and names. These multiple search criteria allow for unconventional and surprising montages whereby the principles of "the association of ideas as distant and right" so often invoked by Godard are fulfilled. By examining the frequent references to Charles Péguy's *Clio*, 1917, in *Histoire(s)*, Lundemo pursues further the selection practices of the archive and the database to discuss mnemotechnical issues.

In "'A Form That Thinks': Godard, Blanchot, Citation", Leslie Hill explores the presence and influence of Maurice Blanchot in Godard's later work, and most specifically the actual figure of Blanchot in the climactic final moments of *Histoire(s)*. Hill brings to bear Blanchot's literary and philosophical work on three central concerns in Godard's cinema: the question of history and the last man; the theme of the ghost in relation to a politics of the film image; and finally Godard's citational practice, which features the constant play with titles, quotations, and other textual fragments. Hill argues that this enormous and spiralling question can best be articulated and analysed by reference to Blanchot's notion of the "neuter".

GODARD'S TWO HISTORIOGRAPHIES

JUNJI HORI Alain Bergala once characterised Godard's overall project as "a refusal, to choose between the two great polarities of cinema: ontology or language, the screen as window or the screen as frame, the being-there of things or montage".[1] I would say that the alternation of these two aesthetic regimes corresponds exactly to two historiographies that coexist in *Histoire(s) du cinéma*, 1998. In addition to the idea of writing history through "montage", Godard develops an idea of saving the atrocities of the Holocaust by the redemptive power of the cinematographic image, inspired by André Bazin's theory and Charles Péguy's singular historiography. The principal idea of this essay is to emphasise that the inexhaustible historiographic power of *Histoire(s)* lies precisely in the incessant alternation between iconophilia and iconoclasm, the religion of image and the science of montage, blindness and clairvoyancy, and, to use Jacques Aumont's dichotomy, the impossible dream of the absolute memory ("mémoire") of the world through what we shall call the "euphoric image" and its transformation into "souvenir" by the operation of montage as Benjaminian "dialectical image".[2]

Montage and history

Whether he treats the history of cinema or the history of the twentieth century, Godard is not interested in their linear progress or their causal system. As Aumont has noted, Godard's history is "a philosophical history that would have lost its Reason; if the universal history Godard speaks of in the history of cinema is rational, its reason is chaos, loss and the withdrawal of the Spirit".[3] It is true that Count Zelten (Hans Zischler) in *Allemagne année 90 neuf zéro*, 1991, translates Hegel, mixing the text of *Lectures on the History of World Philosophy* with that of the French translator's introduction to *La Raison dans l'Histoire*: "In pursuing their interests, human beings make

history and are at the same time 'the means and instruments of a higher purpose and wider enterprise of which they are themselves ignorant and which they nevertheless unconsciously carry out'".[4] But this idea of "universal reason", the idea that reason "exists as an immanent principle within history in which and through which it fulfils itself", is clearly opposed to Godard's historiography.[5]

In replying in Chapter 2A of *Histoire(s)* to Serge Daney's remark that his project can be realised only by someone who belongs to the New Wave, which is situated "in the middle both of the century and of the cinema", Godard produces one of his new aphorisms that exemplifies his anachronic vision of the history of cinema: "the cinema is the affair of the nineteenth century, which was resolved in the twentieth century". The idea of the cinema as a product of the nineteenth century does not indicate simply a series of technical researches that precede the invention of cinematography –from the simple attempt to fix light to the more systematic experiments in decomposing and recomposing movement, among which those of Eadweard Muybridge and Étienne-Jules Marey curiously punctuate Chapters 1B and 3B of *Histoire(s)*. Godard develops this idea in his own way. According to him, cinematography as a "form that thinks", as opposed to the "thought that forms", was born with the advent of modern painting in the middle of the nineteenth century. Baudelaire's "Le Voyage", as well as Charles Cros's "Le collier de griffes", announced what would later be a screen and a perforated film respectively.[6] Quite contrary to the stereotype according to which the cinema is an exemplary art of the twentieth century, Godard, by connecting a series of diverse elements, suggests a totally transdisciplinary and non-linear history of cinema.

We can observe a similar methodology disruptive of time when Godard interprets the history of the twentieth century. In an interview on *Allemagne*

Above: **Godard's** *Introduction à une véritable histoire du cinéma*, **1980, and the 1998 book of "Phrases" derived from** *Allemagne année 90 neuf zéro.*

année 90 neuf zéro, he says as follows: "It always surprises me when journalists […] say that History accelerates when it always slows down […] We said the same thing about the Berlin Wall: it goes quickly. No, it does not go quickly. It took three days to construct it, 40 years to destroy it."[7] Rather than approaching the fall of the Berlin Wall solely in terms of its immediate context (the dissolution of the Soviet Union and the subsequent liberalisation of Eastern Europe, for example), Godard, by juxtaposing "close history" with a "distant history" that dates back to the construction of the Wall, attempts to see the distance, the gap and the echo between the two.

Godard's historiography in *Histoire(s) du cinéma* is based principally on the concept of montage in his idiosyncratic sense of the term. When does his "historical montage" work really critically? At the moment when the concentration camps and pornography are juxtaposed. In Chapter 4A, three images appear successively: a colour pornographic image exhibiting a naked couple in the midst of sexual intercourse, an image from *Freaks*, 1932, where a deformed man guffaws as if he peeps at this erotic scene, and an image of a naked and emaciated prisoner carried away by two SS officers in an extermination camp. We can hardly find a more shocking montage in the entire film. To use Denis de Rougemont's terms in *Penser avec les mains*, 1936, narrated at the same moment, this juxtaposition of death and sensuality marks "the veritable violence" which any act of creation must contain if thought is to escape submission to brutality.

Godard's historiographical method can be observed more clearly when he comments on the Post-War situation of European cinema in Chapter 3A. As for the Polish cinematographic situation, he remarks as follows: "The Poles made two films of expiation, *The Passenger* and *The Last Stop*, and a film of memories, *Kanal*. And then they ended up welcoming Spielberg when 'plus

Above: **Eddie Constantine as Lemmy Caution in** *Allemagne année 90 neuf zéro*, **1991.**

jamais ça' became 'c'est toujours ça'." We shall discuss later the question of expiation. Let us note here that an image of Munk's *The Passenger* cited in the course of this narration is coupled with the scene from a "West German porno film" in which a furious dog violates a woman *a tergo* in the obscurity of the camp.[8] What exactly is the distance between the expiation felt by the Poles for having left the victims of the Holocaust to their fate and the commercial consumption of the camp in an underground pornographic film? What kind of abyss exists between the expiation of the Holocaust and its oblivion? It is precisely such an interval that Godard's montage obliges us to confront.

The same logic is at work when, in Chapter 1A, Godard reflects on the relation between cinema and reality during the Second World War, focusing on the Resistance and the Holocaust. He associates the sequence of the "danse macabre" accompanied by Saint-Saëns in *La Règle du jeu*, 1939, with an anonymous newsreel footage of a defenceless prisoner of the camp (the juxtaposition of a fictive bourgeois masked ball and contemporaneous atrocities), while muttering "history of cinema, history without word, history of the night". Immediately afterwards, we see on the screen a passage from "Le Lilas et la Rose" contained in *Le Crève-cœur*, 1941, an anthology of Aragon's poems on the Resistance published under the Occupation ("Never shall I forget the blood foretold by the crimson of a kiss"), while another poem is hummed on the soundtrack by a faint voice:

> The year thirty-five of my years,
> Just like Villon prisoner,
> Like Cervantes chained up,
> Condemned like André Chénier,
> Before the time of destiny,
> Like others in other times
> On these ill-scrawled leaves
> I begin my testament.[9]

What is at stake in this poem by Robert Brasillach is the poet's self-identification with those famous imprisoned authors who never gave up writing. Brasillach, a fascist writer and collaborationist as well as passionate anti-Semite, condemned to death during the purges of the Liberation, devoted himself to writing a biography of André Chénier while in the prison of Fresnes. We observe here the montage of Aragon and Brasillach, two poets extremely different in the political arena. Moreover, a third element comes to complicate the situation: a man tied to a stake, waiting to be executed shortly afterwards. Which side does this newsreel footage belong to? Does the nameless man who disappeared in a crack of history remind us of Brasillach's words–"Courage!" and "Vive la France!"–uttered at the very moment of his execution? Or does he refer us to a young philosopher featured by Godard in his short film *Le Dernier mot*, 1988, and whom he mentions a little later in the same Chapter, namely Valentin Feldman who cried "Imbeciles, I am dying for you!" when he was shot and whom Aragon defined later as an exemplary "communist man"?[10] The viewer cannot help but feel disoriented by these two possible interpretations.

To establish a constellation between death and sensuality, between the expiation of the Holocaust and its oblivion, and between Aragon, Brasillach and Feldman, and to read a certain kind of truth in the gaps created: this is precisely what Godard is imagining when he states clearly that history is rapprochement and montage.[11] Declaring his intention, at the beginning of Chapter 1A, to tell not only "all the (hi)stories that were" but also "all the (hi)stories that could have been", he tries to "bring together things that have not been brought together before, and do not seem liable to be brought together

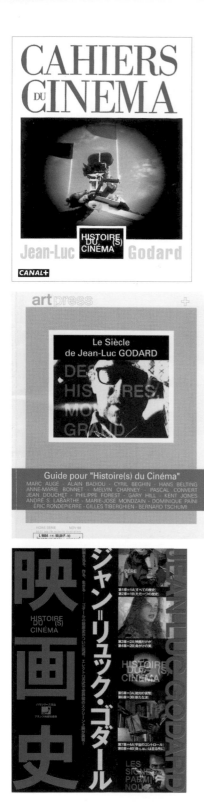

Above: *Histoire(s) du cinéma* special issues of *Cahiers du cinéma* and *Art Press*. Japanese flyer for the series.

at all" (Bresson), such as Copernicus and Vesalius, Rimbaud and Marshall Pétain, Hitler and Zworykin, in order to remind us of the virtual history that would have happened between these terms.[12]

It is possible to describe this method as an attempt to render visible the invisible aspects of history. In the conversation with Daney at the beginning of Chapter 2A, Godard, defining himself as historian, cites an aphorism of Oscar Wilde: "To make a precise description of that which has never happened is the work of the historian." What is important for Godard does not consist in dealing frontally with historical events, but in treating the imperceptible, or even the invisible, of history that would simply not exist in the eyes of serious and reasonable historians. Jan Oort, a Dutch astronomer, concluded from observations that the mass of the Galaxy had to be twice as great as that of optical and visible matter. Godard mentions this famous problem of dark matter both in *Hélas pour moi*, 1993, and in Chapter 4B of *Histoire(s)*. To use this metaphor, he is seeking in the domain of history the Galaxy's "phantom matter, omnipresent but invisible" (4B). It is within a similar framework that Godard, criticising French films such as *Le Chagrin et la pitié*, 1970, by Marcel Ophuls, a film of interviews around a neglected aspect of French history, namely wartime collaboration and Jewish persecution, said that he wanted to shoot "a film that would be called *Ten Years Later or Twenty Years Later* using all the tapes of previous militant films, but to go and refilm the people they filmed ten years later".[13] While Ophuls reconstitutes history from a specific standpoint, Godard wishes to show what lies "between" two periods of history. What matters for him is not simply to follow chronologically a historical past, but to perceive an "echo" between several terms by means of a "cinematographic scan of history".[14]

Godard's approach may be understood as an application of Deleuze's "method of the between" to the historical corpus of the twentieth century. Focusing on *Ici et Ailleurs*, 1974, Deleuze remarks that "in Godard's method, it is not a question of association. Given one image, another image has to be chosen that will induce an interstice between the two".[15] What matters in Godard's historiography is not simply "getting out of the chain or the association", but obliging us thereby to confront the vertiginous interstice and fissure between historical events which serious historians seek never to relate.[16]

The repetition of history, or Godard's meta-historiography

The application of the "method of the between" to the domain of history enables Godard to see the repetition and vicious cycle of history. The clearest example of this is the famous scene in *JLG/JLG: autoportrait de décembre*, 1995, where Godard, drawing in his notebook two triangles that form the Star of David, ponders on the projective and reflective relation between Germany, Israel and Palestine. He is interested here not so much in the historical events themselves as in what he calls during his monologue "the history of history". The attempt to examine an historical relationship that is not simply reduced to historical causality might appropriately be called "meta-historiography".

The reflection on the question of Palestine (and more largely, that of Islam) is also observed in Chapter 4B of *Histoire(s)*. After the Bressonian aphorism on the unexpected association of things, three words are juxtaposed on the screen: Jew, German and Muslim. The word "Muslim" signified, in the context of the concentration camps, those exhausted prisoners on the point of death. The fact that this metaphor belongs to Godard's typical word-play does not weaken its importance as a means of historical interpretation,

Above: **Studies of Godard's historical project.**

because the word constitutes already by itself an historical montage: "when one sees the corpse of a Jew dragged by two Germans in a concentration camp, we can call the corpse 'Muslim' [...] We have to think through both, the camps and Lebanon or Algeria. What happened in Algeria is the aftermath."[17] Godard asserts that not only the Israeli-Palestinian conflict, which dates back to the foundation of Israel, but also the more recent situations in Algeria, Bosnia and Srebrenica, are a kind of repetition of the relations between Jews and Muslims in the death camps. By evoking such rapprochements, he provokes the viewer to interrogate but without the promise of an answer.

At the beginning of Chapter 3A, he also practises the method of "the history of history". He recites first a letter by Victor Hugo dated 29 August 1876, in which Hugo condemns the unanimous silence of Europe on the massacre of the Serbians by the Turks on the eve of the Russo-Turkish War of 1877-1878. He concludes his hoarse reading of this accusatory letter by inscribing a fictional name on Goya's *El general Antonio Ricardos*: "Monsieur le vicomte le laquais d'Orsay". Godard's intentions behind this association of ideas and images is clear: he wants to accuse the servile politics of the French Foreign Office housed at the Quai d'Orsay, which never took action to prevent the barbarisms committed in the former Yugoslavia. He is thus not simply treating the conflict of Yugoslavia in the 1990s, but proposing it as a historical situation that repeats an earlier one more than a century before.

In yet another example from Chapter 4B, Godard superimposes Eisenstein's image of Ivan the Terrible with a newsreel footage of Stalin. This would have been a simple juxtaposition of fiction and documentary of the kind *Histoire(s)* abundantly provides, were it not for the striking close-up shot that follows which shows a bloodstained man in the war in Chechnya.[18] Between the Gulag and Chechnya, are there any resemblances that slip a serious historian's mind? Is Chechnya a repetition of the oppression in the former Soviet Union and of the politics of the Russian Empire? These hypotheses, which emphasise dynamic associations to the detriment of historical exactness, could be considered unsustainable and sometimes misleading. They might hide each historical reality in favour of the interstice of the events, and invent any kind of relation between facts where there would otherwise be no link. Godard's historiography, however, consists precisely in superimposing a "near history" on to a "distant history" in order to produce the intensity of montage at the expense of historical detail.

In *For Ever Mozart*, Godard practises a more dynamic montage of historical events. The essence of this film does not lie in the representation of Sarajevo caught in the whirlpool of war and ethnic cleansing, but in the attempt to consider the conflict in the former Yugoslavia as a repetition of the Algerian War as well as the earlier Spanish Civil War. The reference to the latter appears under various signs throughout the film, such as a poster of Malraux's *Espoir*, a brief mention of *The Invention of Don Quixote* by Manuel Azaña (writer and President of the Republic expelled by Franco), and the number 36 on which the baron bets during roulette. The Algerian War is mentioned notably through two characters: a Muslim maid Djamila, and Camille who believes herself to be a "granddaughter of Albert Camus". Vicky Vitalis (Vicky Messica), a stage director in the film, presents the idea of the repetition of history, citing Juan Goytisolo: "Is not the European history of the 1990s a simple repetition, with slight symphonic variations, of the meanness and confusion of the 1930s (Austria, Ethiopia, Spain, Czechoslovakia...)? A lamentable and interminable Ravel's *Boléro*?"[19]

Above: *For Ever Mozart*, **1996**.

The salvation of reality by the image

At the end of Chapter 2A, an enigmatic phrase appears little by little on the screen: "Only the cinema authorises Orpheus to look back without letting Eurydice die." Needless to say, this maxim is based on a legend in which Orpheus looks back despite the interdiction while bringing Eurydice back from hell, only to lose her forever in the Empire of Death. Among many possible interpretations of this phrase, an explanation from the historiographic viewpoint would be as follows: the proper power of cinema lies in its ability to reestablish the past which it absolutely failed to capture, and to face critical periods of the past, even the slightest glance of which would transform irreversibly its subject as well as object.[20] For Godard, one of the critical periods of the past incarnated by Eurydice, a sublime figure torn between absolute beauty and horror, is the Holocaust. This interpretation is justified by the presence of two collaged images which precede the phrase in question: the first image consists of an archival photo of the liberated Jews in Ebensee camp twinned with a shot from a black and white pornography film; the second shows a boy (Edmund?) wandering solitarily in a road full of corpses (a photograph taken by George Roger), viewed from above by the actress Eileen Sedgwick as she climbs up a ladder. What are the principal characteristics of Godard's attitude toward the Holocaust and its cinematographic representation?

Histoire(s) du cinéma can be interpreted as a meeting place of Godard's two answers to his fundamental question: "What is cinema?" The first answer is his repeatedly proclaimed idea of cinema as a scientific device that enables the scrupulous observation of things. In the dogmatic words of Jean Douchet, Godard is "the filmmaker who tries to adapt cinema to contemporary scientific knowledge" and we can even find "in his films the theory of relativity, quantum physics, the principle of uncertainty, chance and discontinuity, the atomic system and thought".[21] It is true that Godard attributes his confidence to cinema's potential to record rigorously the socio-political mutations of reality, a fact his own work directly attests to, notably the film that announced the events of May 68, *La Chinoise*, 1967: "the events of Nanterre happened a year later, so there was something true; but I filmed it before it really took form".[22] For Godard, the distinction between documentary and fiction is not essential because fiction films, as well as newsreel footages, are documents of the time and place of shooting and preserve metaphorically traces of reality ("égalité et fraternité entre le réel et la fiction"). The essential power of the cinematic apparatus as scrivener and archive of History consists therefore in its documentary capacity to witness historical events, such that it constitutes a "museum of the real" (Chapter 3B).

The second answer to the question "What is cinema?" concerns Christianity, since for Godard cinema functions as a field of salvation in the religious sense of the term. In the cinema auditorium of *Les Carabiniers*, 1963, the screen was torn by Michel-Ange (Albert Juross) who wanted to enter the fictional world. In this way, Godard showed the falseness of cinematic representation. In recent years, however, he often invokes Christian terms to metaphorise the cinematic screen both as the veil with which, according to the Gospel of Nicodemus, Veronica wiped the face of Christ on the way to Calvary and upon which his features were impressed, and as the bandage of the good Samaritan which was offered to a dying traveller robbed by a bandit.[23] Furthermore, a phrase attributed to Saint Paul–"The image will come at the time of the resurrection"–has often appeared as a *leitmotiv* in both his films and interviews of the last 20 years. Finally, when Godard considers the archaeology of projection in Chapter 2A, an image appears from Léonce Perret's *Le Mystère des roches de Kador*, 1912, in which a woman faints in front of an empty white screen. This choice of image is very evocative for the present subject since it indicates the precise moment of the heroine's recovery. Affected by amnesia due to her total–yet false–traumatic conviction of having shot her fiancé, she realises her deceptive memory and completely recovers thanks to the screened reconstitution of her traumatic experience by a professor of cinematographic psychotherapy. Godard emphasises here the almost mystic power of the image's projection on to the screen by implying that artistic activity fufils the role of the promise of salvation played out originally by religion and the Church.

Although we might observe a "conversion" to Catholicism in Godard's films of the 1980s, the motif of "salvation through the image" does not belong to a belief in God but solely to the religion of art which replaced the Church following the announcement of the "death" of God. In Chapter 3B, Godard brings up his frequent visits, at the age of 20, to the Cinémathèque française in the avenue Messine with his future comrades of the New Wave. He confesses that "Langlois confirmed cinema for us" and that for them "true cinema was the one that cannot be seen": "already forgotten, still banned, always invisible, such was our cinema". Godard talks about faith and the cinema in the following terms:

This philosophical basis that cinema is the one that cannot be seen is anchored in an honest and secular Christianity. It reminds me of this phrase by Wittgenstein: "You have there a history, you must believe in it, whatever happens." The cinema, that's it.[24]

It is not a question, therefore, of any religious doctrine but of having faith in the invisible image and in the cinema that cannot be seen. At the same moment in Chapter 3B, Godard says that "the image is first and foremost a matter of redemption [...] the redemption of the real". What enables Godard to redeem reality through the image is precisely his secular faith in images.

The status of the cinema as a scientific apparatus, which constitutes the first answer given by Godard, collapses irreversibly during the Second World

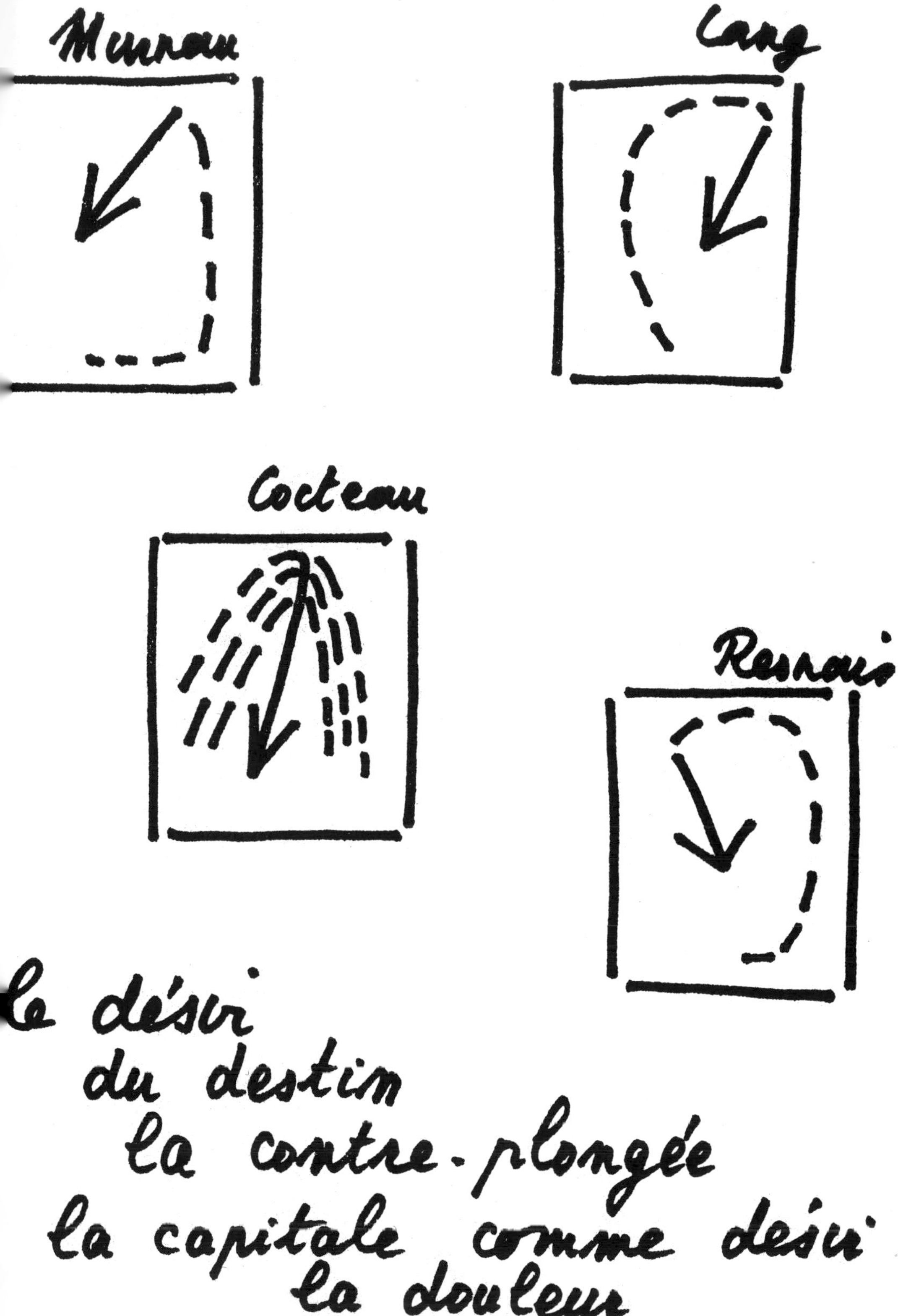

Murnau

Lang

Cocteau

Renais

le désir
      du destin
         la contre-plongée
   la capitale comme désir de
               la douleur
        capitals de l'imprimerie

War because of its failure to film the unique and nodal event of the twentieth century: the concentration camps. According to his thesis repeatedly stated since the 1980s, cinema informed the world of the imminent massacre in the concentration camps by subtly reflecting contemporary circumstances: "Just as Vienna and its music had announced the First World War, so the cinematograph anticipated the Second."[25] The Jewish barber sent to a camp in *The Great Dictator*, 1940 (Chaplin), Erhardt nicknamed "concentration camp" in *To Be Or Not to Be*, 1942 (Lubitsch) and the innocent rabbits massacred by hunters of the high bourgeoisie in *La Règle du jeu*, 1939 (Renoir): these were the "signs amongst us" of the disastrous event. However, as if colluding with the intentions of the Allies never to take the massacre into full account, despite their abundant knowledge of it, the cinema never filmed the concentration camps, thus "totally neglecting its duty" and "totally giving up".[26] Cinema dies for having betrayed its documentary mission to record, and resurrects itself thanks to those few filmmakers who were able to carry it out.

It is at the intersection of these two definitions–the cinema as scientific apparatus (and its collapse) and cinema as Christianity–that a motif emerges of the redemption of the disasters of the Holocaust through the cinematographic image. Godard suggests in his own way a rapprochement of ethics and the sacred when, in Chapter 1A, he matches a colour image of the front gates of Auschwitz with an image of the kneeling sisters in *Les Anges du péché*, 1943, by Bresson. At the end of the same Chapter, we behold an image of Max Linder, a French comedian of the silent era who committed suicide in Austria in 1925. His supposed last words, "Au secours!", are typed on to the screen. At the same time, a passage of oral testimony is heard given in a foreign accent by a female survivor of the Holocaust:

So it's here that what was called the gas "Zyklon B", small crystals, was falling inside, in the columns at first. The gas was coming out of these small crystals, and was starting to go out through the small holes and starting to spread throughout the whole gas chamber. Perhaps those who were next to the columns died in two minutes. Those who were further away, for those who were further away, it lasted ten minutes, a quarter of an hour.

Because it coincides with the ultimate cry of Linder, this testimony both under-lines a call for salvation through the image and stresses its contemporary failure. Furthermore, Godard provides a shot from *Shoah* of Lanzmann in Chapter 1A, where a Polish farmer, in a field near the site of an old concentration camp, repeats the gesture of slitting the throat (he signalled every time with this gesture to the deported Jews). The filmmaker thus highlights the indifference of the Poles towards the camps situated near their dwellings. This emphasis allows us to understand fully the meaning of Godard's interpretation of two Polish films–*The Passenger* and *The Last Stop*–as "expiatory films" (3A): he tries to save, even belatedly, the disasters of the Holocaust by the redemptive power of the cinematographic image.

The immediate trace and the dialectical image
In order to give a proper account of an idea of the redemption of the disasters of the Holocaust by the cinematographic image, and more largely, reality by the image, we have to go back to an aspect of Bazinian theory that lies at the origin of Godard's ideas. Bazin compares the photographic image with the Turin Shroud, "the synthesis of relic and photography", both of which offer authentic and irrefutable proof of what once existed.[27] Bazin develops the idea that reality mirrors itself directly on a non-subjective and decentred image, just as the body of Christ was imprinted, in the manner of an *acheiropoietos* (i.e. not made by human hands), on the sheet which could have enshrouded him at the time of his burial. He perceives an almost

Previous page: *Image from Alain Resnais's L'Année dernière à Marienbad, 1961, reworked in a collage by Godard in 1981.*

Opposite: *La Règle du jeu, Jean Renoir, 1939.*

Above: *Espoir,* André Malraux, 1939-1945.

religious mystery in this process of the immediate impression of a non-subjective image without any artificial reproduction. This is why he appreciates the depth of field and *plan-séquence* shot in the films of Orson Welles and William Wyler, techniques which, by augmenting the quantity of information in a field of vision, demand from us an active and voluntary interpretation. It is on the same basis that he establishes a prohibition against montage: "When the essence of an event is dependent on the simultaneous presence of two or several factors of the action, montage is forbidden."[28]

From the 1980s onwards, Godard has valued Bazin's idea of the immediate trace of the reality on an image, more profoundly even than Truffaut whose attachment for him is rather filial than theoretical. For example, in *Grandeur et décadence d'un petit commerce de cinéma*, 1986, Gaspard Bazin (Jean-Pierre Léaud) remarks that "the grand principle of the classics is to spread a cloth. Yes, because they expect something will come to be impressed", an idea that undoubtedly echoes Bazin's reflection on the Holy Shroud. Godard, who often compares the screen with the veil of Veronica during the production of *Histoire(s)*, remarks in Chapter 1A that "what the light cameras invented by Arnold and Richter retains […] will not be presented on a screen, but on a Shroud". This statement is based on the idea that reality, once it is projected on the sacred screen, is transformed into a mystic image far more brilliant than reality itself.

Godard's interest in Péguy's *Clio*, 1917, can be understood within the framework of his adherence to Bazin's reflections on the image. In Chapter 4B, Godard asks himself what history is. Among the four short answers given by Malraux, Braudel, Cioran and Péguy, Péguy's is particularly important for its relation to Godard's historiography: "history, a sombre fidelity to fallen things".[29] Under the influence of Bergsonism, Péguy condemned the attitude of those modern historians who claim to be capable of reconstructing history from fixed fragments of reality ("fallen things"), thus neglecting the Bergsonian duration of event that involves essentially the process of ageing. In Péguy's terminology, memory, ageing and invention stand prior to history, inscription and inventory. He regarded history as "amateur", "longitudinal" and "parallel" to the event which it considers only from the outside. The heart of the event, however, can be grasped solely by memory, which is "professional", "vertical" and "central" to the event into which it "sinks, plunges and probes".[30] Clio, "the young girl who does the recording", cannot help but swear a "sombre fidelity" to the making of an inventory of historical events (hence her depressed but slightly voluptuous lamentations).[31] On the other hand, Péguy proposed a biblical figure who, by experiencing directly a historical scene of the Crucifixion and by transmitting its immediate trace to posterity, succeeded easily in what Clio never managed to accomplish: Veronica.

Just as Bazin values the immediate trace of reality on an image, so Péguy attaches importance to those who witness a historical event without intermediaries. Godard seems to take this parallelism into account, because when, in Chapter 4B, Anne-Marie Miéville reads a passage by Clio which formulates succinctly the impossibility of the reconstitution of history ("It takes me a day to make the history of one second. It takes me a year to make the history of one minute…"), we also see two photos of Bazin over which are inscribed the phrases: "Montage forbidden by André Bazin" and "the seamless dress of reality".[32] If a photographic image fixes a moment of reality like the Holy Shroud, a cinematographic image preserves the duration of reality. In this sense, it functions as a witness to history *par excellence* and far more privileged than Veronica, since it is the direct trace of history which is able to grasp the duration itself of reality. This is why Godard cites repeatedly the images of *Espoir* which Malraux shot during the Spanish War and which make direct contact with it. It is also why he emphasises the necessity of the documentation of history (and particularly of the Holocaust) by means of the cinematographic image. It is on this level of thought, influenced by Bazin and Péguy, that Godard's idea of the redemption of reality is based.

However, is not this reflection on the image too euphoric and complacent an approach, one that is effective only to those few who believe in advance in the power of authentic images? If the Holocaust had been filmed, what would it have changed? Is it really the case that the montage of concentration camps and pornographic imagery encourages true thinking? In my opinion, Godard's thought on the image is torn between two polarities. If, on the one hand, there is the euphoric image charged with mystery as explained above, on the other there is the quasi-invisible image that bursts through momentarily in the montage of two heterogeneous images. While the former underlies Godard's views on the Holocaust and presupposes a spontaneous faith in images, the latter is deduced from the rapprochement by means of montage, the intensity of which obliges us to experience the limit of the act of seeing. When Godard follows Maurice Blanchot in Chapter 4B and declares that "yes, the image is happiness, but at its side nothingness rests", he must be aware of the duality of his own thought on the image. And, as he adds again citing Blanchot, "the whole power of the image can only be expressed by calling upon [the nothingness]".

What definition of the image is to be deduced from Godard's rapprochement? From an historiographical viewpoint, the Surrealist idea of the heterogeneous image so crucial to Godard since the 1980s (and notably that of the poet Pierre Reverdy, his constant point of reference[33]) is akin to the "dialectical image" as conceived by Walter Benjamin in his last text "On the concept of history", 1940, that is, an image charged with a particular tension and born of an aural and ephemeral encounter with a moment from the past: "The past can be seized only as an image which flashes up at the instant when it can be recognised and is never seen again" (Thesis V).[34] Profound analogies can be observed between Godard and Benjamin far beyond superficial resemblances. Certainly, both thinkers are separated by historical and intellectual contexts. While Benjamin was obliged to live in exile in different countries in Europe between the wars due to the Nazi regime in Germany, Godard, retreating to his atelier in a small Swiss village, has witnessed the post-Cold War world situation with a nostalgia for the intellectual tradition of the Third Republic. Moreover, in *Histoire(s)*, we meet twice (in 2B and 4B) the same text by the young Benjamin, a beautiful fragment on dreams, awakening and love that has nothing to do with the philosophy of history.[35] Despite these differences, however, we can observe nevertheless a considerable affinity between Godard's filmic method and Benjamin's historical materialism. On the one hand, just as, according to Thesis XIV of Benjamin, the French Revolution "cited" Ancient Rome, Godard "cites" the archives of the history of cinema and the twentieth century–fragmented, discontinuous and decontextualised images. He then goes on to produce a shock effect by making them collide with each other through montage, and to bring a moment of the past instantaneously to light, not as it really was but as it could have been. He thus revives its historical and poetic virtuality. All this is marked by the urgency according to which the project is only realisable at this end of the twentieth century. On the other hand, Benjamin's project of historical materialism consists not so much of "recognising the past 'the way it really was'" as in "seizing hold of a memory as it flashes up at a moment of danger". Benjamin formulates the essence of his project as follows: "Historical materialism wishes to retain that image of the past which unexpectedly appears singled out by history at a moment of danger." What is ultimately important to him is the redemption (*Erlösung*) of the virtuality of the past by means of the dialectical image.[36]

The image as happiness which is based on an optimistic belief in images (the Bazin-Péguy side) and the image of nothingness charged with a tension that leads us to the limits of vision (the Reverdy-Benjamin side): it is precisely the incessant alternation between these two regimes of image that renders complex and enriches Godard's reflection on history. Without his almost blind confidence in the cinematographic apparatus or his faith in images, the montage of historical fragments would have been simply a cynical and mocking comment on the ironic repetition of history. If we are really impressed by the fragmentation and recomposition of the visual archives of the twentieth century, it is because the filmmaker profoundly loves the images he destroys. Nevertheless, I would prefer to attach more importance to the redemption of the virtuality of the past through the dialectical image than to the salvation of the disasters of genocide through the image as happiness. Immersed in Post-War French cinephilia, Godard has a predilection for the image charged with an almost religious euphoria. It would, however, be nothing but a simple decadence if he were only to caress, with eschatological melancholy, the image as a mystery of what was there. It is undoubtedly his practice of montage that permits us to glimpse in a blinding sparkle the interstices of historical events charged with the methodological potential of historiography.

THE (IM)POSSIBLE HISTORY

MONICA DALL'ASTA

The solitary history

During his conversation with Serge Daney in Chapter 2A of *Histoire(s) du cinéma*, Godard qualifies his project to make a filmic history of the cinema as simply "unrealisable". In the cryptic mode that is characteristic of Godard, the reason for this impossibility is indicated in the process of reduction that an attempt of this sort would imply. What would be fatally reduced is cinema as "big history": "there is projection/ so I call it big history/ because it can project itself/ the other histories can only reduce themselves". The paradoxical conclusion that one can extract from these assertions is that a cinema history is unachievable because cinema itself is already history. To project its history, in other words, would mean to imagine the projection of history, of cinema as history, that is, the total reproduction of the myriad recordings encapsulated in film and in all the other different technical supports of which cinema is here the emblem. This is why "one would need to make a film lasting a hundred hours", and still this wouldn't be enough, because the History, the One or total History, is much longer than a human life, an immense memory that lies invisible in the archives could never be received as such–certainly not until it remains the one, the big, and therefore solitary history.[1]

To project the history of cinema would mean to condemn a hypothetical spectator to wear out her lifetime in a condition of absolute immobility, and this only to reconstruct an infinitesimal portion of historical time. For, in fact, technical reproducibility multiplies time: as Clio observes in the quote from Péguy included in Chapter 4B: "I need a day/to tell/the story of one second/I need/a year/to tell the story/of one minute/I need/a lifetime/ to tell/the story of one hour/I need an eternity/to tell/ the story/of one day/one can tell everything/except/the story/of what one is doing." Thus

Opposite: *Angelus Novus*, Paul Klee, 1920.

the impossibility of a total reconstruction explains why Godard has moved towards a plural concept of history. If the big history is unachievable, the same is not true for the countless potential histories that it contains. These are possible histories, none of which pretends to be the only possible one, but simply possible. Different versions of an impersonal memory that remains virtual, "reductions" or "cuts" through the incommensurable extension of the invisible History.

In defining what might be labelled "the project of History" as unachievable, Godard meets the thought of Walter Benjamin whose critique of the notion of "universal history" also implied a similar deconstruction of the myth of exhaustiveness. Godard's profound assimilation of this philosopher has left many traces in his work of the last 15 years. For example, fragments of "On the Concept of History" can be found in both *Hélas pour moi*, 1993, and *The Old Place*, 1999, and an allusion to this text of impressive depth was already included in the first version of Chapter 1B of *Histoire(s) du cinéma*, 1988.[2] Here, the citation of an angel drawn by Paul Klee worked as a link to the most famous of Klee's angels, the Angelus Novus that Benjamin describes in Thesis IX of his essay.[3] Though suppressed in the final editing, the reference to the Angelus Novus continues to haunt the whole extension of 1B through the traces of its own effacement. The word "l'ange" printed in red on a frame from Bergman's *The Prison*, 1949, recurs several times in the definitive version, but always with some of its letters partially hidden or cut in a literal re-presentation of the process of elision. The title becomes fully legible only for a moment just before the ending, and precisely between a sentence from the Bible ("Do thyself no harm, for we are all here", Acts of the Apostles, 16:28) and the shot from *Vertigo*, 1958, in which James Stewart dives into the river to rescue Kim Novak. "L'ange" is then inscribed as an anticipation of an image of salvation, which is also the function that the Angelus Novus assumes in Benjamin's essay. Like the characters in Bergman's film–a man and a woman who are watching off-screen, deeply absorbed in the images produced by the projector in the foreground–the Angelus Novus is also staring fixedly at something that we don't see. His face, Benjamin writes, "is turned toward the past. Where we perceive a chain of events, he sees one single catastrophe which keeps piling wreckage and hurls it in front of his feet." This catastrophic movement of history is what the man and the woman in *The Prison* seem to be watching too, since a series of Kuleshov effects create the impression that their glance off-screen is addressed to the images of war and destruction that punctuate the chapter. This frame, in short, stands in the place of the angel, or better–to take literally the message that appears in the caption–it is "l'ange".[4] Yet the explicit content of this image is projection or reproduction, a motif that is further reinforced by three of the four inscriptions to which it is associated during the chapter. Where we don't see "l'ange", we read: "the history of projection", "the Maltese cross" and finally "a solitary history", which translates into a pun the loneliness of "the big history". In sum, what this complicated net of cross references proposes is an equation between cinema-as-projection (i.e. the reproduction of the totality of cinema) and the vision of the Angelus Novus. As Benjamin relates:

the angel would like to stay, awaken the dead, and make whole what has been smashed. But a storm is blowing in from Paradise; it has got caught in his wings with such a violence that the angel can no longer close them. The storm irresistibly propels him into the future to which his back is turned, while the pile of debris before him grows skyward.

But despite his wish for redemption, the angel will never be able to reverse the atrocities of history into an image of happiness. No theological figure could ever accomplish such a decisive task. The redemption of the past is exclusively entrusted to the historical materialist.

The true image of the past

One of the most significant references to the theses "On the Concept of History" appears at the beginning of *Hélas pour moi*. The French version of the enigmatic Thesis II is read by a voice-over during an equally enigmatic *plan-séquence* shot in a park on Lake Geneva. We see a man in the act of spying on a couple while hiding behind the trunk of a "secular" tree. As we watch what might look like a scene of investigation, a road-sweeper crosses the frame horizontally, stopping in the middle to pick up some litter. The invisible speaker pronounces the text in a whisper, as if he wanted to become a transparent medium for the intensity of Benjamin's words.

Is it not the voice of our friends that is sometimes haunted by an echo of the voices that have preceded us on earth? And the beauty of women of another age, does it not resemble that of our friends? It is therefore for us to realize that the past requires a redemption of which a tiny part may be found within our power. There is a mysterious meeting between the defunct generations and the one to which we belong. We have been awaited on earth.[5]

Obscure like a rebus, this passage can only be read allegorically. What it offers is a visual representation of the historiographical method that Benjamin exposes in his essay, written in the months that preceded the Nazi occupation of Paris and just before his suicide in September 1940. Both the investigator and the road-sweeper are emblematic incarnations of a third figure, the historian, whose investigation Benjamin depicts as a search through a mass of detritus, rubble and rags–the material sediments of the past which the historian has to redeem "in the only way possible: that is, by using them".[6] Later in the film, Godard's homage to the theorist of technical reproducibility becomes thoroughly explicit with the appearance of a character called Benjamin. Ironically presented as a clerk in a video-shop, Benjamin is soon associated with the verb *dégager*, a sarcastic comment on what the engaged intellectual becomes in the age of video reproduction.

Benjamin's theory of history has undoubtedly a fundamental role in Godard's late work, and especially in the long-term research for *Histoire(s) du cinéma*. Though the historiographical model for this research is provided by a multiplicity of authors such as André Malraux, Élie Faure, Fernand Braudel, Michel Foucault, Charles Péguy and Jules Michelet, the position that Benjamin occupies within this group is a particurlarly strategic one, for it provides the chance to link–or in Deleuzian terms *agencer*–all these very different names in an intertextual net of quotations.[7] A good example of this function of linkage performed by Benjamin can be found again in the dialogue with Serge Daney in 2A. Echoing Benjamin's contention that "art history does not exist", Godard states: "there has been no history", only to correct himself immediately: "a little bit of/art-history [...] there are indeed bits of a history of painting/which were done by the French/not by others".[8] The reference here is to Élie Faure and André Malraux. The exemplary value they are accorded within art historiography depends on their unconventional use of art reproductions, which do not function in their books as sheer illustrations of what is said in words, but as moments of a pragmatic appropriation of the past that is profoundly consonant with Benjamin's "tactile" conception of technical reproducibility.[9] The proclamation of inexistence by Godard after Benjamin is then to be understood as the

expression of a lack, the desire that an alternative practice of history can finally start to exist.[10] Such an alternative, Benjamin noted, could only emerge from a complete dismissal of the notion of history as a linear development. It is precisely this idea that would later surface in the work of both Foucault and Braudel: Foucault with his insistence on rupture and discontinuity; Braudel with his emphasis on the enduring factors of material life, which he also described–in terms that are surprisingly close to those used by Benjamin in the Theses–as the "losing movements" of history that are made invisible by the mass of the "victorious events".[11] A similar oppositional stance is also at work in Péguy's concern with memory as an experience of time that is systematically denied by "scientific" history.[12] A major reference in *Histoire(s)*, Péguy's work was also very important for Benjamin, who spoke of the "incredible feeling of kinship" and "the sense of community" that the reading of this author had inspired in him, touching him "more closely" than any other written work.[13] As for Michelet, nowhere is Godard's debt towards this author captured as clearly as in a sentence that Benjamin quoted in the opening section of "Paris–the Capital of the Nineteenth Century": "every age dreams the one that follows it".[14] This oneiric, imaginative relation between present and future is what Benjamin tried to express by speaking of the nineteenth century as the "prehistory of modernity", and what *Histoire(s)*, too, repeatedly suggests in its fictional construction of the prehistory of cinema, as, for example, in the use of Baudelaire and Poncelet in order to illustrate the "dream" of projection (Chapter 2A).

Benjamin seems then to function as a privileged entry into a net of quotations, the name that allows–according to the principles of his theory of allegory–to collect around a single conceptual core an otherwise dispersed set of images, or in this case, to gather into a constellation (that could be designated as the anti-historicist constellation) a number of otherwise very different authors. In fact, Godard's constructivist approach to the history of the cinematic century appears as a coherent, self-conscious application of the historiographical method proposed in "On the Concept of History"–the attempt to do with the twentieth century what, in his *Passagen-Werk*, Benjamin had done with the nineteenth.[15]

Like the *Passagen-Werk*, *Histoire(s)* is almost entirely a montage of quotations. In Benjamin's system, this dyad of montage and quotation is attributed the most decisive role in the struggle against historicism, that is to say, against the particular scientific inflection the historical discourse has assumed in modernity under the spell of idealism. What makes historicism so dangerous from a materialistic standpoint is its futile claim to objectivity, its self-representation as a practice of reconstruction. Historicism, Benjamin writes, conceives time only in the form of an "empty, homogeneous continuum" (Thesis XVII), an abstract dimension that always precedes the work of the historian and asks only to be filled with a succession of facts (producing what Braudel would call a "history of events"). The problem with this conception is clearly the same posed by Zenon's paradoxes: once time is spatialised into a homogeneous, or chronological, series of instants, any moment whatever in the past becomes unreachable, irremediably severed from the present by an infinite number of instants. It becomes a dead object of knowledge, a matter that can be endlessly accumulated but will never produce what Benjamin calls the "true picture of the past" (Thesis V).

The project of a "véritable histoire du cinéma" is obviously a different formulation of the same concept.[16] What cannot be mistaken is that "true" works here in opposition to "objective". Insofar as it presupposes the possibility of "knowing the past as it actually was" (Thesis VI), the objective image of the past is bound to be one and the same forever, an eternal, immodifiable version of history. On the contrary, "the true picture of the past flits by", for "the past can be seized only as an image which flashes up at the instant that it can be recognised and is never seen again" (Thesis V). Essentially marked by singularity, the true picture of the past finds its way only in a definite present, to which it is destined: the now of its legibility. Variously defined as "dialectical image" or "*télescopage* of the past through the present", it is an experience of time in which any distance between past and present has been abolished, the effect of a juncture in time.[17] In other words, the true picture of the past is a product of montage.

Historiography as *découpage* and montage

Though never mentioned in the Theses, film is clearly the model of the alternative conception of history that Benjamin developed to contrast the hegemony of historicism. Written only four years after the "Artwork" essay, the Theses show a similar critical move against the illusions of distance in favour of a tactile appropriation of the past based in montage. Whereas the method of historicism is merely additive, Benjamin writes, the movement that the historical materialist performs through time can be compared to a "tiger's leap" (Thesis XIV). The virtual continuum of time has to be systematically disrupted, interrupted, exploded. In short, the materialist writing of history proceeds from an operation of *découpage* in time. Its product is what Benjamin indicates with the term "monad", a piece of time blasted out of the continuum of history's course–that is, very precisely, a quotation:

Historicism rightly culminates in universal history. Materialistic historiography differs from it as to method more clearly than from any other kind. Universal history has no theoretical armature. Its method is additive; it musters a mass of data to fill empty, homogeneous time. Materialist historiography, on the other hand, is based on a constructive principle. Thinking involves not only the flow of thoughts, but their arrest as well. Where thinking suddenly stops in a configuration pregnant with tensions, it gives that configuration a shock, by which it cristallises into a monad. A historical materialist approaches a historical object only where he encounters it as a monad. In this structure he recognises the sign of a Messianic cessation of happening, or, put differently, a revolutionary chance in the fight for the oppressed past. He takes cognisance of it in order to blast a specific era out of the homogenous course of history–blasting a specific life out of the era or a specific work out of the lifework. As a result of this method the lifework is preserved in this work and at the same time cancelled; in the lifework, the era; and in the era, the entire course of history. The nourishing fruit of the historically understood contains time as a precious but tasteless seed. (Thesis XVII)

No text could better describe the functioning of montage in *Histoire(s)*. Each image, that is, each quotation, has in it the vertiginous depth of the monad. Let's take, for instance, the very first picture we see on the screen, the close-up of James Stewart holding the famous photographic camera of *Rear Window*, 1954. As an introduction to an audio-visual history of the cinema, this one image conjures up a number of different motifs. At the most immediate level, by relating film to its historical predecessor, photography, it presents cinema as participating in the history of optical devices, itself a part of the history of technical reproduction. The splitting of vision into two different figures, James Stewart's eyes and the camera lens, implies the inclusion of film in the history of perception, suggesting its decisive role in the deepening and extension of human visual experience. In fact, James Stewart's camera is equipped with a telephoto lens, which he employs to explore the apartments in front of his window and to discover what happened in one of them. Much like Benjamin's "*télescopage* of the past through the present", the telephoto of *Rear Window* serves to discover the truth about a past event, bringing to light what, like the murderer's wife, has disappeared forever. Moreover, the condition of immobility to which James Stewart is confined throughout the whole film qualifies his character as an obvious icon of the spectator. His glance towards an invisible point off-screen marks *Histoire(s)* as a history of the spectator, of both her passion and passivity. And finally, the choice of *Rear Window* is an obvious homage to Alfred Hitchcock, which immediately implies a reference to the *politique des auteurs*. For someone like Godard, to quote a Hitchcock film means in a way to call memory by name, to conjure up the New Wave and its cinephilia as a practice of memory–which in turn could easily take us to *Nouvelle Vague* the film and its echoings of *Vertigo*. But here *Rear Window* also stands as a link to Chapter 4A and to its touching celebration of Hitchcock's acrobatic ability to suspend the flow of time in the immeasurable duration of a moment of danger. A recurring feature in *Histoire(s)*, the stop-frame technique employed to present this picture itself cites the temporal experience generated by Hitchcock's suspense, an experience that is a sort of ideal filmic translation of Benjamin's "Messianic cessation of happening" (and in fact, in Godard's words, Hitchcock has been the only one, with Dreyer, who was able to film a miracle). Indeed, the gesture of interruption that allows the true picture of the past to flash up for a moment before disappearing forever is in no way a freezing or blocking of time–rather, it is a spacing of time, the opening of an interval, or a *durée*, in which memory can finally emerge. That this interval is described by Benjamin as a moment loaded with danger, as it typically appears in movie thrillers, is only another indication of the paradigmatic role that film plays in his theory of history.

What we encounter in this opening quote from *Rear Window*, then, is the inexhaustible temporal density of the monad. Torn from its context and inserted as a flash between two moments of blackness, it is an infinitely explorable image, an implosion of time, the abbreviation or recapitulation of the entire course of history in a single, evanescent picture. It is precisely this monadologic quality of the image that prevents the shock-like montage of *Histoire(s)* from restraining the imaginative production of the spectator within predictable limits, that is, from generating a mental picture that remains identical at each screening. It is on this level that we can measure both the analogy and the difference between Eisenstein and Godard.[18] In fact, the principle of collision on which both authors rely for their editing strategies produces in the two cases very different results. While the "organic" montage of Eisenstein sought to exert a totalising control of the public through a rigorous calculation of the third image to be obtained in the process of collision, Godard's method can instead be labelled, following Deleuze, as "inorganic" or "crystalline", for it aims precisely at losing control of the spectator, positing what Benjamin calls "the death of *intentio*" as the condition for the emergence of involuntary memory.[19] In other words, the functioning of *Histoire(s)* as a memory-machine is in no way subjected to the control of the author's intention. Since monads contain an infinite potential of legibility, the product of their combination can never be predicted and can only appear in the *hic et nunc* of each particular vision. As Benjamin writes, "in now-time truth is laden with time to the point of explosion. The death of *intentio* is nothing else but this explosion, which thus coincides with the birth of historical time, the time of truth."[20]

Above: ***M**, Fritz Lang, 1931.*

The spectacle of history

Working as a setting for the emergence of involuntary memory, *Histoire(s) du cinéma* comes to face a second major issue of the anti-historicist critique, one that invests directly the relationship between history, modernity and film. In 1874, in the essay that inaugurated the basic lines of that critique, Nietzsche already made the point clearly: if historicism fails to provide an authentic comprehension of the past, this is because it presumes that memory is simply a matter of will, the obvious, natural result of its will to remember. This presumption is not just one among many possible ways to conceive of history; it is instead the specific trait that characterises the practice of history in modernity. To demonstrate this point, the essay *On the Use and Abuse of History for Life* develops a metahistorical analysis in which history itself comes to be considered historically, that is, as a product of human thought that changes through the ages. In fact, Nietzsche contended, in the modern world "the constellation of life and history [has] altered, because a powerful and hostile star has interposed itself between them [...] The constellation has truly changed through science, through the demand

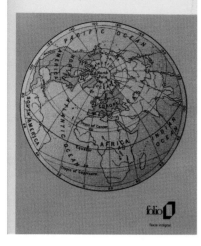

Guy Debord
La Société
du Spectacle

folio

that history is to be a science."[21] Of course, in Nietzsche's mind this change was far from representing the magnificent progress in the knowledge of the past that historicism had put at the core of its programme. The pretension to achieve the ultimate reconstruction of universal history had produced no improvement in the human appreciation of the past; on the contrary, it had managed only to make the modern person even more detached and insensitive in the face of the past.

For Nietzsche, history could be saved only by the extent to which it would be able to serve the forces of life. Its only sense rested in its power to nourish the present, by offering examples to follow (monumental history), images and stories to give the world a familiar appearance and induce a spirit of belonging (antiquarian history), or lessons born from the condemnation of past mistakes (critical history). All of these functions had been displaced by the advent of a new "scientific" concept of history in which the past had become a mere "matter of erudition", an ever growing heap of notions whose accumulation no longer served to enrich the time of life but only to consume it, thus resulting in the paralysis of life. In Nietzsche's view, the spread of the historicist doctrine in nineteenth century Germany had produced an unprecedented inflation of information about the past, a "mass of scholarly data" that had turned people into simple containers of "instructions" or "wandering encyclopedias" unable to act.[22] The "will to remember" was then inexorably leading to the atrophy of life, "for with a certain excess of history, living crumbles away and degenerates"[23] No longer incorporated into a living experience, Nietzsche observed, history now presented itself as a pure spectacle. He wrote: "No generation ever saw such an immense spectacle as is shown now by the science of universal becoming."[24] The "modern person […] has become a spectator […] who continually allows his historical artists to prepare the celebration of a world market fair."[25] The birth of the "historical sense", as Nietzsche despisingly defined the modern inclination toward the past, was strictly coincident with the loss of any ability to make history, for, by becoming a spectator, the subject (or actor) of history had become subject to history, that is "converted into a condition in which even great wars and huge revolutions are hardly able to change anything momentarily".[26] Moreover, the new spectacular form attained by history in modernity was powerfully fostered by the acceleration of technical reproducibility: "The war has not yet ended, and already it is transformed on printed paper a hundred thousand times over; soon it will be promoted as the newest stimulant for the palate of those greedy for history."[27] Reproducibility was thus described as the privileged instrument through which the past came to occupy or colonise the time of life, in a process that would find its ultimate accomplishment in the ever growing dissemination of the recording techniques, such as photography and film. As Guy Debord would later indicate, "in spectacular time, the past dominates the present".[28]

When in Chapter 1B Godard speaks of the world in which cinema suddenly appears as "a world still almost without history" he is implicitly recognising the complicity of film in the spread of the historical sense. Yet in the frame of Nietzsche's critique, the birth of the historical sense is strictly identified with the paralysis of history. A world becomes historical only by losing its faith in the possibility of changing history, or, in Guy Debord's words, "the abandonment of history [has been] built on the foundation of historical time".[29] The passivity of film spectators in front of the atrocities of the twentieth century is certainly one of Godard's major concerns in *Histoire(s)*. Nazism and the war had been clearly announced or even exposed in films such as Lang's *M*, 1931, and *Die Nibelungen*, 1924,

Lubitsch's *To Be Or Not To Be*, 1942, and Chaplin's *The Great Dictator*, 1940, but still the catastrophe was allowed to happen. The prophetic signs that cinema disseminated among us were left without a response. Cinema spoke with a Cassandra voice: according to Godard, the death of Captain de Boieldieu in *La Grande illusion*, 1937, and the death of the little rabbit in *La Règle du jeu*, 1939, were saying something that spectators didn't want to hear, thus revealing their passivity as a form of complicity, for "the forgetting of extermination/is part of the extermination". (Chapter 1A) In this context, an extremely enigmatic quotation attributed to Louis Delluc, both here and in *2x50ans de cinéma français*, 1995, seems to open a dialogue with Guy Debord. More precisely, Delluc's aphorism provides a ready-made inversion or a *détournement* of a phrase contained in the film version of *The Society of the Spectacle*, 1973, a work that certainly represents, as Giorgio Agamben has noted, one of the most direct anticipations of *Histoire(s)*.[30] Where Debord claimed "we must take back from spectacle what it stole from life", Godard (via Delluc) corrects as follows: "if the deaths of Puig and Négus/the death of captain de Boieldieu/the death of the little rabbit/were inaudible/it's because life never/returned to the films what it had stolen from them".

Above: *To Be Or Not To Be*, Ernst Lubitsch, 1942.

So, what would it be that spectators have stolen from films? Everything seems to indicate that it is nothing but memory–the recording, haunting character of what the screen re-presents to the amnesic eyes of the multitudes. Regarding films as pure spectacle, spectators have deprived the recorded images of their character as memory. They have reduced it to a form of entertainment that does not entail any responsibility in terms of action, any practical consequence in their lives. If this is true, the making of *Histoire(s)* can be seen as an attempt to give the *grisbi* back to the cinema. No doubt very ambitious, this programme implies a theoretical as well as methodological answer to one of the most dramatic problems of modernity, that is, the spectator's passivity when faced with the horrors to which the screen tirelessly testifies.

In fact, after the birth of the historical world, it is no longer possible to imagine a situation in which the spectator would be merely replaced by the actor of history. If modernity coincides with the advent of spectatorship in history, the way out of this impasse cannot be a simplistic denial, an apocalyptic condemnation or regressive refusal, of the spectator that we all are. The challenge will instead be to place the spectator in the position of acting as spectator, that is, without removing the passivity by which s/he is fundamentally constituted. But how would it ever be possible to disclose a pragmatic horizon for this figure of passivity, whose advent coincides by definition with the end of praxis? Godard's answer is unequivocal: the only form of action that the spectator can perform while still remaining the passive subject that s/he essentially is will be the making of an audiovisual history of the cinema, a filmic history based on the principle of quotation. While written film histories simply remove the spectator by translating his/her experience into words and then by replacing his/her passive nature with a writer's agency, a filmic history includes the spectatorial experience in the very process of its composition, assuming the visual matter of that experience as the matter of its discourse. This amounts to saying that a filmic history of the cinema automatically includes the spectator in his/her capacity as an author, that it has him/her act as a maker of history. By becoming author, the spectator can now tell the story of his/her own history, a story in which s/he is also the only leading character: the history of passivity, of the beginning of history as spectacle, of the end of history as praxis. In this way, through the absorption of the spectator's passivity into this specifically cinematic form of agency, *Histoire(s)* gives a coherent elaboration of Nietzsche's idea that memory is something that has to be made, not just received; something that must be constantly reorganised, constructed and appropriated by the forces of life. By actively reacting to his/her passivity, the author/spectator of *Histoire(s)* shows that memory is essentially a praxis–or, in other words, that a true cinema history can be made only by making cinema *tout court*.

"The future appears/among memories"

Unlike traditional, bookish film histories, an audiovisual history of the cinema rests on the principle of quotation. And the moment of quotation is precisely the moment when passivity and activity come to coincide, when reading and writing or watching and showing become one and the same thing. While traditional film histories confine themselves to a reconstructive dimension, striving to produce an illusory effect of actualisation, Godard's citational approach can instead be conceived as an activation of the past into the present, where past becomes incorporated into a present praxis. In this sense, quotation appears essentially as a construction of history in the *hic et nunc*. But construction, Benjamin noted, implies destruction. To cite means to produce

Above: **Sergei Eisenstein shooting**
Bezhin lug, **1935-1937.**

a historical object by cutting it out of any linear development, by severing
it from its context, its before and its after, to make it spring directly into the
present. The weight of tradition and cultural heritage, whose effect is, following
Nietzsche, the immobilisation of the subject in a passive position, is displaced
by the freedom of choice implied in construction (extraction and combination),
by the making of history as a dialogue with (rather than a pure reception of)
the past. As Nietzsche suggested, the only remedy for the excess of history in
modernity, the only way for life to affirm its energies in the historical world,
lies in "organising the chaos" produced by the growing information about the
past: choosing my own lineage by jumping at will across the ages, selecting
what in the past specifically talks to me, or what "looks" at me. This is eminently
an operation of montage, and is exactly what Godard accomplishes in *Histoire(s)
du cinéma*.

This notion is explicitly expressed in Chapter 2A during the opening dialogue
between Godard and Daney. Here the New Wave's capacity to make history is
presented as essentially related to its constructivist approach towards the past,
which allowed it to "constitute for itself its own history". If "Baudelaire speaking
of Edgar Poe/is the same as Malraux/speaking of Faulkner/is the same as
Truffaut/speaking of Edgar Ulmer/or Hawks," this is because they all refused
"passively to inherit/the cultural heritage of their art" and decided instead to
"find their own precursors for themselves". But what is more important is the
application of this method to the making of *Histoire(s)* itself. A spectatorial

history, *Histoire(s)* doesn't try to narrate an objective or factual history of the cinema. Rather, it constructs a geneaology by endlessly inventing new relationships between images and sounds, texts, names and circumstances drawn from the most disparate contexts. Moving achronologically through time and space, it reconfigures its material in original combinations, according to the principle borrowed from Bresson and enunciated in 4A: "to bring together things that have not been brought together before, and do not seem liable to be brought together at all". To paraphrase one of Godard's most famous aphorisms, this is not "the just history" but "just a history", a hypothesis of history which thus becomes a (hi)story, or in other words a history that is also a fiction, a fiction with and through history.

As it should be clear by now, this is the only way to make history possible, and also the only way to produce effectively the true history of the cinema. This apparent contradiction surfaces repeatedly in *Histoire(s)*, from the perfectly interchangeable meaning of the quotes drawn from Welles in 1A ("It's all true" as the exact equivalent of "F for Fake"), to the pun "vrai faux-tographe" ("true fake-tographer") in Chapter 2A, to the declared falsifications of film history that Godard exposes with the caption "Erreur" flashed up in red on the screen in 3A. But the contradiction is here the clue to the paradoxical nature that truth assumes in relation to time. As Deleuze demonstrates in his discussion of Leibniz, Nietzsche and Welles in *The Time-Image*, the power of time is essentially a power of falsification.[31] What the flow of time fatally falsifies are the countless alternative futures that each present contains in the form of virtualites, the multitude of futures that will never become present and that time continually sacrifices in forcing the present to become past. To present a "time-image", or to produce a "direct presentation of time"–which, in fact, is only another formulation for the "true picture of the past"–will then mean to appropriate time's power of falsification so as to falsify its own falsifications. This explains why Godard is so insistent in recalling "the films that were never made", a constellation of inexistent works which include the exemplary cases of Eisenstein's *Bezhin Meadow* and Welles's *Don Quixote*, but which is also implied in the allusions to the broken careers of Erich von Stroheim and Jean Vigo. What such references try to communicate is the sense of cinema as it might have been, an experience of the multiple futures encapsulated in the past that the course of time has falsified forever. To disclose these multiple futures is equivalent to falsifying the falsified, that is, to raising the power of the false to its extreme degree. This can never correspond, however, simply to a restoration or reconstruction of the truth, but aspires rather to a creation, an invention, of the truth.[32] And of course, this is a matter of art.

What has never been, what has still to be done or created anew, is then the most intimate truth that the past has left to us to find out. Creation as the extreme power of the false is the "metamorphosis of the true", and it can be effected only by assuming "the point of view of time as becoming [...] a viewpoint that belongs so deeply to its object that the object itself keeps changing according to a becoming that is identical to the viewpoint".[33] In *Histoire(s) du cinéma*, this viewpoint which is endlessly transformed by the object that it transforms is the viewpoint from which cinema looks back on its past while in the process of dying.

Yet there is nothing despairing about this idea. Here, death is posited as the one condition that allows the making of history in the here and now. It is because it is perceived as something that dies that the present can finally reveal its intimate resemblance to the past. And resemblance, the experience of a correspondance through time and in time, is already an epiphany of redemption, as Benjamin's fragment in *Hélas pour moi* allusively suggests. For both Godard and Benjamin, the concept of history as permanent destruction is the condition necessary to seize the present as creative chance, as a praxis able to incorporate the legacy of the past in the very process of creation. In this way film history ceases to be just a cultural heritage: it becomes a memory that lives, transformed at each moment into an entirely new form of cinema, precipitated into a practice that manages to incorporate not only the images but also the experience of over 100 years of cinema: the research on montage of the Soviet authors, the childish gags of silent comedies, Epstein's experiments in slow-motion, the neorealist technique of recording, Hitchcock's suspense, the fictional power of Hollywood cinema, the joy and freedom of the New Wave.... As Benjamin's angel of history, Godard looks backwards and what he sees is an interminable whirl of destruction. But his gaze is not one of pure contemplation. It is a gaze that redeems as it acts, that discloses for us the myriad futures which rest in the womb of the past: what cinema might have been and never was, what it might have become, but above all, the unsuspected novelty that it can still be today.

ANAMNESIS AND BEARING WITNESS: GODARD/LANZMANN

Today it is impossible to eliminate from the image of a body the resonance of the attack on the human image perpetrated in the gas chambers [...] Images are no longer as they were before.[1]

LIBBY SAXTON

"It showed nothing at all."[2] Thus Jean-Luc Godard, always the provocateur, dispatches Claude Lanzmann's nine and a half hour meditation on the Holocaust to the realms of the insignificant–worse, of the unsignifying black hole at the heart of the event which figures and threatens to swallow our most sincere attempts to bear witness. One of the most troubling though under-researched aspects of Godard's condemnations of the development of cinematic history(ies) is that the medium has failed to keep faith with its ethical commitment to presenting the Nazi extermination camps. While the first part of his *Histoire(s) du cinéma* admits a brief citation from *Shoah*, 1985, Godard's reluctance to pay any more than the most cursory lip service to a work that has become an ethical touchstone raises a series of disturbing questions. Such a denial begs justification in the light of the striking convergence of the paths followed by the work of the two filmmakers. Sharing a penchant for polemic and ellipsis, both have consistently created philosophical works which inhabit and probe the very limits of representation, works of resistance and refusal. At a time when new technologies of visual representation are threatening to destabilise our notion of the historical "event" and drain the image of its testimonial power, both directors have abandoned narrativity to explore cinema as a way of rethinking time, memory and history when it is fractured by atrocity. In so doing, they reveal the charged relations between aesthetics and ethics in the wake of a trauma which makes such relations necessary. For both, the moving image remains a privileged witness to the alterity of traumatic experience, producing ethical moments where self-conscious fiction collides with the shock of a real that has yet to be mourned.

Yet the collaborative filmic project recently proposed by Bernard-Henri Lévy for the Arte series *Gauche/Droite* ("Lanzmann–JLG chez BHL", "Le fameux débat", or "Pas un dîner de gala") was intended to give both directors a unique opportunity, in a film where directorial responsibility would be equally shared, to explain and develop their thinking on a deep-rooted dispute that has long been latent between them and begun over the last years to surface. Since Godard's caustic attack on Lanzmann in a 1998 *Les Inrockuptibles* article, where he aligns the Jewish director's position with Adorno's prohibition of art after Auschwitz and the sterile discourses it spawned, interaction between the two directors has been reduced to reciprocal critique, with periodical outbursts on Godard's part met by hostile silence on Lanzmann's.[3] The eventual abandonment of the collaborative film would appear to exemplify not merely the mutual suspicion which progressively reduced all attempts at dialogue to a twisted rhetorical duel, but also a shared conviction that there is simply no common ground between the two that might serve as a point of departure for an encounter.

It is my aim here to test this conviction by staging just such an encounter. Locating a shared anxiety about the ethical–and political–risks of the image at the heart of the work of both directors, I would like to suggest that theirs is much more than a rhetorical game. For the opposing aesthetic and ethical paradigms they defend bring uniquely into focus a wider strand of ethical reflection (preoccupying thinkers as diverse as Adorno and Žižek) which responds to the Shoah in its uneasy relation to visual representation. My concern at this juncture is less to expose the limitations of the position of either director (insofar as their positions can be fixed at all) than to identify certain points of coincidence and difference and their possible ethical stakes. By interrogating *Histoire(s)* and *Shoah* as heuristic lenses through which to view each other, I would like to query the extent to which Godard's attack on cinema's amnesia is redefined by works such as Lanzmann's which privilege a temporal present to cultivate, precisely, the anamnesis or re-membering essential for the mourning of a traumatic past. To rephrase the question using Godard's terms: if only the mournful presentation of the camps could afford the cinematic medium the ethical "redemption" it seeks, what, then, would such a "redemptive" cinema be like, and how different would it be from Lanzmann's *Shoah*?

An ethic of redemption

"Modern cinema was born from those images of the camps [the first images from the Liberation], images which have been ceaselessly at work in it, resurfacing in other forms", writes Antoine de Baecque, identifying the spectral presence of the traumatic real as it returns to haunt the image. His implicit appeal for a cinema that self-consciously seeks out and reflects on those "specifically cinematographic figures that testify to the obsessive presence of the palimpsest that is the residue of the camps", offers a point of orientation and departure for both directors, who respond in opposite ways.[4] Each proceeds to identify and explore a contrasting set of figures of the violence. The possibility that there is something so excessive about this historical reality that it has contaminated every image, that the "documentary" image can no longer remain intact but will always leak into memory-images of the trauma, leads Godard to posit an elliptical narrative of cinematic amnesia, of sin, death and resurrection, couched all the while in ethical-sacred terms. Cinema is put on trial and found guilty, convicted for its failure to bear witness at the moment of agony (or to the persistence and returns of this moment: "You saw nothing at Hiroshima, [...] at Sarajevo").[5] (For the filmmaker, the medium is doubly culpable as it not only "forgot" to film the camps, but also misrecognised that it had (inadvertently) announced their imminent violence.)[6] Repeatedly stressing the connections between escapist narrative and horror, Hollywood and Hitler, Godard's frequently rehearsed verdict identifies a medium whose documentary roots became fatally diseased by the spectacular dictates of Eros and Thanatos ("a film is a girl and a gun"). But "suffering is not a star"–anguish and spectacle make an obscene coupling–and Hitler the movie-star can only be removed from under the sweeping beams of the Twentieth Century Fox klieg lights by a penitent cinema willing to retrace its steps and renew its documentary charge in a long-overdue communion with the traumatic real.

None of this is strikingly new. Godard's ever erudite histories recall and reconfigure not only the Adorno-esque prohibition and a Deleuzian segmentation of cinematic history, but also the latter's analysis of the pleasure in spectacular self-stagings binding cinema to fascism, as well as Paul Virilio's analysis of links between the moving image and warfare.[7] However, I would suggest that the point at which Godard departs from this theoretical heritage is his provocative preservation of the possibility of cinema's self-"redemption" (the term is his own).[8] Amongst the series of ethically and politically charged philosophical claims about the image which underpin *Histoire(s)*, surfacing often in the form of slowly evolving intertextual citations, one of the most persistent refrains is St Paul's thesis from his Biblical epistles, a formula which has punctuated Godard's discourse both on and within his works in various permutations for over a decade: "the image will come at the time of the resurrection". Towards the climax of the opening chapter of *Histoire(s)*, the montage that conflates the horror of Auschwitz and Ravensbrück (condensed in the close-up of a contorted face in a pile of emaciated corpses) with a celestial apparition via the body of a bathing-suit clad Elizabeth Taylor would appear to perform the resurrection that Godard invokes. Here, even more than elsewhere, the production of a semantic excess, obscene yet fertile, at the interstice between images takes away their fascination in order to communicate in compressed form a central thesis of the work. As Godard puts it, "for me, montage is the resurrection of life".[9]

Although the self-deconstructing playfulness of Godard's montage warns us to be wary of taking such pronouncements literally, sequences such as this seem to give them a physical form (to perform them) beyond the realms of figure and metaphor. Not only do the cuts and dissolves suggest that the movie star is also tenderly stroking the victims of the Shoah, but, as Jacques Rancière has pointed out, the original Giotto fresco is fragmented and rotated by 90 degrees, so that the figure of Mary Magdalene is no longer reaching out towards a saviour who rebuffs her–*Noli me tangere* ("Do not touch me")–but down to the earth with an angelic promise of welcome.[10] As Godard's voice completes the links on the soundtrack, an image of separation, absence, an empty tomb, is transfigured, becoming an act of resurrection.

This is one of many sequences in *Histoire(s)* which explores the interpenetration of (and slippage between) ethics and the sacred in visual representation–evidence of what Giorgio Agamben defines as the "messianic" perspective inflecting Godard's more recent work.[11] In the same chapter of *Histoire(s)*, video-editing techniques allow Hollywood nuns to appear to kiss the railway track carrying victims across the iconic threshold of Auschwitz. Such juxtapositions–James S Williams speaks aptly of "sublime crossings and transfigurations"–reconfigure filmic temporality, introducing a tension between the plenitude of the present moment and a "messianism" that orients the images towards an end (a resurrection).[12] And yet this end, both ethical and sacred, is also endless; it already inheres in the present moment, in the very fabric of the montage. For sequences such as the Auschwitz/Taylor/Giotto encounter, where the falsity of the *eidôlon* recruits to itself the truth of the *eikôn*, testify to a faith in the "bleeding", intrinsically multiple "Image" (with a capital "I") produced at the interstice as a vehicle not only of resurrection but also of truth and redemption: "I believe in images", the director proclaims quite simply.[13]

This rhetorical inversion of St Paul's doctrine (for Godard, it is the Image that produces the resurrection) is particularly resonant when the subject of representation is historical trauma. At the heart of Godard's admonishment to Lanzmann lies the conviction that even–and above all–in the case of the Nazi genocide, "it is sufficient to show"; the plenitude of the Image is "capable of denying the void" and is thus sufficient in itself for salvation.[14] This is the sense in which Godard's histoires coincide teleologically (a coincidence reinforced through explicit allusion) with a Proustian narrative of mnemonic recuperation. Such a narrative makes a redemptive claim for art, since time is regained and, in Godard, effectively resurrected into light through projection, allowing its remembering and rediscovery in a moment of pure vision. As it returns the traumatic real to us in fictive fragments, *Histoire(s)* would seem to enact a seductively smooth passage from the amnesia that Jacques Aumont identifies as the condition not only of history and memory but also of montage, which must "forget" certain fragments in order to "remember" others, to anamnesis, as the selected fragments re-member themselves and the forgotten real on screen.[15] In cinema, defined by Godard as "invariably an operation of mourning and of reclaiming life", it would seem that the repetitive impasses of melancholia can be circumvented, the losses mourned and redressed, the image redeemed to realise its true vocation as pure presence, revelation.[16]

Of course, such claims are particularly compelling in a visual era defined, according to Régis Debray, by its capacity to "desacralise the image while pretending to consecrate it".[17] Anything but anachronistic, Godard's eschatological reworking of cinematic history, ironically via video technology, would seem to mark *Histoire(s)* as a utopian, conciliatory project. Besides resurrecting the dead, the miracle-working image is linked through repeated medical metaphors to notions of healing; Godard even goes so far as to suggest that were scientists to learn to practise a cinematic "regard au scalpel" they would find a cure for AIDS: "scientists cannot translate the things they see [...] AIDS has to do with culpability and morality. Cinema exists to make these connections [...]."[18] Yet more problematic than such a controversial diagnosis is the very prematurity of the posited cure. Godard's desire to redeem the image in atonement for cinema's "original sin" is one step beyond the *mal d'archive* (archive fever) identified by Derrida, the desire to restore to memory that is simultaneously created and threatened by the impulse to forget and destroy, but their proximity is nevertheless revealing.[19] Derrida argues via Freud that the archive can never be reduced to mneme or to anamnesis because it is infected and inflected by the death drive, and thus, paradoxically, "takes place at the place of originary and structural breakdown of the said memory": "the archive always and *a priori* works against itself".[20] And indeed, I would suggest that it is in the very feverishness of Godard's compulsive recovery and reconnection of archival fragments in the name of anamnesis that the spectre of amnesia begins to reappear. By linking two critically distinct narratives in *Histoire(s)* (narratives which have tellingly surfaced at similar times in Godardian discourse), a story of cinema's forgetfulness and a story of its redemption, the director neglects the "trouble" of the archive (Derrida) with its self-destructive rifts of death and loss. Instead, he risks reconciling the two narratives into a single consolatory (hi)story of cinema.

This is the point at which the multiplicity of narratives invoked by the bracketed plural in the title of Godard's work threatens to coalesce into a unified History, "une histoire seule", connecting, to cite Charles Tesson's example taken from Chapter 3A of *Histoire(s)*, Manet to Zola to Nana to Berlin to Ufa to Goebbels and Hitler ("the myth").[21] And as Godard's Images are never reducible to the visual, in the meantime, on the soundtrack, deceleration and distortion encourage the "histories with an s" to decompose through phonetic slippage into the unified "histories with an SS". If the coherent story consoles by recuperating unassimilated trauma into positive meaning, then Godard's repeated attempts to locate the horror of the camps, the point at which the narrative universe implodes, within a logical succession of events (and images), incur an ethical risk. And all this despite emphatic warnings–notably from Lanzmann amongst others–about the "obscenity" of such sense-making projects and, indeed, about art's own propensity to undo them.

In short, this is where *Histoire(s)* seem to succumb disturbingly to, even to radicalise, a more widespread impulse in art after Auschwitz to make, in the words of Colin Davis, "habitable meanings out of uninhabitable truths".[22] What is at stake here, indeed, is the ethical question of whether art should attempt to produce meaning at all in such a context. Given the capacity of narrative to provide comfort in its appropriation of difference and erasure of incomprehension, surely cinematic testimony, if it is to explore the inflammatory potential of art in opposition to theories of its conciliatory function which have become uncomfortably common currency, ought to recognise itself instead as the (desperate) attempt to produce meaningless forms? But the metaphors of resurrection which punctuate *Histoire(s)* refuse to surrender the consolation of meaning. Like the aestheticisation and sanitisation of the death of the orphans at the end of Andrzej Wajda's *Korczak*, 1990, where the substitution of white light for gas swathes the unbearable real in an iconic bandage, such metaphors could thus be seen to collude in what Leo Bersani has called a "culture of redemption".[23] Such a culture not only rehearses and hastens the passage from Shoah to Gvurah, from martyrdom to heroism (a central tenet of the traditional Jewish framework of historical interpretation), thereby short-circuiting the real work of mourning. It also expects its art to privilege redemptive values.

This is precisely the expectation met and fuelled by many of the Images offered to us by *Histoire(s)*. What I am resisting here is the seductive urge to endow art with a redemptive authority in the form of a capacity not merely to further but to complete the work of mourning. This urge seems to underlie Godard's discourse of cinematic resurrection: "there can only be an image of a dead brother *after* the mourning work is complete, at the moment when his image is *no longer* an image of pain."[24] For surely such an assertion risks making the image redundant as a vector of memory and testimony? Certainly, in this era of acute media-induced compassion fatigue, it may well be, as Godard suggests, that "an image is not strong because you see a dead person".[25] But how can film of a "musulman" (one of the so-called "living dead") staving off the attacks of an SS dog, even when intercut with the spectacle of dancing skeletons in Jean Renoir's *La Règle du jeu*, 1939, or, in obscene juxtaposition, with the fleshy nakedness of a German porn movie, ever produce anything other than an Image of the irreducible real of unendurable suffering? And, surely, this is a real that has yet to be mourned, redeemed, and resurrected?

The absent real and the missing reel

When Jean-Louis Comolli identifies resurrection as one of the two defining motifs of cinema, he names the other as disguise, arguing that each motif is merely a version of the other.[26] This binding of resurrection to false images, indeed to misrepresentation, highlights further the questions I am raising around the image/redemption equation, questions that have very specific historical roots. For when Godard identifies Lanzmann's *Shoah* with cinema's failure to show, he inadvertently pinpoints something essential about the nature of the Nazi atrocity which casts doubt upon all attempts to accord to a visual regime a privileged redemptive aesthetic. Although Lanzmann has described his most recent film, *Sobibor, 14 octobre 1943, 16 heures*, 2001, as a film of courage and hope which "sanctifies the life [...] at the heart of that kingdom of death", this is a film about resistance, and as such presents itself as the mournful Other of *Shoah*.[27] Instead, the earlier film, Lanzmann's *oeuvre matrice*, gives voice to those who could not resist, and thus works constantly against catharsis, more precisely, against the Image itself, against a Godardian faith in its epiphany at the time of the resurrection.

Ironically, it is Lanzmann who has come under fire for "sacralising" the discourse, accused by Godard, for example, of pronouncing interdictions, taboos, even "book-burning".[28] Strangely, but tellingly, the non-encounter between the two directors has centred around the disputed existence of a tiny fragment of film which Jean-Jacques Delfour has aptly named "la pellicule maudite" ("the accursed reel").[29] Ever since 1985, not insignificantly the release date of *Shoah*, Godard, citing the Nazis' bureaucratic mania for recording every last detail, has been repeating his conviction that this hypothetical footage allegedly shot by Nazis inside a gas chamber to record the very heart of the process of extermination is merely buried in an archive somewhere, "because if it were shown, something would change" (precisely what he never specifies).[30] But his very insistence on the existence of this footage seems to hint at an insecurity with regard to the unimaged real, an anxiety no doubt intensified by current revisionist debate, inspiring a need for vision as proof, as guarantor of truth, where the image alone is the mark of the real. Indeed, it is this concern that explicitly frames some of Godard's reflections on digital technology, as he hypothesises its abuse by Le Pen to retouch images of the camps: "the image will no longer be a proof".[31] As Jean-Michel Frodon and Sylvie Lindeperg have pointed out, such a position would appear disconcertingly to contradict much of the oeuvre of a director notorious for his claims to present "pas une image juste, juste une image" ("not a just image, just an image").[32]

Lanzmann takes as his point of departure a radical refusal of the "logic of proof" that would fetishise the image, a logic more dubious than ever at a time when new technologies of representation are undermining the status of the image as visible evidence, as credible witness.[33] Rethinking the relationship between archive and truth, the director begins to show us how much more than a historical footnote is at stake in the missing Nazi reel. Adamant that images of a working gas chamber could not exist, he has been harshly attacked for his much misinterpreted statement that, were they ever to surface, he would destroy them immediately.[34] For such footage would not only lay bare, to quote Manuel Köppen, "the climax of the unimaginable", "the traumatic-perverse 'primal scene' of the Holocaust", it would also contain and thereby temporarily legitimise the perspective of the Nazi voyeur.[35] And yet it is the staging of this very scene that has produced one of the most ethically charged encounters in the history of the moving image, an encounter which cinema, intrigued by its own limits, has repeatedly figured, erased and reconfigured. Precisely by virtue of the physical absence of the disputed reel, of the documentary "evidence", the view through the spy hole into the gas chamber has come to haunt cinema, where it has been compulsively staged, either–as in Godard–as a redemptive presence, or–as in Lanzmann–as a structuring absence.[36]

Of these traumatic polarities, the former is familiar to us from *Schindler's List*, 1993. Spielberg's zoom through a spy-hole into what, in fact, proves to be simply a shower room exploits the lure of the hidden which is suddenly revealed. It invites a scopophilia, the desire visually to reclaim a trauma framed and contained by the metal circle. Other filmmakers, however, have sought to drain their images of the fascination invoked and pleasure promised by Spielberg. Like Constantin Costa-Gavras's controversial *Amen*, 2002, and Elida Schogt's *Zyklon Portrait*, 1999, which employ the image less to reveal than to allude to its own limits, Leszek Wosiewicz's *Kornblumenblau*, 1988, stages the encounter with the "primal scene" reflexively. Here, shot/reverse shot editing positions the viewer precariously, alternately on the inside amongst the contorted limbs of the dying and on the outside with a young apple-munching SS officer, aligning our perspective with his smug, unflinching gaze. And, in what is (to my knowledge) the only direct cinematic representation of this scene, what we see is no Spielbergian shower room. Instead, we witness something closer to the traumatic return of the *"mise en scène* of suffering", the "tortured body [...] exposed, [...] offered up as spectacle" so movingly described by Foucault in his discussion of public executions in the *âge classique*.[37] In a shot sequence more familiar from horror movies, off-screen space is inhabited not by a fear-inspiring Other but by a voyeur who brings us face to face with our own complicity in an atrocity that is framed as a spectacle. Utterly exterior to the experience of the victims, this framing draws attention both to the sadistic–even pornographic–structure of voyeurism and to the shame it can produce; as Delfour puts it: "the other suffers before my eyes while I myself remain invulnerable."[38] In *Kornblumenblau*, then, while sheer visual overload may mislead us into believing we have finally located the *pellicule maudite*, we are, in fact, viewing its reflexive antidote. Violent and violating, this sequence of unprecedented sadism produces its own self-critique, to cast its viewer-voyeur as both victim and persecutor.

Read thus, this endlessly re-presented filmic moment, the passage across the threshold into the place of death, becomes a privileged figure of the uneasy passage of the Shoah into visual witness, and of the ethical risks incurred by this passage. It can be no coincidence that this is also the figure multiplied and refracted by the kind of film Godard suggests would be the only adequate testimony to the violence:

The only true film to be made about [the camps]–which has never been made and never will be because it would be intolerable–would show a camp from the point of view of the torturers, with their daily problems. How to fit a 2 metre human corpse into a 50 centimetre coffin? [...] How to burn a hundred women with only enough petrol for ten? [...] What would be unendurable is not the horror that would emanate from such scenes, but instead their perfectly normal and human appearance.[39]

Certainly, the implicit equation normal/human would require justification, recalling as it does the "banality of evil" analysed by Hannah Arendt (it could be argued that part of the fascination of Lanzmann's films lies in the way individuals such as Franz Suchomel and Maurice Rossel appear normal yet inhuman).[40] Perhaps the persistence of such debates provides another reason why this project remains, for Godard, unrealisable. More disturbing, however, is the risk that a film which limits itself to the perspective of the executioner (narrating, for example, "the story of the typist who typed 'four gold teeth, five hundred grams of hair' and came back the next day") will merely bottle up symbolic violence.[41] For surely the view through the spy-hole would be inscribed in every image of Godard's hypothetical project. And if so, then how far would it be from a simple–and quite horrific–*mise en scène* of the elusive *pellicule maudite*?

At stake here is the possibility of creating a scopic intersubjective space that does not merely recapitulate the position of a suffering body exposed to the gaze of a Nazi voyeur. What is most compelling–and troubling–about Godard's claims is that they inadvertently identify the spy-hole, an allegory both for the aperture of a camera and for the cinema viewer's capacity to see without being seen, as a heuristic lens, a paradigmatic ethical figure for filmic

representation after, as well as of, the Shoah. And here Godard's claim that cinema failed to bear witness to the camps, a claim contradicted even within *Histoire(s)* (for example by the presence of George Stevens's footage), becomes less elliptical. What actually troubles him is cinema's failure to bear witness to the gas chambers (and here Lanzmann would agree). The level of anxiety created by this failure, not only in Godard, became evident during the debate in the French media triggered by the controversial photographic exhibition in Paris in 2001, *Mémoire des camps*, a debate which has mapped itself–and thereby also shed valuable light–on to the ongoing Godard/Lanzmann stand-off. Georges Didi-Huberman announces his polemical but anxiety-laden agenda from the outset when he insists, citing the Godardian formula, that four of the photographs displayed in the exhibition "save the honour of the real". According to the startling claims of the writer, in contrast to the abundance of archive material from the Liberation, these "four scraps of film snatched from the jaws of hell" finally "make visible" the Shoah itself, the heart of the killing-machine recorded through the spy-hole.[42] Such claims are rather puzzling. Frequently exhibited, these photographs of naked women walking through woods and the incineration of a pile of bodies in an open-air ditch were all taken secretly in Auschwitz by members of the Sonderkommandos in August 1944.[43] What is crucial for Didi-Huberman is the possibility that they were taken from inside Crematorium V at Birkenau; he draws attention to, and reflects on, the significance of a dark frame, suggestive of a window, which, according to certain hypotheses, was situated in one of the gas chambers. Like that of Lanzmann, Didi-Huberman's response to the missing reel is ethically motivated, and yet, with Godard, he draws the opposite conclusion, binding the image to an ethical imperative:

Above: *Pasazerka*, Andrzej Munk. Completed posthumously in 1963 by Witold Lesiewicz, it is frequently cited in Godard's later work.

What the SS wanted to destroy in Auschwitz was not only the life, but also [...] the very form of the human being, and with it its image. In such a context, the act of resisting thus identifies itself as the act of preserving this image in spite of everything [*maintenir cette image malgré tout*] [...].[44]

It is this stubborn, well-intended "malgré tout" reiterated in Didi-Huberman's chosen title, however, that calls attention to the crisis of figurability (the absence of images) that it simultaneously defies. As such, it begs the inevitable question posed by Wajcman in his impassioned riposte: "is there no other remedy to the absence of images than the image?"[45]

Protective shields and veils

It is Lanzmann's constant contention that art should seek less to "remedy" than to diagnose this absence of the image. For to see, to show, to "illustrate" the Shoah may risk using the image itself to paper over the Nazi attack on the image alluded to by Didi-Huberman, replacing absence with a redemptive presence which, as Deleuze has observed, may all too easily operate as a pretext for an escape from the real.[46] Moreover–and contrary to Didi-Huberman's claims and Godardian rhetoric–these photographs no more expose the primal scene of the Shoah, the killing in the gas chamber, than do the archive images of mass graves and bulldozers at Belsen (the metonymic images that have constituted the iconography of the genocide ever since Alain Resnais's *Nuit et brouillard*, 1955). This is where, for Lanzmann, figuration becomes falsification; in the absence of the Nazi reel, the image will only give a reductive account of the real. But the problem runs deeper than degrees of veracity: it is ethical. Given his choice of a visual medium, the most conspicuous of the multiple refusals recorded by *Shoah*, a film created precisely as a rejection of (rather than supplement or antidote to) Godard's elusive *pellicule*, is the absence of all iconic images of the violence. (An intriguing antecedent here is Resnais's suppression, at least in its moving form, of the iconic image of the bombing, the mushroom cloud, in *Hiroshima mon amour*, 1959, despite the fact that it opened Marguerite Duras's original screenplay.) Far from Godard's retrieval and multiplication of archival fragments, for Lanzmann the Shoah lies firmly outside the archive ("I made *Shoah* against all archives"); as the ultimately other, unfixable, unclassifiable event, it resists the archival violence described by Derrida.[47] Not only does this rejection deny the viewer of *Shoah* the dubious visual pleasure promised by so many other filmic presentations of the horror; by casting doubt upon the adequacy of the image as witness, it also forces us to query the ethical status of the image in the context of an event which precipitates a visual medium into crisis.

For the absent reel conceals an absent real; while in one sense the violence became the Nazis' own private spectacle (every camp, it seems, had its own photographic laboratory), the very essence of the project lay in the retroactive self-effacement and amnesia built into it from its very conception.[48] This was the singularity of the atrocity: the so-called *politique nazie du caché* (Nazi politics of the hidden) attempted to master the narratives of history and memory by destroying every trace of its own violence (the Jewish "camouflage commandos" in the camps were a case in point). Robert Antelme has vividly described this experience from the perspective of the inmates, identifying a double negation. *L'Espèce humaine*, 1957, recounts their own efforts to efface their very faces under the SS gaze, to become the unrecognisable, the quasi-invisible.[49] Shoshana Felman's famous insights into testimony point to the implications of such a negation:

The essence of the Nazi scheme is to make itself–and to make the Jews–essentially invisible [...] The Holocaust occurs as the unprecedented, inconceivable historical

Opposite: **Production photograph of the making of *Nuit et brouillard*, Alain Resnais, 1955.**

advent of an event without a witness, an event which historically consists in the scheme of the literal erasure of its witnesses but which, moreover, philosophically consists in an accidenting of perception, in a splitting of eyewitnessing as such; [...] an event which radically annihilates the recourse (and appeal) to visual corroboration [...].[50]

In slaughtering its eye-witnesses and destroying its visual traces, the Shoah produces not only a crisis of witnessing, but also, I would suggest (to para-phrase Felman), an event without an image. Whence Jean-Luc Nancy's claim that "the reality of the camps will have lain firstly in a flattening [*écrasement*] of representation itself, or of the possibility of representation".[51]

This is not to advocate an Adorno-esque silencing of art. On the contrary, and in opposition to Godard's messianic Images, what *Shoah* does show is *l'image absente*, the absolute absence of anything to show except the disappearance of traces in the present. This is the sense in which Lanzmann, with others, is redefining the task of the image, liberating it from the confines of representation and revelation: an image can do more than show. And also vice versa, for precisely as it is erased from the image-track, the "primal scene" beyond the spy-hole comes to haunt every moment of the Sonderkommando testimonies, identified by the film as its absent subject. This is also where the ethical injunction against (mis)representation of the catastrophe becomes irreducible to the religious prohibition of figuration (*Bilderverbot*) with which it is so often equated (and of which Godard falsely accuses Lanzmann). Alain Besançon's recent *L'Image interdite*, 1994, has cogently rethought the history of art as a history of spiritual "iconoclastic crises" born out of multiple (Islamic, Judaic and Christian) attempts–or refusals–to produce a visible image of an invisible divine.[52] For Besançon, both histories–like his commentary–culminate in the radical refusal of representation that defines abstract art (epitomised, of course, by Malevich's *White Square on White*, as a *face-à-face* with a hidden God which reveals only, and precisely, divine invisibility). But such iconoclastic impulses are rendered inadequate by the Shoah, where the invisibility of the subject of representation is doubled by the self-effacement proper to the event itself. Such an event also renders the "iconophiliac" agenda endorsed by Godard's *Histoire(s)* unsustainable.[53] This agenda seems unequivocally present behind the director's insistence on the revelatory potential of montage, for example, at the culmination of the Auschwitz/Taylor/Giotto sequence ("39-44–martyrdom and resurrection of the documentary. Oh what wonder to be able to look at what we cannot see! Oh sweet miracle of our blind eyes!").[54] But while the iconophiliac thesis stems from the reality of the Incarnation (the acceptance of Christ as the visible image/face of an invisible God), and is thus grounded in presence, iconic images of the historical trauma of the Shoah risk merely recuperating an absent (invisible) core into present (visible) meaning. As Elisabeth Pagnoux argues in her critique of Didi-Huberman, "to make us witnesses to this scene [the gas chamber] [...] is to distort the reality of Auschwitz, which was an event without a witness. It is to fill the silence."[55]

Slavoj Žižek has formulated this risk more subversively. The critic draws parallels between the notorious case of Binjamin Wilkomirski, whose best-selling and singularly graphic testimony *Bruchstücke* (Fragments) was later revealed as a fraud, and the experience of soldiers involved in today's "aseptic" technological warfare. Both suffer from forms of False Memory Syndrome, and Žižek, reworking Freud, shows how in both cases the habitual process of generating fantasies to shield the subject from trauma is inverted. While in Roberto Benigni's *La vita è bella*, 1997, what Žižek reads as the benevolent "symbolic fiction" with which Guido protects his son (that the camp is a game, with rules, winners and prizes) invites a reflexive reading of the whole film as a fictional shield designed to protect its spectators, the case of Wilkomirski and the soldiers is more disturbing. Here, rather than a detraumatised fiction of the real, it is the ultimate traumatic experience (for Wilkomirski, life as a child in the camps, and for the soldiers, face-to-face combat) that is itself fantasised as a shield. Each protects himself from trauma with a trauma that was never lived: Wilkomirski was never in a camp, and the soldiers had never encountered the enemy except as a dot on a radar screen. Crucially, their pathological inversion of the protective fiction offers insight into one of the central, and in this context most uncomfortable, lessons of psychoanalysis: that, in Žižek's words, "the images of utter catastrophe, far from giving access to the Real, can function as a protective shield AGAINST the Real."[56]

Once again, then, we find the lure of the redemptive aesthetic, but this time in the more insidious guise of visuals so explicit, so graphic, that we cannot help but be blinded to their consolatory function. When reconfigured in the light of the legacy of the Nazis' self-concealment, however, Žižek's account becomes a warning against the seamless identification of image and truth in the context of such extreme trauma: the more completely we reveal a traumatic reality, the more completely we may be fictionalising–and thereby redeeming–it. This is a warning that runs against the grain of contemporary culture's greed for knowledge (and comfort) through the image. Discerning this greed in Didi-Huberman's polemic, Wajcman radicalises Žižek's argument:

every image of the horror lays a veil over the horror; every image, because it is an image, protects us from the horror [...] at the same time as it uncovers something, it covers it up again just as efficiently; the image diverts us from what it shows us [...] Horror and images repel each other, such is their nature.[57]

As the metaphor slips from a shield to a veil, what in Žižek was a possibility becomes in Wajcman an ontological given. Although his generalising terms verge on the reductive, Wajcman's suspicion of the pacifying power of all images in the face of a real that is resistant to visualisation not only goes some way to accounting for the public success of the *Mémoire des camps* exhibition as an emotional release and salve (it is much easier to begin to mourn an event whose violence has been photographically fixed and contained).[58] It also warns that every filmmaker seeking to reestablish a relation between horror and image must embrace a discourse that is incurably aporetic.

In the light of this aporia of cinema, that the image may conceal as much as it reveals, the task, like that allotted to modern art by Lyotard, becomes to present the fact that the unpresentable exists.[59] To retrieve the event without an image from behind its multiple shields and veils, Lanzmann constructs an entire film around the fading of the traces which Godard collects and multiplies. "The point of departure for the film", Lanzmann explains, "was [...] the disappearance of traces: nothing remains but a void, and it was necessary to make a film out of this void."[60] Thus, as Rancière confirms, "the reality of the genocide that is filmed is the reality of its disappearance."[61] In this way, Lanzmann's rejection of the Godardian *pellicule maudite* comes to figure a broader withdrawal from the consolatory space of representation; the more realistic the representation, he suggests, the more it betrays the notion of an *irreprésentable*, a real that resists representation. (Whence the filmmaker's ethical qualms about the images of geese in *Sobibor* whose deafening cries on the soundtrack compete with, and threaten to overwhelm, the voice of Yehuda Lerner. This is potent *mise en scène*–the Nazis kept geese in the camp to drown the sound of human cries from the gas chambers–provoking Lanzmann to voice his fear of the sequence being "illustrative, thus obscene".)[62] And this movement away from representation is entirely unredemptive. Even in *Sobibor*, in many ways–and in stark opposition to *Shoah*–a skilled driving of the real towards a narrative acting out, closer to myth than to tragedy and invoking notions of suspense, heroism and narrative pleasure, the threat of redemptive closure is undercut in the final moments.[63] A document detailing the convoys of victims arriving at the camp scrolls interminably up the screen, the scandalous absence-presence of those who were not so fortunate displacing Lerner's smile.

For Lanzmann, then, the antidote to iconophilia is not iconophobia. Instead, the catharsis of iconic images must give way to the real of oral testimony. In direct opposition to the "super-production à grand spectacle" ("big-budget spectacular") which Godard has claimed he has always wanted to make about the camps, Lanzmann communicates a traumatic absence in the form of what he calls "fictions du réel" ("fictions of the real").[64] Such fictions produce temporal presences (quite distinct from the Godardian faith in the images of montage as imprints of presence). Whence Lanzmann's refusal to stop filming during Abraham Bomba's breakdown in *Shoah*, for example. Here, the director's unrelenting questions trigger an implosion of the testimonial narrative where, in his words, "the past was resuscitated with such violence that all distance collapsed, producing a pure present, the very opposite of recollection [*souvenir*]", as the real resurfaces through (and against) the fictive detours of *mise en scène*.[65] But rather than facilitating a necessary amnesia as in *Histoire(s)*, Lanzmann's fictions are the vehicles of anamnesis (as distinct from souvenirs), as a pair of scissors and a barber's shop or the startling cries of geese transport the witness back to the threshold of the gas chamber. For what erupts in the midst of these fictions is precisely the Real in the Lacanian sense of an insistent but indecipherable message–the Real of a trauma that returns and resists figuration. And while Godard's montage performs the processes of memory, the passage to anamnesis via the amnesic detour, to truth via fiction's selectiveness, Lanzmann's time-images imitate memory's very temporalities. These temporalities are multiple: momentary paroxysms of pure anamnesis, where the repetition of a gesture (in Bomba's case, the simple act of cutting hair) precipitates the witness's "re-enactment" of the past in the present, alternate with long tracking shots of desolate "non-lieux de mémoire" ("non-sites of memory") that mirror a more nostalgic mode, where living presence is replaced by loss.[66] For, in *Shoah*, the image, in its attachment to the present, is that which reveals memory while barring history from sight.

Absence vs Excess

Godard's disturbingly perfunctory dismissal of Lanzmann's approach, his defensiveness with regard to the *pellicule maudite*, as well as the redemptive power of images, prompts Wajcman to situate Lanzmann as "the exile, the pariah" of Godard's "Church of the Holy Image". Why? "Because [Godard] believes in the image." In contrast to Spielberg, who has created, in Lanzmann's words, "an illustrated Shoah", Lanzmann remains "the Unbeliever, charged with iconoclasm".[67] While Wajcman's religious analogy is lucid, it is limiting in that it risks reducing the debate to the simple binary couple "image/not image". Certainly, as we have seen, both directors disagree about whether or not an image, particularly a direct image of suffering, can have an ethical effect: the production of, at the very least, the spectatorial autonomy necessary to judge and to refuse. Godard's belief that the image need not necessarily be a mechanism of fascination and thus a negation of its subject is based on his conception of montage as itself constituting the Image. This Lanzmann refuses, a refusal doubled by the effacement that was part of the Nazi project itself, so that the task of cinema becomes to reveal this self-negation. Each position can be criticised yet at the same time defends itself. If we begin to reflect, however, on how little Godard's Image has to do with an image (in the sense of the staple visuals of commercial cinema), and thus how far it is removed from representation, the original binary opposition and the vexed question of the evidentiary status of the image (and its theological-philosophical baggage) open up on to more specific questions of editing.

The two works offer profoundly contrasting viewing experiences. Lanzmann's refusal pits itself against what, in Godard, becomes proliferation pushed to the very limits of sense. "Absence" against "Excess": the two figures of the ineffable proper to the communication of the experience of the camps. Certainly, the ethic of radical heterogeneity and inclusion espoused by *Histoire(s)* might be understood as a warning against a film such as *Shoah*, whose screenings have tended to become ceremonialised and its refusals themselves "sacralised" in such a way as to call into question the ethical legitimacy of every other cinematic approach to the camps.[68] But while Godard's conception of montage as collage, or rather collision, could not be more different from Lanzmann's exploration of the testimonial value of the paroxysm (his patient crescendos to moments of pure anamnesis where terror is not shown but lived, where the intensity of experience is privileged over sight), its critique of representation is equally potent. And it is here, in the reinstatement of the notion of an *irreprésentable*, that the two directors find a point of contact, not only in the critique of Spielberg's presumption to trademark the subject, but in the wider call for a systematic questioning of the obscenity of dominant representational forms.

Such a call gains urgency at a time when new technologies are transforming our relationship to historical trauma, which becomes, through unprecedented visibility, pure media spectacle. Symptomatic of this increasingly spectacular mediation of real violence was the televisual *mise en scène* of the attack in 2001 on the World Trade Center in New York, where the endless and meaning-draining looping of this "spectacle of the real" marked merely the beginning of what has tended to be critiqued as a "war of images".[69] I would suggest, however, that there is an important sense in which this conflict can cogently be situated within the era of "wars *without* images", heralded for Serge Daney by the Gulf War.[70] For the hypervisibility of the September 11 attack concealed invisible trauma. The intrusion of the real of catastrophe into an image-saturated society produced a visual void, both real and physical ("Ground Zero", the absence of images of the dead, Bin Laden as the West's elusive blind-spot) and symbolic, what Žižek names the "desert of the Real" and Frodon has called "a 'silence of images' [...] a hole in the production of images by the most 'iconogenic' society humanity has ever known".[71] Rethought as an operation of effacement, this real would seem–in the face of the excess of witnessing which it produced–to pose a resistance to the image that recalls the visual legacy of the self-negation built into the Nazi project.

Once resituated within this legacy, such resistance reanimates the debate about the ethics of presenting suffering as spectacle famously taken up by Jacques Rivette in his critique of Gillo Pontecorvo's *Kapo*, 1960 (a piece so influential for Godard and Daney), and recapitulated almost verbatim over 30 years later by critics of *Schindler's List*.[72] But the televisual spectacularisation of suffering also marks a new stage in this debate. For what was unprecedented about the images of September 11 was their immediacy; by the second plane crash we had become "real time spectator-witnesses".[73] This eruption of real time into representation fuels contemporary concerns about the dissolution of the "historical event". As Vivian Sobchack puts it in her volume *The Persistence of History*, "event and its representation, immediacy and its mediation, have moved increasingly towards simultaneity [...] Today, history seems to happen right now".[74] Crucially, the simultaneity of reality and representation also eradicates the temporal gap that inhabits–and defines–traumatic experience. Marking the temporal delay that splits the traumatic event from its psychic

impact and defers its figuration (the unstable Freudian concept of *Nachträglichkeit*), such a gap is the first prerequisite for remembering and bearing witness. Inevitably, then, its elision in the live spectacle would seem to threaten to render the image redundant as a vehicle for memory, testimony, and mourning.

It is in implicit resistance to this threat that Godard and Lanzmann find themselves reunited. For at a time when the electronic spectacularisation of real death makes imperative a redefinition of the ethical status of the image, both directors find in cinema a uniquely privileged medium for mnemonic and testimonial work. This is surely one of the senses in which we should understand the famous Godardian formula that television generates forgetting. Rendering the real as spectacle, contemporary media tyrannically collude in the serial production of amnesia by erasing–rather than bearing witness to–the otherness of historical trauma. As Daney has argued, however, the homogenising closure imposed, under the guise of complete transparency, by what he calls "the visual" finds a point of resistance in "the image". The latter is defined and inhabited, in contrast, by lack, and is thus "devoted to bearing witness to a certain alterity" (this is why, for Godard, television does not produce images at all).[75] It is the capacity to reveal this lack, this absence, this unfigurable otherness, that the images of *Shoah* share with the Images of *Histoire(s)*.

Despite his rhetoric of redemption, Godard, just as much as Lanzmann, prevents us from seeking refuge or closure in images of catastrophe. Of course, lack is figured by *Histoire(s)* as excess, and here it is through visual overload that closure is deferred, that the iconography of the Shoah is subverted, and that the image transcends the consolatory impulses that could reduce it to a protective shield or veil. Indeed, both directors identify in the cinematic image

Above: *Kapo*, Gillo Pontecorvo, 1960.

a privileged capacity to bear witness to the Other it lacks, the otherness it cannot represent, in short, to the invisible, more specifically, to traumatic "silences of images". From their shared position of questioning and critique with respect to representation, both recognise a visual regime as best able to render absence by frustrating the desire for presence which it invokes.

One of Lanzmann's most powerful images of spontaneous anamnesis, a wrinkled Henrik Gawkowski leaning out of his locomotive and drawing his finger across his throat in front of a sign announcing "Treblinka", has been seamlessly appropriated by Spielberg and others. But it is only when it is recycled in extreme slow motion by Godard in chapter 1A of *Histoire(s)* that its iconic status is revealed, that we realise that these images have an afterlife, and that Gawkowski, too, has entered the archive. Reconfigured by Godard, this image, in its sinister familiarity, reminds us that an image of the present will always become an image of the past in the archive of the future. It also reminds us just how much of *Shoah*'s anamnesic power comes–despite Lanzmann's claims–from the archive, from the concrete referential images supplied by intertexts which play in our memory but are refused to our eyes as we watch the film.

In this sense, the work of each director could be understood as the correcting –and corrected–image of the other. And while it seems unlikely that they will ever see eye to eye on the question of the ethical charge of the image, perhaps this is also the task in which their competing discourses meet. Despite its redemptive telos, *Histoire(s)*, like *Shoah*, ultimately remains a work in progress, a work of endless resurrection, continuously rewriting and contradicting itself, in which the work of mourning is slowed by the repetitions of melancholia. As such, both works demand (to cite Alain Bergala) an "attentive spectator 'in waiting'", willing to forgo consolation and take the risk of opening him/herself to the alterity of texts fissured by aporias, excess and lack.[76] In issuing this demand, both directors cast their spectator no longer as a child to be protected, but as an ethical subject in crisis. For what s/he takes away from both films is the painful realisation that, as we mourn, our most successful attempts to present the Shoah will always be fallible, lacking, partial at best, finally inadequate, but, for the moment at least, always inscribed with a melancholic margin for revision. Tellingly, this is a margin Godard has begun to explore in recent interviews, as he shows signs of revising his verdict on *Shoah*.[77] For as long as his image is no longer "just an image", "le fameux débat" is set to remain a missed encounter, impoverished testament to that scandalous absence which the image is unable to redeem.

THE INDEX AND ERASURE
GODARD'S APPROACH TO
FILM HISTORY

TROND LUNDEMO For Jean-Luc Godard, montage is something cinema never achieved. In *Histoire(s) du cinéma*, 1998, the lost films and missed opportunities of cinema become a driving force in the narratives of film history. Montage could have been realised at a given time, under given conditions, but it never was. Because the capacity for montage was never realised, cinema bears a measure of grief and remains in mourning:

[…] montage is what made cinema unique and different as compared to painting and the novel. Cinema as it was originally conceived is going to disappear quite quickly, within a lifetime, and something else will take its place. But what made it original, and what will never really have existed, like a plant that has never really left the ground, is montage. The silent movie world felt it very strongly and talked about it a lot. No-one found it. Griffith was looking for something like montage, he discovered the close-up. Eisenstein naturally thought that he had found montage…. But by montage I mean something much more vast.[1]

How could cinema have this predisposition for montage but never attain it? This proposition suggests that cinema is seen as an art form with many virtual forms, where only a few are actualised according to the criteria of its historical, social and aesthetic contexts. Whereas some theorists of cinema such as Jean Epstein, Walter Benjamin and Gilles Deleuze identify how the technology of cinema instigates formal and conceptual ruptures in art and society, Godard seems to believe that montage depends on an artistic practice, and that what is at stake is finding the "right" relation between images. He is more concerned with the work of art than the general media discourses of the time, and this accounts for his work throughout *Histoire(s)*, with categories or series of artworks, films, auteurs and authors, musicians, etc.. True montage could not be achieved because the social conditions

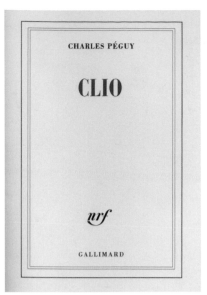

favouring montage retreat from public view quite early in film history. That is why cinema is the right medium at the wrong time, arriving only towards the end of the formation of industrial processes. As Godard states in Chapter 4B, *Les signes parmi nous*: "[…] cinema is the art form of the nineteenth century that gave life to the twentieth, which doesn't exist in its own right."

Yet if montage represents key virtual aspects of cinema that were never actualised, nevertheless, within a historical framework, existing works may enter into relations with social and artistic events to form new relations, and thus reveal new aspects of the works. This is why Godard treats history in the affirmative mode, and why he believes that historical formations actually are possible. *Histoire(s)* may be regarded simply as a meditation on these processes, yet it remains a work of montage. This is because montage is an operation of thought. The compilatory techniques of the series do not reproduce existing forms of montage in the works cited but rearrange the formal and stylistic elements in ways that render them new. Film history becomes a reserve for writing history consisting of preserved as well as lost works, and of actual and virtual events. The basic conception of film history is of a virtual archive, or database, as a material condition for making connections between works and forming new ideas. By treating the familiar images and sounds of film history in ways that make them enter into new relations with each other, Godard focuses on the forgetting of the "original" event as a precondition for the work of montage. For this reason, as we shall see, *Histoire(s)* is one of the most important works for thinking about the logic of the database in computer environments. Indeed, *Histoire(s)* is groundbreaking in its approach to segmentation and serialisation because it employs multiple "search criteria", like iconic matches, movement relations, sound juxtapositions, together with more conventional archival searches based on linguistic criteria and naming. These multiple search criteria allow for unconventional and surprising montages, where the poetic principles of "the association of ideas [as] distant and right" are fulfilled.[2] I wish to pursue this point by analysing the archival properties of *Histoire(s)* as highlighted in Chapter 4A which examines "Hitchcock's method". My point of departure for considering the practices of the archive or the database will be Godard's use of a brief excerpt from *Le Mystère des roches de Kador* from 1912, as well as his repeated citing of Charles Péguy's meditation on the writing of history, *Clio: dialogue de l'histoire et de l'âme païenne*, 1917. As we shall see, the far-reaching compilatory techniques of *Histoire(s)* present the archive as a resource for the rewriting of texts and re-ordering of objects.

Memory demands a support, and I will identify a number of figures of recollection, and consequently of forgetting, by singling out sections or series in the work. I will contend that the discussion of Hitchcock as "master of the universe" is based on the archival powers of distributing memory and forgetting according to the principles of segmentation and indexing. *Histoire(s)* adheres to this strategy in order to foreground the techniques of forgetting at work within its own methods of montage. The concept of the archive serves as a springboard for discussion of how ideas are created through the juxtaposition of images and sounds, and I will argue that this process is always linked to selection and erasure.

Old forms in new contexts?

The new media scholar and artist Lev Manovich observes how computer media seem not to have met the expectation of new forms.[3] It is difficult to identify an "avant-garde" of computer media, in the traditional sense of the term. Computer media productions and applications are rather preoccupied with the re-circulation of the "new forms" characteristic of modernity, and artists' CD-ROMs and DVD installations often deploy the formal experiments of a century ago. Does this mean that the computer is impotent as a creative medium, and that all discourses of creativity and unlimited artistic freedom in computer media prove less productive than those of old technologies like photography and cinema when they were new–that is, when they were repeatedly denounced for their mechanical and reproductive properties? Or does it mean that the very idea of "new forms" is obsolete, and that it is a question embedded in the aesthetics of purity of the modern age, unfit for the hybrid and synthesising operations of the computer? Is not the computer instead engaged in segmenting, indexing and accessing already existing material? These questions about the computer are pertinent because Godard's videographic work in general, and *Histoire(s)* in particular, raises the same issues in relation to montage and the concept of history.

It is in regard to the notion of the archive as a reserve for writing history, for recollection and the emergence of new connections, that Godard's response coincides with Manovich's. It is precisely in segmenting existing material that *Histoire(s)* establishes the principles for recollection. History is conceived through the indexing principles of the archive by implying new criteria for making "searches" in the virtual database. There are no "new forms" in *Histoire(s)*; its work towards new ideas proceeds through montage and juxtapositions. But montage should not be understood simply as mental images resulting from associations of ideas, or the establishment of mental links. Eisenstein's concept of montage always resides in a movement of ideas, that is, a property of signification, and in his theory the mental image always takes priority over the visual level. Contrary to this, the use of existing material in *Histoire(s)* refuses any divisions between mental and visual levels. In Chapter 3B, *Une vague nouvelle*, cinema is accounted for as "a thought that forms, a form that thinks". If montage allows "a form of thought" in cinema, it is because it distributes and erases traces of memory as a prerequisite for a movement of thought. Godard is concerned with cinematic thinking instead of an abstract mental process.

The distribution of patterns of memory is fundamental to classical cinema. One of the most powerful structures for this is the alternation between scenes in parallel editing, crosscutting, shot/reverse shot or point of view shots. A relation between images is established according to a duality between memory and vision, as one image is "stored" while the following one is seen. An alternation of memory between the images is a precondition for all patterns of classical editing. For this reason, classical cinema always invites a high degree of mental activity in making sense of the images. However, this classical form is founded on established notions within idealist divisions between matter and thought. Rather than reproducing these conventional patterns of thought, the video series of *Histoire(s)* confronts these patterns with alternative distributions of memory.

The figure of classical continuity is frequently evoked in the videographical editing in *Histoire(s)*, but it is instead often rearranged as superimpositions. Sometimes the countershot flashes in and out of the centre of the first image. Thus, the memory storage privileging the duality of the seen and the mental image in classical continuity editing is evoked but simultaneously dissolved.[4] Chapter 2B, *Fatale beauté*, superimposes, and shifts aspects between, still images from Hitchcock's *Suspicion* of Joan Fontaine looking and Cary Grant carrying the suspicious glass of milk up the stairs. First, a still from a close-up of Fontaine fills the screen and is subsequently superimposed by a still of Grant carrying the milk. Interestingly, the close-up of Fontaine does not appear in the actual sequence in *Suspicion*, but is obtained from another shot

FAIRE
DESC R IO
PRÉCISE

QUI N'A
S EU LIEU
E LE TRAVAIL
DE L'HISTORIEN

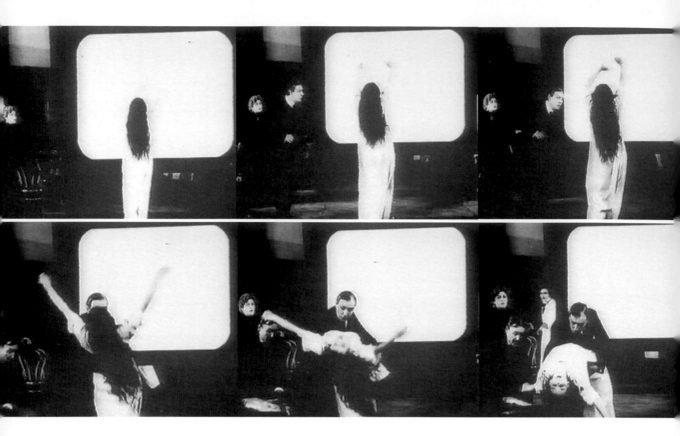

in the film or from a publicity still. A new shot/reverse shot composition is constructed but in the form of a superimposition. The close-up of the glass of milk reappears in Chapter 4A, *Le contrôle de l'univers*, although this time as a moving image. In the same way, many quotes are imperceptibly rearranged and estranged, or repeated in other forms. This technique of quotation and analysis in a single act through decomposition and superimposition is at the very core of Godard's concept of history in the series.

Montage results in an image that contains a virtual reserve, that is more than what it communicates in and of itself. An image that can be edited (in its epistemological sense) is an image that can enter into relation with another image. According to Robert Bresson's *Notes on The Cinematograph*, quoted in Chapter 2B, *Fatale beauté*, images that already carry an interpretation do not act on, or react to, other images, and are useless in the cinematographic system. This is evident in the fragments in *Histoire(s)* which do not seem to carry a meaning of their own. The series rather encourages thinking in images by juxtaposing "things that do not seem liable to be brought together at all" ("rassembler les choses qui ne semblent pas être disposées à l'être"), as it is stated in the series. This points towards what Jacques Rancière claims to be Deleuze's philosophical principle, namely to investigate "a relation of incommensurability".[5] In this sense, the core of the structures of montage in Godard's work is rather the conceptual distance between the elements, and how they refuse to create a meaning. In this sense, Rancière's view that there is no aesthetics in Deleuze's philosophy also holds true for Godard's *Histoire(s)*. There is instead a resistance to the doxa in art. The juxtaposition of images aims at excavating unexpected facets and surprising connections between works and texts rather than to form part of an argument or to convey predetermined ideas. It is for this reason that Godard's method of montage is based on a conception of the archive as a virtual reserve for writing history.

Above: **Suzanne regains her memory in Léonce Perret's *Le Mystère des roches de Kador*, 1912.**

Is is through montage that cinema can form historical expressions. But film history is not simply based on assigning places for works in established categories, or even on forming new historical categorisations. Cinema may interlace quotation and analysis, something that becomes explicit in the decompositions of images in *Histoire(s)*. The temporal displacement between shooting and projection lies behind the claim of the intertitle in Chapter 3B, *Une vague nouvelle*: "the screen is the camera". Cinema allows us to approach history in the present tense but always at the risk of forgetting. The capacity for projection of the past in cinema, and for positioning these images in unexpected correlations, is the historical mode of the series.

The excerpt from Léonce Perret's *Le Mystère des roches de Kador* in 2A, *Seul le cinéma*, elaborates on this. In the film, a young woman, Suzanne, suffers a traumatic experience which causes amnesia. Her cousin, played by the director Perret, is in love with her and writes a letter in her name to set up a meeting with her fiancé, an officer, by the cliffs of Kador. He pours a sleeping potion into her tea and she faints when they reach the cliffs of Kador; he hides in order to shoot the officer as he arrives by boat. Wounded, the officer finds her on the beach and manages to carry her to the boat. They drift ashore and are found without their knowing what happened. In order to heal her, the officer later gets in contact with the psychiatrist Professor Williams who has found a new method for curing amnesia. Williams restages the known events and shoots and edits a film of it. Upon the projection of the film, the woman recollects the missing parts and recovers her memory. In *Histoire(s)*, only a few seconds from the epiphanous moment when she regains her memory are cited. In the lit room, once the projection of Williams's film is over, Suzanne's recollection of the events takes place in front of the blank screen before she eventually passes out. It is via the return of the images in unfamiliar contexts that processes of recollection are triggered. The image never represents the forming of memory, but rather produces a complex process of forgetting and recollection at the core of Godard's concept of montage.

Cinema is portrayed here as a technical prosthesis to memory. The film functions to recall past events but the missing parts condition the process of recollection in the film's projection. A virtual memory of the film is maintained, since the repetitions (the event itself, the shooting and the projection of the film) makes the spectator recall the events that s/he has seen previously in the film without seeing them again. This leaves us with a complex view of cinema's relation to memory: it constitutes the event as a kind of "re-mediation" but simultaneously performs a process of erasure. Memory turns into recollection through elimination, and cinema is viewed as a machine for the selection of images and the distribution of memory. Professor Williams's method of projecting images mirrors that of Godard as historian. As with the amnesiac in *Le Mystère des roches de Kador*, the images from the past in *Histoire(s)* are never of an original event, but rather a rewriting and an erasure.

The media researcher Friedrich Kittler devotes much attention to the psychotechnics of cinema in his 1986 study, *Grammophon, Film, Typewriter*. Following Hugo Münsterberg's *The Photoplay: A Psychological Study*, he argues that whereas psychoanalysis only establishes analogies between cinema and the dream, psychotechnics observes how film enacts the processes of perception and recognition for the viewer.[6] Münsterberg's study was published in 1916, four years after *Le Mystère des roches de Kador* was released, making Dr Münsterberg a pupil and successor to Professor Williams. Attention, recognition, imagination, emotion: all conscious and unconscious processes have their technological correlation–be it the close-up, the flash-back or the split-screen–in Münsterberg's view. According to Kittler, the selections of our mental processes reduce the chaotic noise of everyday life into experience, and this is the process to which Suzanne submits in the screening room. The selections of cinematic technology substitute that of her senses and make the information of the event possible to handle. Her catatonic state is caused by a surplus of emotions and input which is treated by the selections and filtering devices at the core of the technology in "Professor Williams's method".

Godard's brief quote from the end of the screening in *Kador*, when the film is over and the screen is blank, is a telling choice. This shot also appears in *2x50 ans de cinéma français*, made with Anne-Marie Miéville in 1995. It is in the absence of the image that recollection can take place. The quote adheres to the mnemotechnical principle for *Histoire(s)* stated in Chapter 4B: "Who desires to recollect should devote himself to forgetting, at the risk of forgetting absolutely, and to this beautiful coincidence that recollection becomes." Jacques Aumont devotes much attention to this passage in his important study *Amnésies: fictions du cinéma d'après Jean-Luc Godard*, noting that it could be read as a principle for the view of history that informs Godard's entire project.[7] It holds true to the processes of memory portrayed in Lemmy Caution's struggle with the computer in *Alphaville*, 1965 and lies at the core of the process of recollection in *Nouvelle Vague*, 1990. It is only by forgetting, and by having the patience for our memories to come back, that they become true memories. Only upon their return, when they become blood, gaze and gesture, do they become inseparable from us.

Hitchcock's method

Processes of memory depend on the organisational structures of the archive. In Godard's *Histoire(s)*, indexing and segmentation become the precondition for memory and history. In *Le contrôle de l'univers*, Godard identifies Hitchcock's method as one of indexing objects. We have forgotten the logic of the various narratives but we remember the relation between the objects in Hitchcock's films: the windmill turning the wrong way round in *Saboteur*, the cigarette lighter in *Strangers on a Train*, the wine bottle in *Notorious*…. Godard approaches the reserves of film history in a similar way–as an archive of both present and missing objects, where erasure and forgetting result from the indexing of objects. The system of links and selections in Hitchcock's body of work is reworked into Godard's historical project. During a sequence of decomposed quotes from Hitchcock films focusing on the relations between objects, the voice-over states:

We have forgotten why Joan Fontaine leans over a cliff, and what Joel McCrea went to do in Holland; we have forgotten what Montgomery Clift keeps eternally silent about, and why Janet Leigh stops at Bates Motel, and why Theresa Wright is still in love with Uncle Charlie; we have forgotten what Henry Fonda is not entirely guilty of, and exactly why the American government hires Ingrid Bergman. But we remember a handbag, a bus in the desert, a glass of milk, the wings of a windmill, a hairbrush; but we remember a shelf of wine bottles, a pair of glasses, a ring of keys. Because with these Alfred Hitchcock succeeded where Alexander, Julius Cesar, Napoleon and Hitler failed, in taking control of the universe […].

The selection and distribution of images is central to any notion of cinema. In *Histoire(s)*, Hitchcock is portrayed as the master of the universe because he mastered the distribution of relations between signs. Thus, he indicated what should be remembered and what should be forgotten. This is precisely what Deleuze discusses as the mental images coupled to the relation between object and viewer in Hitchcock's films.[8] If parallel editing, as the classical device *par excellence*, implies the memory of an image that is absent, in Hitchcock it simultaneously implies the forgetting of the story. Parallel editing establishes relations between images that are so powerful that they make some objects stand out from their narrative framework and persist as key figures at the expense of narrative cohesion. By encouraging a process of forgetting, some objects and events in Hitchcock's films become icons of a cultural memory. Forgetting allows for memory to turn into recollection, and the eradication of causal relationships in the story places the objects in new connections. In fact, the repetition of the sequences of films, the reiteration of objects, the forgotten causalities, all display the recurrent conjunctions "and... and... and" as defined by Deleuze in Godard's own films.[9] As with Hitchcock, the relations between objects or shots are foregrounded by Godard rather than the objects themselves.

According to Deleuze, Hitchcock stands at the intersection of the "movement-image" and the "time-image" precisely because the relation between the image and the spectator is included in the film. The relation between the events of the film sometimes puts the main character aside and reflects the viewing process as an immobilisation, the suspension of the motor capabilities of the body. This happens to Scotty in *Vertigo*, to Jeffries in *Rear Window*, to Henry Fonda's wife in *The Wrong Man* and to Norman Bates in *Psycho*. When the main character him/herself becomes the spectator of events, Hitchcock's films move from the "movement-image" to the "purely optical and sonorous situations of the time-image". The same claim could be made for the catatonic state of Suzanne in *Le Mystère des roches de Kador*.

Deleuze discusses CS Peirce's classifications of the sign, and "thirdness", as a concept whereby the spectator is figured in the film. These "mental images" are not the result of a free stream of consciousness or an interior monologue, but of a series of relations between objects. Some objects are singled out and contradict the system of the series, and they are elements in this indexing. The distribution of memory that results is probably one of the main reasons why so many artists today engaged in reappropriation take on Hitchcock's work when they refer to cinema.[10] Recollection proceeds through the indexing of objects, forming a catalogue that is key to the understanding of our visual history in general, and, more specifically, to the "montages" resulting from our navigation in new media texts.

Godard's project, as well as Hitchcock's transgression of the classical in the relation between shots, evolves in structures of image retrievals. The "control of the universe" is the power to distribute forgetting and recollection. This is conditioned by the principles employed by the spectator to select images in viewing films, based on the internal relations between images. Hitchcock's indexing of elements according to objects that contradict the logic of a series leads to a figure of thought through its implication of the viewer in the film. As Godard observes, thinking demands memory, but also oblivion. Setting thoughts in motion demands forgetting. Primary memories must be substituted by something more powerful in order to turn them into recollection.[11] The capacity of montage to initiate new ideas depends on its "masking", or rewriting, of memory. This resembles the process whereby the film image achieves movement through the retinal afterimage being masked off by the shutter of the projector.[12] The afterimage alone could never result in movement, as it would only render a blurred image. The virtual aspects of the image, i.e. its movement, could not be actualised unless other aspects were forgotten.

The refraction of light and the selection of images are key elements in Deleuze's film philosophy as well as in the sequences I discuss in *Histoire(s) du cinéma*. The relation between the image, among all the images of the world, and the special image constituted by the spectator's mind, decides the typology of images in the "movement-image". This is achieved according to the delay between the image and its reaction, in the very indetermination or suspension of the action it sets off. The criteria of selection also determine the "time-image", whereby images are distributed according to the transparency that makes them pass unnoticed, and the opaque ones are suspended in passing and reacted with. Even if Godard's film history is less divided by two main

j'étais seul
perdu, comme on dit
dans mes pensées

categories of images than Deleuze's at first may seem to be, he also establishes a point of rupture in the Second World War. Godard and Deleuze, in somewhat different ways, both see Hitchcock's work as the passage between the classical and the modern.

Multiplicities

Godard's video productions establish an analogy between the distribution of shots in Hitchcock's work and the "micromontage" between the photograms in cinematic movement. Montage is the prerequisite for movement and thought in Godard's work in general, and the decomposition of movement submits the shot to its many virtual dimensions. Godard remarks how this technique serves to open up multiple movements: "From the stopping of an image that contains 25 images […] you realise how an image that you have shot, depending on how you stop it, suddenly has billions of possibilities, all the possible permutations between the twenty-five images representing billions of possibilities […] you realise that there are swarms of different worlds inside each movement […]."[13] There is a principle of uncertainty at work in this process, which is linked to the multiple combinations that can be formed between the photograms. This opening of movement is in keeping with the concept of "multiplicities" in Deleuze's philosophy. The concept serves different tasks in different discussions and undergoes important changes in the course of his philosophy. "Multiplicities" are spatial fragments linked in an incalculable possible number of ways, first coined by Georg Riemann in physics and later elaborated in a non-metrical context by Henri Bergson.

Riemann spaces lack any homogeneity […] Every element juxtaposed is thus like a small piece of Euclidian space, but the relation between one space and the following space is not defined, and may be realised according to an infinite number of ways. The most general Riemann space thus presents itself as a collection of amorphous pieces juxtaposed without being connected to each other.[14]

The unpredictability of the connections between the photograms in the decomposed image is parallel to the use of superimpositions in *Histoire(s)*. Considered in this light, the particular elements do not add up to form a whole; multiplicities are selected as actualisations among an event's virtual reserves. The process is linked with the forming of series, as Deleuze suggests regarding music, literature and film. Series are composed of indistinct singularities which change according to where they are linked. Consequently, both in Hitchcock's and Godard's work the conjunction itself is highlighted as the most important element in the serial links. The repetition of images in *Histoire(s)* is central to this approach, as objects, events and shots attain new functions according to where they are linked. The titles of the chapters of *Histoire(s)*, which Godard claimed to be his only script during production, form one such series. This organisational structure explains why the figure of the search engine itself, rather than the separate units of the database, is appropriate for describing image retrievals in the history project.

The notion of the film archive at work in *Histoire(s)* is also constituted by its absent elements: what cinema could have been had it come in the right century, had it achieved montage, had the unmade films been made. Montage must be understood as a process whereby new constellations are continually on the point of becoming, and where a continuous rewriting is taking place through repetitions and erasures. The archive is a field of virtual connections, reserves that exist only in combinations and montages due to changing questions or different search criteria. Modified searches in browsers also result in the same items reappearing in various contexts. In crossing between the moving image and the decomposed, Godard continually moves between the continuous and discrete multiplicities identified by Riemann.[15] Thus, the archive

Opposite and following page: **Working documents for the books of *Histoire(s) du cinéma.***

continually goes from the smooth to the streaked, from the discrete to the indivisibility of the photograms.

The recurrent figure of the editing table in Godard's work, increasingly more central in the later video productions, deploys the virtual aspects of images in Deleuze's philosophy. The presence of the editing table brings together Deleuze's principles for the selection of images based on the transparency and refraction of light and images, and Godard's new juxtapositions of existing images. Its role is at the intersection between shooting and projection, both technologically and in the process of film production, and highlights the analytical approach towards the image. At the core of this figure is the prismatic head of the editing table which secures an intermittent movement in spite of the film-strip's continuous run. One photogram is delayed in its passage until the angle of the prism projects the following photogram instead. The editing table is for this reason a literal image of the crystal in Deleuze's film philosophy, since it grants the coexistence of the actual and the virtual aspects of the image according to which facet of the prism is highlighted. This capacity to project the past in the present tense, to review and decompose existing films, is fundamental to Godard's view of the relationship between history and cinema. The refraction of the light in the prismatic head shifts aspects between images, and could for this reason be regarded as the key figure in Godard's work on montage over the last 20 years.

Iconic search criteria

Godard's project to produce a "true history of cinema" harks back to a planned collaboration with the director of the Cinémathèque française, Henri Langlois. If *Histoire(s)* is a work that is true to its point of departure in the physical film archive, it is still far away from the indexing principles of the traditional archive. The traditional archive proceeds by indexing according to verbal criteria (names of people, places, objects, organisations, etc.), whereas computerised databases allow for searches according to combined or multimedial criteria. New techniques of image compression will unavoidably lead to new indexing principles in visual databases, and consequently also for how we think about images. New data compression standards have made the personal computer a multimedia platform, and prepares the way for indexing according to iconic criteria. Media researcher Wolfgang Ernst foresees that:

images and sounds [...] become calculable and can be subjected to algorithms of pattern recognition–procedures that will "excavate" unexpected optical statements and perspectives out of the audiovisual archive which, for the first time, can organise itself not just according to meta-data but according to its proper criteria–visual memory in its own medium.[16]

Ernst's view that navigation in databases will be submitted to pattern recognition and irrevocably create new montages and "matches" of images is a very important observation. However, cinema has always been a multimedial technology, and to see iconic criteria only as the redemption of the visual database's organisation is incorrect. Cinema, of course, also contains oral and written texts, sounds and music of different kinds, as well as images. Moreover, one should not confuse the indexing of still images with cinema's visual preconditions since cinema consists of movement. Searches in databases according to visual movements are still in the future. The "pictorial turn" in the database may prove prone to discourses of medium specificity and the aesthetics of purity which we have come to associate with modernist art. Instead of hailing the visual, I would rather point to the multiple search combinations made possible by these numerical techniques. With the emergence of multimedia searches, the database offers new and unexpected montages and juxtapositions.

oui, j'étais seul,ce soir
avec mes rêves

Computer media maintain the principles of word searches, for instance, in internet browsers. However, the possibility for searches on audiovisual criteria is being developed, notably through the scanning of images down to pixel level, that creates other possible combinations between image sequences. The random access of digital storage results in new conditions for image retrieval. According to the French philosopher Bernard Stiegler, the digitisation of analogue images (most images in digital media are based on photographic or analogue pictures) leads to the establishment of criteria in the programmes and to standards in the computer's processing of these tasks. The computer's MPEG standard is based on an analysis of images, since the storage of an image sequence actually only stores the changes in a photogram (or its digital equivalent) from the preceding photogram according to a set of parameters and criteria for this difference. This already forms a set of rules for the classification of the elements in an image sequence.

The breakthrough in the capacity to store and process images in the computer raises new questions about image indexing. Transformations in the criteria for indexing and segmenting images go together with changes in our priorities of what should be stored, and which criteria should form the categories in databases. Any historical change in storage techniques, like the one from oral transmission to written text, or from the written manuscript to the printed document, are inevitably accompanied by a loss of information. In very general terms, one could claim that earlier principles for the indexation of images are based on linguistic descriptions, and tend to give priority to semantic categories or names of places and persons. For instance, a general description of the storyline of a film is the major guideline for indexing in film archives, as well as in the programming of television or cinémathèques. This is naturally due to the classical narrative style becoming the dominant mode of cinema, a development connected with the establishment of the written word through the film script in the production process. The institution of the script is a longstanding subject of commentary in Godard's work, and in *Histoire(s)* it implicitly becomes a discourse on indexing and segmentation.

Another work that stands out as a meditation on the conditions for image retrieval in the film archive is Harun Farocki's 1995 video piece, *Arbeiter verlassen die Fabrik*.[17] How image compression techniques lead to new search practices is a question that has informed Farocki's compilation films for some years. In *Bilder der Welt und Inschrift des Krieges*, 1988, and *Gefängnisbilder*, 2001, for instance, the automation of sight allowing for pattern recognition through image analysis is seen in a historical frame stretching back to the Renaissance. In *Arbeiter verlassen die Fabrik*, Farocki describes and investigates how the space in front of the factory has been a field for social and ideological conflicts throughout cinema's history. A logical starting point for this compilation is the 50 seconds often referred to as the first film: *Workers Leaving the Factory* by the Lumière brothers from 1895. Farocki's film juxtaposes sequences from the history of cinema showing the topos of the factory gates in order to discuss the conditions of capitalism and industrialism. As the film acknowledges, the project is itself paradoxical since popular cinema has tended to flee the factory and show the leisure and private life of people instead. Farocki reflects on how the film archive influences, and even produces, this historical topos. The visual archive is the material condition for the writing of history and our memory of a place. For this reason, the principles of image retrieval determine the selections according to which images become physically and mentally accessible.

How does *Arbeiter verlassen die Fabrik* confront the question of the archive's relation to history? A tradition of the documentary genre is to view the film archive as a natural resource for creating a complete or true image of a phenomenon. Farocki instead analyses the indexing principles of the archive. In one of his most famous sequences in *Bilder der Welt und Inschrift des Krieges*, he reveals how the Allied aerial photography of Auschwitz from 1944 could only be identified as images of a concentration camp when these photographs were re-examined in 1977. Until the physical camp had been discovered, the images transmitted no information about Auschwitz. Those who interpreted the photographs had manuals and expertise to interpret the visual information as factories, roads, houses and railways, but not to recognise the concentration camp. Visual perception is conditioned by image archives. The indexing of the information becomes a condition, or even a programme, for what we see in images.

In *Arbeiter verlassen die Fabrik* there is another principle of indexation at work based on iconic criteria. The topos of the factory gates becomes the organisational principle of the compilation project. The space in front of the factory is heterotopic: the film interrogates the different values assigned to the factory, between the homogeneous, strong workers' collectives portrayed in Post-War DDR films, the factory as hell on earth depicted by Weimar cinema, and the phobia of the factory in Hollywood film. *Arbeiter verlassen die Fabrik* gives a fragmentary and lacunary image of the factory instead of a slice of reality. Deleuze comments digressively on the factory when he expands on the conjunctive montage in Godard's cinema and effectively announces Farocki's compilation film: "The factory gate is not the same when I enter as when I leave, or when I pass in front of it if unemployed."[18]

Farocki, of course, addresses the database in a very different way from Godard in *Histoire(s)* since he keeps to a single topos, or a single search command. Still, the principles of montage converge in their attempt to make the familiar images new by positioning them in distant relations to each other, and to find incommensurable relations between them. As with the *bricolage* of early cinema, the shots are subject to permutation and do not establish a continuous space and time, or a logic of cause and effect. There are long passages of silence in both voice-overs, and the ruptures in continuity, light, sound and movement between the passages are highlighted. For this reason, the heterogeneity of the archive itself is analysed, foregrounding the preconditions of the film archive as much as the institution of the factory. As Farocki has claimed, the most important work of a filmmaker is to see the images, and this process is at the core of *Arbeiter verlassen die Fabrik*. Farocki aims at reading familiar and unknown images in a new way: "One should never look for new, unseen images. One should work on the images at hand in a way that renders them new."[19] This perspective also guides the processes of montage in *Histoire(s)*.

Clio and the archive

The privilege given to the editing table, at the intersection between shooting and screening, complies with the overriding view of cinema history as a rewriting, or rather reviewing. This is the sense in which "the screen is the camera", as demonstrated through the recurring references to the opening shot from *Le Mépris* where Raoul Coutard turns the camera on the viewer, a means to forget and recollect. Suzanne's encounter with the images of her own rescue in *Le Mystère des roches de Kador*, coming to life in the moment of the *désoeuvrement* of the projected image, is another instance of this historical mode. The plot is forgotten through the reappearance of objects

Opposite: **Archive imagery used by Harun Farocki in *Arbeiter verlassen die Fabrik*, 1995.**

in Hitchcock's films, and more directly, the attempt to call forward the past and make memory flesh in *Vertigo* is a key element in the Orphic figure of memory and history in *Histoire(s)*. If Hitchcock, along with Dreyer, is the only one to have known how to film a miracle, as it is stated in Chapter 4A, *Le contrôle de l'univers*, this is as true for his distribution of objects to be remembered as it is for his bringing Madeleine back to life. But the very moment the image of Madeleine becomes perfect, she assumes another identity (Judy) and memory becomes recollection. However, as Godard also puts it in *Histoire(s)*, "cinema allows Orpheus to turn around without killing Eurydice". And yet what Scotty sees is a fixed image of memory, as the salts of the photographic emulsion are compared (in 3A, *La monnaie de l'absolu*) to Lot's wife, who turns into a salt statue when she turns round to behold Sodom. The Orphic gaze is a central reference in Godard's work, notably in the relation between the descent, trial and return in *Alphaville*, 1965 and *Allemagne année 90 neuf zéro*, 1991, and especially in the return of Richard Lennox in *Nouvelle Vague*, 1990. But in *Histoire(s)* it becomes a principle for the writing of film history itself, and this is the reason why the series ends, amidst various references to Maurice Blanchot, with a series of quotes from Charles Péguy's *Clio*.

History demands that some documents are forgotten, ignored and lost. This is the insistent and repeated claim made in *Clio*, cited and commented in Chapter 4B, *Les signes parmi nous*, and it is why so many of the texts and images of *Histoire(s)* are incessantly repeated: not to insist on, and to etch in, what one should remember, but on the contrary to demonstrate a process of forgetting where the texts and images become different each time they are repeated since they change their positions in the montage. Because the titles are all repeated in each part, they establish new meanings in each constellation. Appearing different every time, they demonstrate how thought works on the traces of memory. Montage is thus an incitement to forget and to recollect in *Histoire(s)*, just as in Hitchcock's method.

Péguy's meditation on history is in many respects close to Godard's project. In *Clio*, the discussions of history are interlaced with literary analysis, particularly of Victor Hugo, and fragments from poems are constantly repeated in different contexts, just like the film clips in Godard's series. In addition, the dialogue itself is structured in a serial, repetitive form. The reference to *Clio* bears on the nature of the repetitions produced in *Histoire(s)*, where these never insist on what should be remembered but, on the contrary, serve to rewrite history. The repetition of Clio's historical-philosophical theses constitutes in each instance a new beginning for "writing history" without history ever being achieved, parallel to the title of Chapter 1A, *Toutes les histoires*. Before it occurs in *Histoire(s)*, this passage is immediately preceded by the Pompei sequence from *Viaggio in Italia*, 1953, where the traces of history are born from what has turned into dust or from the empty casts of people. The indexical monuments thus double the photographic image and are imbued with death. The following evocation of Blanchot is vital for its description of the image as a reserve for history, since Blanchot states that the image is always "after the fact". The image demands that the thing disappears before it can be reconceived, just as *Histoire(s)* pinpoints the need to forget in order for recollection to take place. Blanchot describes "the image as the thing in its state of withdrawing". Godard quotes from *Clio* the repeated comment on the historical project: "night always falls, holidays end [...]".

According to Clio, history is unattainable and unachievable. Godard cites long passages: "A king may achieve his reign, but never the history of that reign; one may stage a revolution, but one never achieves the history of that revolution".[20] Clio states: "it takes me a day to make the history of one second. It takes me a year to make the history of one minute. It takes me a life to make the history of one hour. It takes an eternity to make the history of one day. One can do anything, except the history of what one does."[21] The role of the document in the writing of history is also discussed. With antiquity there are always too few documents, and more importantly, in the case of contemporary history the documents are always too many. In modern history, the historiographer chokes with documents. Just after the passage cited in *Histoire(s)*, Péguy's dialogue emphasises the need to make selections for missing documents and search criteria, with the result that history becomes art.[22] Clio asks "what if [history] were not about a text but about movement itself, of an idea, of reality, of life [...] Or if it simply were about a text, but where it wasn't about determining it on the basis of words, but on an idea, for instance, or on an intention, on a movement. On a usage."[23] This idea of history as consisting of images, movements and ideas is closely related to the changing selections and the multiple search criteria of the (virtual) archive. The book is too easy, it is too pleasant: "What would it be like if one had to put reality in the book [...] or to put reality in reality? What always happens? Night falls."[24] This cited passage examines exactly the need to set memory in movement through eradication, by introducing life, change, ideas in order for "the beautiful coincidence of recollection to take place". "The one who wants to recollect should devote himself to forgetting, at the risk of forgetting absolutely [...]".

This complex discussion from *Clio* of history beyond the text finds a response in the figure of archival searches on images or on movements deployed in the work's own montage. The questions outlined in the sequence of quotes from *Clio* immediately suggest a series of images of editing tables, from Vertov's *The Man With A Movie Camera*, 1929 and Godard's own *JLG/JLG: autoportrait de décembre*, 1995 and *King Lear*, 1987. Godard's constant reference to Reverdy's "L'Image" turns into his credo when he again proposes the power of the image in its association of ideas that are distant from each other yet correct. The powers of new montages are embedded in selections of multimedial search engines in the archive. A very grainy still of Eisenstein at the editing table is accompanied by the following passage in English from Hollis Frampton: "[...] handling in both hands, the present, the future and the past", which suggests the mnemotechnical properties of cinema and montage. This montage is true to the principle of moving from memory to recollection through forgetting and erasure. Just like Hitchcock, *Histoire(s) du cinéma* proceeds via the selection and distribution of what shall be forgotten.

"A FORM THAT THINKS": GODARD, BLANCHOT, CITATION

Once in a while, take advantage of the fact the sentence isn't finished to begin speaking and begin living.
Jean-Luc Godard, *Passion*, 1981.

LESLIE HILL

Long and varied, as readers will know, is the roll call of filmmakers, poets, novelists, thinkers, critics, actors, and other intellectual or historical figures cited or otherwise mentioned by Jean-Luc Godard in *Histoire(s) du cinéma*, 1998, his eight-part, four and a half hour exploration of the rise and fall of cinema in the course of the last century.[1] Within that list, the part played by the critic and novelist Maurice Blanchot could be said at best to be a tangential one. Indeed, Blanchot is cited, named, and shown on screen only once, seemingly in passing, towards the end of *Les signes parmi nous*, the final chapter in Godard's project. For that reason alone it would surely be misleading to grant the reference to Blanchot any superior or special status. Lack of privilege, however, is no guarantee of insignificance. On the contrary, there is ample evidence elsewhere of the persistence of Godard's dialogue with Blanchot throughout his films of the last decade. Witness, for instance, the statement made by Godard at a press conference in February 1995 to the effect that in making *JLG/JLG: autoportrait de décembre*, 1995, his aim had been "to make a movie like the books I happened to read when I was growing up, by Blanchot, or Bataille".[2]

Press conferences, like all other public or promotional statements, should of course be treated with caution. Godard himself, in *Histoire(s)*, is quick to stress that what counts here are not the impromptu thoughts, or even the considered views of an artist, but the distance travelled by the work itself: "first the works", the viewer is told, "then the people who made them". The text, then, not the person or persona of the author. But it is precisely here that there is ample, albeit discreet confirmation of the enduring nature of Godard's engagement with Blanchot, which finds expression in a pair of notable quotations in two of Godard's most recent films for the cinema: *Hélas pour moi*, 1993, and *For Ever Mozart*, 1996.

Hélas pour moi and *For Ever Mozart* are both multi-layered, dissonant fables. Each draws extensively on an almost limitless archive of literary, philosophical, and filmic material which it recycles and transforms. *Hélas pour moi* takes as one of its subtexts the oft-repeated story of Amphitryon and Alcmena which it recasts as a singular mysterious event occurring like a transfiguration on the shore of Lake Geneva at the end of the afternoon of 23 July 1989. Simon Donnadieu (Gérard Depardieu) leaves on a business trip; his wife Rachel (Laurence Masliah) stays behind, awaiting his return. But during Simon's absence, God–a negative and decidedly post-Christian entity in this film–covertly borrows Simon's identity and body in order to have at least the chance (or so it would appear) of experiencing human desire.[3] But this encounter between divinity and embodiment is an unhappy one, at least from Rachel's point of view. "I learned", she tells the local pastor, spinning a Mallarméan thread initiated shortly before, "that the flesh can be sad". "To be in love", God is informed, in a dialogue Godard later reprises in *Les signes parmi nous*, "you need a body. Without Simon you don't exist." And Rachel goes on: "You can't simply walk in on people's lives like that." The space between God and humanity (whatever such words may be thought to mean at the end of the afternoon of 23 July 1989) has become the site of an irreparable disjunction. This has major implications for the narrative coherence of Godard's film as a whole. Does what has occurred (or not occurred) reach beyond stories and images, or does it somehow precede them? Is the so-called sacred truly transcendent or obstinately immanent? Or neither the one nor the other? At any event, the manifestation of transcendence turns out to be synonymous not with its consecration, but its withdrawal. What happened, the viewer is later told by Simon (or is it God?), was nothing. Is nothing more or less than something? For if transcendence is erased, it is not before immanence in its turn is interrupted. The enigma of anonymous presence remains. And *Hélas pour moi* ends much as it began, with the obscure and unanswerable question of the origin–of the mysterious possibility (or is it impossibility?) of the event itself.

There is, however, a postscript to Godard's film, which explores further the enigmatic evanescence of the event, of the moment which is here and now. This comes in the form of a brief off-screen exchange between Godard's post-theological investigator, Abraham Klimt (Bernard Verley), whose responsibility it is to inquire into what has occurred, and Aude Amiot, the young woman who was witness (it seems) to Simon's substitution by the side of the lake. Spoken over the closing titles (from which the names of the principal actors or stars have been withdrawn), intercut with several blank frames and two or three fixed-frame shots of Rachel and Simon, the text of this dialogue is unattributed. But the spectator soon realises that, like Simon's body, it too has been borrowed for the occasion. As all readers of Blanchot will be aware, it is taken from a famous passage in Blanchot's short narrative (or *récit*) *Au moment voulu* (*When the Time Comes*), first published in 1951 and presumably one of those books by Blanchot read by Godard when growing up.[4]

Close comparison between Blanchot's text and the version given in *Hélas pour moi* reveals, however, that Godard's rendering of the passage falls somewhere short of total accuracy.[5] This comes as no surprise. From the outset, the readiness with which Godard has recourse to literary or philosophical quotations in his films is matched only by the apparent ease with which he edits, alters, reworks, misattributes, and on occasion entirely invents them.[6] This cavalier approach offends against academic norms, but it is less transgressive than might first appear. It is entirely consistent with the possibility of quotation itself. Every text, by dint of being a text, belongs to a given discursive or material context; to withdraw a fragment of text from that context and inscribe it within another is inevitably to transform that text, even if in every other respect the source text is faithfully reproduced. A sentence from Blanchot, transcribed,

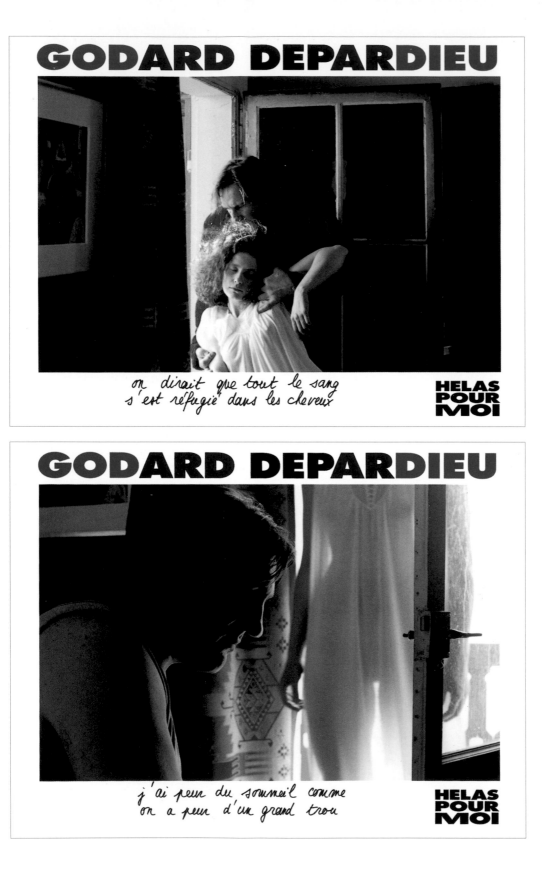

spoken, or otherwise performed in a film by Godard, is no longer simply a sentence from Blanchot. It has at the very least acquired two contexts, two signatures, two functions. It is henceforth divorced from itself, and it is this internal division that gives rise to the many rhetorical or other effects that are inseparable from the history of quotation as such.[7] True, quotation is an age-old practice with many rules and conventions enforced by everything from academic decorum to copyright legislation. But this institutionalisation is deceptive. For what the possibility of quotation confirms, albeit at times almost in spite of itself, is that, however inseparable from its original location it may appear, no text is entirely reducible to that context. Each time it is read, it is reinscribed elsewhere and thereby transformed. Quotation always serves at least two masters, which is a way of saying that it is always liable to refuse to take orders from either. In the realm of quotation the only law that truly holds, one might say, is the law of necessary infidelity.

Quotations, though, are not textual flotsam; they always belong to a specific location. If this were not the case, it would be impossible to quote anything. From one context to the next, whatever its nomadic potential, every quotation, or fragment of quotation, remembers at least one of its previous occurrences. But this fundamental repeatability of all quotations has complex effects. It means that, in addition to recalling whatever it is the quotation says–or may be made to say–about life, love, the universe, each quotation, by presenting itself implicitly or explicitly as a quotation, is thereby already necessarily quoting itself. This self-designation of quotations as quotations is what lies behind the institutional prestige that quotations often acquire and, by that token, their monumental unanswerability. (If this is in St Paul, we say, it must be true, at least in a certain way.) But all such authority is eminently precarious. Any quotation that quotes itself withdraws from itself in order to do so, which is also to say that any quotation, to the extent that it is a quotation, is necessarily marked by the possibility of its own withdrawal as such. And a quotation that quotes itself is always on the verge of parodying itself. Quotations are always liable to become less of an appeal to prior authority than an enigmatic, sometimes even ironic challenge to thought. (Where does St Paul say this? we reply. In what way could it be said to be true? And if it is true, is it still relevant?) Quotations–and this is particularly so in Godard (readers may recall Jeremy Prokosch's little red book from *Le Mépris*)–have a lapidary quality that not only allows them to be repeated from one context to the next but also gives them the status of so many mysterious incitements or provocations to thought. Quotations in Godard constantly enjoin us to think; and though it (unlike others) is not anywhere reprised in Godard's oeuvre, this is how the quotation from *Au moment voulu* functions at the end of *Hélas pour moi*. Moreover, the passage Godard cites is not just any passage, for his citation is a reworking of the extract that is already cited by Blanchot's publisher on the back cover of the 1993 paperback reprint of *Au moment voulu* issued in January 1993, some eight months before the Paris release of Godard's film. Godard's quotation of Blanchot is not just a quotation from Blanchot's story, then; it is a quotation of a quotation from that story. Importantly, then, it belongs not to a completed, authoritative past, but to a repetitive present. What quotation tells us, so to speak, is that the past is never dead; it has not even passed at all.

There is yet another aspect to the question. The self-identity of any quotation is essentially problematic. It is not necessary to attribute quotations; and many are the speakers or writers who use quotations without being able to supply the name of whoever first invented the quotation. Even when (helpfully) a source is indicated, as any spectator of Godard's films soon discovers, this does not necessarily prove anything. When is a quotation a quotation and when is

Opposite: **Lobby cards for Hélas pour moi, 1993.**

it not a quotation? How to tell where a quotation begins or ends? Does it matter whether it comes from Péguy or Renan, or somewhere else? And this is only the beginning. For not only is the presence or identity of a quotation never guaranteed, what it may claim to be the case, with all the institutional authority it can muster, is not by necessity true either. Quotations, then, are not solid points of anchorage, but vanishing points, not moments of stability, but of flight, not tokens of truth, but of errancy. They are by definition always already fragments. And irrepressibly promiscuous, too. As many a modern literary text has shown–take Joyce's *Ulysses* or Pound's *Cantos*–quotations have the eminently democratic virtue of rubbing shoulders with any other fragment of text, of whatever type, in whatever language. Like Coleridge's flower cited (after Borges) at the very end of *Histoire(s)*, quotations may be solitary blossoms; but where they lead is down many a strange alleyway into the garden of forking paths.

This is not all. The possibility of quotation is inseparable from textual repetition in general (of which it is, of course, merely one instance). Repetition itself obeys a perverse and maddening logic. It is itself always at least double. It secures identity, but also erases it. Without repetition no thing can be truly identified as what it is; but no sooner does repetition occur than thought is confronted with two things rather than one, two things that to be recognised as identical must in reality be different from one another. In order, in fact, to be a quotation at all, a quotation must differ from what it was or is. So while it is true that the self-identity of a quotation is reliant on its repeatability, it is equally true that such repetition threatens the identity of any quotation at all by making each occurrence of a text irreducibly different to the one that preceded. To quote a text is to do so here and now; and to quote a text here and now is to quote a different text from the one I quoted a moment ago. Even if a quotation appears to be absolutely identical to what it was elsewhere and at another time, it is nevertheless absolutely different from it. Though it is cited in *Hélas pour moi* as merely one in a banal series of such afternoons, the late afternoon of 23 July 1989 as such is nevertheless unique. It is a singular member in the series which is irreducible to any other member of the series. Which is not to say it is self-identical, since its very singularity derives from its place within that series. The same goes for *Hélas pour moi,* which asks to be viewed not just as a fable about the erasure of transcendence or about quotation as such or even cinema itself, which is of course another word for the same thing, but (more radically) as the mysterious and singular enactment of what occurred on film latc in July 1989 by the lakeside.

Not for nothing in this respect is Godard's film based on a mythological story of repetition and difference; not for nothing does it take as its pretext the most canonic and timeworn of classical domestic plots. Already in 1929 Jean Giraudoux was mocking the story by calling his version of it *Amphitryon 38*, alerting the audience to the prior existence of (at least) 37 other attempts at the material, but also at the same time to the fact that his own version was singular and different. In making *Hélas pour moi*, which borrows dialogue from Giraudoux's play in several places, Godard did the same as his predecessor–and thereby did so differently.

What I have been describing so far, complex though it is, is not an exceptional state of affairs. It is a general condition of all language as such. Indeed, iterability, as Derrida calls it, not only governs so-called natural language; it names the possibility of cinematographic montage too.[8] Quotation and montage in this regard are but two words for the same thing. "Both in terms of art and in terms of creation and invention", Jacques Aumont points out, "there is no getting away from this blatant

FOR EVER
MOZART

for ever godard

20世紀への壮大な鎮魂歌。
戦火のサラエヴォにむかって、映画監督が、若者演劇集団が、
映画が、旅を始める。

フランス映画祭横浜
パルト・リーヌ大作品
bowjapan.com

フォーエヴァー・モーツアルト 監督・脚本：ジャン＝リュック・ゴダール 撮影：クリストフ・ポリック 音楽：フランソワ・ミュリー
出演：マリーナ・ジュラヴニ 編集：イヴァン・ニクラス 録音：ダヴィル・ビョルンスタ, デイヴィッド・ダーリング（THE SEA, ECM1645）、ベート
ーヴェン、モーツアルト（ピアノ協奏曲第27番, K.595） 製作：アラン・サルド、ルート・ヴァルトブルガー 出演：ヴィッキー・メシカ、マデレーヌ・アサス、
ギヨ・ラロウ、ベランジュール・ブロ--、フレデリク・ゼエ 他 1996年 スイス・独合作 製作＝AVVENTURA FILMS-PERIPHERIA-
VEGA FILMS・ECM RECORDS・FRANCE 2 CINEMA・RHONE - ALPES FILMS CANAL +・TELEVISION SUISSE
ROMANDE カラー ドルビー・ステレオ 上映時間：シネマスコープ 配給：TRANS CONTINENTS ©1996 JEAN-LUC GODARD

Above: *For Ever Mozart*, 1996.

Opposite: **Flyer for the Japanese DVD of**
For Ever Mozart.

truth: the filmic signifier, in essential and contingent ways, is a citational signifier."[9] The definition of the one, as supplied in Chapter 4B, courtesy of Robert Bresson–to "bring together things that have not been brought together before, and do not seem liable to be brought together at all"–could serve equally to characterise the possibilities of the other.[10] And what is most singular in Godard's work as a whole in this respect is not only that it treats discourse as though it were an infinite series of discrete fragments, but also that it similarly treats cinema as a form of fragmentary writing. (An early sequence in *Histoire(s)* showing Godard viewing parts of images on his Steenbeck, then sitting at his word processor surrounded by shelves of books, typing out solitary and disjoined words, is eloquent in this regard.) On either side, heterogeneity prevails; and I need say no more at this point to underline how much of Godard's filmmaking relies on the calculated, dynamic interrelationship between separate, often incongruous elements. Ultimately, the only question says Godard in Chapter 4B (and it is an ethical as well as a technical one) is where to begin and end the shot–or the quotation.

It is not that natural language and filmic language are somehow reducible to the same. On the contrary. What both have in common is an absolute commitment to the singularity of the trace. Singularity is not truth, but different. And difference. It resides not in any correspondence between a representation and a fact or *factum*, but in the occurrence of the event of vision, or of invisibility. If citation is portrayed by Godard as a form of resurrection or redemption, then, it is not because it restores an object to its veritable self-identity, but more the reverse. It lingers, transfigures, recodes, reconstitutes. (One recalls a famous cup of coffee in *Deux ou trois choses que je sais d'elle*.) It bears witness to an attempt to address the singular, repetitive nowness of now, what Benjamin, cited in *Hélas pour moi*, famously refers to as "the time of now".[11]

To quote or to make films, then, is to address the moment in its essential repetition and its singularity, in its historicity and its contemporaneity, in relation to both the past and the future. That this is one of Godard's abiding concerns in recent decades is apparent, I think, from *For Ever Mozart*. Here, too, Blanchot has an important part to play. Made three years after *Hélas pour moi*, *For Ever Mozart* is another semi-fictional patchwork essay. It asks the question: what of cinema, here, now, in relation to Sarajevo? To pursue that question, it takes the stories–or better the fragmentary postures, positions, and poses–of what (referring in one fell swoop to the remilitarisation of the Rhineland, the Popular Front, Pirandello, and the inescapability of history and language) Godard calls "36 characters in search of history". That quest–which is also a journey of initiation (Wilhelm Meister, for Godard, is never far)–rapidly turns into a series of variations on the theme of culture and barbarism and the impossibility and necessity of art, mediated at a number of different levels by a manifold of explicit and implicit quotations (from Musset, Cervantes, Camus, Malraux, Ravel, Oliveira, and Mozart, not to mention Duras, Hofmannsthal, and several others).

Part of the film began, Godard explains, as an intervention into a fleeting exchange–or better, non-exchange–between Susan Sontag and Philippe Sollers on the question of the West's response to events in Sarajevo. In protest at the war, Sontag in the summer of 1993 travelled to the Bosnian capital in order to mount a production of *Waiting for Godot*. In an article in *Le Monde* some months later, glimpsed in Godard's film, Sollers commented acerbically that it would have been more appropriate to stage Marivaux's *Le Triomphe de l'amour*. To which Godard responds, in the first part of *For Ever Mozart*, by having a group of characters–Camille (Madeleine Assas), her cousin Jérôme (Frédéric Pierrot), and Djamila (Ghalya Lacroix)–set off for Sarajevo, together with Camille's father, the filmmaker Vicky Vitalis (Vicky Messica) (who, being a filmmaker, is symbolically forced to abandon the journey half-way), in order to stage Musset's *On ne badine pas avec l'amour*, since the local bookshop, as luck would have it, has sold out of Marivaux's *Le Jeu de l'amour et du hasard*.[12] What do Godard's young actors hope to achieve? The answer comes in the words spoken/cited by the novelist (Harry Clever): "A breath of freedom no doubt, that we do not enjoy in our own country."[13]

The parallels between Godard's trio and the roles they are due to take in *On ne badine pas avec l'amour* are plain to see, as are the important differences between them.[14] Apart from Camille's headstrong nature, and the familial or affective relationship she has with the others, there seems little in common between the actors and the shallow, vindictive individuals they intend to play. The congruence between Musset's play and Godard's film is partial at best, and the relationship between them one of ironic dissonance rather than of identification. What is emphasised as a result is the very distance between the parts they are playing in Musset's play (which Godard sporadically cites) and their own aspirations. It is this gap that is largely the subject of the film. And reality intervenes, just as it did in 1940 according to *Histoire(s)*, with a vengeance. Just as in Musset the irresponsible posturing of Camille and Perdican provokes Rosette's death, so in Godard's film, even before Camille, Jérôme, and Djamila have the chance of finding the history they are looking for, history finds them–with the result that Camille and Jérôme are taken hostage by a gang of what (in another spectral inversion of the 1930s) the film calls "international brigands" rather than "international brigades".[15] The pair are duly put to work digging the trench for a mass grave. Shortly after, Djamila is led away, while Camille and Jérôme are killed in the ensuing skirmish.

Moments before her death, roughly mid-way through Godard's film, after 47 of its 84 minutes, Camille, with help from Jérôme, is heard explaining to Djamila (Camille at this point is described as an unemployed philosophy teacher) how philosophy differs from Christianity or Islam. Interrupted all the while by a series of voices speaking in Serbo-Croat and various other noises both on and off, she makes the following (triumphant) declaration, using words that most readers of Blanchot (and Levinas) will instantly recognise. It comes (with minor changes) from a moving tribute by Blanchot to Levinas, and to philosophy, and runs as follows (in Godard's version): "Philosophy would be our companion, for ever, by day and by night, even if it loses its name, even if it absents itself; a clandestine friend in whom we should respect that which does not allow us to be tied to it, even as we sense we are not awake and that what is vigilant in us, even when we sleep, is due to its difficult friendship."[16] The film then cuts, passing from one lakeside, allegedly in Bosnia, to another, in Switzerland (which, of course, the film has never left), moving on to follow the story of Vicky's chaotic shooting of *Le Boléro fatal*, the title of which derives from a remark of Juan Goytisolo, cited in the film, comparing the ineffectual posturing of Western European states around Bosnia in the 1990s to a similar display in the mid-1930s: *pavane*, one might say, *pour une Europe défunte*.

In this context, Godard's appeal to Blanchot may be most easily understood as a gesture of solidarity. For Blanchot's words, written in homage to his life-long friendship with Levinas, are a response to the necessity of remembering and the impossibility of knowing. "How to think philosophically, how to write", Blanchot asks a few paragraphs later, "in memory of Auschwitz, and of those who told us, sometimes in notes buried beside the crematorium: know what has happened, do not forget and yet never will you know."[27] Much of *Histoire(s)* (which I shall come to in a moment) shows, I think, that these words also stand for Godard. In the face of historical disaster–both disaster

C. F. RAMUZ

LES SIGNES
PARMI NOUS

PLAISIR DE LIRE

in history and the disaster of history–how to remember and how to know? How to avoid defeat, but also how to avoid mystification? And how to remain awake amidst the nightmare of history? As a persistent leitmotiv in *For Ever Mozart* puts it, how to turn the page–in the double sense of both witnessing the past and inventing the future?

These questions, says Godard, with provocative hubris, belong to cinema. In two senses: they are, according to Godard, what cinema alone can address; but they are also what fatally cinema, at crucial moments in history and in its own history, was unable to confront. This double claim is what Godard sets out to explore in *Histoire(s)*. And it is this double sense of the power and impotence of cinema that is, I believe, centrally at stake in Godard's engagement with Blanchot in *Histoire(s)* du cinéma, which, as mentioned earlier, comes to a head towards the end of Chapter 4B, *Les signes parmi nous*. It is to this 36$\frac{1}{2}$ minute inquiry into the end of cinema that I now turn.

Godard's title is another quotation, borrowed on this occasion from the novel by CF Ramuz, published shortly after the First World War against the background of the deadly influenza epidemic that followed soon after, causing as it did so even more fatalities than the War itself.[18] Ramuz's novel–and *mutatis mutandis* Godard's film–is a fable. Of apocalypse. Godard confirms as much in numerous ways, inscribing a series of intertitles with words and titles such as "Dies Irae", "Finis terrae", or (in memory of Marguerite Duras whose script for *Hiroshima mon amour* is also briefly evoked) "Les Yeux verts" ("Green Eyes"). But one composite image seen early on can perhaps stand for all the others: it shows the closing title for an unidentified MGM film, signing off with the words: "The End", while superimposing upon it the shadow cast by Max Schreck in the role of Nosferatu the vampire in Murnau's celebrated 1922 film of that name. About two-thirds of the way through the film, a further sequence of intertitles quickly establishes what is at issue both in Ramuz's novel and Godard's film: "There was once a novel/ by Ramuz which told/ how one day a pedlar/ arrived in a village/ by the side of the Rhône/ and made friends/ with everybody/ because he knew how to tell/ a thousand and one stories/ and it so happened a storm broke/ which went on for days and days [repeated twice]/ and then the pedlar announced/ it was the end of the world [repeated three times]/ but the sun eventually came out again/ and the people of the village/ drove the poor pedlar away./ That pedlar was the cinema/ the cinema [repeated]."[19]

This fable of apocalypse condenses several complex motifs. As embodied most famously in the Book of Revelation by Saint John the Divine (relayed here by Jean-Luc the Less-Than-Divine), the figure of apocalypse testifies to the end–of both the world and secular time. It is a moment of revelation, catastrophe, and judgement bringing history (and the New Testament) to a close. It intervenes with blinding, destructive clarity, but also impenetrable obscurity. Apocalyptic fictions, by their nature, are heavy with portents, cryptic messages, and paradoxical or extravagant promises. But they also embody fundamental disenchantment. Apocalypse, Blanchot says somewhere, always disappoints.[20] Apocalyptic statements cannot guarantee the veracity or accuracy of what they assert; they bear within themselves the necessary possibility that what they announce will not come to pass. For if they truly (and seriously) announce the end of history, they must begin by denying themselves the very possibility of doing so. Ends belong to history, and it is only possible to end history by ending the end itself. And it is impossible to end history by declaring it, since to do so defers the end. The paradox is one that Blanchot, at the very end of *Au moment voulu*, powerfully invokes; the modest inhabitants of Ramuz's lakeside Switzerland realise it too, which is why they finally dismiss the pedlar Caille who, like Godard's figure of the cinema, has come to sell them his tracts confidently

Opposite: **Max Schreck in *Nosferatu, eine Symphonie des Grauens*, Friedrich Wilhelm Murnau, 1922.**

HOMMAGE
DE LA FRANCE

A JEAN MOULIN

Discours prononcé par Monsieur André Malraux, Ministre d'Etat,
en présence du Général de Gaulle, Président de la République Française.

RTF

telling them of the impending end. His animadversions are not to be taken seriously. Life goes on. (The situation, be it said in passing, is not very different from the structure of quotations: quotations are always delivered with something approaching finality, and their purpose is often to put an end to discussion; but such gestures simply invite further debate. Ending is, in fact, impossible; it is simply another way of beginning.)

The history of the present cannot be written. Godard concedes as much towards the end of Chapter 4B by citing Péguy's *Clio* who makes precisely that point: "one can do everything", she says, "except the history of what one is doing".[21] The present exists, not as a continuation of the past but as an interruption, a hiatus, a caesura. Godard's thinking of the end–the end of history, time, and cinema–in Chapter 4B is not simply a lament for cinema's heroic past. It is because history is always over; and because, if it is over, it is only because it is not over. The present is not a time for nostalgia. As the motif of apocalypse tells us, it is a time for judgement and decision.

This is the strange temporality of the space to which Godard takes us in the closing episode of *Histoire(s)*. Like its predecessors, *Les signes parmi nous* is full of quotations, and of many different kinds of quotation. There are quotations canonic and obscure, new and old, faithful and imagined; there are quotations from sound documents, musical works, paintings, drawings, cartoons, and films, some ancient, some relatively recent, some instantly recognisable, some mere traces of photograms at the limit of visibility itself, and all of them reprocessed, altered, reinscribed, transfigured within Godard's text. Even to attempt to analyse Chapter 4B in the historical and archival detail that would be necessary is a task that far exceeds what it is possible to envisage here. Let me instead follow the thread I have pursuing so far and concentrate on the closing five or six minutes of the film, and in particular–at almost the very

Above: **Recording of André Malraux's homage to Jean Moulin, 1964.**

end of this ending film about the end or ending of film–on Godard's use of the figure of Maurice Blanchot. For some four and a half minutes before the very end of *Histoire(s)*, Blanchot's name appears on screen in an intertitle, shortly followed by a reproduction of a notorious–and unique–photograph of Blanchot which then dissolves into a celebrated still of the figure of the vampire (played by Max Schreck) in Murnau's *Nosferatu*.

This unexpected appeal to Blanchot is part of a complex network of visual and textual motifs, which may be grouped summarily under three broad headings. First, in these closing minutes of *Les signes parmi nous*, Godard provides a series of variations on the theme of ending: of politics, history, cinema itself. Earlier sequences had already explored similar material, with Godard citing, for instance, the death of Eisenstein's *Ivan The Terrible*, intercut with shots of the death of Stalin, and taking an image of Chaplin only to make it dissolve into one of Adolf Hitler. Other documents feature solely on the soundtrack, with Godard reproducing, for example, the trembling voice of André Malraux paying homage to the tortured Resistance leader Jean Moulin in 1964, or of Paul Celan reading from his poem "Todesfuge". About five minutes before the end of the film, together with a flickering, poorly projected sequence from Feuillade's *Vendémiaire*, 1918, Godard reproduces (to accompany the voice of its lead actor, Christopher Plummer) two extracts from Nicholas Ray's fraught chronicle of disenchantment with the American dream, *Wind Across the Everglades*, 1958, the one a shot of an early victim of spectacularisation in the shape of a local sea-bird hunted for its feathers, the other the face of one of Ray's immigrants increasingly effaced from the movie. Godard then cites a brief sequence from Cassavetes's *Faces*, 1968; this shows one of the leading characters in the film, Maria Forst (Lynn Carlin), shortly before she attempts suicide, in despair at the collapse of her dysfunctional marriage by way of a non-too-indirect indictment of American society itself in the mid-to-late 1960s. Shot on ends of reels of 16mm film, with a hand-held camera and makeshift cast, in the director's apartment (and his mother-in-law's), Cassavetes' film, revisited by Godard (who intensifies the contrast and surrounds Maria with a vignette effect), does plausible duty as an image of cinema's own ending, shot by itself.[22] This theme of the end of cinema is, of course, omnipresent. It receives a further, canonic illustration in this ending section of the film with a famous sequence from the ending of Chaplin's 1951 film, *Limelight*, showing the frenetic last performance of the clown Calvero (Chaplin), aided on-screen by Buster Keaton. Again, what is seen on screen mimics what was happening off it. *Limelight* was Chaplin's own swansong as a performer; but it was also the last film he was to make in the United States before being denied residence in the country because of his communist sympathies and alleged immoral behaviour. (Images of Chaplin are also prominent in the early episodes of *Histoire(s)*.)

Another series of images in this closing section explores faces and hands. Here, too, much earlier material and argument is reprised, notably the sequence based on Denis de Rougemont's *Penser avec les mains* in Chapter 4A. And here, too, eschatology is what is at issue, with the viewer allowed to witness a sequence of enigmatic and at times barely distinguishable images showing hands–hands involved in prayer, love-making, violence, in reaching out, and showing. To emphasise this last motif, just before the end of the film, a visual quotation from *JLG/JLG* shows Godard (albeit barely recognisable with his face in darkness) sitting alongside the unsighted film editor he has just hired. (An intertitle recalls Vladimir Jankélévitch's definition of the object of philosophy, already used in *For Ever Mozart*: "Le je-ne-sais-quoi et le presque-rien", "the I'm-not-sure-what and the almost-nothing".) Film here, it seems, is at the limit of what can in fact be seen. "True cinema", we were told in

Chapter 3B, "is the cinema that cannot be seen." At the end of *Les signes parmi nous*, these words are brought to an enigmatic if paradoxical conclusion; for if true cinema is that which is not visible, it is because cinema belongs not to vision but to the invisible world of touch–and montage (otherwise known as citation).

A third series of references pay tribute to what might best be called the power of the image. Endings, of course, can often be made to serve as mythic beginnings, and Godard next provides at least three instances of this, by showing the tumultuous arrival of the Red Army in Berlin in 1945 (from Mikhail Chiaureli's 1949 Soviet film *Berlinfall*), followed by a famous piece of newsreel footage from 14 June 1944, showing de Gaulle in the streets of Bayeux on his return to France for the first time since the beginning of the Occupation (the same footage is also cited in Chapter 1A).[23] A third image showing the 17 year-old Rimbaud reminds the viewer it is not only poets who enjoy mythic status, but politicians, too. "Men and women used to believe in prophets", we are told, "now they believe in politicians." At which point Godard reads a passage, attributed by an intertitle to Georges Bataille (and reprised by Godard in *L'Origine du vingt et unième siècle* and *Éloge de l'amour*), the burden of which is to insist on the incompatibility between love and the State, and therefore on the limits of the political as such, which Godard illustrates by way of two images from Picasso: the first a charcoal sketch of Stalin that initially appeared as an obituary in the French Communist Party weekly *Les Lettres françaises* in 1953, the second a lithograph entitled "Jeunesse" (Youth) from three years earlier, depicting two lovers, and first designed for the "Rencontre internationale de Nice pour l'interdiction absolue de l'arme atomique".

It is at this precise moment that Godard cites Blanchot's name on screen, and shows the photograph of Blanchot, which quickly dissolves into the instantly recognisable image of Max Schreck from *Nosferatu*. What motivates this startling, incongruous juxtaposition of Maurice Blanchot and Murnau's vampire? Various circumstantial possibilities suggest themselves. First, throughout *Histoire(s)*, Murnau, like Blanchot, is a persistent, albeit discreet point of reference. Images from *Faust* and *Sunrise* appear in Chapters 1A, 2B, and 3B and from *Nosferatu* in Chapters 1A and 1B, as well as twice earlier in 4B. It is no doubt also relevant that, because of his untimely death in 1931 in a car crash, Murnau's career, stretching from the early Weimar Republic to the end of silent pictures in Hollywood, is almost exactly co-extensive with the rise and fall of early cinema itself. And there is the vague physical similarity, particularly in the shot selected by Godard, between the figure of Nosferatu and the 78 year-old Blanchot, photographed in 1985 without his consent (and for the first time in public since the late 1920s) by a team of paparazzi hired by the magazine *Lire*.[24] Murnau, too, according to Lotte Eisner, was also very tall with a slight stoop.[25] And there is the odd coincidence, in this film about the ending of film, that Blanchot is the author of a story or *récit* entitled *Le Dernier Homme* (The Last Man), 1957, and Murnau the director of a virtuoso 1924 film entitled *Der Letzte Mann* (better known in English as *The Last Laugh* and in French as *Le Dernier des Hommes*).

Arguably more important than such trivial associations as these (but is it not one of the distinguishing traits of memory as such, as Proust and Perec tell us, that it refuses to distinguish between the contingent and the essential, the secondary and the primary?) is the fact that these two images–that of Blanchot, that of Max Schreck as Nosferatu–present two fundamental variations on the theme of the power of the image, the two versions, if you will, of the filmic imaginary. The first, the quotation of the photograph from *Lire*, testifies to the relentless spectacularisation of contemporary culture, to the attempt (on the part of the media) to use images to control the invisible, in this case

Above: **Emil Jannings in *Der Letzte Mann*,**
Friedrich Wilhelm Murnau, 1924.

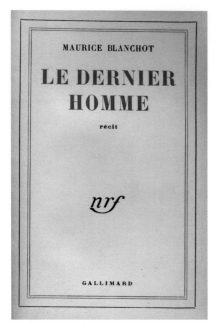

to subjugate a writing (that of Blanchot) which rigorously resisted the reduction of language (and art) to the status of a fantasmatic, mythic image. (Some moments earlier, shortly before the extract from *Faces*, Godard had implied as much by the emblematic and unannounced appearance on screen of a photograph of Guy Debord.) "Speaking is not seeing", writes Blanchot in *L'Entretien infini*; to which Godard's film responds in (paradoxical) agreement: showing an image is not to say anything, since it is montage that speaks, not the image as such. The visual quotation from Murnau that immediately follows, by its very juxtaposition with the photograph from *Lire*, illustrates the point Godard is making, for it offers proof of the possibility (and impossibility) of a contrary ambition: that of redeeming reality by recourse to an image. It is clear from other sequences in *Histoire(s)* that the figure of Nosferatu (unsurprisingly, since Godard has read Lotte Eisner and Siegfried Kracauer) serves as a kind of cinematographic shorthand for the powers of darkness that were to engulf Germany 11 short years after the making of Murnau's film. Indeed, in Chapter 2B Godard argues as much himself by attributing to Murnau and Karl Freund (who worked as cameraman on a number of influential films of the period, including *Der Letzte Mann*, but not in fact either *Faust* or *Nosferatu*) the responsibility for designing–before the fact–the lighting arrangements later to be exploited in the Nuremberg rallies.[26] But Murnau's film itself, though it may anticipate them, refuses this turn of events. For the movie ends when Nosferatu is induced to linger by the side of Hutter's wife, Ellen, as a result of her singular devotion, till after the cock crows, which is the time when images of the dark are dissipated by the dawn, at which point–magically, impossibly, and in a manner that owes nothing to reality and everything to cinematic montage–he simply disappears... in a puff of smoke.

The exploitative violence of spectacularisation on the one hand, then, and the grace (without grace) of impossible redemption on the other–there is perhaps no better summary of Godard's history of cinema as a whole, and the irreducible ambiguity to which it bears witness. Power and virtue, then, in the words of Godard's *King Lear*. Or rather: power versus virtue.

But perhaps even more compelling than the dynamic interplay between the two still images mentioned so far is a third, moving image that immediately follows the picture of Nosferatu and occupies the bottom three-quarters of the screen, during which time the head of the vampire remains briefly visible, before it too fades away. This third visual element is unidentified and its source uncertain (though it may be derived, as Bernard Eisenschitz suggests, from an unnamed Soviet colour documentary). But at this stage attribution seems hardly necessary. For the implications of the shot are unmistakeable. Those who are now glimpsed on screen, in washed-out blues and greys, flared with patches of red, are like the victims of the forces of darkness themselves, the anonymous and faceless undead, proceeding in serried ranks towards the viewer, their gait slowed down, interrupted, decomposed by the citational effects of slow-motion video processing, itself a form of internal, contestatory montage.

The end, indeed. The Gulag. Or the final solution.
But if disaster threatens, Godard's film endeavours to respond. It does so by recourse to a series of tutelary emblems, all of which speak from the edge of darkness. These include, among others, accompanying a pseudo-quotation from the anonymous, posthumous, invisible poetry of Emily Dickinson, a reproduction of Gabriele Münter's famous painting *Jawlensky und Werefkin* from 1908 (it, too, the work of a prominent yet neglected female artist, and which happened to be painted–trivia upon trivia–in the Bavarian village of

Murnau), which then bleeds into a vestigial photogram, reframed, vignetted, and bleached of detail, more fragmentary inscription than image, taken from Robert Wiene's 1919 classic *Das Cabinet des Dr. Caligari*, showing the sleepwalker Cesare (Conrad Veidt), carrying the female protagonist (Lil Dagover) over the rooftops, in what is plainly another case of disaster narrowly averted through love; a reframed shot (taken from Welles's *Mr. Arkadin* of 1955) of Flea Professor Rodzinski in Copenhagen (Mischa Auer), peering down through a magnifying glass at the strange behaviour of the footballing insects under his command and bearing witness to the paradoxical indelibility of the sublunary archive, of that trace of history which Arkadin himself is so keen to erase but which necessarily, and irredeemably, betrays his project of annihilation; a mysterious, barely decipherable extract from the opening sequence of Buñuel's *Un Chien andalou*, paying tribute to the virtues of the cut, or montage, and the blindness that inhabits cinematic vision itself; the deft hands of the unsighted film editor from *JLG/JLG*, counting out lengths of celluloid like so many structures of spatial articulation that precisely no longer belong to the visible world as such, but to montage; the ancient, gravelly voice of Ezra Pound, washed up like a survivor from another history of fascism and the media (radio in his case), perhaps remembering his own lethal fascination with Circe (the "Circé tyrannique" first mentioned in Baudelaire's poem "Le Voyage" read by Julie Delpy in Chapter 2A), and sonorously invoking, in a passage from the first of the *Cantos*, the sorry, drunken fate of Homer's Elpenor (from *The Odyssey*, Books X and XI), of whom all that is known–and in this context it is something rather than nothing–is that, like so many others, he died unburied and unmourned; a fast and furious montage sequence (incorporating half a dozen or more separate shots) from Welles's *Othello*, in which actor and director (like Mischa Auer's Professor, and much like the shot of James Stewart in the role of LB Jeffries peering over an extreme telephoto lens in Hitchcock's *Rear Window* which opens the credits in Chapter 1A) is seen seeing but unseen ("don't show every side of things, keep for yourself a margin of undefinability", Godard had warned in Chapter 1A, again borrowing from Bresson); and the Borges story, "La flor de Coleridge", quoted by Godard at the end, overlaid with a reproduction of Francis Bacon's *Study for Portrait of Van Gogh II*, 1957, and accompanied with frames from Godard's *Allemagne année 90 neuf zéro* and *JLG/JLG*, all telling, in their separate and distinct ways, of the labyrinthine mystery of time–which holds out the promise of redemption only insofar as it simultaneously withdraws it.[27]

Cinema, then, the art of space and montage, is also the art of the invisible, the unspoken, the unburied, and the unreconciled. Immediately before this final sequence, read over the three images described earlier, comes a quotation from Blanchot, spoken by Godard, which is as follows:

Cinema thus had nothing to fear from others or from itself. It was not sheltered from time, but was a shelter for time. Yes, the image is joy, but alongside it nothingness lingers, and the entire power of the image can be expressed only by appealing to that nothingness. One ought perhaps also to add: that the image, which has the capacity to negate nothingness, is also the gaze of nothingness upon us. The image is light, and nothingness immeasurably heavy; the image glimmers, while nothingness is the diffuse impenetrability in which nothing shows up.[28]

Blanchot's intervention at this stage is, I think, decisive. Context is all-important. The words cited by Godard first appeared in 1951, shortly before *Au moment voulu*, in a discussion by Blanchot of the three volumes of Malraux's *Essais de psychologie de l'art* (*Le Musée imaginaire*, *La Création artistique*, and *La Monnaie de l'Absolu*) and of his study of Goya, *Saturne*. Readers familiar with *Histoire(s)* will know that the figure of Malraux looms large in Godard's film, both as the writer and director of *Espoir*, and as the author of such works as *Le Musée imaginaire*, the *Esquisse d'une psychologie du cinéma*, and *Antimémoires*.[29] And it is Malraux who is the most immediate inspiration for the contention that it is montage, or *découpage*, not the moving image as such, that constitutes cinema as art. As Malraux explains in the *Esquisse*, "cinema's means of reproduction was the moving image, but its means of expression is the sequence of shots". "The division into shots", he adds, "that is to say, the independence of cameraman and director with regard to the scene itself, is what gives rise to cinema's expressive possibilities and is responsible for the birth of cinema as art."[30]

But for all the emphasis placed on the autonomy of cinematographic language, which Godard seems largely to endorse, Malraux's schema of artistic development follows a ruthless teleology. The end of art, for Malraux, is myth. Its purpose or destiny is the salvation of man, civilisation, history. In the imaginary museum, metamorphosis rules: not contingency, but transcendence; not death itself, but death put to work, elevated, erected, embodied in the twin emblems of the Sphinx and the Great Pyramid.[31] But myth, as Malraux is well aware, is nothing if not ambiguous. "Cinema addresses the masses", he writes in the *Esquisse*, "and the masses love myth, for both good and ill." Godard quotes these words (together with the passage that follows) in a crucial section of Chapter 1A, not once, but twice over, first by reading them on the soundtrack, then second by displaying them (in ironically degraded form) as a series of intertitles explaining that the film's success is "because crowds love/ myth/ and cinema addresses crowds". In both versions, however, it is noticeable that Godard omits Malraux's ominous closing words (for good and ill, "en bien et en mal"). Godard's purpose, though, is not to minimise the ambiguity of myth.[32] On the contrary, in Godard's text, the passage is accompanied by a powerful series of quotations comprising (among others) shots from Bresson (*Les Anges du péché*, *Les Dames du Bois de Boulogne*), Chaplin (*The Great Dictator*), Lang (*Die Nibelungen*), and Fassbinder (*Lili Marleen*), together with material from Goya and others, not to mention various archive documents, including footage of the Nuremberg rallies, Hitler, the assault on Poland, the Franco-German armistice, and a famous wartime sound recording of de Gaulle in London.

The combined effect of this material is complex; but it brings sharply into relief at least three distinct, but related motifs: the horrors of war, the extent of cinema's resistance to fascism, but also, and more problematically, the complicity of film in the political events of the 1930s and after. True, this is nothing new from Godard. Already in 1963, *Le Mépris* was drawing attention to the paradoxical situation of Fritz Lang, forced to leave Nazi Germany not to escape oppression, but to elude the more sinister fate of being co-opted by Goebbels into the Nazi propaganda machine. (In some ways, the fate endured by Eisenstein was little different, and Godard's citation of the death of Ivan in Chapter 4B, alongside that of Stalin, serves to underline the filmmaker's own complicity in constructing the myth of Stalin, even as he was voicing strong indirect criticism of it.) "The myths on the basis of which we live", interjects an unidentified voice, "are contradictory." Myth, a Nietzschean intertitle confirms, leads "beyond good and evil", "par-delà bien et mal". For every Hynkel, it seems, there is a Hitler, for every Lubitsch (*To Be Or Not to Be*) a Heidegger (*Dasein oder nicht Dasein*). Myth, though it may feed men's dreams, also supplies their nightmares. *Histoire(s)*, with an S, is the History of Cinema, with an SS.

Above: *Die Nibelungen*, Fritz Lang, 1924.

It is here that Godard's appeal to Blanchot at the end of *Histoire(s)* finds its rationale, for Blanchot is singularly aware of the ambiguity underlying Malraux's reliance on myth as both the justification and secret essence of art. This leads him in his explication of Malraux's thinking to disjoin two separate moments in the logic of the work of art. It is these which Godard condenses and appropriates for his own purposes in the passage read in Chapter 4B. The first moment has to do with the temporality of the work itself as a process of constant metamorphosis. Malraux calls this time the present. Blanchot however protests. The temporality of art no more belongs to the present, he says, than it does to the eternal; the time of art is the time of the absence of time, and this is why, in the passage quoted in *Les signes parmi nous*, art–or cinema, as Godard rephrases it–does not shelter from time, but shelters time itself. And this is what grounds the joy–the chance, the felicity–that is art. But this, Blanchot adds, is merely the perspective on art found in traditional aesthetics, to which Malraux in spite of himself remains profoundly indebted. There is something else too, however, an additional, supplementary dimension that exceeds the work itself, does not give rise to religion, does not save humanity or art, is indifferent to heroism, and refuses all monumentality and all spectacularisation. (The argument here closely parallels Godard's thinking on the so-called divine as explored in *Hélas pour moi*.) This other dimension is what (with Bataille) we might provisionally call the unemployed negativity of the image itself, its fundamental and irreducible darkness, which cannot be mediated or bound dialectically, and inhabits all images–in particular, as Godard knows, all cinematographic images–as their common space of both possibility and impossibility. If it is indeed the case, as Bruno (Michel Subor) ironically claims in *Le Petit soldat*, brandishing his Leica, that "cinema is truth 24 times per second", it is only because each of those 24 frames is separated from the one that precedes or follows by a strip of black leader, like a margin of darkness–a darkness that, taken to its logical conclusion, would threaten the very possibility of the film image as such. The image, then, is not only plenitude, but emptiness, not only luminosity, but the repetitive and inescapable movement of night itself. Like death, it makes clear; but like death it also brings the human world to a realisation of its endless, unmasterable impotence. And this is why, Blanchot concludes, in lines that immediately follow those quoted by Godard, "the image seems so deep and empty, so threatening and fascinating, always richer in meaning than we find it possible to attribute to it, and also poor, null and silent, since what greets us in the image is the dark and unmasterable impotence of death as rebeginning".[33]

In his engagement with Malraux, then, Blanchot supplies an essential corrective to the humanist theology of the image culminating in Malraux's imaginary museum. But he also does something more. He provides Godard, at least implicitly, with that theory of cinema which, paradoxically, cinema itself is alone able to supply. For everything I have said so far about quotation, citation, montage in *Histoire(s)* has in reality been no more than a meagre commentary on the (non-)concept of the *neutre* or neuter, elaborated in Blanchot's own writing.[34] In a variety of ways. First, by thematising the movement of effacement and inscription that is another name for textuality in general, the *neutre* names the very possibility of quotation as such. Which is how–this is the second point–the *neutre* underwrites the possibility of the imaginary museum while transforming or displacing it, no longer subordinating it (as does Malraux) to value-laden teleology, but affirming it as an awareness of art's obstinate refusal to coincide with itself and of its essential relationship (as Blanchot puts it) with its own singular inessentiality.

The *neutre* also says something which has quite particular pertinence for *Histoire(s)*. By conceiving the image not as self-identity but as repetition and difference, the *neutre* also names that fold–not to be confused with self-reflexivity–by which cinema (among others), by dint of montage, is able to withdraw from itself to allow the singularity of its own trace to appear (or disappear). This movement of withdrawal and reinscription which the *neutre* designates in Blanchot simultaneously demands thought and resists it. It thereby affirms, so to speak, the necessary excess of textuality over positionality, of image and sound over thesis or argument. This excess is crucial. Without it, Godard's whole project of telling (and retelling) the history and histories of cinema by manipulating the historical archive would not be possible at all. By the same token, such a history cannot aspire to finality or closure. If film, as Godard phrases it in Chapter 3A, is "une forme qui pense" ("a form that thinks"), i.e. a form that does not take its orders from "a thought that forms", this is because it always outstrips the possible limits of the historical, sublunary archive. And it is this that gives cinema, in Godard's eyes, its weakly messianic force. Like Benjamin's *Passagen-Werk*, which, at least according to Adorno, was to have consisted almost exclusively of quotations interacting with one another in dramatic, shock-like interlocution in the style of *Histoire(s)*, Godard's history is unfinished, and unfinishable.[35] Is it therefore even a history? To cite in my turn the title of Jean-Marie Straub's 1965 film, loosely based on Heinrich Böll's *Billard um halbzehn* which it cites rather than it adapts, elaborating in the process a radical poetics and politics of citation, the fate of history in Godard is to remain separated from itself, unquiet, and unreconciled: *nicht versöhnt*.

But that nothing is yet decided is, of course, in itself best proof of the enduring demand that decisions be taken. To cite, Godard's *Histoire(s) du cinéma* reminds us, also means to summon as a witness for the defence or the prosecution, and the fragmentary and undecidable status of Godard's many quotations can do no other in their turn than summon us to judgement, and invite us–incite us–to respond. This is no doubt one of the ways in which, with a force and resilience that (as Blanchot argues) comes from its radical nullity, from its status not as potent presence but as spectral vestige, the image continues to gaze upon us–and one of the ways in which Godard's history of cinema demands of us, its audience, that we engage not only with the historical past, where ghosts reside, but also with the unhistorical future, the time without time when ghosts are always liable to return–to haunt us and recall us to our responsibilities.

NOTES

WORK AND WORKS

DANEY

1. Originally published as Serge Daney, "Le paradoxe de Godard", *Revue Belge du Cinéma*, 22-23, 1986, p. 7.

READER

1. Bennington, Geoffrey, and Derrida, Jacques, *Jacques Derrida*, Paris: Seuil, 1991, p. 269.
2. Witt, Michael, "The death(s) of cinema according to Godard", *Screen*, 40:3, Autumn 1999, pp. 331-346 (p. 334).
3. Silverman, Kaja, and Farocki, Harun, *Speaking About Godard*, New York: New York University Press, 1998, pp. 188 and 183.
4. Silverman and Farocki, p. 177.
5. Temple, Michael and Williams, James S, eds., *The Cinema Alone: essays on the work of Jean-Luc Godard, 1985-2000*, Amsterdam: University of Amsterdam Press, 2000, p. 11.
6. Prédal, René, ed., *CinémAction*, 52, "Le cinéma selon Godard", July 1989, p. 7.
7. Prédal, p. 94.
8. Prédal, p. 9.
9. Debord, Guy, *La Société du spectacle*, Paris: Champ Libre, 1971, pp. 133-134.
10. Amengual, Barthélémy, *Bande à part*, Brussels: Yellow Now, 1993, p. 11.
11. Amengual, p. 28.
12. Amengual, p. 14.
13. I use the term "deconstruction" here in a would-be precise sense, analogous to what Roland Barthes does in *S/Z* when he shows how Balzac's short story *Sarrasine* calls the foundations of its own realism into question.
14. For a comprehensive overview of the events and views of their significance, see Keith Reader with Khursheed Wadia, *The May 1968 Events in France: Reproductions and Interpretations*, London: Macmillan, 1993.
15. Melville's *L'Armée des ombres*, 1969, and Tavernier's *Laissez-passer*, 2002, are examples of such fictionalisations of the Resistance.
16. Jeancolas, Jean-Pierre, *Le Cinéma des Français: La Vème République*, 1958-1978, Paris: Stock, 1979, p. 112.
17. The (by its nature) loosely defined term "gauchisme" referred to movements–variously Maoist, Trotskyist or anarcho-syndicalist in inspiration–that sought to outflank the Communist Party on its left, advocating revolutionary rather than electoral or reformist means to bring about the transformation of society.
18. Roud, Richard, *A Biographical Dictionary of Cinema*, London: Secker and Warburg, 1980, II, p. 841.
19. See for instance François Poulle, *Renoir 1938 ou Jean Renoir pour rien?*, Paris: Cerf, 1969.
20. Lefèvre, Raymond, *"Numéro Deux"*, *Revue du cinéma*, 300, 1975, pp. 98-99 (p. 99).
21. Bergala, Alain, ed., *Jean-Luc Godard par Jean-Luc Godard*, Paris: Cahiers du Cinéma, 1985, pp. 379-380 (p. 379).
22. Bergala, Alain, "La beauté du geste", *Cahiers du cinéma*, 385, 1986, pp. 57-58 (p. 58).

GRANT

1. The epigraphs are taken from an interview with Jean-Luc Godard in *Libération*, 27 December 2000, and Sherry Turkle, "Who am we?", *Wired*, January 1996, p. 148. All translations from French are my own (including film dialogue) unless I am quoting from written sources published entirely in English. This chapter benefited from comments made when it was read at a conference on the work of Anne-Marie Miéville organised by Vicki Callahan at the University of Wisconsin-Milwaukee, 13 September 2003. My thanks to all those who participated in the discussion, especially Jane Gallop, Kelley Conway, Tami Williams, and Cecilia Condit.
2. Ginette Vincendeau writes: "Huillet and Straub work as a co-scripting and co-directing team, their equal collaboration so close that it is scarcely meaningful to separate the roles (Huillet has, however, indicated that she tends to be in charge of sound and editing, while Straub does most of the camerawork)": Vincendeau, Ginette, "Huillet, Danièle and Straub, Jean-Marie", in *Encyclopedia of European Cinema*, Ginette Vincendeau ed., London: British Film Institute, 1995, p. 210.
3. I have opted to concentrate on some of their work made on film for cinematic distribution and not on the vast body of video projects for which Godard and Miéville are also well known. This is because, as I shall make clear in my chapter, the film work, with its industrial context, has provoked a particular kind of discourse about their authorial collaboration as a couple which distinguishes it from discussion of the video work, the latter tending to sideline issues concerning the degree of individual contribution and influence. In any case, some highly impressive studies of the collaborative video work already exist, most notably those by Michael Witt: "On Communication: The Work of Anne-Marie Miéville and Jean-Luc Godard as 'Sonimage' from 1973 to 1979", unpublished PhD Dissertation, University of Bath, 1998; and "Going Through the Motions: Unconscious Optics and Corporal Resistance in Miéville and Godard's *France/tour/détour/deux/enfants*", in *Gender and French Cinema*, Alex Hughes and James S Williams eds., Oxford: Berg, 2001, pp. 171-194.
4. The theoretical underpinning of my approach to questions of film authorship is set out more fully in the following three articles: "Secret Agents: Feminist Theories of Women's Film Authorship", *Feminist Theory*, 2:1, 2001, pp. 113-130; "www.auteur.com?", *Screen*, 41:1, Spring 2000, pp. 101-108; and "Recognising *Billy Budd* in *Beau Travail*: Epistemology and Hermeneutics of an Auteurist 'Free' Adaptation", *Screen*, 43:1, Spring 2002, pp. 57-73.
5. See "Introduction to the Mysteries of Cinema, 1985-2000", in *The Cinema Alone: essays on the work of Jean-Luc Godard, 1985-2000*, Michael Temple and James S Williams eds., Amsterdam:

Amsterdam University Press, 2000, pp. 9-32 (p. 9).

6. Anne-Marie Miéville worked as a stills photographer on this film.

7. "Anne-Marie Miéville: une cinéaste qui sait prendre le retour", in *Le Monde* (édition électronique), 26 December 2000: http://www.lemonde.fr/article_impression/ 0,2322,130094,00.htm.

8. As Kaja Silverman puts it: "Significantly, the categories 'direction' and 'writing' are now absent [from *Numéro Deux*'s credits], and have been replaced by the much more labour-significant 'production', which is credited to not one, but four names: *Number Two*: a film produced by Anne-Marie Miéville and J-L Godard with S Battistella, P Oudry and Others." In Silverman, Kaja and Farocki, Harun, *Speaking about Godard*, New York: New York University Press, 1998, p. 145. Silverman and Farocki engage, nonetheless, in speaking of *Numéro Deux* exclusively as Godard's work. In *Numéro Deux*, most of the images are shot on video, displayed on two video monitors, and then shot again on 35mm as they are played out. "Full" 35mm images are shown of Godard at work in the studio, at the beginning and end of the film.

9. MacCabe, Colin, with Eaton, Mick and Mulvey, Laura, *Godard: Images, Sounds, Politics*, London: Macmillan, 1980, p. 24.

10. Godard, Jean-Luc, "Préface" (extracts of an interview by Godard with Freddy Buache on 14 July 1989), in Buache, Freddy, *Le Cinéma Français des Années 70*, Renens: Hatier/5 Continents, 1990, pp. 5-7; pp. 6-7. Cited by Witt in "On Communication: The Work of Anne-Marie Miéville and Jean-Luc Godard as 'Sonimage'", p. 201.

11. Witt, "Going Through the Motions", pp. 174-175. Winston Wheeler Dixon makes similar points in his survey of Godard's work, *The Films of Jean-Luc Godard*, Albany: State University of New York Press, 1997.

12. With this metaphor, the credit hints that Godard has not "directed" the film (the usual "major" role), but that he has constructed or arranged it, through a particular combination and emphasis, as with a piece of music.

13. Little interest has been expressed by critics or researchers in the contribution of this other co-scenarist, Jean-Claude Carrière, to the scripting process. One exception to this is Michael Witt who notes that Carrière co-scripted several of Luis Buñuel's films. Witt argues that *Sauve qui peut* is highly reminiscent of some of the late films by the Spanish director, despite Godard's claims not to have seen his work. See Witt, "On Communication: The Work of Anne-Marie Miéville and Jean-Luc Godard as 'Sonimage'", p. 193; p. 281, footnote 68. Another argument about Carrière's contribution might depart from the possibility that he was brought into the film's production as a highly experienced commercial art cinema screenwriter, a "safe" pair of hands, by the film's other producers and financiers (apart from Sonimage): Alain Sarde, Sara Films, MK2, Saga Productions, CNC, ZDF, SSR, ORF.

14. Pajaczkowska, Claire, "Liberté! Égalité! Paternité!: Jean-Luc Godard's *Sauve qui peut (la vie)*", in *French Film: Texts and Contexts*, Susan Hayward and Ginette Vincendeau eds., London: Routledge, 1990, pp. 241-255 (p. 241). Pajaczkowska fails to give a source for this quotation, but its frequent repetition by other writers (quoting from her) bespeaks a certain need for its 'truth'.

15. In an interview with Colin MacCabe, Godard states, in his characteristic intriguing fashion: "You know that picture by Cassavetes, *A Woman under the Influence*? Well, all my films are

made under the influence. Perhaps it's the weather, perhaps it's... *Numéro Deux* was made under the influence of Miéville. She wasn't there and she was angry because I'd taken a lot from her and I said I'd always done that. If I make a picture of the sun I'd take from the sun. I can't produce things from myself. I don't know how other filmmakers do it. I'm always taking, I never invent": MacCabe, *Godard: Images, Sounds, Politics*, p. 103. There is too much Godardian playfulness here to take this entirely seriously but the traps laid are highly suggestive: Miéville co-produced the film, but wasn't "there"; Godard took from her as he takes from whatever he's making a picture of, so is *Numéro Deux* to be taken as a "picture" of Miéville, his influential "number two", or of femininity more generally, the "number two" sex, as many commentators, including MacCabe, have argued?

16. Peter Harcourt writes that "it is very different from *Numéro Deux*. *Numéro Deux* situated Godard himself within the problematic of his film both through his self-dismemberment at the opening (his head separated from the rest of his body and isolated on a tiny television screen) and through his powerlessness at the end, his head on his arms, his hands clutching the switches of his sound-mixing machine": "Le nouveau Godard: An exploration of *Sauve qui peut (la vie)*", *Film Quarterly*, 35:2, Winter 1981-1982, pp. 17-27 (p. 25). One might argue that the endings of both films show that, ultimately, they share themes of masculine "self-effacement", and "authorial divestiture", as Kaja Silverman writes of *Numéro Deux* in her article "The Author as Receiver", *October*, 96, Spring 2001, pp. 17-34 (p. 21). See my discussion of Silverman's work later in this chapter.

17. Patton, Paul, "Godard/Deleuze: *Sauve qui peut (la vie)*", *Frogger*, 20, 1986. Available online at http://www.film-philosophy.com/portal/writings/patton.

18. Harcourt, "Le nouveau Godard", p. 20.

19. The Editors (Janet Bergstrom, Elisabeth Lyon and Constance Penley), "Introduction", *Camera Obscura: A Journal of Feminism and Film Theory*, 8-9-10, Fall 1982, p. 5.

20. The Editors, "Introduction", p. 5.

21. The special issue does carry an interview with Godard, the transcription of a public debate he carried out with film critic Pauline Kael in the US: "The Economics of Film Criticism: A Debate–Jean-Luc Godard and Pauline Kael", pp. 163-184. The only mention of Miéville comes when a member of the audience asks him how he makes his money, and he playfully replies: "Well, I have a company I formed 20 years ago. There are two of us in the company (Sonimage), me and Anne-Marie Miéville. We tried to live together and we failed, so we now have two separate apartments. The apartments are three-room apartments or condominiums you call them here. They are very small. Since we live separately, we have two cars which belong to the company. She has a small car and I have a bigger one (laughter; Godard pulls a calculator out of his pocket)", pp. 179-180.

22. Until fairly recently, Miéville has been interviewed only very rarely by journalists and other writers. To my knowledge, she has never responded to requests from researchers (at least those unknown to her) for the kind of information about her collaboration with Godard that the *Camera Obscura* collective attempted to elicit.

23. Some filmographies cite a Miéville project made without Godard's credited collaboration, the 1977 short television film

Papa comme maman. See Witt, "On Communication: The Work of Anne-Marie Miéville and Jean-Luc Godard as 'Sonimage'", p. 344. Witt states in addition that Miéville had also co-scripted some other work for Swiss television separately from her partner.

24. Interestingly, some of these contradictions are also evident in the reviews section later in the special issue which includes Jacques Aumont's critique of MacCabe's *Godard: Images, Sounds, Politics*. In it, the French writer gently berates the book for its "implicit belief in the unity of Godard as *cinéaste*, as a promise for its ultimate coherence": Aumont, "Godard: Images, Sounds, Politics", *Camera Obscura*, Fall 1982, 8-9-10, pp. 211-215 (p. 215). Aumont adds: "A few years ago it would have been impossible to use the notion of the *auteur* in such a direct and unproblematic fashion. Remember Mark Nash's book on Dreyer [...] which refused to refer to the filmmaker other than as "the Dreyer text". MacCabe's fresh confidence in the integrity of the *auteur* might be an unwilling symptom of the opposite tendency" (p. 215).

25. Penley, Constance, "Pornography, Eroticism", *Camera Obscura*, 8-9-10, Fall 1982, pp. 13-18 (p. 14; p. 17).

26. Penley, "Pornography, Eroticism", p. 18.

27. In her other article on Godard/Miéville's work for the collection, Penley touches unconsciously, perhaps, on questions of Miéville's influence on the way that Sonimage introduce feminist questions into their work, though once again in critical terms. She writes of the way a woman's voiceover (she does not mention that it is, in fact, Miéville's voice) accuses Godard of sexism in *Ici et Ailleurs* (his is the male voiceover in the characteristic masculine/feminine, Godard/Miéville style of voiceover "turn-taking" which is now very familiar from much of their video work together): "To assign a censoring and denunciatory role to a woman's voice that is narratively one step from the diegesis is to make of feminism a superior, authoritative truth that stands as a corrective to the sexism of men. It is to make feminism into a moral truth rather than a political theory and set of strategies. Endowing feminism with such inordinate power presumes a masochistic relation for men to that excessive potency. That a masochistic fantasy is at work here can be seen most conspicuously at the end of *Every Man for Himself* when the *mise en scène* requires the "Paul Godard" character to die under (as a result of?) the disaffected gazes of the women in his life": "Les Enfants de la Patrie", *Camera Obscura*, 8-9-10, Fall 1982, pp. 33-58 (p. 51).

28. Bergstrom, Janet, "Violence and Enunciation", *Camera Obscura*, 8-9-10, Fall 1982, pp. 21-30 (p. 21).

29. Bergstrom, "Violence and Enunciation", p. 21.

30. Bergstrom, "Violence and Enunciation", p. 28.

31. Bergstrom, "Violence and Enunciation", p. 28.

32. Strangely, Bergstrom leaves out co-editing from her list of Miéville's known activities in the making of *Sauve qui peut*. This is curious because the particular use of slow motion and stop-action has been viewed as perhaps the film's most radical departure from Godard's earlier film work, and it has since received attention as a methodology which is well established in the co-authored video work for showing male and female bodies. See Witt, "Going Through the Motions".

33. Pajaczkowska, "Liberté! Égalité! Paternité!", p. 244.

34. Pajaczkowska, "Liberté! Égalité! Paternité!", p. 253.

35. Apart from the following passing reference: "*Numéro Deux*, 1975, represents an even more concerted attempt at authorial divestiture–an attempt to create a film in whose production not only Anne-Marie Miéville but also the actors participated and which is at least to some degree spoken by a female voice": Silverman, "The Author as Receiver", p. 21.

36. Silverman, "The Author as Receiver", p. 24. This is similar to the argument towards which Pajaczkowska is gesturing at the end of her study of *Sauve qui peut*, though it remains undeveloped in that work.

37. Silverman, "The Author as Receiver", p. 24.

38. Silverman, "The Author as Receiver", p. 34.

39. Smith, Gavin, "Jean-Luc Godard", in *Jean-Luc Godard: Interviews*, David Sterritt ed., Jackson: University of Mississippi Press, 1998, p. 183. Cited by Silverman in "The Author as Receiver", p. 18.

40. Godard quoted in *L'Avant-Scène Cinéma*, 171-172, p. 52. Cited by MacCabe, *Godard: Images, Sounds, Politics*, p. 23.

41. By 1985 Miéville had made two 35mm short films: *How Can I Love (A Man When I Know He Don't Want Me)*, 1984, and *Le Livre de Marie*, 1985. Much has been made of the collaboration on *Soft and Hard* in discussions of Miéville's influence on Godard. Critics have argued that the film's form, in particular the use of clips from Hollywood films, as well as contemporary television programmes, acts as a kind of template, or a "preparatory sketch", for some of Godard's later work, including *Histoire(s) du cinéma*, as well as the co-directed video films, *Le Rapport Darty*, 1989, *2x50 ans de cinéma français*, 1995, and *The Old Place*, 1999. See Witt, "On Communication: The Work of Anne-Marie Miéville and Jean-Luc Godard as 'Sonimage'"; Witt, "Going Through the Motions"; Temple and Williams, "Introduction to the Mysteries of Cinema", p. 31; and Michael Temple and James S Williams, "Jean-Luc Godard: Images, Words, Histories", *Dalhousie French Studies*, 45, 1998, pp. 99-110.

42. The *mise en scène* is fascinating in the final part of the film, which shows their "conversation". Godard's body dominates the frame, sitting on a sofa with his back to us (we can't really see his face). Miéville, sitting behind him frame-left, struggles to be seen, her body frequently tensed and stretching up into the field of vision, sometimes relaxing back into her allotted space with an intoxicating smile, which defuses some of the most intense moments of confrontation with her partner.

43. Temple and Williams, "Godard: Images, Words, Histories", p. 104.

44. Nor do her short films: *How Can I Love (A Man When I Know He Don't Want Me)*, *Faire la fête*, 1987, and *Le Livre de Marie*. Godard is not credited with collaboration on any of the shorts or the first two feature-length films, though all Miéville's short films and some of the features are produced by JLG Films (the successor company to Sonimage).

45. *Après la réconciliation* was released just before Godard's *Éloge de l'amour* was completed. The casting of Godard is likely to have helped in raising finance for both Miéville's films. Interestingly, *Nous sommes tous encore ici* opens with an off-screen dialogue between Lui (Godard) and Elle in which he encourages her to make the film, despite a low budget.

46. Miéville's 1997 film opens with a dialogue from Plato's *Gorgias*, between Callicles (Bernadette Lafont), and Socrates (Aurore Clément), here "performed" by a suburban housewife and her female friend. Then in the second part of the film, with little filmic exposition to explain his character, Godard

walks out on to a stage to deliver in monologue a passage from Hannah Arendt's *The Origins of Totalitarianism*. He reappears in the final part as one half of a couple–Lui and Elle (Clément)–who bicker and argue about literature, love and their lives until they are briefly reconciled at the end.

47. There is a similar story circulated to explain Miéville's casting of herself in *Après la réconciliation*.

48. "Godard et les lycéens, un cérémonial pédagogique ambigu et pourtant fécond", in *Le Monde* Interactif, 11 November 2000: http://www.lemonde.fr/article_impression/0,2322,116229,00.htm. Godard here makes similar though less categorical disavowals about his character Robert in *Après la réconciliation*: "Robert, who isn't me, but whom I accompanied a little way along the road."

49. Vassé, Claire, "*Nous sommes tous encore ici*: conversations intimes", *Positif*, 434, April 1997, pp. 40-41.

50. Godard interviewed in "Jean-Luc a insisté pour jouer", *Libération* Cinéma, 27 December 2000, available online at: http://www.liberation.fr/cinema/200012/20000122/reconci.html.

51. Godard in "Godard et les lycéens, un cérémonial pédagogique ambigu at pourtant fécond".

52. Miéville interviewed in "Jean-Luc a insisté pour jouer".

53. The prologue lasts eight and a half minutes. Over the years, Godard and Miéville have made several of these "scénario-vidéos": *Scénario vidéo de Sauve qui peut (la vie)*, 1979; *Passion, le travail et l'amour: introduction à un scenario*, 1981; *Scénario du film Passion*, 1982.

54. Miéville says: "What can one do, nothing at all, there's no solution, it's necessary to see and to accept that it's just like that, but it's very difficult, you need a whole lifetime. He says: it's not a question of renouncing your desires, you just need to free yourself of them."

55. At the end of the film, however, Godard's character admires the artistry of his onscreen partner: "You tell it well, with images." (My thanks to Elizabeth Cowie for pointing this out to me.) This might indicate to us that the acts of authorial divestiture performed by Godard and Miéville in their careers are not equal. In Miéville's work such acts against "herself" should be seen as much less violent and much more ambivalent than Godard's in his films. The "death of the author" must, of course, have a different valency for women filmmakers who haven't had much of a life (as authors) yet, than it does for male artists. Femme 1's sometimes crushing treatment of Godard's character in this film might be interpreted in the light of these personal and impersonal politics.

56. This echoes a similar sequence in *Nous sommes tous encore ici*, where Elle picks up the piano-player who had earlier performed in the restaurant during her meal with Lui.

57. This is Femme 1's characterisation of the "couple", drawn from the film dialogue.

58. In *Lou n'a pas dit non*, for example, we are given a foundational story of sexual difference in the film's prologue. In *Mon cher sujet*, the narrative harks back to *Sauve qui peut* in its almost comic portrayal of the numerous ways in which men casually subject women to sexist abuse. Even in *Nous sommes tous encore ici* there is irony pointed up in the way that the female "philosophers" at the beginning voice the ancient words of men, on the subject of men and the value of their work, even as they engage in forms of women's domestic work.

59. If less obviously political, in a narrow sense at least.

60. This is a line taken from the poet's correspondence with his lover Lou Andréas Salomé.

61. Witt, "On Communication: The Work of Anne-Marie Miéville and Jean-Luc Godard as 'Sonimage'", p. 10.

62. I would strongly argue that we should explore the totality of their productions (films, videos, performances, published words, and other utterances) as a kind of ongoing, collaborative "installation work" which constantly interacts with its reception by audiences. Not in a teleological way, as my reference to its beginnings might suggest, but nonetheless as a reasonably definable site or space which does have certain practical, human limits of actual duration, and of physical, intellectual and emotional proximity or distance. This is my approach to questions of (film) authorship in general, but it is particularly fruitful in the case of such self-reflective artists as Miéville and Godard.

63. Witt, "On Communication: The Work of Anne-Marie Miéville and Jean-Luc Godard as 'Sonimage'", p. 199.

QUANDT

1. Perhaps the proximity of the two projects forced a reading, but the traversal of the Godard retrospective soon after the exhibition conclusively revealed that the latter has inexorably displaced Renoir as Godard's mentor-god. Bresson's influence was apparent in Godard's work as early as *Le Petit soldat* and *Les Carabiniers*, and Godard's recent films pay frequent, extended and often direct homage to Bresson, for instance quoting the final line of *Pickpocket*, 1959, before a close-up of a Balthazar-like donkey in the last reel of *Je vous salue, Marie*, calling *Les Dames du Bois du Boulogne*, 1945, "the only French film of the Resistance" in *Histoire(s) du cinéma*, interpolating lengthy clips from *Les Dames* and *Les Anges du péché*, 1944, in *The Old Place*, and lingering on a poster for *Pickpocket* and quoting extensively from Bresson's *Notes sur le cinématographe* in *Éloge de l'amour*. Indeed, as Godard has acknowledged, *Histoire(s)* proceeds from a Bresson axiom in the Notes: "Don't show all aspects of things. Leave a margin of the undefined." (Godard's motif of hands, often shackled, also seems derived from Bresson, or perhaps from Delacroix: "I want to work like a painter with images and details", Godard said in 1993, "Delacroix painted five hundred hands before drawing a full human figure.")

2. Rosenbaum, Jonathan, "Eight Obstacles to the Appreciation of Godard in the United States," in *Jean-Luc Godard, Son+Image, 1974-1991*, Raymond Bellour and Mary Lea Bandy eds., New York: The Museum of Modern Art, 1992, p. 201.

3. See, for instance, Rosenbaum, Jonathan, "Godard in the Nineties: An Interview, Argument, and Scrapbook," *Film Comment*, 34:5, 1998, pp. 52-63.

4. See "Gall/Godard: Autour d'une métamorphose," *Cahiers du cinéma*, 581, 2003, pp. 61-69.

5. Censorious and imprecise subtitles are frequent in English prints of Godard films (although not in Jackie Raynal's largely superb translation of *Numéro Deux*). A provocative commentary by a local book critic pointed out a problem with the worn 16mm print of *La Chinoise* we were forced to show when the film's rights-holder refused to sell us a new copy because of fears of piracy. In *The Toronto Star*, Philip Marchand wrote:

> A few months ago, I went to see some Jean-Luc Godard films from the 1960s at Cinematheque [sic]. One of them was *La Chinoise*, a 1967 movie about a group of student Maoists in Paris. It's a bizarre

film because Godard, on the one hand, can't help ridiculing these bourgeois revolutionaries. On the other hand, he agrees with them. He really does subscribe to their radical critiques of Western capitalist society.

In the middle of a characteristic rant, one of the main characters denounces the "homosexuals" of the Comédie Française, the major national theatre in Paris. When I first saw the film on its release, the English subtitles translated this remark literally. In the print of the movie I saw a few months ago, however, the English subtitles substituted the word "actors" for "homosexuals". A viewer of the movie who spoke no French would have no idea that these idealistic young people on the screen entertained standard Maoist views of homosexuality as a decadent bourgeois perversion.

This bowdlerisation of the movie on the part of the writer of the subtitles was no accident. It was simply too embarrassing to remind audiences today that Godard, the supreme emblem of cinematic cool, Godard, the subversive and transgressive, was a homophobe way back then. It's possible, of course, to maintain that Godard viewed the denunciation of homosexual actors with much the same irony and mockery as he viewed the protagonists as a whole, but no one who sees the movie will believe it.

6. When Raoul Coutard presented *Passion* in Toronto not long after it was made, I asked him in what aspect ratio it should be shown. He made a square with his fingers, indicating 1.33, although the film had been shown commercially in its prescribed ratio, 1.85.

7. The digital image is, however, stable and durable compared to that of aging video. The subtitled videos of *France/tour/détour/deux/enfants*, 1979, *Soft and Hard*, 1985, and *Six fois deux (Sur et sous la communication)*, 1976, are now fuzzy and speckled with static from overuse and deterioration, the images more soft than hard, so to speak. The degradation of the video image actually adds a plaintive counterpoint to these works, as if the very means and medium of communication are slowly dissolving before our eyes.

8. It may be churlish to note that Godard's reactionary rejection of contemporary art in *The Old Place* is concomitant with his increasingly conservative taste in painting: the bourgeois marzipan of Renoir *père*, for example, and the timid abstraction of Nicolas de Staël, ironically the last of the School of Paris painters who had an influence on American painting (and a suicide at the age of forty) before New York displaced Paris as the art capital. It is also striking that Godard's use of fragmented Beethoven (in *Deux ou trois choses*, for instance) and the roughly played Mozart in *Week-end* seems much more modernist than his recent reliance on "pretty" twentieth century music: the lovely miniaturism of Mompou (often called the Spanish Satie), the ingenuous serenity of Hans Otte, whose *Das Buch der Klänge* is celebrated for its curative powers, and the easy-listening mysticism of Arvo Pärt. Perhaps, like Renoir *fils*, who declared "I'm getting old, now I play Mozart", Godard equates senescence with *dégagement*.

9. Temple, Michael, "Big Rhythm and the Power of Metamorphosis," in *The Cinema Alone: essays on the work of Jean-Luc Godard 1985-2000*, Michael Temple and James S Williams eds., Amsterdam: Amsterdam University Press, 2000, pp. 77-95 (p. 79).

FORM AND FIGURE

HEDIGER

1. Godard also has a knack for self-promotion equalled only by such masters of the craft as Alfred Hitchcock or Cecil B DeMille. One must not forget, too, his ear for film titles which rivals that of Rainer Werner Fassbinder.
2. Rancière, Jacques, *La Fable cinématographique*, Paris: Seuil, 2001, p. 221.
3. All indications about stylistic feature of trailers are drawn from Hediger, Vinzenz, *Verführung zum Film. Der amerikanische Kinotrailer seit 1912*, Marburg: Schüren, 2001.
4. Bellour, Raymond, "L'autre cinéaste: Godard écrivain", in *L'Entre-Images 2: Mots, Images*, Paris: POL, 1999, p. 126.
5. See Albéra, François, "Écriture et image. Notes sur les intertitres dans le cinéma muet", *Dialectiques* 9, 1975, p. 28.
6. Sterritt, David, *Jean-Luc Godard: Interviews*, Jackson: University of Mississippi Press, 1998, p. 188.
7. Bellour, "Godard écrivain", p. 135.
8. Silverman, Kaja, "The Author as Receiver", *October*, 96, Spring 2001, p. 21.
9. Klerk, Nico de, "Das Programmformat. Bruchstücke einer Geschichte", *Kintop*, 11, Frankfurt: Stroemfeld, 2002, p. 16.
10. See, for instance, Wilson, John, "Impresario of the Movie Teaser", *Los Angeles Times*, 20 June 1977, and Klady, Leonard, "Truth About Trailers: They Work", *Variety*, 28 November 1994, pp. 13-24.
11. Cited in Büttner, Elisabeth, *Projektion. Montage. Politik. Die Praxis der Ideen von Jean-Luc Godard und Gilles Deleuze*, Vienna: Synema, 1999, p. 9. My translation.
12. Aumont, Jacques, *Amnésies: Fictions du cinéma d'après Jean-Luc Godard*, Paris: POL, 1999, p. 56.
13. See Schmitt, Carl, *Politische Romantik*, Berlin: Duncker and Humblot, 1919, p. 115-152, and *Novalis: Aphorismen*, Michael Brucker ed., Munich/Leipzig: Insel, 1992, p. 27. My translation.
14. The French original reads: "On peut tout mettre dans un film. On doit tout mettre dans un film" (Godard, Jean-Luc, *Godard par Godard: Les années Karina*, Paris: Flammarion, 1990, p. 167).
15. Bellour, Raymond, "L'utopie vidéo", in *L'Entre-Images: Photo. Cinéma. Vidéo.*, Paris: La Différence, 1990, pp. 53-65.
16. Rancière, *La Fable cinématographique*, p. 226.
17. Lacan, Jacques, *Werke. Band III*, Olten: Walter, 1980, p. 808.
18. Hediger, *Verführung zum Film*, p. 225.
19. Godard, Jean-Luc, *Histoire(s) du cinéma*, 4 vols., Paris: Gallimard, 1998, I, pp. 78-85.
20. Aumont, *Amnésies*, p. 33.
21. See Hegel, G W F, *Werke*, Eva Moldenhauer and Karl Markus Michel eds., Frankfurt: Suhrkamp, 1986, vol. 13, p. 92, and Schmitt, *Politische Romantik*.
22. Bohrer, Karl-Heinz, *Die Kritik der Romantik*, Frankfurt: Suhrkamp, 1989, p. 138.
23. See also Bohrer, *Die Kritik der Romantik*, p. 304.
24. Interview with Andrew Kuehn, Los Angeles, 7 December 1997. Andrew Kuehn is the owner of Kaleidoscope Films, the US film industry's most important provider of "coming attraction" trailers. Kuehn has been in the business since 1960 and was responsible for the trailers of such films as *Dr. Zhivago*, 1966, *Jaws*, 1975, and *Titanic*, 1998.

BRENEZ

1. I would like to express my deep thanks to Anne Bergé with whom I have shared a fertile dialogue on Godard over the last 10 years, from which this essay derives.
2. Godard, Jean-Luc, *Introduction à une véritable histoire du cinéma*, Paris: Albatros, 1980, p. 254.
3. Merleau-Ponty, Maurice, *Éloge de la philosophie*, Paris: Gallimard, 1983, p. 45.
4. Merleau-Ponty, *Éloge*, p. 53.
5. Merleau-Ponty, *Éloge*, p. 43
6. See Bresson, Robert, *Notes sur le cinématographe*, Paris: Gallimard, 1979, p. 93, and Adorno, Theodor, *Théorie esthétique*, Paris: Klincksieck, 1989, pp. 176-177.
7. Merleau-Ponty, *Éloge*, p. 73.

BLÜMLINGER

1. See the list in the *Catalogue général des films Lumière*, 1907 (Lumière production ceased in 1905), which contains the following examples: *Nice: Défilé d'automobiles* (1128), *Défilé des cyclistes* (634), *Défilé d'un régiment d'artillerie* (790), and *Défilé des jeunes filles au lycée* (36). See Chardère, Bernard, *Lumières sur Lumière*, Lyons: Institut Lumière/PUL, 1987.
2. The film bears the number 1099 and was probably shot in 1897. The first screening was in 1899. See Chardère, *Lumières sur Lumière*, p. 228.
3. Numerous studies of the performative nature of rituals refer specifically to this paradox. The fact that ritual does not effect a construction of meaning is set out, for example, by Jack Goody. See Goody, Jack, "Against Ritual. Loosely Structured Thoughts on a Loosely Defined Topic", in *Secular Ritual*, Sally Falk Moore and Barbara G Myerhoff eds., Assen: Van Gorcum, 1977, pp. 25-35.
4. In the context of the metapsychological analyses of the 1970s, of Christian Metz and Jean-Louis Baudry for example, the cinematographic *dispositif* has an ideological function: it is that which is no longer seen, but which is the prerequisite for seeing. For theoreticians like Jean-Louis Comolli, Pascal Bonitzer or Stephen Heath this *dispositif* can only be understood as the realm of the aesthetic and the technical and, at the same time, as an ideological expectation. Recent discussions on the *dispositifs* of more current images stress, on the contrary, the historical dimension of the *dispositifs* of the image in the different media, and relativise the universalising notions of the *dispositif* of cinema. Today these comparative theories of the *dispositifs* of the image tend to take Foucault as a starting point in order to understand the *dispositif* as a strategic, technical arrangement to orient the gaze, or as a means of establishing a relationship between the spectator and the image within a symbolic, architectonic or mechanistic context.
5. See Thierry Kuntzel's "Le Défilement" in Dominique Noguez ed., *Cinéma: Théories, Lectures*, Paris: Klincksieck, 1973, pp. 97-110.
6. Daney, Serge, "Du défilement au défilé", *La recherche photographique*, 7, 1989, pp. 49-51 (available in English as "From Movies to Moving", *documentadocuments*, 2, 1996).
7. In relation to early cinema Gunning speaks of a "cinema of attractions". This means a discontinuous mode of representation born out of the work of the showman: "Presenting attractions rather than telling stories. Film emerged in vaudeville, its most important venue until around

1905, as one of the attractions on the programme, surrounded by a series of unconnected numbers in a non-narrative, indeed almost illogical sequence of presentations." (Short films also demonstrated this variety style at a later date in the Nickelodeons, where animated films were shown alongside illustrated songs and topical films. See Gunning, Tom, "The Cinema of Attractions. Early film, its spectator and the avant-garde", *Wide Angle*, 8:3-4, 1986.
8. Daney, Serge, "La dernière image", in *Passages de l'image*, Raymond Bellour, Catherine David and Christine Van Assche eds., Paris: Éditions Centre Georges Pompidou, 1989, p. 57.
9. See Daney, "La dernière image", pp. 58-59.
10. See Daney, "La dernière image", p. 58.
11. This is Lumière's film no. 316, which bears the title *Lausanne/Soldats*. I am grateful to Vinzenz Hediger for drawing my attention to it.
12. See, for example, Daney, "Du Défilement au défilé"; Bellour, Raymond, "Six films en passant", in *L'Entre-Images: Photo. Cinéma. Video.*, Paris: Éditions de la Différence, 1990, p. 143; and Deleuze, Gilles, *Cinéma 2: L'Image-Temps*, Paris: Éditions de Minuit, 1985, p. 254.
13. Deleuze, *L'Image-Temps*, p. 254.
14. Bellour, Raymond, "Moi, je suis une image", in *L'Entre-Images*, p. 105.
15. See Bellour, Raymond, "L'interruption, l'instant", in *L'Entre-Images*, p. 126.
16. See Bellour, *L'Entre-Images*, pp. 131 and footnote 102.
17. See "L'autre cinéaste. Godard écrivain", in Bellour, Raymond, *L'Entre-Images 2: Mots, Images*, Paris: POL, 1999, pp. 123-124 (English version: "(Not) Just an other filmmaker", in Raymond Bellour, and Mary Lea Bandy eds., *Jean-Luc Godard: Son+Image, 1974-1991*, New York: MOMA, 1992, pp. 215-231).
18. In this second *défilé* scene the individual figures step up to the camera again and again. In its repetitive and circular form the passing by of the bodies here constitutes a game between presence and absence. The sequence of figure elements results in a whole: one or more sentences. In the course of this second casting scene the relationship between figure, image and word is thus emphasised, as the homology between the chain of linguistic elements and the chain of figures and images. This could be described using Christian Metz's terminology as the homology between the syntagmatic structure of literary and cinematographic narration.
19. Deleuze, *Cinéma 2*, p. 251.
20. This is a constellation that Deleuze has called the time-image. The exhaustion behind the scream is incidentally also to be found in Antonioni's *Il grido*. See Deleuze, *Cinéma 2*, p. 247.
21. See Daney, "Du défilement au défilé", p. 51, and "La dernière image", p. 59.
22. See the analysis of *Puissance de la parole* by Raymond Bellour in *L'Entre-Images 2*, pp. 91-97.
23. Leutrat analyses Godard's dissection of the words, "Un coup de dé(filé) abolira toujours le hasard", which appears as an epigraph to the video, as well as the meaning of the Latin word *angustia* (from which the French word *angoisse* is derived) which Godard associates with *défilé* in its original sense, i.e. in the sense of a natural defile which is so narrow that one can only pass through it in single file (*à la file*). See Leutrat, Jean-Louis, "The Power of Language: Notes on *Puissance de la parole*, *Le Dernier mot*, and *On s'est tous défilé*", in Michael Temple and James S Williams eds., *The Cinema Alone:*

essays on the work of Jean-Luc Godard, 1985-2000, Amsterdam: Amsterdam University Press, 2000, pp. 179-188, here pp. 183ff.

CALLAHAN

1. See Draper, Ellen, "An Alternative to Godard's Metaphysics: Cinematic Presence in Miéville's *Le Livre de Marie*", in *HAIL MARY: Women and the Sacred in Film*, Maryel Locke and Charles Warren eds., Carbondale: Southern Illinois Press, 1993, p. 67.
2. Kandinsky, Wassily, *Concerning the Spiritual in Art*, M Sadler trans., New York: Dover, 1977, p. 29.
3. Kandinsky, *Concerning the Spiritual in Art*, p. 57.
4. One interesting invocation of the artist by Godard occurs in Chapter 3A of *Histoire(s) du cinéma*. A static shot of Kandinsky's *Murnau, view with railway and castle*, 1909, is presented with a moving image of a train superimposed over the painting. The movements of the two trains are in opposite directions and the image is preceded by a cross-cut, which juxtaposes the fate of the writer Irène Némirovsky with that of various French cinema stars working with the German industry during the war years. While the stars, in newsreel footage, happily take a promotional trip to Berlin, Némirovsky (whose 1930 novel *Le Bal* was adapted in 1931 for the French screen) departs via train for Auschwitz.
5. See Witt, Michael, "Montage, My Beautiful Care, or Histories of the Cinematograph", in *The Cinema Alone: essays on the work of Jean-Luc Godard, 1985-2000*, Michael Temple and James S Williams eds., Amsterdam: Amsterdam University Press, 2000, pp. 33-50 (p. 35).
6. In a fascinating session of the *For Ever Godard* conference held in June 2001 at Tate Modern in London, Gérard Fromanger discussed Godard's drawing lessons with him during the late 1960s. Godard became fixed on the question of the line in a design and asked him, "Does the line exist?" As Fromanger noted, the lessons produced for Godard the important discovery that the line was merely a construction or abstraction by the artist.
7. See Dube, Wolf-Dieter, *The Expressionists*, Mary Whittall trans., London: Thames and Hudson, 1972, p. 38.
8. See Deleuze, Gilles, "Three Questions on Six Times Two", in *Negotiations 1972-1990*, Martin Joughin trans., New York: Columbia University Press, 1995, p. 45.
9. See Williams, James S, "European culture and artistic resistance in *Histoire(s) du cinéma* Chapter 3A, *La Monnaie de l'absolu*", in Temple and Williams, *The Cinema Alone*, pp. 113-139 (p. 134), and Farocki, Harun and Silverman, Kaja, *Speaking about Godard*, New York: New York University Press, 1998, esp. Chapter 7, "Moving Pictures" (pp. 173-196).
10. Godard states that the quotation is from St Paul (noted in Williams, "European Culture and Artistic Resistance", p. 128).
11. The repetition of the drowning sequence in *Nouvelle Vague* also appears to indicate a gesture to Hitchcock, especially with the sublime moment encountered with the rescue(s). In the case of both Judy's and Elena's drowning, a certain element of "performance" is in play, and while their rescues are essentially unnecessary since they can swim, the effort made by their beloved requires an extension, and potential loss, of the self–either with a plunge or with a hand extended. The drownings also suggest the 1945 Technicolor noir classic, *Leave Her to Heaven*, where Ellen Berent (Gene Tierney) mercilessly lets the younger brother of her husband drown to ensure her central role in the family. Thus, when Elena performs the second drowning, playing out Roger's earlier dilemma, her "rescue" signifies her own transformation in the film for she has shed the role of femme fatale in exchange for Roger's place in the narrative.
12. Draper, "An Alternative to Godard's Metaphysics", p. 67.
13. For a good overview of the feminist responses to both films, see Locke and Warren, *HAIL MARY: Women and the Sacred in Film*.
14. Deleuze, Gilles, "Control and Becoming", in *Negotiations 1972-1990*, p. 67.

WITT

An earlier version of this chapter was published as "Going Through the Motions: Unconscious Optics And Corporal Resistance in Miéville and Godard's *France/tour/détour/deux/enfants*", in *Gender and French Cinema*, Alex Hughes and James S Williams eds, Oxford: Berg, 2001, pp. 171-194.
All translations from the French are mine unless otherwise stated.
1. Mulvey, Laura, "The Hole and the Zero: The Janus Face of the Feminine in Godard", in Raymond Bellour and Mary Lea Bandy eds., *Jean-Luc Godard: Son+Image, 1974-1991*, New York: The Museum of Modern Art, 1992, pp. 75-88 (p. 81).
2. Godard, Jean-Luc, "Ailleurs", *Cahiers du cinéma*, 89, 1958. In Jean-Luc Godard, *Jean-Luc Godard par Jean-Luc Godard*, Alain Bergala ed., Paris: Cahiers du Cinéma/Éditions de l'Étoile, 1985, pp. 146-149 (p. 149).
3. Godard, Jean-Luc, "Propos rompus", *Cahiers du cinéma*, 316, 1980. In *Godard par Godard*, pp. 458-471 (pp. 461-462).
4. Aumont, Jacques, *L'Oeil Interminable: Cinéma et Peinture*, Paris: Séguier, 1989, pp. 241-242.
5. Godard, Jean-Luc, "Jean-Luc Godard, télévision-cinéma-vidéo-images: paroles...", *Téléciné*, 202, 1975, pp. 11-13 (p. 12).
6. Williams, Raymond, *Television: Technology and Cultural Form*, London: Fontana, 1974.
7. Godard, Jean-Luc, "La chance de repartir pour un tour", *Les Nouvelles Littéraires*, 30 May 1980. In *Godard par Godard*, pp. 407-412 (p. 410).
8. Fargier, Jean-Paul, "Le grand méchant loup", *Les Nouvelles Littéraires*, 30 May 1980, p. 36.
9. Reported in Bruneau, Pierre, "Un drôle de 'tour' avec Godard", *Minute*, 2-8 April 1980, p. 28.
10. Godard, Jean-Luc, "Jean-Luc Godard: 'La pellicule, c'est complètement chiant!'", *Télé-Ciné-Vidéo*, December 1980, pp. 34-35.
11. MacCabe, Colin, "Betaville", *American Film*, 10, 1985, pp. 61-63 (p. 61).
12. The combination of interviews with children and videographic slow motion in the prologue to *Après la réconciliation*, followed by the exchange between the unnamed woman (Miéville) and Robert (Godard) around the creative intensity of an earlier encounter and collaboration, invokes *France/tour*. Imagery of the children manipulating the microphone or video camera at the beginning of each movement is equated in *Histoire(s)* with the power of the cinematograph as a nascent art-form.
13. Godard, "Propos rompus", p. 471.
14. See Willener, Alfred, Milliard, Guy and Gantry, Alex, *Videology and Utopia: Explorations in a New Medium*, Diana Burfield trans., London: Routledge and Kegan Paul, 1976.

15. See Philippe Dubois's suggestive term *vidéo-scalpel*, in Dubois, Philippe, "L'Image à la vitesse de la pensée", *Cahiers du cinéma* (November supplement), 437, 1990, pp. 76-77 (p. 76).

16. Vertov, Dziga, *Kino-Eye: The Writings of Dziga Vertov*, Annette Michelson ed., Kevin O'Brien trans., London: Pluto, 1984, p. 15.

17. Godard, Jean-Luc, *Introduction à une véritable histoire du cinéma*, Paris: Albatros, 1980, p. 309.

18. Benjamin, Walter, "The Work of Art in the Age of Mechanical Reproduction", in *Illuminations*, Hannah Arendt ed., London: Fontana, 1973, pp. 211-244 (pp. 229-230).

19. Marey, Étienne-Jules, *La Machine animale: locomotion terrestre et aérienne*, Paris: Germer Baillière, 1873.

20. Marey, Étienne-Jules, *Le Mouvement*, Nîmes: Jacqueline Chambon, 1994, p. 319.

21. Marey, Étienne-Jules, *La Chronophotographie*, Paris: Gauthier-Villars, 1899, p. 5.

22. Godard, "Propos rompus", p. 467.

23. See Marey, Étienne-Jules, *Étude sur la locomotion animale par la chrono-photographie*, Paris: Association Française pour l'Avancement des Sciences, 1886.

24. Illich, Ivan, *Deschooling Society*, London: Calder and Boyars, 1971, p. 11.

25. Penley, Constance, "Les Enfants de la Patrie", *Camera Obscura*, 8-9-10, Fall 982, pp. 33-58 (p. 52). Ariès, Philippe, *Centuries of Childhood*, Harmondsworth: Penguin, 1979.

26. Foucault, Michel, *Discipline and Punish: The Birth of the Prison*, Alan Sheridan trans., Harmondsworth: Penguin, 1979.

27. Bruno, G, *Le Tour de la France par Deux Enfants: Devoir et Patrie*, Paris: Eugène Belin, 1884. Reprinted by Firmin Didot in 1975.

28. Foucault, *Discipline and Punish*, pp. 137-138.

29. See de la Salle, M, *Traité sur les obligations des frères des écoles chrétiennes*, Rouen: Imp de Veuve Laurent Dumesnil, 1783.

30. Foucault, *Discipline and Punish*, p. 228.

31. Deleuze, Gilles, "Three questions about 'Six fois deux'", R Bowlby trans., in Bellour and Bandy, *Jean-Luc Godard: Son+Image*, pp. 35-41 (p. 41).

32. Penley, "Les Enfants de la Patrie", p. 34.

33. Godard, "La chance de repartir pour un tour", p. 410.

34. Reynaud, Bérénice, "'Impure Cinema': Adaption and Quotation at the 1985 New York Film Festival", *Afterimage*, 13, 1986, pp. 9-11 (p. 11).

RANCIÈRE

1. Epstein, Jean, "Bonjour cinema", Tom Milne trans., in Richard Abel ed., *French Film Theory and Criticism, 1907-1939*, Princeton: Princeton University Press, 1998, vol. I, p. 242.

2. See Godard's comments on Hitchcock's death in Jean-Luc Godard, *Jean-Luc Godard par Jean-Luc Godard*, Alain Bergala ed., 2 vols., Paris: Cahiers du Cinéma, 1998, I, pp. 412-416.

3. See Païni, Dominique and Cogeval, Guy eds., *Hitchcock et l'art: coïncidences fatales*, Paris: Centre Georges Pompidou/Mazzota, 2000. For a pertinent discussion of the Godard/Hitchcock relation, see Jacques Aumont's essay "Paradoxal et innocent" in the same volume.

4. I address this issue in my book, *La Fable cinématographique*, Paris: Seuil, 2001, p. 165; p. 185.

SOUND AND MUSIC

MARTIN

1. Ropars-Wuilleumier, Marie-Claire, "Form and Substance, or the Avatars of the Narrative", in *Focus on Godard*, Royal S Brown ed., Englewood Cliffs: Prentice-Hall, 1972, p. 99.

2. See my essay "Godard: The Musical", in *CinemaScope*, June 2001, and "Musical Mutations: Before, Beyond and Against Hollywood", in *Movie Mutations*, Adrian Martin and Jonathan Rosenbaum eds., London: British Film Institute, 2003.

3. Durgnat, Raymond, "Jean-Luc Godard: His Crucifixion and Resurrection", *Monthly Film Bulletin*, 620, September 1985, pp. 268-271 (p. 270).

4. See my "Scanning Godard", *Screening the Past*, 2000, www.latrobe.edu.au/screeningthepast/reviews/rev0600/ambr10a.htm.

5. Guarner, José Luis, *"Pierrot le fou"*, in *The Films of Jean-Luc Godard*, Ian Cameron ed., London: Studio Vista, 1969, p. 98.

6. The translation of Apollinaire is by AS Kline, 2002, www.tonkyline.free-online.co.uk/Apollinaire.htm.

7. See Jean-Luc Godard, *Godard on Godard*, Tom Milne ed., London: Secker and Warburg, 1972, p. 247.

8. See Wollen, Peter, *Paris-Hollywood: Writings on Film*, London: Verso, 2002, p. 74.

9. See Ropars-Wuilleumier, Marie-Claire, "The Graphic in Filmic Writing: *À bout de souffle* or The Erratic Alphabet", *Enclitic*, 5-6, 1982, pp. 147-161.

10. See Rohmer, Éric, *The Taste for Beauty*, Carol Volk trans., Cambridge: Cambridge University Press, 1989, pp. 53-58; Demeure, Jacques, *Positif*, 500, October 2002, p. 96 (my translation).

11. Ropars-Wuilleumier, "Form and Substance", p. 100.

12. See Perez, Gilberto, *The Material Ghost: Films and Their Medium*, Baltimore: Johns Hopkins University Press, 1998, pp. 353-360.

13. Ta voix, tes yeux, tes mains, tes lèvres. Nos silences, nos paroles. La lumière qui s'en va, la lumière qui revient. Un seul sourire pour nos deux. Pas besoin de savoir. J'ai vu la nuit créer le jour sans que nous changions d'apparence. Ô bien aimée de tous, bien aimée d'un seul. En silence ta bouche a promis d'être heureuse. De loin en loin dit la haine, de proche en proche en proche dit l'amour. Par la caresse nous sortons de notre enfance. Je vois de mieux en mieux la forme humaine, comme un dialogue d'amoureux. Le coeur n'a qu'une seule bouche. Toutes les choses au hasard, tous les mots dits sans y penser. Les sentiments à la dérive. Les hommes tournent dans la ville. Les regards, la parole. Le fait que je t'aime, tout est en mouvement. Il suffit d'avancer pour vivre, d'aller droit devant soi vers tous ceux que l'on aime. J'allais vers toi. J'allais vers la lumière. Si tu souris, c'est pour mieux m'envahir. Les rayons de tes bras entrouvraient le brouillard.
I have selected what I regard as the best available English translations from the subtitles of the Criterion DVD edition of the film (USA) and the SBS television b15. broadcast (Australia).

14. See Farocki, Harun and Silverman, Kaja, *Speaking about Godard*, New York: New York University Press, 1998, pp. 232. These authors refer, as do I, to Richard Weisman's English translation, *Capital of Pain*, New York: Grossman Press, 1973.

15. Abrigeon, Julien d', *Jean-Luc Godard, cinéaste écrivain: De la citation à la création, présence et rôle de la littérature dans le cinéma de JLG de 1959 à 1967*, http://tapin.free.fr/godard/.

I acknowledge my general debt to this excellent thesis from 1995.

16. Chen, Su-Shuan, Protas, Meredith and Doberne, Leah, "Les Trois Médias Surréalistes: La Musique de Satie, La Poésie d'Éluard, La Peinture de Miro", http://www.french.pomona.edu/msaigal/classes/FR102/Spring99/susan-meredith-leah/webpage.html.

17. Amengual, Barthélémy, *Bande à part*, Brussels: Yellow Now, 1993, pp. 37-38.

18. Amengual, *Bande à part*, p. 133.

19. Amengual, *Bande à part*, p. 131.

20. Ropars-Wuilleumier, "Form and Substance", p. 99.

JULLIER

1. The working title of this film currently in production in Sarajevo is *Notre Musique*.

2. *Les écrans sonores de Jean-Luc Godard*, radio interview by Thierry Jousse, released as a CD by Radio France/France Culture (collection "Signature"), 2000.

3. Gualandi, Alberto, *Lyotard*, Paris: Belles Lettres, 1999, p. 65. Gualandi also demonstrates that this argument already existed in Plato's *The Sophist*. According to Sophists, there is no truth, only conventions, rules and word games (see Alain Badiou, cited in Gualandi, *Lyotard*, p. 18). Lyotard refuses to espouse completely Sophist theory, but he does not wish to jettison it either (that would lead to "theoretical terror"). Instead, he tends to favour the pragmatic and paralogical approach.

4. Lyotard, Jean-François, *La Condition postmoderne*, Paris: Éditions de Minuit, 1979.

5. Lyotard, Jean-François, *L'Inhumain*, Paris: Galilée, 1988, p. 151 and p. 134.

6. Lyotard, Jean-François, *Discours, figure,* Paris: Klincksieck, 1971, p. 52.

7. Gualandi, *Lyotard*, p. 24.

8. Szersnovicz, Patrick, "Création: la musique d'aujourd'hui n'est pas née d'hier", *Le Monde de la musique*, 246, February 2000, p. 54.

9. Adorno, Theodor W, *Quasi una fantasia* [1963], Paris: Gallimard, 1982, p. 199.

10. Dambricourt, Jean-Pierre, "L'épuisement de la musique/La saturation des pseudo-universaux dans les œuvres de Michael Nyman", in *Les Universaux en musique*, Costin Miereanu and Xavier Hascher eds., Paris: Publications de la Sorbonne, 1998, pp. 318-319.

11. Eco, Umberto, "Diables en musique", in the CD booklet of *In cerca di cibo* by Gianluigi Travesi and Gianni Coscia, ECM Records, 2000.

12. EMI-Classics CD booklet, 1979.

13. Tillmann, Barbara, Bharucha, Jamshed J and Bigand, Emmanuel, "Implicit learning of tonality: a self-organizing approach", *Psychological Review*, 107:4, 2000, p. 908.

14. The anti-gravity muscles are measurably activated. See Besson, Mireille, "Meaning, structure and time in language and music", *Cahiers de psychologie cognitive*, 17:4-5, 1998, pp. 921-950.

15. Young, James O, "The cognitive value of music", *The Journal of Aesthetics and Art Criticism*, 57:1, 1999, p. 45.

16. Young, "The cognitive value of music", p. 48.

17. Young, "The cognitive value of music", p. 51.

18. Besson, "Meaning, structure and time in language and music", p. 923.

19. See Rousseau's *Essai sur l'origine des langues*, 1791.

20. See Peretz, Isabelle, Gagnon, Lise and Bouchard, Bernard, "Music and emotion: perceptual determinants, immediacy and isolation after brain damage", *Cognition*, 68:2, 1998, pp. 111-141.

21. Peretz, Gagnon and Bouchard, "Music and emotion", p. 123 and p. 135.

22. Adorno, *Quasi una fantasia*, p. 232.

23. Adorno, *Quasi una fantasia*, p. 276.

24. Adorno, *Quasi una fantasia*, p. 283.

25. Cited by Adorno in *Quasi una fantasia*, p. 277.

26. Adorno, *Quasi una fantasia*, p. 278.

27. Adorno, *Quasi una fantasia*, p. 284.

28. "Rejecting as illusory any immanent law that is said to govern music", Adorno, *Quasi una fantasia*, p. 278.

29. Adorno, *Quasi una fantasia*, p. 287.

30. Adorno, *Quasi una fantasia*, p. 281.

31. Pekkilä, Erkki, "On musical signification in television commercials", in Miereanu and Hasher, *Les Universaux en musique*, p. 325.

32. Aumont, Jacques, *À quoi pensent les films*, Paris: Séguier, 1996, pp. 265-266.

33. Aumont, *À quoi pensent les films*, p. 269.

34. Aumont, *À quoi pensent les films*, p. 266.

35. Adorno, *Quasi una fantasia*, p. 28.

36. Carroll, Noël, *Theorizing the Moving Image*, New York: Cambridge University Press, 1996, p. 142.

37. Godard, Jean-Luc, *Godard par Godard: Des années Mao aux années 80*, Paris: Flammarion, 1991, p. 73.

38. Godard, *Godard par Godard*, p. 83.

39. Booklet for the CD by H-K Jungheinrich on ECM Records.

40. *Weekend*, a film without images, was directed by Walter Ruttmann in 1930, and was released as a CD in 1994 by the French label Métamkine based in Grenoble. Another example of a soundtrack release that includes music as well as dialogue and noise is *Eraserhead*, produced by Alan R Splett and David Lynch for the London label Alternative Tentacles Records (half of the original soundtrack features on the disc). *Apocalypse Now* was also released in 1979 on a vinyl double-LP.

41. Gracyk, Theodore, "Listening to music: performances and recordings", *The Journal of Aesthetics and Art Criticism*, 57:2, 1999, p. 140.

42. See the discussion between Gracyk ("Play it again, Sam: a response to Niblock", *The Journal of Aesthetics and Art Criticism*, 57:3, 1999, pp. 368-370) and Howard Niblock ("Musical recordings and performances: a response to Theodore Gracyk", *The Journal of Aesthetics and Art Criticism*, 57:3, 1999, pp. 366-368).

43. See Brown, Lee B, "Phonography, rock records and the ontology of recorded music", *The Journal of Aesthetics and Art Criticism*, 58:4, 2000, pp. 362-372.

44. Gracyk, "Listening to music", p. 147.

45. Niblock, "Musical recordings and performances", p. 367.

46. Gracyk, "Play it again, Sam", p. 369.

47. See Schaeffer, Pierre, *Traité des objets musicaux*, Paris: Seuil, 1966.

48. Barthes, Roland, *Oeuvres complètes, tome I 1942-1965*, Eric Marty ed., Paris: Seuil, 1993, p. 565.

49. Aumont, *À quoi pensent les films*, p. 270.

50. Fano, Michel, "Montage et composition sonore", *Le technicien du film et de la vidéo*, 367, April 1988, pp. 36-37.

51. Cage, John, *Journal*, Paris: Maurice Nadeau/Papyrus, 1983.

52. See Dalhaus, Carl, "La crise de l'expérimentation", *Contrechamps*, 3 ("Avant-garde et tradition"), September 1984, pp. 111-112. Dalhaus seems to deny that some noises are not replicas, and only grants a didactic quality to concrete music (intended to teach how to listen to the daily sounds of life), not an artistic one.

53. "Now all these pulverised voices make a new, single voice for me" (Bartoli, Claire, "Interior View", booklet for the CD *Nouvelle Vague*, ECM Records, 1997, pp. 29-30).

54. Godard in 1975 on *Numéro Deux* (*Godard par Godard*, p. 148).

55. Hujic, Lida, "'I hope you're enjoying your party': MTV In wartorn Bosnia", *Screen*, 37:3, 1996. p. 269.

56. See Jullier, Laurent, "Bande-son: attention travaux", in *Godard et le métier d'artiste*, Gilles Delavaud, Jean-Pierre Esquenazi and Marie-Françoise Grange eds., Paris: L'Harmattan, 2001.

57. Godard, *Godard par Godard*, p. 143.

58. Note that Schaeffer in his *Journal de la musique concrète*, 5 May 1948, uses almost exactly the same words as Lyotard 30 years later: "It would be great to know how to find and to taste, in a mechanical monotonous sound, the interplay of a few atoms of freedom, the imperceptible improvisations of chance" (*Pierre Schaeffer: l'œuvre musicale*, François Bayle, ed., Paris: INA-GRM/Librairie Séguier, 1990, p. 29).

59. Of course, since this is postmodern elitism and/or allusion, Coleridge is not quoted. But we can note, since Godard seems to like this kind of coincidence (combining, for example, Stravinsky's *Le Sacre du printemps* with Louis Feuillade's *Les Vampires* because both were made in the same year), that *Anima Poetae* was first published in 1895, the year of the Lumière brothers' *cinématographe*.

60. Adorno, *Quasi una fantasia*, p. 29 and p. 48.

61. Adorno, *Quasi una fantasia*, p. 55 and p. 56.

62. Young, "The cognitive value of music", p. 50, on the subject of Hindemith's *Trauermusik*.

63. I would like to express my thanks to the cognicitians who answered my questions about the concept of tonality–Mireille Besson (CNRS-CNRC), Emmanuel Bigand (CNRS-Université de Bourgogne), Isabelle Peretz (Université de Montréal)–and to my interlocutors at ECM Records, Julia Emmer and Florian Ganslmeier.

WILLIAMS

1. See *Les écrans sonores de Jean-Luc Godard*, Paris: Radio France/France Culture (collection "Signature"), 2000.

2. This chapter was nearing completion in spring 2003 when Godard began production in Sarajevo of a film in collaboration with Eicher. The provisional title, *Notre Musique*, would at first glance appear to dispel the idea that Godard cannot, or will not, translate his feelings about music into discourse. Moreover, in a short written "Project" effectively proposing *Notre Musique* as a tribute to Manfred Eicher and his ECM family of musicians and composers, Godard raises issues about music that will preoccupy us in this chapter, namely that music is a vehicle of hope and can speak to us in a way that television and the press no longer can, with honesty and fervour, and also, more suggestively, that music might itself constitute an entire film. (My thanks to Laurent Jullier for providing access to this document.) The truth will become clear once the film is complete, but first reports of the shoot do little to disprove my opening premise. According to Alain Bergala who directly cites Godard, the film will actually take the structural form of a medieval triptych and feature writers reading their own work. In other words, it will be a film revolving principally around text and image. What music there is will be restricted to "a little piano" accompanying at times silent images of war. See Alain Bergala, "Godard tourne à Sarajevo", *Cahiers du cinéma*, July-August 2003, pp. 37-39 (p. 38).

3. For example, in my own examination of Chapter 3A of *Histoire(s)*, an immensely rich musical episode, I make mention only in passing of Hindemith. See "European culture and artistic resistance in Chapter 3A, *La Monnaie de l'absolu*", in *The Cinema Alone: essays on the work of Jean-Luc Godard, 1985-2000*, Michael Temple and James S Williams eds., Amsterdam: Amsterdam University Press, 2000, pp. 113-139. Exceptions to this critical norm include: Delvaux, Claudine, "Godard musicien", *Revue Belge du Cinéma*, 1988, pp. 51-53; Jousse, Thierry, "Godard à l'oreille", in "Numéro Spécial Godard–Trente ans depuis", *Cahiers du cinéma*, 1991, pp. 40-45; Aumont, Jacques, "Lumière de la musique", in "Numéro Spécial Godard–Trente ans depuis", *Cahiers du cinéma*, 1991, pp. 46-48; Jullier, Laurent, "Bande-son: attention travaux", in *Godard et le métier d'artiste*, Gilles Delavaud, Jean-Pierre Esquenazi and Marie-Françoise Grange eds., Paris: L'Harmattan, 2001: Jullier, Laurent, "JLG/ECM" (in the present volume).

4. Cited in Claire Bartoli's "Interior View", in the booklet to *Nouvelle Vague*, Munich: ECM Records, 1997, p. 69.

5. For a succinct analysis of some of the strategies of fragmentation employed by Godard in his early films, for example, preventing a melody from developing and randomly cutting into it to give it an analytical charge, see Aumont, Jacques, *À quoi pensent les films*, Paris: Séguier, 1996, pp. 265-269.

6. See Alex Ross's fascinating article, "Ghost Sonata: What happened to German music?", *The New Yorker*, 24 March 2003, pp. 64-71, which argues that German composers still fetishise and make a virtue out of ugly dissonance (the comfort of C Major, for example, is taboo), so keen are they to forget the recent past, the fact, for example, that Hitler had Beethoven played in the camps.

7. In *For Ever Mozart*, where the section devoted to music takes pride of place at the end, the actual playing of Mozart by Les Jeunes de Fribourg is very limited. Indeed, the faint, muffled cello sounds of Darling quickly arrive with the final credits to function almost as a safety curtain.

8. Cited in Douin, Jean-Luc, *Jean-Luc Godard*, Paris: Rivages, 1994, pp. 99-100.

9. See Aumont, "Lumière de la musique", p. 47. Aumont interprets the end of *Sauve qui peut* as music's revenge after having been kept too much at a distance. This is a specifically feminine and maternal revenge, since Godard's alter ego will be eternally irritated by what he will hear finally as the music of his own death.

10. Unlike Jullier, who in "JLG/ECM" focuses on Godard's primary attraction for tonal music (in particular its ECM "postmodern" variant) as opposed to modernist atonal music, I shall not be making any real distinction between different forms of classical and modern music in Godard's work. Indeed,

I will argue that what is crucial is not the particular music Godard chooses but rather how he uses it. On a related note, Jullier posits in the form of a rhetorical question that Godard chose ECM's melodic tracks, and edited and transposed them more spectacularly, so as to highlight his own manipulation of them. The implication here of a deliberately soft musical backdrop to Godard's later work also lies behind the idea articulated by James Quandt in "Projecting Godard: Here and Elsewhere" (in the present volume) that Godard's predilection for contemporary (ECM) composers like Pärt and Mompou (employed at length in *L'Origine du vingt et unième siècle*, 2000) indicates a conservative sensibility in art and music (see endnote 8). As we shall see, however, if Godard were actually to engage with more avant-garde contemporary composers such as Luciano Berio (for example, his *Sinfonia*, 1968-1969, which takes the form of a complex collage in which spoken and sung texts in many languages are combined with a highly intricate orchestral score), this could potentially duplicate and cancel out the particular weft and warp of his own compound sound textures.

11. See Katherine Dieckmann's interview with Godard in *HAIL MARY: Women and the Sacred in Film*, Maryel Locke and Charles Warren eds., Carbondale: Southern Illinois Press, 1994, p. 121.

12. Locke and Warren, *HAIL MARY*, p. 120.

13. Locke and Warren, *HAIL MARY*, p. 121.

14. Locke and Warren, *HAIL MARY*, p. 121.

15. See Williams, "European culture and artistic resistance", p. 137.

16. "La musique est la plus forte [...] c'est elle qui soutient tout", *Jean-Luc Godard par Jean-Luc Godard*, 2 vols., Alain Bergala ed., Paris: Cahiers du Cinéma, 1998, II, p. 390.

17. Bartoli, "Interior View", pp. 76-77.

18. See Swed, Mark, "Sharing Sound Theories on Filmmaking", *LA Times*, 6 August 2000 (included in Jean-Luc Godard, *Histoire(s) du cinéma*, Munich: ECM Records, 2000, a promotional dossier containing reviews and interviews).

19. Paul Hindemith (1895-1963), hounded in Germany by the Nazis, was eventually forced into exile in the United States (via Switzerland): Béla Bartók (1881-1945) left Hungary in 1940 when the Horthy government aligned itself with the Nazis and died from leukemia in straitened circumstances in exile in the US; Anton Webern (1883-1945) was shot dead by friendly fire in Mittersill at the end of the war; Dmitri Shostakovich (1906-1975) was constrained for much of his life and career by a totalitarian regime.

20. See Godard's interview with Michèle Halberstadt, "The artistic act is an act of resistance", *Enthusiam*, 5, Winter 2002, pp. 2-7, where Godard talks of cinema as essentially a lyrical artform. For an analysis of the lyrical in Godard's work, see Adrian Martin's chapter "Recital: Three Lyrical Interludes in Godard" in the present volume.

21. This is the subtitle of Godard's very frank interview with Jean-Pierre Dufreigne around *Éloge de l'amour* in *L'Express*, 4 May 2001.

22. Kaja Silverman and Harun Farocki argue persuasively that since this gift cannot be possessed, it neither bankrupts the one who gives nor indebts the one who receives. The giver gladly gives, and the receiver gladly receives. They even propose *Nouvelle Vague* as Godard's account of heterosexuality at the end of the twentieth century. See "The Same, yet Other", *Speaking about Godard*, New York: New York University Press, 1998, pp. 197-227. (Strangely, they barely mention the use and value of music in *Nouvelle Vague*, simply recording the fact that Godard uses only the initial nineteenth century part of Schoenberg's *The Transfigured Night*.) In a separate later article, Silverman also describes *JLG/JLG* in terms of the gift, arguing that in this film existence is effectively defined as the giver, the world as the gift, and the author as the receiver. Godard, she suggests, will attempt to become the blank surface in which the world inscribes itself; hence, "The Author as Receiver", *October*, 96, 2001, pp. 17-34.

23. See Žižek, Slavoj, *The Ticklish Subject: The Absent Centre of Political Ontology*, London and New York: Verso, 1999, esp. "The Politics of Truth, or, Alain Badiou as a Reader of St Paul", pp. 127-170, and *The Fragile Absolute–or, why is the Christian legacy worth fighting for?*", London and New York: Verso, 2000, esp. "The Breakout", pp. 143-160. Žižek bases his argument on his reading of Alain Badiou's *L'être et l'événement*, Paris: Seuil, 1988, and *Saint Paul. La Fondation de l'universalisme*, Paris: PUF, 1997. For Žižek, Badiou's four main génériques –love, art, science, politics–are ways of reinscribing the encounter with the Real Thing on to the symbolic texture. Interestingly, when Badiou writes specifically about *Histoire(s)* in "Le plus-de-voir", *Art Press*, hors série, November 1998, pp. 86-91, he makes no attempt to relate his theories of the Truth-Event to Godard's work.

24. Žižek, *The Ticklish Subject*, p. 212.

25. Žižek, *The Ticklish Subject*, p. 162.

26. Žižek, *The Ticklish Subject*, p. 212.

27. Cited in *SOMA* (San Francisco), 17:1, 2003, p. 39.

28. "Jean-Luc Godard rencontre Régis Debray", in *Godard par Godard*, II, pp. 423-431 (p. 429).

29. See Žižek, Slavoj, *The Fright of Real Tears: Krzysztof Kiéslowski. Between Theory and Post-Theory*, London: BFI, 2001, pp. 134-135.

30. See Guerin, Marie Anne, "L'amour enfui", *Trafic*, 39, Autumn 2001, pp. 5-15 (p. 11). Guerin also makes the following highly suggestive statement: "There is no-one other [than Godard] to give actors this chance to know nothing of the story or mystery they are playing or figure in, yet still be sure of the art and beauty in the director's look and the period they are playing" (p. 15).

31. See Taubin, Amy, "In the Shadow of Memory", *Film Comment*, 38:1, January-February 2002, pp. 50-52 (p. 52). Taubin observes correctly that if the images depend on variety and surprise (the framings are nearly always unexpected), there is rarely any cutting on movement and each image retains its identity. We might add that the dazzling black and white documentary views of Paris, which appear so free and spontaneous when intercut with black spacing, each acquire the status of a visual event and allow the viewer to see Paris as if for the first time.

32. This is not completely the case, however. The last thing we hear is a fragmented and slightly altered version of Edgar's opening voiceover text to the actress. What was: "and then again/ the first moment/ you remember the names/ no, no/ perhaps it wasn't said" (leading to: "and if we asked you/ that it was you/ that you had the choice..."), becomes in a solitary voiceover by Edgar: "if we asked you/ that it was you/ that you had the choice [...] and then, well,/ the first moment/ you remember the names/ perhaps/ it wasn't said/ perhaps it

wasn't/ said." The last phrase is repeated altogether four times by Edgar and recited over the final instance of black spacing.

33. Compare this result with that of the contemporaneous short by Godard and Miéville, *Dans le noir du temps*, 2002. There, the continuous playing of Pärt's slow, miniaturist composition for piano and cello, *Spiegel im Spiegel*, 1978, which is interrupted only temporarily by a brief extract from a song by Miéville, has a smothering and chilling effect on the film as a whole. Indeed, the blanket use of Pärt chimes very uncomfortably with the pathos of the image with its stuttering "last visions" and Godard's spoken plea for compassion.

34. The quote in full from Bataille, which recurs in different forms throughout the film and is wrongly attributed to *Le Bleu du ciel*, is as follows:

> Nothing could be farther from the image of the loved one than that of the State whose reason is opposed to the sovereign value of love. The State does not have, or it has lost, the power to embrace before us the whole of the world, that totality of the universe which is given at once outside, in the loved one as object, and inside, in the lover as subject.

Douglas Morrey has also underlined the significance of this quote in a fine discussion of history and resistance in *Éloge*, but the conclusions he draws for our understanding of love in the film are a little different. Morrey states that:

> love can only be known as a kind of grieving memory for a promise never fulfilled, whose trace remains in those indefinable alterations we notice in ourselves. In the same way, the total view of history is forever deferred by the work of history that is never finished, since it endlessly generates more history and thus more work, even as the effects of history begin to shape our lives. Love and history, then, bring us into contact with our necessary failure to attain them, and it is this painful consciousness of the limits of our thought that drives thought inexorably forwards.

Douglas Morrey, "History of resistance/resistance of history: Godard's *Éloge de l'amour* (2001)", *Studies in French Cinema*, 3:2, 2003, pp. 121-130 (p. 128). While Morrey is certainly right to make parallels between love and history in terms of an unattainable "absolute vision", I am suggesting in addition that the performance of music in *Éloge* (which Morrey does not explore) redefines history as memory and serves to transport love to a different level, that of the potential uniting of self and other through music which, with each successive note, is continually delivering on its promise.

LACK

1. Borges, Jorge Luis, "Two English Poems", in *Oeuvres complètes*, Paris: Gallimard-Pléiade, 1999, II, p. 72.

2. To hear Godard's voice on the subject of voice, "see" Thierry Jousse's interview on CD with Godard, *Les écrans sonores de Jean-Luc Godard*, Paris: Radio France/France Culture (collection "Signature"), 2000, esp. section 2, "La voix, l'objet sonore".

3. If we all went blind, we would still have his "sound screens"("écrans sonores")–the EP of *Charlotte et son Jules*, the LP of *Une femme est une femme*, the CD of *Nouvelle Vague* (and of course the five-CD set of *Histoire(s)*)–to tell us what Godard's cinema had been. Derek Jarman's *Blue*, 1993, might survive as a film, at least until we have all forgotten what the colour blue looks like.

4. From *Prénom Carmen*, 1983, and *Soigne ta droite*, 1987.

5. André Marcon performing Valère Novarina's *Le discours aux animaux*, Paris: POL, 1987: "I am the living error. I am Jean, who has always played the Living One despite himself." The

same voice is heard again in *Histoire(s)* 3B in a passage about Jean Epstein, establishing a similar identification.

6. The story is from *Salutation paysanne*, 1921; the recording was made much later, possibly in 1941, and can be found on the LP, *C-F Ramuz par lui-même*, Éditions Rencontre, 1976.

7. These vocal exercises are developed in the sequence that immediately follows: the singing lesson scene from *Citizen Kane*.

8. "Conférence de presse" for *Prénom Carmen*, Venice 1983.

9. Compared, for example, to Godard's cameo in Rivette's *Paris nous appartient*, 1961, where voice and body combine to reinforce the stereotypes of his already formed media image.

10. Body and voice are similarly masked in Godard's performance as Professor Pluggy in *King Lear*, 1987.

11. "Le dernier à parler" is Blanchot's phrase regarding Paul Celan, an earlier speaker in *Histoire(s)*.

12. This essay has concentrated on feature films and left unmentioned, regretfully, several shorter works where Godard's voice is a primary signifier: *Une histoire d'eau*, 1958, *Letter to Jane*, 1972, *Ici et Ailleurs*, 1974, *Scénario vidéo de Sauve qui peut (la vie)*, 1979, *Lettre à Freddy Buache*, 1982, *Scénario du film Passion*, 1982, *Changer d'image*, 1982, *Petites notes à propos du film Je vous salue Marie*, 1983, *Meetin' WA*, 1986, *Le Rapport Darty*, 1989, *Les Enfants jouent à la Russie*, 1993, *2x50 ans de cinéma français*, 1995, *Adieu au TNS*, 1996, *The Old Place*, 1999.

13. For a theoretical approach to "sa voix" (to which I am much indebted), see Bellour, Raymond, *L'Entre-Images 2*, Paris: POL, 1999: "Above all there is voice. Voices. Their irrepressible multiplicity. Their reverberation at the heart of a dispersed centre. His voice" (p. 119).

14. Compare these unattributed citations with the discussion of the same source text in *Éloge de l'amour*: "Parrain m'a dit de te donner ce livre, il paraît qu'il est extraordinaire./ Qu'est-ce que c'est?/ Robert Bresson, *Notes sur le cinématographe*" (Godfather told me to give you this book, apparently it's extraordinary./ What is it?/ Robert Bresson, *Notes on the cinematograph*).

15. A recording of Malraux's speech for the reception of Jean Moulin's ashes into the Panthéon, in 1964, released on LP as *Hommage de la France à Jean Moulin*, RTF, 1965.

16. A curious variant of this overlaying of languages occurs in the version for Swiss television of *King Lear*, where the English spoken by actors (including Godard himself) is overlaid with a narrating voice (Godard's) translating (not quite) simultaneously into French.

17. At least it can seem so in the mix of the 1998 video set. The clearer sound of the ECM CD, 1999, and the Cinefil DVD, 2001, allow us to hear more exactly Freud's words. The original recording was made in London in December 1938 (see: http://web.utk.edu/~wmorgan/psy470/freudvoi.htm). Godard's editing has carefully extracted the essence of Freud's remarks: "[...] I discovered some new and important facts about the unconscious [...] Out of these findings grew a new science, Psycho-Analysis [...] I had to pay heavily for this bit of good luck [...] Resistance was strong and unrelenting. In the end I succeeded [...] But this struggle is not yet over [...] My name is Sigmund Freud."

18. "Could it be that the u in *produire* prevents *produire* from having *dire* in it", Godard, Jean-Luc, *Histoire(s) du cinéma*, Paris: Éditions Gallimard-Gaumont, 4 vols., 1, p. 32.

19. Lessons in ventriloquism were provided by Cocteau, who

in *Orphée* supplies the voice when Cégeste is seen speaking into a radio transmitter.

20. It is clear, from the use in the montaged newspaper of a studio portrait of the actor, that this sequence is reading the media image of the parties involved alongside their image as characters in a fiction.

21. This is a strictly literal translation. A more poetic rendering of Aragon's "Elsa I Love You" is offered by Rolfe Humphries and Malcolm Cowley in *Aragon, Poet of Resurgent France*, Hannah Josephson and Malcolm Cowley eds., London: Pilot Press, 1946, p. 48: "Bevelled by every kiss/ The years wear down too fast/ Beware, beware of this/ Sad breakage of the past."

22. The death scene in *À bout de souffle* alludes obliquely to Aragon by taking place in the rue Campagne-Première, where Aragon and Elsa Triolet lived in the 1930s.

23. The use a few minutes later of an image from *Nuit et Brouillard* supports the suggestion.

24. It also made a mockery of the EP soundtrack marketed at the time with Belmondo's image on the cover, although his voice was not on the record.

25. Earlier in *Vivre sa vie*, the extract from Dreyer's 1928 silent film *La Passion de Jeanne d'Arc* had foregrounded the gap between voice and image by contrasting the original expression of synchronicity, where words spoken are delivered in an interpolated intertitle, with those of the 1950s' re-editor of Dreyer's film, Lo Duca, superimposing subtitles on the image of the speaker. This opposition is invoked as a premiss of the "Oval portrait" sequence, since before Godard's voice replaces Kassowitz's, subtitles are used to represent the exchange between Nana and the young man.

26. The title of Godard's 1988 film for France Telecom, adapting Poe's philosophical dialogue "The Power of Words".

27. See the oval portrait shown in *Bande à part* as a reference to *Vivre sa vie*, Godard's preceding film with Karina.

28. It can also be heard in extracts from other films (*Le Mépris* in 1B, *King Lear* in 3B, *JLG/JLG* in 4B).

29. These figures may not be absolutely exact. On the screen the titles of books and films are also listed, with a similar falling away after the first chapter of *Histoire(s)* (102 in 1A and 1B; only 52 in the remaining six chapters). There is no arbitrariness, however, in the choice of the screen titles. Often they identify or serve as commentary on an image shown or text spoken.

30. Renoir's *La Règle du jeu* seems to be replaced by Leiris's autobiographical work of the same name.

31. Overall 2B differs from 1A and 1B in the variety of illustration supplied: hands for *Les mains sales*; a landscape with mountains for *La montagne magique*; a Courbet painting of two children on a beach for *Les enfants du capitaine Grant*. My thanks to Briony Fer for the identification.

32. The first dialogue sequence lasts nine minutes; a return to the dialogue later in this episode lasts three minutes, and is framed slightly differently, though the objects before the camera (Godard, Daney, video-monitor, window) remain the same.

33. In fact a reprise of the opening mention in 1A.

34. A fragment from a third dialogue follows: "Ça tourne"/ "Alors dix secondes après, bon allez-y, allez-y, allez-y." This exchange between director and crew echoes the opening words of the earlier dialogue with Daney: "Tu dis dix

secondes. Quand tu veux…" ("They're rolling"/ "Then ten seconds after, good, let's go…"; "You say ten seconds. When you want….")

35. In an extract from *JLG/JLG* shown in 4B: "Cela ne se dit pas […] cela s'enregistre" ("That isn't spoken […] it's recorded") (though the ECM translation has "filmed" for "s'enregistre", which clearly misses a technical detail).

36. In the theatrical trailer for *À bout de souffle* the tape recorder is shown in close-up and named as a constituent element of the film to come.

37. For a more detailed discussion of these broadcasts, see Lack, Roland-François, "The Point in Time: Precise Chronology in Early Godard", *Studies in French Cinema*, 3:2, 2003, pp. 101-109.

38. Marc Paillet's 1964 film, *Gauche année zéro*, made irrelevant by de Gaulle's presidential victory in 1965.

39. See also the image and dialogue (with Belmondo) from *Une femme est une femme* shown in Chapter 3B, recalling Karina's status as, in the words of *Paris-Match*, "the New Wave bride". Her voice and image make more explicit autobiographical reference than Godard's from the same period (of which there is indeed only what we see and hear of him in the scene from *Le Mépris*).

40. In the book of *Histoire(s)* the Karina-Belmondo still is the first image shown. This exaggerates, perhaps, the importance of the sentimental motif, though in 3B Karina's words in *Pierrot le fou* are reproduced as text on screen: "tu me parles avec des mots et je te regarde avec des sentiments" ("you speak to me with words and I look at you with feelings").

41. Godard had previously compared Karina with Leslie Caron. She is described in *Le Petit soldat* as having "the same kind of mouth as Leslie Caron", and Godard's description of his characters in *Bande à part* says of Karina's character: "For a minute, Odile is Leslie Caron in *Orvet* or *Lili*…".

42. "I was that man."

43. My translation.

44. The title of Robert Antelme's memoir of the death camps, *L'Espèce humaine*, appears on the screen in 4B.

45. "Que dire alors?", in the French version of Borges: "What should one say, then?".

46. "Une boucle bouclée": interview with Alain Bergala, in *Jean-Luc Godard par Jean-Luc Godard*, 2 vols., Alain Bergala ed., Paris: Cahiers du Cinéma, 1998, II, p. 41: "I can say then: 'I was that man, and the cinema was that flower.'"

47. The scene with Chaplin at the piano holding a white rose is unused footage from *The Cure*, 1917, first shown in Brownlow and Gill's 1983 documentary *Unknown Chaplin*.

48. Borges, "Une rose jaune", in *Oeuvres complètes*, II, p. 17 (my translation of the French translation from the Spanish).

49. As are the first images of 4B: alternating photographic portraits forming a rather odd screen couple, Jewish Simone Signoret and Fascist Robert le Vigan (accompanied on the screen by "L'amour").

50. A phrase typed on the screen at the end of 1B, quoting Saint Paul in the Acts of the Apostles, invokes the title of a 1997 film by Miéville: "Do thyself no harm, for we are all here".

51. Reference to a literary couple, Robert Antelme and Marguerite Duras, clearly informs the catalogue of horror in this episode.

52. *Much Ado About Nothing*, II.ii. The speech from which the line compares, in terms echoed in *Histoire(s)*, the difference

between love and friendship: "Friendship is constant in all other things/ Save in the office and affairs of love:/ Therefore all hearts in love use their own tongues;/ Let every eye negotiate for itself/ And trust no agent; for beauty is a witch/ Against whose charms faith melteth into blood."

53. As Philippe Sollers comments, in *Femmes*, Paris: Gallimard, 1983, p. 281: "What was Sartre's most famous phrase? The one at the end of *Les Mots*? The one that the schoolchildren of the future will have to copy out a hundred times so that they properly assimilate the new humanism?" (my translation) All such pertinent remarks in *Femmes* should interest us, since that text is the source of the phrase most frequently cited by Godard since the mid-1980s, the one that begins "Yes, night has fallen, another world is awakening, hard, cynical, illiterate, amnesiac...." My thanks to Jean-Louis Leutrat for the reference.

54. Astruc, Alexandre, *La Tête la première*, Paris: Olivier Orban, 1975, p. 123.

55. Of *La Belle et la Bête*, perhaps, where the colour of the Beast's rose is unspecified.

56. For a close reading of this identification in *Histoire(s)* 4B, see Robbins, Alex, "'Ce colporteur c'était le cinéma': Remembrance and Rebirth in Jean-Luc Godard's *Les Signes parmi nous*", *French Studies Bulletin*, 87, 2003, pp. 2-8.

57. It is just possible that the painting was looted rather than destroyed. I am grateful to Tobias von Elsner, curator of the Kulturhistorisches Museum in Magdeburg, for details regarding the fate of the Van Gogh painting. I would also like to thank Jann Matlock for help with identifying images discussed in this essay, and for her invaluable comments on my first draft.

HISTORY AND MEMORY

HORI

1. Bergala, Alain, "Filmer un plan" [1989], in *Nul mieux que Godard*, Paris: Cahiers du Cinéma, 1999, p. 83.

2. Aumont, Jacques, *Amnésies: Fictions du cinéma d'après Jean-Luc Godard*, Paris: POL, 1999, pp. 25-26.

3. Aumont, *Amnésies*, p. 145.

4. Papaioannou, Kostas, "Hegel et la philosophie de l'histoire", in Hegel, WF, *La Raison dans l'Histoire*, Paris: Union Générale d'Éditions, 1979, p. 19. See also Hegel, *Lectures on the Philosophy of World History: Introduction: Reason in History*, HB Nisbet trans., Cambridge: Cambridge University Press, 1975, p. 74.

5. Hegel, *Introduction: Reason in History*, p. 74.

6. See Godard, Jean-Luc and Ishaghpour, Youssef, *Archéologie du cinéma et mémoire du siècle*, Tours: Farrago, 2000, pp 45-46.

7. Godard, Jean-Luc, "La solitude de l'Histoire", *Le Monde*, 5 September 1991, p. 34.

8. See Godard, Jean-Luc, "La légende du siècle": interview with Frédéric Bonnaud and Arnaud Viviant, *Les Inrockuptibles*, 170, 21-27 October 1998, pp. 20-28 (p. 28).

9. Brasillach, Robert, "Le testament d'un condamné", in *Oeuvres Complètes de Robert Brasillach*, Paris: Au Club de l'Honnête Homme, 1964, vol. IX, p. 94. (I am indebted to Roland-François Lack for the identification of this poem.) In *Éloge de l'amour*, 2001, Edgar (Bruno Putzulu), not satisfied

with the reading by an old lady he tests in the audition, demands his servant Philippe Loyrette to sing this Brasillach poem, which he also sang in Jean-Luc Rossignol's short film *Testament d'un condamné*, 1993.

10. See Aragon, Louis, *L'homme communiste*, vol. I, Paris: Gallimard, 1946, p. 42.

11. Godard, Jean-Luc, "À propos de cinéma et d'histoire", in *Jean-Luc Godard par Jean-Luc Godard*, 2 vols., Alain Bergala ed., Paris: Cahiers du Cinéma, 1998, II, pp. 401-405 (p. 402).

12. Godard, "À propos de cinéma et d'histoire", p. 402. In an interview with Régis Debray, Godard mentions Vladimir Kosma Zworykin as follows: "The television tube, the iconoscope, was invented by a German-Jew, Zworykin, at the moment of the coming to power of Hitler, in 1932 [1933]. My history of cinema shows these kinds of small things." (*Godard par Godard*, II, p. 426.) Moreover, the iconoscope was used experimentally in the Olympic Games in Berlin, 1936, which were partly shot by Leni Riefenstahl. It is probably on this "constellation" that the montage of Hitler's photo and the word "ICONOSCOPE" at the end of Chapter 1B is based.

13. Godard, Jean-Luc, *Introduction à une véritable histoire du cinéma*, Paris: Albatros, 1980, p. 244.

14. Godard, "La légende du siècle", p. 28.

15. Deleuze, Gilles, *Cinema 2: The Time-Image*, Hugh Tomlinson and Robert Galeta trans., Minneapolis: University of Minnesota Press, 1989, p. 179.

16. Deleuze, *Cinema 2*, p. 180.

17. Godard, Jean-Luc, "Une boucle bouclée: Nouvel entretien avec Jean-Luc Godard par Alain Bergala", in *Godard par Godard*, II, pp. 8-41 (p. 11).

18. Godard was one of the first signatories to an international appeal against the war in Chechen. See "Grozny rasée, corps torturés, peuple écrasé... Une horreur hante l'Europe", *Le Monde*, 23 March 2000.

19. Goytisolo, Juan, *Cahier de Sarajevo*, François Maspéro trans., Strasbourg: La Nuée bleue, 1993, p. 74.

20. Aumont exhaustively interprets this phrase from historical, poetic, cultural and mythic viewpoints. See the chapter entitled "Orphée se retournant" in *Amnésies*, pp. 33-66.

21. Douchet, Jean, "Le théorème de Godard", "Numéro Spécial Godard–Trente ans depuis", *Cahiers du cinéma*, 1991, p. 12.

22. Godard, *Introduction à une véritable histoire du cinéma*, p. 175.

23. See Godard, "À propos de cinéma et d'histoire", p. 402.

24. Godard, "À propos de cinéma et d'histoire", p. 429. Wittgenstein's phrase also appears in Chapter 1B, when Godard introduces a theme of "cinema as Christianity".

25. Godard, "À propos de cinéma et d'histoire", p. 404.

26. Godard, Jean-Luc, "Le cinéma n'a pas su remplir son rôle": interview with Jean-Pierre Lavoignat and Christophe d'Yvoire, in *Godard par Godard*, II, pp. 335-343 (p. 336).

27. Bazin, André, "Ontologie de l'image photographique" [1945], in *Qu'est-ce que le cinéma?*, Paris: Les Éditions du Cerf, 1985, p. 14.

28. Bazin, "Montage interdit" [1953, 1957], in *Qu'est-ce que le cinéma?*, p. 59.

29. Péguy, Charles, *Oeuvres en prose complètes*, vol. III, Paris: Gallimard-La Pléiade, 1992, p. 997.

30. Péguy, *Oeuvres en prose complètes*, pp. 1177-8. It is on the same logic that his praise of Jules Michelet is based: "When he [Michelet] says that history is a resurrection [...], he shows his

genius and we must understand that from history, inscription and historical history itself he returns to memorialist history, [...] memory and aging" (Péguy, *Oeuvres en prose complètes*, pp. 1176-7). Michelet is one of the historians that implicitly inspired Godard's method. According to an interview, he proposed, on the occasion of the bicentenary of the French Revolution, to film Madame de Lamballe's death on the basis of Michelet's description (see "Le bon plaisir de Jean-Luc Godard", *Godard par Godard*, II, pp. 305-322 (p. 316).

31. Péguy, *Oeuvres en prose complètes*, III, p. 1114.

32. Péguy, *Oeuvres en prose complètes*, III, p. 1147.

33. For a useful discussion of Reverdy in the context of Godard's long and evolving practice of montage, see Witt, Michael, "Montage, My Beautiful Care, or Histories of the Cinematograph", in Michael Temple and James S Williams eds., *The Cinema Alone: essays on the work of Jean-Luc Godard 1985-2000*, Amsterdam: Amsterdam University Press, 2000, pp. 33-50, esp. 49-50.

34. For an English translation, see Benjamin, *Illuminations*, Hannah Arendt ed., Harry Zohn trans., London: Fontana, 1992.

35. The fragment cited by Godard is entitled "The Ball", part of "The Metaphysics of Youth", 1913-14. "Youth" does not correspond so much to adolescence as to a state of mind which always seeks to determine one's own destiny. "The ball", on the other hand, designates a place of escape where those who are tired of the pursuit of "youth" meet each other. By associating the fragment with a euphoric scene of Ermanno Olmi's *The Engagement*, 1962, Godard emphasises its poetic and graceful atmosphere.

36. In analysing the last sequence of Chapter 1B, Bergala considers Benjamin's work on history as the key text for understanding Godard's historical project of the last twenty years. See Bergala, "L'Ange de l'Histoire", in *Nul mieux que Godard*, pp. 221-249 (pp. 221-224).

DALL'ASTA

1. "Une boucle bouclée: Nouvel entretien avec Jean-Luc Godard par Alain Bergala", in *Jean-Luc Godard par Jean-Luc Godard*, 2 vols., Alain Bergala ed., Paris: Cahiers du Cinéma, 1998, II, p. 15.

2. Further references to Benjamin's theory of history can be found in Godard, Jean-Luc, "À propos de cinéma et d'histoire", *Trafic*, 18, 1996, pp. 28-32, and in the dialogue with Youssef Ishaghpour, "Archéologie du cinéma et mémoire du siècle", *Trafic*, 29-30, 1999, pp. 16-35 and pp. 34-53.

3. For a discussion of this image, see "L'Ange de l'histoire", in Bergala, Alain, *Nul mieux que Godard*, Paris: Cahiers du Cinéma, 1999, pp. 221-249. According to Bergala, the theses entitled "On the Concept of History" constitute "the most crucial text for the understanding of Godard's project of the last twenty years". Also known as "Theses on the Philosophy of History", the English translation (by Harry Zohn) of Benjamin's essay can be found in the classical anthology edited by Hannah Arendt in 1968, *Illuminations*, London: Fontana, 1992, pp. 245-256.

4. The displacement of meaning is the semiotic movement that is characteristic of allegory. A lucid description of the functioning of allegory is provided by Gershom Scholem:

> Allegory consists of an infinite network of meanings and correlations in which everything can become a representation of everything else, but all within the limits of language and expression. To that extent it is possible to speak of allegorical immanence. That which is expressed by and in the allegorical sign is in the first instance something which has its own meaningful context, but by becoming allegorical this something loses its own meaning and becomes the vehicle of something else. Indeed the allegory arises, as it were, from the gap which at this point opens between the form and its meaning. The two are no longer indissolubly welded together; the meaning is no longer restricted to that particular form, nor the form any longer to that particular meaningful content. What appears in the allegory, in short, is the infinity of meaning which attaches to every representation.

Quoted in Buck-Morss, Susan, *The Dialectic of Seeing: Walter Benjamin and the Arcade Project*, Cambridge, MA: MIT Press, 1991, p. 236. This formulation is obviously indebted to Benjamin's own discussion of allegory in *The Origin of German Tragic Drama*, John Osborne trans., London: NLB, 1973 (a text concluded in 1925). One of Benjamin's closest friends, Scholem, is cited in Chapter 3A of *Histoire(s)* through a fragment of his "Ten Unhistorical Statements about the Kabbalah" from 1958, although it was first published in English in *Modern Judaism*, 5, 1985. The quote is reprised from *Hélas pour moi*, where Scholem's text is re-titled as "Dix propositions historiques sur l'Ancien Testament".

5. Slightly different from the German version, the French version "Sur le concept d'histoire" (translated by the author himself) can be found in Benjamin, Walter, *Écrits français*, Paris: Gallimard, 1997. In the English translation (in *Illuminations*, p. 245) the German version of Thesis II reads as follows:

> "One of the most remarkable characteristics of human nature", writes Lotze, "is, alongside so much selfishness in specific instances, the freedom from envy which the present displays toward the future". Reflection shows us that our image of happiness is thoroughly coloured by the time to which the course of our own existence has assigned us. The kind of happiness that could arouse envy in us exists only in the air we have breathed, among people we could have talked to, women who could have given themselves to us. In other words, our image of happiness is indissolubly bound up with the image of redemption. The same applies to our view of the past, which is the concern of history. The past carries with it a temporal index by which it is referred to redemption. There is a secret agreement between past generations and the present one. Our coming was expected on earth. Like every generation that preceded us, we have been endowed with a weak Messianic power, a power to which the past has a claim. That claim cannot be settled cheaply. Historical materialists are aware of that.

6. Benjamin, *Gesammelte Schriften, vol. V: Passagen-Werk*, Rolf Tiedemann ed., Frankfurt am Main: Suhrkamp Verlag, 1972, p. 574 (N 1a, 8).

7. In fact, the use of montage and quotation in *Histoire(s)* can usefully be interpreted as a method to produce an *agencement collectif d'énonciation*, in the sense given to this expression by Gilles Deleuze and Félix Guattari in *Mille plateaux. Capitalisme et schizophrénie*, Paris: Éditions de Minuit, 1980, esp. chapter 4, "20 novembre 1923. Postulats de la linguistique".

8. Benjamin in a letter to Florens Christian Rang, 9 December 1923. Quoted in Didi-Huberman, Georges, *Devant le temps: Histoire de l'art et anachronisme de l'image*, Paris: Éditions de Minuit, 2000, p. 87.

9. Benjamin, Walter, "The Work of Art in the Age of

Mechanical Reproduction" [1936], in *Illuminations*, pp. 211-244. As it has been repeatedly noted, the expression "mechanical reproduction" in this classical English translation by Harry Zohn does not correspond to the meaning of *technischen Reproduzierbarkeit* in the original text, which can be rendered without difficulties with "technical reproducibility". In *Introduction à une véritable histoire du cinéma*, Paris: Albatros, 1980, Godard explicitly interprets the use of art reproductions in the books of Faure and Malraux as a form of visual criticism:

> I don't see how one can be a film critic; a music critic, yes; if you're a music critic or an art critic, you can put two paintings together and take a photograph, you can bring together two or three paintings and make a relationship visible, and you can make use of language, too, if you want. That's what some critics have done, not many. In France, Élie Faure a bit, and Malraux a bit, I can't think of any others; but, in fact, the innovation of Malraux in art history, where he had a lot of success, was simply the fact that he used a lot of photos: at least you could see what he was talking about; whereas with films you can't do that.

But the method of this criticism by means of images was not simply illustrative, otherwise it would have been identical to the use of stills in film history books, on which Godard comments as follows:

> I am always surprised, in film history books, by the way the pictures are placed, arranged, on the page. The photos are generally used as illustrations of the theses that are already established in prose. They place a photo of a Griffith film next to the page where they discuss Griffith, which seems a bit simplistic; you don't learn much that way. Perhaps the writer has seen something, I'm not denying that, but the things that Sadoul or Bazin have seen, in my opinion, when I read their books later, I've no way of seeing what they have seen; that's what bothers me.

Godard, Jean-Luc, "Les Cinémathèques et l'Histoire du Cinéma", *Travelling*, 56-57, 1980, p. 125. On the contrary, Godard suggests, the images in the books of Faure and Malraux allow the viewer to appropriate the vision of another. On the role played by the works of Faure and Malraux in the conception of *Histoire(s)*, see Temple, Michael, "Big Rhythm and the Power of Metamorphosis: Some Models and Precursors for *Histoire(s) du cinéma*", in *The Cinema Alone: essays on the work of Jean-Luc Godard 1985-2000*, Michael Temple and James S Williams eds., Amsterdam: Amsterdam University Press, 2000, pp. 77-95.

10. This is how Benjamin's contention is interpreted by Georges Didi-Huberman in *Devant le temps*: "When Benjamin writes that 'there's no history of art', it isn't to express a judgement of inexistence. It's to express a need, a desire: that art history should at last begin to exist in the form of a history of the works themselves." (p. 87) This new form of history will have to break with "the familiar and fallacious connection of 'causes' and 'effects'. Art history ends up denying the temporality of its object by relating art 'only by means of causality', in the usual historicist way. But art works, says Benjamin, have their 'specific historicity', which is not expressed in the 'extensive mode' of a causal or familial narrative like you find in Vasari. It expresses itself in multiple ways, in the 'intensive mode', which between works 'brings out connections that are atemporal without being ahistorical' [...] or in the monadic mode–in the Leibnizian sense–of that historicity specific to art works."

11. Braudel, Fernand, "Pour une économie historique" [1950], in *Écrits sur l'histoire*, Paris: Flammarion, 1969.

12. This is, for instance, how Clio describes herself in the eponymous text by Péguy:

> In the sense they have given to the word science when they want me to be a science, or I am a science in the sense they understand the word, and as they wish, in which case I cannot even begin the beginning of my beginning, or I betray, even by an atom, being a science, their science, and since they have made me incapable of being an art, I am no longer able to do anything at all [...] People pretend there's only one history, in fact there are two, Clio and history, we have seen it ourselves by the way. For ancient times, for ancient peoples, for ancient man, for ancient events, for ancient worlds, I am Clio, I lack documents. For modern times, for modern peoples, for modern man, for modern events, for modern worlds, I am history, and I lack a lack of documents. That's where the metaphysics of history was born.

Péguy, Charles, "Clio: dialogue de l'histoire et de l'âme païenne", in *Oeuvres en prose complètes*, vol. II, Paris: Gallimard, 1992, pp. 1148-9.

13. Arendt, Hannah, "Walter Benjamin: 1892-1940", in Benjamin, *Illuminations*, p. 27.

14. Quoted in Benjamin, "Paris–the Capital of the Nineteenth Century" [1935], Quintin Hoare trans., in *Charles Baudelaire. A Lyrical Poet in the Age of High Capitalism*, London: Verso, 1983, p. 158.

15. On the analogy between *Histoire(s) du cinéma* and the *Passagen-Werk*, see Païni, Dominique, "Que peut le cinéma?", *Art Press* (hors série), 1998, pp. 4-7.

16. See Godard, *Introduction à une véritable histoire du cinéma*, which contains a transcription of the lectures given by the author at the Conservatoire d'art cinématographique in Montreal in 1979 and represents the most extensive documentation of the first stage in his articulation of the project.

17. "The dialectical image is a flash of ball lightning covering the whole horizon of past", Benjamin, *Gesammelte Schriften*, I, p. 1233 (Ms 491). The expression "*télescopage* of the past through the present" appears in vol. V of the *Gesammelte Schriften* (1982), p. 588 (N 7a, 3). In the *Dictionnaire historique de la langue française*, Paris: Dictionnaires Le Robert, 1992, the entry "télescoper" is defined as follows: "the verb *télescoper* is primarily used in French intransitively for 'collapsing into each other in a collision like the different parts of a telescope', today mainly used pronominally as *se télescoper*. It is used transitively for 'shunt into' (1893, firstly for a railway accident) and the pronominal usage has developed in the figurative sense, 'crash violently into' and 'crash violently together'."

18. The frame for this comparison is provided by Deleuze, Gilles, *Cinéma 2: L'Image-Temps*, Paris: Éditions de Minuit, 1985, Chapter VII, §3. On Godard's relationship to both Eisenstein and Vertov, see Witt, Michael, "Montage, My Beautiful Care, or Histories of the Cinematograph," in Temple and Williams, *The Cinema Alone*, pp. 33-50.

19. For an exemplary discussion of the theme of involuntary memory in *Histoire(s)* at the intersection of Proust and Benjamin, see Ricciardi, Alessia, "Cinema Regained: Godard Between Proust and Benjamin", *Modernism/Modernity*, 4, 2001, pp. 643-661.

20. Benjamin, *Gesammelte Schriften*, vol. V, p. 576 (N 3, 1).

21. Nietzsche, Friedrich, *On the Use and Abuse of History for Life*, Ian Johnston trans., text in the public domain, released September 1998, www.mala.bc.ca/~johnstoi/Nietzsche/history.htm, §IV.

22. Nietzsche, www.mala.bc.ca/~johnstoi/Nietzsche/history.htm.

23. Nietzsche, www.mala.bc.ca/~johnstoi/Nietzsche/history.htm, §I.

24. Nietzsche, www.mala.bc.ca/~johnstoi/Nietzsche/history.htm, §IV.

25. Nietzsche, www.mala.bc.ca/~johnstoi/Nietzsche/history.htm, §V.

26. Nietzsche, www.mala.bc.ca/~johnstoi/Nietzsche/history.htm, §V.

27. Nietzsche, www.mala.bc.ca/~johnstoi/Nietzsche/history.htm, §V.

28. Debord, Guy, *La Société du spectacle*, Paris: Buchet-Chastel, 1967, Chapter 6, §156 (*The Society of Spectacle*, Freddy Perlman trans., text in the public domain, http://situationist.cjb.net).

29. Debord, *La Société du spectacle*, Chapter 6, §158.

30. What kind of history is this? One needs to be clear that it's not a chronological history, but truly a messianic one. Messianic history is defined above all by two characteristics. It's a history of Salvation, something must be saved. And it's an ultimate history, an eschatological history, where something must be accomplished, judged, but in another time, and it must therefore be removed from chronology, without entering another world. This is why messianic history is incalculable [...] for the arrival of the Messiah is incalculable. But at the same time each historical moment is the moment of his arrival, the Messiah has always already arrived, he is always already there. Each moment, each image is charged with history, because it is the little door through which the Messiah enters. It is this messianic situation of cinema that Debord shares with the Godard of *Histoire(s) du cinéma*. Despite their ancient rivalry–Debord said in 1968 that Godard was the most stupid of the pro-Chinese Swiss–Godard has found the same paradigm that Debord was the first to establish.

See "Le cinéma de Guy Debord" in Agamben, Giorgio, *Image et mémoire*, Paris: Hoëbeke, 1998, pp. 67-68.

31. Deleuze, *Cinéma 2*, Chapter VI, §1.

32. The analogy between Benjamin and Deleuze on this point–the contradictory character that truth assumes in relation to the past–can be explained through the philosophical genealogy that they both choose for their reflections: Leibniz, Nietzsche and Bergson. In fact, the duplicity of Deleuze's "crystal-image", which involves the simultanous perception of a "virtual image" and an "actual image", corresponds exactly to the dialectical structure of the "monad" which Benjamin also defines as a "*télescopage* of the past through the present". The similitude is particularly striking since monads constitute themselves in a process that Benjamin describes through the metaphor of crystallisation (see Thesis XVII cited above). Both concepts result from two distinct, but not incompatible, elaborations of the philosophy of Henri Bergson.

33. Benjamin, Thesis XVII.

SAXTON

1. Wajcman, Gérard, *L'Objet du siècle*, Lagrasse: Verdier, 1998, p. 25. Sections of this chapter have appeared in an earlier form in an article in *Trafic*, 47, Autumn 2003, pp. 48-66. I would like to thank the Arts and Humanities Research Board of the British Academy for their support in funding the research that has led to this piece, and Jean Khalfa, Raymond Bellour, Jean-Michel Frodon, Chris Darke and James S Williams for their invaluable comments on draft versions.

2. Godard, Jean-Luc, *Jean-Luc Godard par Jean-Luc Godard*, 2 vols., Alain Bergala ed., Paris: Cahiers du Cinéma, 1998, II, p. 146.

3. Godard, Jean-Luc, "La légende du siècle", interview with Frédéric Bonnaud and Arnaud Viviant, *Les Inrockuptibles*, 170, 21-27 October 1998, pp. 20-28. For a more detailed account of much of the history of the proposed joint project and some of its implications, see Frodon, Jean-Michel, "'Le fameux débat' Lanzmann–Godard: le parti des mots contre le parti des images", *Le Monde* (Supplément Télévision), 28 June 1999, p. 5.

4. Baecque, Antoine de, "Premières images des camps: Quel cinéma après Auschwitz?", *Cahiers du cinéma*, hors-série ("Le siècle du cinéma"), November 2000, pp. 62-66 (p. 66).

5. *Histoire(s) du cinéma* (video), Paris: Gaumont, 1998, Chapter 4B.

6. Godard refers here to certain moments, read by him as prophetic, in films which just predate the discovery of the camps, such as the rabbit hunt and death dance in Jean Renoir's *La Règle du jeu*, 1939, and the round-ups in Charles Chaplin's *The Great Dictator*, 1940.

7. Deleuze remarks, for example, that "up to the end Nazism thinks of itself in competition with Hollywood", in *Cinéma 2: L'Image-Temps*, Paris: Éditions de Minuit, 1985, p. 344. Lending weight to Godard's theory of cinema's culpability, this is the sense in which films about fascism inevitably invite self-referential readings, an inevitability most famously explored and exploited by Hans Jürgen Syberberg in *Hitler: Ein Film aus Deutschland*, 1977.

8. See, for example, *Godard par Godard*, II, p. 316.

9. *Godard par Godard*, II, p. 246. For two of the most important analyses of the Auschwitz/Taylor encounter so far, analyses to which the present discussion is indebted, see Williams, James S, "European Culture and Artistic Resistance in *Histoire(s) du cinéma* Chapter 3A, *La Monnaie de l'absolu*", and Wright, Alan, "Elizabeth Taylor at Auschwitz: JLG and the Real Object of Montage", both in *The Cinema Alone: essays on the work of Jean-Luc Godard 1985-2000*, Michael Temple and James S Williams eds., Amsterdam: Amsterdam University Press, 2000, pp. 113-139 (pp. 134-137); pp. 51-60. For both critics, this moment is central to an understanding of the whole work: Williams finds in it a "metapoetic comment on Godard's own process", and Wright a precise representation of the director's "unattainable" idea of montage.

10. Rancière, Jacques, "La Sainte et l'héritière: À propos des *Histoire(s) du cinéma*", *Cahiers du cinéma*, 537, July-August 1999, 58-61 (p. 60). ("The Saint and the Heiress: Apropos of Godard's *Histoire(s) du cinéma*", TS Murphy trans., *Discourse* 24:1, Winter 2002, pp. 113-149). For Rancière, as for Williams and Wright, Godard's entire project is emblematised by this sequence.

11. Agamben, Giorgio, "Face au cinéma et à l'Histoire, à propos de Jean-Luc Godard", *Le Monde* (Supplément Livres), 6 October 1995, I, X-XI (p. XI).

12. Williams, "European Culture and Artistic Resistance", p. 135.

13. Godard, cited in Carr, Jay, "A Muted Godard Awaits US Bow of *Hail Mary*", *Boston Globe*, 7 October 1985, p. 28. While both the Greek terms here signify a "likeness", an "image", *eikôn* implies a truthful representation in contrast to the false image implied by *eidôlon*.

14. *Godard par Godard*, II, p. 146; *Histoire(s) du cinéma*, Chapter 4B.

15. Aumont, Jacques, *Amnésies: Fictions du cinéma d'après Jean-Luc Godard*, Paris: POL, 1999. For Aumont, this is another way in which the operations of montage, as "a tool of forgetting", reflect the processes of thinking: unpacking the Godardian ellipses, he speaks of the "difficult and painful work of forgetting that, all by itself, constitutes the Memory on which thought exists", p. 26.

16. *Godard par Godard*, II, p. 387.

17 Debray, Régis, *Vie et mort de l'image: Une histoire du regard en Occident*, Paris: Gallimard, 1992, pp. 61-62.

18. *Godard par Godard*, II, pp. 427-30.

19. The term is Wajcman's, in "'Saint Paul' Godard versus 'Moïse' Lanzmann, le match", *L'Infini*, 65, 1999, pp. 121-127 (p. 123).

20. Derrida, Jacques, *Mal d'archive: Une impression freudienne*, Paris: Galilée, 1995, pp. 26-27.

21. See Tesson, Charles, "Une machine à montrer l'invisible: conversation avec Bernard Eisenschitz à propos des *Histoire(s) du cinéma*", *Cahiers du cinéma*, 529, 1998, pp. 52-56 (p. 53).

22. Davis, Colin, "Understanding the Concentration Camps: Elien Wiesel's *La Nuit* and Jorge Semprun's *Quel beau dimanche!*", *Australian Journal of French Studies*, 28:3, 1991, pp. 291-304 (p. 302).

23. Bersani, Leo, *The Culture of Redemption*, Cambridge, MA: Harvard University Press, 1990.

24. *Godard par Godard*, II, p. 430 (my emphasis).

25. In Smith, Gavin, "Jean-Luc Godard" (interview), *Film Comment*, 32: 2, March-April 1996, pp. 31-41 (p. 38).

26. In Comolli, Jean-Louis and Rancière, Jacques, *Arrêt sur histoire*, Paris: Éditions du Centre Pompidou, 1997, p. 35, p. 38.

27. Lanzmann, Claude, "'The Disaster'", *Les Temps Modernes*, 615-6, September-October 2001, pp. 1-3 (p. 1).

28. Godard, "La légende du siècle", p. 28.

29. Delfour, Jean-Jacques, "La Pellicule maudite. Sur la figuration du réel de la Shoah", *L'Arche*, 508, June 2000, pp. 14-17.

30. Godard, in an interview with Antoine Dulaure and Claire Parnet, *L'Autre Journal*, 2, January 1985, p. 21. For similar claims see also, for example, *Godard par Godard*, II, p. 247, and "La légende du siècle", p. 28.

31. Godard, cited in Niney, François, *L'Épreuve du réel à l'écran: Essai sur le principe de réalité documentaire*, Brussels: De Boeck, 2000, p. 303.

32. Frodon, "'Le fameux débat' Lanzmann–Godard"; Lindeperg, Sylvie, *Clio de 5 à 7. Les Actualités filmées de la Libération: archives du futur*, Paris: Éditions CNRS, 2000, p. 268.

33. Arnaud des Pallières, whose film *Drancy Avenir*, 1996, has received rare praise from Lanzmann, makes particularly insightful contributions to this debate. Deconstructing the notion of photographic proof, des Pallières uncovers an art which is "anxious for truth" and yet which simultaneously exempts itself from proof by producing singularities ("L'Art, puissance de vérité", in Lindeperg, *Clio de 5 á 7*, pp. 270-273 (p. 272)).

34. Lanzmann, Claude, "Holocauste, la représentation impossible", *Le Monde* (Supplément Arts-Spectacles), 3 March 1994, p. i, p. vii, (p. vii).

35. Köppen, Manuel, "Von Effekten des Authentischen–*Schindler's List*: Film und Holocaust', in *Bilder des Holocaust: Literatur, Film, bildende Kunst*, Manuel Köppen and Klaus R Scherpe eds., Köln: Böhlau, 1997, pp. 145-170 (pp. 160, 162; my translation).

36. Besides the films discussed below, this scene has also notably been staged by films such as Claude Lelouch's *Les Uns et les Autres*, 1981, and Robert Enrico's *Au nom de tous les miens*, 1983, as well as by the notorious American TV series *Holocaust*, 1978.

37. Foucault, Michel, *Surveiller et punir: naissance de la prison*, Paris: Gallimard, 1975, p. 21, p. 14.

38. Delfour, "La Pellicule maudite", p. 15.

39. Godard, Jean-Luc, "Feu sur *Les Carabiniers*", *Cahiers du cinéma*, 146, August 1963, pp. 1-4 (p. 2).

40. This is a position which is being subjected to renewed critical scrutiny, for example, in Lanzmann's critique of Eyal Sivan's *Un Spécialiste, portrait d'un criminel moderne*, 1999, a thought-provoking film about the Eichmann trial, which Lanzmann opposes to *Shoah*.

41. Godard, Jean-Luc, *Introduction à une véritable histoire du cinéma*, Paris: Albatros, 1980, p. 321.

42. Didi-Huberman, Georges, "images malgré tout", in *Mémoire des camps, photographies des camps de concentration et d'extermination nazies (1933-1999)* (catalogue for the exhibition at the Hôtel de Sully, Paris, 12 January-25 March 2001), Clément Chéroux ed., Paris: Marval, 2001, pp. 219-241 (p. 219).

43. The Sonderkommando Jews were unfortunate enough to be forced to work in and around the gas chambers and crematoria, and their unique position as eye-witnesses–they had seen the horror from the inside–meant they were generally executed after a few months.

44. Didi-Huberman, "images malgré tout", p. 239.

45. Wajcman, Gérard, "De la croyance photographique", *Les Temps Modernes*, 613, March-May 2001, pp. 47-83 (p. 55).

46. Deleuze, *Cinéma 2*, pp. 31-32.

47. Lanzmann, Claude, "La question n'est pas celle du document, mais celle de la vérité", *Le Monde*, 19 January 2001 (this is the interview that generated the argument between Wajcman and Didi-Huberman); Derrida, *Mal d'archive*, p. 19. Lanzmann's refusal of archive material also extends (with rare exceptions such as the famous industrial memorandum sequence) to written documents.

48. For discussion of some of the uses to which the SS put the photographic image, from anthropometric portraiture to medical experiments, see About, Ilsen, "La Photographie au service du système concentrationnaire national-socialiste (1933-1945)", in *Mémoire des camps*, pp. 29-53.

49. Antelme, Robert, *L'Espèce humaine*, Paris: Gallimard, 1957, pp. 57-58. This experience is described from an alternative perspective in another of Lanzmann's more recent films, *Un Vivant qui passe*, 1997. Rossel's repeated admission that he can no longer picture one of the victims–"Non, je ne le vois pas" ("No, I cannot see him", but the pronoun *le* could also mean "it", referring to the broader picture)–recapitulates the central thesis of a film that explores the voluntary blindness of certain witnesses to the atrocity taking place before their eyes (Rossel, in Lanzmann, Claude, *Un Vivant qui passe: Auschwitz 1943–Theresienstadt 1944*, Paris: Mille et une nuits (ARTE Éditions), 1997, p. 58).

50. Felman, Shoshana, "À l'âge du témoignage: *Shoah* de Claude Lanzmann", in *Au sujet de Shoah, le film de Claude Lanzmann*, Michel Deguy ed., Paris: Belin, 1990, pp. 55-145 (p. 61, p. 63).

51. Nancy, Jean-Luc, "La Représentation interdite", in "L'Art

et la mémoire des camps: Représenter exterminer", Jean-Luc Nancy ed., *Le Genre humain*, 36, 2001, pp. 13-39 (p. 20).

52. Besançon, Alain, *L'Image interdite: une histoire intellectuelle de l'iconoclasme*, Paris: Gallimard-Folio, 1994.

53. The term "iconophilia" was suggested by Raymond Bellour to describe the tone of some of Godard's more recent rhetoric, and was radicalised into "idolatry" by Frodon (during panel discussions at *For Ever Godard*, conference held at Tate Modern, London, 21-24 June 2001).

54. *Histoire(s) du cinéma*, Chapter 1A.

55. Pagnoux, Elisabeth, "Reporter photographe à Auschwitz", *Les Temps Modernes*, 613, March-May 2001, pp. 84-108 (p. 106).

56. Žižek, Slavoj, *The Art of the Ridiculous Sublime: On David Lynch's Lost Highway*, University of Washington, Seattle: Walter Chapin Simpson Center for the Humanities, 2000, p. 34.

57. Wajcman, "De la croyance photographique", p. 68.

58. Wajcman opens himself here to the criticism of neglecting the value of certain kinds of photography (for example Holocaust-related photographic art) in other directions, a value insightfully explored by Andrea Liss in her *Trespassing through Shadows: Memory, Photography, and the Holocaust*, Minneapolis: University of Minnesota Press, 1998.

59. Lyotard, Jean-François, "Réponse à la question: qu'est-ce que le postmoderne?", *Critique*, 38:419, April 1982, pp. 357-367 (p. 364).

60. Lanzmann, in *Au sujet de Shoah*, p. 295.

61. Rancière, Jacques, "S'il y a de l'irreprésentable", in Nancy, *L'Art et la mémoire des camps*, pp. 81-102 (p. 95).

62. Cited in Savigneau, Josyane, "Claude Lanzmann et 'la réappropriation de la violence par les juifs'", *Le Monde*, 16 May 2001, p. 26.

63. The description "a mythological film" (adopted by Lanzmann from Wajcman) appears in the opening text, and is lucid in its necessary contrast with the privileging of tragedy over myth in *Shoah* (justified by Lanzmann in *Au sujet de Shoah*, p. 304, pp. 315-316). In the same vein, commentators have taken their lead from the director in discussing *Sobibor* in terms more habitually associated with Hollywood: "Hitchcockian suspense", "heroism", "a kind of quintessence of the action movie" (see, for example, Nouchi, Frank, "Le jour où fut sauvée l'humanité", *Cahiers du cinéma*, 558, June 2001, p. 20).

64. Godard, *Introduction à une véritable histoire du cinéma*, p. 321 (it is worth noting this claim predates *Schindler's List*); Lanzmann, in *Au sujet de Shoah*, p. 301.

65. Lanzmann, preface to Müller, Filip, *Trois Ans dans une chambre à gaz d'Auschwitz*, Paris: Pygmalion/Gérard Watelet, 1980, pp. 9-17 (p. 10).

66. Lanzmann, in *Au sujet de Shoah*, pp. 280-292.

67. Wajcman, "'Saint Paul' Godard versus 'Moïse' Lanzmann, le match", p. 125; Lanzmann, "Holocauste, la représentation impossible", p. vii.

68. The risk of ceremonialisation is also run by *Nuit et brouillard*, another film about the refusal of representation. Reflecting on the role of cinema as witness, Serge Daney recalls that the reflex reaction of the government to the Touvier Affair and Carpentras was to order state TV to screen Resnais's film. Here Daney's history of cinema contradicts those of Godard: for Daney, the Shoah is one of those twentieth century events that only cinema has seen (see

Daney, Serge, "Journal de l'an passé", *Trafic*, 1, 1992, p. 5).

69. This is the expression employed by Thierry Jousse, and with a significant qualification: "No previous war has ever been to this extent a war of images [*guerre de l'image*], *whether these images are visible or invisible*" (Jousse, Thierry, "De Kaboul à New York", *Cahiers du cinéma*, 563, December 2001, pp. 10-11 (p. 10; my emphasis)).

70. Daney, Serge, *Devant la recrudescence des vols de sacs à main: cinéma, télévision, information*, Lyon: Aléas, 1991, pp. 191-192 (my emphasis).

71. Žižek, Slavoj, *Welcome to the Desert of the Real: Five Essays on September 11 and Related Dates*, London: Verso, 2002; Frodon, Jean-Michel, "L'Éphémère silence des images", *Le Monde*, 13 November 2001, p. 18. Frodon argues astutely that the attacks have confronted Hollywood with the invisible Other which threaten its (visual) hegemony, and yet on which it feeds: this alterity is habitually figured and fictionalised, not by the cinema of the real preferred by Lanzmann, but by the horror film.

72. Rivette, Jacques, "De l'abjection", *Cahiers du cinéma*, 120, 1961, pp. 54-55. Compare, for example, Rivette's claim that "every traditional approach to the 'spectacle' [of the camps] is a matter of voyeurism and pornography" (p. 54) with Jill Godmilow's critique of Spielberg for producing "out of all that veracity […] only a pornography of the real" (Godmilow, Jill, "How Real is the Reality in Documentary Film?", *History and Theory*, 4:36, 1997, pp. 80-101 (p. 93).

73. Tesson, Charles, "Retour à l'envoyeur", *Cahiers du cinéma*, 561, October 2001, pp. 42-44 (p. 44).

74. Sobchack, Vivian ed., *The Persistence of History: Cinema, Television, and the Modern Event*, New York and London: Routledge, 1996, p. 5.

75. Daney, *Devant des recrudescence des vols de sacs à main*, p. 193.

76. Bergala, Alain, *Nul mieux que Godard*, Paris: Cahiers du Cinéma, 1999, p. 11.

77. See, for example, "Godard: la grandeur d'un petit commerce de cinéma", *Epok*, 16, May 2001, pp. 8-15 (p. 10).

LUNDEMO

1. Godard, Jean-Luc, "Le montage, la solitude et la liberté", *Confrontations: les mardis de la FEMIS*, Paris: FEMIS, 1990. All translations in this text, both from *Histoire(s)* as well as written sources, are my own.

2. Godard quotes this passage from the surrealist poet Pierre Reverdy's poem "L'image" in *Passion, JLG/JLG: autoportrait de décembre* and *Histoire(s)*, and makes alterations to the original text in some instances. See Pierre Reverdy, "L'image", *Nord-Sud*, 13, March 1918 (reprinted in *Plupart du temps: Poèmes 1915-1922*, Paris: Flammarion, 1967, p. 410).

3. Manovich, Lev, "Avant-Garde as Software", in *Ostranenie*, Stephen Kovats ed., Frankfurt: Campus, 1999.

4. This is why Dan Graham's *Installation for Viewing Videos* in Kassel 1997 made such an appropriate screening for the series (even if Graham himself rejected the idea). Each of the eight parts of the series was screened on monitors in separate compartments of a glass construction, where the glass walls formed oblique angles in each compartment. This made the images of the different monitors superimpose and reflect themselves in each compartment, and *Histoire(s)* was thus submitted to its own approach to film history, allowing for interlacing and reflecting images in each other.

5. Rancière, Jacques, "L'inoubliable", in Comolli, Jean-Louis and Rancière, Jacques, *Arrêt sur histoire*, Paris: Éditions du Centre Pompidou, 1997, p. 63.

6. Kittler, Friedrich, *Gramophone, Film, Typewriter* [1986], Stanford: Stanford University Press, 1999, pp. 159-163. Münsterberg, Hugo, *The Photoplay; A Psychological Study* [1916], New York: Dover, 1970.

7. Aumont, Jacques, *Amnésies: Fictions du cinema d'après Jean-Luc Godard*, Paris: POL, 1999.

8. Deleuze, Gilles, *Cinéma 1: L'Image-Mouvement*, Paris: Éditions de Minuit, 1983, pp. 273-276.

9. Deleuze identifies the conjunction as the key element in Godard's cinema in an interview entitled "Trois questions sur 'Six fois deux'", *Cahiers du cinéma*, 271, 1976 (reprinted in *Pourparlers*, Paris: Éditions de Minuit, 1990, pp. 64-65).

10. Pierre Huyghe, Douglas Gordon, Victor Burgin, Chris Marker and many others work with references to Hitchcock in the gallery context.

11. I follow here the distinction between "*mémoire*" and "*souvenir*" (which I translate as "memory" and "recollection" respectively) suggested by Aumont, and which is central to the whole of my argument. See Aumont, *Amnésies*, pp. 25-26.

12. Aumont, *Amnésies*, p. 25.

13. Godard, Jean-Luc, "Propos rompus", *Cahiers du cinéma*, 316, October 1980 (reprinted in *Jean-Luc Godard par Jean-Luc Godard*, Alain Bergala ed., Paris: Éditions de l'Etoile/Cahiers du Cinéma 1985, p. 462).

14. Deleuze, Gilles and Guattari, Félix, *Mille plateaux: Capitalisme et schizophrénie II*, Paris: Éditions de Minuit, 1980, p. 606. The concept of "multiplicity" is interestingly downplayed in Deleuze's books on the cinema, but the selections of images follow the same principles. Deleuze discusses these principles as "crystalline space" and "hodological space" in *Cinéma 2: L'Image-Temps*, Paris: Éditions de Minuit, 1985, pp. 167-170.

15. Deleuze and Guattari, *Mille plateaux*, p. 46.

16. Ernst, Wolfgang, "A Visual Archive of Cinematographical Topoi: Navigating Images on The Borderline of Digital Addressability", http.//www.suchbilder.de (accessed 14 January 2003).

17. See Farocki, Harun, "Obdachlose am Flughafen; Sprache und Film, Filmsprache", *Jungle World*, 46, 2000, www.nadir.org/nadir/periodika/jungle_world/_2000/46/15a. htm (accessed 14 January 2003). Farocki expands here on the archival properties of his work. Farocki was also part of the research project, together with Friedrich Kittler and Wolfgang Ernst, on the emerging image retrieval techniques in computer media.

18. Deleuze, "Trois questions sur 'Six fois deux'", p. 65.

19. Kriest, Ulrich, "'Freiheit, die Lohnarbeit heisst'", *Der Ärger mit den Bildern; Die Filme von Harun Farocki*, Rolf Aurich and Ulrich Kriest eds., Konstanz: UVK Medien, 1998, p. 287.

20. Péguy, Charles, *Clio: dialogue de l'histoire et de l'âme païenne*, Paris: NRF, 1917, p. 238.

21. Péguy, *Clio*, p. 239.

22. Péguy, *Clio*, pp. 241-243.

23. Péguy, *Clio*, p 239. This passage is also cited in *Histoire(s)*.

24. Péguy, *Clio*, p. 239.

HILL

1. The discussion that follows is based on the video version of Godard's *Histoire(s) du cinéma* produced by Gaumont in 1998. I am grateful to Douglas Morrey for helpful comments on an earlier version of this essay; I should also like to thank Philippe-Emmanuel Sorlin and the work of Bernard Eisenschitz for helping in the identification of some of the source material used by Godard in *Histoire(s)*.

2. Godard, Jean-Luc, *Jean-Luc Godard par Jean-Luc Godard*, 2 vols., Alain Bergala ed., Paris: Cahiers du Cinéma, 1998, II, p. 301.

3. For an illuminating account of Godard's often enigmatic film, see Bergala, Alain, *Nul mieux que Godard*, Paris: Cahiers du Cinéma, 1999, pp. 171-182; much useful information is also to be found in Fieschi-Vivet, Laetitia, "Investigation of a Mystery: Cinema and the Sacred in *Hélas pour moi*", *The Cinema Alone: essays on the work of Jean-Luc Godard, 1985-2000*, Michael Temple and James S Williams eds., Amsterdam: Amsterdam University Press, 2000, pp. 189-206.

4. See Blanchot, Maurice, *Au moment voulu*, Paris: Gallimard, 1951, pp. 151-152; *When The Time Comes*, Lydia Davis trans., *The Station Hill Blanchot Reader*, Barrytown: Station Hill, 1999, p. 255. Godard, born in 1930, is presumably exaggerating the limits of his adolescence! On Blanchot's shorter fiction in general, see my *Blanchot: Extreme Contemporary*, London: Routledge, 1997.

5. In Blanchot's *récit*, the passage cited by Godard (which is not in the form of a dialogue) reads thus:

> La nuit, dans le Sud, quand je me lève, je sais qu'il ne s'agit ni du proche, ni du lointain, ni d'un événement m'appartenant, ni d'une vérité capable de parler, ce n'est pas une scène, ni le commencement de quelque chose. Une image, mais vaine, un instant, mais stérile, quelqu'un pour qui je ne suis rien et qui ne m'est rien–sans lien, sans début, sans but–, un point, et hors de ce point, rien, dans le monde, qui ne me soit étranger. Une figure? mais privée de nom, sans biographie, que refuse la mémoire, qui ne désire pas être racontée, qui ne veut pas survivre; présente, mais elle n'est pas là; absente, et cependant nullement ailleurs, ici; vraie? tout à fait en dehors du véritable. Si l'on dit: elle est liée à la nuit, je le nie; la nuit ne la connaît pas. Si l'on me demande: mais de quoi parlez-vous? je réponds: alors, il n'y a personne pour me le demander.

Lydia Davis translates as follows:

> At night, in the South, when I get up, I know that it isn't a question of proximity, or of distance, or of an event belonging to me, or of a truth capable of speaking, this is not a scene, or the beginning of something. An image, but a futile one, an instant, but a sterile one, someone for whom I am nothing and who is nothing to me–without bonds, without beginning, without end–a point, and outside this point, nothing, in the world, that is foreign to me. A face? But one deprived of a name, without a biography, one that is rejected by memory, that does not want to be recounted, that does not want to survive; present, but she is not there; absent, yet in no way elsewhere, here; true? altogether outside of what is true. If someone says, she is bound to the night, I deny it; the night doesn't know her. If someone asks me, but what are you talking about? I answer, well, there is no one to ask me that. (p. 255)

Citing the passage, Godard divides it up for male (M) and female (F) voice as follows:

> [F:] La nuit, quand je me lève, je sais qu'il ne s'agit ni du proche, ni du lointain, ni d'un événement m'appartenant, ni d'une vérité

capable de parler, ce n'est pas une scène, ni le commencement de quelque chose. [M:] Une image. [F:] Oui, un instant, mais stérile, quelqu'un pour qui je ne suis rien et qui ne m'est rien, un point, et hors de ce point… [M:] Une figure? [F:] …rien, dans le monde, qui ne me soit étranger. Oui, mais privée de nom, sans biographie, qui [sic] refuse la mémoire, qui ne désire pas être racontée; présente, mais elle n'est pas là; absente, et cependant nullement ailleurs. [M:] Tout à fait en dehors du véritable, donc. [F:] Si l'on dit: elle est liée à la nuit, je dis non; la nuit ne la connaît pas. [M:] Mais de quoi parlez-vous, mademoiselle? [F:] Si on me demande, je réponds: alors, il n'y a personne pour me le demander.

6. Bergala points out, for instance, that the famous sentence attributed to Bazin in *Le Mépris*, and used in *For Ever Mozart* and Chapter 1A of *Histoire(s)* (that "le cinéma substitue à notre regard un monde qui s'accorde à nos désirs"), is not by Bazin at all, but based on a remark by Michel Mourlet. See Bergala, *Nul mieux que Godard*, p. 20.

7. For an analysis of the structure and history of quotation, see Compagnon, Antoine, *La Seconde main*, Paris: Seuil, 1979.

8. On iterability, see Derrida, Jacques, *Marges: de la philosophie*, Paris: Éditions de Minuit, 1972, pp. 367-393; *Margins of Philosophy*, Alan Bass trans., Chicago, University of Chicago Press, 1982, pp. 307-330.

9. Aumont, Jacques, *Amnésies: Fictions du cinéma d'après Jean-Luc Godard*, Paris: POL, 1999, p. 60.

10. See Bresson, Robert, *Notes sur le cinématographe*, Paris: Gallimard-Folio, 1975, p. 52. The range of the term "montage" in Godard is vast, as Michael Witt shows in "Montage, My Beautiful Care, or Histories of the Cinematograph", in Temple and Williams, *The Cinema Alone*, pp. 33-50.

11. See Benjamin, Walter, *Gesammelte Schriften*, Rolf Tiedemann and Hermann Schweppenhaüser trans., 7 vols., Frankfurt: Suhrkamp, 1991, I, p. 2, p. 701. Importantly, Benjamin links the *Jetztzeit* precisely to the redemptive function of citation, and illustrates the point by citing the figure of Robespierre citing ancient Rome. As Benjamin explains some pages earlier: "the past becomes quotable in each of its lived moments only for redeemed humanity. Each lived moment turns into a mention in dispatches [*citation à l'ordre du jour*] for the day that is the day of judgement," (p. 694). On Godard's familiarity with this text, see Bergala, *Nul mieux que Godard*, pp. 221-222.

12. See *Godard par Godard*, II, p. 372. Sontag's attempt to stage Beckett's play in Bosnia was widely reported at the time; see for instance "En attendant Godot à Sarajevo", *Le Monde*, 25 August 1993. Sollers's reply (in the course of a review of Marivaux's plays) appeared in *Le Monde*, 20 May 1994, and is reproduced in *La Guerre du goût*, Paris: Gallimard-Folio, 1996, pp. 546-550.

13. See Godard, Jean-Luc, *For Ever Mozart: phrases*, Paris: POL, 1996, p. 46.

14. In Musset's play, Camille and Perdican (like Camille and Jérôme in Godard's film) are cousins; Perdican's father wishes his son and niece to marry; the pair play a series of bittersweet games with this possibility, with Camille threatening to return to her convent and Perdican intending to marry Camille's foster-sister, Rosette (to be played in Godard's version of the play by Djamila, Vicky's maid). By heartlessly involving Rosette in their games, the pair provoke her death.

15. Godard, *For Ever Mozart*, pp. 56-57.

16. "La philosophie serait notre compagne, à jamais, le jour, et la nuit, même si elle perd son nom, même si elle s'absente, une amie clandestine dont nous respectons ce qui ne nous permet pas d'être liés à elle, tout en pressentant que nous ne sommes pas réveillés, que ce qu'il y a de vigilant en nous, même dans le sommeil, est dû à son amitié difficile." Blanchot's essay first appeared under the title "Notre compagne clandestine" in *Textes pour Emmanuel Lévinas*, François Laruelle ed., Paris: Jean-Michel Place, 1980, pp. 79-87. The passage quoted appears in Godard, *For Ever Mozart*, pp. 65-66. Oddly, in an interview with Alain Bergala and Serge Toubiana (in *Godard par Godard*, II, p. 379), Godard attributes the quotation to Levinas. One of the few commentators to notice the quotation was Christophe Bident, in *Maurice Blanchot: partenaire invisible*, Seyssel: Champ Vallon, 1998, p. 458. The original text (slightly modified by Godard) is as follows: "La philosophie serait notre compagne à jamais, de jour, de nuit, fût-ce en perdant son nom, devenant littérature, savoir, non-savoir, ou s'absentant, notre amie clandestine dont nous respections–aimions–ce qui ne nous permettait pas d'être liés à elle, tout en pressentant qu'il n'y avait rien d'éveillé en nous, de vigilant jusque dans le sommeil, qui ne fût dû à son amitié difficile". (p. 80)

17. Blanchot, "Notre compagne clandestine", pp. 86-87. The solidarity between Blanchot and Godard is not limited to the challenge of remembering the Shoah. It also extends to their denunciation of the French colonial presence in Algeria. It is now widely known that Blanchot was largely responsible for drafting the text of the *Manifeste des 121*, which at the time Godard admittedly failed to sign, but which he goes on to cite elsewhere, notably in *Masculin Féminin* ("one of the 121 French talking movies of which only three or four are ever made", according to the opening title) and in *JLG/JLG*; see Godard, Jean-Luc, *JLG/JLG: phrases*, Paris: POL, 1996, p. 24. Blanchot and Godard, in different ways, were also closely involved in the *événements* of May 68. More recently, together with Godard and Miéville, Blanchot was a signatory of a petition against French laws on immigration initiated by Pascale Ferrand and Arnaud Desplechin in February 1997; see Phil Powrie, "Heritage, History, and 'New Realism'", in *French Cinema in the 1990s*, Phil Powrie ed., Oxford: Oxford University Press, 1999, pp. 10-14.

18. See CF Ramuz, *Oeuvres complètes*, Gustave Roud and Daniel Simond eds., 20 vols., Lausanne: Éditions Rencontre, 1967, IX, pp. 7-134.

19. It goes without saying that nowhere in Ramuz's novel is the cinema in fact mentioned! An outline for a film based on the book appeared in the special 1991 issue of *Cahiers du cinéma* on Godard, "Trente ans depuis" (p. 10).

20. Blanchot, Maurice, *L'Amitié*, Paris: Gallimard, 1971, p. 118; *Friendship*, Elizabeth Rottenberg trans., Stanford: Stanford University Press, 1997, p. 101.

21. Péguy, Charles, *Oeuvres en prose 1909-1914*, Marcel Péguy ed., Paris: Gallimard-Pléiade, 1961, p. 242.

22. On the making of *Faces*, see Carney, Ray, *The Films of John Cassavetes*, Cambridge: Cambridge University Press, 1994, pp. 74-113. Godard dedicates Chapter 1B, *Une histoire seule*, to Cassavetes (and Glauber Rocha).

23. For de Gaulle's own account of the visit to Bayeux, which marked his transformation from wartime general to future political leader, see *Mémoires de guerre, II: L'Unité 1942-44*, Paris: Plon, 1956, pp. 229-232.

24. On the background to the photograph, see Bident, *Maurice Blanchot: partenaire invisible*, pp. 535-536. Blanchot comments on his refusal to be photographed in public in a letter to Blandine Jeanson published the following year, in which he declined the invitation to contribute a photograph to the exhibition catalogue *Photographes en quête d'auteur: 66 portraits de la littérature francophone contemporaine*, Paris: Agence Vu, 1986. In a text reproduced in facsimile in the volume, he explains as follows: "I have always tried, with more or less good reason, to appear in public as little as possible, not in order to glorify my books, but to avoid the presence of an author who might lay claim to an existence of his own."

25. See Eisner, Lotte H, *FW Murnau*, Paris: Le Terrain Vague, 1964, p. 16. The book is dedicated to Henri Langlois.

26. It will be remembered that already in *Alphaville* in 1965 the French-speaking Nazi-Soviet-American dictator, Professor Léonard Von Braun (Howard Vernon), is addressed by Lemmy Caution (Eddie Constantine) as Monsieur Nosferatu.

27. See Bresson, *Notes sur le cinématographe*, p. 104: "Ne pas montrer tous les côtés des choses. Marge d'indéfini."

28. See Blanchot, *L'Amitié*, p. 48, pp. 50-51; *Friendship*, p. 37, p. 40 (translation modified). In quoting from Blanchot, Godard again makes changes, substituting cinema for Blanchot's work [*oeuvre*], and deleting some two-and-a-half pages between the second and third sentences, as well as several sub-clauses and a number of other expressions. Blanchot's original essay, "Le Musée, l'art et le temps", was the third in a sequence of essays on Malraux from 1946 onwards and first appeared in two parts in *Critique*, 43, December 1950, pp. 195-208, and 44, January 1951, pp. 30-42. The argument closely resembles that presented in the essay "Les Deux Versions de l'Imaginaire", written the same year, and republished four years later in *L'Espace littéraire*, Paris: Gallimard, 1955, pp. 266-277; *The Space of Literature*, Ann Smock trans., Lincoln and London, University of Nebraska Press, 1982, pp. 254-263. Blanchot's dialogue with Malraux is implicit in a number of the writer's Post-War fictional texts, too, as I argue in my *Bataille, Klossowski, Blanchot: Writing at the Limit*, Oxford: Oxford University Press, 2001, pp. 189-191. For a discussion of Godard's borrowing from Blanchot, which he reprises in *The Old Place* made in collaboration with Anne-Marie Miéville in 1999 (in which the same unidentified shot of the undead also recurs, followed soon after by a quotation from Henry James which itself is probably drawn from an essay by Blanchot published in *Le Monde* for 22 July 1983), and in the second half of *Éloge de l'amour*, 2001, see Godard, Jean-Luc and Ishaghpour, Youssef, *Archéologie du cinéma et mémoire du siècle*, Tours: Farrago, 2000, pp. 82-83.

29. On the uses to which Malraux is put in *Histoire(s)*, see Temple, Michael, "Big Rhythm and the Power of Metamorphosis", in Temple and Williams, *The Cinema Alone*, pp. 77-95.

30. Malraux, André, in *Esquisse d'une psychologie du cinéma*, Paris: Gallimard, 1946, n.p. The passage recurs in Malraux, *Le Musée imaginaire*, Paris: Gallimard-Folio, 1965, p. 86. Other points of convergence between Malraux and Godard include the condemnation of sound and the rejection of filmed theatre. Godard's attacks on television follow much the same logic as Malraux's attack on talking pictures.

31. On the importance of these two Egyptian monuments for Malraux's aesthetic theory, see Malraux, *Antimémoires*, Paris: Gallimard-Folio, 1972, pp. 45-47.

32. The ambiguity of myth, as Godard will have been aware, is an abiding theme in Pre-War ethnographic and anthropological thinking in France; see for instance Roger Caillois's classic study *L'Homme et le sacré*, Paris: Gallimard-Folio, 1950 [1939].

33. Blanchot, *L'Amitié*, p. 51, *Friendship*, p. 40 (translation modified).

34. On the neutre in Blanchot, see my *Blanchot: Extreme Contemporary*, pp. 127-142. On the image in Blanchot, see Marie-Claire Ropars-Wuilleumier, "Sur le désoeuvrement: l'image dans l'écrire selon Blanchot", *Littérature*, 94, May 1994, pp. 113-124; and for a suggestive discussion of Blanchot's two versions of the imaginary, see Wall, Thomas Carl, *Radical Passivity, Levinas, Blanchot, and Agamben*, Albany: State University of New York Press, 1999.

35. See Adorno, TW, *Gesammelte Schriften, 10, 1: Kulturkritik und Gesellschaft I*, Frankfurt: Suhrkamp, 1977, p. 250. As readers will know, Adorno remained sceptical as to whether an analysis exclusively made up of quotations, which is how (perhaps inaccurately) he presents Benjamin's project, was feasible at all. Adorno's question is one that must no doubt be asked of *Histoire(s)*, albeit that Godard's text is not exclusively made up of quotations, far from it, but which similarly, at least on occasion, ascribes to montage (and cinema) alone the capacity to think, to make propositions, and construct arguments. On some of the parallels between *Histoire(s)* and Benjamin's *Passagen-Werk*, see Godard and Ishaghpour, *Archéologie du cinéma et mémoire du siècle*, pp. 18-19. Crucial here, of course, is the status of Godard's own commentary on the materials cited and reworked in *Histoire(s)*: authoritative intervention, whimsical gloss, or provocatively abysmal self-citation?

SELECTIVE BIBLIOGRAPHY

Works by Jean-Luc Godard, including short texts not included in *Jean-Luc Godard par Jean-Luc Godard* I and II

——and Macha, Méril, *Journal d'une femme mariée*, Paris: Denoël, 1965.

The Married Woman, New York: Berkley Medallion, 1965.

"Présentation de *La Chinoise*", in Collet, Jean, *Jean-Luc Godard*, Paris: Séghers, 1968, pp. 104-107.

"Présentation de Week-end", in Collet, Jean, *Jean-Luc Godard*, Paris: Séghers, 1968, pp. 116-119.

"Pas de vrai plaisir sans Perrier", *J'accuse*, 1, 15 January 1971, p. 11.

"Nantes-Batignolles: Un bond en avant", *J'accuse*, 2, 15 February 1971, p. 4.

Special Issue of *Cahiers du cinéma*, 300, May 1979.

Introduction à une véritable histoire du cinéma, Paris: Éditions Albatros, 1980.

"*France/tour/détour/deux/enfants*: Déclaration à l'intention des héritiers", *Caméra Stylo*, September 1983, pp. 64-65.

Jean-Luc Godard par Jean-Luc Godard I (1950-1984), Alain Bergala ed., Paris: Cahiers du Cinéma/Éditions de l'Étoile, 1985. (Includes and supplements material published earlier in three parts by Flammarion under the general title *Godard par Godard*: *Les années Cahiers, Les années Karina, Des années Mao aux années 80*.) Reprinted in 1998 with an additional text, "Le cercle rouge".

Godard on Godard [1972], Tom Milne and Jean Narboni trans. and eds., New York: Da Capo, 1986 (texts from 1950 to 1968).

"Notes parmi d'autres", *Le Monde Radio-Télévision*, 22-23 June 1986, p. 17.

"Lettre numéro un aux membres de la commission d'avance sur recettes. Premières remarques sur la production et la réalisation du film *Sauve qui peut (la vie)*", *Cahiers du cinéma*, 477, March 1994 [1979], p. 58.

"Dernière Minute", *Cinématographe*, 1995, pp. 32-33.

JLG/JLG: phrases, Paris: POL, 1996.

For Ever Mozart: phrases, Paris: POL, 1996.

"Lettre aux *Cahiers*", *Cahiers du Cinéma*, 508, 1996, pp. 14-27.

"Sans-papiers: avant qu'il ne soit trop tard" (with Patrice Chéreau, Anne-Marie Miéville and Stanislas Nordey), *Le Monde*, 13 May 1998, p. 1.

2x50 ans de cinéma français: phrases, Paris: POL, 1998.

Allemagne neuf zéro: phrases, Paris: POL, 1998.

Les enfants jouent à la Russie: phrases, Paris: POL, 1998.

Jean-Luc Godard par Jean-Luc Godard II (1984-1998), Alain Bergala ed., Paris: Cahiers du cinéma, 1998.

Histoire(s) du cinéma, 4 vols., Paris: Gallimard-Gaumont, 1998.

——and Youssef Ishaghpour, *Archéologie du cinéma et mémoire du siècle*, Tours: Farrago, 2000.

Éloge de l'amour: phrases, Paris: POL, 2001.

——and Emmanuel Burdeau, Christiane Meyer-Thoss and Charles Tesston, *The Future(s) of Film: Three Interviews 2000/01*, Constance Lotz ed., John O' Toole trans., Bern: Gachnang & Springer, 2002.

Critical Works on Jean-Luc Godard

Achard, Maurice, *Vous avez dit Godard?*, Paris: Libres-Halliers, 1980.

Albéra, François ed., *Jean-Luc Godard*, Munich: Carl Hanser Verlag, 1979.

Amengual, Barthélémy, *Bande à part*, Brussels: Yellow Now, 1993.

Andrew, Dudley, ed. *Breathless*, New Brunswick: Rutgers University Press, 1995.

Aumont, Jacques, "Godard peintre, ou l'avant-dernier artiste", in *L'Oeil Interminable: Cinéma et Peinture*, Paris: Séguier, 1989, pp. 223-247.

——, "La mort de Dante", *Cinémas* (Canada), 8:1-2, 1997, pp. 125-145.

——*Amnésies: Fictions du cinéma d'après Jean-Luc Godard*, Paris: POL, 1999.

Bellour, Raymond, *L'Entre-Images: Photo. Cinéma. Vidéo.*, Paris: La Différence, 1990, pp. 327-387.

——and Mary Lea Bandy eds., *Jean-Luc Godard: Son+Image 1974-1991*, New York: Museum of Modern Art, 1992.

——*L'Entre-Images 2: Mots, Images*, Paris: POL, 1999.

Bergala, Alain, *Nul mieux que Godard*, Paris: Cahiers du Cinéma, 1999.

Bersani, Leo, *Forming Couples: Godard's Contempt*, Oxford: European Humanities Research Centre, 2004.

——and Ulysse Dutoit, *Forms of Being: Cinema, Aesthetics, Subjectivity*, London: British Film Institute, 2004.

Brown, Royal S ed., *Focus on Godard*, Englewood Cliffs, NJ: Prentice-Hall, 1972.

Buache, Freddy, "De Godard à Jean-Luc", *Revue Belge du Cinéma*, Winter 1985, pp. 50-62.

——"Jean-Luc Godard et Anne-Marie Miéville", in *Trente ans de cinéma suisse 1965-1995*, Paris: Centre Georges Pompidou, 1995, pp. 117-123.

——"La rumeur des distances traversées", *Cinémathèque*, 8, 1995, pp. 43-49.

Cameron, Ian ed., *The Films of Jean-Luc Godard*, London: Studio Vista, 1967.

Cannon, Steve, "Godard, the Groupe Dziga Vertov and the myth of 'Counter-Cinema'", *Nottingham French Studies*, 32:1, Spring 1993, pp. 74-83.

Cerisuelo, Marc, *Jean-Luc Godard*, Paris: Lherminier/Quatre-Vents, 1989.

Collet, Jean, *Jean-Luc Godard: An Investigation into his Films and Philosophy*, New York: Crown, 1970.

Coureau, Didier, *Jean-Luc Godard 1990-1995: Nouvelle Vague, Hélas pour moi, JLG/JLG. Complexité esthétique, esthétique de la complexité*, Paris: Presses Universitaires du Septentrion, 2000.

Cunningham, Stuart, and Ross Harley, "The Logic of the Virgin Mother", *Screen*, 28:1, Winter 1987, pp. 62-76.

Daney, Serge, "Le thérrorisé (pédagogie godardienne)", *Cahiers du cinéma*, 262-3, 1976, pp. 32-39.

Deleuze, Gilles, *Cinema 2: The Time-Image* [1985], Hugh Tomlinson and Robert Galeta trans., London: Athlone Press, 1989.

Delavaud, Gilles, Jean-Pierre Esquenazi and Marie-Françoise Grange eds., *Godard et le métier d'artiste* (Actes du colloque de Cerisy), Paris: L'Harmattan, 2001.

Desbarats, Carole, and Jean-Pierre Gorce eds., *L'Effet-Godard*, Toulouse: Éditions Milan, 1989.

Dior, Julie, "À la poursuite du je: *JLG/JLG*", *Cinémathèque*, 12, 1998, pp. 24-33.

Dixon, Wheeler Winston, *The Films of Jean-Luc Godard*, Albany: State University of New York Press, 1997.

Douin, Jean-Luc, *Godard*, Paris: Rivages, 1989.

Durgnat, Raymond, "Jean-Luc Godard: His Crucifixion and Resurrection", *Monthly Film Bulletin*, 620, September 1985, pp. 268-271.

Eisenschitz, Bernard, "'Une machine à montrer l'invisible': Conversation à propos des *Histoire(s) du cinéma*", *Cahiers du cinéma*, 529, 1998, pp. 52-56.

Farber, Manny, "Jean-Luc Godard", in *Negative Space: Manny Farber on the Movies*, New York: Da Capo Press, 1998, pp. 259-268.

Gervais, Marc, "Jean-Luc Godard 1985: These Are Not The Days", *Sight and Sound*, 53:4, Autumn 1985, pp. 278-283.

Giannetti, Louis, *Godard and Others: Essays on Film Form*, New Jersey: Associated University Presses, 1975.

Guzzetti, Alfred, *Two or Three Things I know about Her: Analysis of a film by Godard*, London and Cambridge MA: Harvard University Press, 1981.

Harcourt, Peter, "Le nouveau Godard: An exploration of *Sauve qui peut (la vie)*", *Film Quarterly*, 35:2, Winter 1981-1982, pp. 17-27.

——"Calculated Approximations of Possibilities: Rhetorical strategies in the late films of Jean-Luc Godard", *Cineaction*, 48, 1998, pp. 8-17.

Henderson, Brian, "Towards a Non-Bourgeois Camera Style", *Film Quarterly*, 24:2, Winter 1970-1971, pp. 2-14.

Ipacki, David, "Le Verbe ressuscité et l'image crucifiée: *JLG/JLG* de Jean-Luc Godard", *Cinémathèque*, 8, 1995, pp. 33-42.

Jameson, Fredric, "High-Tech Collectives in Late Godard", in *The Geopolitical Aesthetic: cinema and space in the world system*, Bloomington, Indianapolis and London: Indiana University Press/British Film Institute, 1992, pp. 158-185.

Kreidl, John Francis, *Jean-Luc Godard*, Boston: Twayne, 1980.

Kwietniowski, Richard, "Between Love and Labour", *Screen*, 24:6, November-December 1983, pp. 52-69.

Lack, Roland-François, "The Point in Time: Precise Chronology in Early Godard", *Studies in French Cinema*, 3:2, 2003, pp. 101-109.

Leblanc, Gérard, "godard: valeur d'usage ou valeur d'échange", *Cinéthique*, 5, September-October 1969, p. 22.

Lefèvre, Raymond, *Jean-Luc Godard*, Paris: Edilig, 1983.

Lesage, Julia, *Jean-Luc Godard: a guide to references and resources*, Boston: GK Hall, 1979.

Leutrat, Jean-Louis, *Des traces qui nous ressemblent: Passion de Jean-Luc Godard*, Seyssel: Éditions Comp'Act, 1990.

——"*Histoire(s) du cinéma*, ou comment devenir maître d'un souvenir", *Cinémathèque*, 5, 1994, pp. 19-24.

——*Jean-Luc Godard, un cinéaste mallarméen*, Paris: Schena-Didier Érudition, 1998.

Locke, Maryel and Charles Warren eds., *HAIL MARY: Women and the Sacred in Film*, Carbondale: Southern Illinois Press, 1993.

Loshitzky, Yosefa, *The Radical Faces of Godard and Bertolucci*, Detroit: Wayne State University Press, 1995.

MacBean, James Roy, *Film and Revolution*, Bloomington: Indiana University Press, 1975.

MacCabe, Colin, "The Politics of Separation", *Screen*, 16:4, Winter 1975-1976, pp. 46-61.

——(with Mick Eaton and Laura Mulvey), *Godard: Images, Sounds, Politics*, London: British Film Institute/MacMillan, 1980.

——*Godard: A Portrait of the Artist at 70*, London: Bloomsbury, 2003.

Marie, Michel, "'It really makes you sick!': Jean-Luc Godard's *À bout de souffle* (1959)", in *French Film: Texts and Contents*, Susan Hayward and Ginette Vincendeau eds., London: Routledge, 1990, pp. 201-215.

——*Le Mépris: Jean-Luc Godard–étude critique*, Paris: Nathan, 1990.

——*À bout de souffle: Jean-Luc Godard–étude critique*, Paris: Nathan, 1999.

Martin, Adrian, "Godard: The Musical", *CinemaScope*, June 2001.

——"Scanning Godard", *Screening the Past*, 2000, www.latrobe.edu.au/screeningthepast/reviews/rev0600/ambr10a.htm.

Milne, Tom ed., *Godard on Godard*, London: Secker and Warburg, 1972.

Monaco, James, *The New Wave: Truffaut, Godard, Chabrol, Rohmer, Rivette*, New York: Oxford University Press, 1976.

Morrey, Douglas, "History of resistance/resistance of history: Godard's *Éloge de l'amour* (2001)", *Studies in French Cinema*, 3:2, 2003, 121-130.

Moullet, Luc, "Jean-Luc Godard", *Cahiers du cinéma*, 106, 1960, pp. 25-36.

Mussman, Toby ed., *Jean-Luc Godard: a critical anthology*, New York: EP Dutton, 1968.

Nesbitt, Molly, "History Without Object", in *Art and Film Since 1945: Hall of Mirrors*, Kerry Brougher ed., New York: Monacelli Press/Los Angeles: Museum of Contemporary Art, 1996, pp. 280-297.

Pajaczkowska, Claire, "Liberté! Égalité! Paternité!: Jean-Luc Godard's *Sauve qui peut (la vie)*", in *French Film: Texts and Contexts*, Susan Hayward and Ginette Vincendeau eds., London: Routledge, 1990, pp. 241-255.

Rafferty, Terrence, "Double Godard: The director revisits *Alphaville* and presents a self-portrait", *The New Yorker*, 6 February 1995, pp. 92-96.

Rancière, Jacques, "La sainte et l'héritière: À propos des *Histoire(s) du cinéma*", *Cahiers du cinéma*, 536, 1999, pp. 58-61. Translated by TS Murphy as "The Saint and the Heiress: A propos of Godard's *Histoire(s) du cinéma*", *Discourse*, 24:1, 2002, pp. 113-119.

Robbins, Alex, "'Ce colporteur c'était le cinéma': Remembrance and Rebirth in Jean-Luc Godard's *Les Signes parmi nous*", *French Studies Bulletin*, 87, 2003, pp. 2-8.

Robinson, Marc, "Resurrected Images: Godard's *King Lear*", *Performing Arts Journal*, 11:1, 1988, pp. 20-26.

Roloff, Volkor and Scarlett Winter eds., *Godard Intermedial*, Tübingen: Stauffenburg, 1997.

Ropars-Wuilleumier, Marie-Claire, "Totalité et fragmentaire: La réécriture selon Godard", *Hors Cadre*, 6, 1988, pp. 193-207.

Rosenbaum, Jonathan, "Theory and Practice: The criticism of Jean-Luc Godard", *Sight and Sound*, 41:3, Summer 1972, pp. 124-126.

——"*Numéro deux*", *Sight and Sound*, 45:2, Spring 1976, pp. 124-125.

——"Trailer for Godard's *Histoire(s) du cinéma*", *Vertigo*, 7, 1997, pp 12-20.

——"Godard in the 90s: an interview, argument, and scrapbook", *Film Comment*, 34:5, September/October 1998, pp. 52-61.

——"Le vrai coupable: two kinds of criticism in Godard's work", *Screen*, 40:3, Autumn 1999, pp. 316-322.

Roud, Richard, *Jean-Luc Godard*, Bloomington: Indiana University Press, 1969.

Sanbar, Elias, "Vingt et un ans après", *Trafic*, 1, Winter 1991, pp. 109-119.

Shafto, Sally, "Saut dans le vide: Godard et le peintre", *Cinémathèque*, 16, 1999, pp. 92-107.

Silverman, Kaja, "The Author as Receiver", *October*, 96, 2001, pp. 17-34.

——and Harun Farocki, *Speaking about Godard*, New York: New York University Press, 1998.

Skoller, Jeffrey, "Reinventing Time, Or The continuing Adventures of Lemmy Caution in Godard's *Germany Year 90 nine zero*", *Film Quarterly*, 3:3, 1999, pp. 35-42.

Sollers, Philippe, "*JLG/JLG*: un cinéma de l'être-là", *Cahiers du cinéma*, 489, 1994, pp. 37-39.

Sontag, Susan, "Going to the movies: Godard", *Partisan Review*, Spring 1968, 2, pp. 290-313.

——"Godard", in *Styles of Radical Will*, New York: Farrar, Strauss and Giroux, 1969, pp. 147-185.

Stam, Robert, *Reflexivity in Film and Literature: From Don Quixote to Jean-Luc Godard*, New York: Columbia University Press, 1992.

Sterritt, David ed., *Jean-Luc Godard: Interviews*, Jackson: University of Mississippi Press, 1998.

——*The Films of Jean-Luc Godard: Seeing the Invisible*, New York: Cambridge University Press, 1999.

Taubin, Amy, "In the Shadow of Memory", *Film Comment*, 38:1, January-February 2002, pp. 50-52.

Temple, Michael, "It will be worth it", *Sight and Sound*, 8:1, January 1998, pp. 20-23.

——and James S Williams, "Jean-Luc Godard: Images, Words, Histories", *Dalhousie French Studies*, 45, Winter 1998, pp. 99-110.

——"The Nutty Professor: teaching film with Jean-Luc Godard", *Screen*, 40:3, Autumn 1999, pp. 323-330.

Theweleit, Klaus, *One+One*, Berlin: Brinkmann & Bose, 1995.

Toffetti, Sergio ed., *Jean-Luc Godard*, Turin: Centre Culturel Français de Turin, 1990.

Touratier, Jean-Marie and Daniel Busto eds., *Jean-Luc Godard–Télévision/Ecritures*, Paris: Galilée, 1979.

Vianey, Michel, *En attendant Godard*, Paris: Grasset, 1966.

Wacjman, Gérard, "'Saint Paul' Godard contre 'Moïse' Lanzmann, le match", *l'Infini*, 65, 1999, pp. 121-127.

White, Armond, "Double Helix: Jean-Luc Godard", *Film Comment*, 32:2, March-April 1996, pp. 26-30.

Wills, David ed., *Jean-Luc Godard's* Pierrot le fou, Cambridge: Cambridge University Press, 2000.

Williams, Christopher, "Politics and Production: Some pointers through the work of Jean-Luc Godard", *Screen*, 12:4, 1977, pp. 62-80.

Williams, James S, "The Signs Amongst Us: Jean-Luc Godard's *Histoire(s) du cinéma*", *Screen*, 40:3, Autumn 1999, pp. 306-315.

——"Beyond the Cinematic Body: human emotion vs. digital technology in Jean-Luc Godard's *Histoire(s) du cinéma*", in *Inhuman Reflections*, Scott Brewster, John J Joughin, David Owen and Richard Walker eds., Manchester: Manchester University Press, 2000, pp. 188-202.

——and Michael Temple eds., *The Cinema Alone: essays on the work of Jean-Luc Godard* 1985-2000, Amsterdam: Amsterdam University Press, 2000.

Witt, Michael, "Godard, le cinéma et l'ethnologie: ou l'objet et sa reproduction", in Christopher Thompson ed., *L'Autre et le sacré: surréalisme, cinéma, ethnologie*, Paris: L'Harmattan, 1995, pp. 369-378.

——"On Communication: The Work of Anne-Marie Miéville and Jean-Luc Godard as 'Sonimage' from 1973 to 1979", unpublished PhD Dissertation, University of Bath, 1998.

——"On Gilles Deleuze on Jean-Luc Godard: an Interrogation of 'la méthode du ENTRE'", *Australian Journal of French Studies*, 36:1, 1999, pp. 110-124.

——"The death(s) of cinema according to Godard", *Screen*, 40:3, Autumn 1999, pp. 331-346.

——"Qu'était-ce que le cinéma, Jean-Luc Godard? An analysis of the cinema(s) at work in and around Godard's *Histoire(s) du cinéma*", in *France in Focus: Cinema and National Identity*, Elizabeth Ezra and Susan Harris eds., Oxford: Berg, 2000 pp. 23-41.

——"In praise of JLG", *Sight and Sound*, 14:2, February 2004, pp. 8-9

Wollen, Peter, *Readings and Writings: Semiotic Counter Strategies*, London: Verso, 1982.

——, 'JLG', in *Paris-Hollywood: Writings on Film*, London, Verso, 2002, pp. 74-92.

Wood, Robin, "Jean-Luc Godard", *New Left Review*, 39, November-December 1966, pp. 77-83

——"In Defense of Art", *Film Comment*, 11:4, July-August 1975, pp. 44-51.

Periodicals: special issues on Jean-Luc Godard

"Jean-Luc Godard: au-delà du récit", *Études cinématographiques*, 57-61, 1967.

"Jean-Luc Godard", *Image et Son*, 211, December 1967.

"Jean-Luc Godard", *Wide Angle*, 1:3, 1976, pp. 4-52.

"Jean-Luc Godard and Anne-Marie Miéville", *Camera Obscura: A Journal of Feminism and Film Theory*, 8-9-10, Fall, 1982.

"Dossier: Jean-Luc Godard", *Cinématographe* (Paris), 95, 1983.

"Godard" (Special Issue 4), *Art Press*, December 1984-February 1985.

"Godard", *L'Avant-Scène Cinéma*, 323-4, 1984.

"Jean-Luc Godard: les Films", *Revue Belge du Cinéma*, 16, 1986.

"Jean-Luc Godard: Le Cinéma", *Revue Belge du Cinéma*, 22-23, 1988.

"Le Cinéma selon Jean-Luc Godard", *CinémAction*, 52, 1989.

"Spécial Godard–Trente ans depuis", *Cahiers du cinéma* (hors série), November 1990.

"Godard", *Blimp*, 21, Autumn 1992.

"Jean-Luc Godard: Au-delà de l'image", *Études cinématographiques*, 194-202, 1993.

"*Histoire(s) du cinéma* de Jean-Luc Godard", *Cahiers du cinéma*, 513, May 1997.

"JLG", *Vertigo*, 7, Autumn 1997.

"Godard, toutes les histoire(s) qu'il y aurait", *Cahiers du cinéma*, 529, November 1998.

"Le Siècle de Jean-Luc Godard: Guide pour *Histoire(s) du cinéma*", *Art Press*, hors série, November 1998.

"Spécial *Histoire(s) du cinéma*", *Cahiers du cinéma*, 537, July-August 1999.

"The Godard dossier", *Screen*, 40:3, Autumn 1999.

"Où en est le God-Art?", *CinémAction*, 109, 2003.

PICTURE CREDITS

p. 31 (b): *La Chinoise*, 1967. Directed by Jean-Luc Godard. Production: Anouchka Films, Les Productions de la Guéville, Athos Films, Parc Films, Simar Films. Collection *L'Avant-Scène Cinéma*.

p. 32 (a): *Caméra-oeil*, 1967. Directed by Jean-Luc Godard. Produced by Chris Marker. Production: SLON. Collection *L'Avant-Scène Cinéma*.

p. 32 (b): *L'Aller et retour andate e ritorno des enfants prodigues dei figli prodighi*, 1967. Directed by Jean-Luc Godard. Produced by Carlo Lizzani. Production: Castoro Films, Anouchka Films. Collection *L'Avant-Scène Cinéma*.

p. 33 (a): *Week-end*, 1967. Directed by Jean-Luc Godard. Production: Films Copernic, Ascot Cineraïd, Comacico, Lira Films. Collection *L'Avant-Scène Cinéma*.

p. 33 (b): Double page from Jean-Luc Godard, *le gai savoir (mot-à-mot d'un film encore trop réviso)*, Paris: Union des Écrivains, 1969. Collection Michael Witt.

p. 34 (a): *Ciné-tract*, 1968. Directed by Jean-Luc Godard.

p. 34 (b): *Un film comme les autres*, 1968. Directed by Jean-Luc Godard. Production: Anouchka Films. Collection Philippe Dubois.

p. 35 (a): *One Plus One*, 1968. Directed by Jean-Luc Godard. Produced by Iain Quarrier and Michael Pearson. Production: Cupid Productions. Collection *L'Avant-Scène Cinéma*.

p. 35 (b): Production photograph depicting Richard Leacock and Jean-Luc Godard during the making of *One American Movie*, 1968. Collection *Cahiers du cinéma*.

p. 36 (a): *British Sounds*, 1969. Directed by Jean-Luc Godard and Jean-Henri Roger. Produced by Irving Teitelbaum and Kenith Trodd. Production: Kestrel Productions for LWT. Collection Philippe Dubois.

p. 36 (b): *Pravda*, 1969. Directed by Paul Bourron, Jean-Luc Godard, and Jean-Henri Roger. Produced by Claude Nedjar. Production: Centre Européen Cinéma-Radio-Télévision. Collection Philippe Dubois.

p. 37 (a): *Vent d'est*, 1969. Directed by Jean-Luc Godard, Jean-Pierre Gorin, and Gérard Martin. Production: CCC, Poli Film Kunst, Anouchka Films. Collection Philippe Dubois.

p. 37 (b): *Lotte in Italia*, 1969. Directed by Jean-Luc Godard and Jean-Pierre Gorin. Production: Anouchka Films, Cosmoseion for Radiotelevisione Italiana. Collection Philippe Dubois.

p. 38 (a): *Vladimir et Rosa*, 1971. Directed by Jean-Luc Godard and Jean-Pierre Gorin. Production: Munich Tele-Pool, Grove Press Evergreen Films. Collection Philippe Dubois.

p. 38 (b): Lobby card for *Tout va bien*, 1972. Directed by Jean-Luc Godard and Jean-Pierre Gorin. Distributed by Gaumont. Collection Steve Cannon.

p. 39 (a): Sequence of portraits used in *Letter to Jane*, 1972. Produced and directed by Jean-Luc Godard and Jean-Pierre Gorin. Collection BFI Stills.

p. 39 (b): Extract from the storyboard for *Jusqu'à la victoire*. Authors: Jean-Luc Godard and Jean-Pierre Gorin. First published in *Take One*, 2/11, 1970, pp. 7-9. Collection Roland-François Lack.

p. 39 (c): *Ici et Ailleurs*, 1974. Directed by Jean-Luc Godard and Anne-Marie Miéville. A Gaumont production. Courtesy Gaumont.

p. 40 (a): U.K. poster for *Numéro Deux*, 1975. Directed by Jean-Luc Godard. Distributed by The Other Cinema. Collection Michael Temple.

p. 40 (b): *Comment ça va?*, 1975. Directed by Jean-Luc Godard and Anne-Marie Miéville. Produced by Jean-Luc Godard, Anne-Marie Miéville, and Jean-Pierre Rassam. Production: Sonimage, Bela, SNC. Photographs: Michael Witt.

p. 41 (a): *Six fois deux (Sur et sous la communication)*, 1976. Directed by Jean-Luc Godard and Anne-Marie Miéville. Produced by Jean-Luc Godard and Michel Raux. Production: Institut National de l'Audiovisuel, Sonimage. Photographs: Michael Witt.

p. 41 (b): "Faut pas rêver" by Patrick Juvet. Released by Barclay, 1976. Cover: Philippe Morillon. Collection Michael Temple.

p. 42 (a): *France/tour/détour/deux/enfants*, 1978. Directed by Jean-Luc Godard and Anne-Marie Miéville. Production: Institut National de l'Audiovisuel, Sonimage. Photographs: Michael Witt.

p. 42 (b): *Scénario vidéo de Sauve qui peut (la vie)*, 1979. Directed by Jean-Luc Godard. Production: Sonimage, Télévision Suisse Romande. Collection Philippe Dubois.

p. 43 (a): Publicity document for Aäton cameras, 1979. Courtesy Aäton.

p. 43 (b): *Passion, le travail et l'amour: introduction à un scenario*, 1979. Directed by Jean-Luc Godard. Production: Sonimage. Photograph: Jean-Jacques Henry. Collection *Cahiers du cinéma*.

p. 44 (a): Set of Godard playing cards distributed at the time of the release of *Lettre à Freddy Buache*, 1982. Photograph: Michael Witt. Collection Muriel Tinel.

p. 44 (b): Production photograph taken during the making of *Passion*, 1982. Directed by Jean-Luc Godard. Photograph: Anne-Marie Miéville. Collection *Cahiers du cinéma*.

p. 45 (a): *Scénario du film Passion*, 1982. Directed by Jean-Luc Godard. Production: Télévision Romande, JLG Films. Collection Philippe Dubois.

p. 45 (b): *Changer d'image*, 1982. Directed by Jean-Luc Godard. Production: Institut National de l'Audiovisuel, Sonimage. Photographs: Michael Witt.

p. 46 (a): Lobby card for *Prénom Carmen*, 1983. Directed by Jean-Luc Godard. Distributed by Parafrance. Collection Michael Witt.

p. 46 (b): *Petites notes à propos du film Je vous salue, Marie*, 1983. Directed by Jean-Luc Godard. Production: JLG Films. Photograph: Michael Witt.

p. 47 (a): U.K. poster for *Je vous salue, Marie*, 1985. Distributed by The Other Cinema. Collection Michael Witt.

p. 47 (b): U.K. poster for *Détective*, 1985. Distributed by Artificial Eye. Collection Michael Witt.

p. 48 (a): *Soft and Hard*, 1985. Directed by Jean-Luc Godard and Anne-Marie Miéville. Production: Deptford Beach Production, Channel 4, JLG Films. Photographs: Michael Witt.

p. 48 (b): Production photograph taken during the making of *Grandeur et décadence d'un petit commerce de cinéma*, 1986. Directed by Jean-Luc Godard. Photograph: TF1/Patrick Roche. Collection Michael Witt.

p. 49 (a): *Meetin' WA*, 1986. Directed by Jean-Luc Godard. Production: JLG Films. Photographs: Michael Witt.

p. 49 (b): Press book for *Aria*, 1987. Produced by Don Boyd. Distributed by Virgin. Collection Michael Witt.

p. 50 (a): *Soigne ta droite*, 1987. Directed by Jean-Luc Godard. A Gaumont production. Collection Michael Temple. Courtesy Gaumont.

p. 50 (b): Lobby card for *King Lear*, 1987. Directed by Jean-Luc Godard. Distributed by Bodega Films. Collection Michael Temple.

p. 50 (c): Japanese flyer for *King Lear*, 1987. Collection Michael Temple.

p. 51 (a): *Closed*, 1988. Directed by Jean-Luc Godard. Production: JLG Films, Marithé et François Girbaud Design. Photographs: Michael Witt.

p. 51 (b): Marithé et François Girbaud press book. Collection Michael Witt.

p. 51 (c): *On s'est tous défilé*, 1988. Directed by Jean-Luc Godard. Produced by Marithé et François Girbaud Design. Photographs: Michael Witt.

p. 52 (a): *Puissance de la parole*, 1988. Directed by Jean-Luc Godard. Production: France Télécom, JLG Films, Gaumont. Collection *Cahiers du cinéma*.

p. 52 (b): *Le Dernier mot*, 1988. Directed by Jean-Luc Godard.

Produced by Anne-Marie Miéville. Production: Erato Films, Socpresse, JLG Films, *Le Figaro magazine*, Antenne 2. Photographs: Michael Witt.

p. 53 (a): *Histoire(s) du cinéma*, 1998. Directed by Jean-Luc Godard. A Gaumont production. Courtesy Gaumont.

p. 53 (b): *Le Rapport Darty*, 1989. Directed by Jean-Luc Godard and Anne-Marie Miéville. Production: JLG Films, Gaumont. Photographs: Michael Witt.

p. 54 (a): Press book for *Nouvelle Vague*, 1990. Directed by Jean-Luc Godard. Distributed by AMLF. Collection Michael Witt.

p. 54 (b): *L'Enfance de l'art*, 1991. Directed by Jean-Luc Godard and Anne-Marie Miéville. Production: JLG Films, UNICEF. Photographs: Michael Witt.

p. 55 (a): *Allemagne année 90 neuf zero*, 1991. Directed by Jean-Luc Godard. Produced by Nicole Ruelle. Production: Antenne 2, Brainstorm, Gaumont, Périphéria. Collection BFI Stills.

p. 55 (b): *Pour Thomas Wainggai*, 1991. Directed by Jean-Luc Godard and Anne-Marie Miéville. Produced by Amnesty International, Vega Film. Photographs: Michael Witt.

p. 56 (a): Lobby card for *Hélas pour moi*, 1993. Directed by Jean-Luc Godard. Distributed by Pan Européenne. Collection Michael Temple.

p. 56 (b): *Les Enfants jouent à la Russie*, 1993. Directed by Jean-Luc Godard. Produced by Alessandro Cecconi, Ira Barmak, and Ruth Waldburger. Production: Worldvision Enterprises (N.Y.), Cecco Films, RTR. Photographs: Michael Witt.

p. 57 (a): *Je vous salue, Sarajevo*, 1994. Produced and directed by Jean-Luc Godard. Photographs: Michael Witt.

p. 57 (b): *JLG/JLG: autoportrait de décembre*, 1995. Directed by Jean-Luc Godard. A Gaumont production. Courtesy Gaumont.

p. 58 (a): *2x50 ans de cinéma français*, 1995. Directed by Jean-Luc Godard and Anne-Marie Miéville. Produced by Colin MacCabe. Production: British Film Institute, Périphéria, Bob Last. Photographs: Michael Witt.

p. 58 (b): Untitled, 1996. Produced and directed by Jean-Luc Godard. Photographs: Michael Witt.

p. 59: French poster for *For Ever Mozart*, 1996. Directed by Jean-Luc Godard. Distributed by Les Films du Losange. Collection Michael Temple.

p. 60 (a): *Plus Oh!*, 1996. Directed by Jean-Luc Godard.

p. 60 (b): Japanese flyer for *Histoire(s) du cinéma*. Collection Michael Temple.

p. 61 (a): *The Old Place*, 1999. Directed by Jean-Luc Godard and Anne-Marie Miéville. Produced by Mary Lea Bandy and

Colin MacCabe. Production: Museum of Modern Art, New York. Photographs: Michael Witt.

p. 61 (b): *L'Origine du vingt et unième siècle*, 2000. Directed by Jean-Luc Godard. Production: Canal Plus, Vega Film. Photographs: Michael Witt.

p. 62 (a): French poster for *Éloge de l'amour*, 2001. Directed by Jean-Luc Godard. Distributed by ARP Sélection. Design: Caractères. Collection Michael Witt.

p. 62 (b): Japanese flyer for *Ten Minutes Older*, 2002. Collection Michael Witt.

p. 63 (a): *Liberté et Patrie*, 2002. Directed by Jean-Luc Godard and Anne-Marie Miéville. Producer: Ruth Waldburger. Production: Vega Film, Périphéria.

p. 63 (b): *Histoire(s) du cinéma*, 1998. Directed by Jean-Luc Godard. A Gaumont production. Courtesy Gaumont.

p. 69 (a): Orson Welles. Collection BFI Stills.

p. 69 (b): Roberto Rossellini. Collection BFI Stills.

p. 69 (c): Marguerite Duras, 1977. Collection BFI Stills.

p. 69 (d): François Truffaut, 1959. Collection BFI Stills.

p. 70: NP Abramov, *Dziga Vertov*, Lyon: SERDOC, 1965 (volume 35 of *Premier Plan*). Collection Michael Temple.

p. 73: *Opus International*, No. 2, July 1967. Cover design: Roman Cieslewicz. Collection Michael Witt.

p. 74: *L'Avant-Scène Cinéma*, 171-172, July-September 1976. Courtesy *L'Avant-Scène Cinéma*.

p. 76: Japanese flyers for *Les Carabiniers*. Collection Michael Temple.

p. 77: *Bande à part*, 1964. Produced and directed by Jean-Luc Godard. Production: Anouchka Films, Orsay Films. Collection *L'Avant-Scène Cinéma*.

p. 78: *Les Carabiniers*, 1963. Directed by Jean-Luc Godard. Produced by Georges de Beauregard and Carlo Ponti. Production: Rome-Paris Films, Laetitia, Les Films Marceau. Collection *L'Avant-Scène Cinéma*.

p. 80: Photograph depicting Geneviève Galéa and Catherine Ribeiro during the making of *Les Carabiniers*. Collection Michael Witt.

p. 82: *Au hasard Balthazar*, 1966. Directed by Robert Bresson. Production: Parc Film, Argos Films, Athos Films, Svensk Filmindustri, Swedish Film Institute, Mag Bodard. Collection BFI Stills.

p. 84: *Week-end*, 1967. Directed by Jean-Luc Godard. Production: Films Copernic, Ascot Cineraïd, Comacico, Lira Films. Collection *L'Avant-Scène Cinéma*.

p. 85 (a): German poster for *La Chinoise*. Directed by Jean-Luc Godard. Design: Hans Hillmann. Collection Michael Temple.

p. 85 (b): Godard special issue of the Hungarian film journal *Metropolis* published in Winter 1999. Courtesy *Metropolis*.

pp. 86-87: *Opus International*, July 1967, pp.14-15. Collection Michael Witt.

p. 89: *Numéro Deux*, 1975. Directed by Jean-Luc Godard. A Gaumont production. Courtesy Gaumont.

p. 90: French poster for *Numéro Deux*. Directed by Jean-Luc Godard. Distributed in France by SNC Paris. Collection Michael Witt.

p. 92: Production photograph of *Grandeur et décadence d'un petit commerce de cinéma*, 1986. Directed by Jean-Luc Godard. Photograph: TF1/Patrick Roche. Collection Michael Witt.

p. 95: Outline of the "Images of Britain" project. Collection Colin MacCabe.

p. 96: Proposal for *2x50 ans de cinéma français*. Collection Colin MacCabe.

p. 98 (a): Japanese flyer for *Le Mépris*. Collection Michael Temple.

p. 98 (b): Alberto Moravia, *Le Mépris*, Claude Poncet, trans., Paris: Flammarion, 1955. Courtesy Flammarion. Collection Roland-François Lack.

p. 98 (c): *Le Mépris*, 1963. Directed by Jean-Luc Godard. Produced by Joseph Levine and Carlo Ponti. Production: Rome-Paris Films, Les Films Concordia, Compagnia Cinematografica Champion. Collection *L'Avant-Scène Cinéma*.

p. 100: January 2001 Cinémathèque de Toulouse programme. Programme design: Compagnie Bernard Baissait, Bernard Lagacé. Courtesy Cinémathèque de Toulouse. Collection Michael Witt.

p. 101: Miéville and Godard during the making of *Sauve qui peut (la vie)* in 1979. Collection *Cahiers du cinéma*.

p. 102: Miéville and Godard at the Sarlat Festival in 2000. Photograph: Emmanuelle Barbaras. Collection *Cahiers du cinéma*.

p. 103: Production photograph of *Dalla Nube alla Resistenza (From the Clouds to the Resistance)*, 1979. Directed by Jean-Marie Straub and Danièle Huillet. Collection *Cahiers du cinéma*.

p. 104: *Nous trois*, episode 5a of *Six fois deux (Sur et sous la communication)*, 1976. Directed by Jean-Luc Godard and Anne-Marie Miéville. Produced by Jean-Luc Godard and Michel Raux. Production: Institut National de l'Audiovisuel, Sonimage. Photographs: Michael Witt.

p. 105: UK poster for *Sauve qui peut (la vie)*. Directed by Jean-Luc Godard. Distributed by Artificial Eye. Collection Michael Witt.

p. 106: *Sauve qui peut (la vie)*, 1980. Directed by Jean-Luc Godard. Production: Sara Films, MK2, Saga Productions, MK2, Sonimage, CNC, ZDF, SSR, ORF. Photographer: Anne-Marie Miéville. Collection Michael Temple.

p. 107 (a): *How Can I Love (A Man When I Know He Don't Want Me)*, 1984. Directed by Anne-Marie Miéville. Production: JLG Films, Sonimage Suisse. Photographer: Anne-Marie Miéville. Collection *Cahiers du cinéma*.

p. 107 (b): *Mon cher sujet*, 1989. Directed by Anne-Marie Miéville. Production: La Cinq, CNC, Les Films du Jeudi, JLG Films, Xanadu, Radio Télévision Suisse Romande. Photographer: Anne-Marie Miéville. Collection *Cahiers du cinéma*.

p. 111: *Soft and Hard*, 1985. Directed by Jean-Luc Godard and Anne-Marie Miéville. Production: Deptford Beach Production, Channel 4, JLG Films. Photographs: Michael Witt.

p. 112: Poster for *Après la reconciliation*, 2000. Directed by Anne-Marie Miéville. Distributed by Velvet Films. Design: Nuit de Chine. Collection Michael Temple.

p. 114: Poster for *Nous sommes tous encore ici*, 1997. Directed by Anne-Marie Miéville. Distributed by Les Films du Losange. Design: Kilimandjaro. Collection Michael Temple.

p. 116: *Lou n'a pas dit non*, 1994. Directed by Anne-Marie Miéville. Production: DF1, Sara Films, Périphéria, Vega Film, Canal Plus, CNC, BVF, Radio Télévision Suisse Romande. Collection *Cahiers du cinéma*.

p. 118: *Wide Angle: A Film Quarterly of Theory, Criticism and Practice*, Vol. 1, No. 3, 1976. Cover design: Karen Nulf. Collection Michael Witt.

p. 119: *Bande à part*, 1964. Produced and directed by Jean-Luc Godard. Production: Anouchka Films, Orsay Films. Collection *L'Avant-Scène Cinéma*.

p. 120: André Malraux and Sergei Eisenstein in Moscow. Collection *Cahiers du cinéma*.

p. 123: Frame enlargement from *L'Arrivée d'un train à La Ciotat*, Auguste and Louis Lumière, 1895. Collection *Cahiers du cinéma*.

p. 124: *Cahiers du cinéma*, 200-201, April-May 1968. Cover drawing: Gabriel Pascalini. Courtesy *Cahiers du cinéma*.

p. 127: Cinematheque Ontario programme guides. Volume 12, Number 1, Fall 2001: cover and p.12. Volume 12, Number 2, Winter 2002: cover and p.6. Courtesy Cinematheque Ontario.

p. 128 (a): Programme booklet for the "Tout Godard" retrospective, Paris, January-February 1989. Design: Com'Images, Hervé Tissot. Collection Michael Witt.

p. 128 (b): Poster for the 52nd International Berlin Film Festival "European 60s: Revolte, Phantasie & Utopie" retrospective, February 2002. Collection Michael Temple.

p. 131 (a): "For Ever Godard" conference pack, Tate Modern, June 2001. Sponsored by *agnès b.*.

p. 131 (b): Catalogue published to accompany the retrospective mounted by the Centre Culturel Français de Turin and the Museo Nazionale del Cinema de Turin in 1990. Edited by Sergio Toffetti. Graphics: Silvio Cocco. Collection Michael Witt.

p. 131 (c): Catalogue published to coincide with the "The Jean-Luc Godard Film Forum", Hull, October 1973. Collection Michael Witt.

p. 132 (a): Programme booklet for the Godard and Miéville retrospective held at the Cinémathèque Suisse, Lausanne, from December 1991 to February 1992. Edited by Freddy Buache. Cover: Werner Jeker. Courtesy Cinémathèque Suisse. Collection Michael Witt.

p. 132 (b): Catalogue published to accompany the retrospective mounted by the Viennale Vienna International Film Festival in collaboration with the Österreichisches Filmmuseum in October 1998. Graphics: Perndi Büro für Grafik. Collection Michael Temple.

p. 132 (c): Programme booklet for the "Jean-Luc Godard 1967-1979: années politiques, années oubliées" retrospective organised by the "la vie est à nous" association at Le Cinématographe cinema, Nantes, February 2003.

p. 135 (a): Robert Bresson, *Notes sur le cinématographe*, Paris: Gallimard, 1975. Courtesy Gallimard.

p. 135 (b): Jean Cocteau, *Du cinématographe*, André Bernard and Claude Gauteur, eds., Paris: Belfond, 1973.

p. 136: Poster for the "Sur Jean-Luc Godard" exhibition held at the *agnès b.* Galérie du Jour in Paris, January-February 1986. Design: *agnès b.*.

p. 138 (a): *Revue Belge du Cinéma*, 22/23, 1988. The first edition of this special issue was published to coincide with the Godard retrospective held in Brussels in 1986. Both issues edited by Philippe Dubois.

p. 138 (b): Programme booklet for the "God Art" retrospective organised by the Cinéma Le Méliès and the Musée d'Art Moderne, Saint-Étienne, April 1991. Collection Michael Witt.

p. 138 (c): Programme booklet for the touring version of the British Film Institute retrospective held at the National Film Theatre, London, July-October 2001. Courtesy BFI.

p. 145: Trailer for *À bout de souffle*, directed by Jean-Luc Godard.

p. 148: Trailer for *Détective*, directed by Jean-Luc Godard.

p. 149: Press book for *Détective*, 1985. Directed by Jean-Luc Godard. Distributed by Acteurs Auteurs Associés. Collection Michael Witt.

p. 150: Trailer for *Éloge de l'amour*, directed by Jean-Luc Godard.

p. 152: Trailer for *Le Mépris*, directed by Jean-Luc Godard.

p. 158: Poster for *Hélas pour moi*, 1993. Directed by Jean-Luc Godard. Distributed by Pan Européenne. Design: Cole & Baltimore/AH AH. Collection Michael Temple.

p. 161: *Faut pas rêver*, 1978. Directed by Jean-Luc Godard.

p. 162: *Vladimir et Rosa*, 1971. Directed by Jean-Luc Godard and Jean-Pierre Gorin. Produced by Claude Nedjar. Production: Munich Tele-Pool, Grove Press Evergreen Films. Collection Philippe Dubois.

p. 163: *Soigne ta droite*, 1987. Directed by Jean-Luc Godard. A Gaumont production. Collection Philippe Dubois. Courtesy Gaumont.

p. 164 (a): *Tous les garçons s'appellent Patrick*, 1957. Directed by Jean-Luc Godard. Produced by Pierre Braunberger. Production: Les Films de la Pléiade. Collection *L'Avant-Scène Cinéma*.

p. 164 (b): *Pierrot le fou*, 1965. Directed by Jean-Luc Godard. Produced by Georges de Beauregard and Dino de Laurentiis. Production: Productions Georges de Beauregard, Rome-Paris Films, Dino de Laurentiis Cinematografica. Collection *L'Avant-Scène Cinéma*.

p. 166 (a): *La Chinoise*, 1967. Directed by Jean-Luc Godard. Production: Anouchka Films, Les Productions de la Guéville, Athos Films, Parc Films, Simar Films. Collection *L'Avant-Scène Cinéma*.

p. 166 (b): *Le Grand escroc*, 1964. Directed by Jean-Luc Godard. Produced by Pierre Roustang. Production: Ulysse Productions, LUX-CCF, Primex Films, Vides Cinematografica, Toho-Towo, Caesar Film Productie. Collection *L'Avant-Scène Cinéma*.

p. 167: *Alphaville*, 1965. Directed by Jean-Luc Godard. Producer: André Michelin. Production: Chaumiane, Filmstudio. Collection Philippe Dubois.

p. 168: Lobby card for *Le Joli mai*, 1963. Directed by Chris Marker. Distributed by Ursulines Distribution. Collection Michael Temple.

p. 169: Jean Rouch and Edgar Morin during the making of *Chronique d'un été*, 1961. Collection BFI Stills.

p. 170: Godard, René Thom, "Louison", and Marcel Reymond in episodes 2b (*Jean-Luc*), 5b (*René(e)s*), 1b (*Louison*), and 3b (*Marcel*) of *Six fois deux (Sur et sous la communication)*, 1976. Directed by Jean-Luc Godard and Anne-Marie Miéville. Produced by Jean-Luc Godard and Michel Raux. Production: Institut National de l'Audiovisuel, Sonimage. Photographs: Michael Witt.

p. 171: *Le Petit soldat*, 1960. Directed by Jean-Luc Godard. Produced by Georges de Beauregard. Production: Productions Georges de Beauregard, Société Nouvelle de Cinéma. Collection *L'Avant-Scène Cinéma*.

p. 172: *Masculin Féminin*, 1966. Directed by Jean-Luc Godard. Produced by Anatole Dauman. Production: Anouchka Films, Argos Films, Svensk Filmindustri, Sandrews. Collection *L'Avant-Scène Cinéma*.

p. 173 (a): Press release for *Tystnaden* (*The Silence*), 1963. Directed by Ingmar Bergman. Distributed by Cocinor. Collection Michael Witt.

p. 173 (b): Japanese flyer for *Masculin Féminin*, 1966. Collection Michael Temple.

p. 176: *Éloge de l'amour*, 2001. Directed by Jean-Luc Godard. Produced by Alain Sarde. Production: Périphéria, Télévision Suisse Romande, Arte France Cinéma, Avventura Films, Vega Film, Canal Plus. Collection BFI Stills. Courtesy Wild Bunch.

p. 179: *Tout va bien*, 1972. Directed by Jean-Luc Godard and Jean-Pierre Gorin. A Gaumont production. Courtesy Gaumont.

p. 181: *On s'est tous défilé*, 1988. Directed by Jean-Luc Godard. Produced by Marithé et François Girbaud Design.

p. 182: *Ici et Ailleurs*, 1974. Directed by Jean-Luc Godard and Anne-Marie Miéville. A Gaumont production. Courtesy Gaumont.

p. 183: *Grandeur et décadence d'un petit commerce de cinéma*, 1986. Directed by Jean-Luc Godard. Produced by Pierre Grimblat. Production: TF1, Hamster Productions, Télévision Suisse Romande, Radio Télévision Lausanne, JLG Films.

p. 184: Cécile Tanner in *Sauve qui peut (la vie)*, 1980. Directed by Jean-Luc Godard. Produced by Sara Films, MK2, Saga Productions, MK2, Sonimage, CNC, ZDF, SSR, ORF. Photographs: Sonimage/Anne-Marie Miéville. Collection Michael Temple.

p. 185: *Grandeur et décadence d'un petit commerce de cinéma*, 1986. Directed by Jean-Luc Godard. Produced by Pierre Grimblat. Production: TF1, Hamster Productions, Télévision Suisse Romande, Radio Télévision Lausanne, JLG Films.

p. 186: Mexican lobby card for *L'Avventura*, 1959. Directed by Michelangelo Antonioni. Distributed by Galatea, S.p. A. Collection Michael Witt.

pp. 190-192: *JLG/JLG: autoportrait de décembre*, 1995. Directed by Jean-Luc Godard. A Gaumont production. Courtesy Gaumont.

p. 193: *Nouvelle Vague*, 1990. Directed by Jean-Luc Godard. Produced by Alain Sarde. Production: Sara Films, Périphéria, Canal Plus, Vega Film, Télévision Suisse Romande, Films Antenne 2, CNC, DFI, Sofica.

p. 194: *Histoire(s) du cinéma*, 1998. Directed by Jean-Luc Godard. A Gaumont production. Courtesy Gaumont.

p. 195 (a): Japanese flyer for *JLG/JLG: autoportrait de décembre*, 1995. Collection Michael Temple.

p. 195 (b): Italian poster for *Nouvelle Vague*, 1990. Directed by Jean-Luc Godard. Distributed by Penta Classic Distribuzione. Collection Michael Temple.

p. 196 (a): *Je vous salue, Marie*, 1985. Directed by Jean-Luc Godard. A Gaumont production. Courtesy Gaumont.

p. 196 (b, c): *JLG/JLG: autoportrait de décembre*, 1995. Directed by Jean-Luc Godard. A Gaumont production. Courtesy Gaumont.

p. 197: *JLG/JLG: autoportrait de décembre*, 1995. Directed by Jean-Luc Godard. A Gaumont production. Courtesy Gaumont.

p. 198: Lobby cards for *Passion*, 1982. Directed by Jean-Luc Godard. Distributed by Parafrance. Collection Michael Witt.

p. 201: *Une vie*, 1958. Directed by Alexandre Astruc. Produced by Annie Dorfmann. Production: Agnès Delahaye Productions, Nepi Films. Collection *Cahiers du cinéma*.

p. 204: *The Man with a Movie Camera*, 1929. Directed by Dziga Vertov. Production: VUFKU. Collection BFI Stills. Courtesy Öesterreichisches Filmmuseum, Vienna.

p. 205: *France/tour/détour/deux/enfants*. Directed by Jean-Luc Godard and Anne-Marie Miéville. Production: Institut National de l'Audiovisuel, Sonimage, 1978.

p. 206 (a): Chronophotograph by Étienne-Jules Marey, 1890. Collection BFI Stills. Courtesy Science Museum, London.

p. 206 (b): Serial photograph by Eadweard Muybridge, 1887. Courtesy Kingston Museum and Heritage Service, Kingston-upon-Thames.

pp. 208-209: *France/tour/détour/deux/enfants*. Directed by Jean-Luc Godard and Anne-Marie Miéville. Production: Institut National de l'Audiovisuel, Sonimage, 1978.

p. 210: *Cahiers du cinéma*, 271, November 1976. Courtesy *Cahiers du cinéma*.

p. 211: *France/tour/détour/deux/enfants*. Directed by Jean-Luc Godard and Anne-Marie Miéville. Production: Institut National de l'Audiovisuel, Sonimage, 1978.

p. 212: *Marcel*, episode 3b of *Six fois deux (Sur et sous la communication)*, 1976. Directed by Jean-Luc Godard and Anne-Marie Miéville. Produced by Jean-Luc Godard and Michel Raux. Production: Institut National de l'Audiovisuel, Sonimage.

p. 213: *À nous la liberté*, 1931. Directed by René Clair. Produced by Frank Clifford. Production: Société des Films Sonores Tobis. Collection *Cahiers du cinéma*.

p. 215: *Une femme mariée*, 1964. Produced and directed by Jean-Luc Godard. Production: Anouchka Films, Orsay Films. Collection Philippe Dubois.

pp. 218-219: Macha Méril and Jean-Luc Godard, *Journal d'une femme mariée*, Paris: Denoël, 1965, pp. 78-79.

pp. 222-223: Collage by Godard, 1979. First published in Jean-Luc Godard ed., *Cahiers du cinéma*, 300, May 1979, pp. 14-15. Collection *Cahiers du cinéma*.

pp. 228-229: Collage by Godard, 1980. First published in Jean-Luc Godard, *Introduction à une véritable histoire du cinéma*, Paris: Albatros, 1980, pp. 248-249.

p. 230: *Going Forth By Day*, Bill Viola, 2002. Photograph: Kira Perov. Courtesy Bill Viola Studio and Guggenheim Museum, New York.

p. 234: *Bande à part*, *À bout de souffle*, *Le Petit soldat*. All images in this chapter are from Philippe Dubois's collection.

p. 235: *Une femme est une femme*, *Une femme mariée*.

p. 236: *Les Carabiniers*, *Alphaville*.

p. 237: *Masculin Féminin*, *Deux ou trois choses que je sais d'elle*.

p. 238: *La Chinoise*, *Le Gai savoir*.

p. 239: *Un film comme les autres*, *One Plus One*.

p. 240: *British Sounds*, *Lotte in Italia*, *Vent d'est*.

p. 241: *Vladimir et Rosa*, *Tout va bien*.

p. 242: *Six fois deux (Sur et sous la communication)*, *France/tour/détour/deux/enfants*.

p. 243: *Numéro Deux*, *Comment ça va?*

p. 244: *Lettre à Freddy Buache*, *Prénom Carmen*.

p. 245: *Passion*.

p. 246: *Scénario du film Passion*, *Je vous salue, Marie*.

p. 247: *Soigne ta droite*, *Scénario vidéo de Sauve qui peut (la vie)*, *Histoire(s) du cinéma*.

p. 253: Mexican lobby card for *À bout de souffle*, 1960. Distributed by Cinematografica Azteca S.A. Collection Michael Temple.

p. 254: Production photograph taken during the making of *Westbound*, 1959. Directed by Budd Boetticher. Collection *Cahiers du cinéma*.

p. 257: *À bout de souffle*, 1960. Directed by Jean-Luc Godard. Produced by Georges de Beauregard. Production: Société Nouvelle de Cinéma. Collection *L'Avant-Scène Cinéma*.

p. 259: Spanish poster for *Alphaville*, 1965. Designer: Fuencisla del Amo. Collection Michael Temple.

pp. 260-261: *Alphaville*, 1965. Directed by Jean-Luc Godard. Produced by André Michelin. Production: Chaumiane, Filmstudio. Collection *L'Avant-Scène Cinéma*.

p. 262: *Alphaville*, 1965. Directed by Jean-Luc Godard. Producer: André Michelin. Production: Chaumiane, Filmstudio. Collection Philippe Dubois.

p. 266: *Bande à part*, 1964. Produced and directed by Jean-Luc Godard. Production: Anouchka Films, Orsay Films. Collection *L'Avant-Scène Cinéma*.

p. 273 (a): Cover of the ECM press book for the *Histoire(s) du cinéma* 5-CD box-set. Cover photograph: Richard Dumas. Courtesy ECM Records.

p. 273 (b): Cover of the *Histoire(s) du cinéma* 5-CD box-set, 1999. ECM New Series 1706 - 10 465151-2. Courtesy ECM Records.

p. 275 (a): Meredith Monk and Vocal Ensemble, *Do You Be*, 1987. ECM 1336 831 782-2. Courtesy ECM Records.

p. 275 (b): Arvo Pärt, *Miserere*, 1991. ECM New Series 1430 847 539-2. Courtesy ECM Records.

p. 276 (a): David Darling, *Cello*, 1992. ECM 1464 511 982-2. Courtesy ECM Records.

p. 276 (b): Giya Kancheli, *Abii ne viderem*, 1995. ECM New Series 1510 445 941-2. Courtesy ECM Records.

p. 276 (c): Ketil Bjørnstad, David Darling, Jon Christensen, Terje Rypdal, *The Sea II*, ECM 1633 CD 537 341-2. Courtesy ECM Records.

p. 276 (d): Dino Saluzzi, *Andina*, 1988. ECM 1375 837 186-2. Courtesy ECM Records.

pp. 280-281: Macha Méril and Jean-Luc Godard, *Journal d'une femme mariée*, Paris: Denoël, 1965, pp. 48-49.

p. 285: Publicity photograph for *The Great Dictator*, 1940. Directed by Charles Chaplin. Distributed by United Artists. Collection BFI Stills.

p. 286: *Prénom Carmen*, 1983. Directed by Jean-Luc Godard. Produced by Alain Sarde. Production: Sara Films, JLG Films, Films Antenne 2. Collection Philippe Dubois.

p. 289: *Le Rouge*, Gérard Fromanger, 1968. Courtesy Gérard Fromanger.

pp. 290-291: *Prénom Carmen*, 1983. Directed by Jean-Luc Godard. Produced by Alain Sarde. Production: Sara Films, JLG Films, Films Antenne 2. Collection *Cahiers du cinéma*.

p. 293: *Masculin Féminin*, 1966. Directed by Jean-Luc Godard. Produced by Anatole Dauman. Production: Anouchka Films, Argos Films, Svensk Filmindustri, Sandrews. Collection *Cahiers du cinéma*.

p. 294: Production photograph for *Armide*, 1987. Directed by Jean-Luc Godard. Collection *Cahiers du cinéma*.

p. 295: *Lettre à Freddy Buache*, 1981. Directed by Jean-Luc Godard. Production: Sonimage, Film et Vidéo Production Lausanne. Photographs: Michael Witt.

p. 296: Japanese press book for *Je vous salue, Marie*, 1985. Collection Michael Witt.

p. 299: *Je vous salue, Marie*, 1985. Directed by Jean-Luc Godard. A Gaumont production. Collection Philippe Dubois. Courtesy Gaumont.

p. 300: *Je vous salue, Marie*, 1985. Directed by Jean-Luc Godard. A Gaumont production. Courtesy Gaumont.

p. 301: Cover and track-listing of the *Nouvelle Vague* box-set, ECM Records, 1997. ECM New Series 1600/01 449 891-2. Courtesy ECM Records.

p. 302: *Nouvelle Vague*, 1990. Directed by Jean-Luc Godard. Produced by Alain Sarde. Production: Sara Film, Périphéria, Canal Plus, Vega Film, Télévision Suisse Romande, Antenne 2, CNC, DFI, Sofica Investimage, Sofica Creations.

p. 307: Publicity photograph for *Nouvelle Vague*, 1990. Directed by Jean-Luc Godard. Distributed by AMLF. Collection Michael Witt.

p. 308: *Éloge de l'amour*, 2001. Directed by Jean-Luc Godard. Produced by Alain Sarde. Production: Avventura Film, Périphéria, Canal Plus, Arte, Vega Film, Télévision Suisse Romande. Collection BFI Stills. Courtesy Wild Bunch.

p. 313: *Le Gai savoir*, 1968. Directed by Jean-Luc Godard. Production: ORTF, Anouchka Films, Gambit, Bavaria Atelier. Collection *L'Avant-Scène Cinéma*.

p. 314 (a): Lobby card for *Prénom Carmen*, 1983. Directed by Jean-Luc Godard. Distributed by Parafrance. Collection Michael Witt.

p. 314 (b): *Numéro Deux*, 1975. Directed by Jean-Luc Godard. A Gaumont production. Collection Philippe Dubois. Courtesy Gaumont.

p. 314 (c): Poster for *King Lear*, 1987. Directed by Jean-Luc Godard. Distributed by Cannon Releasing Corporation. Collection Michael Temple.

p. 315 (a): *Vivre sa vie*, 1962. Directed by Jean-Luc Godard. Produced by Pierre Braunberger. Production: Les Films de la Pléiade. Collection Philippe Dubois.

p. 315 (b): *L'Avant-Scène Cinéma*, 19, November 1962. Courtesy *L'Avant-Scène Cinéma*.

p. 315 (c): Marcel Sacotte, *Où en est la prostitution?*, Paris: Buchet-Chastel, 1959. Collection Roland-François Lack.

p. 316 (a): Production photograph of *L'Atalante*, 1934. Directed by Jean Vigo. Collection Michael Temple.

p. 316 (b): *Le Testament d'Orphée*, 1960. Directed by Jean Cocteau. Produced by Jean Thuillier. Production: Éditions Cinégraphiques. Collection Michael Temple.

p. 316 (c): Godard and Jean Renoir in 1968. Collection *Cahiers du cinéma*.

p. 316 (d): Jean Epstein circa 1946. Collection *Cahiers du cinéma*.

p. 319 (a): Japanese flyer for *Le Petit soldat*, 1960. Collection Michael Temple.

p. 319 (b): Publicity photograph of Michel Subor. Collection Roland-François Lack.

p. 321: *Le Petit soldat*, 1960. Directed by Jean-Luc Godard. Produced by Georges de Beauregard. Production: Productions Georges de Beauregard, Société Nouvelle de Cinéma. Collection *L'Avant-Scène Cinéma*.

p. 324: *Made in USA*, 1966. Directed by Jean-Luc Godard. Produced by Georges de Beauregard. Production: Anouchka Films, Rome-Paris Films, SEPIC. Collection *L'Avant-Scène Cinéma*.

p. 325: Jean-Luc Godard, *Made in USA*, London: Lorrimer, 1967.

p. 327: Lobby card for *Pierrot le fou*, 1965. Directed by Jean-Luc Godard. Distributed by SNC. Collection Nicole Brenez.

p. 328: Tobias von Elsner, *Alles verbrannt? Die verlorene Gemäldegalerie des Kaiser Friedrich Museums Magdeburg*, Magdeburg: Magdeburger Museen, 1995. Courtesy Magdeburger Museen.

p. 335 (a): Jean-Luc Godard, *Introduction à une véritable histoire du cinéma*, Paris: Albatros, 1980.

p. 335 (b): Jean-Luc Godard, *Allemagne neuf zéro: phrases*, Paris: POL, 1998. Courtesy POL.

p. 336: *Allemagne année 90 neuf zéro*, 1991. Directed by Jean-Luc Godard. Produced by Nicole Ruelle. Production: Antenne 2, Brainstorm, Gaumont, Périphéria. Collection *Cahiers du cinéma*.

p. 338 (a): Supplement to *Cahiers du cinéma*, 537, July-August 1999. Courtesy *Cahiers du cinéma*.

p. 338 (b): *Art Press* special issue, November 1998. Courtesy *Art Press*.

p. 338 (c): Japanese flyer for *Histoire(s) du cinéma*. Collection Michael Temple.

p. 339 (a): Michael Temple and James S Williams eds., *The Cinema Alone: essays on the work of Jean-Luc Godard 1985-2000*, Amsterdam: Amsterdam University Press, 2000. Courtesy Amsterdam University Press.

p. 339 (b): Inuhiko Yomoto and Junji Hori eds., *Godard, Image, History*, Tokyo: Sangyo-Tosho, 2001. Courtesy Sangyo-Tosho.

p. 339 (c): Jacques Aumont, *Amnésies: Fictions du cinéma d'après Jean-Luc Godard*, Paris: POL, 1999. Courtesy POL.

p. 340: *For Ever Mozart*, 1996. Directed by Jean-Luc Godard. Produced by Alain Sarde. Production: Avventura Films, Périphéria, Vega Film, CEC Rhône Alpes, France 2 Cinéma, Canal Plus, CNC, Télévision Suisse Romande, Eurimages, DFI. Collection *Cahiers du cinéma*.

pp. 342-343: Collage by Godard, 1981. First published in Jean-Luc Godard, *Introduction à une véritable histoire du cinéma*, Paris: Albatros, 1980, pp. 118-119.

p. 344: Lobby card for *La Règle du jeu*, 1939. Directed by Jean Renoir. Distributed by La Nouvelle Édition Française. Collection *Cahiers du cinéma*.

pp. 346-347: *Espoir*, 1939-1945. Directed by André Malraux. Produced by Edouard Corniglion-Molinier. Production: Productions Corniglion-Molinier. Collection *Cahiers du cinéma*. Courtesy Les Grands Films Classiques.

p. 351: *Angelus Novus*, Paul Klee, 1920. Collection The Israel Museum, Jerusalem. Photograph: The Israel Museum/David Harris. (c) DACS 2003.

p. 352: Walter Benjamin, *The Arcades Project*, Howard Eiland and Kevin McLaughlin, trans., Cambridge MA: Belknap Press for Harvard University Press, 1999.

p. 354: Fernand Braudel, *Écrits sur l'histoire*, Paris: Flammarion, 1969. Courtesy Flammarion.

p. 356: Friedrich Nietzsche, *On the Use and Abuse of History*, New York: Library of Liberal Arts/Macmillan, 1957.

p. 357: *M*, 1931. Directed by Fritz Lang. Produced by Seymour Nebenzahl. Production: Nero-Film. Collection BFI Stills.

p. 358: Guy Debord, *La Société du spectacle*, Paris: Gallimard, 1992. Courtesy Gallimard.

p. 359: *To Be Or Not To Be*, 1942. Produced and directed by Ernst Lubitsch. Production: Romaine Film Corporation. Collection BFI Stills.

p. 361: Sergei Eisenstein shooting *Bezhin lug* (*Bezhin Meadow*), 1935-1937. Photograph: Jay Leyda. Collection BFI Stills.

p. 371: *Pasazerka* (*The Passenger*), 1963. Directed by Andrzej Munk and Witold Lesiewicz. Produced by Wilhelm Hollender. Production: Film Polski, Zespól Filmowy "Kamera". Collection *Cahiers du cinéma*.

pp. 372-373: Production photograph of *Nuit et brouillard*, 1955. Directed by Alain Resnais. Collection BFI Stills.

p. 378: *Kapo*, 1960. Directed by Gillo Pontecorvo. Production: Vides Cinematografica, Zebra Films, Cineris, Francinex, Lovcén Film. Collection BFI Stills.

p. 381: Charles Péguy, *Clio*, Paris: Gallimard, 1932. Courtesy Gallimard.

p. 383: Collage by Godard for the books of *Histoire(s) du cinéma*, 1998. Collection Gaumont.

p. 384: *Le Mystère des roches de Kador*, 1912. Directed by Léonce Perret. A Gaumont production. Courtesy Gaumont.

p. 388: Collage by Godard for the books of *Histoire(s) du cinéma*, 1998. Collection Gaumont.

p. 391: Collage by Godard for the books of *Histoire(s) du cinéma*, 1998. Collection Gaumont.

p. 392: *Arbeiter verlassen die Fabrik* (*Workers Leaving the Factory*), 1995. Directed by Harun Farocki. Produced by Harun Farocki. Production: Harun Farocki Filmproduktion, WDR, ORF, Dr. Heinrich Mis/LAPSUS, Christian Baute/DRIFT, Chris Hoover. Courtesy Harun Farocki.

p. 398: Lobby cards for *Hélas pour moi*, 1993. Directed by Jean-Luc Godard. Distributed by Pan Européenne. Collection Michael Temple.

p. 400: Flyer for the Japanese DVD of *For Ever Mozart*. Collection Michael Temple.

p. 401: *For Ever Mozart*, 1996. Directed by Jean-Luc Godard. Produced by Alain Sarde. Production: Avventura Films, Périphéria, Vega Film, CEC Rhône Alpes, France 2 Cinéma, Canal Plus, CNC, Télévision Suisse Romande, Eurimages, DFI. Collection *Cahiers du cinéma*.

p. 404: *Nosferatu, eine Symphonie des Grauens*, 1922. Directed by Friedrich Wilhelm Murnau. Produced by Albin Grau, Enrico Dieckmann. Production: Prana-Film. Collection BFI Stills.

p. 405: CF Ramuz, *Les Signes parmi nous*, Lausanne: Plaisir de lire, 1953. Collection Roland-François Lack.

p. 406: André Malraux, *Hommage de la France à Jean Moulin*, RTF, 1964. Collection Roland-François Lack.

p. 409: *Der Letzte Mann*, 1924. Directed by Friedrich Wilhelm Murnau. Produced by Erich Pommer. Production: Ufa. Collection BFI Stills.

p. 410: Maurice Blanchot, *Le Dernier homme*, Paris: Gallimard, 1957. Courtesy Gallimard.

p. 413: *Die Nibelungen*, 1924. Directed by Fritz Lang. Produced by Erich Pommer. Production: Decla Filmgesellschaft/Ufa. Collection BFI Stills.

INDEX

454